American Literary Scholarship   1989

American Literary Scholarship
An Annual 1989

Edited by David J. Nordloh

Essays by David M. Robinson, Frederick Newberry,

Benjamin Franklin Fisher IV, Brian Higgins,

John Carlos Rowe, Robert Sattelmeyer, Richard A. Hocks,

Reed Way Dasenbrock, Ladell Payne, Susan F. Beegel,

William J. Scheick, Alice Hall Petry, Gary Scharnhorst,

Jerome Klinkowitz, Melody M. Zajdel, Richard J. Calhoun,

Peter A. Davis, Michael J. Hoffman, F. Lyra,

Michel Gresset, Rolf Meyn, Massimo Bacigalupo,

Keiko Beppu, Jan Nordby Gretlund, Elisabeth Herion-

Sarafidis, and Hans Skei

Duke University Press   *Durham and London*   1991

© 1991 Duke University Press
LC 65–19450   ISBN 0–8223–1139–9
Printed in the United States of America
by Heritage Printers, Inc.

Table of Contents

Foreword

With this volume of *American Literary Scholarship*, Louis Owens and I take over as coeditors of the series. We face the challenge of maintaining its reputation for thoroughness and fairness even as the continuing explosion of the canon and the proliferation of published work complicate the task. But we have the 27-year example of our predecessors, James Woodress and J. Albert Robbins, to guide us, and we have their generous expressions of support to fall back on.

Like the study of American literature itself, ALS mixes tradition and innovation. Alterations will be necessary soon because of shifts in interest in the major authors treated in Part I and the continuing expansion demanded of those genre chapters in Part II which must cover material to the present. Meanwhile, the present volume is different from the previous one for other reasons. There's no chapter on "Fiction: 1900 to the 1930s" because I was unable to commission a contributor in time; Professor Jo Ann Middleton has agreed to prepare it for ALS *1990* and to cover both 1989 and 1990 publications. Professor José Antonio Gurpegui, who supplied "Spanish Contributions" for the "Foreign Scholarship" chapter last year, was interrupted in the task by illness this year, but will return. And the chapter on "Black Literature," which has had a shaky history since the mid-1980s, does not appear in this volume. The immediate occasion of its disappearance is the failure of the assigned contributor to complete the work, but there are two more significant reasons. One, the amount of publication dealing with black writers is becoming so great that a single chapter assembled by a single contributor is becoming impossible. Two, it's simply inappropriate to treat black writers in a separate chapter while discussing other "groups"—minorities, Native Americans, ethnics—in the regular genre-period chapters. Professor Owens and I agree in eliminating the distinction and the "Black Literature" chapter and having *all* relevant writers treated in the genre-period chapters.

Several new contributors have joined the team that will produce ALS *1990*. John Wenke, Salisbury State University, Maryland, re-

places Brian Higgins as author of the chapter on "Melville." Bruce
Fogelman, University of Tennessee, takes over for Reed Way Dasen-
brock in covering "Pound and Eliot." M. Thomas Inge, Randolph-
Macon College, returns to the "Faulkner" chapter after a year's sab-
batical during which Ladell Payne ably stood in. Gary Scharnhorst,
University of New Mexico, who prepared "Fiction: The 1930s to the
1960s" this year, will move to "19th-Century Literature," replacing
Alice Hall Petry; and Charlotte Hadella, Arkansas State University,
will fill Scharnhorst's original slot. Lee Bartlett, University of New
Mexico, takes over "Poetry: 1900 to the 1940s" from Melody Zajdel.
Michael Fischer, University of New Mexico, assumes "Themes, Topics, Criticism" from Michael J. Hoffman.

We want to express our gratitude to the retiring contributors for
their faithful service, and particularly Michael J. Hoffman, who since
1973 has done the very difficult chapter on "Themes, Topics, Criticism" some 14 times. Our gratitude as well to the many departmental
and university-level administrators at Indiana University and the
University of California, Santa Cruz, for their support of the coeditors, and to the able and unflappable editorial staff of Duke University Press who oversee production of this volume.

Professor Louis Owens will edit *ALS 1990*. Authors are invited
to forward 1990 publications to him at Porter College, University of
California, Santa Cruz, CA 95064. To simplify matters for publishers,
I will continue to process review copies of books for all *ALS* volumes;
my address is Department of English, Indiana University, Bloomington, IN 47405.

David J. Nordloh

Indiana University

Key to Abbreviations

Festschriften, Essay Collections .and Books Discussed in More Than One Chapter

Afro-American Women Writers / Ann Allen Shockley, ed., *Afro-American Women Writers, 1746–1933: An Anthology and Critical Guide* (Hall 1988)

Aliens Tongues / Elizabeth Klosty Beaujour, *Alien Tongues: Bilingual Russian Writers of the 'First' Emigration* (Cornell)

Americana & Hungarica / Charlotte Kretzoi, ed., *Americana & Hungarica* (Budapest: Department of English, L. Eötvos University)

The American Epic / John P. McWilliams, Jr., *The American Epic: Transforming a Genre, 1770–1860* (Cambridge)

American Horror Fiction / Brian Docherty, ed., *American Horror Fiction* (St. Martin's)

American Unitarianism / Conrad Edick Wright, ed., *American Unitarianism, 1805–1861* (Northeastern)

The American Writer and the University / Ben Siegel, ed., *The American Writer and the University* (Delaware)

Architects of the Abyss / Dennis Pahl, *Architects of the Abyss: The Indeterminate Fictions of Poe, Hawthorne, and Melville* (Missouri)

Bardic Ethos / Jeffrey Walker, *Bardic Ethos and the American Epic Form: Whitman, Pound, Crane, Williams, Olson* (LSU)

The Complex Image / Joseph Fichtelberg, *The Complex Image: Faith and Method in American Autobiography* (Penn.)

Conspiracy and Romance / Robert Levine, *Conspiracy and Romance:*

Studies in Brockden Brown, Cooper, Hawthorne, and Melville (Cambridge)

Dark Eden / David C. Miller, *Dark Eden: The Swamp in Nineteenth-Century American Culture* (Cambridge)

Daughters and Fathers / Lynda E. Boose and Betty S. Flowers, eds., *Daughters and Fathers* (Hopkins)

Determined Fictions / Lee Clark Mitchell, *Determined Fictions: American Literary Naturalism* (Columbia)

Discovering Ourselves in Whitman / Thomas Gardner, *Discovering Ourselves in Whitman: The Contemporary Long Poem* (Illinois)

Ecological Revolutions / Carolyn Merchant, *Ecological Revolutions: Nature, Gender, and Science in New England* (No. Car.)

The Edge of the Swamp / Louis D. Rubin, Jr., *The Edge of the Swamp: A Study in the Literature and Society of the Old South* (LSU)

Engendering the Word / Temma F. Berg et al., eds, *Engendering the Word: Feminist Essays in Psychosexual Poetics* (Illinois)

Essays for Richard Ellmann / Susan Dick et al., eds., *Essays for Richard Ellmann: Omnium Gatherum* (McGill-Queens)

Faulkner and the Craft of Fiction / Doreen Fowler and Ann J. Abadie, eds., *Faulkner and the Craft of Fiction: Faulkner and Yoknapatawpha, 1987* (Miss.)

Faulkner's Discourse / Lothor Hönnighausen, ed., *Faulkner's Dis-*

course: An International Symposium (Niemeyer)

Feminism and Psychoanalysis / Richard Feldstein and Judith Roof, eds., *Feminism and Psychoanalysis* (Cornell)

Fiction and Historical Consciousness / Emily Miller Budick, *Fiction and Historical Consciousness* (Yale)

Figures of Speech / R. Jackson Wilson, *Figures of Speech: American Writers and the Literary Marketplace, from Benjamin Franklin to Emily Dickinson* (Knopf)

First Person Singular / A. Robert Lee, ed., *First Person Singular: Studies in American Autobiography* (St. Martin's, 1988)

Forever There / Elizabeth I. Hansen, *Forever There: Race and Gender in Contemporary Native American Fiction* (Peter Lang)

The Frontier Experience and the American Dream / David Mogen et al., eds., *The Frontier Experience and the American Dream: Essays on American Literature* (Texas A & M)

Gender, Race, and Region / Helen Taylor, *Gender, Race, and Region in the Writings of Grace King, Ruth McEnery Stuart, and Kate Chopin* (LSU)

Girls Who Went Wrong / Laura Hapke, *Girls Who Went Wrong: Prostitutes in American Fiction, 1885–1917* (Bowling Green)

Gothic Fiction/Gothic Form / George E. Haggerty, *Gothic Fiction/ Gothic Form* (Penn. State)

Gott und Politik in U.S.A. / Klaus-M. Kodalle, ed., *Gott und Politik in U.S.A.* (Athenäum, 1988)

The Great Prairie Fact and Literary Imagination / Robert Thacker, *The Great Prairie Fact and Literary Imagination* (New Mexico)

The Green American Tradition / H. Daniel Peck, *The Green American Tradition: Essays and Poems for Sherman Paul* (LSU)

Hemingway's Neglected Short Fiction / Susan F. Beegel, ed., *Heming-*

way's Neglected Short Fiction: New Perspectives (UMI Research Press)

High Resolution / Henry S. Sussman, *High Resolution: Critical Theory and the Problem of Literacy* (Oxford)

Intertextuality and Contemporary American Fiction / Patrick O'Donnell and Robert Con Davis, *Intertextuality and Contemporary American Fiction* (Hopkins)

The Invention of Ethnicity / Werner Sollors, ed., *The Invention of Ethnicity* (Oxford)

Jason's Voyage / Klaus Lanzinger, *Jason's Voyage: The Search for the Old World in American Literature* (Peter Lang)

The Language of Modernism / Randy Malamud, *The Language of Modernism* (UMI Research Press)

Literary Nonfiction / Chris Anderson, ed., *Literary Nonfiction: Theory, Criticism, Pedagogy* (So. Ill.)

Literature and War / David Bevan, ed., *Literature and War* (Rodopi)

Manhood and the American Renaissance / David Leverenz, *Manhood and the American Renaissance* (Cornell)

Marx and Modern Fiction / Edward J. Ahearn, *Marx and Modern Fiction* (Yale)

Measuring the Moment / Keith A. Sandiford, *Measuring the Moment: Strategies of Protest in Eighteenth-Century Afro-English Writing* (Susquehanna)

Modern American Fiction / Thomas Daniel Young, ed., *Modern American Fiction: Form and Function* (LSU)

The Modern American Novella / A. Robert Lee, ed., *The Modern American Novella* (St. Martin's)

'Murder Will Out' / T. J. Binyon, *'Murder Will Out'* (Oxford)

Nature Transfigured / John Christie and Sally Shuttleworth, eds., *Nature Transfigured: Science and Literature, 1700–1900* (Manchester)

New Ground / A. Carl Bredahl, Jr.,
*New Ground: Western American
Narrative and the Literary Canon*
(No. Car.)

Painterly Abstraction / Charles Altieri,
*Painterly Abstraction in Modern
American Poetry* (Cambridge)

The Poetic Fantastic / Patrick D.
Murphy and Vernon Hyles, eds.,
The Poetic Fantastic (Greenwood)

Poetry and the Fine Arts / Roland
Hagenbuchle and Jacqueline S.
Ollier, *Poetry and the Fine Arts*
(Pustet)

Politics and the Muse / Adam J. Sorkin,
*Politics and the Muse: Studies in
the Politics of Recent American
Literature* (Bowling Green)

Reading in America / Cathy N. Davidson, ed., *Reading in America: Literature and Social History*
(Hopkins)

Reading Narrative / James Phelan, ed.,
*Reading Narrative: Form, Ethics,
Ideology* (Ohio State)

Recovering Literature's Lost Ground
/ James M. Cox, *Recovering Lit-
erature's Lost Ground: Essays in
American Autobiography* (LSU)

Redefining the American Gothic /
Louis S. Gross, *Redefining the
American Gothic: from Wieland
to Day of the Dead* (UMI Research Press)

Refiguring the Father / Patricia Yea-
ger and Beth Kowaleski-Wallace,
eds., *Refiguring the Father: New
Feminist Readings of Patriarchy*
(So. Ill.)

Representation of the Self / Jeffrey
Steele, *The Representation of the
Self in the American Renaissance*
(No. Car.)

Re-reading the Short Story / Clare
Hanson, ed., *Re-reading the Short
Story* (St. Martin's)

Rewriting the Good Fight / Frieda
Brown et al., eds., *Rewriting the
Good Fight: Critical Essays on the
Literature of the Spanish Civil
War* (Mich. State)

The Rights of Nature / Roderick
Frazier Nash, *The Rights of Nature:*

*A History of Environmental
Ethics* (Wisconsin)

The Romance of Failure / Jonathan
Auerbach, *The Romance of Fail-
ure: First-person Fictions of Poe,
Hawthorne, and James* (Oxford)

Romantic Foundations / Leon Chai,
*The Romantic Foundations of the
American Renaissance* (Cornell,
1987)

Second Stories / Cynthia S. Jordan,
*Second Stories: The Politics of
Language, Form, and Gender in
Early American Fictions* (No.
Car.)

Self and Form in Modern Narrative /
Vincent P. Pecora, *Self and Form
in Modern Narrative* (Hopkins)

Sexchanges / Sandra M. Gilbert and
Susan Gubar, *Sexchanges* (Yale)

The Short Story Cycle / Susan Garland Mann, *The Short Story Cycle:
A Genre Companion and Reference Guide* (Greenwood)

Short Story Theory at a Crossroads /
Susan Lohafer and Jo Ellyn
Clarey, eds., *Short Story Theory at
a Crossroads* (LSU)

Slavery and the Literary Imagination
/ Deborah E. McDowell and
Arnold Rampersad, *Slavery and the
Literary Imagination: Selected
Papers of the English Institute
1987* (Hopkins)

Spiritual Autobiography in America /
Daniel B. Shea, *Spiritual Autobiography in America* (Wisconsin,
1988)

*Stanley Cavell and Literary Skepti-
cism* / Michael Fischer, *Stanley
Cavell and Literary Skepticism*
(Cornell)

The Still Performance / James Mc-
Corkle, *The Still Performance:
Writing, Self, and Interconnection
in Five Postmodern American
Writers* (Virginia)

The Theory of the American Romance
/ William Ellis, *The Theory of the
American Romance: An Ideology
in American Intellectual History*
(UMI Research Press)

The Thirsty Muse / Tom Dardis, *The Thirsty Muse: Alcohol and the American Writer* (Ticknor and Fields)

This Incomperable Lande / Thomas J. Lyon, *This Incomperable Lande: A Book of American Nature Writing* (Houghton Mifflin)

Uncanny American Fiction / Allan Gardner Lloyd-Smith, *Uncanny American Fiction* (St. Martin's)

Wege amerikanischer Kultur / Renate von Bardeleben, ed., *Wege amerikanischer Kultur: Aufsätze zu Ehren von Gustav H. Blanke. Ways and Byways of American Culture: Essays in Honor of Gustav H. Blanke* (Frankfurt: Peter Lang)

Witness Through the Imagination / S. Lillian Kremer, *Witness Through the Imagination: Jewish American Holocaust Literature* (Wayne State)

Women and Sisters / Jean Fagan Yellin, *Women and Sisters: The Anti-Slavery Feminists in American Culture* (Yale)

Women on the Color Line / Anna Shannon Elfenbein, *Women on the Color Line: Evolving Stereotypes and the Writings of George Washington Cable, Grace King, Kate Chopin* (Virginia)

Writing Realism / Daniel H. Borus, *Writing Realism: Howells, James, and Norris in the Mass Market* (No. Car.)

Zen in American Life and Letters / Robert S. Ellwood, ed., *Zen in American Life and Letters* (Undena, 1987)

Periodicals, Annuals, and Series

Agenda

AI / *American Imago*

AIQ / *American Indian Quarterly*

AL / *American Literature*

ALR / *American Literary Realism, 1870–1910*

Americana (Univ. de Paris IV)

American Art Journal

American Jewish Archives

AmerP / *American Poetry*

AmLH / *American Literary History*

Amst / *Amerikastudien*

Anais: An International Journal

AN&Q / *American Notes and Queries*

Annales du CRAA / Centre de Recherches sur l'Amérique Anglophone (Univ. de Bordeaux III)

Anuari d'Angles (Barcelona)

APR / *American Poetry Review*

AQ / *American Quarterly*

AR / *Antioch Review*

ArAA / *Arbeiten aus Anglistik und Amerikanistik*

ARLR / *American Renaissance Literary Report*

ArmD / *Armchair Detective: A Quarterly Journal Devoted to the Appreciation of Mystery, Detective, and Suspense Fiction*

ArQ / *Arizona Quarterly*

ATQ / *American Transcendental Quarterly*

Baker Street Miscellany

BALF / *Black American Literature Forum*

BB / *Bulletin of Bibliography*

BC / *Book Collector*

Black Ice (Boulder, Col.)

BSUF / *Ball State University Forum*

BSWWS / *Boise State University Western Writers Series*

Caliban (Toulouse Le Mirail)

California History

CCTEP / *Conference of College Teachers of English Studies*

CCur / *Cross Currents*

CCV / *Cahiers Charles V* (Univ. de Paris VII)

CdS / *Corriere della Sera* (Milan)

CentR / *Centennial Review*

ChildL / *Children's Literature*

CIEFLB / *Central Institute of English and Foreign Languages Bulletin*

Cithara: Essays in the Judaeo-Christian Tradition

CLAJ / *College Language Assn. Journal*

CLC / *Columbia Library Columns*

ClioI / CLIO: A Journal of Literature, History, and the Philosophy of History
CLQ / Colby Library Quarterly
Clues: A Journal of Detection
CML / Classical and Modern Literature
CollL / College Literature
Columbia: A Magazine of Poetry and Prose
ConL / Contemporary Literature
Connecticut Review
Conradiana: A Journal of Joseph Conrad Studies
Costerus: Essays in English and American Language and Literature
CQ / Cambridge Quarterly
Cresset (Valparaiso, Indiana)
CRevAS / Canadian Review of American Studies
Crit / Critique: Studies in Modern Fiction
CritI / Critical Inquiry
Criticism: A Quarterly for Literature and the Arts
CS /Concord Saunterer
Cycnos (Univ. de Nice)
DicS / Dickinson Studies: Emily Dickinson (1830–86), U.S. Poet
DLB / Dictionary of Literary Biography
DNR / Dime Novel Roundup
Documentary Editing
DQ / Denver Quarterly
DR / Dalhousie Review
EAL / Early American Literature
EIC / Essays in Criticism (Oxford, England)
EigoS / Eigo Seinen (Tokyo)
EIHC / Essex Institute Historical Collections
EiP / Essays in Poetics: The Journal of the British Neo-Formalist School
EiT / Essays in Theatre
ELH / [formerly Journal of English Literary History]
ELN / English Language Notes
ELWIU / Essays in Literature (Western Ill. Univ.)
Enclitic
EONR / Eugene O'Neill Review

ESQ: A Journal of the American Renaissance
EuWN / Eudora Welty Newsletter
Expl / Explicator
Extrapolation: A Journal of Science Fiction and Fantasy
FCB / Flannery O'Connor Bulletin
FJ / Faulkner Journal
FNS / Frank Norris Studies
FSt / Feminist Studies
Genders
Genre
GN / Germanic Notes
GrandS / Grand Street
HC / Hollins Critic
HDN / H. D. Newsletter
HJR / Henry James Review
HLB / Harvard Library Bulletin
HLQ / Huntington Library Quarterly
HN / Hemingway Review
HofP / Horns of Plenty: Malcolm Cowley and His Generation
Horisont (Malmoe, Sweden)
HTR / Harvard Theological Review
Interspace (Nice)
Iowa Journal of Literary Studies
IowaR / Iowa Review
JAC / Journal of American Culture (Bowling Green State Univ. Press)
JADT / Journal of American Drama and Theatre
JAmS / Journal of American Studies
JASAT / Journal of the American Studies Assn. of Texas
JDN / James Dickey Newsletter
JEP / Journal of Evolutionary Psychology
JEthS / Journal of Ethnic Studies
JHI / Journal of the History of Ideas
JILS / Journal of Interdisciplinary Literary Studies
JMGS / Journal of Modern Greek Studies
JML / Journal of Modern Literature
JMMLA / Journal of the Midwest Modern Language Assn.
JNT / Journal of Narrative Technique
JPSP /Journal of Personality and Social Psychology
JSSE / Journal of the Short Story in English

JWMS / Journal of the William Morris Society
KAL / Kyushu American Literature
KR / Kenyon Review
L&P / Literature and Psychology (Teaneck, N. J.)
Legacy: A Journal of Nineteenth-Century American Women Writers
LFQ / Literature/Film Quarterly
LGJ / Lost Generation Journal
LHY / Literary Half-Yearly
LIT / Literature Interpretation Theory
LitR / Literary Review: An International Journal Devoted to English Studies
Mark Twain Circular
MD / Modern Drama
MELUS: The Journal of the Society for the Study of Multi-Ethnic Literature of the United States
MFS / Modern Fiction Studies
MHLS / Mid-Hudson Language Studies
MissQ / Mississippi Quarterly
MLQ / Modern Language Quarterly
MLS / Modern Language Studies
Mosaic: A Journal for the Interdisciplinary Study of Literature
MQ / Midwest Quarterly: A Journal of Contemporary Thought (Pittsburg, Kans.)
MR/ Massachusetts Review
MSEx / Melville Society Extracts
MStrR / Mickle Street Review
MTJ / Mark Twain Journal
Nabokovian
NCL / Nineteenth-Century Literature
NConL / Notes on Contemporary Literature
NCP / Nineteenth Century Prose
NDQ / North Dakota Quarterly
NEQ / New England Quarterly
NewC / New Criterion
NewComp / New Comparison: A Journal of Comparative and General Literary Studies
NHR / Nathaniel Hawthorne Review
NLA / La Nouvelle de langue anglaise (Univ. de Paris III)
NMW / Notes on Mississippi Writers
NOQ / Northwest Ohio Quarterly

NOR / New Orleans Review
Novel: A Forum on Fiction
NYRB / New York Review of Books
NYTBR / New York Times Book Review
Obsidian II: Black Literature in Review
OL / Orbis Litterarum: International Review of Literary Studies
OLR / Oxford Literary Review
Oregon Historical Quarterly
Paideuma: A Journal Devoted to Ezra Pound Scholarship
Palimpsest
P&L / Philosophy and Literature
PAPA / Publications of the Arkansas Philological Society
Parnassus: Poetry in Review
PBSA / Papers of the Bibliographical Society of America
Pennsylvania History
PLL / Papers on Language and Literature
Ploughshares
PMHB / Pennsylvania Magazine of History and Biography
PMLA: Publications of the Modern Language Assn.
PNotes / Pynchon Notes
PoeS / Poe Studies
PQ / Philological Quarterly (Iowa City, Iowa)
Prospects: An Annual Journal of American Cultural Studies
Proteus: A Journal of Ideas
PSA Newsletter / Poe Studies Assn. Newsletter
PubHist / Publishing History
PUUHS / Proceedings of the Unitarian Universalist Historical Society
QJS / Quarterly Journal of Speech
RANAM / Recherches Anglaises et Américaines
R&L / Religion and Literature
RCF / Review of Contemporary Fiction
REAL / RE Arts & Letters: A Liberal Arts Forum
Rendezvous: Journal of Arts and Letters (Pocatello, Idaho)
Representations
RES / Review of English Studies
Restant: Tijdschrift voor Recente

Semiotische Teorievorming en de Analyse van Teksten / Review for Semiotic Theories and the Analysis of Texts

Rev / *Review* (Blacksburg, Va.)

RFEA / *Revue Française d'Etudes Américaines*

RSA: *Rivista di Studi Americani*

SAF / *Studies in American Fiction*

Sage: *A Scholarly Journal on Black Women* (Georgia State Univ.)

Sagetrieb: *A Journal Devoted to Poets in the Pound-H.D.-Williams Tradition*

SAJL / *Studies in American Jewish Literature*

SALit / *Chu-Shikoku Studies in American Literature*

SAQ / *South Atlantic Quarterly*

SAR / *Studies in the American Renaissance*

SB / *Studies in Bibliography*

SBHC / *Studies in Browning and His Circle*

SBN / *Saul Bellow Journal*

SCR / *South Carolina Review*

SCRev / *South Central Review: The Journal of the South Central Modern Language Assn.*

SDR / *South Dakota Review*

Il Secolo XIX (Genoa)

SEEJ / *Slavic and East European Journal*

SELit / *Studies in English Literature* (Tokyo)

Seven: *An Anglo-American Literary Review*

SFS / *Science-Fiction Studies*

Shenandoah

ShLR / *Shoin Literary Review*

SHR / *Southern Humanities Review*

SJS / *San Jose Studies*

SLJ / *Southern Literary Journal*

SN / *Studia Neophilologica*

SNNTS / *Studies in the Novel* (North Texas State Univ.)

SoAR / *South Atlantic Review*

Social Text

SoQ / *Southern Quarterly*

SoR / *Southern Review*

SoSt /*Southern Studies*

SPAN: *Newsletter of the South Pacific Assn. for Commonwealth Literature and Language Studies*

SR / *Sewanee Review*

SSEng / *Sydney Studies in English*

SSF / *Studies in Short Fiction*

StAH / *Studies in American Humor*

La Stampa (Turin)

StQ / *Steinbeck Quarterly*

Style

SWR / *Southwest Review*

TCL / *Twentieth-Century Literature*

TJ / *Theater Journal*

TkR / *Tamkang Review*

TLe / *Théorie, Littérature, enseignement* (Univ. de Paris VIII)

TLS / (London) *Times Literary Supplement*

TPB / *Tennessee Philological Bulletin*

TPQ / *Text and Performance Quarterly*

TSLL / *Texas Studies in Language and Literature*

TUSAS / Twayne's United States Authors Series

TWN / *Thomas Wolfe Review*

UDR / *University of Dayton Review*

UMSE / *University of Mississippi Studies in English*

UTQ / *University of Toronto Quarterly*

VIJ / *Victorians Institute Journal*

VQR / *Virginia Quarterly Review*

WAL / *West American Literature*

W&I / *Word and Image: A Journal of Verbal/Visual Enquiry*

Witness (Farmington Hills, Mich.)

WMQ / *William and Mary Quarterly*

WS / *Women's Studies*

WSJour / *Wallace Stevens Journal*

WVUPP / *West Virginia University Philological Papers*

WWR / *Walt Whitman Quarterly Review*

YER / *Yeats Eliot Review*

YFS / *Yale French Studies*

YULG / *Yale University Library Gazette*

Publishers

Abrams / New York: Harry N. Abrams

Algonquin / Chapel Hill, No. Car.: Algonquin Books of Chapel Hill (div. of Workman Publishing)

Almquist and Wiksell / Stockholm: Almquist and Wiksell

Applause / New York: Applause Theatre Books

Ardis / Ann Arbor, Mich.: Ardis Publications

Arte Público / Houston, Tex.: Arte Público Press (div. of Univ. of Houston)

Athenäum / Frankfurt: Athenäum

Atheneum / New York: Atheneum (imprint of Macmillan Publishing Co.)

Barnes and Noble / New York: Harper & Row Publishers, Inc.

Benjamins / Philadelphia: John Benjamins North America, Inc.

Blackwell / Oxford: Basil Blackwell, Ltd.

Boise State / Boise, Idaho: Boise State Univ.

Bompiani / Milan: Gruppo Editoriale Fabbri, Bompiani, Sonzogno, Etas

Bouvier / Bonn: Bouvier

Bowling Green / Bowling Green, Ohio: Bowling Green State Univ. Popular Press

Calif. / Berkeley: Univ. of California Press

Cambridge / New York: Cambridge Univ. Press

Capra / Santa Barbara, Calif.: Capra Press

Carroll / New York: Carroll & Graf (dist. by Publishers Group West)

Catholic / Washington, D. C.: Catholic Univ. Press of America

Chelsea / New York: Chelsea House Publishers (div. of Main Line Book Co.)

Chicago / Chicago: Univ. of Chicago Press

Chronicle Books / San Francisco: Chronicle Books (div. of Chronicle Publishing)

Clarendon / Oxford: Clarendon Press

Columbia / New York: Columbia Univ. Press

Continuum / New York: Continuum Publishing Co. (dist. by Harper & Row Pubs., Inc.)

Cornell / Ithaca, N. Y.: Cornell Univ. Press

Da Capo / New York: Da Capo Press (div. of Plenum Publishing Corp.)

Delaware / Newark: Univ of Delaware Press (dist. by Associated Univ. Presses)

Duke / Durham, N. C.: Duke Univ. Press

Envoy / New York: Envoy Press

Erlbaum / Hillsdale, N. J.: Lawrence Erlbaum Associates

ETC / Palm Springs, Calif.: ETC Publications

Facts on File / New York: Facts on File, Inc.

Fairleigh Dickinson / Teaneck, N. J.: Fairleigh Dickinson Univ. Press (dist. by Associated Univ. Presses)

Farrar / New York: Farrar, Straus & Giroux, Inc.

Fawcett / New York: Fawcett Book Group (div. of Ballantine Books/ Random House)

Florida / Gainesville: Univ. of Florida Press

Fordham / New York: Fordham Univ. Press

Gale / Detroit: Gale Research, Inc. (subs. of International Thompson Publishing, Inc.)

Garland / New York: Garland Publishing, Inc.

Georgia / Athens: Univ. of Georgia Press

Greenwood / Westport, Conn.: Greenwood Press, Inc.

Grove / New York: Grove Press (dist. by Random House, Inc.)

Gunter Narr / Tübingen: Gunter Narr Verlag

Hall / Boston: G. K. Hall & Co. (div. of Macmillan Publishing Co.)

Harcourt / San Diego, Calif.: Harcourt Brace Jovanovich, Inc.

Harvard / Cambridge: Harvard Univ. Press

Hawaii / Honolulu: Univ. of Hawaii Press

Heath / Boston: Heath

Hodder / London: Hodder & Stoughton

Holt / New York: Henry Holt & Co. (subs. of Verlagsgruppe Georg Von Holtzbrinck)

Hopkins / Baltimore: Johns Hopkins Univ. Press

Houghton Mifflin / Boston: Houghton Mifflin Co.

Illinois / Champaign: Univ of Illinois Press

Indiana / Bloomington: Indiana Univ. Press

Institute / Williamsburg, Va.: Institute of Early American History and Culture (dist. by Univ. of North Carolina Press)

Iowa / Iowa City: Univ. of Iowa Press

Iowa State / Ames: Iowa State Univ. Press

I.U.O. / Naples: Istituto Universitario Orientale

Kansas / Lawrence: Univ. Press of Kansas

Kent State / Kent, Ohio: Kent State Univ. Press

Kentucky / Lexington: Univ. Press of Kentucky

Knopf / New York: Alfred A. Knopf, Inc. (subs. of Random House, Inc.)

Lehigh / Bethlehem, Pa.: Lehigh Univ. Press (dist. by Associated Univ. Presses)

Library of America / New York: Library of America (dist. by Viking Penguin, Inc.)

Little, Brown / Boston: Little, Brown & Co. (div. of Time, Inc.)

Living Batch / Albuquerque, N. M.: Living Batch Books (dist. by Univ. of New Mexico Press)

Locust Hill / West Cornwall, Conn.: Locust Hill Press

Loyola / Chicago: Loyola Univ. Press

LSU / Baton Rouge: Louisiana State Univ. Press

McFarland / Jefferson, No. Car.: McFarland & Co., Inc.

McGill-Queens: Toronto: McGill-Queens Univ. Press (imprint of Univ. of Toronto Press)

Macmillan / London: Macmillan Publishers, Ltd.

Maisonneuve / Washington, D. C.: Maisonneuve Press (div. of Institute for Advanced Cultural Studies)

Manchester / Manchester: Manchester Univ. Press (dist. by St. Martin's Press, Inc., subs. of Macmillan Publishing Co.)

Mass. / Amherst: Univ. of Massachusetts Press

Mass. Studies / Westfield, Mass.: Institute for Massachusetts Studies, Westfield State College

Meckler / Westport, Conn.: Meckler Publishing Corp.

Mellen / Lewiston, N. Y.: Edwin Mellen Press

Mercer / Macon, Ga.: Mercer Univ. Press

Methuen / New York: Routledge, Chapman & Hall, Inc.

Michigan / Ann Arbor: Univ. of Michigan Press

Mich. State / East Lansing: Michigan State Univ. Press

Minnesota / Minneapolis: Univ. of Minnesota Press

Miss. / Jackson: Univ. Press of Mississippi

Missouri / Columbia: Univ. of Missouri Press

Morrow / New York: William Morrow & Co., Inc. (subs. of Hearst Corp.)

NAL / New York: New American Library (subs. of Pearson, Inc.)

Nanundo (Tokyo)

Nebraska / Lincoln: Univ. of Nebraska Press

Nevada / Reno: Univ. of Nevada Press

New Directions / New York: New Directions Publishing Corp. (dist. by W. W. Norton & Co., Inc.)

New Engand / Hanover, N. H.: University Press of New England

New Mexico / Albuquerque: Univ. of New Mexico Press

Niemeyer (Tübingen)

No. Car. / Chapel Hill: Univ. of North Carolina Press

Noonday / New York: Noonday Books (imprint of Farrar, Straus & Giroux)

Northeastern / Boston: Northeastern Univ. Press

Northwestern / Evanston, Ill.: Northwestern Univ. Press

Norton / New York: W. W. Norton & Co., Inc.

NYU / New York: New York Univ. Press

Ohio / Athens: Ohio Univ. Press

Ohio State / Columbus: Ohio State Univ. Press

Okla. / Norman: Univ. of Oklahoma Press

Oxford / New York: Oxford Univ. Press, Inc.

Paulist / Mahwah, N. J.: Paulist Press

Penguin / New York: Penguin Books

Penn. / Philadelphia: Univ. of Pennsylvania Press

Penn. State / University Park: Pennsylvania State Univ. Press

Peter Lang / New York: Peter Lang Publishing, Inc. (subs. of Verlag Peter Lang AG [Switzerland])

Pittsburgh / Pittsburgh: Univ. of Pittsburgh Press

Praeger / New York: Praeger Publishers

Princeton / Princeton, N. J.: Princeton Univ. Press

Pustet / Regensburg: Verlag Friedrich Pustet

Putnam / New York: G. P. Putnam's Sons

Rodopi / Amsterdam: Editions Rodopi BV

Routledge / New York: Routledge, Chapman & Hall, Inc.

Rutgers / New Brunswick, N. J.: Rutgers Univ. Press

St. Martin's / New York: St. Martin's Press, Inc. (subs. of Macmillan Publishing Co.)

Scarecrow / Metuchen, N. J.: Scarecrow Press, Inc. (subs. of Grolier Educational Corp.)

Scribner's / New York: Charles Scribner's Sons

Simon & Schuster / New York: Simon & Schuster, Inc. (div. of Paramount Communications, Inc.)

Smithsonian / Washington, D. C.: Smithsonian Institution Press

So. Car. / Columbia: Univ. of South Carolina Press

So. Ill. / Carbondale: Southern Illinois Univ. Press

Stanford / Stanford, Calif.: Stanford Univ. Press

Steinbeck Society / Muncie, Ind.: Steinbeck Research Institute, Dept. of English, Ball State Univ.

Story Line / Santa Cruz, Calif.: Story Line Press

Susquehanna / Selinsgrove, Pa.: Susquehanna Univ. Press (dist. by Associated Univ. Presses)

Syracuse / Syracuse, N. Y.: Syracuse Univ. Press

Texas A & M / College Station: Texas A & M Univ. Press

Third World / Chicago: Third World Press

Ticknor and Fields / Boston: Ticknor and Fields

Tor / Carmel, Calif.: Tor House Press

Twayne / Boston: Twayne Publishers (imprint of G. K. Hall & Co., div. of Macmillan Publishing Co.)

UMI / Ann Arbor, Mich.: University Microfilms International (div. of Bell & Howell)

UMI Research Press / Ann Arbor, Mich.: UMI Research Press (affil. of UMI)

Undena / Shafter, Calif.: Undena Publications

Ungar / New York: Ungar Publishing Co.

Union / Schenectady, N. Y.: Union College Press

Univ. Press / Lanham, Md.: University Press of America

Unwin Hyman / London and Boston: Unwin Hyman

Vendome / New York: Vendome Press

Viking / New York: Viking Penguin, Inc.

Virginia / Charlottesville: Univ. Press of Virginia

Vision / London: Vision Books (dist. by St. Martin's Press, Inc.)

Washington / Seattle: Univ. of Washington Press

Wayne State / Detroit: Wayne State Univ. Press

Weidenfeld & Nicolson / New York: Weidenfeld & Nicolson (dist. by Random House)

White Rose / Memphis, Tenn.: White Rose Press

Whitston / Troy, N. Y.: Whitston Publishing Co.

Winter / Heidelberg: Carl Winter

Wisconsin / Madison: Univ. of Wisconsin Press

Wyndham Hall / Bristol, Ind.: Wyndham Hall Press

Yale / New Haven, Conn.: Yale Univ. Press

York / Fredericton, N. B., Can.: York Press

Part I

1. Emerson, Thoreau, and Transcendentalism

David M. Robinson

Nineteen eighty-nine will have to be reckoned a landmark year for studies of Emerson's early career. The first volume of his *Complete Sermons* appeared, along with four significant new monographs on his early development and a collection of new essays on his intellectual milieu, 19th-century Unitarianism. When this work is assimilated, it will change the grounds of our understanding of Emerson's development, and by implication the origins of Transcendentalism. The year's work was also marked by several significant studies of Emerson and Thoreau in what we might broadly term social and political contexts.

i. General Studies

Cornel West's history of American pragmatism, *The American Evasion of Philosophy: A Genealogy of Pragmatism* (Wisconsin), begins with a chapter on Emerson (pp. 9–41) as an "organic intellectual" committed to human empowerment, individual experiment, and a universe of flux, whose work carries significant political promise "as a form of cultural criticism." Although West is frank about the racial and cultural circumscriptions of the Emersonian "self," and the way his "moral criticisms" can become "politically impotent," these limitations do not overshadow the prophetic promise of the "Emersonian culture of creative democracy." West finds the key to Emerson's influence in his "evasion of epistemology-centered philosophy," an enabling act for the pragmatist tradition. Compelling as his portrait of the engaged Emerson is, it overlooks the epistemological fuel of some of Emerson's most significant work, for, as much of the best Emerson criticism has shown us, his philosophy developed through his intense interest in questions of perception—hardly the Dewey-like "evasion" of epistemology that West describes. Even so, West's philosophical concern for political and economic justice, his sense of Emerson's prophetic quality, and his incisive critique of Foucault's anti-utopianism, will make his book an influential contribution to the debate on Emerson's political availability. James Hoopes's *Consciousness in New England: From Puritanism and Ideas to Psychoanalysis and Semiotic* (Hopkins) ably traces the development and decline in New England of the "consciousness concept," the idea of consciousness as produced by or contained within a self. Hoopes argues that the rise of that concept had a major impact on the conception of conversion within Puritan Calvinism. The Transcendentalists, particularly Orestes Brownson ("the most philosophically acute thinker in America in the period between Edwards and Peirce"), extended the concept, hoping to collapse the barrier between self and God, thus reclaiming an earlier Puritan sense of humiliation in the Deity. Peirce, the key figure in Hoopes's narrative, countered the consciousness concept with the insistence that personality is the product of thought, and that "thought is not experienced or perceived but only inferred from signs." David Leverenz's *Manhood and the American Renaissance* is an engagingly written study of the literary patterns of accommodation and resistance to the definition of "male self-worth" through "work-place competition." Leverenz's sensitivity to gender-based power in relationships is demonstrated in brilliant analyses of Hawthorne and Stowe, but his thesis is not supple enough to account effectively for the spiritual vocabulary of Transcendentalism, and his impatience with such discourse narrows the range of his critical response—reading Emerson, he says, is like "body-surfing in the cosmos." "Experience," a benchmark text for Emerson studies (see Cavell, section *ii.b.*, below), is thus reduced to an essay of "self-avoidance," something "annoying, petulant, and evasive at almost every turn." Such lapses, however, do not overshadow Leverenz's generally attentive and revealing engagements with the texts. His depiction of the restricting definitions of manhood, more effective in his reading of fiction, is a useful contribution to the dialogue on gender and culture.

ii. Emerson

a. **Early Career.** Albert J. von Frank's edition of volume 1 of *The Complete Sermons of Ralph Waldo Emerson* (Missouri) presents the first 42 sermons (three more volumes are under way) with annotations, textual notes, and a detailed chronology for the years 1826–29, as Emerson rose from a supply preacher to minister of Boston's Second

Church. The sermons are presented in a clear-text version, based on editorial principles similar to those used in the *Early Lectures*. Most of Emerson's revisions were completed before his first delivery and are therefore incorporated in the texts, unless evidence places them after the initial delivery. My historical introduction to the *Complete Sermons* (pp. 1–32) attempts to locate the sermons in the context of the Unitarian pietist tradition and emphasizes Emerson's exposition of the doctrine of "probation" as part of the liberal response to Calvinism, and an initial step in his development of the doctrine of self-culture. Wesley T. Mott's *"The Strains of Eloquence": Emerson and His Sermons* (Penn. State), the first book-length critical study of the sermons, considers them "touchstones in [Emerson's] personal, vocational and literary growth" and effectively places them in the context of New England theological culture. Of particular importance is Mott's groundbreaking discussion of the gradual process by which Emerson adapted Unitarian discourse on the "internal evidences" of Christianity into a sense of the inward quality of religious truth. With this observation Mott further problematizes the Transcendentalist "break" with Unitarianism and qualifies Emerson's reputation as a mystic (for a contrasting view, see Hodder, below). Mott's Emerson is less an antinomian enthusiast than an inheritor of a more widely shared Puritan mission of balancing ecstasy and otherworldliness with an ethical imperative.

Mott notes that the ministry gave Emerson access to "rhetorical masks and personae that would veil his vulnerable real self." The psychological stress attendant on his assuming the vocation of his father and the consequent struggle for personal maturity are the subjects of Evelyn Barish's *Emerson: The Roots of Prophecy* (Princeton). Barish argues that the early death of his father left Emerson with an unresolved Oedipal struggle that largely accounts for the difficult and at times painful course of his early development. Barish has made perceptive use of the Emerson family letters, and her treatment of Mary Moody Emerson will confirm the growing consensus that she was Emerson's most crucial early intellectual model. Although Barish's depiction of Emerson's struggle with his father's legacy leads to some problems in relative emphasis, it is nonetheless a helpful model, if not pushed too hard. Barish expands Emerson's somewhat diffident attitude toward authority into sullen rebelliousness, and treats his adolescent fantasy writings ("fandango effusions," as Charles Emerson termed them) with too much high-serious prominence. But these cavils are minor when compared with Barish's larger accomplishments, which include her telling discussion of Emerson's battle with Hume (see also John Michael's related discussion, *ALS 1988*, pp. 8–9), and the integration of her valuable research into Emerson's tubercular condition (see *ALS 1982*, p. 9) with the other circumstances of his personal development.

Mary Kupiec Cayton's *Emerson's Emergence: Self and Society in the Transformation of New England, 1800–1845* (No. Car.) traces the evolution of Emerson's "cosmic organicism" from "the cultural hegemony of the social organicist ideal that Unitarianism represented." Cayton is in solid command of New England theological and social history, and persuasive in grounding Emerson in that context. But on an interpretive level, Cayton's tendency to reduce religious discourse to a form of masked politics is at points troubling, making Emerson too much the unwitting tool of the hegemonic order, his tradition a crippling rather than an enabling one. The complexity of 19th-century religious discourse generated moral imperatives that could be either crippling or liberating, a duality that does not correspond readily to divisions of social class. Thus when Cayton's description of theological development is keenest, as in her excellent account of Lyman Beecher's assault on Boston Unitarianism, I felt the limits of her argument most acutely. Cayton describes Beecherite Calvinism with overtones of populist insurgency, but also documents its rigid social conformity, leaving it a troubling alternative to Unitarian liberalism. Despite this difference over the political significance of religious forms, I was impressed with Cayton's sympathetic depiction of Emerson as a representative American intellectual struggling for "moral independence" in a culture that blinded one "to all but a self-defeating, very narrowly defined self-interest." In *Emerson's Rhetoric of Revelation* (Penn. State), Alan R. Hodder argues that *Nature* is best understood as Emerson's transferral inward of the biblical concept of apocalypse. Hodder's well-written study expands our sense of the range of Emerson's sources, but his rhetoric can become narrowing, as when he pairs the mystical roots of *Nature* against Emerson's early reading in science, emphases that are better seen as complementary. Hodder is generally less persuasive in accounting for the genesis of *Nature* than in describing its form—a "grainy texture" which rejects "continuous rhetoric," generating a dialectical reading experience that moves between mental self-possession and an "emptiness," or divesting, of the mind. This illuminating analysis might have been brought into closer dialogue with previous essays on the structure of *Nature*, such as those by Richard Lee Francis and Barry Wood (see *ALS 1967*, p. 14, and *ALS 1976*, p. 7).

The outpouring of interest in early Emerson and his milieu also included Sarah Wider's " 'Most Glorious Sermons': Anna Tilden's Sermon Notes, 1824–1831" (*SAR*, pp. 1–93), a transcription of week-by-week accounts of preaching at Channing's Federal Street Church, with a useful introduction and extensive notes. Wider focuses on Tilden's reactions to Emerson's preaching in "What Did the Minister Mean: Emerson's Sermons and Their Audience" (*ESQ* 34[1988]: 1–21), emphasizing the gaps between Emerson's intentions and Tilden's interpretations. Susan L. Roberson's "Beauty and the Soul: The Beginnings of Emerson's Aesthetics" (*JASAT* 19[1988]:23–33) describes the interplay between Emerson's religious and aesthetic development as revealed in the sermons, showing that the concept of the "man-made self" culminates both aspects of his thought. In "Emerson and the Spirit of Theory" (*R&L* 21, iii:17–42), Roger Lundin views Emerson's resignation from the ministry as a key enactment of the "Cartesian paradigm" of skepticism about all forms of "the Other." Lundin argues that this skepticism has conditioned much contemporary literary theory and proposes philosophical hermeneutics of Heidegger and Ricoeur as an alternative. In "Emerson's Sicily: History and Origins" (*ESQ* 34[1988]:23–36), Robert D. Richardson, Jr., examines Emerson's tour of Sicily, the first part of the journey which punctuated his break from the ministry, noting its preparatory function for the pivotal moment at the Jardin des Plantes in Paris. Richardson notes the imaginative influence of Plutarch in helping Emerson come into possession of his Sicilian experiences. In "Composing the World: Emerson and the Cabinet of Natural History" (*NCL* 44:18–44), Elizabeth A. Dant deepens our understanding of Emerson's experience at the Jardin des Plantes by perceptively explaining the cabinet of natural history as "a device that answered [Emerson's] desire to create a world-encompassing encyclopedic genre." Dant describes the lyceum movement as a cultural manifestation of the same impulse and traces Emerson's attempt to embody this principle in "The American Scholar." Robert Burkholder's "The Radical Emerson: Politics in 'The American Scholar' " (*ESQ* 34[1988]:37–57) dismantles quite convincingly Holmes's characterization of the address as our "intellectual Declaration of Independence"—"the finest bit of historical fiction that one can find in all of the venerable history of Emerson studies." Similar nationalist rhetoric, Burkholder finds, was standard for previous Phi Beta Kappa orations. In "Poetry, Personality, and the Divinity School Address" (*HTR* 82:185–99), I argue that Emerson's call for a poetic gospel answered a Unitarian search for religious emotion that would tally with that of evangelicalism. The most representative Unitarian response to the Divinity School Address was not the attack of Andrews Norton, but Henry Ware, Jr.'s defense of the personal deity, a critique that accelerated Emerson's exploration of the "soul" as a locus of his philosophy. In "Revisionism and the Structure of Emersonian Action" (*AmLH* 1:404–31), Richard Grusin offers welcome attention to Emerson's overlooked 1838 "Letter to President Martin Van Buren." The letter demonstrates Emerson's conception of action as representative and bipolar and provides Grusin with a basis for assessing recent interpretations of Emerson's political availability.

These essays on the maturing Emerson were complemented by several studies of *Essays: First Series*. In " 'The Turn of His Sentences': The Open Form of *Essays: First Series*" (*ESQ* 34[1988]:59–75), Martin Bickman describes the "turn" that denotes the structure of each essay, opening it to further self-reflexive analysis and preventing its "hardening" or premature closure. "Circles" with its "perpetual self-qualification and expansion" is an important exemplification of this pattern. My essay "Grace and Works: Emerson's Essays in Theological Perspective" (*American Unitarianism*, pp. 121–42) traces the interplay of grace and works as spiritual means in "Self-Reliance," "Spiritual Laws," and "The Transcendentalist," noting that in 1841–42 Emerson's reliance on ecstatic experience was becoming increasingly problematic. In "Two Gardens: Emerson's Philosophy of History" (*The Green American Tradition*, pp. 21–38), Richard Hutson argues perceptively that *Essays: First Series* "may be understood as Emerson's philosophy of history." In correcting the assumption that Emerson is ahistorical, Hutson locates Emerson's grounding in "the memory of the New England town," which functioned for him imaginatively as an ideal community and formed the basis of his assessment of contemporary reform movements. In "A Dialogue with Death: An Examination of Emerson's 'Friendship'" (*SAR*, pp. 219–39), George Sebouhian finds that Emerson was "not cool and distant" as his reputation suggests, but a man whose relationships were colored by the repeated losses of loved ones and the resulting conviction that experience is "transitional." This argument provides Sebouhian with a different perspective on the Emerson-Fuller friendship—it was Fuller, and not Emerson, who was attempting to make friendship an idealized and static concept.

b. **Later Career and Influence.** Most notable among the work on later Emerson was *This New Yet Unapproachable America: Lectures After Emerson and Wittgenstein* (Living Batch), Stanley Cavell's engagement with "Experience," a "breakthrough" essay in its articulation of Emerson's struggle with skepticism. Cavell sees the essay's "recommendations to ignorance" as crucial "not as an excuse but as the space, the better possibility, of our action." Cavell plays the essay's elegaic strand against its projection of possibilities, arguing that the "testament" of "Experience" is "young Waldo's promise, as kept or founded in the old Waldo." Cavell is Emersonian in his interest in the stimulative possibilities of the text, which in plainer language means that he sometimes takes a passage beyond what I think can be reasonably inferred about Emerson's intentions—most notably in a strained tracing of the essay's images of pregnancy. But these excursions always—well, almost always—are worth the detour. I found most intriguing the way that the form of Cavell's lectures echoes that of "Experience" in a progression from proposed solution to attendant dilemma in a seemingly endless progression. Of related interest is Michael Fischer's *Stanley Cavell and Literary Skepticism*, a discussion of Cavell's relation to recent literary theory, and Charles Crittenden's "The Suchness of Things: In Zen Buddhism, American Transcendentalism and Ordinary Language Philosophy" (*Zen in American Life and Letters*, pp. 51–67), which aligns Zen Buddhism with Cavell's earlier synthesis of the Transcendentalists and Wittgenstein. In "Emerson's Rhetoric of War" (*Prospects* 12[1987]:293–320), Michael Lopez uses Foucault's description of 19th-century discourse on the individual to argue that a "philosophy of power" was Emerson's defining characteristic. Lopez cautions against an overly literal interpretation of Emerson's extravagant and aggressive rhetoric, noting its relation to his self-conception as an artist, and its relevance to modern discourse on the problem of the "self." In "De-Transcendentalizing Emerson" (*ESQ* 34[1988]:77–139), Lopez cogently describes the uneasiness in recent criticism about "claims to unity or resolution" in Transcendentalist discourse—the "de-transcendentalizing" of Emerson, as Lawrence Buell has termed it. Lopez situates Emerson in the larger context of Hegelian philosophy and suggests that Emerson be reconceived as a "post-idealist." Two important essays by Christina

Zwarg focus on later Emerson texts in light of the Emerson-Fuller friendship. In "Emerson as 'Mythologist' in *Memoirs of Margaret Fuller Ossoli*" (*Criticism* 31:213–33), Zwarg uses Emerson's biographical account of Fuller to show how they found in each other important mutual self-representation. "Fuller's plight as a female critic was not only filled with difficulty, but also," Emerson discovered, "much like his own." In "Emerson's 'Scene' Before the Women: The Feminist Poetics of Paraphernalia" (*Social Text* 18[1987–88]:129–44), Zwarg examines Fuller's impact on Emerson's address to the Woman's Rights Convention of 1855, a reversal of "the assumption even among feminist critics . . . that Emerson held sway over Fuller." Zwarg notes that the speech was "one of the first lectures in support of the woman's movement to be given by a major literary figure" and offers a persuasive account of the significance to feminist theory of Emerson's belief "that you do not liberate women by giving them the 'freedom' of men." Zwarg's essays give us a subtler and more engaged Emerson than we have realized, and a much more challenging Fuller. In "Emerson's *English Traits*: 'The Mechanics of Conversation' " (*ATQ* n.s. 3:153–67), Benjamin Goluboff explains how Emerson's ambivalence about England was transmuted through his conversational form into a "creative dialogue on British civilization." David W. Hill's "God, Wolf, and Law: Emerson's Indeterminant 'Fate' " (*ESQ* 34[1988]:229–55) is a well-informed explanation of the structural movement of "Fate," from its emphasis on fate as limit to a changing stress on fate as power, and finally to Emerson's articulation of a "self-conscious sensitivity to apparent opposites." Although I think Hill gives undue emphasis to the essay's references to Norse mythology, he is astute in tracing the compositional layers of the essay and unwilling to reduce them to a simple linear progression. Students of late Emerson should also take note of Ronald A. Bosco's " 'Poetry for the World of Readers' and 'Poetry for Bards Proper': Theory and Textual Integrity in Emerson's *Parnassus*" (*SAR*, pp. 257–312), an instructive examination of the tangled problem of "Emerson's precise role" in editing the collection. Bosco's work has wide importance because *Parnassus* presents an extreme form of a problem with many later Emerson texts. Bosco adduces the close relation of "Poetry and Imagination" to *Parnassus* and calls attention to that essay as "the unrecognized fullest statement by Emerson of poetic theory."

Len Gougeon's broadly informed "Emerson, Carlyle, and the Civil War" (*NEQ* 62:403–23) traces Emerson's and Carlyle's increasingly divergent views on slavery, which eventuated in Emerson's public denunciation of Carlyle's position in his 1863 lecture "Fortune of the Republic." Gougeon emphasizes the sense of abandonment that Emerson and other New England intellectuals felt over the lack of English support for the Civil War. In a related essay, "Emerson, Poetry, and Reform" (*MLS* 19:38–49), Gougeon argues that a series of forgotten poems published in an antislavery annual represent Emerson's initial reaction to the Fugitive Slave Act. It was the actual arrest of slaves somewhat later that prompted his impassioned address of 1851. Further information on Emerson's complicated relation to the reform movements is brought forward in Irving H. Bartlett's "The Philosopher and the Activist: New Letters from Emerson to Wendell Phillips" (*NEQ* 62:280–96), which illustrates how Phillips nudged the sometimes obtuse Emerson along in progressive causes. Nina Baym's "Early Histories of American Literature: A Chapter in the Institution of New England" (*AmLH* 1:459–88) is a thorough and critical account of the construction of a late 19th-century narrative of "the virtues and achievements of an Anglo-Saxon United States founded by New England Puritans." Noting the importance accorded to Emerson in this narrative, Baym comments that Emerson's "centralization is not, as many present-day Americanists believe, a twentieth-century construction." S. Nagarajan's "Emerson and Advaita: Some Comparisons and Contrasts" (*ATQ* n.s. 3:325–36) argues that despite clear affinities, Emerson's philosophy lacks the attention to practical discipline central to Advaita.

Emerson continues to be a magnet for influence studies such as Virginia M. Kouidis's "Prison into Prism: Emerson's 'Many-Colored Lenses' and the Woman Writer of Early Modernism" (*The Green American Tradition*, pp. 115–34), which traces "Emerson's relevance to the woman writer," with reference to Kate Chopin, Dorothy Richardson, Marianne Moore, and Mina Loy. George J. Leonard ("Emerson, Whitman, and Conceptual Art," *P&L* 13:297–306) argues that Emerson anticipated conceptual art's denigration of the importance of the object. Another essay linking Emerson to the modern visual arts is Ralph F. Bogardus's "The Twilight of Transcendentalism: Ralph Waldo Emerson, Edward Weston, and the End of Nineteenth-Century Literary Nature" (*Prospects* 12[1987]:347–64), which finds Weston an intellectual "heir" to "transcendentalism in general, and Emerson in particular." The most instructive comment on Emerson's modern influence, though I would have wished for a fuller exposition, was Charles Simic's "Visionaries and Anti-Visionaries" (*DQ* 24:114–23), which portrays Emerson, whether endorsed or rejected, as the key influence in American poetry. Simic is most interested in the "visionary skeptics," Dickinson, Frost, and Stevens, who "accept Emerson's experience [in *Nature*] but not his interpretation."

iii. Thoreau

Much of the year's work on Thoreau concentrated on historical reconstructions of his milieu, intellectual and social, with an important cluster of studies investigating his contribution to ecological thinking. Leonard N. Neufeldt's *The Economist: Henry Thoreau and Enterprise* (Oxford) persuasively places Thoreau's works within his culture's larger discourse on "enterprise," stressing his "appropriation and manipulation of economic vernacular." Neufeldt traces Thoreau's struggle to redefine the language, and thus the values, embodied in the flourishing genres of the ethical guidebook and success manual, and points out the "serious parody" of this discourse in *Walden*. One of Neufeldt's most significant accomplishments is to redirect us to *Walden* as an economic document; a corollary of this emphasis is the elevation of "Life Without Principle" as the key successor to *Walden* among Thoreau's works. Neufeldt's demonstration of Thoreau's achievement in "refashioning words and displacing meanings," a tactic which I find characteristic of the work of Emerson and Fuller as well, is an important extension of the political availability of the entire Transcendentalist movement. Beneath the surface of Neufeldt's study is the sense of Thoreau's personal struggles with vocation and success, a narrative opened further in his " 'We Never Agreed . . . in Hardly Anything': Henry Thoreau and Joseph Hosmer" (*ESQ* 35:85–107). Neufeldt finds that Thoreau's 1852 journal comments on the "hearteating" entrapment of rural life, exemplified in his boyhood friend Hosmer, suggest the layers of complexity in Thoreau's view of his presumably beloved Concord countryside. I found Robert Sattelmeyer's account of the cooling of another friendship, " 'When He Became My Enemy': Emerson and Thoreau, 1848–49" (*NEQ* 62:187–204), informative and quite moving. With the help of a fragmentary journal of 1848–49, Sattelmeyer locates the crisis point in the friendship at Emerson's return from his lecture tour of England. Unspoken tensions had been building throughout the 1840s, but these were exacerbated by Emerson's "sense of his own success in the world" after the

tour, Thoreau's complicated sympathies for Lidian, and his overly
sensitive rejection of Emerson's apparent attempt to voice their difficulties directly. This article will, I believe, attain status as one of the
classic essays in our field. I was also hooked by Sattelmeyer's " 'The
True Industry for Poets': Fishing With Thoreau" (*ESQ* 33[1987]:189–
201), which presents a more genial Thoreau at ease with the fishermen
around Concord, but struggling with inner conflict about the social
and psychological implications of fishing. Sattelmeyer provides an
informative discussion of fishing as cultural practice and a persuasive
account of its pivotal role at key moments in *Walden*. Bait fishermen
and other humble folk will take heart at his description of Thoreau's
fishing for trout with sapling poles and salt pork. Walter Harding's
"Thoreau's Text and Murphy's Law" (*ESQ* 33[1987]:202–10) is an informative and at points amusing account of the history of the editing
of Thoreau, with Franklin B. Sanborn the story's chief villain. Harding's essay will make teachers grateful for the new paperback edition
of the Princeton *Walden*, with J. Lyndon Shanley's authoritative text.
Francis B. Dedmond's " 'Many Things to Many People': Thoreau in
His Time and Ours" (*BSUF* 30:60–69), the keynote address at Ball
State's 1986 Thoreau Symposium, offers an overview of the changes in
Thoreau's reputation, contrasting the political readings of Thoreau's
significance with several recent psychological studies. In "Thoreau,
Slavery, and Resistance to Civil Government" (*MR* 30:535–65), Barry
Kritzberg surveys Thoreau's growing antislavery involvement, ex-
plaining how the Anthony Burns case led Thoreau to doubt the ade-
quacy of individualism as a response to the crisis. Kent Ljungquist
(" 'Meteor of the War': Melville, Thoreau, and Whitman Respond to
John Brown," *AL* 61:674–80) finds that Thoreau's depiction of Brown's
career was affected by newspaper accounts of meteor activity after
Brown's arrest. Henry Petroski's *The Pencil: A History of Design and
Circumstance* (Knopf [1990]) contains an interesting description of
an often-overlooked aspect of Thoreau's life, his innovation and skill
as a pencil-maker.

Three essays, in addition to those of Neufeldt and Sattelmeyer discussed above, suggest the growing critical importance of Thoreau's
Journal. In "Roots, Leaves, and Method: Henry Thoreau and Nineteenth-Century Natural Science" (*JASAT* 19[1988]:1–22), William
Rossi analyzes an 1851 entry in which Thoreau pursues the analogy of
the dual development of the plant, in branches and root, and of the
mind, with its penetrating roots of knowing. Rossi effectively places

the discussion in the context of Thoreau's struggles with the growing positivism of 19th-century science, seeing Thoreau's metaphor of the search for deeper meaning as an alternative conception of scientific knowledge comparable to Polanyi's conception of knowledge as "indwelling." In "Killing Time/Keeping Time: Thoreau's Journal and the Art of Memory" (*The Green American Tradition*, pp. 39–57), H. Daniel Peck argues that the *Journal* is not, as Perry Miller decribed it, a shield for Thoreau's retreat from public failure, but "a kind of surrogate memory" which attained its value through its potential for "commemorating experience." Thoreau's *Journal* becomes the battleground between epistemologically and politically oriented criticism in David S. Gross's "Deconstruction and the Denial of Meaning: On Sharon Cameron's *Writing Nature: Henry Thoreau's Journal*" (*Genre* 21[1988]:93–106). Gross commends Cameron's presentation of the *Journal* as "fluid, complex, problematized," but argues that "her interpretive strategies obscure social and ideological issues of great concern to Thoreau."

Thoreau's continuing cultural influence is the subject of Lawrence Buell's "The Thoreauvian Pilgrimage: The Structure of an American Cult" (*AL* 61:175–99), a groundbreaking consideration of "canonical investment" in terms of the structure of a religious pilgrimage. Buell describes the historical process by which Concord and Walden Pond have become sacralized, and Thoreau himself invested with sainthood, a development informed by "the interlinked values of pastoralism and counter-culturalism." Buell's essay helps explain Thoreau's continuing presence in ecological thinking, and the corresponding presence of ecological concern in Thoreau criticism. Buell's sense of the cultural reverence for the Walden area is confirmed in Thomas Blanding's "Historic Walden Woods" (*CS* 20[1988]:3–74), a survey of the history of the Walden Woods area and the cultural significance of its connection to Thoreau. In "American Pastoral Ideology Reappraised" *AmLH* 1:1–29), Buell proposes a useful frame of reference for the intersection of ecological and literary concerns by critically reconsidering recent assessments of the American pastoral as "conservative and hegemonic." Buell argues instead for the "ideological multivalence" of the pastoral, noting that it includes both consensual and oppositional qualities. Thoreau is one of a wide range of pastoral writers who suggest that in our present cultural situation the pastoral will "take on increasingly radical forms for some time to come." The oppositional qualities of Thoreau's work are confirmed in several ecologically oriented studies of larger American cultural trends. In a useful charting of recent ecological discourse, *The Rights of Nature*, Roderick Frazier Nash describes Thoreau's "unprecedented" formulation of an environmental ethic which by implication extended "rights" into nature. In *Ecological Revolutions*, an impressive study of two revolutions in land-use changes in New England's history, Carolyn Merchant finds ecologically important elements of animism in Thoreau's consciousness and calls his work "a wide-ranging radical critique of the market revolution." Thoreau is also given prominence in Thomas J. Lyon's *This Incomperable Lande*, which includes an important taxonomy and historical survey of nature writing. In "Deriving a Biocentric History: Evidence from the Journal of Henry David Thoreau" (*Environmental Review* 12[1988]:117–26), Robert Kuhn McGregor sees Thoreau's journal as both a source and an example for a new history informed by a "biocentric world view."

iv. The Transcendentalist Movement

The interest in Emerson's genesis was supplemented by several important essays in *American Unitarianism* that probe the doctrinal continuum between Unitarianism and Transcendentalism. Perhaps the most revisionary of these is Lilian Handlin's "*Babylon est delenda*— the Young Andrews Norton" (pp. 53–85), an essay which presents Norton without his usual black hat, an embattled liberal and ultimately a "defeated radical," who had failed to convince his Unitarian colleagues of the necessity of an aggressive confrontation with Calvinism early in the century. Handlin's essay complicates the received view of Norton as a rigid conservative and effectively delineates some of the internal complexities of the liberal movement. Conrad Wright ("Institutional Reconstruction in the Unitarian Controversy," pp. 3–30) calls attention to institutional changes in such areas as pulpit exchange, Christian fellowship, ecclesiastical councils, and church-parish relations which conditioned the later theological debates of the Transcendentalist Controversy. Wright's essay is grounded in an examination of parish controversy in Dorchester. Joseph Conforti ("Edwardsians, Unitarians, and the Memory of the Great Awakening, 1800–1840," pp. 31–52) demonstrates how the shadow of the Great Awakening colored the Unitarian perception of Orthodoxy, conditioning its reaction to Transcendentalism. Like Cayton (see above), Conforti stresses the importance of Lyman Beecher's evangelical crusade in Boston. Daniel Walker Howe ("The Cambridge Platonists of Old England and the Cambridge Platonists of New England," pp. 87–120) traces a pietistic strand within liberalism to the Cambridge Platonists, arguing convincingly that later Unitarians "*made use*" of this tradition in their project of theological reformation. This element of liberalism "helped lay the groundwork for the reception of the philosophy of Kant by the Transcendentalist Unitarians," an observation that qualifies Emerson's characterization of Transcendentalism as a new surge of idealism. Jane H. Pease and William H. Pease ("Whose Right Hand of Fellowship? Pew and Pulpit in Shaping New England Practice," pp. 181–206) offer a valuable portrait of the divided social ethic of 19th-century Unitarian congregations, noting that "entrepreneurially oriented and powerfully elite congregations generated responses at odds with a denomination understood to be socially progressive and theologically innovative." Gary L. Collison ("'A True Toleration': Harvard Divinity School Students and Unitarianism, 1830–1859," pp. 209–37) uses records of two student groups, the Philanthropic Society and the Debating Society, to describe the atmosphere of intellectual vitality and growing social activism at Harvard Divinity School during the Transcendentalist Controversy. Collison sees the school as central to the progressive evolution of Unitarianism, and Henry Ware, Jr., emerges as "a model of toleration and progressive sympathies." Lawrence Buell ("The Literary Significance of the Unitarian Movement," pp. 163–79) argues that literary scholars, like late-19th-century Unitarian historians, often "reduce early Unitarian discourse to aesthetic impressionism." Ironically though, this image of a purely literary Unitarianism has not altered the more general tendency to treat it as "a benighted state of cultural privation from which the really important New England writers had to break away in order to accomplish anything interesting." The collection also includes valuable bibliographical essays by Peter Drummey ("Materials at the Massachusetts Historical Society for the Study of Unitarian History," pp. 241–51) and Alan Seaburg ("Unitarian Resources at Harvard University," pp. 253–61).

Further focus on the Unitarian context was included in Guy R. Woodall's investigation of "Convers Francis, The Transcendentalists, and the Boston Association of Ministers" (*PUUHS* 21:41–48), which reveals Francis's general dismay with the more conservative Unitarian reactions to Transcendentalism, and helps identify in more detail the leaders of the resistance to it. Woodall's "William Henry Furness'

Remarks on the Four Gospels in the '*Annus Mirabilis*' " (*ATQ* n.s. 3: 233–44) adds further detail on the emergence of Transcendentalism from its Unitarian context with a consideration of the argument and reception of Furness's controversial book. Woodall explains that Furness regarded the biblical miracles as real, but not "evidences" of Christianity, a position that accords with Mott's description (see above) of the Unitarian theory of "internal" evidences of Christianity. Leonard Neufeldt's " 'Self-Culture': Ein Grundbegriff der Unitarier in der ersten Hälfte des 19. Jahrhunderts" (*Gott und Politik in U.S.A.*, pp. 257–77—text in German) surveys and extends recent scholarly work on Unitarian and Transcendentalist conceptions of self-culture, with particular emphasis on its development from religious into ethical and political discourse.

Robert Gross's "The Machine-Readable Transcendentalists: Cultural History on the Computer" (*AQ* 41:501–15) is commendable for both its stimulating description of an important experiment in teaching (I would wish for more such discussions of innovative teaching) and its contribution to our sense of 19th-century Concord's social patterns. He describes how computer analyses of the 1850 census of Amherst and Concord reveal patterns of family life, householding, and consumption, and cogently explains the relevance of such information to the cultural context of Transcendentalism. There were two significant articles on Fuller in addition to the essays by Zwarg and Seboulian noted above. In " 'A Tale of Mizraim': A Forgotten Story by Margaret Fuller" (*NEQ* 62:82–104), Jeffrey Steele identifies with what seems to me a conclusive attribution Fuller's only known short story, one of a series that she had projected on Hebrew history. Robert N. Hudspeth's solid assessment of Fuller's critical achievement in " 'A Higher Standard in Thought and Action': Margaret Fuller and the Idea of Criticism" (*American Unitarianism*, pp. 145–60) reminds us that her writing on feminism and social issues was possible because of her development of "a coherent critical vision." Hudspeth notes that given her restricted vocational alternatives, Fuller became a literary critic "almost by default," but found in the work "intellectual freedom" and "a potent means of self-culture." Francis B. Dedmond's edition of "The Selected Letters of William Ellery Channing The Younger (Part One)" (*SAR*, pp. 115–218) includes a thorough introduction, chronology, calendar of Channing's extant letters, and detailed annotations. Dedmond's selection gives us more information on the complex web of friendships among the Transcendentalists, and some sense of Channing's troubled personality. Another new source of insight into the Concord world is *The Journals of Louisa May Alcott*, ed. Joel Myerson and Daniel Shealy (Little, Brown), which includes a solid introduction (pp. 3–39) by Madeleine B. Stern. In "The Peabody Family and the Jones Very 'Insanity': Two Letters of Mary Peabody" (*HLB* 35[1987]:218–29), Helen R. Deese presents Mary Peabody's sympathetic accounts of Jones Very after his discharge from McLean Asylum, which suggest that Very's sense of being persecuted was not entirely without foundation. Deese describes the tangled situation of Very's texts, and her procedure in editing them, in "The Presumptuous Task of Editing the 'Holy Spirit': The Jones Very Edition" (*Documentary Editing* 11:5–9). Alfred G. Litton's "The Development of the Mind and the Role of the Scholar in the Early Works of Frederic Henry Hedge" (*SAR*, pp. 95–114) views "Conservatism and Reform," with its stress on authority and social involvement, as an alternative to the Emersonian view of the scholar and helpfully weighs the significance of several essays that preceded it. The letters in Mathew Fisher's "Emerson Remembered: Nine Letters by Frederic Henry Hedge" (*SAR*, pp. 313–28), occasioned by James E. Cabot's preparation of the Emerson *Memoir*, include Hedge's memorable description of the Transcendental Club—"no club, properly speaking, no organization, no presiding officer, no vote ever taken on any question."

Oregon State University

2. Hawthorne

Frederick Newberry

An extraordinary number of fine studies appeared in 1989, led by Luther S. Luedtke's book on Oriental influences in Hawthorne's work. The larger merit of Luedtke's work emerges from his suggesting the cultural dimensions of New England's cultivated knowledge of Oriental literature and lore. Luedtke therefore historicizes Oriental matters once taken for granted in Hawthorne's New England but less available to us over the years through oversight or neglect. Such historicizing distinguishes most if not the best Hawthorne scholarship in 1989. Theorizing, apart from historical contexts, was definitely out. Facts—and extrapolations from them—were in. Likewise, *The Marble Faun* entirely gave way to *The Blithedale Romance*. In this regard, the work of Lauren Berlant, Robert S. Levine, Jonathan Auerbach, and Richard Brodhead deserves special mention. In recent years, of course, *Blithedale* has steadily assumed greater importance in the canon; but because of these four writers the gap between it and *The Scarlet Letter* for preeminence is appreciably narrowed. Perhaps Robert Browning's estimation of the novel will achieve widespread endorsement after all. Finally, two splendid essays by Lauren Berlant, part of a forthcoming book that promises to be a milestone, should be singled out.

i. General Studies

a. **Books.** Original and meticulous in scholarship, Luther S. Luedtke's *Nathaniel Hawthorne and the Romance of the Orient* (Indiana) reorients our assumptions about Hawthorne's imaginative geography from the privileged Occidental world to the "mysterious east." Indeed, Luedtke's Hawthorne reveals our ignorance of manifold Oriental sources of western fables and myths, an ignorance not shared by Hawthorne's contemporaries or seafaring ancestors. Relating the travel journals of Hawthorne's father to the fantasies and reading of young Nathaniel, Luedtke delineates and documents the sources of Oriental references and allusions throughout Hawthorne's works. A crucial implication of Hawthorne's eastern lore bears upon his conception of fantasy: his fairyland, like that of Spenser and later romantic poets, owes considerable debt to such works as *The Arabian Nights*. Luedtke therefore historicizes Hawthorne's attraction to the Orient through popular 19th-century exploration accounts, travel narratives, and scholarship on the East. Most interpretive applications of this research are convincing. In "Rappaccini's Daughter," for example, the Islamic *Jannat al Ferdaws* must surely be a pretext for the garden's sensuous imagery; and the Arabian manuscripts that foreground *Secretum Secretorum, or, De Regimine Principum* contain the original poisoned damsel motif. Other valuable source readings are those on "The Wives of the Dead," "Drowne's Wooden Image," and the major novels—most richly, *The Blithedale Romance*. The Oriental influences in *Fanshawe*, however, seem strained.

Regrettably unrewarding, Edward Wagenknecht's *Nathaniel Hawthorne: The Man, His Tales and Romances* (Continuum) has no thesis, no declared critical approach, no sustained or cogent analysis—whether old or new. The opening biographical chapter seems perfunctory, while the next two chapters, devoted to familiar tales and the four novels, merely review critical studies of the 1960s and 1970s. For example, in discussing eight historical tales (in 17 pages), Wagenknecht ignores the contributions of Michael J. Colacurcio on all eight. This neglect, combined with plot summaries and a distillation of Wagenknecht's 1961 book in the last chapter, lends the impression that the book is uncommonly dated. Even as an introduction to Hawthorne for uninformed readers it lacks the reliability of Terence Martin's revised *Nathaniel Hawthorne* (TUSAS 75, 1983). The exception is Wagenknecht's chapter on the unfinished romances, which, for its brevity, offers a judicious overview of Hawthorne's waning powers.

Elissa Greenwald's *Realism and the Romance: Nathaniel Hawthorne, Henry James, and American Fiction* (UMI Research Press) poses an odd difficulty, because it frequently scraps its generic methodology. Greenwald says Richard H. Brodhead's *The School of Hawthorne* (1986) "has deeply influenced" her but, while its "focus is on the cultural significance of the Hawthorne-James relation," her "concerns are more formalistic." Though such concerns may obtain in some dim or finely nuanced way, Greenwald more often sacrifices attention to formalistic strands for the interlacing of paired works and the unifying of sequential parts of her thesis—that Hawthorne and James exploit a psychological zone between romance and novel. Greenwald does have sparkling insights on separate novels; and she presents more fully than anyone else the four stages in James's evolving, complicated views of Hawthorne. Still, for a coherent analysis of the link between Hawthorne and James, Brodhead's book remains unchallenged.

Emily Miller Budick's *Fiction and Historical Consciousness* devotes four chapters and additional commentary to Hawthorne, with excellent readings of "Young Goodman Brown," "Roger Malvin's Burial," and *Gables*. Budick posits that "American historical romances insist on the reality of history and society in order to cast doubt on the mind's autonomy and to force the imagination to consider something outside itself." That "something" in "Roger Malvin's Burial" is the quotidian world ignored by Reuben in favor of an inherited biblical typology that leads to psychic collapse. When Reuben returns to the scene of Malvin's death, he fails to see "the differences that prevent likeness from being sameness." He becomes a false historian, as does Goodman Brown, who, failing to question the demonic affiliation of his ancestors, evidently believes their specters are strictly for his own moral intellection. History may indeed be spectral, but proper history "does not abandon the world to the solipsistic self-indulgence and egocentrism of an ahistorical Goodman Brown." Through Brown, Hawthorne rejects Puritan literalizations and self-righteousness by means of a sympathy and Christian charity lacking in the Puritans. With such readings, Budick returns to a moral criticism, sometimes equaling that of Colacurcio, to whom she is indebted.

Frederick Crews has permitted reissue of his 1966 *The Sins of the Fathers: Hawthorne's Psychological Themes* (Calif.), for which he provides an afterword (pp. 273–86) assessing the strengths, weaknesses, and relevance of the book both then and now. As he has made clear in several essays since 1975, Crews no longer subscribes to the circular logic and reductiveness of Freudian "pseudoscience." In *Sins*, of course, Crews incurred an appreciable debt to Freud, passing up, he now thinks, "an opportunity to pursue determinate biographical considerations [in Hawthorne's life] as opposed to dogmatizing about the universal Oedipus complex." While cautioning a younger generation of critics against Freudian reductiveness, he clearly closes the gap between himself and Roy Male in their once notorious debate. If he were to rewrite the book he would now "insist on Hawthorne's diffidence, slyness, and suggestiveness"; and he would "give less attention to the author's putative struggle with his unconscious and correspondingly more to his deliberate toying with his readers' expectations, . . . the extraordinary self-control with which he simultaneously manipulated literary conventions and ironically distanced himself from them." This psychic and literary command is precisely the point of Budick (above) and Auerbach (below).

b. **Essays.** The year's most hyperbolic essay is Evan Carton's " 'A Daughter of the Puritans' and Her Old Master: Hawthorne, Una, and the Sexuality of Romance" (*Daughters and Fathers*, pp. 208–32), which begins, "Tortured family relations and ambivalent representations of women are the heart of Hawthorne's fiction and have supplied the lifeblood of its critical history." Many readers would disagree with this essentialist reduction and with excesses in Carton's methodology. For example, quoting Hawthorne's remark from the preface to *Snow-Image* that "You must make quite another kind of inquest, and look through the whole range of [an author's] fictitious characters, both good and evil, in order to detect any of his essential traits," Carton declares, "Hawthorne writes 'good and evil' here, but he implies, and might more revealingly have written, 'male and female.' " No such implication exists. But Carton needs a rhetorical purchase for an analysis of what he proposes is Hawthorne's divided sexuality, read particularly in Hawthorne's relationship with Una, wherein father sees in daughter his own inconsistent nature. In arguing that Hawthorne enjoys and then denies an intimacy with Una but without specifying the conduits of that intimacy, Carton wrenches texts to plumb Hawthorne's supposed neuroses. A reduced version of the essay appears as "Paternal Guilt and Rebellious Daughters: Hawthorne, Una, and *The Marble Faun*" (*EIHC* 125:92–103).

Of the two chapters on Hawthorne in David Leverenz's *Manhood and the American Renaissance*, "Devious Men: Hawthorne," pp. 227–58, is printed for the first time. Leverenz says middle-class writers like Hawthorne struggled with contemporaneous definitions of manhood derived from competition and the market economy. In several stories and *Blithedale*, Leverenz traces "Hawthorne's fascination with malice and humiliation"; and, sometimes wiser than Carton, he does not find guilty self-reflection in Hawthorne so much as in us. Hence, in trying to discover a sexual secret in Parson Hooper after the example of Poe, we aggressively violate men possessing "quasi-female sympathy"; and Hawthorne's text, by way of Milton, "indicts" our own complicity, guilt, and sin. "In so doing, Hawthorne dramatizes the entrepreneurial ideology of manhood he found all about him. . . . From 'My Kinsman, Major Molineux' through *The Scarlet Letter,* Hawthorne builds his tales around spectacles of public humiliation, as strong men collectively try to shame weaker, yet nobler individuals." But having suggested that Hawthorne always exceeds our prescience, Leverenz, like Carton, pushes on to discover neurosis at the root of Hawthorne's insight: in this case, the fear of homosexual rape. Hence the old story of Hawthorne's having slept with Uncle Robert Manning in that terribly narrow bed. This unnecessary tack sullies Leverenz's otherwise extraordinary reading of Hawthorne's mind and craft.

Gentle, half-aware of the scholarship, and rather marvelously immune to the acrimonious debate, James J. Waite in "Nathaniel Hawthorne and the Feminine Ethos" (*JAC* 11, iv[1988]:23–33) joins an earnest squad (mostly male enlistees) in defense against feminist-minded attacks on Hawthorne's treatment of women. He also enters another skirmish by asserting that Hawthorne expresses his commendably androgynous nature in a "singular concern [for] women," a concern that "never diminished his own masculinity." Though I'm inclined to agree on both counts, the fray is a long way from being over and the outcome uncertain.

In the best treatment of the subject to date, Alfred H. Marks's "Hawthorne, Tieck, and Hoffmann: Adding to the Improbabilities of a Marvellous Tale" (*ESQ* 35:1–21) details, through Scott and others, the influence of Ludwig Tieck and E. T. A. Hoffmann on several tales, *The Marble Faun,* and Hawthorne's art of the romance generally. Tieck helped Hawthorne to shape his fiction and critical theories, and Hoffmann provided "an elastic definition that fits not only with Hawthorne's association of romance and retelling but also with almost every statement Hawthorne made on the *romance.*" Remarkably lucid and sensible, Michael Dunne's "Varieties of Narrative Authority in Hawthorne's *Twice-Told Tales* (1837)" (*SoAR* 54, iv:33–49) undertakes the fullest analysis yet of Hawthorne's early narrative techniques, focusing on the eight tales not recounted by first-person or "quasi-omniscient third-person narrators."

Another essay focusing on Hawthorne's consummate control, John McWilliams's "The Politics of Isolation" (*NHR* 15, i:1–7), will persuade almost everybody that Hawthorne exploits his isolation, self-deprecation, and literary marginalization as a maneuver to emphasize his centrality. Skillfully analyzing Hawthorne's use of "idle," McWilliams adds a formidable voice to the revisionist argument that Hawthorne held immense respect for his profession and his own craft. Fritz Gysin's "Paintings in the House of Fiction: The Example of Hawthorne" (*W&I* 5:159–72) sets out to examine Hawthorne's use of painting from the vantage of Wendy Steiner's definition of *ecphrasis*. But the reader is led away from this definition through one errant shift after another. Gysin nevertheless presents a fascinating cinematic reviewing of the Judge's death scene in *The House of the Seven Gables*, and he gives a perceptive reading of the moment when Colonel Pyncheon's portrait falls on its face: "Holgrave, the artist, unwillingly becomes the agent of the portrait's curious self-execution."

Alfred Weber's "The Outlines of 'The Story Teller,' the Major Work of Hawthorne's Early Years" (*NHR* 15, i:14–19), radically distills his 1972 monograph on the same subject, arguing for the circumstances, aim, and contents of Hawthorne's aborted third collection of tales, "a framed story-cycle of a special kind." To read from disparaging and inaccurate points of view that Hawthorne saw himself as "the artist of Puritanism" does not augur well for Susan Manning's "Nathaniel Hawthorne" (*CQ* 17:109–25). Manning archly refuses Hawthorne admission to the pantheon of great writers because of his limited vision, intellectual poverty, and failure to touch real experience. But with an anomalous turnabout, she finds in Hawthorne's complex perspectives a wisdom for our time: his "prose substitutes for the diversity of actuality a dense verbal texture which re-establishes the imaginative relations of observation to belief, and so sustains the complexity of human possibility against the puritan polarities from which it springs."

ii. Essays on the Novels

a. The Scarlet Letter. In "Hester's Revenge: The Power of Silence in *The Scarlet Letter*" (*NCL* 43:465–83), Leland S. Person, Jr., probes the major characters' exploitation of silence for power and revenge. Arguing for the formative effects of Hester's silent complicity in Chillingworth's plot, Person sees Hester as a disguised though active seeker of power and punishment through whom Hawthorne can sublimate "his own desire to enact revenge upon his political enemies, the Salem Whigs." Exceedingly well done, the argument nevertheless requires some caution, as when Person says "it is reasonable to examine the novel itself for traces of revenge," because it was written soon after Hawthorne had lost his job and because he had vowed revenge on those responsible. Hester's refusal to name Dimmesdale at the outset is not really much different, then, from her failure to disclose Chillingworth's identity: both result in a vengeful punishment of her lover. But, on Hester's part, no motive is offered for Hester's act—indeed, Person says all of her motives are secret. We seem left with a presupposition that Hester should want revenge because her creator does.

Cynthia S. Jordan's "Inhabiting the Second Story: Hawthorne's Houses," in *Second Stories*, pp. 152–79, argues that Hawthorne "equates his own verbal art ... with unofficial and subversive accounts of American experience—at times, literally with 'feminine' modes of creative expression." Unlike Person, Jordan views Hester's opening silence as a "safer mode of self-defense," a "double victimization ... both culturally and self-imposed." Like Person, Jordan sees Hester complying with patriarchal power, unfortunately transmitting to Pearl the lessen to "hush" and thus compromising Hawthorne's cultural hope for mutuality of the sexes. Crucial new readings of familiar scenes highlight Jordan's uneven essay. She connects Dimmesdale's patriarchal triumph in his election sermon to Chillingworth's when the leech sees the minister's breast. And no one, I think, has noticed before Jordan that while recalling his parents, Dimmesdale witnesses "maternal estrangement" when his mother turns away, prefiguring the reactionary choice to deny his feminine side in favor of patriarchal control.

Differing with Person and Jordan, Richard Hull, " 'I Have no Heavenly Father': Foucauldian Epistemes in *The Scarlet Letter*" (*ATQ* n.s. 3:309–23), claims that "for Hester to have named Dimmesdale would have vindicated the classical confidence" of the Puritans that iniquity could be exposed. "But in demonstrating that Puritan authority is powerless to expose iniquity, she demonstrates the modern opacity of relations." Much else appears in this valuable study of Hawthorne as a "harbinger" of Foucault in representing three historical epistemes of language. Edward Schamberger's "The Failure of 'a citty upon a hill': Architectural Images in *The Scarlet Letter*" (*EIHC* 125:9–23) erratically fulfills its promise, but the historical data on Salem's customhouse save the essay from familiarity.

In a book arguing compellingly against the validity of formal distinctions between novel and romance, William Ellis's "The Case of

Hawthorne: History, Manners and the Idea of Community," in *The Theory of American Romance*, pp. 105–13, discusses form and movement in *The Scarlet Letter* to support A. N. Kaul's thesis on the realistic, communitarian American novel. My "A Red-Hot *A* and a Lusting Divine: Sources for *The Scarlet Letter*" (*NEQ* 60[1987]:256–64) submits sources for Hawthorne's potential knowledge of a woman in Maine who, while married to a former Puritan minister associated with adulterous behavior, had a cheek branded with an "A"; the novel's references to the letter's heat and its being a brand may therefore have been based on fact. Well-researched in possible sources but occasionally strained in their application, David C. Cody's " 'The Dead Live Again': Hawthorne's Palingenic Art" (*ESQ* 35:23–41) proffers the pseudoscience of palingenesis (the resurrection of once living things from their ashes) as the creative impetus for reviving the past in "The Custom-House." The relevance of palingenesis to "Ethan Brand," however, is certain. Aladar Sarbu's "The Topicality of *The Scarlet Letter*," in *Americana & Hungarica*, pp. 35–55, raises familiar issues, mostly in dialogue with critics two and more decades ago. David Van Leer's "Hawthorne's Alchemy: The Language of Science in *The Scarlet Letter*," in *Nature Transfigured*, pp. 102–20, is an admitted extract from a previous essay (see *ALS* 85); but with Van Leer's new introduction, the case for Hawthorne's seeing scientific language as a disastrous influence on modern discourse acquires cogency.

b. **The House of the Seven Gables.**   A good piece of historical scholarship, David H. Watters's "Hawthorne Possessed: Material Culture and the Familiar Spirit of *The House of the Seven Gables*" (*EIHC* 125:25–44) delivers actual 17th-century chairs on which the Pyncheon chair is based. Watters explores the chair as "a mediator between seventeenth- and nineteenth-century attitudes toward the armchair as a signifier of authority," and he opposes the comfortable, contemporaneous symbolism of such artifacts with the novel's republican stance toward status, matrilineal descent, and history as a narrow teleology. Drawing from "the cult of domesticity and the particular conventions of the domestic novel," Susan Van Zanten Gallagher's "A Domestic Reading of *The House of the Seven Gables*" (*SNNTS* 21:1–13) essays with moderate success to re-create the context within which Hawthorne's contemporaries could appreciate the novel as his best work.

c. **The Blithedale Romance.** Perhaps nothing more outstanding has been written on *Blithedale* than Lauren Berlant's "Fantasies of Utopia in *The Blithedale Romance*" (*AmLH* 1:30–62). The essay examines how the metaphor of the "unwedded bride," the "virgin's untouched hymen," reflects a personal fantasy of life as a failed emplotment of love and how this fantasy was implicated in a collective vision of hope and failure that existed in American historiography at the outset of Puritan experience. Both failures derive from the "masculine libidinal will to power," no matter how unconscious or well-intended. In one way or another the principal characters are all motivated by personal love, suggesting that Coverdale is not so eccentric after all. Though Berlant identifies the theories of Fourier behind the novel's personal and communal love plots, her treatment of John Eliot's relation to American utopian experiments may be the essay's finest contribution. Eliot's story is Coverdale's "touchstone," providing the rationale for Berlant's "historical archaeology," an excavation of the kinship shared by Hollingsworth and Eliot. Devoted to a principle of love, both are motivated by a preexisting personal commitment translated into power. This theoretical and practical convergence becomes the monstrous in Hollingsworth so appalling to Coverdale. Hence the tragic "trajectory of history that relies fully on the personal story," and hence too Coverdale's feelings that "utopia is a totalitarian state." One of Berlant's several concluding insights is that "Coverdale's reading of his love plot, evident in his juxtaposition of the 'hitherto unwedded bride' with the buried events of American history, is that its failure grows from the failure of American political praxis to appropriate and incorporate his, and others', visionary passion; his retrospective bitterness about the failure of Fourierism on the farm grows from his inability to find an alternative discourse to that of love within which he might even imagine gratification." This essay must become required reading on *Blithedale*.

Robert S. Levine's "'A Confusion of Popish and Protestant Emblems': Insiders and Outsiders in Nathaniel Hawthorne's *The Blithedale Romance*," in *Conspiracy and Romance*, pp. 104–64, historicizes the novel within antebellum movements notable for conspiratorial fears expressed by nativist anti-Catholics. Responding to countersubversive strategies in convent literature, *Blithedale* converts the utopian experiment into a typical conflict between Protestant-democratic insiders and subversive Catholic outsiders. Hollingsworth, the priestly outsider, has "the mesmerical powers that anti-Catholic alarmists

ascribed to priests in the confessional." Through infiltration and seduction, he seeks to establish a subcommunity of converts, in accord
with a plot of flight and entrapment. Coverdale, the countersubversive
confessor, intends to protect innocent Priscilla from Zenobia, the
"lascivious nun," and from priest-crafty Hollingsworth and Wester-
velt. A host of double identities, the characters finally enact Protestant-
Catholic, conservative-revolutionary tensions hearkening back to the
regicide of Charles I and to the Reformation generally. Levine's essay
is an important addition to the novel's historical moment and memory.

Equally significant in observing the historical context of *Blithedale*, Richard Brodhead's "Veiled Ladies: Toward a History of Antebellum Entertainment" (*AmLH* 1:273–94) concentrates on Priscilla as
a medium through which to notice the mid-century moment when
certain women appeared in the public limelight from behind domestic
veils, accompanied by proleptic showbiz managers. The "Veiled Lady
registers the creation of a newly publicized world of popular entertainment taking place simultaneously with the creation of a newly
privatized world of woman's domestic life." Manipulated by Wester-
velt for public viewing, Priscilla can be likened to Jenny Lind and
Fanny Fern, whose public selves were managed respectively by P. T.
Barnum and the Mason Brothers. Brodhead admits that Hawthorne
"shows no grasp of the enabling side of the publicity that he knows as
new at this time," but he establishes Hawthorne's awareness that
women writers and performers successfully won a massive audience
because they satisfied vicarious desires of deprived, intimidated, and
inhibited individuals. *Blithedale* records, even if it does not understand, how the entertainment industry develops from a privatized domestic ideal of woman that creates the need for a spectatorial entertainment in the "consumable form of *other* or *represented* life."

Jonathan Auerbach's "Hawthorne's *The Blithedale Romance* and
the Death of Enchantment," in *The Romance of Failure*, pp. 71–117,
cogently investigates Coverdale's first-person narrative as it implicates
Hawthorne's "best efforts at self-concealment" and "his inability to restore enchantment [of literary romance] to its proper place" in a world
of appearances forbidding access to the human heart. Drawing from
Michel Butor, Auerbach pronounces the psychological criticism on
Coverdale's unreliability as a spurious distraction from "the main
point of Hawthorne's preface, namely, that fiction can offer only the
illusion of mimesis, not mimesis itself, and that the search for an ideal

congruence therefore is bound to fail." We have no special vantage from which to determine the validity of Coverdale's troubling narrative, because "his is the only story we have." Whereas the characters' masked, multiple roles problematize interpretation, they nevertheless constitute Hawthorne's "realistic" effort to confront epistemological questions influential on later writers. Since Coverdale is unable to live the Blithedale experiment, his self-alienating focus on writing itself "is part of a larger problem of alienation at Blithedale that extends beyond the first person's unique responsibilities as narrator; . . . for the first person is a form particularly well suited to dramatize the dangers of an all-consuming 'I.'" Though risking his own entrapment, Hawthorne expresses the need to resist self-reflexivity through the failure of Blithedale and a unified narrative, both of which are a product of egotism. Auerbach's study demands the attention of all readers who would approach the novel's central concerns.

Challenging the equation of Coverdale's hostility to women's ambitions with Hawthorne's own, Robert Miles's "*The Blithedale Romance*, Rousseau, and the Feminine Art of Dress" (*TSLL* 31:215–36) intelligently argues that the novel "offers a self-conscious critique of 'gender,' by seeing it as mutable, as something not only subject to discourse, but *as* discourse." Finding useful similarities between *Blithedale* and Rousseau's *Émile*, Miles notes how Zenobia's choice of dress disrupts her observers' efforts to read her body, producing "a moment of 'aporia' in which the feminine art of dress, and its imprisoning discourse, is reduced to a shambles"—a fallout akin to the collapse of characters in Coverdale's narrative. On behalf of Zenobia and Coverdale, Hawthorne is perfectly aware of both moments through his sensitivity "to the play and power of language"; and because of this awareness he more nearly represents the historical conditions that create misogyny than he does his private, "proper person" who may mistrust feminine aspirations.

Less provocative but of interest, Ken Egan, Jr.'s, "Hawthorne's Anti-Romance: *Blithedale* and Sentimental Culture" (*JAC* 11, iv:45–52) argues that Hawthorne implicitly criticizes Coverdale for adhering to a sentimental genre from which some women writers had already broken free. Of special note is Egan's equating the novel's cultural critique with Andrew Jackson Downing's biting comments on the pastoral, "cottage house" vogue of architecture in the antebellum period. Mason I. Lowance's "Hawthorne and Brook Farm: The

Politics of *The Blithedale Romance*" (*EIHC* 125:65–91) amounts to
a refresher course in the lures and dangers of drawing analogies between the novel (including Hawthorne's preface) and actual experience. Excepting Lowance's belief that the representations of characters show Hawthorne's sensitivity to women's rights, the essay
treads familiar ground. Quite problematically, Mark Holland's "Miles
Coverdale: Hawthorne's Presentation of the *Puer Aeternus* Arche-
type" (*JEP* 9, March:17–24) proposes that Coverdale suffers "under
the negative influence of the *puer*," whereby his desire to mature and
achieve artistic success is thwarted by childish fantasy and the mother
complex. Coverdale continually experiences a vicious circle of *puer*
entrapment, which Holland analyzes in three scenes.

iii. Essays on Major Tales

According to John N. Miller's "The Pageantry of Revolt in 'My Kinsman, Major Molineux' " (*SAF* 17:51–64), the story "demands no allegorical or elaborate historical exegesis." Almost literally, albeit richly,
Miller examines the tale's trifold pattern of revolts against authority,
rationality, and familial control. Hawthorne "reveals no intention of
exploring the guilt or morality of revolution in American history, or
of preaching the importance of historical consciousness," though Miller also affirms that "to recognize the historical and political basis of
the story is to protect its experiential complexity against the imposition
of timeless allegorical constructs." Miller unmasks the carnivalesque
"insurrection" against Robin's rationality as it parallels Boston's grotesque rebellion against the Major. Overall, "whether formalized into
Puritan processions, corrupted into the counterfeit merriment of aging Maypolers, or conscripted for nocturnal mob rebelliousness, pageantry in Hawthorne's historical fiction has lost its ritual innocence
and become noticeably different from festive celebrations of older
civilizations." Aside from Miller's treatment of the Old-World associations of the carnivalesque, the arguments and historicizing have
been anticipated by Q. D. Leavis, Peter Shaw, Colacurcio, and me.

Dennis Pahl's "The Poison of Interpretation: Giovanni's Reading
of Rappaccini's Daughter," in *Architects of the Abyss*, pp. 59–77,
dwells on epistemological uncertainty, providing no access to character or events. Pahl concludes that in "attributing the original authorship of the story to Aubépine (a fictional self), Hawthorne . . . places

himself in the position of translator of his 'own' work," which makes the story "but another of his many 'twice-told' tales." Hence, Pahl draws a metacritical reduction: the story is an infinitely regressive series of unauthored texts.

In challenging counterpoint, John Downton Hazlett's "Re-reading 'Rappaccini's Daughter': Giovanni and the Seduction of the Transcendental Reader" (*ESQ* 35:43–68) succeeds in untangling the tale's epistemological and narrative points of view. Hazlett says "the tale's allegory . . . concerns the difference between art and life. In art . . . writers and their audiences establish symbolizing conventions to unravel narrative or aesthetic meaning, but in real life, we apply these same conventions only at our peril." Hawthorne's target is a fideistic or a transcendental habit of equating outward appearance with inward reality. Giovanni's resistance to a heterodox, gothic version of this habit is actually a narrative trap promoting the equation. The tale's editor (Hawthorne himself) affords vantage of the narrator's accessory commission of "manslaughter," in the performance of which he and other men in the tale use transcendental "fancy" and literary conventions to kill a woman whose inward reality remains largely unavailable to them.

Contrarily, George E. Haggerty's "Hawthorne's Gothic Garden," in *Gothic Fiction/Gothic Form*, pp. 105–37, investigates Hawthorne's unequaled divination of mental regions that earlier practitioners of the Gothic scarcely approached. But Haggerty discovers no locus from which to moralize on "Rappaccini's Daughter" because the true gothic horror resides not so much in the tale as in our world and our minds. Hawthorne's ambiguous allegory therefore depends on "the limitless reaches of our own private worlds." The essay's decided strengths are jeopardized by a tendency to claim too much, such as "Hawthorne's fictional method centers . . . on that area of experience the Gothic novelists first examined"—an incautious reduction in the manner of Carton (above). And it seems to me too insistent in dismissing historical and psychological explanations in order to substitute its own subjective one. I would especially quarrel with the statement that "it has taken so long for historical readings to be introduced [into readings of Hawthorne's fiction] because history is lost in subjective response, and that is as Hawthorne thinks it should be." It may well be, as several writers who have been mentioned in this chapter allow, that much of Hawthorne's fiction seems intent on warning against epistemological and psychological dangers of self-reflexivity. But as Haggerty evidently sees it, Hawthorne's gothicism has no serious philosophical or theological moorings.

My "The Biblical Veil: Sources and Typology in Hawthorne's 'The Minister's Black Veil'" (*TSLL* 31:169–95) submits the origins of Hawthorne's information on the Reverends Samuel and Joseph Moody upon whom Parson Hooper is modeled. Beyond sources, the essay examines the implications of Hooper's veil from the vantage of the Old and New Testaments, especially 2 Cor. 3:7–17. I caution against Colacurcio's exclusive emphasis on the Great Awakening context of the tale. Hooper's literalistic investment in Puritan typology and historiography represents Hawthorne's critique of Puritanism generally, an exaggerated reification of Israel in the service of its errand and millennial expectation. Thus Hooper's misguided adoption of the Mosaic veil "amounts to a profound anachronism whose emphasis on the Old Adam essentially renounces the availability of redemption through Christ's only historical appearance."

Conceivably the best essay on Hawthorne in 1989, Lauren Berlant's "America, Post-Utopia: Body, Landscape, and National Fantasy in Hawthorne's *Native Land*" (*ArQ* 44, iv:14–54) rivals Colacurcio's treatment of "Alice Doane's Appeal" as it sweepingly undertakes a multi-eral historicizing of the "National Symbolic," defined as "the order of discursive practices whose reign within a national space performs, and also refers to, the 'law' in which the accident of birth within a geographic/political boundary transforms individuals into subjects of a collectively-held history." Berlant begins analyzing the dynamic of symbolic acculturation consistent with the Statue of Liberty, deriving implications for "transcoding the national scene along gender lines," which, in conjunction with spatial considerations, provides "a powerful relay between the utopian and the political prospects of national identity." While the process of the National Symbolic homogenizes individual and group differences through a conception of America as a neutral territory removed from political activity, "Hawthorne's expression of the Nation is a search to create a space of cultural critique that is not appropriable by the will-to-absorb-difference or contradiction that characterizes a dominant strain of liberal-idealist 'utopian' ideology." Thus Berlant opposes Sacvan Bercovitch's thesis that Hawthorne is a consensus liberal. A salient point indicative of Berlant's complex examination of the tale is this: "As with the Statue of Liberty, discourse about history, society, and knowledge is organized around the nonrepresentability of Alice, her discourse, her impassive hymen; it passes through her, she embodies it as she is disembodied by it through her non-representation in the configuration of the national narrative."

Ellen E. Westbrook's "Probable Improbabilities: Verisimilar Romance in Hawthorne's 'The Birth-mark' " (*ATQ* n.s. 3:203–17) separates the mixed narrative conventions in the tale, predictably arriving at the unexciting conclusion that they portray a world licensed by romance. Georgiana is "a near-perfected representative of our imperfect sisters," while Aylmer is "a near-perfected representative of our less imperfect brothers." Also unexciting, A. James Wohlpart's "The Status of the Artist in Hawthorne's 'The Artist of the Beautiful' " (*ATQ* n.s. 3:245–56) revives the romantic issue of the artist as divine creator in order to argue that both Owen and his butterfly are really part of this humanly tainted world.

Sometimes tough to read, Alan O. Weltzien's "The Picture of History in 'The May-Pole of Merry Mount' " (*ArQ* 45, i:29–48) undertakes a valuable deconstruction of the ofttold stories and histories that appear in the multiple and intermixed generic sections of the tale, giving privileged attention to the middle (ostensibly historical) narrative that leaves Edith and Edgar suspended between jollity and gloom. Although taking the historical studies of the tale seriously, Weltzien finally believes that "historical actuality recedes behind multiple acts of narration." But, unlike Haggerty (above), he does not wish to elevate story at the expense of history, or, indeed, to feel obliged to take sides in any of the tale's allegorical contests. Instead, he aims to negotiate a mediation between them by "redefining history as story, and story as the potential meeting ground, if not marriage, of history and romance, the actual and the imaginary." With such a marriage, he concludes, "the moment time imprisons timelessness, and lends it thereby some structure, is the moment life and great art both become possible."

iv. Miscellaneous

Admirably researched and poised, Jean Fagan Yellin's "Hawthorne and the American National Sin," in *Green American Tradition*, pp. 75–97, gathers a wealth of old and new evidence for Hawthorne's knowledge of black slavery and probes his averting the subject of slavery in his works, as well as his potentially disbelieving in the humanity of blacks. Hawthorne's failure to analyze his racial responses is, says Yellin, inconsistent with his self-scrutiny in relation to other pressing issues of his time. While Hawthorne's distrust of reformers generally and abolitionists particularly must explain a measure of his evasion, Yellin suggests, drawing on a passage in "Chiefly About War Matters," that the only way Hawthorne could imaginatively appreciate the significance of slavery was by projecting himself into the future from whence to consider it in the past.

Clearing up confusion begun last century, James Bense's "Nathaniel Hawthorne's Intention in 'Chiefly About War Matters'" (*AL* 61:200–214) peels away the layers of scholarship and primary evidence to reveal the existence of footnoted commentary in the essay before James T. Fields asked for deletions before *Atlantic* publication. Hawthorne originally conceived the essay "in great part as a censorship hoax," creating an ironic framework in which to represent censorship at a passionate moment of national crisis and to "illustrate the dialectic of freedom of speech."

Rita K. Gollin's " 'Pegasus in the Pound': The Editor, the Author, Their Wives, and *The Atlantic Monthly*" (*EIHC* 125:104–22) is an admirable investigation of Nathaniel's and Sophia's personal and professional relationship with James T. and Annie Fields in the early 1860s. From correspondence and other sources, Gollin argues that Sophia and the Fieldses did their utmost to provide an environment in which Hawthorne might write and maintain his health. Despite the falling out between Sophia and the Fieldses after Hawthorne's death, Gollin believes that Fields himself was always generous to Hawthorne in friendship, practical and financial support, and encouragement to produce, even if his motives may have occasionally included the pecuniary. Margaret B. Moore's "Hawthorne and the Five-Dollar School" (*Publication of the Philological Association of the Carolinas* no. 6:1–9) details the reputation of Samuel Archer, Hawthorne's schoolmaster in Salem (1819–20), the curriculum of the school, and the possible influence Archer had on Hawthorne's attending college.

Richard Boyd's "The Politics of Exclusion: Hawthorne's *Life of Franklin Pierce*" (*ATQ* n.s. 3:337–51) evidently takes "political" and "partisan" to be synonymous, invalidly calls on Colacurcio and Brodhead in support of this grafting, insupportably charges Hawthorne with incessantly indulging in strident political rhetoric, and yet, if one tones down the exaggerations, makes a plausible case for Hawthorne's having been so intent on saving the federal union through moderation that he implicitly commits in his rhetoric—his indirect attacks on abolitionists—the same kind of sacrificial violence that the mob commits on the scapegoat effigy of Lady Eleanore in the tale bearing her name.

Thomas Woodson's "Sophia Hawthorne's Diary for June 1861" (*NHR* 15, ii:1–5) includes an extract from the full diary of 1861, along with an exemplary preface suffused with helpful facts and contexts for the diary's cryptic entries. Also exemplary, Gary Scharnhorst's " 'Now You Can Write Your Book': Two Myths in Hawthorne Biography" (*NHR* 15, ii:6–9) briefly but meticulously unravels the authority and lack thereof for Sophia's buoyant response to Hawthorne's dismissal from the Custom House and for the existence of an autobiographical memorandum sent by Hawthorne to R. H. Stoddard. Although Julian Hawthorne has been faulted for fabricating the facts involved in both instances, Scharnhorst finds the accounts somewhat reliable. In "Divine Childhood in the Hawthorne Household" (*EIHC* 125:45–54), T. Walter Herbert, Jr., traces the evolution of the Hawthornes' unworldly marriage to the production of Una whom, until the terrible twos, the parents saw as a reflection of romantic purity but then came to see as a worldly creature of mystifying origins. Through this latter image of the child, and through Sophia's description of her, Herbert unites Una with the conception of Pearl more convincingly than anyone else.

Essaying to discover characters' motives to vivify or revivify "dead materials," William Crisman's " 'The Snow-Image' as a Key to Hawthorne's Biotechnology Tales" (*ATQ* n.s. 3:169–87) tracks fascinating parallels between "Snow-Image" and several tales. Though written later, and though having biographical roots that Crisman ignores, "Snow-Image" fills in "the gaps of childhood experience that Hawthorne's tales of mature biotechnical experimentation merely hint at or simply suppress." One of these gaps is the childlike urge to re-form a mother's "willingness to acknowledge her children by abandoning her exclusive claim to creation." A problem with the essay as it stands is Crisman's finessing the classification of "Drowne's Wooden Image" under the rubric of biotechnology tales, to which his rhetoric implicitly confesses. Mary Jane Hurst's "The Language of Children in 'The Snow-Image' " (*EIHC* 125:55–64) credibly relates the behavior and speech of Hawthorne's children to those of Violet and Peony, affirming the tale's original place in American fiction owing to the dependence of plot and theme on the nonsexist discourse of children.

A profitable reevaluation of Hawthorne's so-called minor tales, Michael Dunne's "Diegesis and the Narrative Voice in Hawthorne's 'Foot-prints on the Sea-shore'" (*TPB*, 26:30–37) claims that Hawthorne's pronouns, verb tenses, and direct addresses to the narratee create "an illusion of equivalent reality for the narrator and the reader." This reality anticipates Gérard Genette's *diegesis*—the encompassing voice synonymous with fiction. Ronald St. Pierre's "'The Married of Eternity': Hawthorne's 'The Wedding-Knell'" (*ShLR* 20 [1986]:87–10) is a limited New Critical reading of "a marriage of 'immortal souls' who in marrying turn away from worldliness, triumph over the funereal aspects of marriage and mock both life and death by passing beyond the limits of Time and entering the realm of Eternity."

A timely essay on a disregarded work, Laura Laffrado's "'If We Have Any Little Girls among Our Readers': Gender and Education in Hawthorne's 'Queen Christina'" (*ChildL* 17:124–34) argues that "the life of Christina overcomes the gender-based rigidities" of the story's narrator, who allows Hawthorne to mediate his own ambivalence over Christina's gender-based isolation but also to tell "a personal truth: that miseries awaited one whose education led toward estrangement from society, perhaps as an artist, perhaps as a woman." Laffrado's "Fear of Cultural Excision: Narration as Rhetorical Strategy in 'The Gorgon's Head'" (*NHR* 15, i:7–11) discovers adult seriousness in yet another of Hawthorne's children's stories: "Hawthorne uses sight in 'The Gorgon's Head' to illustrate the movement from inexperience (blindness) to the ability to 'see,' to control one's own narration, become one's own author." Laffrado has fine insights on the story's Chinese box of narrators and their authority.

Duquesne University

3. Poe

Benjamin Franklin Fisher IV

The year's work once again reveals the diversity pervasive in the Poe world. Books are few, criticism of the poems scanty. Gothicism and the detective fiction draw repeated attention, as do several less familiar nonfictional works, which provide bases for illuminating studies.

i. Textual, Bibliographic, Attribution Studies

Richard Kopley has passed along responsibilities for compiling the valuable "International Poe Bibliography" to Susan F. Beegel, who ably compiles that for 1988 (*PoeS* 22:10–21). Burton R. Pollin also continues a familiar line of research in "Poe's Word Coinages: Supplement II" (*PoeS* 22:40–42), which, listing 36 new items, brings his total to 1,063.

"Outis" (see *ALS 1987*, p. 36; and *ALS 1988*, pp. 37–38) keeps promoting controversy, witness the letters by Burton R. Pollin and Dwight Thomas in the *PSA Newsletter* (17:6–7). At this point Poe himself does not stand up well as the strongest candidate, and Thomas's opinion that other writers from the era might as plausibly be considered should not be taken lightly. In addition, Edward J. Piacentino reprints a neglected supplemental document, by "T.," from 1845, in "The Poe-Longfellow Plagiarism Controversy: A New Critical Notice in *The Southern Chronicle*" (*MissQ* 42:173–82). According to T., Poe did not make the case for Longfellow as plagiarist.

The "Bibliographical Essay" in *ANQ* for July 1988 (n.s. 1:105–12), Eric W. Carlson's "Poe: II, New Critical Studies," evaluates eight items. Carlson's own—at times over-structured—"frames of reference" to Poe tend to diminish the established recognition of Poe's comic successes, e. g., by G. R. Thompson in the *Columbia Literary History of the United States.*

ii. General Accounts: Books and Parts of Books

Michael J. Deas's *The Portraits and Daguerreotypes of Edgar Allan Poe* (Virginia) furnishes a systematic, thoughtful survey. Taking account of extant genuine and spurious likenesses, and those known though no longer available, Deas follows leads established by Denise B. Bethel to demolish considerable nonsense in much biographical-legendary interpretation of Poe and to offer original, stimulating thoughts concerning the relevance of the portraits to Poe the man and artist. The first volume of Elizabeth S. Wiley's concordance to Poe's writings (in this case, to the poems) supersedes that by Booth and Jones, but it is discussed in detail elsewhere in *ALS 1989*.

Poe as a Southern literary figure, the topic of G. R. Thompson's *Columbia Literary History* chapter (*ALS 1988*, pp. 39–40), also occupies Louis D. Rubin, Jr., in chapter 4 of *The Edge of the Swamp* (pp. 127–89). Rubin distinguishes Poe from other antebellum Southern writers, notably W. G. Simms, because of Poe's repeated uses of psychological, or interior, states. Rubin seems to be as teased as many others have been in viewing Poe as Southern author, so he devotes considerable space to Poe's themes of slavery as they tie in with madness, sexual anxieties, and live burial. Rubin casts doubts on Poe's authorship of the famous *Southern Literary Messenger* review of Paulding's *Slavery in the United States* and the anonymous *The South Vindicated*, and, just as interesting, he inclines toward ascribing "A Dream," a prose fantasy, to Poe. Poe's creation of city nightmares at a time when other Americans generally turned their eyes elsewhere makes him our first important urban writer, in the estimate of Rubin, who closes with an analysis of "Hop-Frog" that brings together many features of what he discerns as the Poesque. Much of Rubin's information is not new, although many of his suggestions about it are (but see Rosenthal, cited below, for a more sympathetic opinion about Poe's departures from tragedy). The proofreading lacks care.

Two complimentary critiques of seminal Poesque motifs neatly dovetail. Charles A. Huttar's "Poe's Angels," in *Essays for Richard Ellmann*, pp. 82–84, 445, informs us how tension-filled is Poe's angel symbolism, which touches on his ideal, elusive worlds, on a "spiritual consummation whose price is the rejection of the physical world," and on the role of the creative artist. Poe does not attempt to reduce such tensions, but, in making them "the very soul of his poetry," he manifests an antagonism toward transcendental thought and a kinship with the

Victorian James Thomson. Poe's ambivalent angels appealed to the French Symbolists and also cropped up in the poetry of Wallace Stevens. Adjunct reading appears in my "Fantasy Figures in Poe's Poems," in *The Poetic Fantastic*, pp. 43–51, which contrasts demon creatures who inhabit shadowy regions (notably in "The Raven," "Tamerlane," "Alone," "The Assignation," and "Silence—A Fable") with less frightening figures who function amid radiant, comforting light (especially those in "To Helen" [1831] and "Eldorado"). Following leads suggested to me by Richard P. Benton, I address rich thematic and technical similarities between "To Helen" and "The Assignation." My essay also builds on work by Todorov, Marder, and Griffith. George E. Haggerty's statement that Poe "was the first American to write a truly sophisticated Gothic fiction" may seem commonplace, but his treatment of Poe's theories about and handling of the "tale," especially in "Metzengerstein," "The Pit and the Pendulum," and "Usher," in *Gothic Fiction/Gothic Form*, pp. 81–106, offers refreshing perspectives. Poe's mockery of terror tales, Haggerty contends, is calculated to make us aware how time-honored substance can be used to achieve "a more effective Gothicism"—at its best in the tale as opposed to longer fiction; what may often seem to be limitations in matters of setting and characterization transform through Poe's creativity into superior, plausible art that centers in terror, horror, and passion. Thus Poe far outdistances the explained supernaturalism of Mrs. Radcliffe and her disciples. More on Poe's Gothicism—notably in its ramifications into vampirism, incest, and madness as vehicles for "alienation and dissociation" among questing but ever uncertain narrators—is sensibly analyzed throughout *Redefining the American Gothic*, by Louis S. Gross, whose chief attention encompasses "Morella," "Ligeia," and "Usher." A contrasting view appears in Manuel Aguirre's "The Eye and the House: The 19th Century Symbolism of Edgar Allan Poe" (*Restant* 16[1988]:21–32), where we learn that motifs of the Evil Eye and the haunted house in "The Tell-Tale Heart" and "Usher" are means of surpassing mere staple themes and types in order to explore the numinous and its relationship to the real world. Amplified coverage of such thematics may be found in Allan Gardner Lloyd-Smith's *Uncanny American Fiction*, pp. 35–52, where numbers of Poe's tales, *Pym*, *Rodman*, and several poems are treated in terms of the Freudian "*Unheimliche*" (what ought to have remained secret but has come to light). We find here a deft probing of borders where reality and supernaturalism intertwine, especially as such mergers involve that Poesque mainstay, the will. Not everyone else will agree with certain opinions set forth here (e. g., calling the narrator in "Ligeia" an opium addict, or distinguishing animal imagery in "Metzengerstein" from that in several other pieces), nor will the many typos delight readers. Nevertheless, Lloyd-Smith's thinking should spark additional studies of Poe's uses of psychology. A deft overview of Poe's successes with all-too-human, rather than supernatural, horrifics (in which comedy is an inescapable element, as it is in the productions of the other best horror-fiction writers) appears in John M. Ford's "Edgar Allan Poe: Tales of Mystery and Imagination," in *Horror: 100 Best Books*, ed. Stephen Jones and Kim Newman (Carroll & Graf [1988], pp. 30–32). Ford's title, of course, derives from what has become a warhorse British collection of Poe's fiction (1852), although he does not specifically cite it. Eric W. Carlson's "Edgar Allan Poe," in Bobby Ellen Kimbel, ed., *American Short Story Writers Before 1880* (*DLB* 74[1988], pp. 303–22), furnishes a serviceable biography, a survey of the tales, with side-glances at other works, and conclusions about Poe's contributions to the short story. In the main sensible, Carlson's remarks are at times undercut by his championing a Poe closer to Emersonian Transcendentalism than many others would allow. Thus humorous textures in certain tales are distorted, e. g., in the section on "The Assignation," which seems to bifurcate sober from comic too severely (and is this tale a parody of Sir Thomas More or Tom Moore?), or in the contradictions about hoax/non-hoax in "Hans Pfaall" (pp. 311, 318). I would be among the last to define Poe's tales as nothing other than unmitigated mirth; at times, however, his blending of comic and serious actually adds greater subtlety, as attested by Mabbott, Gargano, Cox, Pollin, Thompson, and many others. Such features must be noted because Carlson's is a work of reference that will be used by many unacquainted with Poe and Poe scholarship.

iii. Critical Studies

a. **Poems.**   M. L. Rosenthal cites "The City in the Sea" as an example of daringly hypnotic lyric techniques that mingle beauty with horror. Claiming that all literary creations might well be called "poems," Rosenthal, in "Hurrah for Longinus! Lyric Structure and Inductive Analysis" (*SoR* 25:30–51), also turns his attention to *Pym*,

"Ligeia," and "Usher" as works in which lyrical movement and effect supplant narrative. In these and in other Poe works we encounter patterned tonal units or centers that may be termed "affects." Inward and outward emotional pressures are exquisitely dramatized by means of such patterning. Quite rightly, Rosenthal perceives the nearness of gravity and buffoonery as characterizing Poe's writings. Poe fashions a "melodramatic assumption of fatality, unsupported by the deeply shared sacred traditions underlying the works of the classical tragic playwrights. Yet the psychological terror remains." The essay's revelations about Poe's blending of poetry with prose, about seriocomic features, and about his comparability with Hawthorne and Faulkner make it a must for anyone seriously studying Poe. Likewise, Brad Howard's thoughtful critique, " 'The Conqueror Worm': Dramatizing Aesthetics in 'Ligeia' " (*PoeS* 21[1988]:36–43), intensifies our awareness of Poe's interminglings of poetry with fiction. Howard's "meta-reading" supplements and extends opinion about the poem's merits and its relation to the general theme of human opposition of mortality to supernal yearning. Addressing a longer poem as one essentially about origin, R. C. De Prospo gives close attention to "Al Aaraaf" in regard to theme, phonetics and prosody—especially the last two as they function in the title—in taking on the ideas of Floyd Stovall, G. R. Thompson, Jefferson Humphries, Mutlu Konuk Blasing (who is "she," and not "he"), and Michael J. S. Williams to look at the larger area of "modern humanist discourse" in "Poe's Alpha Poem: The Title of 'Al Aaraaf' " (*PoeS* 22:35–39). One is uncertain whether the intention is to zap previous ideas of prosody, of deconstruction, or of language in even more abstract contexts. This critique will promote controversy, I suspect.

b. **Tales, Sketches, *Pym*.** Poe's establishment of the superhero detective is evaluated sympathetically in "Tales of Mystery and Imagination," in H. R. F. Keating's *Crime & Mystery: The 100 Best Books* (Carroll [1987], pp. 11–12). Of course, Poe's detective tales had appeared in hardcover as early as 1845, in *Tales*, a fact often overlooked by crime-fiction enthusiasts. T. J. Binyon also reminds us, in chapter 1 of *'Murder Will Out'* (Oxford), that although Poe may not have intended to do so, he created the "first proper fictional detective and the first proper detective stories." Dupin is the prototype for all succeeding fictional detectives, although he was an amateur, and so only with the debut of Emile Gaboriau's Lecoq came the first professional detective who took center stage in the stories where he appeared. The sleuths who intervened—Dickens's Inspector Bucket and Collins's Sergeant Cuff—were lesser characters in large casts. Binyon's statement that "certainly Poe's detective stories remain the only ones to have been written by a literary genius" (p. 4) will assuredly raise the hackles of afficionadoes.

John T. Irwin, in "Handedness and the Self: Poe's Chess Player," turns to "Maelzel's Chess Player" as a forerunner of the detective tales (*ArQ* 45, i:1–28). In the essay, Poe initiates chess-playing analogies for portraiture of inner and outer, physical and psychological, phenomena; these analogies enhance crucial analytic powers in the subsequent tales. In illustrating his own points, Irwin ranges from Poe's likenesses in these works to Aristotle on Pythagorean principles and to Leibniz and Locke. Matters of right- and left-handedness and of mirroring in Poe's strategies are also perceptively brought forth. Gameplaying, the resolvent-analytic, signification—all as components in Poe's fascination with the mysteries of language as they are reflected in his ratiocinative fiction—are also primary facets in Shawn Rosenheim's "The King of 'Secret Readers': Edgar Poe, Cryptography, and the Origins of the Detective Story" (*ELH* 56:375–400). Great weight attaches to Poe's writings on cryptography and conondrums (in *Alexander's Weekly Messenger*, December 1839) as origins for the detective tales, thinks Rosenheim, who also concludes that the "W. B. Tyler" associated with this body of writing was none other than Poe himself, hoaxing.

Revaluating Poe's first Dupin tale, Terry J. Martin will cause outcries among many devotees. His "Detection, Imagination, and the Introduction to 'The Murders in the Rue Morgue'" (*MLS* 20:31–45) explores possibilities that, instead of displaying genuine analytical powers (those associated with imagination and creativity), Dupin merely evinces a simple ingenuity—and therefore Martin runs counter to much else that has been thought and published about "Murders." His hypotheses are, however, clearly articulated, strongly bolstered by primary and secondary materials, and deserving of a hearing.

Another turn of the imaginative-rational screw occurs in Martin Roth's "Mysteries of 'The Mystery of Marie Roget'" (*PoeS* 22:27–34), an attempt to "foreground the drifts and collapses of its text," particularly as they "disturb the reader's interpretive relationship to the narrative." On foundations in Lacan, Derrida, and Schorr Roth erects an elaborate, close reading of the tale, one in which the matter of the unusual as opposed to the rational and ordinary accords to Dupin greater imaginative powers than he wins from Martin. In many ways Roth's reading (particularly when he touches on aspects of the sensual) is challenging. In his opening statements about the privileging of just one voice in Poe's text, though, Roth overlooks Richard P. Benton's "defense" of the tale (1969) and Richard Fusco's analysis of Poe's revisions (1978).

Moving away from the ratiocinative fiction, but with critical theory still in mind, we come to Ib Johansen's "The Madness of the Text: Deconstruction of Narrative Logic in 'Usher,' 'Berenice,' and 'Dr. Tarr and Professor Fether'" (*PoeS* 22:1–9), which offers a combined view of madness in theme and textuality, hopefully to engender additional studies of a critical-theory nature. Madness-cum-reading (in which libraries play significant roles) is certainly an interesting topic in Poe's three tales, although Johansen strains our credibility in locating a library analogous to Roderick Usher's studio in "Tarr and Fether" and in having the narrator in that tale ultimately lost "inside the labyrinth of the text." The feminine "Other" Johansen proposes is also forgotten when it comes to "Tarr and Fether." The article is weakened, too, because Johansen ignores many important publications about the selected three tales which, had they been drawn in, might sharpen some of the suggestions—or show that some are not so original as they may first appear.

In "Entropic Imagination in Poe's 'The Masque of the Red Death'" (*CollL* 16:210–18), Hubert Zapf draws on "entropy" (a combination of energy and transformation) to demonstrate how the world in this tale operates as "a cultural artifact that consumes itself in the same way in which the fictional categories that are used by Poe to communicate this world—i. e., space, time, characters, action, and symbolism—consume themselves in the process of the text." The initial differences between Prince Prospero and the "Red Death" disappear, and they seem to be much more alike, by the close of the tale. Richard D. Slick's explication, that "Masque" prefigures the contemporary AIDS epidemic and its resulting upheavals, is less persuasive ("Poe's 'The Masque of the Red Death,'" *Expl* 47:24–26).

Poe's humor keeps waving a beckoning hand. New light is shed on "How to Write a Blackwood Article/A Predicament" by Jonathan Auerbach, in *The Romance of Failure*, pp. 3–11, who deftly argues how we might read this pair of tales as signal commentary on Poe's own role in his works because they embody transferences of power

from author to character(s). For Auerbach, the role of the writer in
these pieces assumes far more serious dimensions than the satiric
textures might immediately convey. Harry M. Bayne's succinct "Poe's
'Never Bet the Devil Your Head' and Southwest Humor" (*ARLR* 3:
278–79) convincingly places this tale against important background,
a relationship which, if followed up thoroughly, may alert us to much
in the way of Poe's grotesquerie. Poe drew substantially on southwestern features of games, tall tales, "innovative or shocking language," and humor related to the physical. Hitting at the Transcendentalists, Poe turned on them the artillery of another mode in
American literary expression. Bayne's study takes a merited place in
ranks with Fred Madden's critique of "A Descent into the Maelstrom"
(*ALS 1988*, p. 45) and Alfred H. Marks's equally relevant "Hawthorne,
Tieck, and Hoffmann: Adding to the Improbabilities of a Marvellous
Tale" *ESQ* 35:1–21). Marks alerts us to common patterns of extravagance in fiction by the Germans, Hawthorne, and Poe.

"Usher" also continues to yield diverse facets, as demonstrated,
first, in Robert Hoggard's plausible thesis that Roderick and Madeline's incest produces horrendous results from her becoming *enceinte*
with his child: "Pregnant Thoughts on 'The Fall of the House of
Usher'" (*UMSE* n.s. 7:118–20). Hoggard's "Red Moon Rising: A
Marxist View of 'The Fall of the House of Usher'" (*ARLR* 3:280–81)—
a takeoff on extremes in one variety of recent critical theory—in its
consideration of how Madeline's ascent from a feudal dungeon may
reflect the rise of the economically, socially, and sexually oppressed
is, like "Pregnant Thoughts," sure to provoke those who want their
Poe only in terms of unmitigated horrors or sobriety. A different note
sounds in Jack G. Voller's reminder that Poe's awareness of and negativity toward the Kantian Sublime in "Usher" should not be ignored
just because his response to Burkean aesthetics constitutes another
major feature ("The Power of Terror: Burke and Kant in the House
of Usher," *PoeS* 21[1988]:27–36), and that the consequences, as well
as the sources, of terror are implicit in Poe's great tale. Voller supplements the solid work on "Usher" by Darrel Abel, Craig Howes, and
Kent Ljungquist.

Somewhat different Poesque seriousness is the mainstay in Leonard W. Engel's "Claustrophobia, the Gothic Enclosure and Poe"
(*Clues* 10:107–18). Another Engel analysis of enclosure, this one takes
up "The Premature Burial," "MS. Found," and *Pym*. Modifying practices of many other gothicists, Poe makes enclosure the principal focus

in his fiction. Typically, such isolation from the normal world as is reflected in this method spurs the affected character to dwell on emotions that he has tried to suppress. The conclusion of "The Premature Burial" is positive, with implications of the narrator's being freed from fear of enclosure and death, as are the endings in "MS. Found," "A Descent," and *Pym*, which hint at rebirths in identities. Symbolism of premature burial, more important in matters of psyche than of physique, infuses these works, and Poe's enclosure devices impart "a thematic unity and an artistic integrity they would not otherwise have." Though such pieces may reflect Poe's personal obsessions, as Engel submits, that hypothesis will occasion disputes. To turn to Robert E. Seaman's "Lacan, Poe, and the Descent of the Self" (*TSLL* 31:196–214), another interpretation of "A Descent," is a downward journey for readers, who will rapidly detect that Seaman should have familiarized himself with more of the work on "A Descent" before preparing his own rather pedestrian critique.

Solid, readable material about another gothic warhorse gives appeal to Curtis Fukuchi's "Poe's 'Berenice' and the Skull Beneath the Skin" (*UMSE* n.s. 7:98–108), a penetrating reading of this tale (and of "Usher," which resembles it) as a rendering of man's fears about death coupled with ambivalences "toward sensuality and physical life in general." Egaeus creates his own miseries because he does not sufficiently resist his life-denying visions. We come away from this study with a strong sense of how Poe renewed leases on many gothic properties in arrears.

Akin to such doubts and misgivings related to the senses versus the spirit are those probed in Curtis Dahl's sprightly, but thoughtful, consideration of the food and drink, "Port Wine, Roast Mutton, and Pickled Olives: Gourmet Food in Poe's *The Narrative of Arthur Gordon Pym*" (*UMSE* n.s. 7:109–17). Placing *Pym*, in part, as a recognizable 19th-century narrative of a "gentleman's son afloat," Dahl reminds us that its overt gastronomical details differentiate it from more customary specimens. He adds that, in all honesty, no single, exclusive meaning emerges from the profusion of eatables and drinkables, although he does keep steadily before us a host of tantalizing possibilities underlying this "highly worked artifice that engulfs us in its ironic, absurd, and horrific ambience." I propose here that *Pym* as an outgrowth of the Folio Club scheme should not be overlooked in this respect, and that the very multiplicity of possibilities relevant to the food and drink may only point up Poe's uncertainties as he com-

menced writing a novel. Equally straightforward in suggesting that
not all of the ambiguities in a Poe work are resolvable is Tracy Ware's
"The Two Stories of 'William Wilson' " (*SSF* 26:43–48). Contending
that Todorov's and Siebers's conceptions of the fantastic are limited
in dealing with Poe's fantastic tale, Ware goes on to discuss three
problems inherent in the piece—narrative unreliability, whether a
second Wilson exists, and the ending, which, clouded as it is, makes
unclear how the story can be told at all. Ware also balks at acceptance
of the tale as allegory. The hesitancy of the storyteller resembles our
own as we read "William Wilson," and so we must conclude that, after
all has been said (and Ware commands the secondary bibliography
with ease), the tale is a paradox beyond solution.

iv. Sources and Influences, Miscellaneous

Selma B. Brody's "Poe's Use of Brewster's *Letters on Natural Magic*"
(*ELN* 28:50–54) convincingly demonstrates Poe's mining of this work
of popular science for the optical effects in many of his writings.
Among more specialized studies, J. Lasley Dameron reveals that William Scoresby's *Journal of a Voyage to the Northern Whale-Fishery*
(1823) inspired the visionary city, in "Another Source for Poe's 'City
in the Sea' " (*PoeS* 22:43–44). Adeline Tintner's information, in "Fire
of the Heart in 'Al Aaraaf': Beckford and Byron as Source" (*PoeS* 22:
47–48)—that Poe's poem has ancestry in *Vathek* and *The Giaour*—
should have paid further respects anent Beckford to Mabbott's notes
for other Poe titles in the *Collected Works*, Kenneth Graham's 1985
study of Beckford and Poe (*ALS 1985*, p. 46), and pertinent items in
my *The Gothic's Gothic* (1988), which cover some of the same territory. Tintner is stronger on Poe's Byron-Moore origins. Peter J. Soren-
son's explanatorily titled "William Morgan, Freemasonry, and 'The
Cask of Amontillado' " (*PoeS* 22:45–47) reasonably names Morgan's
Illustrations of Masonry (1826) as a likely inspiration for the murder,
the trowel incident, and the fate of Fortunato. With as strong persuasion, Kent Ljungquist specifies an anonymous tale, "The Pirate's
Treasure," in the New York *Rover* (1845) as background for "The
Gold-Bug." He corrects the idea that Poe may have used Mrs. G. A. H.
Sherburne's tale of the same title, and he links Poe once again with a
strong candidate for identification as "Outis," Lawrence Labree, who
referred to the *Rover* publication (" 'The Gold-Bug' and 'The Pirate's
Treasure': A Correction and Addition," *PoeS* 21[1988]:47–48).

Poe's significance for illustrators receives ample treatment in Burton R. Pollin's *Images of Poe's Works* (Greenwood), a "comprehensive descriptive catalogue of illustrations." Poe's illustrators have long interested Pollin, and this book brings together the fruits of his researches in fine form. Individual illustration of Poe's writings in periodicals, those in collections of his works, as well as those in other graphics, such as paintings and films, in many nations and with foreign-language letterpress as well as English—all receive just dues. Given that Poe and the visual arts has been a subject of repeated interest, this book should serve many cross-disciplinary uses. For one, it may stimulate critical study similar to that connecting the Hudson River School of painters and American writers, or to that on Pre-Raphaelitism and its impact on literature and graphics among 1890s figures and beyond. Pollin's explanatory matter also makes readily accessible the crosscurrents in the book. One could wish for more examples, and some in color, of the illustrations themselves, but such absences do not detract from the main purpose.

Several additional windings and turnings of the Poesque are worth note. Andrew Tudor's remarks on Poe and horror films supplement some of Pollin's observations and listings, although *Monsters and Mad Scientists* (Blackwell) places Poe as one of many whose horrors have enlivened the film medium. Tudor keeps us aware that Poe's literary melodramatics naturally attract filmmakers, as is evident in Roger Corman's *Fall of the House of Usher, The Pit and the Pendulum, The Premature Burial, Tomb of Ligeia,* and *The Masque of the Red Death,* in which overstatement, supernaturalism, and madness are uppermost—as they were earlier in films of "The Black Cat," which take great liberties with Poe's tale (*ALS 1988,* p. 51).

More distinctly literary influences are charted in William Carter's *Conversations with Shelby Foote* (Miss.) and the late W. T. Bandy's "Allen Tate's Juvenilia" (*SoR* 25:86–94). Foote recalls that in his childhood "American literature consisted of a flock of New England writers with Edgar Allan Poe sort of thrown in to leaven the lump." The "great writers," according to this prescription, were Lowell, Whittier, Longfellow, and Emerson—all, excepting Emerson, bad in Foote's estimation. Commenting on Tate's youthful admiration for Poe, Bandy reprints from the 1921 Vanderbilt student yearbook, *Commodore,* a takeoff on "The Bells," entitled "The Girls," which adroitly mimics Poe's stanzaic pattern and sound effects. These essays indicate how Poe's shadow fell across the imaginations of many later

Southern writers. Tate's parody dovetails nicely with that in Burton R. Pollin's "The 'Raven' Parody that Captivated Abe Lincoln" (*UMSE* n.s. 7:121–29), which reprints "The Pole-Cat," from the Quincy [Illinois] *Whig*, March 18, 1846, along with valuable commentary on lampoons of Poe's renowned poem. Lincoln's amusement with "The Pole-Cat" has been recorded, but no previous reprinting seems to exist, nor has anyone else proposed, as Pollin does, Andrew Johnston, editor of the paper, as author. Finally, Edward J. Piacentino corrects "An Error in Poe's Review of *Rienzi*" (*ANQ*, n.s. 1[1988]:136–37). Poe mistakenly identified Petrarch as a major character in the Bulwer-Lytton novel, although elsewhere he keeps more reliable command of information relating to the Italian, who often occupied his thoughts.

University of Mississippi

4. Melville

Brian Higgins

i. Editions

While deconstructionist and New Historicist approaches to literature had a major impact on Melville studies in the 1980s, the most important development in the last decade—in terms of lasting influence—will undoubtedly prove to be the Northwestern-Newberry Edition's resumption of publication after the long hiatus of the 1970s. Five volumes have appeared since 1982, and only four of the total 15 now remain to be published: volume 11, *Published Poems*; volume 12, *Clarel*; volume 13, *Billy Budd, Sailor, and Other Late Manuscripts*; and volume 14, *Correspondence*. All are scheduled to appear within the next four years. Nineteen eighty-nine saw publication of volume 15, *Journals*, which prints the journals Melville kept on his travels to England and Europe in 1849–50, to England, the Near East, and Europe in 1856–57, and on his voyage around Cape Horn to San Francisco in 1860. The texts of the journals have been newly edited by Howard C. Horsford, with Lynn Horth, from the manuscript journals "in close collation with earlier editions," notably Eleanor Melville Metcalf's edition of *Journal of a Visit to London and the Continent* (1948) and Horsford's edition of *Journal of a Visit to Europe and the Levant* (1955). As a result of Horsford's and Horth's labors, the texts differ from the earlier editions in wording at some 100 points—and in spelling, punctuation, and capitalization at many more. The difficulties of reading Melville's handwriting in the journals are amply illustrated by reproductions of many pages and passages, including all words the editors were unable to decipher to their satisfaction. Horsford's "Historical Note" succinctly places the journals in the context of Melville's career as an author and discusses the literary use he made of them later, notably in *Moby-Dick*, the stories, and *Clarel*. Horsford and Horth's annotations of the journal entries provide a mine of information about the places Melville visited, the people he met, and the works of art he saw. The annotations are handsomely illustrated with maps and reproductions of contemporary paintings and engravings. A section of additional documents (prepared by Harrison Hayford) includes Melville's notes in Hawthorne's *Mosses*. The *Journals* will be indispensable for the study of crucial periods in Melville's life; the volume is also a delight just to browse in.

Gordon Poole's attractive edition of "At the Hostelry" and "Naples in the Time of Bomba" (I.U.O.) will shortly be superseded by volume 13 of the Northwestern-Newberry edition, which will print the pieces as part of Melville's unfinished *Burgundy Club* book and also contain a more detailed discussion of the growth of the *Burgundy Club* manuscript and its incomplete state than the one Poole provides in his introduction to the two poems. (See also section *ix*, below.) Poole's edition, nonetheless, will continue to be valuable for its explanatory notes.

ii. General

Norwood Andrews, Jr.'s *Melville's Camões* (Bouvier) goes a long way toward compensating for the scant attention Melvilleans have paid to Melville's high regard for the Portuguese poet. Displaying an impressive knowledge of Camões and relevant Melville scholarship, Andrews, a professor of Portuguese, focuses mainly on *White-Jacket*, *Moby-Dick*, and the poems "In a Garret" and "Camoens" to show how Melville "put to his own artistic use a Camões whom he knew as thoroughly as the translations and biographies he read permitted and whom he admired greatly for more than half a century." Andrews's persistent wrangling with other critics at times lessens the force of his demonstration (though he often provides lucid correctives), but he establishes nonetheless the importance of the "sometimes completely overlooked Camonian content" in the works he treats. (Alexandrino Eusébio Severino's recent article on Camões and *Moby-Dick* [see *ALS 1988*, pp. 59–60] should be added to Andrews's account of previous commentary on Melville and Camões.)

Two book-length New Historicist readings of Melville appeared in 1989. In *Empire for Liberty: Melville and the Poetics of Individualism* (Princeton) Wai-chee Dimock argues that the "textual governance" of Melville's writings "cannot be divorced from the social governance of antebellum America." (By "textual governance" she means "the formal logic by which Melville executes his authorial dictates, supervises and legitimizes, affixes meanings and assigns destinies.")

Authorship for Melville, she contends, was "almost exclusively an exercise in freedom, an attempt to proclaim the self's sovereignty over and against the world's"; his "authorial enterprise" can be seen as "a miniature version of the national enterprise," more specifically as a miniature version of Manifest Destiny and its "informing logic of freedom and dominion." His works thus dramatize "the very juncture" where "the imperial self of Jacksonian individualism recapitulates the logic of Jacksonian imperialism."

In Dimock's analysis, Melville "speaks for and with his contemporaries"—most of all "when he imagines himself to be above them, apart from them, opposed to them." The Melville of John Samson's *White Lies: Melville's Narratives of Facts* (Cornell) more knowingly resists the ideology and "myths" of his culture. Less thesis-ridden than Dimock's book, *White Lies* examines *Typee, Omoo, Redburn, White-Jacket, Israel Potter,* and *Billy Budd* as Melville's "vital rewritings" of his sources. Melville does not simply adopt the sources' "formal and intellectual characteristics," Samson argues; rather, he examines their ideological assumptions, sees their "facts" as less than true (as "white lies"), and in his own narratives controverts them. Each of Melville's narrators, Samson maintains, typifies an attitude held by the narrators of exploration literature; Melville exposes the contradictions and biases within his narrator's ideology and his "evasion or denial of experiences in conflict with his ideology." Like the narrators in his sources, Melville's narrators cling primarily to 18th-century ideas, trying "to carry over into the troubled nineteenth century some of the Enlightenment's confidence in racial, cultural, political, and religious superiority."

James Duban's "Chipping with a Chisel: The Ideology of *Melville's* Narrators" (*TSLL* 31:341–85), the lead article in a special issue edited by Duban on "Melville and His Narrators," quarrels with a number of recent New Historicist accounts of Melville, including Dimock's, finding a "selective inattention to narrative" in their portrayal of Melville's "unwitting participation in consensus ideology." Duban's own position is closer to Samson's: drawing frequently on his *Melville's Major Fiction* (see *ALS 1983*, p. 65), he argues at length that Melville "seems less to perpetuate" than "to critique the ideological assumptions of nineteenth-century America." As early as *Typee*, Duban holds, Melville displayed a "sophisticated grasp of the relation between narration and consensus ideology" and, starting with Tommo, created narrators "whose own susceptibility to ideology serves to define and expose the often harmful moral tendencies of consensus outlooks." Duban's and Samson's attempts to dissociate Melville from his narrators at times seem about equally labored. A more incisive account of the shortcomings of recent New Historicist criticism that is pertinent to Dimock can be found in an essay Duban cites, Frederick Crews's "Whose American Renaissance?" (*NYRB* 27 Oct. 1988:75–79).

Less trendy and less sophisticated than Dimock's and Samson's studies, Bruce L. Grenberg's *Some Other World to Find: Quest and Negation in the Works of Herman Melville* (Illinois) gives a rather old-fashioned account of Melville's "developing mind and art," incorporating a good deal of routine (and often banal) commentary on the "continuity of thought, theme, and character" in Melville's works from *Typee* to *Billy Budd*. Melville's first six books, Grenberg tells us, are all built around their protagonists' quests—quests for "completion," or wholeness, in a mutable and infinite world—and all of the quests fail. Book by book, Melville "draws ever-constricting definitions of the individual's capacity for wholeness, until in *Moby-Dick* and *Pierre* the self is defined expressly by its tragic alienation from the world, from all humanity and, finally, from any certain sense of its own identity." The theme of all the late works is "the unrelieved isolation of the individual." In response to "more and more specialized" Melville scholarship and criticism, Grenberg seeks to restore a sense of the "whole" Melville, yet (apart from a few pages he devotes to *Clarel*) he ignores Melville's poetry, lectures, journals, and letters.

An example of that more specialized scholarship, which nonetheless contributes to our sense of the "whole" Melville, is Leon Chai's treatment in *Romantic Foundations* (Cornell, 1987), which focuses on passages in *Mardi, Moby-Dick, Pierre, The Confidence-Man, Billy Budd*, and Melville's letters to illustrate his affinities with (and differences from) Goethe, Coleridge, Shelley, and Balzac.

iii. Miscellaneous

Readers familiar with Lewis Mumford's *Herman Melville* (1929) will be interested in Donald L. Miller's account of Mumford's work (and limited research) on Melville and his friendship with Henry A. Murray in *Lewis Mumford: A Life* (Weidenfeld & Nicolson, pp. 263–91). Miller contends that Mumford was primarily writing about himself in the biography, "explaining nearly every critical point of Melville's forming in terms of his own life experience." (See *ALS 1979*, p. 49,

for discussion of Mumford's autobiography.) Merton M. Sealts, Jr.'s
" 'An utter idler and a savage': Melville in the Spring of 1852" (*MSEx*
79:1–3) adds a little to our knowledge of Melville's activities after his
completion of *Pierre* by reproducing and transcribing Augusta Melville's memoranda of several "excursions" in the Berkshires that he
made that spring with various members of his family.

iv. *Typee* to *White-Jacket*

Bryan C. Short's " 'The Author at the Time': Tommo and Melville's
Self-Discovery in *Typee*" (*TSLL* 31:386–405) contends that the
"central experience" narrated in *Typee* is "the compelling tale of
Melville's self-discovery as a writer." In order to "break into voice,"
Short argues, Melville must imagine a realm, Typee Valley, "where
the charms of inarticulate experience and linguistic authority coexist";
what Tommo "seeks to escape from is Melville's own entrapment in
a mute and impotent past." Short also maintains that Melville's ex-
cisions for the revised edition of *Typee* reflect his "own growing
authorial identity"; they "have the effect of simplifying both the language and the world of *Typee*, and of giving freer play to Melville's
dominant style." In "Melville's *Mardi*: Narrative Self-Fashioning and
the Play of Possibility" (*TSLL* 31:406–25), John Wenke deftly analyzes a number of episodes to show that in *Mardi* "action essentially
provides the excuse or point of departure for presenting the narrator's
experience of his own consciousness." (The narrator's "overreaching
philosophical self" appears "full-blown" at the book's outset, Wenke
maintains.) Melville's concern here is "to make knowledge of the self
through knowledge of the world the locus of interest." *Mardi* fully
dramatizes for the first time, Wenke argues, Melville's "ongoing attempt" to "present as explicit fictional subject the protean qualities of
human consciousness, with the distinct expectation that the formulation of one moment might be undone by the next." Wenke also distinguishes in *Mardi* "two distinctly identifiable narrative voices that
stand in dialectical tension"—the voices of "a fraternal genialist and a
solipsistic isolationist."

Margaret E. Stewart finds another kind of tension in *White-
Jacket*—tension between Melville's "yearning for rebellion" and his
"recoiling from it" ("The 'Romance' vs. the 'Narrative of Facts':
Representational Mode and Political Ambivalence in Melville's *White-
Jacket*," *ATQ* n.s. 3:189–202). Her view of this political ambivalence

as an outgrowth of the book's competing realistic and romantic modes seems based on a hazy concept of what constitutes realistic and romantic representation.

v. Moby-Dick

Larry J. Reynolds's *European Revolutions and the American Literary Renaissance* (Yale, 1988) valuably documents the paramount importance the European revolutions of 1848–49 held for American writers of the time, and his chapter on Melville (pp. 97–124) provides a welcome treatment of an underexplored topic—the many references to France and French affairs in Melville's writings. On the evidence Reynolds presents, however, it seems doubtful that Melville's alleged "lifelong obsession with revolution in France" helped to shape *Moby-Dick* as drastically as he contends, and his claim that Napoleon served as prototype and paradigm for Ahab also arouses skepticism. The chapter will probably occasion considerable debate nonetheless; as Reynolds notes, his findings call into question Marxist and New Left interpretations that dwell on Melville's sympathies for the proletariat. According to Reynolds, *Moby-Dick* incorporates "a damning commentary on current French political radicalism" that expresses Melville's "distrust of the 'people' and his revulsion at their capacity for self-destructive violence."

David Leverenz's "coercively kinky" reading of *Moby-Dick* in *Manhood and the American Renaissance* (pp. 279–306) is livelier and crankier than most recent writing on the book. Leverenz argues that Ishmael and Ahab are twinned "in their desire to be beaten": their "beating fantasies" displace a self-loathing "expressed primarily as a craving to be dominated by unloving power"; specifically, "they fear and crave being dominated by a stronger man." According to Leverenz, *Moby-Dick* is "the most extravagant projection of male penis envy in our literature," though the whale ultimately looks "as much like a wandering womb or a malevolent breast as a castrating penis."

The year's remaining essays on *Moby-Dick* were slight. Carol Bebee Collins in "Ahab and Steelkilt: Opposite Sides of the Same (Gold) Coin" (*ATQ* n.s. 3:219–27) proposes that "The *Town-Ho's* Story" and parallels between Steelkilt and Ahab enable the reader to understand what is grand about Ahab and what would happen to him if he lost the opportunity to attain that grandeur (he would lose his identity and his mythic status). Michael Hollister in "Melville's Gam with Poe in *Moby-Dick*: Bulkington and Pym" (*SNNTS* 21:279–91) claims that through Bulkington (who is supposedly "swept overboard by a storm" and drowned) Melville "acknowledges" Poe's *The Narrative of Arthur Gordon Pym,* "while contrasting his own vision"; and in "*Moby-Dick's* Ishmael, Burke, and Schopenhauer" (*MQ* 30:161–78), Christopher S. Durer briefly examines Ishmael in relation to Burke's ideas on the sublime and attempts to show that, "without realizing it," Ishmael becomes a spokesman for Schopenhauer's ideas and "is cast in the Schopenhauerian mold."

vi. Pierre

Jeffrey Steele's discussion of *Pierre* in *Representation of the Self* (pp. 159–71) adds to our sense of the ways in which Melville's "critique of psychological idealism" measures his "distance" from Emerson. Melville does not accept the unconscious as a "benign creative force" over which an individual exercises "the Apollonian control" imagined by Emerson, Steele notes, and by "turning away from idealizations of the unconscious toward the recognition of the mind's physical basis," he "anticipates all those later writers—ranging from Nietzsche to Derrida—who see self-representation as a fictional activity rather than as a Neoplatonic memory of essential truth."

Anne French Dalke's "The Sensational Fiction of Hawthorne and Melville" (*SAF* 16[1988]:195–207) focuses on elements of *Pierre* common in popular fiction of the day. Dalke finds that midway through the book Melville shifts from the sentimental "mode of fiction" to the sensational; his "bipartite depiction" of the two modes counterposes "the false sentimentality of the female fictional world" against "the bleak economics of the male." In Lee E. Heller's deconstructive reading, "The Stranger in the Mirror: Incest, Text, and the Making of Meaning in *Pierre*" (*SNNTS* 21:389–99) the image of the stranger in the mirror is central to *Pierre.* According to Heller, characters, text, and author "all become obsessed with issues of the repetition of familial identity, the definition of the individual via likeness, and the act of representation itself"; the second half of the text raises "questions about imposture and textual incestuousness as the writer makes his book into an extension of himself, conflating the crises in personal and aesthetic meaning."

vii. Stories

Nineteen eighty-nine provided welcome relief from the spate of new readings of "Bartleby" published in recent years. Dan McCall in *The Silence of* Bartleby (Cornell) has sensible things to say about the "Bartleby Industry," in particular about the many "source" studies of the story and those studies that set out to "prove" that Bartleby or the narrator *is* Hawthorne or Dickens or Poe or Emerson or Thoreau or Irving or Evert Duyckinck or Lemuel Shaw or whoever. McCall is often perceptive, too, in his commentary on the narrator, though in arguing that the narrator is reliable he glosses over parts of the story and fails to address some of the grounds on which other critics have detected unreliability. McCall is also somewhat overconfident in claiming that it was Melville who eliminated the "three lines of by-play about Mrs. Cutlets" from the *Piazza Tales* text (see the discussion notes to "Bartleby" in the Northwestern-Newberry edition of *The Piazza Tales and Other Prose Pieces, 1839–1860*) and in omitting them from the version of the original *Putnam's Monthly* text that he prints at the end of the book. It is worth remembering, too, that "Bartleby" was probably not Melville's first short story, as McCall claims a number of times, even if we discount the early "Fragments from a Writing Desk" (see the "Historical Note" to the NN edition, pp. 485–87). McCall is not always reliable in other biographical details and not always accurate in his quotations.

Robert S. Levine's informative chapter on "Benito Cereno" in *Conspiracy and Romance* (pp. 165–230) investigates ways in which contemporary debates on slavery and reform institutions found expression in antebellum sea narratives, "texts that typically imaged the seaman as slave and prisoner, the captain as slave driver and prisonkeeper, and the ship as plantation and prison." The issues central to the sea narratives and to "the transsectional debate on institutionalism" are central to "Benito Cereno," Levine argues; in his representation of the revolt aboard the *San Dominick* Melville appropriates "key alarmist tropes" that betray "some of his own anxieties about the potentially violent consequences of America's racial situation." Levine's complex argument attempts to reconcile a "new historical" reading of "Benito Cereno" that implicates Melville in the "containment strategies" of his culture, and a "dialogical" reading, following Bakhtin, that places Melville "at an ironic and critical distance from such strategies."

In the year's one general essay on *The Piazza Tales*, Louise K.

Barnett gives a sketchy account of "the withdrawal of the Melvillian protagonist from speech" ("'Truth is Voiceless': Speech and Silence in Melville's *Piazza Tales,*" *PLL* 25:59–66); in the tales, she claims, "speech moves toward silence because experience is too horrible or incomprehensible to find expression in words or because the bad faith of speakers makes communication impossible." Thomas Pribek's "'Between Democritus and Cotton Mather': Narrative Irony in 'The Apple-Tree Table'" (*SAR*:241–55) is more informative. Pribek examines "The Apple-Tree Table" in the context of Melville's reading about Democritus and shows "some analogous references to Democritus in contemporary writers, both English and American, in order to demonstrate that Melville's narrator uses Democritus with conscious irony."

Frank Pisano's "Melville's 'Great Haven': A Look at Fort Tompkins" (*SAF* 17:111–13) adds details to Philip Young's interpretation of Daniel Orme as Melville's self-portrait (see *ALS 1988*, p. 65), plausibly identifying the site of Orme's death as Fort Tompkins, the fort described in *Redburn,* chapter 7.

viii. *Israel Potter* and *The Confidence-Man*

Hennig Cohen's "Melville's *Israel Potter* and Temple Church" (*MSEx* 76:9–13) examines ways in which Melville in *Israel Potter* put to use his "considerable interest" in the Knights Templars and Temple Church, London, and drew upon Charles G. Addison's *The History of the Knights Templars* ("either directly or by way of another writer who had borrowed from it"). Less convincingly, Daniel Reagan's "Melville's *Israel Potter* and the Nature of Biography" (*ATQ* n.s. 3: 257–76) tries to show that in *Israel Potter* Melville "adopts and critiques" the idea that biography should represent the lives of great men, the view of biography formulated by Carlyle and Emerson, "popularized in the pages of *Putnam's, Harper's,* and other periodicals, and practiced by such noted biographers as Jared Sparks." According to Reagan, Melville criticizes this view "for its tendency to ignore the common man as a viable subject and productive force of history"; through his technique of "dialectical description" he suggests "ways of reintegrating the common man into the events and the texts of history."

The year's offerings on *The Confidence-Man* were meager. Jonathan Cook in "Melville's Man in Gold Sleeve Buttons: Chief Justice

Lemuel Shaw" (*ESQ* 34[1988]:257–81) argues that the dress and characterization of the man in gold sleeve buttons in chapter 7 could reflect the close relationship between Shaw and Daniel Webster, since the gold sleeve buttons are "possibly patterned after the attire" of Webster. The man in gold sleeve buttons, Cook maintains, "would seem to be Lemuel Shaw wearing Daniel Webster's coat, that is, Shaw enforcing the Fugitive Slave Law while wearing the apparel of the man who was instrumental in its formulation and enactment." Cook has little to support the identification beyond those buttons. Cecilia Konchar Farr in "The Philosopher with the Brass Plate: Melville's Quarrel with Mormonism in *The Confidence-Man*," (*ATQ* n.s. 3: 353–61) struggles to show that references to Mormon theology inform chapter 22.

ix. Poetry

Melville's poetry attracted an unusually high number of essays in 1989. *Battle-Pieces* received its most substantial treatment in recent years in Robert Milder's "The Rhetoric of Melville's *Battle-Pieces*" (*NCL* 44: 173–200), which focuses on the strategies by which the volume attempts to convert its readers "to the prospect of a wise and magnanimous America reestablished on the bedrock of tragic vision." The achievement of *Battle-Pieces*, Milder argues, "lies in the artfulness of design by which Melville patterns his readers' shared experience of the war into national myth and leads his audience, without their knowing it, toward an understanding of history and experience." The redemption through suffering that *Battle-Pieces* imagines for America is linked in Milder's view to the "vocational recovery" Melville sought for himself—and to his belief that he might "guide the nation in a time of crisis and in so doing rescue himself from impotence and obscurity."

David Cody's " 'So, then, Solidity's a crust': Melville's 'The Apparition' and the Explosion of the Petersburg Mine" (*MSEx* 78:1, 4–8) shows the relevance of passages in Carlyle's *Sartor Resartus* and *The French Revolution* to "The Apparition" and presents strong evidence that Melville "owed the germ" of the poem "to a contemporary account [in *Harper's Weekly*] of the famous explosion of the mine at Petersburg, Virginia, on July 30, 1864." R. D. Madison's "Melville's Sherman Poems: A Problem in Source Study" (*MSEx* 78:8–11) calls into question the extent of Melville's use of a previously cited source,

George Ward Nichols's *The Story of the Great March*. Madison suggests that Melville may have drawn more on "miscellaneous newspaper reports or common knowledge," while Nichols's book may have made "a significant but nevertheless small contribution" to the poems. Kent Ljungquist's " 'Meteor of the War': Melville, Thoreau, and Whitman Respond to John Brown" (*AL* 61:674–80) links the last line in "The Portent" to a meteor shower that was widely covered in the press in November 1859; Ljungquist notes that Melville, Thoreau, and Whitman all "responded to the same natural phenomenon by endowing it with metaphysical significance."

In "The Small Voice of Silence: Melville's Narrative Voices in *Clarel*" (*TSLL* 31:451–73), Stan Goldman distinguishes four narrative voices. The first three—an "obtrusive organizing" voice, a "participating" voice, and a "reverent" voice—prepare the way, according to Goldman, for the fourth, an "inner narrative voice of divine immanence." This inner voice, "a quiet, unobtrusive revelation of the divinity within a person," suggests "the validity of subjective truth, the hope of immortality, and the possibility of spiritual peace" and, "by showing the other side of death and despair, prepares the reader for the Epilogue of hope." This "theology of hope," Goldman maintains, "counters the themes of hiddenness, silence, death, suffering, and despair that most critics read from the poem."

Vernon Shetley's "Melville's 'After the Pleasure Party': Venus and Virgin" (*PLL* 25:425–42) sheds new light on the poem by relating it to "a substantial body of imagery and writing on the subject of cloistral life for women" and more significantly to "a body of discussion, in nineteenth century America, on the relations among art, life, and sexuality" (though the "body of discussion" Shetley cites is rather limited). In his reading of the poem, Shetley identifies the narrator not with Melville but with "that group of voices that tell us the stories of Bartleby and much of the uncollected magazine fiction: complacent sentimentalists whose desire to point morals blinds them to the human significance of the stories they tell."

In " 'House of the Tragic Poet': Melville's Draft of a Preface to His Unfinished Burgundy Club Book" (*MSEx* 79:1, 4–7), Robert A. Sandberg prints his transcription of a previously unpublished essay by an "anonymous, self-effacing editor," who in Sandberg's view "becomes, de facto, the most important single unifying rhetorical force" informing the unfinished manuscript. Sandberg's " 'The Adjustment of Screens': Putative Narrators, Authors, and Editors in Melville's Un-

finished *Burgundy Club* Book" (*TSLL* 31:426–50) focuses on this un-
named "putative" editor, his introductory essay, "House of the Tragic
Poet," and the stages of the book's composition—"as far as these have
been defined"—to elucidate "the rhetorical design Melville might
have finally used" to inform the book.

x. *Billy Budd, Sailor*

The reprinted material in *Critical Essays on Melville's* Billy Budd,
Sailor, ed. Robert Milder (Hall), quite properly begins with Hayford
and Sealts's account of the growth of the manuscript; the collection
then conveniently brings together much of the best-known criticism
of the last 65 years. In his introduction Milder ably surveys developments in criticism since the first estimates of the book in the 1920s
and points to the most promising areas for future investigation.
Hershel Parker has frequently lamented the failure of most critics
to come to terms with the story's compositional history (see *ALS,
1972–1980*), and Milder rightly states that Hayford and Sealts's
Genetic Text still raises by far "the most crucial questions yet to be
explored" (though nearly 30 years have passed since its first publication). As Milder notes, "not only does the compositional evidence
subvert particular readings of the story, but it challenges the premise
of aesthetic unity on which nearly all readings are based." Milder
builds on boggy ground when he argues that *Billy Budd* can nonetheless be said to have some sort of unity, even if not in "the strict New
Critical sense"; but he gives a lucid account of the shortcomings of
most *Billy Budd* criticism (including much of what he reprints): "an
intention operative at one or another stage of composition and surviving in the published text as a major regional emphasis is identified
with Melville's governing idea and allowed to control the reading of
the entire story to the distortion or neglect of other regionally dominant emphases." Milder's introduction and his prominent inclusion of
Hayford and Sealts's work may have the welcome effect of causing
writers on *Billy Budd* to pay more attention to the critical implications
of the compositional evidence.

In the one new essay in Milder's collection, "*Billy Budd, Sailor*:
Melville's Last Romance" (pp. 223–37), James McIntosh argues that
Billy Budd is a development of the romance as Hawthorne conceived
it—as "a hybrid form, combining the actual and the imaginary, fact
and fable, the probable and the marvelous, and the historical and the

mysterious," and intent on revealing "the truth of the human heart." McIntosh makes more of a case than Dennis Pahl, who relates the story to Nietzsche's "genealogy of morals" in his chapter on *Billy Budd* in *Architects of the Abyss* (pp. 81–106). According to Pahl, Melville is less interested in telling the truth of a certain story than in telling the story of "truth" itself. *Billy Budd* "dramatizes how all truth becomes merely a product of those forces that have, by a will to power, come into positions of authority"; it makes clear that the "forms" of truth "are maintained only through the same surges of violence and disorder they purport to regulate and control." In Pahl's reading, the narrator of *Billy Budd* and Captain Vere share a similar lust for power. Emily Miller Budick in *Fiction and Historical Consciousness* (pp. 58–62) attributes Vere's "failure" to his "peculiarly literalistic imagination," to "his belief in typological cosmic relationships and his special antitypological historiography." The story supposedly presents Melville's version of "America's wildly erring, antitypological, ahistorical concept of self."

John F. Hennedy in "Federations in the Fancy: Traces of *Measure for Measure* in *Billy Budd*" (*MSEx* 77:1, 7–13) offers grounds for thinking that *Measure for Measure* "influenced *Billy Budd* at least as significantly as did *Othello*." Episodes "of a spiritually innocent young man's preparation for death, arguments by an authority figure for the necessity of applying the law to its severest limits, and resemblances between Shakespeare's Angelo and Melville's Claggart" are the main parallels that Hennedy cites.

University of Illinois at Chicago

5. Whitman and Dickinson

John Carlos Rowe

This year's work on Whitman is characterized by the general effort to reaffirm the poet as politically avant-garde and as a model for subsequent cultural and ideological criticism. One focus for these defenses of Whitman's political commitments is predictably his utopian theories of the body, a topic of considerable interest in theoretical circles these days, thanks in part to the general cultural anxiety about the body, occasioned not only by feminist challenges but also by scientific developments in human engineering. A more direct consideration of these recent theories (Scarry, Derrida, Chodorow, Cixous, et al.) would have made these approaches more cogent and relevant.

Dickinson criticism still struggles with the lack of historical information so that the effort to "historicize" continues to tumble back into her texts and often reproduce just those New Critical aesthetic values such historicism hopes to overcome. There are some promising solutions to this problem in this year's work, as well as a turn away from mere celebration of Dickinson's poetic "rebellion" against patriarchy and toward a more historical consideration of her identity as a conflicted 19th-century woman writer.

i. Walt Whitman

a. **Bibliography, Editing.** Ed Folsom's "Walt Whitman: A Current Bibliography" (*WWR* 63:140–43, 206–09; 7:38–40, 7:93–95) includes good mini-reviews of books and essays, literary and literate items not certain to show up in standard scholarly searches, especially to books not devoted exclusively to Whitman.

Owen Hawley's "The Centenary of 'Horace's Book': *Camden's Compliments to Walt Whitman*" (*WWR* 7:79–87) reconstructs the history of the publication of Horace Traubel's collection of memories

Erik Curren assisted me in the research for this review—JCR.

from the 70th anniversary party given for Whitman in Camden. Especially interesting is Hawley's account of the aging and ailing Whitman participating in plans for the little book's subscription and circulation to assure that this "combination of eulogistic propaganda and personal letter" would add its slender contribution to his reputation.

b. **Biography.** George Hutchinson's " 'The Laughing Philosopher': Whitman's Comic Repose" (*WWR* 6:172–88) is hard to classify because it is both biography and general criticism. This ambivalence also makes it interesting for subsequent biographers because Hutchinson takes seriously the commonplace that Whitman worked hard to the end of his life to construct his public image. Whitman in the 1880s is Hutchinson's concern here (as it is in several other pieces this year, perhaps prompted by the 1992 centenary of Whitman's death). Hutchinson argues that Whitman carefully modeled himself after the later Stoics, who shared his sense of the "fundamentally comic intimations of immortality" and of the sort of comedy that comes from inexplicable "faith" (perhaps like that which appears so unexpectedly at the end of Melville's *Clarel*). For Hutchinson, this alignment of comic sensibility and stoicism distinguishes the later poetry and public personality.

In keeping with the year's emphasis on feminist issues, Marion Walker Alcaro's "Walt Whitman and Mrs. G." (*WWR* 6:153–71) is a revaluation of Whitman's relationship with Anne Gilchrist. Alcaro argues against Edwin Haviland Miller's assessment in the Whitman *Correspondence* that she was a "pathetic Victorian lady" by portraying Gilchrist, author of "A Woman's Estimate of Walt Whitman," as a literate woman who shared many of Whitman's poetic and philosophical values. It is too bad that Alcaro does not generalize a bit about such intellectual friendships in the Victorian period. Gilchrist's relationship with Whitman between 1876 and 1878 (as well as in the years before, when she claims to have "fallen in love" with him simply by reading his poetry) resembles nothing so much as the "intellectual friendships" celebrated by Margaret Fuller in *Woman in the Nineteenth Century*.

Sherry Ceniza's "Walt Whitman and Abby Price" (*WWR* 7:49–67) is equally important feminist reconstruction. Committed Fourierist socialist and women's rights activist, Abby Price also recalls some of the ideals for women outlined by Fuller. Ceniza carefully traces

Whitman's early knowledge of Price's writings, which he knew before he met her, and the general effect of women's rights activism on the 1856 edition of *Leaves of Grass*. Once again, Whitman's relations with intellectual and—in the case of Price and her circle—politically activist women are notable for their egalitarianism: "The nature of Price and Whitman's friendship is striking in its reciprocity. In the letters, he never condescends; she doesn't defer. They spoke to each other as the best of friends do—in a direct manner."

Randall Waldron's "Jessie Louisa Whitman: Memories of Uncle Walt, et al., 1939–1943" (*WWR* 7:15–27) is a sort of biographical footnote to Waldron's *Mattie: The Letters of Martha Mitchell Whitman* (1977), an edition of the letters of Jessie's sister, Whitman's other niece. The information is based primarily on an interview with Jessie conducted in 1939 by Ralph L. Fansler, "a passionate Whitman enthusiast." The interview is part of The Fansler Collection at Northwestern, which also includes Whitman memorabilia that Jessie gave Fansler sometime between 1939 and 1942. Jessie's memories are the typically defensive responses of a family member, and have little scholarly value.

Carolyn Kinder Carr's "A Friendship and a Photograph: Sophia Williams, Talcott Williams, and Walt Whitman" (*American Art Journal* 31:3–12) offers substantial historical and material evidence that the September 1886 photograph of Whitman in Camden used by Thomas Eakins for his 1887–88 portrait of the ailing poet was taken not by Eakins himself but by his friend Sophia Williams, a writer and photographer in her own right, who with her husband, Talcott, visited Whitman in 1886. The essay provides yet further evidence for the feminist argument that women's accomplishments in the arts are often neglected or, as in this case, simply "stolen" in the misattributions of scholars blind to their own patriarchal assumptions.

c. Criticism: General. With four new critical studies devoted to Whitman and two other books in which Whitman plays a major role, 1989 was an important year for Whitman scholarship and criticism.

The reissue by Da Capo of Walter Lowenfels's 1960 *Walt Whitman's Civil War* indicates the centrality of political concerns in recent scholarship on Whitman. It's good to have this well-organized anthology of Whitman's responses to the Civil War available again, although the new edition might have included some of Whitman's journalism and notebook entries to indicate that his views on race, abolition, and the prospect of war were not so unequivocally liberal as Lowenfels's anthology suggests. In short, the book is dated.

Vivian Pollak anticipated me by discussing at length Betsy Erkkila's *Whitman the Political Poet* (Oxford) in *ALS 1988*. I should add only that the book, which appeared in 1989, is yet another indication of how recent critics have been intent on refurbishing Whitman's reputation as a politically committed poet and person. Erkkila generally defends Whitman against charges of racism and antiabolitionist sentiments, and as Pollak pointed out avoids some of the more troublesome details of his relations with women. In the main, however, *Whitman the Political Poet* offers a more direct treatment of Whitman and his political contradictions than previous studies.

Thomas Gardner's *Discovering Ourselves in Whitman* traces Whitman's influence on modern to postmodern poets writing the middle-length and long poem. Separate chapters are devoted to Berryman, Kinnell, Roethke, Duncan, Ashbery, and Merrill. This is a poetic history, distinguished by its thesis (à la Harold Bloom) that the influence of Whitman in the 20th-century long poem is present everywhere and yet rarely "traced back to him," offered by Gardner in evidence that "Whitman's influence has been generalized now as one set of tensions within our cultural heritage." Gardner's conclusions are more specific to the modernist tradition than to either Whitman's own period or our own postmodernity (even though Ashbery and Merrill are nominally treated as "postmoderns"). A less literary treatment of Whitman as cultural institution would have better engaged the book in the current scholarly conversation about his politics.

David Kuebrich's *Minor Prophecy: Walt Whitman's New American Religion* (Indiana) demonstrates the value of newer religious approaches to a poet, like Whitman, who had obvious ambitions as religious prophet. Kuebrich recognizes that the "prophetic Whitman" has become something of a dead issue in recent years, and he is rather defensive in his insistence that a "close analysis of Whitman's spirituality" will "resurrect the earlier prophetic reading of Whitman's intention." For Kuebrich, the "principal poem" is the 1855 *Leaves of Grass*, which is to be read as Whitman's modern Bible. This, too, is not entirely original, and the readings it produces are somewhat conventional. Kuebrich's crucial section is chapter eight, "Poetry and Politics: A New Public Faith," but this does not talk about the various circles Whitman drew around him, instead simply acknowledging that he was not "successful in the virtually superhuman task . . . of forging an alternative to the Judeo-Christian world view." Kuebrich connects this utopian theology to Whitman's liberated views on sexuality, gender, and politics, but he stresses too much the "millennial perfectionism" in Whitman without considering how central such values are to the more secular philosophy of liberal progressivism with its attendant economic and social forces. Kuebrich's book reminds us that religious studies have much to offer in assessing romantic and modern poets, especially those with prophetic social and intellectual aims, but it also shows how religious studies continue to follow their own version of literary formalism, caught in a version of *Geistesgeschichte* in considerable need of historicist criticism if not deconstruction.

M. Jimmie Killingworth's *Whitman's Poetry of the Body: Sexuality, Politics and the Text* (No. Car.) attempts to fashion Whitman in terms of our contemporary critical debates, especially feminist, gay, and textualist ones, and does so in a way he himself characterizes as "New Historicist." In some cases this description of the method is accurate, especially when Killingworth links Whitman's poetic advocacy of "erotic physical morality" with 19th-century women's rights activism and advocacy of free love. But the overall treatment remains firmly focused on the first three editions of *Leaves of Grass* and on a postbellum "aftermath" (1865–1891) that Killingworth reads rather traditionally as Whitman's descent into aesthetics. Once again, the youthful Whitman is affirmed and the later Whitman reviled for abstraction and ideological surrender. There is little to refute in the poetic readings, but they chart a familiar "poetic career" and thus do not fulfill Killingworth's initial promise to describe a Whitman different from the ones offered by the old literary histories and formalist readings.

Among the books with substantial sections on Whitman published in 1989, I want to include Larry Reynolds's *European Revolutions and the American Literary Renaissance* (Yale), which was not mentioned in this chapter last year. It is an important study of U.S. literary responses to the European revolutions of 1848–49, as well as to the general context for revolution in Europe in the 19th century. The chapter on Whitman is especially important, because Reynolds quite forthrightly acknowledges Whitman's early criticism of abolitionists, "low opinion of Negroes," and other views incompatible with the prevailing view of him as politically avant-garde. Reynolds argues that it was more Whitman's sympathy with the French, especially the French

Revolution, that shaped his prophetic poetry and its call for a revolution in social behavior and values in the 1850s. Carefully reading
Whitman's journalism for the Brooklyn *Daily Eagle* during 1846 and
1847, Reynolds shows how Whitman, like Margaret Fuller, "anticipated the 1848–1849 upheavals on the Continent and stood ready to
applaud and justify them." Despite Whitman's reputation as the 19th-
century poet of "American nationalism," Reynolds argues convincingly that Whitman rejected a "narrow nationalism," envisioned a
more international social order, and aspired to become "a poet of all
nations." It is a theme that Whitman would revive later in his career,
especially in his poetry of the 1870s, and suggests that Whitman both
anticipated social directions and the internationalism of the high
modernists.

Joseph Fichtelberg's *The Complex Image* is an interesting contribution to the theory of autobiography. It is nominally concerned with
"American" autobiography, but Fichtelberg's theoretical models are
drawn from critics known for positions that exceed national boundaries—James Olney, Louis Renza, and Michael Sprinker—as does his
prototype for the radical autobiographer, Friedrich Nietzsche, the
subject of the first chapter. What interests Fichtelberg is the struggle
of modern thinkers to construct a functional *textual* self amid a world
increasingly hostile to the willful, unique self. Whitman's problem in
Leaves of Grass is, somewhat predictably, comparable to Nietzsche's.
Following Bercovitch's *Puritan Origins of the American Self*, Fichtelberg works out the heritage of the "tension between the communal
and the isolated self" that is at once the "American" intellectual heritage *and* the European rationalist tradition. In his own way, Fichtelberg offers an intellectual history for Whitman that resembles Reynolds's more material one: it reconnects Whitman to his European
sources.

Among the general essays on Whitman, Mark DeLancey's "Texts,
Interpretations, and Whitman's 'Song of Myself' " (*AL* 61:359–81)
establishes some of the contexts for this year's scholarship because his
rhetorical approach focuses on consensus as the essential issue of
Whitman's poetics. With so much recent criticism revolving around
Whitman's abilities to address the great political issues of his time—
race and slavery, gender, sexuality—that approach ought to yield a
defining essay. Unfortunately, DeLancey has little to say about specific political and historical issues. Instead, he treats Whitman as the
poet of modernity in reconciling Wordsworthian and Emersonian ver-

sions of romantic idealism. Although DeLancey often refers to Whitman's "democracy," what he means by Whitman's modernity is simply the adaptability of his poetry to a deconstructive theory of the sign and thus of knowledge as rhetoric. DeLancey's combination of Derrida, Harold Bloom, Stanley Fish, and other contemporary theorists only reminds us how limited such "theoretical history" looks these days.

Michael Moon's "Disseminating Whitman" (*SAQ* 88:247–65) is part of Moon's larger project on the ways Whitman, Alger, and James "engage questions of the history and theory of homosexuality" in the United States that challenge traditional conceptions of that "theme" in American literature. In his adaptation of deconstruction to gay criticism, Moon analyzes Whitman's critique of phallogocentrism; he focuses on motifs of liquidity in Whitman—"drinking, spilling, weeping, sweating, soaking, and flooding"—as indirect expressions of homosexual and onanistic desires. Such figuration, like the more familiar imagery of men bathing, spraying, and sousing in *Leaves of Grass*, is part of what Moon considers Whitman's effort to poetically construct an alternative "body" beyond the constraints and boundaries of patriarchal rationality. His reading of Whitman (with interesting links to the other figures in his longer project) suggests a more fantastic and less literal use of literature to express alternative configurations of the subject, the body, and sexuality. But Moon's own slide from literary figurations of the body and sexuality to the debate between realism and romance in current approaches to the 19th century is not very convincing, in part because it is predicated on such a conventional definition of "realism."

My impression that much of the general criticism on Whitman for 1989 centers on issues of gender and sexuality may be shaped in part by the special emphasis on these topics in the *Mickle Street Review*. Sandra Gilbert's " 'Now in a moment I know what I am for': Rituals of Initiation in Whitman and Dickinson" (discussed in the Dickinson section, below), David S. Reynolds's "Whitman and Nineteenth-Century Views of Gender and Sexuality" (11:9–16), William H. Shurr's "Whitman and the Seduction of the Reader" (11:71–79), and Louis Simpson's "Strategies of Sex in Whitman's Poetry" (11:34–45) focus on Whitman's response to 19th-century attitudes toward gender and sexuality, generally arguing that Whitman's poetry refunctions contemporary conventions for the sake of alternative conceptions informed by the inherent erotics of poetry and the imagination. Jerome

Loving's "Whitman's Idea of Women" (*MStrR* 11:17–33) is more traditionally thematic in its effort to link Whitman's homosexuality with
feminist issues, but like Moon's essay sees Whitman's poetry concerned with alternative conceptions of gender and thus the *process* of
maternity and homosexual *desire* as predicates of such a new subjectivity and physicality. Loving's effort to show that Whitman's
homosexuality allows him to overcome the masculine domination and
commodification of women, especially through sexual reproduction,
seems a little too neatly political in the current effort to redeem Whitman. For example, it does not answer the feminist criticism (see
Vivian Pollak, below) that Whitman represented eroticism far more
frequently in terms of men than women.

An interesting short essay by Robert Leigh Davis, "Wound-
Dressers and House Calls: Medical Representations in Whitman and
Williams" (*WWR* 6:133–39), casts a somewhat different light on
Whitman's "radical" reformulation of the body. Focusing on *Specimen
Days* and *Drum-Taps* (and William Carlos Williams's *Spring and
All*), Davis argues that for Whitman "medical attention restores the
coherence and social interconnection lost in deep injury." Davis relates the nurse, reader, and poet to a "healing" of the wounds of war
that effectively cover over the monstrosity of the wound. Davis misses
the best instance of this in *Drum-Taps*, "Vigil Strange I Kept on the
Field One Night," but the general argument is an important qualifica-
tion of the somewhat overoptimistic efforts to "save" Whitman by way
of his radical reconceptualizations of the body.

Karen Sanchez-Eppler's "To Stand Between: A Political Perspective on Whitman's Poetics of Merger and Embodiment" (*ELH* 56:
923–46) aims to redeem Whitman from political objection, especially
of his sparse poetic treatment of slavery and race. Beginning with the
notebook lines for what would become section 21 of "Song of Myself,"
she notes the important deletions from the final draft of such crucial
lines as "I am the poet of slaves and of masters of slaves" and "I go
with the slaves of the earth equally with the masters / And I will stand
between the masters and the slaves." These and similar deletions, in
which Whitman explicitly inaugurates his poetic project as one committed to the political issues of slavery, is for Sanchez-Eppler finally
Whitman's "consistent" strategy of "decontextualizing" his imagery
of its political referents. Too quickly, Derridean *différance* becomes
Sanchez-Eppler's strategy of mediation: bisexuality, miscegenation,
and homosexuality, among other issues in Whitman's poetry and for

his times, are read under the governing trope of poetic metaphor itself, which is that "site where difference meets." Would that it were true, thus solving at a stroke Whitman's neglect, repression (see Pollak, below), or feigned mastery (see Davis, above) of complex political issues sketchily treated in his poetry. In fact, decontextualization means *depoliticization*, contrary to Sanchez-Eppler's conclusions.

Katherine Kinney's "Whitman's 'Word of the Modern' and the First Modern War" (*WWR* 7:1–14) tries to address Whitman's response to the Civil War and its issues by connecting his homosexuality to a prophetic vision of a utopian democracy in which democracy both en masse and in the individual might be reconciled. Kinney, who also studies American literature dealing with the Vietnam War, is an empathetic reader of Whitman's war poems in *Drum-Taps*, and perhaps for that reason can see nothing but hope in his effort to individualize the suffering of soldiers otherwise dehumanized as the machinery of the first modern war. She thus misses the demonized qualities of *Drum-Taps* tentatively addressed by Davis (above).

d. **Criticism: Individual Works.** Vivian Pollak's "Death as Repression, Repression as Death: A Reading of Whitman's 'Calamus' Poems" (*MStrR* 11:56–70) convincingly interprets Whitman's "apparently perverse attraction to death" as part of his paradoxical effort "to deny the fulfillment of his eroticism and to affirm its vitality in the face of social and psychological oppression." For Pollak, Whitman's repression of his own homosexuality seems to be the principal aim of his tropes on death, and she virtually equates "death" with what Whitman considers forbidden eroticism. Reading Whitman in terms of his own anxieties regarding his homosexuality strikes me as a useful corrective to criticism that praises him for his frank expression of homoeroticism. Unfortunately, Pollak tries to resolve such an insuperable problem for Whitman in his times by offering a tidy solution in Art itself: "Whitman anticipates a heroic death that will liberate him from the death-in-life which he associates with erotic bereavement and with sexual repression."

Kent Ljungquist's "'Meteor of War': Melville, Thoreau, and Whitman Respond to John Brown" (*AL* 61:674–80) adds interesting historical material to the argument that Whitman characteristically transformed political into poetic issues. Ljungquist demonstrates that associations of Brown's raid on Harper's Ferry in 1859 with meteors are based in part on accounts in the press of a meteor shower that ap-

peared in the Northeast after the raid and before Brown's execution
that same year. "In typical Whitman fashion," Ljungquist writes of
"Year of Meteors," "he appropriates this image to the 'I' of the poem
and asks: 'What am I myself but one of your meteors?'" Once again,
the role of Whitman's egotistical sublime in his aestheticization of the
political questions leading up to the Civil War here seems to gain
warrant as a critical and scholarly question of importance.

Paul Diehl's "'A Noiseless Patient Spider': Whitman's Beauty—
Blood and Brain" (*WWR* 6:117–32) and Geoffrey Sill's "'You Tides
with Ceaseless Swell': A Reading of the Manuscript" (*WWR* 6:189–
97) contribute to our understanding of the genesis of the poetry.
Examining drafts in the 1862–64 notebook, the 1868 version, and the
final and finest form in the 1881 *Leaves of Grass*, Diehl shows concretely how Whitman joined "physical and semantic acts of language"
in the effort to approach the "impossibility" of the spiritual world.
Sill's essay is more conventional genetic scholarship; the critical argument follows Roger Asselineau's thesis in *The Evolution of Walt
Whitman* (1962) that Whitman in his later years was particularly attentive to formal poetic matters. Like so much genetic criticism, both
essays conclude predictably that the last version is the best. I don't
debate their conclusions regarding these particular poems, but wonder about the frequency of the argument. Isn't there an ideology implicit in all of this that the "great writer" is *bound* to improve whatever he revises? There are exceptions, of course, but they are sparse
in Whitman criticism. Wouldn't it be fun for someone to argue:
"Yegads! That 1881 *Leaves of Grass* is a disgrace! He should have left
the poems alone!"

e. **Affinities and Influences.** George Hutchinson's "Whitman and
the Black Poet: Kelly Miller's Speech to the Walt Whitman Fellowship" (*AL* 61:46–58) attempts to save Whitman from increasing
scrutiny of his sometimes troublesome attitudes toward slavery and
race by reconstructing the origins of his influence on modern African-
American writers. For Hutchinson, the "recorded black response to
Whitman" begins with a speech by Kelly Miller, dean of the College
of Arts and Sciences at Howard University and later a minor figure in
the Harlem Renaissance, to the Walt Whitman Fellowship on 31 May
1895. Hutchinson argues that "the audience Miller addressed was,
from both literary and political standpoints, the forebear of various
types of white audiences during the Harlem Renaissance." Miller's

reading of Whitman positions him as a black writer and thinker "vis-à-vis western literary tradition," a role that Hutchinson claims Whitman "would serve for many black writers and critics to come." Hutchinson traces the line of influence from Miller's Whitman to the voice of Whitman in Langston Hughes and in Houston Baker's *Blues, Ideology, and Afro-American Literature*.

George Leonard's "Emerson, Whitman, and Conceptual Art" (*P&L* 13:297–306) explores the residual influences of Emerson's and Whitman's idealism on the emergence of conceptual art as a new avant-garde at the end of the 1960s. Leonard argues that Emerson and Whitman attacked the "art object" even more thoroughly than postmodern conceptual radicals like Joseph Kosuth. Yet the Hegelianism that Leonard correctly finds at the heart of the transcendentalist aesthetic has a way of reinstituting aesthetic hierarchies that are just as insidious as the fetishism of the "artwork." Arguments like Leonard's that an avant-garde art movement, like conceptual art, is not so new after all and may have been done even better by its precursors have a tendency to ignore historical differences. The fake artworks of the 19th-century "classical revival," for example, are not the same as the modernist high-cultural forms criticized by conceptual artists more than a century later. Indeed, Emerson's and Whitman's romantic idealism was by then another "cultural fetish," in considerable need of New Left aesthetic critique.

ii. Emily Dickinson

a. **Bibliography and Editing.** *Emily Dickinson's Reception in the 1890s,* ed. Willis J. Buckingham (Pittsburgh) may be the most important publication of the year in Dickinson studies because its collection of more than 600 notices and reviews tells us so much about both the invention of Dickinson as modern poet and the fin-de-siècle culture to which her "strangeness" so appealed. For those interested in reconstructing 19th-century norms for literary reading this is a rich source, although it must be added that the book deals with the *late* 19th century—a period far more similar to our own than the mid-century United States that prompted Dickinson's first writings. In the introduction Buckingham tries to summarize the significance of the material for scholars and critics. I only wish there could be more of such discussion, but the volume itself is already very long—and, at $120, very expensive.

Barbara Kelly's "ED Checklist, annotated (1985–1988)" (*DicS* 71: 18–35) is extremely useful, thanks to Kelly's fine and often witty annotations. Other features in *Dickinson Studies* include "Foreign Bibliography," such as Niels Kjaer's "Danish" and Carlos Daghlian's "Portuguese" in the same issue as Kelly's checklist. But *Dickinson Studies* could use some help in learning the elementary rules of desktop publishing and the common sense of readable layout.

b. **Criticism: General.** Barbara Kelly in her annotations to the Dickinson checklist (see above) points out that the relative lack of biographical and historical information about Dickinson encourages textual considerations that only with great difficulty avoid New Critical methods and values. I take this as my organizing principle for this year's review; feminist and deconstructive approaches continue to enliven Dickinson studies, as they have throughout the 1980s, and these are just the approaches most likely to find text-centered interpretation the most constraining. There are still, however, a fair number of essays concerned with explicating individual Dickinson poems or reading "themes" in certain "groups" of her poems. The latter are often the most aggravating, because the "groupings" are so transparently contrived by the critic, unconstrained by more specific historical information about conditions of production. Thus Adrian Richwell's "Poetic Immortality: Dickinson's 'Flood Subject' Reconsidered (A Reading of Emily Dickinson's Poetry about Literary Fame)" (*DicS* 69:1–31) treats Dickinson's work as some critical *combinatoire*. Ditto for so many of the explications published in the *Explicator*. They are not really scholarship or criticism designed for a national audience of professionals, but classroom "exercises."

Some indication of the "textualist problem" in the criticism is the variety of efforts to treat Dickinson's poetry in relation to pedagogy. Few of these efforts succeed in overcoming the traditional uses of Dickinson's lyrics in the classroom. As short, rhetorically complex works, the poems are eminently "teachable," unfortunately in terms that tend to reinforce New Critical fetishes: irony, defamiliarization, "poetic thinking" (as opposed to rationality), and lyric "voice." A good example of adapting this aesthetic to pedagogy is Lee J. Richmond's "Teaching Emily Dickinson and Metaphor: Towards Modern Poetry Practice" (*DicS* 72:33–43); over the years such essays have been legion. Even the methods avowedly opposed to New Criticism end by being caught in its trap. Thus Robin Riley Fast and Christine Mack

Gordon's collection, *Approaches to Teaching Dickinson's Poetry* (MLA), and George Hillocks's "Literary Texts in Classrooms" in Phillip Jackson and Sophie Haroutounian-Gordon's *From Socrates to Software: The Teacher as Text and the Text as Teacher* (Chicago: National Society for the Study of Education) struggle in very different ways to develop alternative approaches to teaching literature but end up reaffirming the categories that could be found alphabetized in M. H. Abrams's old glossary of *Literary Terms.*

More interesting in this vein is *Emily Dickinson: A Celebration for Readers,* ed. Suzanne Juhasz and Cristanne Miller, the entire volume 16 of *Women's Studies* devoted to the proceedings of a conference held at the Claremont Colleges in September, 1986, the year of the Dickinson centennial. The proceedings reproduce six workshops, each devoted to one Dickinson poem (numbers 271, 315, 656, 754, 1581, and 1651); each workshop was conducted by three scholars, each offering a brief reading of the poem that led to discussion. The aim was to make the conference a participatory experience—in effect, a subversion of the customary model of "speaker" and "audience," which is often enough the model for the classroom ("teacher" and "students"). Obviously modeled after feminist collaborative research projects and less scholarly, decentered "communal" activities, these workshops do manage to get beyond formalist approaches to Dickinson's poetry. Their limitations are also an effect of their strength: spontaneity makes careful historical and scholarly work difficult, even though some extraordinarily qualified scholars and critics participated. Cheryl Walker's keynote address (alas, an exception to the workshop rule) is particularly noteworthy, because it tries to turn Dickinson studies from the "fashionable" celebration of Dickinson's "cleverness in avoiding various forms of social oppression" experienced by many 19th-century women and toward the contradictions in Dickinson's life and poetry. Although Walker terms this a "form of post-structuralism," it looks today more like cultural criticism under the worthy motto "No privileged texts!" Even so, the conference and its proceedings remain text-bound, with some notable exceptions in the discussions, and even collaborative work cannot dissipate the ghosts of Irony and the Logic of Metaphor. Perhaps it is time to apply cultural criticism to Dickinson *as* formalist, not just in her invention by critics but in her own construction of her poetic self.

One of the critics represented in *Emily Dickinson: A Celebration for Readers* is Joanne Dobson, whose *Dickinson and the Strategies*

of Reticence: The Woman Writer in Nineteenth-Century America
(Indiana) promises to revise the protomodernist (and often New
Critical) Dickinson by interpreting the poetry in terms of her contemporaries. Reading Dickinson in conjunction with Lydia Huntley
Sigourney, Maria Sedgwick, Harriet Beecher Stowe, Susan Warner,
Rebecca Harding Davis, Fanny Fern, Louisa May Alcott and a wide
range of other 19th-century women writers, Dobson does the work of
historical reconstruction that has been one of the hallmarks of feminist criticism over the past 20 years. As much as Dobson wants to
situate Dickinson in the company and traditions of 19th-century
women writers, she acknowledges that certain negative consequences
follow. Many of these successful writers demonstrate that Dickinson's withdrawal from the world "was *not* the inevitable response
of a woman writer (even a brilliant one) to her talent and social
position." This book provides the "other direction" away from formalist analysis of Dickinson's writings that so many other critics
desperately want but claim is "unavailable" due to the paucity of
biographical materials. In fact, there is another, rich "history" for
Dickinson, albeit not always in the best interests of her reputation for
"uniqueness," in this other history.

Another, somewhat more conventional, way to "historicize" Dickinson is Virginia H. Oliver's *Apocalypse of Green: A Study of Emily
Dickinson's Eschatology* (Peter Lang). Oliver's careful study of Dickinson's religious themes in terms of contemporary 19th-century theological debates, especially in the response to rapid scientific developments, is recognizable "intellectual history" with an emphasis on
religious studies. It is not quite "history of religion," since Oliver's
sources range from traditional theologians to Transcendentalists like
Emerson and Thoreau. Oliver's most interesting discussions are those
devoted to Dickinson's anticipation of modern theories of time in her
effort to reconcile "eternity" with scientific theories of "infinity." Alas,
this gives us yet another "protomodern" Dickinson, albeit one who
carries over the religious traditions of two centuries.

Bettina L. Knapp's *Emily Dickinson* (Continuum) is a kind of
"introduction and interpretation" volume that reinforces the New
Critical Dickinson. Repeatedly connecting Dickinson with the symbolists, the later surrealists, and other proto- or high-modern writers
and movements, Knapp does little to revise Dickinson. With insistent
references to poetic mysticism, she turns her into a kind of vatic seer.
This is a book designed for undergraduates, and for that reason all the

more aggravating for its platitudes. Much of the scholarship cited is now very old or just unreliable.

R. Jackson Wilson is a historian, not a literary critic, and his *Figures of Speech* is a good example of the new importance historians have accorded literary production in the 19th century. Dickinson would seem to be a strange figure in such a history, given the posthumous publication of her poetry, but Wilson makes an interesting case for her as a protomodernist in her correspondence with Higginson. Wilson argues that Dickinson's modesty regarding her own work was a convention of the time, also adopted by Irving, Garrison, and Emerson. It was, of course, a pose of false modesty; their "relinquishment of fame" was intended to establish "credentials that gave them a claim on the moral and aesthetic high ground." For writers earlier in the century, such credentials were bolstered by associations with established institutions for moral authority: the ruling class (through patronage), a political party, or the church. Dickinson's correspondence with Higginson marks a change in this conception of literary authority and the marketplace; it is for Wilson the beginning of an independent "literary market," in which publication and complex valuations of "circulation" (not just "sales") would assume ever greater centrality in the constitution of the "literary life" and the authority of its producers. Of course, this Dickinson anticipates the high moderns, arguably the first generation of Western writers forced to reconcile the moral and aesthetic demands of "serious literature" with the problem of earning their keep. His approach to Dickinson is yet another promising way of historicizing her, short of some unexpected discovery of a trunk of documents.

Joanne Feit Diehl is represented with a brief reading of poem 1651 in *Emily Dickinson: A Celebration for Readers* (see above) and a major essay, "Murderous Poetics: Dickinson, the Father, and the Text," (*Daughters and Fathers*, pp. 326–43). Diehl incorporates the convention of "female self-sacrifice" in a reading of Dickinson's poetic defenses as the poet's means of investing herself with "purgative, aggressive power." Nevertheless, the "consequences of such hard-won freedom may be a kind of purity that betrays at best a mutilated independence," in which "mutilated" suggests the limitation of either pure aesthetics or a purely religious independence. Like other critics this year, Diehl qualifies the often overenthusiastic "celebration" of Dickinson's rebellion as a woman poet. The Other against whom her poetry struggles is various, at times omnipresent, and—like U.S. hegemony—

pervasively phallic: Father/God/Lover/Precursor. The "murder" in
the title is thus double: toward the conventional feminine "self" (or
role model) but also against the Name-of-the-Law-that-is-the-Father
(Lacan). This is post-structuralist Dickinson at its best, because Diehl
keeps the terms carefully aligned within the religious, domestic, and
ideological conventions of Dickinson's culture. Text-centered as this
essay is, it overcomes the formalist inclinations of so many other
readings.

Thomas Hockersmith's " 'Into Degreeless Noon': Time, Consciousness, and Oblivion in Emily Dickinson" (*ATQ* n.s. 3:278–95) is a carefully argued treatment of Dickinson as existentialist. For Hockersmith,
this is evident in her rejection of transcendence and thus, presumably,
the more spiritual drifts of Transcendentalism, but it ignores the traditional connection between international romanticism and modern
existentialism: "Dickinson evokes the sense of fear and helplessness
that characterizes the ordeal of life. At the same time, she reveals the
magnificence of its struggle. For Dickinson, this struggle is the essence
of life itself." Well, yes, if you're middle-class, white, have leisure time
and disposable income for pens and paper.

Janet Buell's " 'A Slow Solace': Emily Dickinson and Consolation"
(*NEQ* 62:323—45) did not have the benefit of Joanne Dobson's book,
and that's a pity. Following Gilbert and Gubar's argument in *The
Madwoman in the Attic*—a thesis that their recent *No Man's Land*
revises considerably—Buell argues that Dickinson typifies the plight
of the "female artist" of her class and time who "had no choice but
actively to elect deprivation in order to achieve the unconventional
aims of art." Dobson points out that there were scores of successful
women writers in the 19th century who demonstrably achieved artistic excellence without "actively" choosing this sort of self-sacrifice.
Undoubtedly, "Emily Dickinson's form of spinsterhood required courage," but such courage pales before the efforts of Harriet Jacobs to
earn the money to "buy" her children out of slavery by writing *Incidents in the Life of a Slave Girl* or those of women writers who raised
children as single parents by writing in the late-night hours. The
sources for Dickinson's elegiac strangeness should be sought elsewhere than in her middle-class domesticity.

Every year there are several belletristic essays on Dickinson by
poets and writers. Usually they are thinly veiled "advertisements for
myself." Charles Simic's "Visionaries and Anti-Visionaries" (*Denver
Quarterly* 24:114–23) is obviously Simic's effort to create a tradition

for himself. He builds it from poets "like Dickinson, Frost, and Stevens who have a lover's quarrel with Emerson and his transcendentalism." What he says about these three poets (four, counting himself) is roughly accurate: "For them Nature is opaque, inert, mute, and often malevolent." Of course, they are moderns, like Simic, who tells us that "the American poet is the high trapeze artist in a visionary circus where the lights have been turned off." Let's face it: late modernism is bad modernism at this stage of the 20th century. Far more interesting is Alice Fulton's effort to construct a "Dickinsonian" tradition for modern and contemporary poets in "Her Moment of Brocade: The Reconstruction of Emily Dickinson" (*Parnassus* 15:9–44). This long essay is marred by its author's apparent unfamiliarity with scholarship and criticism since the late 1970s, particularly the feminist "reconstruction" of Dickinson's 19th-century cultural contexts. But Fulton's argument that Dickinson ought to be treated as a 19th-century origin, in the manner of Whitman, for 20th-century American poets deserves attention. The tradition she sketches too quickly is the real interest of this essay: A. R. Ammons, Robert Creeley, Heather McHugh, Phyllis Janowitz, May Swenson, Denise Levertov, and Charles Simic (see above). Yes, they're mostly "late moderns," too, but Fulton's "construction" of a Dickinsonian tradition that includes men and women poets is quite promising and should be pursued.

Linda Munk's " 'Musicians Wrestle Everywhere': Emily Dickinson, Carl G. Jung and the Myth of Poetic Creation" (*DicS* 72:3–16) is another in a sinking raft of Jungian studies of U.S. literature. Jung's archetypes are about as useful (and useless) as poetic metaphors or literary archetypes in articulating certain norms that we might say have something to do with a "collective unconscious." But Jung was discredited long ago for his neglect of the specific social and historical circumstances shaping these archetypes; he's as much a formalist as Northrop Frye.

c. **Criticism: Individual Works.** Douglass Robinson's "Two Dickinson Readings" (*DicS* 70:25–35) interprets poems 657 and 303 as occasions for revising Harold Bloom's *Map of Misreading* as the map of "Amerika." The Bloomian "anxiety" that Robinson finds in Dickinson, however, is one that serves his own argument in *American Apocalypses: The Image of the End of the World in American Literature* (1985). His aim is to establish a productive dialogue between the optative Emerson and the apocalyptic Poe, and his project is perfectly

Bloomian. Alas, he misses the obvious feminist point, which is that Dickinson "fits" such a model only insofar as she is made to reenact a "family romance" that is fundamentally masculine.

d. **Affinities and Influences.** Sandra Gilbert's " 'Now in a Moment I Know What I Am For': Rituals of Initiation in Whitman and Dickinson" (*MStrR* VI:46–55) is a major contribution to our understanding of the differences between Whitman and Dickinson, especially important in light of the efforts to read Whitman as the 19th-century U.S. male poet most sympathetic to feminist politics and gender issues. Gilbert argues convincingly that the generic conventions of "Out of the Cradle Endlessly Rocking," for example, suggest "rituals of initiation" like those "defined and discussed by Arnold van Gennep and Victor Turner," which are demonstrably *patriarchal* initiation rites. Dickinson, on the other hand, works toward "*bewilderment* and *subversion*" rather than the conventions of socialization (into cultures ruled by men) that Gilbert finds in Whitman. Rather than arguing that Dickinson fully constituted a *woman's rite de passage* (à la Chodorow, for example), Gilbert suggests simply that Dickinson problematized the convention of the *rite de passage* so relentlessly enacted by literature in modern societies.

University of California, Irvine

6. Mark Twain

Robert Sattelmeyer

Cultural criticism of Mark Twain reigned in 1989. Led by Susan Gillman's *Dark Twins*, many of the most interesting and important works carried on the tradition (albeit with upgraded methodology and vocabulary) of regarding Mark Twain as a peculiarly sensitive if often unwitting register—a kind of distinguished coal miner's canary—of the ills of late 19th-century American culture. These challenging forays into the negative isms of our collective past shared the spotlight with two books issued by the Mark Twain Project, the second volume of *Mark Twain's Letters* and *Huck Finn and Tom Sawyer Among the Indians, and Other Unfinished Stories.*

i. Biography

While there were no major biographical studies this year, both Susan Gillman's book and the "Biographical Directory" in *Huck Finn and Tom Sawyer Among the Indians,* both discussed below, have significant biographical implications. The most interesting biographical article was not about Mark Twain himself but about Van Wyck Brooks. Turning the psychoanalytic tables, Andrew Abarbanel, in "The 'Ordeal' of Van Wyck Brooks" (*L&P* 35:89–104), accounts for Brooks's misreading of Twain by examining the similarities between Brooks's family and Twain's, and concluding that "each of Brooks' parents and brother, then, was in some way a caricature of the worst traits of the corresponding members of Samuel Clemens' family. This fact facilitated in Brooks an unconscious identification of himself as a caricature of some of the worst traits of Mark Twain himself. . . . this allowed Brooks to use and abuse the image of Twain as the whipping boy for his own vulnerable ego at the hands of his own particularly fastidious super-ego." Abarbanel describes Brooks's thwarted creativity during the first half of his career, when *The Ordeal of Mark Twain* was produced and when Brooks was "floridly psychotic for months on end," and promises in future studies to investigate the contrasting functions of Twain's creative process.

Two articles in the Fall 1987 issue of *MTJ* extend our knowledge of visits Mark Twain made to Newport and Annapolis. John Roche's "Making a Reputation: Mark Twain in Newport" (25:23–27) describes Twain's trip during the summer of 1875 as a stage in his acceptance in the world of the Eastern literary establishment. In "Mark Twain's Visit to Annapolis" (25:2–8), Charles J. Nolan, Jr., and David O. Tomlinson chronicle Twain's movements during a May 1907 visit, during which he gave an "entertainment" for the benefit of a Presbyterian church and was repeatedly told to put out his cigar. Not surprisingly, he cut his visit short. In the same issue Nick Karanovich provides additional details on "Sixty Books in Mark Twain's Library" (25:9–20) that were sold at auctions of the Doheny collection between 1987 and 1989, and Alison Ensor explores "The Favorite Hymns of Sam and Livy Clemens" (25:21–22).

ii. Editions and Bibliography

Volume 2 of the *Mark Twain's Letters* (Calif.) appeared from the Mark Twain Project (see Hamlin Hill's review of volume 1 in *ALS 1988*), covering 1867 and 1868. Edited by Harriet Elinor Smith, Richard Bucci, and Lin Salamo, the letters and accompanying documents richly chronicle Mark Twain's life during one of its busiest periods—one that saw him leave San Francisco for New York (surviving a cholera epidemic on the way), travel to Europe and the Middle East on the *Quaker City* excursion, begin to establish himself as a successful lecturer in the East, write *The Innocents Abroad*, and fall in love with Olivia Langdon. The letters are printed in "plain text," with Clemens's alterations indicated by simple typographic signs, and there are numerous reproductions of important letters and textual cruxes. The volume is accompanied by several useful appendices, including genealogies of the Clemens and Langdon families, a register of the passengers and crew of the *Quaker City*, and Mark Twain's lecture schedule for 1868–69. In the tradition established by volume 1, the letters are meticulously annotated, providing a virtual documentary biography of Mark Twain for this period. This has the makings of a magnificent edition.

Huck Finn and Tom Sawyer Among the Indians, and Other Unfinished Stories (Calif.) gathers a number of "Matter of Hannibal" fragments, most of which, including the title piece, were published in *Mark Twain's Hannibal, Huck, and Tom*, edited for the Mark Twain Papers by Walter Blair in 1969: "Villagers 1840–3," "Jane Lampton Clemens," "Tupperville-Dobbsville," "Clairvoyant," "Tom Sawyer's Conspiracy," and "Huck Finn" (called "Doughface" in the Blair volume). Also included are Mark Twain's 6 February 1870 letter to Will Bowen, and the following from other volumes of the Mark Twain Project: "Boy's Manuscript" (*The Adventures of Tom Sawyer*), "Hellfire Hotchkiss" (*Satires and Burlesques*), and "Schoolhouse Hill" (*Mysterious Stranger Manuscripts*). Collectively, they make widely available for the first time a group of sketches and incomplete works that richly amplify and complicate Twain's portrait of his boyhood home and its people. New and noteworthy in the collection is the complete version of "Villagers 1840–3," Twain's remarkable recollections of more than a hundred of his townspeople, many of whom would be candidates for roles in "Twin Peaks." The editors' "Biographical Directory," providing corrections and additional details of the lives of these and other Hannibal residents, is about twice the length of the original in *Hannibal, Huck, and Tom*, and correspondingly more detailed and valuable.

The year's only significant bibliographical work, J. C. B. Kinch's *Mark Twain's German Critical Reception 1875–1986* (Greenwood), is a comprehensive annotated bibliography of writings about Mark Twain in German. This very useful and carefully prepared volume includes monographs, journal articles, substantial newspaper articles, dissertations, excerpts from literary histories, and introductions and afterwords to selected editions of Twain's works in German. Mark Twain had a special relationship with Germany, the Germans, and their language, and this book amply demonstrates that the interest has been more than mutual. Its basic chronological organization could provide the raw material for very interesting studies using Hans Robert Jauss's theories of the aesthetics of reception, and other methods of organization and possibilities for searching are built into the comprehensive 50-page index. The nonevaluative annotations are both unusually full (often ranging up to 500 words) and lucidly written.

iii. General Interpretations

Easily the most significant critical book of the year was Susan Gillman's *Dark Twins: Imposture and Identity in Mark Twain's America*

(Chicago). Informed by recent theory in cultural studies, Gillman takes Mark Twain's pervasive concern with twins, doubling, and impersonations—his "most apparently unique and idiosyncratic representations of problematic identity"—and shows how they "engage with late-nineteenth-century efforts to classify human behavior within biological, sexual, racial, and psychological parameters." This constellation of issues is for Gillman, as she claims it was for Mark Twain, less a set of literary than of social concerns. Consequently, it is neither Twain the literary artist nor Twain the humorist who appears in this book but rather Twain as "representative man" (gender emphasized) of his age.

If much (some might say most) of Mark Twain is missing in this work of cultural pathology, much is also revealed. Gillman does not disregard Mark Twain the writer, but rather examines his career as necessarily involving him in contradictions that rendered identity confusing. As humorist cum serious writer, he was alternately the perpetrator and exposer of various shams and hoaxes (not forgetting the primal creative act of inventing Mark Twain himself), and to the extent that he participated aggressively in the developments and transformations in both authorship and the publishing industry during his age he was peculiarly susceptible to the conflicts that W. D. Howells called "the lot of the hybrid class of post-Civil War authors."

Having described Mark Twain's problematic identity as a literary man/entrepreneur/publisher, Gillman focuses on three groups of texts, setting each one in a distinct yet interrelated cultural context and tracing a development from "literal, external, and conscious" forms of doubling to forms that are increasingly "metaphysical, abstract, and speculative." The first is *Pudd'nhead Wilson and Those Extraordinary Twins*, which Gillman rejoins at the hip to disclose a tangle of questions involving the legal basis of racial identity. The "farce" of the twins revolves around the absurdity of determining identity and responsibility by law, setting up the "tragedy" of *Pudd'n-head Wilson*, where Wilson's courtroom triumph gives way to the tragic uncertainties of Tom Driscoll and Valet de Chambre's real (as socially and economically constituted) versus their legal status.

The second group are "Tales of Sexual Identity," including *Following the Equator*, *Joan of Arc*, "Why Not Abolish It?" (a magazine piece on the "age of consent"), and a group of fragmentary and relatively little-known "transvestite tales," particularly the most fully realized of these, "Wapping Alice," which was not published until

1981. These are "set in dialogue" (to use Gillman's terminology) with late 19th-century cultural attitudes about sexual identity and appropriate gender roles. Twain affirms traditional stereotypes of sexual difference having to do with "female purity" and dependence in his "age of consent" piece, and, somewhat paradoxically, in *Joan of Arc* finds the apotheosis of the feminine in the figure of the Maid of Orleans, who remained pure and girlish despite donning armor and leading an army into battle. During the same period, however, he also produced a set of writings that call restrictive gender boundaries into question. He admires the androgynous appearance and flowing garments of both sexes of Ceylonese natives in *Following the Equator*, and in the "transvestite tales," notably "Wapping Alice," he enacts "an open-ended confounding of sexual categories." But what he could entertain in his fiction he tended to deny in life, as Gillman demonstrates by considering "Wapping Alice" in the context of the notorious 1907 trial of Harry K. Thaw for murdering his wife's alleged seducer. Twain's final version of the story was dictated during the trial, which raised many of the same contradictory issues of female seductiveness versus female dependence, and his willingness to exploit these ambiguities theatrically in his own fictional courtroom was countermanded by his conventional response to the trial. Whatever dissolution of sexual boundaries he yearned for imaginatively, he shared his culture's "Dementia Americana," a term coined by Thaw's lawyer to characterize the temporary insanity induced in his client from learning of the violation of his wife's honor and purity.

The last group of texts treated are the "Dream Writings," late, fragmentary tales of fantasy and epistemological speculation—"voyages to alternate worlds in decentered time and space"—which are set in the context of psychical research and formulations of theories of the unconscious. Gillman argues convincingly that these tales, notably *The Mysterious Stranger* manuscripts, reflect a "deeply engaged interaction with contemporary psychological theories"; and that as a writer long troubled by questions of individual identity, the nature of creativity, and authorial control, Mark Twain was inevitably drawn to and affected by the many topics investigated and debated under the aegis of the Society for Psychical Research during the last two decades of his life. In this context, "No. 44" is less a satire on the damned human race than a catalog of psychical phenomena through which Twain examined the nature of his own creativity and imagination. The performances of "No. 44" are entertaining, and through them

Twain celebrates the fictive impulse and comes close to accepting that "subliminal self" that was paradoxically both evolutive and dissolutive in his own psyche. The other late fantasy tales, in *Mark Twain's "Which Was the Dream?" and Other Symbolic Writings of the Later Years*, represent voyages into an alien "cosmic environment" which "reject their own epistemological project of locating an authoritative foundation for knowledge, and instead opt for a totally decentered, relativized vision of experience," even though they simultaneously return us, via satire, to the world of the early 20th century.

The "deeply historicized" Mark Twain who emerges from (or perhaps is submerged in) Gillman's book is vigorously attacked by Frederick Crews in "The Parting of the Twains" (*NYRB* 20 July:39–44). In his view, Gillman's Mark Twain is a product of "social constructionism," the latest form of infidelity which denies literature a privileged status and regards it as one of many forms of cultural discourse. It also tends to deny the author artistic control over his text, demonstrating instead how Mark Twain merely "fell in with the self-protective mental strategies of his day." Crews accuses this mode of criticism of presumption in claiming exclusive rights to a skeptical apprehension of history, and—hurling the ultimate insult nowadays—naiveté: "Where they really part company with traditionalists is in their puritanical concern to maintain a politically correct position—one that will be guiltless of sexism, racism, economic individualism, and other distortions of a presumed state of nature. In practice, this spirit of post-Sixties conformism translates into a perpetually scandalized relation to the past—a phobic manner that is the very reverse of historiographic sophistication."

Unreconstructed intentionalists may share Crews's skepticism about the theoretical bases of some New Historicist interpretations of American literature, but there is nevertheless much to admire in Gillman's book. The issue of artistic autonomy is at least deferred by her focus on works that testify to a lack of artistic control—although one may question the centrality of an interpretation which rests mostly on false starts and fragments. Actually, the deterministic "social constructionism" of her methodology correlates highly with Twain's own disavowal of conscious control over his writings. Disregarding for the moment the issue of *her* intention, her focus on the culturally determined nature of this writing observes the spirit in which it was conceived. And her argument is, finally, always interesting and characterized by a breadth of learning and appreciation of nuance. If the book does not treat Mark Twain's humor—a fact that may fatally compromise it to some—it does treat in an illuminating way humor's dark twin: the conflicts and anxieties that enable and engender the humorous in the first place. *Dark Twins* is a book to be reckoned with.

A study which needs to be set in dialogue with Gillman's is Henry Nash Smith's *How True Are Dreams?: The Theme of Fantasy in Mark Twain's Later Work*, a paper originally given at Elmira in 1985 and the first in a series of "Quarry Farm Papers" published by the Elmira College Center for Mark Twain Studies under the general editorship of Darryl Baskin. Edited by Alan Gribben, with a gracious foreword commemorating Smith's contributions to American letters, *How True Are Dreams?* has a kind of neo-Brooksian emphasis on "the damage done to Mark Twain's career as a writer by the conflict of forces in American culture of his day." Smith sees Mark Twain's interest in dreams late in his career as a potentially potent literary innovation, an "intuition that the fictional use of dreams could open up the virtually unexplored realms of the unconscious as material for fiction" and as a potential "release from the determinism that haunted him." Unlike Gillman, however, Smith believes that Mark Twain's allegiance to a Genteel Tradition convention which linked dreams to the Ideal prevented him from making a real breakthrough: "He apparently sees no connection between his reading in current psychological research that recognized dreams as an avenue of communication between levels of consciousness, and the essentially trivial notion of dreams embodied in literary conventions." The formal innovation that Mark Twain did achieve, according to Smith, lay in the free-association method of his autobiographical dictations, but it was too little and too late.

Less consequential among general interpretations is another posthumously published study, John Q. Hays's *Mark Twain and Religion: A Mirror of American Eclecticism*, ed. Fred A. Rodewald (Peter Lang), another attempt to show that Twain's final years were not really so bitter and pessimistic as they were cracked up to be. Hays maintains that Mark Twain's religious belief or lack of it was conditioned by his exposure to four different and contradictory "philosophies" during his early and middle years—Calvinism, Deism, Romanticism, and scientific determinism—and that each continued to exert a varying pull on him throughout life. While there is doubtless a strain of truth in this thesis, it is rather broad and the book never gets much beyond handbook definitions of these influences. As a result, tracing their interrelations becomes a kind of shell game played in slow motion—it is no mystery where the pea of his religious belief may be found at a particular time. And throughout there is a tendency to accept uncritically the many fictional and rhetorical poses in Mark Twain's work as representing authentically the state of his beliefs at a given time. *Mark Twain and Religion* does provide a compendium of passages that comment directly or indirectly on religion, but otherwise it is not essential to Mark Twain scholarship.

On the other hand, an article which points out an aspect of his career actually needing study is Marlene Boyd Vallin, "Mark Twain, Platform Artist: A Nineteenth-Century Preview of Twentieth-Century Performance Theory" (*TPQ* 9:322–33). Vallin is concerned to show how Twain's theories and practices as a platform artist anticipate the developments of modern speech theory, but for literary scholars her description of the ways his performances self-consciously diverged from prevailing 19th-century elocution theory and practice will be even more suggestive. She points out the importance of Mark Twain's public performances to his overall career and notes that most studies tend to chronicle rather than analyze them. If we are to understand Mark Twain's participation in the culture of his age, his contemporary reception, and his dialogic relation with his audiences, these performances will need further study. Finally, among general interpretations, Thomas Bulger's transparently titled "Mark Twain's Ambivalent Utopianism" (*SAF* 17:235–42) surveys "The Curious Republic of Gondour," "Captain Stormfield's Visit to Heaven," and *Connecticut Yankee* for evidence that Twain's ambivalence about utopian possibilities runs throughout his career.

iv. Individual Works Through 1885

In "Verbally *Roughing It*: The West of Words" (*NCL* 44:67–92), Lee Clark Mitchell deftly explores the book's language as not merely an anticipation of Twain's later style but the feature which most distinguishes it from earlier depictions of the West. These depictions had emphasized the region's unique physical grandeur, but *Roughing It* "draws our attention instead to the unparalleled idiosyncrasies of its language." In part, this exuberance exists by way of its well-understood contrast to highly conventionalized "Eastern discourse"; but its more important function is to point out how that language is really constitutive of the distinctive reality of the West. The book's tall tales, which "draw our attention to their own fictionality," epitomize this process, constantly deferring or displacing expectations of formulated truth with entertaining fictions. The differences between West and East "are finally less physical than discursive," and the conceptual mode for apprehending this "is best achieved by disrupting conventional discourse."

Like Mitchell, Drewey Wayne Gunn attends to an undervalued aspect of the book, analyzing "The Monomythic Structure of *Roughing It*" (*AL* 61:563–85) and finding a carefully structured recapitulation of the heroic journey that leads to self-knowledge. Fitting the novel into this pattern is dreary work, though, reducing humorous incidents into sober stages on the way to individuation. Even the travelers' encounter with the "sociable heifer" who rained dislocated grammar and decomposed pronunciation on them in the stagecoach is full of mythic import: "The passengers are joined by a woman, a 'grim Sphynx' that presides over the first stage of the journey. She tries to tempt them to turn aside from their mission, but they easily resist." Although acknowledging its lapses, Gunn finds *Roughing It* possessed of a "remarkably unified structure" and "psychologically more mature than even *Adventures of Huckleberry Finn*" because the protagonist "manifests a human's normal growth from childhood into responsible adulthood."

In "Four Ways to Inscribe a Mackerel: Mark Twain and Laura Hawkins" (*SNNTS* 21:138–53), Susan K. Harris finds something fishy both in Twain's portrayal of the heroine of *The Gilded Age* and in the way critics have interpreted it. Contesting the view that Mark Twain was merely parodying women's sentimental fiction in Laura, Harris shows that by the 1870s many of the most popular women novelists had provided very different portraits and models of female protagonists. Conversely, she argues that Mark Twain inscribed Laura in four different modes as the story progressed: "as a figure of fallen innocence, as a victim of male power fantasies, as an American culture hero, and as a Mark Twain alter-ego." When she reached this most interesting last role (signaled, in part, by her prospective career as a lecturer), Mark Twain recoiled and, to reassert his authority over the text, returned her to the figure of fallen innocence and killed her, as he told Mary Fairbanks, dead as a mackerel. Harris does not consider Charles Dudley Warner's role in this process, although he wrote many of the chapters which carry Laura's story.

Tom Sawyer enjoyed a respite from the lickings administered in recent years; no studies were devoted to his book in 1989, although

two earlier articles turned up. In *"The Adventures of Tom Sawyer,*
Play Theory, and the Critic's Job of Work"* (*MQ* 29[1988]:357–65),
Sanford Pinsker reminds us—via Huizinga's *Homo Ludens*—how important an element play is in the novel. Pinsker sees Tom enlivening
the boring, workaday world of St. Petersburg and, ultimately, showing
how "play can thwart figures of adult authority." From a different
corner of the academic universe, George F. Mahl, "Everyday Speech
Disturbances in *Tom Sawyer*" (*Explorations in Nonverbal and Vocal
Behavior* [Erlbaum, 1987], pp. 286–309), studies such phenomena as
stuttering, hesitation, and so on, in the novel and finds that they are
generally associated with Tom's feigned struggles with his memory
and that they decrease dramatically in the concluding portion of the
novel written after Mark Twain had put the manuscript aside for two
years.

Adventures of Huckleberry Finn was, as customary, the subject of
a number of articles from a number of perspectives, more or less
illuminating. Two of the most thoughtful essays engaged the novel
through the psychological and social pressures presumed to operate
on Huck. Ernest D. Mason's "Attraction and Repulsion: Huck Finn,
'Nigger' Jim, and Black Americans Revisited" (*CLAJ* 33:36–48) takes
up the issue of racism freshly, examining Huck's attraction to Jim as
a "combination of revulsion and fascination, intimacy and remoteness,
attraction and repulsion." The genuine ambivalence of Huck's relationship with Jim—and Twain's portrayal of it—derives from the
fact that Huck's real affection for Jim is made possible by his having
"internalized the racist and paternalistic view that blacks are children
all their lives long." Their relationship historically considered is
further complicated because often "the very act of saving a black
man from slavery is simply another expression of restoration of the
ideology of white supremacy." The novel's humor is rooted in our
helplessness in the face of racism: "The stillness [*sic*], cruelty, and
absurdity of racism are all laughable precisely because we can't cope
with them. Their various subtleties and numerous forms are literally
infinite." In another essay examining the conflicting sources of his
ethical sense, "Motherless Child: Huck Finn and a Theory of Moral
Development" (*ALR* 22, i:31–42), Mark Altschuler employs concepts
from Robert Coles's *The Moral Life of Children* to examine Huck's
relationship to Mary Jane Wilks, which becomes a key to understanding how it is that he "can take a moral stand without being 'brung up
to it.'" Even more than Jim, Altschuler argues, Mary Jane fulfills

Huck's emotional and psychological needs, embodying in one figure "mother, victim, and orphan—the three most powerful psychic images for Huck." Especially as mother figure she offers Huck the sort of "unearned nurturing" he needs to become morally self-reliant, and her banishment of his deepest guilt (when she insists that he not blame himself for the loss of the money) enables him to do the right thing not only in the Wilks episode but also shortly afterward when he vows to help Jim escape.

Richard E. Peck's "The Campaign that . . . Succeeded" (*ALR* 21, iii:3–11) usefully considers the reciprocal relations of Mark Twain's Civil War narratives and *Huck Finn*. Peck argues that not only did the novel influence "The Private History of a Campaign that Failed" (as Tom Quirk has recently shown) by providing Twain with a dramatic model for the memoir's conclusion, but also that an earlier version of the narrative, an 1877 address printed as "Mark Twain's War Experiences," influenced the composition of the novel itself: in it Twain and his friend Ben Tupper "are clearly prototypes of Tom and Huck" as they engage in nighttime escapades on the farm, and the common-sensical Ben opposes Clemens's romantic notions of military conduct and finally deserts.

The Huck Finn and Strange Bedfellows category is represented this year by Thomas Matchie's "The Land of the Free, or the Home of the Brave?—Three 19th Century Cultural Rebels" (*JAC* 11, iv:7–13), which matches Huck with Kate Chopin's Edna Pointellier and Mari Sandoz's Crazy Horse as a trio of politically correct, race- and gender-balanced subversives. More farfetched but more interesting is Charles Rowan Beye's "Gilgamesh, Lolita, and Huckleberry Finn" (*CML* 9[1988]:39–50). He sees the relationship of Huck and Jim as serving the same purpose as male friendships in *Gilgamesh* and the *Iliad*, "the creation of a composite whole masculine psyche."

Finally, two notes address longstanding if minor problems of identification and location. Alison Ensor (*Expl* 48:32–35) argues that the name "St. Petersburg" should not be understood as primarily suggesting heaven but rather as an example of the custom of naming midwestern towns after European capitals. And in "The Delicate Art of Geography: The Whereabouts of the Phelps Plantation in *Huckleberry Finn*" (*ELN* 26, iv:63–66), Gerald Hoag suggests that internal evidence in the text and the rate of the Mississippi current would place the plantation farther south than southern Arkansas, where Twain and most scholars have placed it.

In keeping with this year's emphasis on unfinished or unpublished works, Stephen H. Sumida's "Reevaluating Mark Twain's Novel of Hawaii" (*AL* 61:586–609) lucidly surveys the surviving evidence about this 1884 project and hypothesizes its themes, characters, implications, and relations to other work of this period, especially *Connecticut Yankee*. Apparently never completed, despite Mark Twain's request that Mary Fairbanks read a "finished" manuscript, the Hawaii book involved the author in a "complex pastoral" with a mixed-race protagonist whose life spanned the era of European colonization and missionarying. Sumida disputes Fred W. Lorch's argument that Twain would have sided with the missionaries against the "primitive" native religion, and believes that he intended it "as a somehow balanced elegy for all that had passed away: for the virtues of the ancient Hawaiian religion and culture, for the good works and intentions of the missionaries, as well as for Bill Ragsdale [the hero] himself and the contemporary, lively, and tragic Hawaii he embodied."

v. Individual Works After 1885

In "An American Tragedy, or the Promise of American Life" (*Representations* 25:71–98), Walter Benn Michaels undertakes to "trace the transformations undergone by the opposition between the individual and the social during the Progressive period, or rather . . . to show how that opposition disappeared," using as his illustrative texts *A Connecticut Yankee in King Arthur's Court*, *Looking Backward*, and *An American Tragedy*. A tall order, but, like that of his earlier *The Gold Standard and the Logic of Naturalism*, Michaels's argument here bears careful attention, not only for its vertiginous reversals of received wisdom but also for its delivery of what Hank Morgan would call some real "lifters." As figures of cultural transformation, Michaels's writers seem inevitably to mean the opposite of what they say, particularly if they think they are engaged in a critique of their culture. In *The Gold Standard* he maintains that *Sister Carrie*, despite its sympathetic depiction of an underclass, constitutes an unequivocal endorsement of unrestrained capitalism, so we are not perhaps surprised to find that "*A Connecticut Yankee* does not, then, express an attitude toward technology, either the optimistic one of a Mark Twain who loved machines or the pessimistic one of a Mark Twain who was getting nervous about the Paige Compositor and beginning to worry about the ultimate value of machine culture. Rather it embodies a commitment to the essential likeness of persons and machines, a commitment embodied also in Twain's own identification with the Paige and in his vision of himself as a kind of writing machine." Mark Twain could only imagine "atomistic" individualism, which could not be altered except by destroying it (thus the obliteration of the knights at the end), but this individualism was essentially mechanical and inflexible, and ultimately, setting out to defend individuals, "he prepares them for the factory."

Where Michaels sees *Connecticut Yankee* as a prophecy of the machine age, David R. Sewell explores its backward look to 6th-century Britain as a colonization fantasy in "Hank Morgan and the Colonization of Utopia" (*ATQ* n.s. 3:28–44). Once again, however, the ostensible subjects (satire of aristocracy, the Church, faith in technology, etc.) are displaced under analysis into personal fantasies or projections that bespeak the ills of the writer's age: "The relation between Hank's progressivism and Camelot's backwardness is structurally identical to the dichotomy between 'civilization' and 'savagism' that provided nineteenth-century America with an ideology, an anthropology, and a literary myth." Moreover, the "most radical implication" of the novel "is that utopian narrative is a variety of literary imperialism—that Utopia is always a colony." On a lighter note, Gary Scharnhorst, in "Mark Twain and the Millerites: Notes on *A Connecticut Yankee in King Arthur's Court*" (*ATQ* n.s. 3:297–304), detects in Hank Morgan's apocalyptic theatricals a satiric echo of the Millerites, whose expectation that the world would end on 22 October 1844 Twain recalled from his childhood. In particular, Scharnhorst believes, Twain modeled his conclusion "on the end of the world as prophesied by the pre-millenialist William Miller—the very prophecies he had repeatedly satirized in the same work."

An essay which cogently relates *Tom Sawyer Abroad* to the political and psychological themes of such works as *Pudd'nhead Wilson* and *Connecticut Yankee* is Earl F. Briden, "Twainian Epistemology and the Satiric Design of *Tom Sawyer Abroad*" (*ALR* 22, i:43–52). Briden demonstrates how Mark Twain's developing determinist epistemology—expressed fully in *What Is Man?*—explains the debates of the characters and informs the satire of political and economic nationalism in the novel.

Pudd'nhead Wilson continued to be the focus of ambitious projects to analyze race relations in late-19th-century American culture. Nancy Fredricks's "Twain's Indelible Twins" (*NCL* 43:484–99) can profitably be read in conjunction with Gillman's book, since she too treats the socially constituted nature of racial identity and deemphasizes questions of intent and motivation in favor of regarding the novel as an autonomously functioning "textual machine." Her argument stresses the image of "tangled twins"—both Luigi and Angelo and *Pudd'nhead Wilson* and *Those Extraordinary Twins*—that hangs over the text and "sets in motion an elaborate, if tortuous, textual ballet involving structures of language, kinship, and political economy." The residents of Dawson's Landing demand a language that "functions symbolically as a transparent medium capable of revealing the truth of the world" in order to make the arbitrary distinctions that structure their society seem natural and inevitable. Self-protectively, they eschew irony, which discloses the discontinuity of language and experience and is capable of subverting the symbolic order. The irony of Pudd'nhead Wilson's calendar is discontinuous from the text itself, and Wilson upholds the symbolic order by introducing a high-tech method—fingerprinting—to confirm it.

Brook Thomas's "Tragedies of Race, Training, Birth, and Communities of Competent Pudd'nheads" (*AmLH* 1:754–85) is a long, complex, and rewarding essay that more than delivers on its title's promise. Skillfully mediating among current critical approaches, and contrasting *Pudd'nhead Wilson* to Albion Tourgée's antiracist *Pactolus Prime*, Thomas claims that the novel's "power to speak to us today can best be understood by examining changes occurring in American society in the late nineteenth century at the same time that its continuing capacity to implicate us in a cultural tragedy helps us better understand the consequences of those changes." Chief among these changes were a shift away from a neo-Lamarckian linkage of heredity and environment in the nature/nurture debate among scientists, a conflict among republican, laissez-faire, and progressive/liberal interpretations of the Civil War amendments to the Constitution (culminating in *Plessy* v. *Ferguson*), and the concomitant rise of the scientific professionalism and society's increasing dependence on it to resolve complex legal and social issues. All these come to bear on matters of race in *Pudd'nhead Wilson* in a world where training is everything, community standards drive the law, and Wilson himself is a representative of the newly professionalized scientific community. Mark Twain exposes the tragedy without offering a solution: "If Pudd'nhead makes fingerprints tangible, Twain makes visible the cultural narrative in which Pudd'nhead's scientific professionalism objectively helps to restore order temporarily disrupted by a black woman's attempt to advance her son. Insofar as our society continues to grant authority to Pudd'nhead's scientifically trained professionalism, Twain's narrative invites us to scrutinize its accepted standards of reasonableness even if it offers us no guarantee as to what the results of that scrutiny will be."

Blake Allmendinger's "Murder in Retrospect: Henry's Death in Samuel Clemens's *Autobiography*" (*ALR* 21, iii:13–24) analyzes Mark Twain's successive refashionings of the 1858 *Pennsylvania* disaster in *Life on the Mississippi* and the *Autobiography*. He argues that in these autobiographical accounts Twain first accepted responsibility for Henry's death and then shifted it to the doctors attending Henry and to Henry himself. His argument might be usefully complicated by reference to chapter 4 of *The Gilded Age*, Mark Twain's newspaper account of his brother's death, and two 1985 studies, Edgar M. Branch's *Men Call Me Lucky: Mark Twain and the "Pennsylvania"* and Jay Martin's "The Genie in the Bottle."

A more general reading of the *Autobiography* is Warren L. Chernaik's "The Ever-Receding Dream: Henry Adams and Mark Twain as Autobiographers" (*First Person Singular*, pp. 72–103). Like other recent critics, Chernaik sees that Adams and Twain, diametrically opposed in so many obvious ways, have some striking affinities. His nicely turned essay explores the sense of failure that rules both works, contrasts their formal principles, and sees them both as "profoundly political in their concerns. Each work is an essay in demythologizing, which mounts a coherent critique of the capitalist ethos as it had developed in America in the later nineteenth century."

There were a scattering of notes and essays on other works of Mark Twain's last decade. Louis J. Budd's "Another Stab at the Origin of No. 44 as a Name" (*Mark Twain Circular* 3, vii–viii:1–3) plausibly conjectures that it comes from a godlike hero by that name in *Dziady*, a drama-pageant by the Polish writer Adam Mickiewicz which Mark Twain could have learned about in 1897–98 in Vienna from Clara's Polish piano teacher Teodor Leszetycki. Wesley Britton, "Tom Paine and Mark Twain: 'Common Sense' as Source for 'The War Prayer' " (*CCTEP* 54, Sept.: 13–19), posits this influence on the basis of similarities of rhetorical structure, subject, and use of biblical analogues. Finally, a hopeful but dubious reading of "The Great Dark" is G. K.

Watkins, *God and Circumstances: A Lineal Study of Intent in Edgar Allan Poe's "The Narrative of Arthur Gordon Pym" and Mark Twain's "The Great Dark"* (Peter Lang). Watkins sees both tales as symbolic fables that are "intensely life affirming," each offering a vision of the need for Americans to transcend reason, materialism, and science through reliance upon the unconscious.

Georgia State University

7. Henry James

Richard A. Hocks

Who would have thought that 1989 would be the year of the "book" on Henry James after so many books already? Yet James studies exploded in 1989 with 15 more books, among them major studies by Alfred Habegger, David McWhirter, Sharon Cameron, Lynda Boren, Adeline R. Tintner, Peter Beidler, Terry Heller, Bonny MacDonald, and Elissa Greenwald, and highlighted by longtime *ALS* contributor Robert Gale, (now supposedly retired). Meanwhile, articles seem to appear in thematic volumes almost as often as in journals. Interesting new developments include an increasing number of gender studies, less deconstruction, more Lacan-influenced criticism. The works most frequently analyzed are *The Bostonians, The Princess Casamassima*, and easily in first place (will this ever change?) "The Turn of the Screw."

i. Editions, Reference Works, Biographical Studies

If there is one indispensable James book for 1989, it is undoubtedly Robert L. Gale's *A Henry James Encyclopedia* (Greenwood) described with total accuracy by Daniel M. Fogel in his foreword as "the greatest single compilation of knowledge about Henry James and about James's world since the completion of Leon Edel's *Life of Henry James*." Gale calls his massive volume "a labor of love," but I would call it the labors of Hercules, all the more amazing in that Gale created it in three years (Edel needed almost 20 for his five-volume *Life*). Those familiar with Gale's decade of *ALS* chapters (1976–85), his *Plots and Characters* (1965), his revision of *Eight American Authors* (1971), *The Caught Image* (1964), or, say, his *DLB* entries already know his veritable genius for concision. But even such admirers will be surprised by the monumentality of this alphabetical, cross-referenced sequence of 3,000 entries, whose 800 pages convey the informational heft of 3,000, whose 12 convenient appendices categorize their subjects like an index, and whose entries are often astonishingly thick with the ambience of James's milieu or the network of his associations, whether intellectual or personal—the rich entries on George Eliot, Howells, Flaubert, Maupassant, even Emerson, for example. Although Gale conceives his *Encyclopedia* as an "overture, an extended preface" to James, it is especially delightful and useful to the seasoned Jamesian, both for the innumerable items one did not know as well as for checking back on those never-ending matters one is half-sure about. To give a personal testimony: in a recent critical book on James's short fiction, I found myself revising the length of several of his tales in line with Gale's more reliable word counts (all entries on James's fiction include word counts), thereby affecting my classification of certain tales as "nouvelle," "anecdote," and such. What cannot be counted are all the times other scholars will benefit similarly from this wonderful work of scholarship, or else find it just plain addictive.

Todd K. Bender's *A Concordance to Henry James's* The Awkward Age and Erika Hulpke and Todd K. Bender's *A Concordance to Henry James's* What Maisie Knew (Garland) succeed last year's volumes on "The Turn of the Screw" and *The Spoils of Poynton* in a projected series of concordances of the complete works. Like their predecessors, these two are based on the New York Edition text. The Library of America adds to its splendid collection of James's works a new volume comprising the novels from 1886 to 1890, *The Princess Casamassima, The Reverberator,* and *The Tragic Muse.* Editor Daniel M. Fogel has elected to print the Macmillan texts; he supplies annotation, a typically informative and articulate "Note on the Texts," and a superb chronology.

A welcome reprint of John L. Sweeney's 1956 edition of *The Painter's Eye* (Wisconsin) comprises 30 of James's essays and notes on the pictorial arts and features a fine new foreword by Susan M. Griffin with corrected versions of Sweeney's helpful appendices. Griffin points to James's "pragmatic cognizance of the dynamic interrelationship of critic, artist, audience, market, and object," as well as his "imaginative recreation of the artist's act of creation." Griffin elsewhere combines sharp psychoanalytic and critical acumen in "The Jamesian Body: Two Oral Tales" (*VIJ* 17:125–40), claiming convincingly that James's perennial fondness for "Hop O' My Thumb" reveals his self-projection as the resourceful child who overcomes father and mother and competes successfully with siblings by eventually telling tales. Griffin's further analysis of James's and heroine Catherine Sloper's corpulence as issuing in gender-based "narrative ambiguity" nicely complements this essay's preoccupation with various levels of James's psychic "nourishment."

Finally, Miranda Seymour's *A Ring of Conspirators: Henry James and His Literary Circle, 1895–1915* (Hodder, 1988) is a mistitled anecdotal account of James's relations with Crane, Wells, Conrad, Ford Madox Ford, Wharton, and William James. For the student of James there is here only diversion and derivative journalism. Indeed, in "Duplicity in Sussex" (*NewC* 8, iv:66–72), James Tuttleton comments appropriately on Seymour's "inquisitorial" conceit that James's circle of "strained friendships" with Wells, Crane, and Conrad, all of whom lived close to Rye, constituted a "ring of foreign conspirators," all plotters against British letters because they were, in Seymour's terms, "all deceitful men who praised their rivals publicly while slandering them in private."

ii. Sources, Influences, Parallels

With *The Pop World of Henry James: From Fairy Tales to Science Fiction* (UMI Research Press), Adeline R. Tintner conveys still another layer of James's fertile "transmuting" imagination and rounds out her trilogy of specialized yet inevitably intertextual genetic criticism. All Jamesians know well Tintner's methodology of unearthing sources "appropriated" by James, but this time her range extends to fairy tales—especially Perrault *contes*—to legends, scandals, the cult of Orientalism, even his own jury duty (Tintner exemplifies her method by showing the connection of "The Given Case" to a divorce hearing). Other sources are English and American popular literature, although the English include high-culture authors like Dickens, Wells, and Kipling. Perhaps the most intriguing matter suggested by this study is an evaluation of James opposing that of Alfred Habegger (to be discussed shortly), since Tintner, like Habegger, cites James's use of material by American women writers Maria Cummins and Louisa May Alcott. Where Tintner's James is "always imitating and always original," an author with "catholicity" of interests, Habegger's James is condescending and almost hypocritically misogynist. One argument for Tintner's view is that *The Museum World* (1986), *The Book World* (1987), and now *The Pop World* cumulatively suggest that Habegger's focus of sources and analogues—though only one significant part of his argument—may be too narrow. Tintner's "iconic voyages" into "popular subliterature" tell us that "James lived in the world."

In "Hamlet and Henry James's First Fiction" (*ANQ* n.s. 2:137–38), W. R. Martin briefly observes the yet unnoticed appearance of Shakespeare's "Mousetrap," the play-within-a-play, in James's earliest story, "The Story of the Year." Hilton Anderson, "Daisy Miller and 'The Hotel Child': A Jamesian Influence on F. Scott Fitzgerald" (*SAF* 17:213–18), proposes that, although Fitzgerald modeled his story on James's nouvelle, Fitzgerald's tale does not succeed because he lacks James's "extensive knowledge of international society and its nuances."

David Ellis's "Henry James's Autobiography: The Education of a Novelist" (*First Person Singular*, pp. 104–24) compares James's autobiographical tracings about the growth of his artistic mind to Wordsworth's *Prelude*. The main difference is that James in portraying the development of a novelist rather than a poet finds his "chief agency" not in Nature but the endless variety of "human appearances." Ellis's essay also focuses on James's contrasting meetings with Tennyson, who was surprisingly complimentary of James's work, and G. H. Lewes, who (interestingly in view of recent scholarship) was very disparaging. Frederick Nies and John Kimmey, "*David Copperfield* and *The Princess Casamassima*" (*HJR* 10:179–84), show the various parallels in settings, scenes, names, and wordings in these two major novels, a tribute from one master to his elder "master."

Noting their similar backgrounds as American expatriates and James's influences on Eliot's poetry, Hirofumi Iwamatsu in "Henry James: *The Portrait of a Lady* in Relation to T. S. Eliot" (*KAL* 30:57–66) suggests that both Eliot and James share "the strain of the Puritanical moralists": Isabel is (in Matthiessen's phrase) "the granddaughter" of the Puritans in her "moral integrity." Iwamatsu observes that Eliot's criticism points to James's intense spiritual awareness despite an apparent indifference to religious dogma. Similarly, Russell J. Reising, "Condensing the James Novel: *The American* in *Hugh Selwyn Mauberley*" (*JML* 15:17–34), follows initial investigations (by Kenner, Espey, Donoghue, and Bell) of verbal echoes from other James novels in Pound and writes convincingly of *The American* in *Mauberley*, indeed proposing that *Mauberley* "works on, perhaps 'translates' . . . not only *The American*" but the "James novel broadly conceived." Reising also reiterates the well-known consanguinity of

James's and Pound's shared vision of tyrannical structures inhibiting human freedom.

"Telepathy: From Jane Austen and Henry James (*OLR* 10. i–ii: [1988]:43–60) by Nicholas Royle explores a concept taken from Derrida's essay of the same name, as well as Foucault's "discursive formation." He defines "telepathy" as communication between minds outside normal channels and "discursive formation" as "roots, cords, lines" that connect ideas and minds. Both *Emma* and "Turn of the Screw" share "uncanny correspondences" narratologically and stylistically at a distance "which cannot be measured" or explained except by telepathy.

iii. Critical Books

There are several contenders for the major critical book of 1989. Two of them are David McWhirter's *Desire and Love in Henry James* (Cambridge) and Sharon Cameron's *Thinking in Henry James* (Chicago), both ambitious reconceptions of the character of the late fiction. McWhirter's mostly thematic study problematizes authentic love in late James by juxtaposing it to specious desire, "the imagination of loving" or "intransitive figuration" analogous to Freud's pleasure principle in excess of the limitations of reality—reality as posed by Sartre and Denis de Rougement, for example, two of McWhirter's moral and intellectual mentors. The core theme is that James's last three novels progress from a desire-laden "unfulfilled solipsim" epitomized in Strether, on to Milly's more "transitive syntax" of action in *Wings of the Dove*, a positive step confirmed by James's new use of counterpointing centers of consciousness. *The Golden Bowl*, however, is the complete "breakthrough," with Maggie Verver's love issuing in action and the "reality principle," and James himself as "metonymic author" instead of mere "metaphoric writer," thus taking control in the guise of the Bloomsbury shopman "directing" the plot. One problem with McWhirter's claim is that the earlier corpus is too rich and complex to be viewed tacitly as mere testing ground or prelude for the achievement of his first—and last—great novel. Another problem is that his study means to be dialectical (between love and desire) but tends to make them binary oppositions. Yet McWhirter's book is far better than its own thesis; the readings of the major novels are brimming with humanistic insight augmented by perceptive parallels between James and Stendhal, Ricoeur, Girard, and many others.

Cameron's difficult *Thinking in Henry James* is strong just where McWhirter seems weak—in conceptual rigor and philosophical sophistication. Her core thesis is that whereas "James's Prefaces psychologize the idea of consciousness by imagining it as centered, subjective, internal, and unitary" (or a "self"), the novels themselves "contradict" that idea. For James consciousness is not "dismissed or deconstructed," however, but rather "disseminated." That is, Jamesian thought is "exteriorized"; he "moves it between persons." Thinking, especially in *The Golden Bowl* and *Wings of the Dove*, is "not the dictate of consciousness's interiority but rather the dictation of what is in another's mind." All Jamesians interested in the rich tradition of philosophical analysis from, say, Dorothea Krook to Paul Armstrong can profit from Cameron's conceptual reorientation. Yet for all its sophistication, Cameron's high conceptual gloss does not conceal certain flaws. Debunking the psychological approach to Jamesian consciousness is bracing but not altogether successful. A number of her claims may be accounted for by William James's own "later phase" redefinition of consciousness as functional rather than as entity, a position Cameron herself almost acknowledges but veers from brilliantly. Furthermore, she never explains *why* James so misconstrued his artistic consciousness time and again in his Prefaces; the "unreliability factor" for an issue like this is different from, say, his claims about a germ or his judgment of a novel's success or failure. In any case, a critic should try to account for such a major disparity. For additional problems with this study and simply a fuller treatment of both Cameron and McWhirter, see my recent review in *Nineteenth-Century Literature*.

One might argue that the most important 1989 book is *Henry James and the "Woman Business"* by Alfred Habegger (Cambridge). This historically thick account tells how James first absorbed, then rewrote, popular women's domestic fiction as well as that of the "women agonists"—Maria Cummins, Susan Warner, Augusta J. Evans, Elizabeth Stoddard, Anne Moncure Crane, Louisa May Alcott, and others—into his own earlier fiction. But in doing so he imposed "reactionary ideals" and "authoritarian doctrines" handed down from Henry Sr., whose noxious "angel" views of women and marriage Habegger recounts with massive archival evidence. The result, in this feminist/psychological study, is a deeply bifurcated James, whose instinctive feeling for the orphan heroine of women's fiction is implacably quelled by a dutiful adherence to his father's bizarre views of women—as seen especially in *Watch and Ward, Portrait of a Lady,* and *The Bostonians.* Habegger also drastically reinterprets James's relationship with Minnie Temple in line with his polemic; I say "polemic," because his iconoclastic study is also possibly the most berating, contentious attack I have read in tandem with an otherwise impressive sifting of historical research. Habegger's "rehistorizing" of James will appeal to many in the academy interested in canon reformation and culture studies. It will appeal less to those who do not find meaning in Jamesian texts univocal with the biographical James, or who prefer greater critical sophistication. An example: Habegger thinks *The Portrait* is "banal" and built on contradiction, since it "represents marriage as a house of bondage yet never supports the obvious idea that Isabel would be wise to escape." Some readers would find that "obvious" version the banal one. Yet this is a truly major work, not only on James (and his family) but of cultural history. I only wish the thesis *about* the "divided" James were reflected in Habegger's own presentation of him.

I greatly recommend that, immediately after Habegger, any reader who can should read Lynda S. Boren's *Eurydice Reclaimed: Language, Gender, and Voice in Henry James* (UMI Research Press), for it shows vividly how two minds can deal with the same locus of issues and arrive at different conclusions. Boren's passionate interest is in the distinctive musical form of James's narrative voice (even her chapter titles suggest a musical score), but she approaches this issue through psycholinguistics, drawing heavily not only on Bakhtin but also Lacan, together with very brief but illuminating interdisciplinary forays into Locke, Saussure, Jakobson, even Diderot. What makes her psychoanalytic approach such a contrast to Habegger's is that she looks at the same three novels, *Match and Ward, The Portrait,* and *The Bostonians,* and finds in James's dialogic or polyphonic voices the "feminine position" and principle; she also finds Eurydicean "linguistic allegory" in *What Maisie Knew* (Habegger's preferred late James novel). Boren perceives in James's distinctive lyricism and "hieroglyphic mode" the "lack" born of desire, the search and intermittent reclaiming of the lost subconscious voice of Eurydice by James's constant "fractur[ing] of patriarchal language." Henry James is never more nonlinear than in this study, and the study itself is free-associative and open-ended—again, in striking contrast to Habegger,

who never loses the tight grip on his thesis. And yet, these two critics
finally do converge over James's late condescending views on women's
American speech: for Boren, however, an important aspect of James's
phallocentrism; for Habegger, the veritable apotheosis of his lifelong
opinion of women.

Despite all the fine work in recent years on the James/Hawthorne
connection by Gordon Hutner (see *ALS 1988*, p. 100), Richard Brodhead (*ALS 1987*, p. 97), John Rowe (*ALS 1983*, pp. 44–45), and
others, Elissa Greenwald's *Realism and the Romance: Nathaniel
Hawthorne, Henry James, and American Fiction* (UMI Research
Press) is a genuine contribution charting the evolution of Hawthorne
on James's imagination. Greenwald admirably revisits romanticism
and realism to show their interfusion in James, uses the 1904 Centenary Essay as a rich locus for James's conceptual frame, and includes fine "Hawthornian" readings of *The Portrait, The Bostonians,
Wings of the Dove, The Golden Bowl*, and segments of *The American
Scene*. The claim that James embodies the "romantic real" is hardly
new, but Greenwald's reformulation of that conception is compulsory
reading. *Henry James's Portrait of the Writer as Hero* by Sara S.
Chapman (St. Martin's) is an informed overview and analysis of
James's major body of fiction about writers—from "The Author of
Beltraffio" (1884) to *The Sacred Fount* (1901)—together with his
"most complete dramatisation of the writer-as-hero" in the later Prefaces, wherein he collaborates with "the reader-as-ideal-critic." Chapman's theme of the "reader-writer" relationship in James underscores
the connection, found increasingly in James studies, between his creative credo, modernism, and reader-response theory. Finally, Bonny
MacDonald explores with rare acuity James's 40 years of Italian writings in *Henry James's* Italian Hours: *Revelatory and Resistant Impressions* (UMI Research Press). Her intricately focused thesis is that
James's youthful "receptive vision" to Italy in 1869–70 carries the
force of a humbling revelation borne of "multiplicity of impression,
tactile experience," transcribed by a style which parallels the "gestalt"
account of perception enunciated by William James and phenomenol-
ogists. MacDonald further argues that late James "reclaims" his Italy
by responding to its impenetrable "magic," which "resists" mastery by
even his late style: she thus builds a bridge—far too infrequent in
James studies—between the early "pictorial" style and the late "constructing" style.

iv. Criticism: General Essays

Charles Caramello's "Portrait Narration: Generals James and Stein" (*Intertextuality and Contemporary American Fiction*, pp. 103–20) recounts once again that Stein dubbed James her "forerunner" because he had anticipated her own strategy in realistic character portrayal. In her portrait narration "Four Americans," she even uses the conceit of James as a general; her wordplay coordinates James's "being a general" with his being a "general type of autobiographical writer for his reader," allowing her, then, to explore James's compositional method in his memoirs as well as her own "reading of them." James K. Folsom analyzes some of James's "questing characters" (mostly women) in "Imaginative Safety Valves: Frontier Themes in the Literature of the Gilded Age" (*The Frontier Experience and the American Dream*, pp. 87–94). James's seekers like Isabel Archer hope for "a new start" or new life in Europe. The irony is that "beginning anew is impossible," since the characters' old selves are never left behind.

Rayburn S. Moore, "Up to Scratch in Vulgar Parlance: The Colloquial in Henry James's Letters" (*PAPA* 15:121–30), asserts that James's letters offer not only the best exhibition of his colloquial style but an excellent means of examining the artist's public and private personality. In "Literary Pornographics: Henry James's Politics of Suppression" (*HJR* 10:185–96), Catherine Vieilledent proposes that James wished to counter the charge that virtually all literature is pornographic, that novels are dishonest, and that realism and romanticism are separate categories. He especially blurs such oppositions in "The Story in It," where " 'the honorable' woman gets her romance" and remains honest.

The late J. A. Ward thoughtfully shows the different ways James conceives portraiture in "The Portraits of Henry James" (*HJR* 10: 1–14). James's concern in *Portrait* is with "psychological and dramatic rendering of character," whereas in *Portraits of Places* and *Partial Portraits* he represents geographical sites and literary works in some sense "as human characters." The portrayal of Venice, too, is like a portrait of a lady, and his literary criticism most frequently becomes an analysis of "persons rather than of artists."

Although obviously not an article, Daniel H. Borus's *Writing Realism* is the case of a book saturated in the historical milieu of realism but far less focused on James than its title might imply. The treatment is discursive and contextual, even in Borus's comments on the "realist political" novel, *The Princess Casamassima*. This is the sort of book that reminds us that historically minded scholars take realism seriously in a way critics and theorists seldom do. Of similar stamp is Tom Quirk's perspicacious essay, "Realism, the 'Real,' and the Poet of Reality: Some Reflections on American Realism and the Poetry of Wallace Stevens" (*ALR* 21, ii:34–53). Quirk mentions Henry James only briefly, but his intelligent revaluation on behalf of a more supple understanding of American Realism indicates the crucial bridge between both Henry and William James and Stevens.

George F. Haggerty's "James's Ghostly Impressions" in his study *Gothic Fiction/Gothic Form* (pp. 139–68) argues (as have others) that James revises the ideas of predecessors Hawthorne and Poe about the gothic tale, "without diluting them in intensity or fierceness." The focus in stories like "Owen Wingrave," "Sir Edmund Orme," "Turn of The Screw," and "The Jolly Corner" is on painting pictures of "the common objects of life" which become pictures of ourselves, but not through a direct presentation of the supernatural. Haggerty's approach suggests an evolution from haunted houses and personalities in the two earlier tales, to a whole questioning of the nature of subjectivity and the fusion of subject with object in "Turn of the Screw," to a more congenial view of "confrontation" and "accommodation" in "The Jolly Corner."

Michael Irwin explores ambiguity and form in "Henry James and the Vague *Nouvelle*" (*The Modern American Novella*, pp. 13–29). Works like "Daisy Miller," "Turn of the Screw," and "Figure in the Carpet" are "intriguing," but "elusive and indistinct," which readers can find irritating—"as by the instability of a wobbling table." Yet Irvin believes "In the Cage" has more substance, density, and texture. James's novellas deal generally with characters often "impotent, shirking the encounter with reality and allowing experience to dissolve into theory." I much appreciate Irwin's point about "In the Cage," but surely that story, steeped in codes, is also theoretical. Klaus Lanzinger's long chapter on James, "The Passionate Pilgrim," from his *Jason's Voyage* (pp. 113–62), basically surveys without surprise James's variations on his international theme in the early fiction. In "A Conversation with Louis Auchincloss on Henry James (*HJR* 10: 61–67), David A. Leeming (interviewer) discovers that even though Auchincloss obviously is closely associated with James and deeply admires the master's style, he feels that he does not "really write like James" at all because James is unique in such a way he would be dangerous to imitate. The interview also touches on James's artistic and moral development as a novelist.

Several general essays this past year could be grouped under the category "Gender Studies" and/or "Homoeroticism." First, "Henry James and the Battle of the Sexes" (*SWR* 74, ii:176–99) by Wendy Lesser offers a perceptive analysis of James's ambiguous portrayal of his female characters whose moral development relates to the polar tensions of sympathy and discrimination, passivity and energetic will-fulness, wit and seriousness, knowledge and innocence. Although Lesser deals with the gender issue in such works as *The Golden Bowl*, *Portrait*, *Spoils* and others, she really focuses her attention on the sexual battles—and various critics' "misrepresentation" of them—in *The Bostonians*. James's novels, she says, compel the reader to place sympathies, but every choice involves a loss—we, as readers, cannot have "everything our way."

"The Beast of the Closet: Homosociality and the Pathology of Manhood" (*CritI* 15:587–605) by David Van Leer voices his disagreement with Eve K. Sedgwick's desire to connect homosexuality to the larger issues of society and sexuality, and her further suggestion that "homophobia and homosexual/homosocial bonds" undergird "homosexual panic." Van Leer uses "The Beast in the Jungle" to illustrate that Sedgwick operates from the same position of power she attributes to May Bartram—really knowing Marcher's secret "beast," his "male panic"—yet she herself never commits "the majority's homophobic sin of 'really knowing' homosexuality." Sedgwick, says Van Leer, names male bonding as neurotic, "thereby empowering the woman" who is saved from such a fate. But in "Tide and Trust" (*CritI* 15:745–57), Sedgwick responds disbelievingly to what she deems Van Leer's misreading of her work and intention, objecting to his "allegorical practice" of defining all questions of gay male "identity, history, theory, politics, and definition" as internal issues and woman's place in relation to them as "outside." She believes such "narrative scapegoating" is a negative position historically foisted on both women and gay men, and worries that it may "foreclose or deny certain spaces of vitalizing difference."

Michael Moon's "Disseminating Whitman" (*SAQ* 88:247–65) discusses the relationship between the works of Walt Whitman, Horatio Alger, and Henry James. Moon contends that these three figures with their divergent interests and practices all "engage the questions of the history and theory of homosexuality." He uncovers Jamesian homoeroticism in Miles's being sent from school in "Turn of the Screw," as well as various "homophobic implications" in tales like "the Pupil" and "The Author of Beltraffio."

Scott S. Derrick explores the metaphor of "ease" and its relationship with "inter- and intra-gender" masculinity in "A Small Boy and the Ease of Others: The Structure of Masculinity and the Autobiography of Henry James" (*ArQ* 45, iv:25–56). Derrick highlights in James's autobiography those elements associated by Melanie Klein with "ease"—envy, nourishment, and disease. James envied the "ease" of other males (their masculinity), an envy bound up with feelings of "emptiness, hunger and deprivation." To still his hunger, James "gorged himself with impressions that never satiate." Susan M. Griffin, "Screening the Father: The Strategy of Obedience in Early James" (*Refiguring the Father*, pp. 39–57), uses James's familial relationship with his weak father as a means of exploring the thematics of James's fictional daughters struggling with a parent about the question of seeking a husband. Griffin argues that such parents are reluctant to speak with authority, a lesson in familial behavior James learned at home. Through his stories James the son "plots to simultaneously mask and unmask the father weakened by desire."

Julie Rivkin offers a perceptive analysis (and self-analysis) regarding the opposition between the gender-reading theories of Felman and Fetterley in "Resisting Readers and Reading Effects: Some Speculative Reading on Gender," in *Narrative Poetics: Innovations, Limits, Challenges*, ed. James Phelan (Ohio State, 1988, pp. 11–22). Rivkin revisits *Maisie* because of the way it "raises questions of reading, gender, and doubleness" for the feminist (female) reader, since this novel is itself about the act of reading. Maisie is both "a model female reader and a model of unreadability" because she is "a reading subject herself."

v. Criticism: Individual Novels

Manfred Mackenzie in "The Way Home" (*SPAN* 28:63–84) compares *Roderick Hudson* with H. H. Richardson's *Maurice Guest*, showing that both engage in the "symbolic labour" and ultimately sacrificial act of reclaiming the Old World in order to rediscover the New World. Edwin Fussell analyzes the political climate and the physical topography of Paris in their relation to James's early, international (and geographical) novel in his "Time and Topography in *The American*" (*HJR* 10:167–78). The novelist exhibits his consciousness of American tourism within the domain of this novel by showing far more than most tourists can see of Paris.

Barbara Rasmussen, "Re-producing 'James': Marxism, Phallocentrism and "Washington Square" (*JAmS* 23:63–67), debates current Marxist readings of the work by adding a psychoanalytic feminist perspective. Asserting that phallic "masculinity" in the novel is equated with fullness, while femininity is equated with the lack of it, she cites Jacqueline Rose's Lacanian view—that "femininity can only be understood in terms of its *construction* (that is, that there is no essence of woman)"—as being of "crucial importance, especially taken together with [Lacan's] concomitant stress on the phallus as mere signifier of an always already-lost wholeness." Thus a feminist critic faced with a text like *Washington Square* cannot hope to avoid "entering into phallic relations—the have and have-not dyad."

In "The Marriages of Henry James and Henrietta Stackpole" (*HJR* 10:15–31), Elise Miller offers an intelligent analysis of James's ambivalence about marriage as it is played out in the relationship between Isabel, representing Emersonian idealism, and Henrietta, who represents both James himself and the marriage of the masculine with the feminine, as her name suggests. Whereas Isabel approaches her marriage idealistically and discovers it to be a caged prison, Henrietta approaches marriage "aggressively and realistically," and eagerly awaits her forthcoming union at the end of the novel. Sarah B. Daugherty, in "Henry James and George Eliot: The Price of Mastery" (*HJR* 10:153–66), makes another good case for James's debt to and competition with George Eliot, especially in the way James builds the character of Isabel with reference to Eliot's female protagonists like Maggie, Rosamond, and Gwendolen. Daugherty also proposes that both James and his "lady" pay a great price for their myth of mastery—in James's case he only assuages his "masculine insecurity."

Claire Kahane thoroughly analyzes Freud's theory of "Hysteria, Feminism, and the Case of *The Bostonians*" (*Feminism and Psychoanalysis*, pp. 280–97). Kahane claims that, like Freud's relationship with Dora, James had to identify with his subject Olive in order to represent her, and this representation was "extremely disturbing" to him. He renders the source of her morbidity as the "hysterical fantasy of violation," which "equates speaking with potency and silencing with being raped and castrated"—a fantasy Kahane believes James shared with or projects onto his character. In "The Curious Case of Doctor Prance" (*HJR* 10:32–41), Ian F. A. Bell claims that, although *The Bostonians* is "beset by schisms," male vs. female, public vs. private, North vs. South (to name a few), Dr. Prance eludes these schisms by her "drab" manner and thus becomes a "profoundly disturbing" element in the novel, one that disrupts "the antimonies that structure the other characters." Also, Sarah B. Daugherty, "Henry James, George Sand, and *The Bostonians*: Another Curious Chapter in the Literary History of Feminism" (*HJR* 10:42–49), notes that Verena is a "caricature" of George Sand, while Basil is taken from James himself; but, unlike Basil, James retains the role of "insightful" critic of Sand's work: although he expresses certain chauvinistic prejudices toward her writing, he was deeply drawn to her life, style, and spontaneity.

Merla Wolk interestingly presents Verena as an "artist/child" whose gift of expression elicits a desire for repression from the "powerful parent figures" of Olive and Basil in "Family Plot in *The Bostonians*: Silencing the Artist's Voice" (*HJR* 10:50–59). Wolk also draws a parallel between Verena's gift at public speaking and James's failure at the public art of writing successful drama. A rigorous analysis by Rudiger Bittner of Verena's conduct to Olive is "Understanding a Self-Deceiver," in *Perspectives On Self-Deception*, eds. Brian P. McLaughlin and Amelie Oksenberg Rorty (Calif., 1988, pp. 535–51). Bittner first considers several theories of self-deception, only to reject them through logical analysis. His determination is that Verena simply went wrong—"like getting into a rut," not a "state she chose" but a "condition she got entangled in." The focus perforce then shifts to Olive, who assumes Verena to be guilty of self-deception in order to blame her because Olive has been hurt by her action.

Merete Licht reconsiders the textual evidence that James used Vernon Lee as his model for Christina Light in "Henry James's Portrait of a Lady: Vernon Lee in *The Princess Casamassima*," from *A Literary Miscellany Presented to Eric Jacobsen*, eds. Graham D. Caie and Holger Norgaard (University of Copenhagen, 1988, pp. 285–303). Edel believes there is no evidence that James met Lee before the publication of *Roderick Hudson*, where Christina first appears, yet Licht wonders why Lee "retaliates" against *The Princess* in "Lady Tal," when James had been kind and encouraging. Licht suggests the reason was not James's portrait of Christina, but rather the Muni-

ments and their entourage. "The Princess Casamassima's 'Sudden Incarnation' and Octave Feuillet" (*TSLL* 31:257–72) by Pierre A. Walker
proposes that the allusion to Feuillet gives a significant clue to understanding the novel, especially the friendship between Hyacinth and
the princess, her "capricious" personality, and the ending of the novel.
This allusion creates an intertextual intrigue which can lead a reader
from *The Princess* to *Roderick Hudson* to *Histoire d'une Parisienne,
La Veuve* in order to discover the princess's true desire for revenge.

Nicholas Tingle's "Realism, Naturalism, and Formalism: James
and *The Princess Casamassima* (*ALR* 21, ii:54–66) reveals that James's
work, if judged with "a realistic epistemology" or, to a lesser degree,
with "naturalistic criteria for arriving at knowledge," causes misunderstanding because such interpretations misread realism and naturalism into the texts. The paradox, though, is that James's fiction both
undercuts and depends on "this privileged epistemological stand-
point," while he waged a "formalistic battle" throughout his career,
especially in works like *The Princess* and the experimental work of the
1890s.

"What Everybody Knew Versus What Maisie Knew: The Change
in Epistemological Perspective from the Prologue to the Opening of
Chapter 1 in *What Maisie Knew*" (*Style* 23:197–212) is Mary Galbraith's deft Bakhtinian analysis of the many voices James presents
in the prologue of this story. However, as readers of the first sentence,
we are asked to "bracket what we know" (what everyone else has said)
about Maisie's situation in order to enter into her world as she might
perceive it. Galbraith's insight is that Maisie's epistemological state is
that of nonexistent enigma, an "experiencer" trapped in her own subjectivity until her surprising final act.

"The Social Vision of *The Spoils of Poynton* (*AL* 61:59–77) by
Richard S. Lyons is one of the more thoughtful discussions in recent
years of this perennially intriguing book. Lyons shows with acuity
how James's "residual social themes" enunciated in the *Notebooks* but
missing from the later Preface—especially the problematic of "inheritance," or "coming into possession"—persist in the completed text,
though they begin to assume a level recessive to James's newer interest
in consciousness. Lyons illuminates the place of *Spoils* in "the curve of
James's career," with many contextual insights vis-à-vis James's other
fiction of the 1880s and 1890s. The essay is a model of how a cordial
mind need not denigrate familiar readings to make a worthy new
point. Chris Brown explores several parallels in "Wagner and *The*

Spoils of Poynton" (*CLQ* 25:227–36). Mona Brigstock's physical appearance suggests the Valkyrian Rhine Maidens because she is repeatedly "romping," "strong willed," and attired in men's patent-leather shoes, whereas Fleda is slim, pale, and black-haired—"no good at all," according to Mrs. Gereth. Brown even sees a structural "aesthetic enmity" in that each work has its realm of radiance (Valhalla and Poynton) and "frumps" (the caves and Waterbath). Another parallel lies in the melodramatic endings, great scenes involving fires.

Susan L. Marshall explores with perceptive intricacy the Jamesian contingencies, inversions, and inevitable compromises between art and life in " 'Framed in Death': *The Sense of the Past* and the Limits of Revision" (*HJR* 10:197–209). Ralph Pendrel's faith in the "magic of art" is controverted by his complicating experiences in the world of 1820, and despite James's projected "secure" ending proposed in his Notes, the novel's unfinished state underscores the "wavering margin" that cannot be dispensed with—a "step forward in [James's] exploration of the limits of creation."

Douglas Paschall's "Complicit Manoeuvers: The Form of *The Wings of the Dove* (*Modern American Fiction*, pp. 13–27) is exactly what the title indicates, a close analysis of how all three major characters in *Wings* are equally complicit in their roles, thereby displaying through James's art the ineluctable moral complexity of the human predicament as well as the novel's "essential intelligibility." In " 'The Language of the House' in *The Wings of the Dove*" (*EIC* 39:116–36), Michiel Heyns demonstrates how semiotic theory can enhance our knowledge about such elements as setting, "without relegating them to the realm of the illusory." Heyns claims that the various settings and houses in James's book act as a "*parole* within the *langue* generated by the novel."

William Righter, "Golden Rules and Golden Bowls" (*P&L* 13:262–81), does a nice job of transposing the moral ambiguity of *The Golden Bowl* into philosophical/ethical terms, showing that both the "aesthetic" and "ethical" positions associated with major characters "multiply their forms" and blur clear divisions, creating at once a "tragedy and a romance." Maggie in particular is a "Foucaultian heroine" with "tissues of pressure," and her resolution makes difficult "any underlying principle . . . involved in the consensus that concludes the book." For James, then, unlike, say, Tolstoy, the "law of successive aspects" renders impossible any Kantian maxims. This essay covers familiar territory, yet is elevated and freshly articulate. Arlene Young presents a rhetorical equivalent to Righter's philosophical stance in "Hypothetical Discourse as Ficelle in *The Golden Bowl* (*AL* 61:382–97), a fine essay that probes the implications of James's well-known "unuttered utterances" and extends them to the "indeterminacy" through discourse of the novel itself; the ficelle function of the Assinghams is repeated by all the hypothetical language of the main characters, creating "a model for the relationship between the narrator and the reader," and exacerbating the novel's "inherent problems of interpretation."

vi. Criticism: Tales

"The Hermes in Henry James's 'The Last of the Valerii' " (*HJR* 10: 210–13) by Michael Clark notes that James's underlying emphasis in this story is the conflict between sexuality and the civilizing process, and suggests that the reference to Hermes points to Valerio's pagan lust within marriage. W. R. Martin and Warren U. Ober in "Captain Diamond and Old Hickory: Realities and Ambivalence in Henry James's 'The Ghostly Rental' " (*SSF* 26:1–9) propose that central to this puzzling early tale is James's use of disguise, allegory, and his own ambivalence as artist and Europeanized American. In "Reading Over Endless Histories: Henry James's *Altar of the Dead*" (*YFS* 74 [1988]:261–84), Andrzej Warminski rereads this story as an allegory about what has been happening on the critical scene over the past 15 years with the onset of deconstructive criticism. Though the tale has often been considered "nasty business" for many critics, it teaches us about the materiality and interpretation of texts: for it is a text about alter egos, the other (*autre*), and "alternative associates"—a story about a self, "whether it be Stransom's, James's, or the reader's," which cannot recognize itself in its own text.

In the "Epilogue" to his *Architects of the Abyss* (pp. 107–14), Dennis Pahl superbly deconstructs James's view of the artist as organic and unifying "center" by showing with discrimination how the critic-narrator of "The Aspern Papers" and James himself in the late Preface similarly "decenter" themselves from the truth and the past by "composing" their own "papers" and encountering barriers and obstacles at every turn in the form of "garden walls and impenetrable chambers."

Although I complain constantly about the unending crush of articles on "The Turn of the Screw," I am rather surprised by two new book-length studies which enhance our appreciation of it. Peter G. Beidler's *Ghosts, Demons, and Henry James: The Turn of the Screw at the Turn of the Century* (Missouri) returns the tale to its historical context as part of the vast number of "ghost narratives" and "spiritualistic phenomena" at once popular and of continual interest to the flourishing Society for Psychical Research. Stocked with published reports and case histories, Beidler re-creates the environment out of which the major features of James's tale emerge in a way analogous to Alfred Habegger's treatment of James and women's domestic fiction. F. W. Meyers's fascinating assessment of James's story in a letter to a fellow researcher and James's own reading of a paper by William to the society (which Oscar Cargil, however, pointed out long before the present generation of James scholars) are but two highlights in Beidler's impressive array of contemporary analogues. Ultimately, he does propose a "revisionist" view in claiming that Miles and Flora are at times possessed by Quint and Jessel, and that we can trust most of what the governess tells us happened at Bly. At the same time, he does a very nice job of explaining James's originality as the imaginative combination of "three separate traditions—the romantic, the scientific, and the demonic."

Nothing could be more different from Beidler's historical approach than Terry Heller's The Turn of the Screw: *Bewildered Vision* (Twayne). Exquisite is the way Heller, within the frame of the Twayne Masterworks format, fashions a fine theoretical approach to the tale by using post-Freudian psychoanalysis (Lacan) in tandem with some strategic reader-response theory—the "implied re-reader" of the prologue, for example. Although in part he teases out a familiar theme of ultimate ambiguity, Heller never gets bogged down with the mountainous scholarship and discussion of the work, because, finally, his key insights are Lacanian: for example, the governess is not driven by sexual desire but by the desire for "wholeness"; her status as "novice authority" betokens absence in Victorian society of the father's name; her language of the "unspeakable" bespeaks her unconscious desire to see for herself what she believes the children see, and so forth. Heller even claims that James's tale "criticizes ideology" and thereby imposes an "etiquette of imposing meaning." Among its many accomplishments, this little gem of a book is also a fine application of Christine Brooke-Rose's *Rhetoric of the Unreal* (1981).

Now to the more usual spate of yearly "Screw" essays: Richard Dillworth Rust explores the concept of "liminality," or the "thresh-

old," in "Liminality in *The Turn of the Screw*" (*SSF* 25 [1988]:441–
45). "Liminal" persons in the tale include the "orphan children, who
lack status; the 20-year-old governess, who is in a transitional age at
the edge of adulthood; and Peter Quint, who, when living, was the
servant made the master." Rust points to liminal scenes on "nearly
every page," arguing that the "threshold is a place or condition of
great power, but also the locus of the horrible." The one problem with
this essay is that possibly Rust sees too much liminality—like the governess herself. In "Henry James and India: A Historical Reading of
The Turn of the Screw," (*ClioI* 18[1988]:23–40), Graham McMaster
offers a Marxist approach, claiming that the tale "reveals its generic
heritage by handling class and national problems, and . . . displaying
the specific imperialism in the mid-1890s." His Jamesian germ is that
the children *and* the uncle (of the revised text) are Indian orphans
and thus part of the 19th-century novel's function to "fix anxieties and
expectations about displacement and promotion and the reapportion-
ing of communal product." Reading the whole work against the context of James's concern about empire and the "transmission of property" is a good impulse, but one wonders if such massive historicity
arises from the tiny textual reference.

J. S. Leonard in "James's Ghosts and the Art of Fiction" (*WVUPP*
35:46–51) connects James's statements from "The Art of Fiction" about
the relationship of "impressions" to experience with the ghostly ap-
paritions in both "Turn of the Screw" and "The Jolly Corner." In both
tales the impressions create the reality; however, in the first, Miles's
naming exorcises the ghost and makes it vanish, whereas in the second
the ghost materializes only when Brydon "gives up the search." Leonard thus suggests that both stories are about interpreting experience
through narrative "gaps" in the "trace of an impression." Don Anderson recounts what Wayne Booth calls the "critical disagreements"
swirling around the story in "A Fury of Intention: The Scandal of
Henry James's 'The Turn of the Screw' " (*SSEng* 15:140–52). In tracing the scholarship from Wilson and Abrams through Edel to Gass
and Felman, his thesis is basic: "The tale has not been exhausted,
though much criticism of it now is. And there is *nothing scandal-
ous* about that." Finally, Vincent P. Pecora's "Reflection Rendered:
James's *The Turn of the Screw*" (*Self and Form in Modern Narrative*,
pp. 176–213) sets the tale in a sociocultural context by affirming that
"the notion of independent bourgeois agency itself" is at stake in
such modernist narratives. The absent master's "art of life," the

orphaned children's "trusting innocence," and the governess's "ordinary human virtue"—all such "textual machinery" provides a "deceptive openness" which conceals the static issues of distant uncles and rivalry for inheritance. Pecora points, appropriately, both to Rowe and Felman as correctly identifying the core issue of mastery and its relationship to authority.

Bruce Fogelman, in "John Marcher's Journey for Knowledge: The Heroic Background of 'The Beast in the Jungle'" (*HJR* 10:68–73), parallels "the thunderstorm incident" in James's tale to Book IV of the *Aeneid* when Dido and Aeneas fatefully come together. Using the epic as a backdrop provides "an implicit standard of self-realization" which is unfulfilled in the character of Marcher.

vii. Festchriften, Conference Proceedings

The Magic Circle of Henry James: Essays in Honour of Darshan Singh Maini, eds. Amritjit Singh and K. Ayyappa Paniker (Envoy) is a substantial volume of 24 contributions, including an introductory overview essay and a lovely "Portrait" of the honoree by the editors ("a large soul housed in a medium-sized body"), dedicated to the foremost Indian scholar of James. Ten of the essays are reprinted in whole or part, and 12 are new. The new essays range from a severe critique of James's moral liberalism, his limitations as theoretician, and his unsatisfactory ending in *The Portrait*, to more frequent but equally familiar topics: his connections with American naturalists, his revisioning of the Daisy Miller type, his theory of representation, his darker visions in *The Wings* and *The Golden Bowl*, his parallelisms with brother William, with Graham Greene, and Virginia Woolf. Only Adeline Tintner's claim in "The Jamesian Tradition in *The Book Class*: Louis Auchincloss's *A Small Boy and Others*" (pp. 326–41) that James's influence on Auchincloss is the equivalent of Balzac's on James may be said to be a new subject, but it is obviously familiar methodological minting from Tintner's realm. Though not generally new subjects, then, the essays are rather uniformly well presented. Readers of the volume should not ignore the reprinted essays, several of which are very strong pieces by noted Jamesians. This book also gives me the occasion to point out something which I reluctantly omitted last year, the reprinting in 1988 by UMI of Professor Maini's major study, *Henry James: The Indirect Vision*.

Finally, there probably is no better index of the unabated vitality of James studies than the astonishing number of conference sessions devoted to his work each year. Fortunately, *The Henry James Review* (10, ii) gives over an entire issue to reprinting some 16 papers chosen from three recent events, the James Society meetings in San Francisco (1987) and New Orleans (1988), with presentations on "The James Family" and "The Late James," and a symposium in Dallas convened in conjunction with the world premiere of Dominick Argento's opera *The Aspern Papers*—by no means the full complement of good papers given nor meetings held during that period. Those selected authors, including Leon Edel, are known James scholars whose work is regularly reviewed in *ALS*. It is most enjoyable to "hear" all these papers without scholarly apparatus, especially since so many are still so good; such satisfying change of pace is characteristic of Daniel M. Fogel's animated leadership of *HJR*.

University of Missouri

8. Pound and Eliot

Reed Way Dasenbrock

Pound volume was substantially exceeded by Eliot volume this year, to use the stock market phrase. The sheer quantity of work done on Eliot, even if some of the surge may stem from the previous year's centennial celebrations, is a sharp reversal of the situation of just a few years earlier. In contrast, less work (and less important work) was done on Pound than in any year in the 1980s. Eliot is hard to write about, however, and I didn't find this year's work as substantive or innovative as that of 1988.

i. Pound

a. **Text, Biography, and Bibliography.** The major event of the year in this category was the publication of *Elektra* (Princeton), a translation of the Sophocles play done by Pound and Rudd Fleming in 1949. Pound's *Elektra*—aside from being interesting in itself—sheds light on Pound's other translation projects in the St. Elizabeths years, *The Confucian Odes* as well as more obviously *The Women of Trachis*. It has been capably edited by Richard Reid, though I would have preferred Reid's introduction to have been more informative on the circumstances of the play's translation and subsequent nonpublication.

New Directions also issued the 11th edition of *The Cantos*, which though without major new additions moves Cantos 72–73 from the end of the poem to between 71 and 74. A major conference on the text of *The Cantos* was held at Yale in October, and though none of the results of this conference has yet seen print, I predict that the text of *The Cantos* is about to become the next major issue in Pound criticism.

Also published this year was "On America and World War I" (*Paideuma* 18, i–ii:205–14), which includes a previously unpublished article and a previously uncollected 1916 *TLS* review on the war presented by Timothy Materer.

Pound's biographers took a rest this year, and the one contribution to bibliography was Thomas A. Goldwasser's "Ezra Pound's *A Lume Spento*: A Preliminary Census" (*PBSA* 83:17–42), listing all known copies of Pound's first and rarest book.

b. **General Studies.** Wendy Stallard Flory's *The American Ezra Pound* (Yale) is probably the most substantial contribution to Pound studies this year, a detailed examination of Pound's relation to his native land, particularly in the 1930s, that makes good use of the correspondence and other material in the Pound Archive at Yale. I'm not very impressed by Flory's overall argument, however, that Pound's commitment to American issues somehow mitigates or lessens his commitment to Fascism. As the title *Jefferson and/or Mussolini* should tell us, Pound's Italian politics were closely intertwined with his American ones in ways that Flory does not help us understand.

Pound is one of the central figures in Charles Altieri's *Painterly Abstraction*, a fascinating and deeply rewarding study that defies easy summary. Among its multiple foci are the influence of modernist painting on modernist poetry, the role of abstraction in modernism, an eloquent defense of modernism against a variety of postmodernist critiques of modernism, and—as always in Altieri's work—a defense of literature. What Altieri has to say about Pound doesn't fit neatly into the ongoing project of Pound criticism; he isn't filling any obvious "holes." I therefore wouldn't hand *Painterly Abstraction* to anyone seeking help with *The Cantos*; but his chapter on Pound and discussions elsewhere in the book demand careful and sustained consideration by Pound scholars. Altieri's discussion of the Early Cantos focuses on the way Pound wants to get the first person back into the epic; there is also a fascinating discussion of translation and how this relates to Pound's "constructivist ethos" and epic.

Several other books include Pound in their itineraries. There is a good idea behind James F. Knapp's *Literary Modernism and the Transformation of Work* (Northwestern, 1988), which is to see that modernism is much more directly connected to changes in society and in work than has been acknowledged; modernism in Knapp's vision is engaged in a dialogue with Taylorism and other forms of rationalization in the workplace. Knapp's study, however, doesn't realize its promise. Most of the book is made up of fairly conventional close readings of major modernist texts that are curiously uncontextualized and therefore unfaithful to his general presuppositions. He also misses the modernist writer most relevant to his subject, Wyndham Lewis.

Finally, he is committed to seeing only the ways in which modernism anticipates his own critical position on technology; but that is to capture half the picture, since the modernists were fascinated by some of these developments as well. The chapter and a half on Pound has some interesting things to say about *Mauberley* as a text resisting Taylorization; the discussion of *The Cantos* is less rewarding and rather diffuse. Also having trouble fitting a traditional reading into a book with ambitions toward social relevance is Henry S. Sussman in *High Resolution.* A long chapter on "The Economies of Modern American Poetry" (pp. 115–96) that is mostly about *The Cantos* never connects up with the larger themes of literacy that interest Sussman; nor does it have much that is new to say about Pound, though I did like the suggestion in passing that Spenser is an important forerunner. A much more satisfactory book in its treatment of Pound is James G. Nelson's *Elkin Mathews: Publisher to Yeats, Joyce, Pound* (Wisconsin), which has an informative chapter on Pound's relations with Mathews. Nelson's tone is much more old-fashioned than that of Knapp or Sussman, but in fact his emphasis on publishing history gives us a much richer sense of the social context of the literary work than either.

The aesthetics of modernism is the subject of several articles this year. Patricia Rae's "From Mystical Gaze to Pragmatic Game: Representations of Truth in Vorticist Art" (*ELH* 56:689–720) is an original and persuasive look at vorticist aesthetics, placing Pound's and Lewis's "conceptions of the cognitive capacities of the arts" in a number of intellectual contexts, including the pragmatism of William James. Jacob Korg's "The Dialogic Nature of Collage" (*Mosaic* 22, ii:95–109) and Bruce E. Fleming's "The Ideogram in Pound and Eisenstein: Sketch for a Theory of Modernism" (*SWR* 74:87–97), respectively, compare Pound's aesthetic to cubism and the work of Sergei Eisenstein; neither article breaks much new ground, though each seems convinced that it does. An interesting look at the evolution of modernism after the glory years is provided by Massimo Bacigalupo's "Compound Ghosts: The Modernists' Canon in the Thirties and Forties" (*Interspace* 4:35–42); Bacigalupo's theme is the turn toward politics made by the major modernists in these years, and he has some suggestive remarks on Pound's interests in Dante and Cavalcanti in these years. Finally, Pound's relations to two journals are studied in two good articles in *American Poetry.* Robert von Hallberg usefully points out through a study of the relations between "Ezra Pound and the

Mercure de France" (6, ii:11–14) that Pound wasn't purely an oppositional or avant-garde writer; he had his aspirations toward the mainstream when they were at all encouraged. In contrast, Richard
Sieburth's "Pound's *Dial* Letters: Between Modernism and the Avant-
Garde" (6, ii:3–10) discusses how Pound's relations with the *Dial*
were more strained than Eliot's precisely because of Pound's more
avant-garde conception of modernism.

The relation of Pound to various of his intellectual and political
heroes is explored in several articles. Thomas Cody looks at Pound's
interest in "Adams, Mussolini and the Personality of Genius" (*Paideuma* 18, iii:77–103). This essay is useful in the way it distinguishes
Pound's sense of textuality from that of Riddel and Derrida and in
its focus on Pound's interest in the "great man," but it is weakened by
its failure to cite virtually any previous Pound scholarship. Fresher
comparisons are drawn by E. P. Walkiewicz and Robert Casillo.
Walkiewicz's "And Agassiz for Gestalt Seed: Pound's American Taxonomy" (*KR* 11, iv:116–22) relates Agassiz's rejection of Darwinism
to Pound's "lack of tolerance for variation," while Casillo's "The Italian
Renaissance: Pound's Problematic Debt to Burckhardt" (*Mosaic* 22,
iv:13–29) shows how Pound used Burckhardt but doesn't show anything especially problematic about it.

Two essays in *Paideuma* engage in what I find to be the frustrating
genre of summarizing a correspondence rather than providing us with
it, but both articles are nevertheless quite interesting. Philip J. Burns
in " 'Dear Uncle George': The Pound-Tinkham Letters" (18, i–ii:35–
65) gives an informative survey of Pound's correspondence with Con-
gressman Tinkham of Massachusetts, one of the few public figures
who actually wrote Pound back, combined with a less informative survey of Pound's political ideas. " 'Five Years I Wrote to You . . .' : An
Unknown Correspondent of Ezra Pound" (18, i–ii:161–83) is a detailed summary by Rodney Symington of the correspondence in St.
Elizabeths between Pound and Else Seel, a German writer living in
British Columbia.

Probably the final manifestation of Pound's centennial to be dis-
cussed in *ALS* is the special issue of *Rendezvous* (22, i[1986]) devoted
to some of the offerings at the 1985 Pound Centennial Conference in
Hailey, including papers and talks by Mary de Rachewiltz, Scott
Thomas Eastham, Rick Ardinger, Peter Dale Scott, Bernard K. Duffy,
Ford Swetnam, Carroll Terrell, Hank Nuwer, and Kevin Oderman.
Eastham's "Hear/Say: Ezra Pound and the Ten Voices of Tradition"

(pp. 8–25) has some interesting remarks connecting Pound's interest in religious and literary traditions to "ancestor worship" in Asia and Africa. Scott's "Man of Anger, Man of Peace: The Poetic Politics of Ezra Pound" (pp. 34–47) is an unconvincing defense of Pound's "essentially benign" "long-range visionary politics," which Scott unsuccessfully tries to dissociate from Pound's "problematic voice of anger." And Kevin Oderman's "A Profession of Folly" (pp. 81–87) looks at themes of metamorphosis and transformation in Pound's poetry, particularly the early poem, "The Tree."

Finally, Pound's prose and prose translations were the subject of just two articles this year. In "Modernism and Science: The Case of Pound's *ABC of Reading*" (*Paideuma* 18, i–ii:187–96), Paul Douglass criticizes Pound's use of scientific analogies in the *ABC* and argues that they are indebted to Bergson's "philosophical scientism." Mary P. Cheadle's focus is "The Vision of Light in Ezra Pound's *The Unwobbling Pivot*" (*TCL* 35:113–30), informative about Pound's two translations of this work and relating Pound's Confucianism to Neoplatonism.

c. **Relation to Other Writers.** An interesting backlighting of Pound's relation to William Carlos Williams is found in the many comments by Williams on Pound in *William Carlos Williams and James Laughlin: Selected Letters* (Norton), an attractive volume ably and unobtrusively edited by Hugh Witemeyer. Jeffrey Walker's *Bardic Ethos* is also concerned with the "Pound-Williams tradition," as it has come to be called, but readers of Pound will find little of interest in this badly focused study. Walker is more interested in the "bardic ethos," whatever that might be, than he is in the "American epic form," and he never succeeds in identifying the two. He then compounds the problem by looking at poets who were obviously interested in epic forms, both new and old, without getting much said about these forms. Nothing here advances beyond or revises Michael André Bernstein's *The Tale of the Tribe* (1980).

The articles in this category this year focus more on Pound's influence than influences on him. One exception is Walter Baumann's study of the relation between "Ezra Pound and Heinrich Heine" (*Paideuma* 18, iii:59–75), which doesn't have a sharp focus though it is informative on Pound's translation of Heine in *Canzoni*. Willard Bohn's "Thoughts that Join Like Spokes: Pound's Image of Apollinaire" (*Paideuma* 18, i–ii:129–45) is similarly informative without being argumentative, providing a detailed discussion of Pound's references to Apollinaire.

The most substantial study of Pound's relation to his contemporaries is Frank Lentricchia's "Lyric in the Culture of Capitalism" (*AmLH* 1:63–88), which despite its grandiloquent title is a reading of Pound's and Frost's contrasting responses to the situation of publishing poetry in the magazines of their day. This is a good, contextually informed piece of criticism. David Roessel's "Pound, Lawrence, and 'The Earthly Paradise' " (*Paideuma* 18, i–ii:227–30) argues persuasively that Pound influenced Lawrence's going to Lago di Garda in 1913. David Gordon quotes a letter to Pound from James Laughlin quoting Moore's admiring comments on his *Confucius* in "And Moore: Marianne on Ezra's *Confucius*" (*Paideuma* 18, iii:149–50). Albert Cook's "Projections of Measure: The Continued Synergies of Pound and Williams" (*ArQ* 45, ii:35–61) stresses the continuity between the metrics of Pound and Williams and those of Olson and Creeley; Cook sees Pound's invention of an "anti-Propertian" metric in *Propertius* as a crucial breakthrough for Pound. Finally, the best article on Pound's relation to other writers and critics this year is Christopher Beach's "Ezra Pound and Harold Bloom: Influences, Canons, Traditions and the Making of Modern Poetry" (*ELH* 56:463–83), which expertly contrasts Bloom's theories about the anxiety of influence with Pound's much less anxious theories and practice and argues that it is Pound—not Bloom—who enables us to make sense of contemporary American poetry.

d. **The Shorter Poems.** Not much at all was written about Pound's poetry except for *The Cantos* this year, but *Hugh Selwyn Mauberley* and, more surprisingly, *The Confucian Odes* are the subject of several good articles each. Massimo Bacigalupo explicates some of the references to "Art and Artists in Ezra Pound's *Mauberley*" (*Poetry and the Fine Arts*, pp. 135–51). In "Irony and Common Sense: The Genre of *Mauberley*" (*Paideuma* 18, i–ii:147–60), Stephen J. Adams argues against the traditional view that the poem is a dramatic monologue spoken by Mauberley; according to Adams, it is instead satire. Brian G. Caraher's "Reading Pound with Bakhtin: Sculpting the Social Languages of *Hugh Selwyn Mauberley*'s 'Mere Surface' " (*MLQ* 49[1988]:38–64) uses several ideas of Bakhtin as a way to explore the complexity of *Mauberley*. This looked like the kind of article I dread reading, an inappropriate application of a currently fashionable theorist, but I was pleasantly surprised: Caraher sensitively applies his theorist here, exploring the relevance of Bakhtin's ideas about the lyric undergoing "novelization" only to find that other ideas of Bakhtin about polyphonic discourse are more appropriate to the poem. This is well worth reading.

Eugene Eoyang's "Waley or Pound? The Dynamics of Genre in Translation" (*TkR* 29:441–65) is a welcome comparison by a Sinologist of Pound and Waley's translations of the *Shih Ching*. Eoyang argues for a difference in the intended audience of the two translators: Waley's "contingent" translation aims at the student of Chinese; Pound's "surrogate" translation aims at an audience of general readers and readers of poetry. The bulk of Eoyang's article is an examination of the translators' respective versions of four of the *Odes*; Eoyang gives Pound a hard time for the inaccuracy of some of his translations, but praises the quality of others. And it is interesting to find a learned reader confirming one's sense of the unevenness but occasional brilliance of Pound's translation. Finally, Mary Cheadle's "Defining Ode 65 in 'Relation to Life' " (*Paideuma* 18, i–ii:231–43) is a close look at one poem in *The Confucian Odes* with an explicit allusion to Thomas Hardy. Cheadle is less concerned with these poems as translations than as poems by Pound. *The Confucian Odes* remains one of Pound's least appreciated, understood, or studied works, and since Cheadle makes good sense of this one ode, she should be encouraged to go on to the rest.

e. **The Cantos.** The slowdown in Pound studies can be felt in work on *The Cantos* as well, even though increasingly Pound is seen above all as the author of *The Cantos*. One sign of this perception is the inclusion of the poem in a series of Cambridge books devoted to "Landmarks of World Literature." George Kearns faced an admittedly hard task accomplishing this in *Pound: The Cantos* (Cambridge), and his brief study is full of sensible advice about how to tackle the poem. But the novice reader is still better off, in my judgment, tackling the poem with the help of Kearns's earlier *Guide to Ezra Pound's Selected Cantos* (1980) than with this kind of summary.

Ronald Bush's 1976 book, *The Genesis of Ezra Pound's Cantos*, has been republished by Princeton University Press with a new introduction by the author, and Bush's study remains a model of the kind of detailed textual and contextual studies we need of the whole poem. A very different kind of piece is Carroll F. Terrell's "Canto Thirty-Six, from *Dark and Light*" (*Paideuma* 18, i–ii:215–26). Described by the author as versified footnotes to *The Cantos*, this contains a number of extremely perceptive observations about the structure of the poem. I don't take *The Cantos* to be as perfectly organized as Terrell finds it to be, but we all ought to ponder the organization he finds there and see if we are convinced by it.

A number of general studies of the poem are concerned with Pound and the occult. Angela Elliott's "The Word Comprehensive: Gnostic Light in *The Cantos*" (*Paideuma* 18, iii:7–57) is a terrible essay, reminiscent of some of the worst excesses of Yeats criticism. She produces no real evidence that Pound had any direct acquaintance with Gnosticism and ignores all the collateral traditions Pound did know something about. Demetres P. Tryphonopoulos's "*The Cantos* as Palingenesis" (*Paideuma* 18, i–ii:7–33) is a better essay along the same lines; concerned with establishing Pound's acquaintance with this material, he has some interesting remarks about Ovid. Philip Kuberski's "Pound's Sacred Technology" (*Paideuma* 18, iii:105–19) is the best of these three essays, as it gives us a less reductive explanation of Pound's concern with metaphysics and myth.

Just three essays this year focus on sections of *The Cantos*. The best is Lawrence S. Rainey's fine "The Malatesta *Cantos* and the Making of Ideology" (*AmerP* 6, ii:15–27). Rainey argues that the Malatesta Cantos are part of a turning point in Pound's career which Rainey places in and relates to Pound's residence in Paris in the early 1920s. More specifically, Rainey argues for the importance for Pound of a 1912 book on Malatesta, Beltramelli's *Un tempio d'amore*. The fact that Beltramelli wrote the first biography of Mussolini (in 1923) enables Rainey to make some nice and persuasive points about the place of Malatesta in Pound's political evolution. Carol H. Cantrell and Ward Swinson's "Cantos LII–LXXI: Pound's Textbook for Princes" (*Paideuma* 18, i–ii:67–128), a continuation of an earlier essay (*Paideuma* 17, ii–iii[1988]), argues for a shift between the Chinese History Cantos and the Adams Cantos that is greater than any shift between the Adams Cantos and *The Pisan Cantos*. This fails to account for Cantos 72–73, which Cantrell and Swinson think are still unavailable, cantos that carry forward everything these critics object to in Cantos 52–61. In "Pound's Rendering of Abstraction in the *Pisan Cantos*" (*Paideuma* 18, iii:137–46), James Lowe argues that Pound was somehow struggling with abstraction in Pisa, an argument that makes little sense of the most concrete section of the poem.

Larry R. Michaels provides three "Addenda to Terrell's *A Companion to the Cantos of Ezra Pound*" (*AN&Q* n.s. 1[1988]:142–43), which offers two useful corrections to Terrell concerning the reference to Shivers and Alfalfa in Canto 93 and a less persuasive correction concerning the Brothers Adams in Canto 84. But the absence of other detailed studies of *The Cantos* of the kind more numerous in recent years is just one sign that Pound criticism seems in general to be on hold. Important issues remain to be fully tackled, among them the text of *The Cantos* and the relation of *The Cantos* to Pound's political involvements.

ii. Eliot

a. **Text, Biography and Bibliography.** Eliot textual studies return to their slumber this year after the publications of the *Letters* last year. The major contribution to Eliot's biography is E. W. F. Tomlin's *T. S. Eliot: A Friendship* (Routledge). Tomlin's memoir is a detailed and affecting account of a friendship with Eliot that, though not close, lasted more than 30 years. Consciously designed, I suspect, as a corrective to recent trends in Eliot biographies, it tends toward the hagiographic on occasion in its attempt to portray Eliot as a good man as well as a great poet. Eliot's attention to younger writers and critics such as Tomlin was extraordinary, however, and is an aspect of his career that we may not take enough note of.

Casey Herrick has compiled an annotated bibliography of recent secondary work on *Four Quartets* in "*Four Quartets*: An Annotated Bibliographical Supplement, 1980–1986" (*BB* 46:122–28). And William Baker describes "Some T. S. Eliot Inscribed Copies—An Addendum" (*BC* 38:253–57), which lets us know primarily that the Possum didn't give away much useful information while inscribing his own books.

b. **General Studies.** Eric Sigg's *The American T. S. Eliot: A Study of the Early Writings* (Cambridge) was, I expect, an impressive dissertation; it is now a stimulating but not totally successful book. It is oddly organized, as it seems to start over again with each chapter, and the themes Sigg has not quite woven together are not of equal value. A perceptive treatment of "American aestheticism," the work of Henry Adams, Henry James, and Santayana, as a context for Eliot's work and of Eliot's sense of himself as a member of an American elite struggles for attention with a very odd discussion of Protestantism and Eliot's reaction to it. Sigg's sense of Unitarianism seems derived wholly from Eliot's dismissive remarks about his religious upbringing, and this won't quite do.

More important studies are John Mayer's *T. S. Eliot's Silent Voices* (Oxford) and Jeffrey M. Perl's *Skepticism and Modern Enmity: Before and After Eliot* (Hopkins), though each in its own way reflects the coercive pressure put on Eliot studies by the Eliot Estate. Mayer's work takes off from a close study of Eliot's unpublished poetry notebook in the Berg Collection and argues that his work there and in the early poetry constitutes the development of a new poetic genre, the "psychic monologue." What he has to say about these poems sounds sensible enough; unfortunately, he hasn't been given permission to quote any unpublished work, which makes some of this book—for the majority of readers who haven't been to the Berg Collection—a little like reading a discussion of the sculptures of Phidias. However, despite this absurd limitation, what Mayer has to say sheds fresh and important light on the published poems from "Prufrock" to "Gerontion" that he also discusses. I don't think the concluding discussion of *The Waste Land* is the culmination of the book in quite the way Mayer intends it to be, however, since I'm not persuaded that *The Waste Land* is "Eliot's most dazzling psychic monologue" so much as the beginning of something else. Mayer here is in keeping with recent criticism in stressing both the autobiographical nature of the poem and the existence of a voice behind the multiple voices of the poem, but one can go too far in that direction, canceling the other voices in a search to get behind them.

Perl's *Skepticism and Modern Enmity* is more ambitious, seeking to make a contribution to the history of modern culture as well as to Eliot studies. It has many fine things in it, a marvelous discussion of how indebted critics attacking Eliot such as Bloom and J. Hillis Miller are to him, an original discussion of how Eliot responded to World War II in his prose and plays, and a good central theme about how Eliot—in philosophy and in politics—always sought to get beyond either/or polarities and find a middle way. The connections drawn here between Eliot's skepticism and his subsequent commitment to Christianity are important and convincing. However, Perl's book also features a more conventional source study—about what Eliot's unpublished philosophical notebooks from his Harvard education can tell us about his attitude toward philosophy—and I find this material less impressive. Here, the Eliot Estate has violated its stated policy and let Perl quote extensively. But it is Mayer's book which really builds on unpublished material and would have benefited from permission to quote. *Skepticism and Modern Enmity* comes just after two important studies, Shusterman's *T. S. Eliot and the Philosophy of Literary Criticism* (1988) and Cleo Kearns's *T. S. Eliot and Indic Traditions* (1987). Perl cites Shusterman's book but hasn't fully responded to its argument, and he does not seem to have seen Kearns's before his went to press. I find these books more authoritative in placing Eliot in relation to, respectively, contemporary philosophy and Buddhism. Perl is an extremely gifted cultural historian and is very good on Eliot's relation to contemporary culture; he is less gifted as a historian of philosophy. But there is still probably more to learn from his book than from any other on Eliot this year.

The themes of Charles Altieri's *Painterly Abstraction* overlap with *Skepticism and Modern Enmity* in that both are interested in showing the indebtedness to modernism of most post-modernist critiques of modernism. Altieri's focus, however, is contemporary poetry, not contemporary criticism. Eliot is less pervasive in *Painterly Abstraction* than Pound or Stevens, but there is a rewarding chapter focusing on the early poetry which offers an interesting counterpoint to Mayer's book, since Altieri's focus is on how the early poetry attempts to escape the condition of the first person. What Altieri says about the use of "you" is suggestive, and it is Altieri's approach—not Mayer's—that enables us to make more sense of *The Waste Land*.

One doesn't learn much that is new about T. S. Eliot in the chapter on his work in David B. Dickens's *Negative Spring: Crisis Imagery in the Works of Brentano, Lenau, Rilke and Eliot* (Peter Lang), unless it is a surprise that Eliot's imagery of the seasons is connected to a personal and religious struggle. It is interesting, however, that "negative spring" is a topos in German-language poetry before Eliot, though Dickens does not make a case for influence. An even less satisfactory book is Randy Malamud's *The Language of Modernism*. Malamud's chapter on Eliot comes between a chapter on Woolf and one on Joyce, and his remarks are generally either unoriginal or unpersuasive (and sometimes both). He writes about the parataxis of modernist writing, including Eliot's, as if no one has mentioned this, and the discussion of quotation and allusion that follows has no more to offer. Anyone who can refer to "the lullingly complacent and pompously confident rhythms of Tennyson" or who after referring to Joyce's "literary disorder" can claim that "there is no ideal vision of society embodied in his literature" cannot be taken seriously as a commentator. This is a dissertation rushed far too quickly into print.

Cynthia Ozick's "T. S. Eliot at 101" (NY [20 Nov.]:119–54) attracted a good deal of attention this year. Her piece should be in a familiar enough vein for Eliot scholars, however, as it describes a Bloom-like rejection of Eliot as the reactionary modernist father, though Ozick demonstrates a much sharper sense of Eliot's real artistic achievement than Bloom ever has. Elisa Kay Sparks discusses the Eliot-Bloom relationship in "Old Father Nile: T. S. Eliot and Harold Bloom on the Creative Process as Spontaneous Generation" (*Engendering the Word*, pp. 51–80). This is mostly a fairly predictable feminist critique of Eliot and Bloom as "phallogocentric" critics, though interesting where it argues for a close parallel between the two. Even more dubious psychologizing can be found in Joseph Browne's "T. S. Eliot: The Poet as Proof-Rock, Old Possum, and Preacher" (*MHLS* 12, i:1–12), in which Eliot's mother is blamed for his failure to develop his "true self."

Other general studies put Eliot in one or another context (or box) with varying degrees of success. Michael Beehler's "Semiotics/Psychoanalysis/Christianity: Eliot's Logic of Alterity" (*ArQ* 45, iv:57–73) argues quite oddly that it is Eliot's Christianity that brings him closest to contemporary thought, to Derrida's "logic of alterity." Constance A. Pedoto, also bent on modernizing Eliot, discusses "Intertextuality in the Works of T. S. Eliot: A Means to Total Readability or to Complete Frustration?" (*YER* 10:31–34), summarizing different perspectives on intertextuality and showing that they can all be exemplified by Eliot's works. Herbert Grabes gives us another essay on "Deliberate Intertextuality: The Function of Quotation and Allusion in the Early Poetry of T. S. Eliot" (in *Multiple Worlds, Multiple Words: Essays in Honour of Irene Simon*, eds. Hena Maes-Jelinek et al. [University of Liege, 1987], pp. 139–52), focusing on the connection between Eliot's allusions and his insistence on the historical sense and tradition. Jonathan Morse's sketch "Toward a History of the Eliot Era" (*YER* 10:9–12) tries in brief compass to suggest a move beyond Kenner's and Bloom's mutually exclusive conceptions of modernism. The best essay among these is Donald J. Childs's "T. S. Eliot: From Varieties of Mysticism to Pragmatic Poesis" (*Mosaic* 22, iv:99–116). Childs shows how Eliot's understanding of mysticism derives from Bergson and Evelyn Underhill; according to Childs, Eliot finally makes sense of mysticism as something to do, as a human practice, in ways that connect up with pragmatism and with the late poetry. Finally, Walter J. Ong's "T. S. Eliot and Today's Ecumenism" (*R&L* 21, ii:1–17) reminds us again that Eliot also has a readership interested in his religious thought, precisely what many critics find most problematic about his work. Ong has an interesting point to make, that Eliot's notion of religion is recuperative, not future-oriented, in contrast not just to his stance in aesthetics but to the thrust of contemporary ecumenism and contemporary theology.

c. Relation to Other Writers. Two books this year treat Eliot's relation to a single predecessor, Gareth Reeves's *T. S. Eliot: A Virgilian Poet* (St. Martin's) and Vinnie-Marie D'Ambrosio's *Eliot Possessed: T. S. Eliot and Fitzgerald's Rubaiyat* (NYU). Reeves's study is quite rewarding, D'Ambrosio's is terrible. The difference is that Reeves knows how to read poetry closely: he can take a familiar passage, unpack the Vergilian echoes underneath, and persuade one that Vergil is indeed a relevant presence in the passage. He discusses a range of Eliot's poems from "La Figlia Che Piange" to *Four Quartets*, has a mastery of Eliot's prose and the secondary work on Vergil that Eliot knew, and never drastically overstates his case. D'Ambrosio, in contrast, reads closely but without effect, as time and again he argues for echoes of Fitzgerald that he fails to make me see. He also does not understand how to build a case for influence; phrases like "it seems unlikely that Eliot would have been unaware of it" punctuate the text. Also published this year was "T. S. Eliot's Virgilian Hauntings: 'La figlia che piange' and the *Aeneid*" (*NewComp* 7:113–24), an earlier draft of Reeves's first chapter. Reeves has built a useful book out of a number of separate articles; D'Ambrosio had a good article but overbuilt on insufficient foundations.

Stephen Sicari's "In Dante's Wake: T. S. Eliot's 'Art of Memory'" (*CCur* 28:413–34) focuses on Eliot's relation to the other poet necessarily present in Reeves's study, Dante. Sensitively exploring the relation between *Four Quartets* and the *Commedia*, Sicari argues that Eliot's poem imitates Dante's in its stress on the redemptive force of memory. But there is still plenty to say about Eliot's relation to the Victorians, as is shown by James Longenbach's "Matthew Arnold and the Modern Apocalypse" (*PMLA* 104: 844–55). Longenbach compares Eliot's rhetoric of crisis to Arnold's and argues that their use of a "rhetorical of finality" contains "its own critique." Longenbach's comparison of Arnold and Eliot is a good deal more persuasive and illuminating than "A Prufrockian Look at Browning's 'The Last Ride Together'" (*SBHC* 16[1988]:106–13) offered by David M. Wilkes, which is a superficial modernization of Browning's poem. Hirofumi Iwamatsu doesn't tell us anything new in "Henry James: *The Portrait of a Lady* in Relation to T. S. Eliot" (*KAL* 30:57–66). With something new to say on a familiar topic, on the other hand, is Timothy Materer in "W. B. Yeats, T. S. Eliot, and the Critique of Occultism in *Four Quartets*" (*YER* 10:1–4); Materer's focus is on how Eliot continues his critique of Yeats even in *Four Quartets*. Less solemnly, but also to the point, Robert F. Fleissner treats the relation between "Another Baskerville Hound and Moriarty Cat: T. S. Eliot and Conan Doyle" (*Baker Street Miscellany* 56 [Winter 1988]:1–13), a discussion of the various echoes of the Sherlock Holmes stories in Eliot's poems and plays. George A. Geevarghese doesn't have much to say about his familiar topic, "T. S. Eliot and F. H. Bradley: A Reconsideration of the Question of Influence" (*CIEFLB* n.s. 1, i:24–32), though I find myself in agreement with his general contention that at times too much has been made of the Eliot-Bradley connection.

Stephen Fredman's "Williams, Eliot, and American Tradition" (*TCL* 35:235–53) presents Williams's sense of tradition as closer to Eliot's than either might have thought. Roderick Beaton stresses the influence of Eliot's "mythic method" on Seferis in "From mythos to logos: The Poetics of George Seferis" (*JMGS* 5[1987]:135–52). Steven Helmling's "T. S. Eliot and Ralph Ellison: Insiders, Outsiders, and Cultural Authority" (*SoR* 25:841–58) describes how Ellison modeled himself on Eliot's literary career and has to an extent been caught in that model. These are all rewarding essays; much less rewarding is Bickford Sylvester's "Hemingway's Italian Waste Land: The Complex Unity of 'Out of Season'" (in *Hemingway's Neglected Short Fiction*, pp. 75–98). Sylvester presents the story—indeed all of *In Our Time*—as modeled on *The Waste Land*; the level of evidence offered can best be shown by his taking the fishing in the story as a reference to the Fisher King. In much the same vein, Dan Vogel unsuccessfully argues for a "near-parodic" relation between *The Waste Land* and *Herzog* in "Bellow, Herzog, and *The Waste Land*" (*Saul Bellow Journal* 8, i:44–50). But I'm more persuaded by the parallels presented in Colette Lindroth's "*The Waste Land* Revisited: 'Sammy and Rosie Get Laid'" (*LFQ* 17:95–98). One wonders what "Westminster Abbey" himself—as Wyndham Lewis called Eliot—would have thought of a graffiti-covered bus with lines from *The Waste Land* written all over it, but this at least gives Lindroth some solid evidence to work with. But why do such studies seem fatally compelled to overstate their case? Eliot's poem is surely not *the key* to Kureishi and Frears's film any more than *From Ritual to Romance* is the key to *The Waste Land*. Works of art are not locks or doors or secret passages, so there is no reason to assume a missing key. Finally, Seamus Heaney describes his own process of "Learning from Eliot" (*Agenda* 27, i:17–31).

d. **Poetry and Plays.** Most of the work on the early poetry this year focuses on the poems in Eliot's first book. Ludmila Gruzewska-Wojtas discusses the opposition between "The Street and 'The Drawing Room': The Poetic Universe of T. S. Eliot's *Prufrock and Other Observations*" (*EiP* 14, ii:65–82), making the perceptive observation that the lower-class urban landscape of the streets and the upper-class drawing rooms are for Eliot ultimately more similar—in their lack of vitality and value—than dissimilar. The two articles that discuss "Prufrock" on its own are less enlightening: Robert F. Fleissner finds some improbable and unnecessary sources for what he terms "The Germanic Insect Image in *Prufrock*" (*GN* 21, i:2–3), and Henrik Rosenmeier makes some obvious remarks about Boston as "The Setting of 'The Lovesong of J. Alfred Prufrock'" (in *A Literary Miscellany Presented to Eric Jacobsen* [Copenhagen: University of Copenhagen, 1988], pp. 304–14). Robert Coltrane establishes "The Imagist Relationship between Pound's 'Les Millwin' and Eliot's 'Morning at the Window'" (*Paideuma* 18, iii:123–28). The most substantial of these essays is John-Paul Riquelme's "The Transformation of Romantic Tropes in T. S. Eliot's 'Rhapsody on a Windy Night'" (*Style* 23:1–15), a close reading of the poem presenting it as a turn on a number of romantic conventions amounting to a turn on romanticism itself. I like the way this essay builds on recent work relating modernism to romanticism, only to use that to restate a more traditional view of modernist literature as programmatically antiromanticist. In particular, de Man's widely influential attack on modernism must look rather different after what we now know about de Man's involvement with a kind of modernist fascism, and this essay is one step in the direction of a needed reevaluation of de Man's critique.

The only essay on Eliot's second book is Stephen H. Clark's "Testing the Razor: T. S. Eliot's *Poems 1920*" (in *Engendering the Word*, pp. 167–89); according to Clark, these poems should be "read pri-

marily as articulations of a psychology of sexual fear and desired re-
taliation." Clark's essay is an attempt to see what reading these poems
"as a man" might mean, but the theoretical component of the essay is
composed of more questions than answers.

There is remarkably little written specifically on *The Waste Land*
this year. Dennis Ryan's "Marie Lloyd and the Last 'London Letter':
T. S. Eliot's Transmutation of Ideology into Art in *The Waste Land*"
(*YER* 10:35–40) discusses the music hall artist Marie Lloyd and, more
problematically, relates her to the give, sympathize, control passage at
the close of the poem. Donald Beagle's "Eliot's *The Waste Land*"
(*Expl* 47, iii:40–41) contains more about *Dracula* as a source for the
poem's imagery. Leonard Diepeveen's "Shifting Metaphors: Interarts
Comparisons and Analogy" (*W&I* 5:206–13) uses the example of the
relation of *The Waste Land* to cubism to look at the problem of comparing works in different artistic media. Though Eliot's poem is not
extensively discussed, this is a penetrating essay well worth attention.

There are two closely related essays on "The Hollow Men." Venus
Freeman's " 'The Hollow Men': Between the Idea and the Reality"
(*YER* 10:41–43) sees the poems as part of Eliot's religious search
rather than religious despair, as if one needs to make a clear-cut distinction between the two. Leslie Stratyner's "By The Banks of the
Acheron: T. S. Eliot, Dante, and 'The Hollow Men' " (*YER* 10:17–20)
traces the Dante references in the poem to come to a more balanced
perspective on spiritual search and despair.

Of the four quite different essays on *Four Quartets*, only the most
contentious one is worth reading. Cynthia Ho presents nothing new
on the connotations of the poem's title in "Currents of Action: Place-
Name in T. S. Eliot's 'Dry Salvages' " (*RE Arts and Letters* 15, i:5–12).
Laura Severin's " 'In My End is My Beginning': Mother as Saviour in
Four Quartets" (*YER* 10:25–27) discusses the uses of Julian of Nor-
wich in "Little Gidding," developing from that a claim that the poem
is about the "Mother God." This is full of dubious psychologizing.
W. G. Bebbington's "Four *Quartets*?" (*EIC* 39: 234–41) is both distinctly British and quite entertaining in its willingness to call all the
critics and Eliot himself idiotic. An attempt to take the title seriously,
it criticizes all previous attempts to draw analogies between music
and Eliot's poem as not well-founded in music theory. Bebbington
considers the title "at worst the result of ignorance and presumption,"
and he makes the useful point that the usual talk about the four poems
relating to four seasons, elements, and so on should logically make it

one quartet, not four of them. Bebbington shows us that we don't understand the title of the poem, which is a useful enough exercise; what he doesn't do is point us to any more useful understanding, mostly because he doesn't think there is one to be had. Robert C. Schweik might have supplied such an understanding in his "T. S. Eliot's *Four Quartets* and the Uses of 'Referred Forms'" (*Cithara* 28, ii:43–64), as he advances the term "referred form" for titles of modern art works that refer to another art form such as *Four Quartets*. But Schweik just uses *Four Quartets* as an example, and there is unfortunately no sustained discussion of Eliot's title.

Dorothy Lindemann's "Old Possum's Book of Practical Cats" (*YER* 10:28–30) takes these poems altogether too solemnly.

There are four articles and one book on the plays. R. J. Cloughterty, Jr.'s "T. S. Eliot's *Murder in the Cathedral*: A Chorus Divided" (*YER* 10:13–16) discusses a production copy of the play in which the chorus is divided and given specific lines, something anyone producing the play would certainly want to know. Martha C. Carpenter's "Orestes in the Drawing Room: Aeschylean Parallels in T. S. Eliot's 'The Family Reunion'" (*TCL* 35:17–42) is a detailed comparison of *The Family Reunion* with the *Oresteia* arguing for an exact parallelism between the plays. Theresa M. Towner's "From Romance to Ritual: The Evidence of *The Family Reunion*" (*SCRev* 6, i:62–74) is a more interesting and more analytical essay, concerned with describing Eliot's ritualistic and purgative designs on his audience. Finally, William Errett Kinnison's "'Why, damme, it's too bad!': The Structure of Comedy and the Strictures of the Doubting Game in T. S. Eliot's *The Confidential Clerk*" (*YER* 10:21–24) is a good discussion of the way Eliot plays off skepticism and belief as reflections of different audiences of his play. William Tydeman's Murder in the Cathedral *and* The Cocktail Party (Macmillan, 1988) is yet another of the recent British introductory books on Eliot; this one is eminently forgettable, a very general survey with little that is new to say and an overly defensive tone about Eliot's dramatic achievement.

e. **The Criticism.** David Huisman's "Title and Subject in *The Sacred Wood*" (*EIC* 39:217–33) argues that Eliot's title comes not from *The Golden Bough* but from Vergil through Petronius. Richard Shusterman's "Eliot's Pragmatist Philosophy of Practical Wisdom" (*RES* 40:72–92) is yet another fine article on Eliot's criticism from the philosopher who is becoming the master of the subject. Shusterman discusses Aristotle's concept of *phronesis* and Eliot's interest in it as a form of knowledge not imitative of science. He makes good (and original) use of Eliot's study of Aristotle with Joachim at Oxford and usefully contrasts Eliot's "Aristotelian" pragmatism to that of contemporary neopragmatists such as Rorty and Fish. This article should be read.

Readers of research tools such as *ALS* benefit from hearing more than one voice, so I've decided that this is going to be my final *ALS* chapter. The four years I have been reviewing work on Pound and Eliot have shown a decided reassertion of the centrality of Eliot for the period and for modern literature, despite some resistance to his politics and continued confusion about how, given his ambiguous national status, he fits into our nationalistically defined institutions of literary study. I find it more than a little odd that for the moment these issues seem to be somewhat less problematic for Pound: he is considered clearly an American writer, even though virtually all the time he spent in the United States as an adult he spent confined in an insane asylum; his politics are also possibly less and certainly no more of an obstacle to his serious consideration than Eliot's. But of course controversy guarantees continued attention, as readers of de Man have discovered, and perhaps our coming to a kind of consensus about Pound has helped lead to the measurable recent decline in the amount of work done on him. I predict renewed controversy and renewed attention, however, as Pound's texts come under scrutiny in the wake of Yeats and Joyce; and I don't think the matter of Pound's politics— surely a more central issue for his work than for Eliot's—has been at all settled.

New Mexico State University

9. Faulkner

Ladell Payne

All will agree that 1989 was a banner year in Faulkner studies. More than 20 books of criticism and scholarship were published, including a substantial new biography and the reissuing of an established classic study. Nearly 100 essays appeared, two-thirds of them in collected volumes. In terms of merit, however, there will be less agreement. An uncivil war continues between the advancing armies of semiotics and deconstruction and those who defend an unreconstructed New Criticism. Few prisoners are taken, fewer wounds bound, and the critical house is still divided against itself.

i. Bibliographies, Editions, and Manuscripts

With the continuing help of William Boozer's quarterly checklists in *The Faulkner Newsletter & Yoknapatawpha Review*, the annual checklists of scholarship on Southern literature in *Mississippi Quarterly*, and the annual *MLA* bibliography, students are well able to keep abreast of Faulkner studies. In addition, John E. Bassett provides a review of the last decade's criticism in "Faulkner in the Eighties: Crosscurrents in Criticism" (*CollL* 16:1–27). Bassett describes the traditional formalistic, thematic, and bibliographic studies which have continued to appear and also sympathetically traces the growing importance of newer modes of criticism grounded in rhetoric and semiotics. The late Calvin S. Brown gives a less sympathetic review in his "Faulkner: The Unabated Spate" (*SR* 97:556–72). Looking at nine books published from 1986 through 1988, Brown is quite willing to call a spate a spate—or worse—and he is relentlessly critical of those who lose themselves "in the more pretentious artificial jingles of contemporary literary criticism."

I am pleased to note the appearance of the first three of a 20-volume series of "notes" intended to assist the Faulkner reader in

understanding obscure or difficult words and passages, including literary allusions, dialect, and historical events, prepared under the general editorship of James B. Meriwether and published as The Garland
Faulkner Annotation Series (Garland). The volumes are *Annotations
to William Faulkner's* Mosquitoes by Edwin T. Arnold, and similarly
titled volumes on *Sanctuary* by Melinda McLeod Fousselle and *Pylon*
by Susie Paul Johnson. Equally welcome is the news that a regular
department in *MissQ* will be devoted to notes, queries, addenda, and
corrigenda to the series.

Noel Polk and John D. Hart's two-volume Absalom, Absalom!: *A
Concordance to the Novel* and one-volume Pylon: *A Concordance to
the Novel* (UMI) constitute the 11th and 12th volumes in the extremely valuable series issued by the Faulkner Concordance Advisory
Board. *Volume V: Manuscripts and Documents of Faulkner: A Comprehensive Guide to the Brodsky Collection* (Miss.), edited by Louis
Daniel Brodsky and Robert W. Hamblin, includes early cartoons, 41
poems written between 1916 and 1925, holograph and typescript
drafts of *Requiem for a Nun* and *A Fable*, the typescript of "By the
People," fragments from *Big Woods*, and "Weekend Revisited," a
version of *The Wishing Tree*, several versions of "Wash," a chapter of
Absalom, Absalom!, all but one of Faulkner's 14 major speeches, vari-
ant texts of essays, and a polemical foreword on the evils of racism.
Among the plays are a version of *Requiem for a Nun* and the one-act
comedy "Innocents Return" identifying—probably inaccurately—Joan
Williams as joint author. Also appearing this year were two unpub-
lished letters. Philip Cohen's "A Previously Unpublished Faulkner
Letter" (*CollL* 16:103–05) discusses an undated holograph to Ben
Wasson urging him to try to get a better price for Faulkner's stories.
Joan St. C. Crane's "William Faulkner to Eudora Welty: A Letter"
(*MissQ* 42:223–27) reproduces the only known letter from him to
her.

Neither a bibliography, an edition, nor a manuscript, but certainly
related to all three is Beth Dyer Biron's "Word Without a Word: How
the French Translators of Faulkner's Texts Don't Always Fit What
They're Trying to Say At" (*Faulkner and the Craft of Fiction*, pp. 194–
210). Biron argues convincingly that "the present French translations
do not reflect the culture of the South . . . as Faulkner described it,
and they do not have as compelling a mythic dimension as do the
original texts."

ii. Biography

The major biographical work published this year was Frederick Karl's 1,131-page *William Faulkner: American Writer* (Weidenfeld & Nicolson). Drawing upon Joseph Blotner's two-volume life, Karl has written a psychological assessment of the writer and examined the ways in which Faulkner used family, friends, and townspeople as the bases for his fictional characters. Karl sees Faulkner's youthful insecurity, his unhappy marriage, and his alcoholism as fundamental to much that is in the novels. Those who accept the methodology will find Karl's book insightful; those who do not will find it excessively speculative. (Indeed, the accuracy of Karl's emphasis on Faulkner's misery has already been challenged in a review by Dean Faulkner Wells in *The Faulkner Newsletter* 9, iii:2). I for one regret its dense, repetitious nature and wish the author had more completely mastered the English plain style.

Several studies look at particular aspects of Faulkner's life. Tom Dardis's chapter on Faulkner in *The Thirsty Muse* is a carefully considered evaluation of the biographical and anecdotal information about Faulkner's drinking problem. Dardis concludes that Faulkner was an alcoholic whose work was seriously hampered by his drinking. Using conversations he recorded in 1985, 1986, and 1987, Louis Daniel Brodsky ("The Faulkners, the Franklins, and the Fieldens: A Conversation with Victoria Fielden Johnson," *SoR* 25:93–131) describes the relationships among William and Estelle Faulkner, Estelle's first husband Cornell Franklin, and all of their children and grandchildren, especially those who grew up at Rowan Oak, as remembered by Estelle and Cornell Franklin's granddaughter. While acknowledging the difficulties brought on by alcohol, infidelity, insecurity, and fame, the account stresses a sense of family love and caring and should be read as a counterview to the darker visions of Karl and Dardis.

Joan St. C. Crane looks at the extant copies of the postal inspector's letter to Faulkner enumerating his shortcomings as a postmaster and despite conflicting evidence surmises that the letter was probably a hoax perpetuated by Phil Stone (" 'Case No. 133733-C': The Inspector's Letter to Postmaster William Falkner," *MissQ* 42: 229–45). Stephen Hahn in "William Faulkner on Privacy" (*CLC* 38, iii:27–35) carefully documents Faulkner's insistence on preserving his personal privacy during the 1940s and 1950s and suggests a relationship be-

tween this personal trait and Faulkner's fictional technique. Hahn
does not address the implications of Faulkner's later very public years
and his cooperation with biographer Joseph Blotner.

iii. Criticism: General

Except for two interesting chapters by Barbara Alberson Morris examining the attitudes toward his own ancestors implicit in Faulkner's
treatment of genealogy (especially that of the McCaslins and Sarto-
rises), *Reading Faulkner* (Wisconsin) is primarily the work of Wesley
Morris. He views Faulkner's work not as a series of novels which can
be read formalistically but as an entire fictional universe, a single narrative. With a high level of self-assurance unmitigated by modesty,
Morris argues that any critical approach which rejects concerns with
social history, influence, biography, intentionality, and representation
leads to erroneous conclusions. His own conclusion is that "Faulkner
incorporates his life as a southern writer into his narratives with uncommon zeal. . . . The subject of his novels is a cultural crisis embedded in a crisis of aesthetics, thematized as a family crisis, expressing a crisis of personal identity."

Michel Gresset's *Fascination: Faulkner's Fiction, 1919–1936*,
adapted from the French by Thomas West (Duke), explores Faulkner's artistic development from his earliest poetry and essays to *The
Reivers*, with special attention to the novels written before *Absalom,
Absalom!* except *The Sound and the Fury*. Six of his 14 chapters are
devoted in whole or in part to *Sanctuary* and *Flags/Sartoris*. Following an intuitive approach based on the psychological and philosophical insights of Freud, Lacan, and Sartre, Gresset argues that
Faulkner's writings were produced from a psychological state and
therefore are not approachable through aesthetics.

Joseph R. Urgo in *Faulkner's Apocrypha: A Fable, Snopes, and the
Spirit of Human Rebellion* (Miss.) accepts uncritically Lawrence H.
Schwartz's thesis in *Creating Faulkner's Reputation* (see *ALS 1988*,
pp. 141–42) that Faulkner's reputation was created by Malcolm Cowley, the New Critics, and the Rockefeller Foundation in the context of
a postwar cultural readjustment. Cowley is especially culpable because he popularized his vision of a "mythical" world of Faulkner,
replacing Faulkner's own view that it was "apocryphal." Urgo's Marxist reading offers the late fiction as a culmination rather than a decline. *The Reivers*, for example, is about "what the representatives

and holders of authority do with symbols of power and with their control of the future: keep them locked away, unexamined, and out of the reach of potential and eventual usurpers." Urgo is clearly correct in seeing the economic and social problems of the American South reflected in Faulkner. I find his thesis that Flem Snopes is somehow the embodiment of Faulknerian values perversely wrongheaded.

While not rejecting the values inherent in New Critical and structural methodology for helping one explore what works of fiction may or may not mean, Stephen M. Ross is much more concerned with *"how"* they express meaning." His goal in *Fiction's Inexhaustible Voice: Speech and Writing in Faulkner* (Georgia) is to apply recent literary theory and theories of discourse. Ross identifies four modes of voice and spends a chapter on each: "A *phenomenal* voice depictive of speech (or writing) as an event or object in the fiction's world; a *mimetic* voice imitative of talk; a *psychic* voice expressive of the silent inner discourse of consciousness; an *intertextual* voice identifiably Faulkner's yet necessarily in touch with other texts, other discourses and other discursive practices in the world at large." Substantially free of jargon, Ross's book is clearly written, its judgments helpful. *Fiction's Inexhaustible Voice* effectively demonstrates the considerable value nonformalistic critical practice affords when clearly presented and not tied to the whims of its practitioners.

In his well-ordered, lucidly written *The Crossing of the Ways* (Rutgers), Karl F. Zender takes as his primary purpose "to analyze the effect on Faulkner's art of the disappearance of a traditional South and of the emergence of a modern, deregionalized America." His secondary but no less important aim is "to add to our understanding of Faulkner's creative process, particularly of its conscious intellectual aspects." The result is a thoughtful, intelligent exploration of Faulkner's novels based on a solid critical reading and a thorough understanding of Faulkner's concerns as a man and as an artist. Arguing that Faulkner's subject was always "himself and the world" and that he was painfully aware of the decline in his creative powers, Zender explores the ways in which Faulkner converted these facts into "a fictional theme, especially in the Snopes trilogy." In my judgment, *The Crossing of the Ways* is one of the more important books on Faulkner published this year.

David Dowling's clearly written *William Faulkner* (St. Martin's), another of the introductory handbooks published in the Modern Novelists series edited by Norman Page, offers solid information and mature critical help for the serious reader. Dowling uses recent scholarship and semiotic criticism to demonstrate that Faulkner's themes are generated within the textual interplay of the novels. He anchors his readings to Faulkner's larger issues, thus creating an introductory study of some sophistication.

Bern Keating, an Oxford acquaintance of Faulkner who was a journalist for *U.S. News and World Report*, has written a personal, anecdotal, book-length essay exploring Faulkner's strengths and weaknesses as a writer, historian, sociologist, and philosopher. Taking his title, *Faulkner's Seacoast of Bohemia* (White Rose), from Shakespeare's geographical lapse, Keating argues that while Faulkner was a wonderful poet, he was a most unreliable historian, geographer, geologist, and philosopher. Therefore, the reader should distrust the "mind-numbing jargon of most Faulkner experts." Faulkner should be seen "as a poet wrestling with an essentially unsolvable problem, the trick of expressing the absurdity of life and man's condemnation to inescapable and eternal ignorance of his place and purpose." In *From Hardy to Faulkner: Wessex to Yoknapatawpha* (St. Martin's), John Rabbetts draws at considerable length the parallels he sees between Hardy and Faulkner. Each created "a fictional microcosm of remote regions." In each he sees "a common attitude of ambivalence . . . toward the rival claims of past and present, tradition and modernity, nature and society. . . ." Always clearly written and sometimes insightful, Rabbetts's work asserts comparability, not influence.

In addition to these book-length studies, seven collections of essays on Faulkner were published, four as books, three as special journal issues. *On Faulkner: The Best from* American Literature, ed. Louis J. Budd and Edwin H. Cady (Duke), reprints 18 Faulkner articles by as many authors in order of first publication in the journal. In contrast, John E. Bassett's *Vision and Revisions: Essays on Faulkner* (Locust Hill) contains 14 essays written over 10 years by one author, only one—"Light in August: The Novel as Open Form" (pp. 107–23)—previously unpublished. The collection is helpful in what it tells us about Faulkner's novels and about the evolution of one of his critics.

Faulkner and the Craft of Fiction prints essays presented at the 14th University of Mississippi-sponsored Faulkner and Yoknapatawpha Conference in 1987, edited by Doreen Fowler and Ann J. Abadie with a competence we now take for granted. Also in 1987 the University of Bonn hosted an International Faulkner Symposium which focused on the process of communication as seen in Faulkner's narrative language. Edited with an introduction by Lothor Hönnighausen under the title *Faulkner's Discourse*, the 29 essays prepared for the occasion are organized into three groups: "The New Impact of Psychoanalysis," "Social Realities and Literary Discourse," and "Problems of Narration." *The Faulkner Journal* (3, i[Fall 1987]), issued in the spring of 1989 and edited by John T. Matthews and James B. Carothers, contains five essays. More distinguished collections appear in the William Faulkner issues of *CollL* (16:1–105), edited by Bernard Oldsey, and *MissQ*, edited by Noel Polk.

In his "Carcassonne in Mississippi: Faulkner's Geography of the Imagination" (*Faulkner and the Craft of Fiction*, pp. 148–71), Robert W. Hamblin argues that Faulkner used the actual world, i.e., Oxford, as no more than a point of departure: "Like the surrealistic painters with whom he has so much in common, Faulkner sought to capture a new realism—a super-realism—that combines elements of the everyday, outer world and the inner world of the artist's creative vision." Arthur F. Kinney in "The Family-Centered Nature of Faulkner's World" (*CollL* 16:83–102) relies (unnecessarily it seems to me) on statements from sociology texts to define the nature of family life in the American South before moving to a discussion of several of the important Faulkner families. His thesis that family graces are important in the world of Faulkner's novels is, however, unassailable.

Taking Faulkner's Nobel speech reference to man's puny, inexhaustible voice and Faulkner's own thin, flat, soft voice as points of departure, Michel Gresset ("Faulkner's Voice," *Faulkner's Discourse*, pp. 184–94) examines voices, especially puny ones, as a recurring motif in Faulkner's fiction. In "Faulkner's Use of Repetition" (*Faulkner and the Craft of Fiction*, pp. 21–47), Donald M. Kartiganer points out that "Faulkner's craft of fiction is to tell stories, and then to tell them again." Drawing upon Kierkegaard's concept of "repetition forward" as "reexperiencing the past in a new key—revisiting its initial meanings" as growth within repetition, Kartiganer argues that except for *The Sound and the Fury*, all of Faulkner's major texts can be read as repetitions forward. And in "Beyond 'Beyond': Aspects of Faulkner's Representation of Death" (*Faulkner's Discourse*, pp. 223–33), Mick Gidley examines Faulkner's depiction of dying in his fiction and concludes that because death is "unknown territory," it can be visited only in metaphor.

iv. Criticism: Special Studies

A number of essays identify ideas and influences in Faulkner's work. In her "Drowsing Maidenhead Symbol's Self: Faulkner and the Fictions of Love" (*Faulkner and the Craft of Fiction*, pp. 124–45), Judith L. Sensibar looks at Faulkner's relationship with his wife, Estelle, and argues that he was not only influenced by her but also "very consciously used the tension and theater of his marriage for imaginative experimentation. His marriage and love affairs functioned somewhat like his role playing." In the same volume ("Faulkner: Master of the Heroic and the Pastoral Modes," pp. 1–20), Cleanth Brooks contends that Faulkner created 20th-century variants of the pastoral in *The Hamlet* and of the heroic in *The Unvanquished*. Although Brooks identifies Ike Snopes as Faulkner's faun and Eula Varner as his love goddess, his primary interest is in demonstrating that, despite its problems, *The Unvanquished* is successful as a heroic novel. In a tightly reasoned essay, "The Scriptural Tradition and Faulkner's Gnostic Style" (*SoR* 25:563–68), John L. Desmond argues that Faulkner's attempt to use the scriptural tradition to affirm the transcendent possibilities of human existence in such characters as Joe Christmas and Ike McCaslin was unsuccessful because he did not accept the analogical validity intrinsic in the Scriptures. He relied instead on "the power of heightened rhetoric . . . to create through language" a sense of the transcendent. Pursuing a similar interest, John Sykes, *The Romance of Innocence and the Myth of History: Faulkner's Religious Critique of Southern Culture* (Mercer), offers a persuasive analysis of Faulkner's attempt to replace the inadequate myths of Southern culture— the white woman as vessel of virtue, the cavalier as Southern founder, Puritanism as a basis for spiritual life—with an "ironic myth" which affirms the spiritual qualities of humanity while insisting that a "larger spiritual reality is all but inaccessible to conscious man."

In *Faulkner's Country Matters: Folklore and Fable in Yoknapatawpha* (LSU), Daniel Hoffman looks at the relationship between the structure and content of Faulkner's novels, especially *The Unvanquished*, *The Hamlet*, and *Go Down, Moses*, and traditional American folk myths, fables, and folktales to place Faulkner in the company of Hawthorne, Melville, and Twain as a writer whose work is informed in a major way by such materials. W. R. Martin identifies Joseph Conrad as a Faulkner source in "Faulkner's Pantaloon and Conrad's Gaspar Ruiz" (*Conradiana* 21:47–51). In "Versions of the

'Primal Scene': Faulkner and *Ulysses*" (*Mosaic* 22, ii:63–77), Michael Zeitlin ingeniously if not always convincingly explores the extent to which Faulkner borrowed episodes and Freudian images from Joyce's *Ulysses*, especially in *Sanctuary* and *Flags in the Dust*. Zeitlin's analysis of a Joycean influence on *Mosquitoes* is more persuasive ("Faulkner in Nighttown: *Mosquitoes* and the 'Circe' Episode," *MissQ* 42: 229–310).

In what was for me a very helpful essay, "Lips by 'Laws Veneris,' Breasts by 'Anactoria,' Anecdote by William Faulkner" (*EiP* 14, i:1–27), Richard Godden compares Faulkner's poetic practice in *A Green Bough* with the theory and practice of Mallarmé, Valéry, Baudelaire, and Swinburne to demonstrate both similarities and differences. In "Faulkner and the Symbolist Novel" (*Modern American Fiction*, pp. 118–35), Carol M. Andrews, also referring to the French Symbolists, looks at the central images Faulkner identified as being the inception of *The Sound and the Fury* and notes that all three represent an absence, a lack of something: Damuddy's death, Caddy's muddy drawers, and Benjy's lack of reason. She sees Caddy's absence as the novel's organizing principle and symbolic center.

In "Faulkner and the Paradoxes of Description" (*Faulkner's Discourse*, pp. 170–83), André Bleikasten examines description as a stylistic technique and finds it analogous to archaeology in Faulkner's hands. In "Visual Motion in Faulkner's Narrative Act" (*Faulkner's Discourse*, pp. 46–52), Wolf Kindermann states that "the identity of the ideal Faulknerian reader emerges from a growing awareness of the epistemological considerations mirrored in the nodal passages of each novel." In "Faulkner's Patriotic Failure: Southern Lyricism versus American Hypervision" (*Faulkner and the Craft of Fiction*, pp. 105–23), William E. H. Meyer, Jr., is just as certain that Faulkner "failed as an American novelist precisely because his art was primarily aural and our culture is dominated by the visual." And in "Faulkner's Narrative: Between Involvement and Distancing" (*Faulkner's Discourse*, pp. 141–48), Sonja Basič looks at the "often paradoxical juxtaposition and merging of extreme reader involvement and extreme distancing" as an important aspect of both modernism and Faulkner.

Exhibiting an interest in both the aural and the visual, Michiko Yoshida ("The Gravity of Silence in Faulkner's Language," *Faulkner's Discourse*, pp. 204–13) examines Faulkner's use of silence in *The Sound and the Fury* to draw interesting parallels between Faulkner's practice and the traditions of haiku and the No theatre. In the same collection, Jacques Pothier explains that his purpose in "Negation in Faulkner: Saying No to Time and Creating One's Own Space" (pp. 38–45) is "to comment on negativity as it is mirrored in the style and to see how the denial of time is achieved through a sanctuary of space."

In "Telling Against Writing: On a Transition in Faulkner's Style" (*Faulkner's Discourse*, pp. 195–203), Kenzaburo Ohashi identifies telling with the native storytelling tradition of American fiction which occurs when "a writer's omniscient narrative consciousness" unites "with that of the point of view character" and "breaks through the fetters of words, of writing, and recaptures the function of telling afresh in the world of fiction." Also in *Faulkner's Discourse*, Michael Millgate and James E. Carothers attempt to define the stylistic differences between Faulkner's early and late work. In "Faulkner: Is There a Late Style?" (pp. 271–74), Millgate answers yes and identifies it with Faulkner's "reduced sense of the need to get down on paper all that he thought and imagined" after receiving the Nobel Prize. In "The Rhetoric of Faulkner's Later Fiction and of Its Critics" (pp. 263–70), Carothers identifies the turning point as occurring in 1942. It "can be seen in his having found a wide, substantial, intelligent audience after that time and not having one before." John T. Matthews takes a different and to me a more interesting view of narrative in "Faulkner's Narrative Frames" (*Faulkner and the Craft of Fiction*, pp. 71–91) by looking at Faulkner's use of Quentin Compson to narrate "Lion," "That Evening Sun," and "A Justice" some years after his fictional suicide in *The Sound and the Fury*, thus giving the later stories a context, a frame of reference, which Matthews sees as analogous to Faulkner's use of multiple narrators to tell the Sutpen story or prose headnotes in *Requiem for a Nun*.

In looking at the techniques Faulkner used to represent thought in his fiction, Stephen Ross looks at "Carcassonne" ("Lying Beneath Speech: Preliminary Notes on the Representation of Thought in 'Carcassonne,'" *Faulkner's Discourse*, pp. 159–69) and identifies four discursive practices: the meditative which releases into epiphany, sleep, or death; the splitting of self and "Other"; the layering of psychic space; and the reification of internal speech into writing. Working a related vein, Myriam Díaz-Diocaretz looks at the various modal strategies Faulkner followed in his several presentations of Temple Drake in *Sanctuary* and *Requiem for a Nun*. The absence of a narrator's modal voice in the latter work allows Faulkner to take the same vantage point as the reader/viewer and thus refuse overtly to judge Temple ("Look What He Has Already Done to Me: Modality and Temple Drake," *Faulkner's Discourse*, pp. 214–22). Dieter Maindl ("Some Epistemological and Esthetic Implications of William Faulkner's Discourse," *Faulkner's Discourse*, pp. 149–58) suggests that the stream-of-consciousness narrative as Faulkner used it depicts a person fixed in life and dead to change, thus constituting a method inappropriate to Faulkner's later view of life as motion. And in "Inadequacies of Style in Some of Faulkner's Short Stories" (*Faulkner's Discourse*, pp. 234–41), Hans Skei finds, not surprisingly, that in some instances the content of Faulkner's stories justifies the long sentences, repetitions, and so on, and in some instances does not.

In " 'Thinking I Was I Was Not Who Was Not Was Not Who': The Vertigo of Faulknerian Identity" (*Faulkner and the Craft of Fiction*, pp. 172–93), Philip M. Weinstein does an excellent job of suggesting a basis for understanding *Absalom, Absalom!* by combining Althusser's view that our sense of uncoerced human behavior comes from our spontaneous assent to the social ideologies which surround us along with Lacan's observations concerning our inability to find our identities in either imaginary mergers or symbolic distinction. Although some may disagree with Weinstein concerning the limitations of the New Criticism, they will be hard-pressed to ignore his contention that "the identity of texts is not essential but contextual; their value is inescapably conditioned by current canons of assessment."

Relying on Freud for his terms and Marx for his reading, Richard C. Moreland, "Compulsive and Revisionary Repetitions in Faulkner's 'Barn Burning' and the Craft of Writing Difference" (*Faulkner and the Craft of Fiction*, pp. 48–70), looks upon the various accounts of Thomas Sutpen as compulsive repetition reflecting "explicit nostalgia for a diseased social structure." Contrarily, the various forms of the story are examples of "revisionary repetition," a practice which repeats in order somehow to alter "a structure and its continuing power."

Karen Ramsey Johnson ("Gender, Sexuality, and the Artist in Faulkner's Novels," *AL* 61:1–15) examines the metaphorical patterns Faulkner associates with artists and the act of creation and finds them to be not only sexual in nature but frequently of "perverse or deviant sexuality, confused or ambiguous gender." She concludes that Faulkner saw artistic creation as simultaneously active and passive and that he suggests this view through a confusion of traditional male and female roles. Another feminist approach is taken by Dawn Trouard,

"Eula's Plot: An Irigarian Reading of Faulkner's Snopes Trilogy" (*MissQ* 42:281–97), who uses the feminist theories of Luce Irigaray to demonstrate that Eula Varner is first, last, and foremost Faulkner's most bitter illustration of the patriarchal subjugation of women in American culture. And the only essay specifically on Faulkner and race this year, Reginald Martin's "Faulkner's Conflicting Views of the Equality of Color" (*Obsidian II* 4, ii:1–11), surveys a number of Faulkner's conflicting public statements concerning blacks in conjunction with conflicting public interpretations of them and concludes that Faulkner was an often troubled man called on to make great moral pronouncements, about which he was not always up to the task.

v. Individual Works to 1929

Little critical attention was paid this year to Faulkner's early novels, although *Mosquitoes, Flags in the Dust*, and *The Sound and the Fury* were each considered. In a clearly written essay, "Story, Myth, Rite of Passage, and *Mosquitoes*" (*FJ* 3, i[1987]:26–38), Chris LaLonde argues for the importance of Faulkner's second novel because it is "the first true instance of Faulkner's work appropriating rites of passage as an organizing principle and as a specific and important theme." Pamela E. Rhodes sees Byron Snopes as emblematic of the poor-white hill men dispossessed of their farms during the cotton crisis of the 1920s pitted against the planter-banker class represented by the Sartoris family. In "'I Remember Them Letters': Byron Snopes and Interference" (*Faulkner's Discourse*, pp. 77–89), she argues that Byron "embodies that whole group of social forces which formalistic esthetics ignores . . . the silent redneck, the excluded other." Philip M. Weinstein offers a deconstructive feminist reading of *The Sound and the Fury* in "'If I Could Say Mother': Construing the Unsayable about Faulknerian Maternity" (*Faulkner's Discourse*, pp. 3–15). He argues that within the representational economy of the novel, Faulkner's rendering of Mrs. Compson is uniquely punitive. He defines her "unsayable" feminist basis as a "portrait of maternity crazily arrested in the 'virginal' phase of the Virgin Mary model. . . . The ideal silent nourisher has degenerated into a non-nourishing, non-stop talker." In "The Rhetoric of Containment in Faulkner" (*Faulkner's Discourse*, pp. 55–67), John T. Matthews states that *The Sound and the Fury* is clearly Marxist in its presentation of the way in which such a person as Quentin Compson can reject the values of antebellum gentility, especially antebellum attitudes toward race, economic exploitation, and the restoration of past fortune and privilege, while failing to see that this vision still conditions both him and others who reject it.

vi. Individual Works, 1930–1939

If relatively scant attention was paid to the novels which appeared prior to 1930, those of the second decade received aplenty. Each novel of the period was the subject of at least one essay, *Light in August* of eight, *Absalom, Absalom!* a total of 11. Carolyn Norman Slaughter's "*As I Lay Dying*: Demise of a Vision" (*AL* 61:16–30) is a stimulating exploration (a "thinking" in her terms) of the novel's explicit treatment of language as "not doing," in contrast to life, which is "doing." In a major contribution to our understanding of Faulkner's narrative practice in *As I Lay Dying*, Dorothy J. Hale ("*As I Lay Dying's* Heterogeneous Discourse," *Novel* 23:5–23) carefully analyzes the interior monologues which form the novel's narrative structure and convincingly suggests the different purposes achieved by the differing levels of public and private discourse represented. Even more, she extrapolates from her analysis to suggest Faulkner's reasons for returning to a more traditional narrative form in *Light in August* and later novels. Less convincingly, Ken Bennett ("Faulkner's *As I Lay Dying*," *Expl* 47:42–44) argues that when Dewey Dell asks Darl "are you going to tell pa and are you going to kill him," the "him" referred to is the fetus, not pa, and that her subsequent hatred of Darl is motivated by Darl's understanding of the situation and refusal to aid her in getting an abortion. And in "Curious Chronology in the Ending of *As I Lay Dying*" (*PAPA* 15:154–65), Charles Chappell discusses a chronological inconsistency.

Offering a reading of *Sanctuary* indebted to Freud, Lacan, and Nietzsche, Homer B. Petty ("Reading and Raping in *Sanctuary*," *FJ* 3, i[1987]:71–84) argues that rape is not only the master trope for understanding what occurs in the novel, but defines the reader's role in interpreting it. Terry Heller ("Mirrored Worlds and the Gothic in Faulkner's *Sanctuary*," *MissQ* 42:247–59) first explores the mirrored structure which reflects *Sanctuary's* respectable and unrespectable social levels and then examines the novel's overt and repressed sexual worlds; he then relates Faulkner's practice to that of the gothic novel. Working a similar vein, David L. Vanderwerken looks at the ways in which this novel's episodes of comic relief reinforce the tragic vision of this roman noir ("Lost in the Whorehouse: The Comic Chapters of *Sanctuary*," *CCTEP* 54:34–38).

Cleanth Brooks takes his lumps in essays by Thomas L. McHaney and Peter Nicolaisen, who disagree with his view of "community" in *Light in August*. In "Problems in Faulkner's Poetics" (*Faulkner's Discourse*, pp. 248–53), McHaney deems Brooks's reading inadequate because it ignores the novel's dark comedic travesties on the Adonis and Diana myths, Jungian archetypes, and Bergsonian "free acts." More, it ignores the diversity of existence in Jefferson in order to stress community. Nicolaisen in "Group Perspective and Group Behavior: Notes on Faulkner's 'Forensic Imagination'" (*Faulkner's Discourse*, pp. 90–98) sees the "community" of *Light in August* both as a generally misinformed observer/chorus and as identifiable groups such as Hightower's congregation and Percy Grimm's platoon.

In "Shadows of Jung: A Psychological Approach to *Light in August*" (*SLJ* 22:80–95), Terrell L. Tebbetts offers a Jungian reading to help "readers understand the interplay of social pressures and free individuals in this novel." One can (and I do) find this well-written essay insightful without sharing Tebbett's certainty that Miss Atkins's tube of toothpaste can only be a surrogate breast, that Joe Christmas lacks courage, or that having characters develop integrated personalities is among the novel's most enduring concerns. Through an analysis of Faulkner's treatment of Lena Grove, Joanna Burden, and Joe Christmas, Deborah Clarke argues in "Gender, Race, and Language in *Light in August*" (*AL* 61:398–413) that the "design of the novel can be traced by the way women are constructed then deconstructed, attesting to creative power but also subverting it in a dialogue between male voice and unknown female tongues." She sees Faulkner as one "who, in testing the limits of language, tests and challenges conventional conceptions of gender, constructing his tale in that challenge." Christopher LaLonde is also interested in gender and language in this novel. In "A Trap Most Magnificently Sprung: The Last Chapter of *Light in August*" (*Faulkner and the Craft of Fiction*, pp. 92–104), he sees evidence in the traveling salesman's narrative that despite Lena Grove's strength and independence, "she travels in the trapped, closed space of male perception, valuation, and figuration." Charles M. Chappell, in "Faulkner's Arch-Villain: Eupheus ('Doc') Hines" (*CollL* 16:66–74), contends that Hines is the principal villain and primary instigating force for violence and tragedy in *Light in August* and perhaps "the most odious character in all of Faulkner's fiction." Jeremy Smith, "Religious Experience and Literary Form: The Interrelation of Perception, Commitment, and Interpretation" (*R&L* 21, iii:61–83), discusses *Light in August* as a novel which evokes perception and value judgment without direct reference to the views of the "real" William Faulkner.

In the only essay published on *Pylon*, John N. Duvall also takes issue with Cleanth Brooks, this time challenging Brooks's view that the novel's primary characters reject the traditional familial relationships celebrated within the community. In "Paternity in *Pylon*: 'Some Little Sign?'" (*FJ* 3, i[1987]:39–51), Duvall avers that *Pylon* "highlights a recurring pattern in Faulkner's fiction of the 1930s—unions of men and women at the margins of the community"—unions which "problematize mainstream critics' assessment of gender."

In "*Absalom, Absalom!*: A Postmodernist Approach" (*Faulkner's Discourse*, pp. 276–92), Gerhard Hoffmann sees the novel as a textbook example of postmodernist attitudes toward the meaning of history. Since history is not seen as having some all-determining, undestandable structure, living in history is the subject of possibility. Faulkner's lesson is that only the imagination can reconstruct history and connect past and present. Concerned with fiction as a representation of social reality comparable to that offered by the social sciences rather than as a meditation on history, Edward J. Ahearn ("Vautrin's Hundred," *Marx and Modern Fiction*, pp. 119–63) demonstrates "through the mediation of Marx's thought the intersection of *Le Pere Goriot* and *Absalom, Absalom!* in the closely linked fields of history, economy, and the family." The intersection of language and gender is Judith Bryant Wittenberg's subject in "Gender and Linguistic Strategies in *Absalom, Absalom!*" (*Faulkner's Discourse*, pp. 99–108). She sees this novel as managing "simultaneously to encode and critique the prevailing masculinist discourse and culture," primarily through Rosa Coldfield's language and her impact on Quentin Compson.

Patrick O'Donnell is interested in both history and Rosa Coldfield. Using the techniques and turgid prose sometimes associated with the deconstructionists, as well as some of Julia Kristeva's insights, he argues ("Sub-Rosa: Voice, Body, and History in *Absalom, Absalom!*" *ColL* 16:28–47) that "the speech that goes under the sign of Rosa's name" is essential "to grasping the content of abjection in *Absalom, Absalom!*." Also concerned with narrative structure in *Absalom, Absalom!*, Bernard Radloff in "Dialogue and Insight: The Priority of the Heritage in *Absalom, Absalom!*" (*MissQ* 42:261–72) sees the oral narrative shared by Quentin and Shreve as constituting the heritage which defines past, present, and future understood by the narrators. Consequently, their explicit attempt to discover the reason for Bon's murder is an implicit attempt to discover the meaning of Quentin's heritage. Deborah Garfield's "To Love as 'Fiery Ancients' Would: Eros, Narrative and Rosa Coldfield in *Absalom, Absalom!*" (*SLJ* 22: 61–79) offers a splendid analysis of the psychological bases of Rosa's love of Charles Bon, her understanding of events both actual and imagined, and her inability ever finally to understand human behavior—especially her own.

In "Litotes and Chiasmus: Cloaking Tropes in *Absalom, Absalom!*" (*Faulkner's Discourse*, pp. 16–24), James A. Snead offers a Freudian reading of Faulkner's use of these narrative and stylistic devices and finds that in his hands moments of unveiling become moments of cloaking, scenes of recognition become scenes of denial. Following Freud's view that negation (repression) both denies and affirms an unacceptable reality, François Pitavy ("Some Remarks on Negation and Denegation in William Faulkner's *Absalom, Absalom!*," *Faulkner's Discourse*, pp. 25–32) examines the narrative and psychological implications of negation and denegation in Rosa Coldfield's and Quentin Compson's understanding and presentation of themselves and Thomas Sutpen. Exploring a similar topic in "The Poetics of Negation in Faulkner's *Absalom, Absalom!*" (*Faulkner's Discourse*, pp. 33–37), Winfred Herget sees Faulkner's extensive use of negation as a means of leaving open an unspecified number of affirmative possibilities: "By positing what never was, fiction becomes a way of negating the impermanence of reality." In "Contemporary History in *Absalom, Absalom!*: Some Directions for Study" (*Faulkner's Discourse*, pp. 132–38), Karl F. Zender considers the novel in the light of the dominant political rhetoric of the 1930s, sees the shadows of John Dewey and progressive education in Quentin's and Shreve's collaborative act of learning, wonders if Faulkner's presentation of the imagination would be illuminated by Freud's *Analyses Terminable and Interminable*, and suggests that a critique of Mr. Compson's letter as a latent presence in *Absalom, Absalom!* can be given only when the novel is read in the light offered by modern literary theory. In a well-written, carefully documented essay ("Being Otherwise: Nature, History, and Tragedy in *Absalom, Absalom!*," *ArQ* 45, iii:47–76), Charles Sherry examines the meanings evoked by the various stories told within the novel and finds the conflict between nature and history fundamental to its meaning.

Susan Garland Mann's "William Faulkner's *The Unvanquished*" and "William Faulkner's *Go Down Moses*" (*The Short Story Cycle*, pp. 107–19, 121–40) are primarily informational, not critical, providing a summary of subject matter and details of composition and publication. In a separate essay, "Seasonal Imagery and the Pattern of Revenge in *The Unvanquished*" (*NMW* 21:4–51), Mann explores the ways in which patterns of seasonal or weather imagery reinforce the revenge theme and its ultimate repudiation. Ursula Brumm looks at "Old Man" as a story separate from *The Wild Palms* in "Theme and Narrative Voice in Faulkner's 'Old Man' " (*Faulkner's Discourse*, pp. 242–47). After she points out its similarities to *Don Quixote*, she examines narrative technique and concludes that "the telling of the story, the narrative mode, becomes part of the plot."

vii. Individual Works, 1940–1949

All but two of the essays devoted to the novels of this decade address *Go Down, Moses*. The exceptions are both studies of *The Hamlet*. In what he describes as a poststructural critique, Richard C. Moreland, "Antisemitism, Humor, and Rage in Faulkner's *The Hamlet*" (*FJ* 3, i[1987]:52–70), looks to the raucous tradition of Southwestern humor as fundamental to Faulkner's achievement. Moreland sees in Ratliff's ability to view Flem Snopes within a context of humor and Mink Snopes's inability to see him except within a context of rage as the difference between achieving and not achieving "humor's always unstable poise under the pressure of constantly changing events." Of greater help is Lynn Snyder's "Doors, Windows, and Peepholes in *The Hamlet*" (*NMW* 21:19–30), which discusses Faulkner's practice of presenting key characters and actions through framing devices.

David Cowart's "Through a Glass Darkly: *Go Down, Moses*" in his *History and the Contemporary Novel* describes Faulkner's novel as "an extremely sophisticated version of a type of historical fiction, the chronicle-novel." In Cowart's well-supported analysis, *Go Down, Moses* finds "an approximation in the past and in the present of the fuller ideal of human community that it manifestly expresses a yearning for in the future." In "Faulkner's 'Was': A Deadlier Purpose than Simple Pleasure" (*AL* 61:414–28), Carl L. Anderson looks closely at the actions and statements of Uncle Buck and Uncle Buddy and argues that Buddy, not Buck, has the moral strength. In "From Old Gold to IOUs: Ike McCaslin's Debased Genealogical Coin" (*FJ* 3, i[1987]:2–25), Stephen Baker sees the replacement of the gold Ike was to have inherited from the McCaslins with worthless Beauchemp IOUs as symbolizing Ike's loss of validation and identity with the past. David Timms's "Contrasts in Form: Hemingway's *The Old Man and the Sea* and Faulkner's 'The Bear' " (*The Modern American Novella*, pp. 97–112) argues that the former is a novella because it is more circumscribed than a novel in its treatment of time, space, and multiplicity of themes, but the latter is something else. At no point does Timms acknowledge the larger context of *Go Down, Moses*.

Identifying the delta-shaped diagram Faulkner included in the text of "Delta Autumn" with a virgin's hymen as well as with what is left of the old woods, Richard Godden ("Iconic Narrative: or, How Faulkner Fought the Second Civil War," *Faulkner's Discourse*, pp. 68–76) argues unconvincingly that Faulkner resisted the agricultural and social revolution in the South during the 1930s with "an iconic enclosure which isolates the land within a natural female function and then modifies the function."

viii. Individual Works, 1950–1962

Of those novels published during Faulkner's last years, only *A Fable* and *The Reivers* were the subject of essays. Noel Polk applies to *A Fable* Roland Barthes's theories concerning the nature of myth and mythic language and Karl Marx's social attitudes. In "Roland Barthes Reads *A Fable*" (*Faulkner's Discourse*, pp. 108–16), Polk sees myth as a means whereby those who have power control the inarticulate, powerless masses. Patrick Samway, S. J., suggests that Bakhtin's observation that the principle of metamorphosis governs *The Golden Ass* of Lucius Apuleius aptly describes *The Reivers* of Faulkner's Lucius Priest. In "Narration and Naming in *The Reivers*" (*Faulkner's Discourse*, pp. 254–62), Samway also suggests that Faulkner uses names relevant to classical mythology and language from the Gospel to St. John to produce "a collection of mythological meanings whose common thread is intense calculated ambiguity." Closer to the mark in my judgment and certainly less ambiguous is Heidi Ziegler's "Faulkner's Rhetoric of the Comic: *The Reivers*" in *Faulkner's Discourse*, pp. 117–26. Drawing upon Bergson and Kant, Ziegler presents

The Reivers as the novel in which Faulkner arrived "at a consistent rhetoric of the comic."

ix. The Stories

In "Silencing Women in 'The Fire and the Hearth' and 'Tomorrow' " (*CollL* 16:75–82), John N. Duvall examines the marginal role of the daughters whose rape, seduction, or amorous relationship has been pertinent to a court action in *Sanctuary* and the stories named in the title. He contends that Faulkner uses the courtroom as a "non-mimetic space that foregrounds the silencing of women by patriarchy and makes the law a silent partner in the father's desire to control his daughter's desire." In "The Language of Stereotype in 'Death Drag' " (*Faulkner's Discourse*, pp. 127–31), Ilse Dusoir Lind finds the stereotypical presentation of Ginsfarb as a dirty, unpatriotic Jew concerned with money undercut by Ginsfarb's being in many respects clearly the opposite of the stereotype. In the contradictions and in superficial parallels between Ginsfarb and Faulkner, she discovers "how the self in its inner turmoil projects its negative feelings on the socially rejected Other at the same time that it binds itself to the Other through psychic identification with it." What oft was thought, perhaps, but ne'er so well repressed.

Hal Blyth in "Faulkner's 'A Rose for Emily' " (*Expl* 47:49–50) just as unconvincingly argues that Miss Emily poisoned Homer Barron because he was a homosexual. Karl F. Zender in "Character and Symbol in 'Barn Burning' " (*CollL* 16:48–59) sees Faulkner's focus as not just on Sarty's growth to maturity through rejecting his father, but also on Ab's attempt to teach Sarty those lessons he must learn to become an adult. Zender regrets Faulkner's failure here and elsewhere to unite a son's need to know with a father's legitimate need to teach. Kathy Cackett also is interested in the relationship between Ab and Sarty. In " 'Barn Burning:' Debating the American Adam" (*NMW* 21, i:1–17), she discusses the ways in which these two embody qualities defined by R. W. B. Lewis. And John Wylie Hall, in "Faulkner's Barn Burners: Ab Snopes and the Duke of Marlborough" (*NMW* 21, ii:65–68), notes that whereas Faulkner drew upon the Victorian judgment of Marlborough as a mean-spirited booty hunter when comparing Ab Snopes to him in "Barn Burning," in *A Fable* he listed the Duke among "the titanic congeries in the long heroic roster who were the milestones of the rise of man."

Edmond L. Volpe gives us two essays which to my taste are more helpful. His " 'Dry September': Metaphor for Despair" (*CollL* 16:60–65) is a concise analysis of the wasteland metaphor as it informs the story. By also examining an earlier handwritten version entitled "Drouth," Volpe shows the degree to which this metaphor dominated Faulkner's vision from the beginning. Similarly, in " 'Elly': Like Gunpower in a Flimsy Vault" (*MissQ* 42:273–80), Volpe compares the published "Elly" with an earlier unpublished version entitled "Selvage" and finds that while Faulkner's revisions do not substantially change the story, they do greatly clarify its meaning.

Randolph-Macon College

10. Fitzgerald and Hemingway

Susan F. Beegel

Chapter 10 of *American Literary Scholarship* has always borne an unfortunate resemblance to the chapter of *A Moveable Feast* wherein Fitzgerald and Hemingway step into the men's room at Michaud's for "a matter of measurements." Fitzgerald's reputation suffers unfairly through this annual measurement of his bibliography against Hemingway's. This year there are only 30-plus entries on Fitzgerald vs. about 100 on Hemingway. However, Hemingway scholars inclined to feel smug should remember that Fitzgerald's death took place 20 years before Hemingway's, and therefore Hemingway studies today are still exploiting materials that Fitzgerald studies have long since exhausted.

i. Text and Bibliography

Edited and with an introduction by Matthew J. Bruccoli, *The Short Stories of F. Scott Fitzgerald: A New Collection* (Scribner's) is this year's major textual event in Fitzgerald studies. The volume replaces the Malcolm Cowley collection of 28 short stories that has long dominated the teaching and study of Fitzgerald. More generous, Bruccoli offers 43 of Fitzgerald's finest, arranged in order of their composition, making his anthology a chronicle of Fitzgerald's development as a short story writer as well as a social history told in magazine stories. He also details sources, publication history, and textual peculiarities. Bruccoli draws his texts from thorough familiarity with all extant versions of each tale. Adoption of this omnibus should see Fitzgerald's short fiction more widely taught and written about.

Henry S. Villard and James Nagel's collaborative effort, *Hemingway in Love and War: The Lost Diary of Agnes von Kurowsky, Her Letters and Correspondence of Ernest Hemingway* (Northeastern), offers both new texts and new biographical information. The primary materials have been carefully arranged, edited, and annotated, and are well-supplemented by Villard's personal memories of 1918 Milan and Nagel's scholarly research. However, Kurowsky herself, who nursed the wounded Hemingway during his World War I hospitalization, is this volume's star. Her diaries and letters reveal a committed nurse thoroughly enjoying her wartime adventures in Italy and the attentions of numerous male admirers. She views both herself and others with an insight and humor that readily explain Hemingway's passion for her. It's refreshing to have a woman's opinion of Ernest Hemingway before anyone *knew* he was Ernest Hemingway, and the unfolding relationship documented in these letters reads like a novel.

Megan Floyd Desnoyers's regular column in *The Hemingway Review*, "News from the Hemingway Collection" (*HN* 8, ii:53–54; 9, i: 96–97), is required reading for textual scholars anxious to keep abreast of the John F. Kennedy Library's acquisitions. Al DeFazio's "Hemingway Bibliography" (*HN* 8, ii:55–65; 9, ii:104–12) canvasses recent popular and academic publications.

ii. Biography

The neotemperance movement sweeping the country has prompted a new effort to understand American writers' remarkable susceptibility to alcoholism. Studies of both Fitzgerald and Hemingway are integral to two books on this subject, Donald Goodwin's *Alcohol and the Writer* (Penguin, 1988) and Tom Dardis's *The Thirsty Muse: Alcohol and the American Writer* (Ticknor and Fields). As an M.D., Goodwin's command of literary biography is shaky, but his grasp of the psychological and physiological implications of alcoholism is considerable. Dardis has the biographical facts under control, but minimal understanding of alcoholism's pathology. There is little new to be said about Fitzgerald's alcoholism, but both Goodwin and Dardis underscore the need for Hemingway's principal biographers to take their subject's lifelong addiction into account.

This year's dose of Hemingway biography should be taken with Jackson J. Benson's "Ernest Hemingway: The Life as Fiction and the Fiction as Life" (*AL* 61:345–58). Hemingway scholars continually bemoan the problems arising from widespread confusion of Hemingway's life and work, but Benson is the first to define what those problems are, to examine how and why they occur, and to prescribe a cure. Contextual scholars may not agree with Benson on all counts, but this thoughtful essay requires careful reading and considered response.

Hemingway: The Paris Years (Blackwell), the second installment of Michael Reynolds's projected five-volume biography, helps make 1989 a vintage year for Hemingway studies. Reynolds embarks on a meticulous reconstruction of historical and cultural milieu, an enterprise balanced by his tempered admiration of Hemingway as a writer and his equally tempered understanding of Hemingway's failings as a man. Although Reynolds sometimes applies novelistic techniques to biography with varying degrees of success, readers steeped in tedious academic prose may welcome the occasional walk on the wild side. His portrait of the young writer grappling with the explosion of artistic expression and sexual licentiousness that was Paris in the '20s is the best explanation we have to date of the making and marring of Ernest Hemingway, writer.

A. E. Hotchner's *Hemingway and His World* (Vendome) is more coffee-table extravaganza than biography. The text is journalistic, enthusiastic, dubious biography—often straying from the facts and offering long, undocumented quotations probably garnered from Hotchner's conversations with Hemingway. The real glory of this folio volume resides in its plentiful and beautifully presented illustrations— not only the usual photographs of Hemingway, but also reproductions of paintings and photos of historic events, bullfight tickets, war posters, movie stills, dust jackets, African landscapes. The handsomest photobiography we've seen to date, *Hemingway and His World* could serve in the classroom to help students visualize historical context.

iii. Influences, Sources, and Parallels

Fitzgerald attracted two notable influence studies this year. A. E. Elmore's comprehensive "*The Great Gatsby* as Well Wrought Urn" (*Modern American Fiction*, pp. 57–92) explores *Gatsby*'s indebtedness to a host of writers from Dante to Wharton, demonstrating how Fitzgerald created a modern novel of compression from a smorgasbord of classic materials. A briefer effort, Hilton Anderson's "*Daisy Miller* and 'The Hotel Child': A Jamesian Influence on F. Scott Fitzgerald" (*SAF* 17:213–18), concludes that Fitzgerald's short story exhibits neither James's "serious concern for his subject matter nor the artistic talent of his finer works." On the cusp, Lionel Kelly's "Hemingway and Fitzgerald: Two Short Stories" (*Re-reading the Short Story*, pp. 98–109) offers conventional interpretations of "Hills Like White Elephants" and "The Lees of Happiness" without developing parallels between them. Still, Fitzgeraldites may wish to consult Kelly on the seldom discussed "Lees."

Fifty years after the Spanish Civil War, scholars seem most interested in influences on Hemingway's Spanish Civil War novel. William Adair's "*For Whom the Bell Tolls* and *The Magic Mountain*: Hemingway's Debt to Thomas Mann" (*TCL* 35: 429–44) deserves applause for developing parallels between these novels' psychic landscapes, dream sequences, attitudes toward time, and cultural metaphors. Erik Nakjavani's "Intellectuals as Militants: Hemingway's *For Whom the Bell Tolls* and Malraux's *L'Espoir*" (*Rewriting the Good Fight*, pp. 199–214) compares the struggles of intellectuals in both novels to square their capacities for "nuanced ethical reflection" with war's violence and political exigencies. A brief note, Joseph Waldmeir's "Chapter Numbering and Meaning in *For Whom the Bell Tolls* (*HN* 8, ii:43–45), demonstrates the indebtedness of the indomitable guerrilla leader Pilar to Gertrude Stein.

Three other studies deserve mention. Well-grounded in contemporary critical theory, David Timms's "Contrasts in Form: Hemingway's *The Old Man and the Sea* and Faulkner's 'The Bear'" (*The Modern American Novella*, pp. 97–112) contrasts technical, thematic, and genre features to reach a working definition of "novella." Alan Price's "'I'm Not an Old Fogey and You're Not a Young Ass': Owen Wister and Ernest Hemingway" (*HN* 9, i:82–90) makes good use of newly available correspondence to develop the Wister-Hemingway relationship. In "The Libel of Dos Passos in *To Have and Have Not*" (*JML* 15, iv: 597–601), Robert Fleming uses a deleted passage from the novel's manuscript to debunk the widely held belief that Hemingway based the character of Philip Gordon on John Dos Passos.

iv. Criticism

a. **Full-Length Studies: Fitzgerald.** The first book-length treatment of its subject in 18 years, Alice Hall Petry's *Fitzgerald's Craft of Short Fiction: The Collected Stories 1920–1935* (UMI Research Press) is most welcome. Petry has chosen to study the four authorized collections of short stories—*Flappers and Philosophers, Tales of the Jazz Age, All the Sad Young Men*, and *Taps at Reveille*—examining through them the author's developing concepts of love, sex, and marriage; self vs. society; free will vs. fate; dreams and disillusionment; the historical sense; and the idea of home. Writing in a biographical frame and with a feminist tang, Petry focuses not only on such oft-criticized stories as "The Ice Palace" and "Babylon Revisited," but gives equally satisfying treatment to overlooked stories like "Benediction" and "Gretchen's Forty Winks." This always interesting and often witty book is an important addition. (Alabama is already planning a paperback reprint, scheduled for 1991 release.)

British-trained critic John B. Chambers, in *The Novels of F. Scott Fitzgerald* (St. Martin's), attacks the widespread, biographically based belief that Fitzgerald was an "emotional rather than a conceptual thinker." Instead of dismissing the early novels *This Side of Paradise* and *The Beautiful and Damned* as ill-conceived and technically flawed, he reads them as displaying "a careful organization based upon a coherent ironic point of view." Chambers then uses that "[not] startlingly innovative" point of view—that life is a cheat, its conditions those of defeat, and its deeper satisfactions arising out of struggle—as a touchstone for interpreting *The Great Gatsby* and *Tender Is the Night*. His willingness to take *This Side of Paradise* and *The Beautiful and Damned* seriously makes his analyses of these novels valuable; however his thesis seems to limit appreciation of the rich complexities of *Gatsby* and *Tender*.

b. Full-Length Studies: Hemingway. Encyclopedic in scope and usefulness, Paul Smith's *A Reader's Guide to the Short Stories of Ernest Hemingway* (Hall) seems destined to become a classic of Hemingway criticism. The book has a chapter on each of the 55 short stories published during Hemingway's lifetime, and each chapter covers, under separate headings, an individual story's composition history, publication history, sources and influences, and critical history. The composition histories are a cornucopia of new factual information about when and how these stories were composed, the publication histories treat Hemingway's relationship to the literary marketplace, and the sections on sources and influences provide a much-needed genealogy of the stories' literary ancestry. Most valuable are the sections titled "Critical Studies." Here Smith provides lively summaries of existing criticism, shrewd judgments about where it has gone wrong, and well-informed insights about where it should head. Anyone currently at work on the short fiction should double-check his or her command of the subject with Smith.

Joseph Flora's tripartite *Ernest Hemingway: A Study of the Short Fiction* (Twayne) first traces the author's development as a short story writer in a 124-page essay that provides an up-to-date overview. He next serves up his own scholarly and valuable edition of Hemingway's "Art of the Short Story" and reprints the author's preface to *The First Forty-Nine*. The book closes with six selections reprinted from recent criticism of the short stories, bringing a variety of approaches to bear on theory and technique rather than on specific stories. Flora's combination of materials results in a solid general sense of Hemingway's achievement.

Half travelogue and half critical study, Edward F. Stanton's *Hemingway and Spain: A Pursuit* (Washington) interleaves chapters recounting Stanton's personal experiences in Spain with chapters exploring Hemingway's experiences and their contributions to his Spanish fiction and nonfiction. Stanton's stated object is to contrast past and present and create a counterpoint between Hemingway's voice and his own. Unfortunately, the personal chapters are written in grating imitation Hemingway, and the critical chapters do not build on existing criticism to achieve new ground. Stanton's admiration for Hemingway and Spanish culture knows no bounds. Always passionate, never detached, this book nevertheless does have some important things to say about the influence of the bullfight and such uniquely Spanish concepts as *ambiente, pundonor*, and *duende* on Hemingway's writing.

c. **Collections: Fitzgerald.**   Editor A. Robert Lee's *F. Scott Fitzgerald: The Promises of Life* (Vision) presents nine new essays by British scholars. Lee's introduction (pp. 7–16) reviews the Fitzgerald myth and calls for "a new round of Fitzgerald interpretation." Well-balanced and workmanlike, the anthology itself provides a solid, carefully researched overview of the Fitzgerald canon and its criticism, as well as many moments of insight.

Four essays treat Fitzgerald's novels. Andrew Hook's "Cases for Reconsideration: Fitzgerald's *This Side of Paradise* and *The Beautiful and Damned*" (pp. 17–36) argues that the generally slighting evaluations of these early novels require review. In " 'A quality of distortion': Imagining *The Great Gatsby*" (pp. 37–60), A. Robert Lee catalogs the "careful, writerly" distortions, the "fantastical and certainly amazed remembering" that characterize Nick Carraway's narration and give *Gatsby* its qualities of dream, myth, and emblematic drama. Harold Beaver, in "*Tender Is the Night*: Fitzgerald's Portrait of a Gentleman" (pp. 61–73), views the novel as Fitzgerald's "most thoroughly Jamesian fiction," a history of "the social anarchy of the Gilded Age," the "triumph of commerce and sex." In "*The Last Tycoon*: Fitzgerald as Projectionist" (pp. 74–93), Robert Giddings asserts that the novel "ranks among Fitzgerald's most glittering prizes" in its transformation of Irving Thalberg into Monroe Stahr and exploration of art's relationship to industry and mass society.

Another two essays treat the short fiction. In " 'All Very Rich and Sad': A Decade of Fitzgerald Short Stories" (pp. 94–112), Herbie Butterfield reviews those written between the May Day riot of 1919 and the stock market crash of October 1929. Taking "May Day" as the symbolic beginning of Fitzgerald's Jazz Age and "Babylon Revisited" as its requiem, Butterfield views stories of the decade as providing "a highly charged and well founded critique" of its "money-making, money-mesmerized ethos." Brian Harding's " 'Made for—or against—the Trade': The Radicalism of Fitzgerald's *Saturday Evening Post* Love Stories" (pp. 113–30) reveals stories that superficially seem to confirm "middle-class fantasies about the lifestyle of the very rich" as parodies of social aspiration.

The last three essays in Lee's anthology strive for "a wider angle of inclusiveness." Elizabeth Kaspar Aldrich, in " 'The most poetical topic in the world': Women in the Novels of F. Scott Fitzgerald" (pp. 131–56), discusses the relationship of Scott and Zelda's actual and artistic struggle over the authorship of Zelda's life to the portrayal of women in the novels. " 'A Touch of Disaster': Fitzgerald, Spengler, and the Decline of the West" (pp. 157–80) by John S. Whitley focuses on works written prior to the 1926 translation of Oswald Spengler's *The Decline of the West* to demonstrate that Fitzgerald's sense of civilization's decay was entirely his own. Finally, Owen Dudley Edwards's "The Lost Teigueen: F. Scott Fitzgerald's Ethics and Ethnicity" (pp. 181–214) views Fitzgerald as an Irish-American and apostate Catholic writer, finding his "Celtic identity . . . in a philosophy of success through failure."

d. Collections: Hemingway. Editor Charles M. Oliver has collected 15 essays on Hemingway films in *A Moving Picture Feast: The Filmgoer's Hemingway* (Praeger). An introduction by Robert W. Lewis (pp. xi–xvi) establishes the theme of the anthology—the complex symbiosis between the box office appeal of the Hemingway name and Hollywood's power to distort popular perceptions of his art. The volume enhances understanding of the Hemingway myth and its

origins, while the collisions of Tinseltown and literature make entertaining reading.

The collection begins with five general essays on the Hemingway/
Hollywood relationship. In "Hemingway's Cinematic Style" (pp. 3–
11), Eugene Kanjo discusses elements of pictorial discourse in the
author's fiction and, with an extended discussion of "Soldier's Home,"
relates them to his quest for new dimensions in prose. Gene D. Phillips's "Novelist versus Screenwriter: The Case for Casey Robinson's
Adaptations of Hemingway's Films" (pp. 12–18) treats the cinematic
exigencies that forced Robinson to make Margot Macomber a romantic heroine, keep Joe Butler from knowledge of his father's dis-
honesty, and give "Snows of Kilimanjaro" a happy ending. In "Hollywood Publicity and Hemingway's Popular Reputation" (pp. 19–25),
Frank M. Laurence examines the Hemingway image promulgated by
movie publicity campaign materials, while in "Death in the Matinee:
The Film Endings of Hemingway's Fiction" (pp. 26–31) Laurence
scrutinizes Hollywood's quest for emotions appropriate to entertainment. The section ends with George Bluestone's "Filming Novels: The
Hemingway Case" (pp. 32–37), arguing that Hollywood adaptations
justifiably softened Hemingway's "narrow, imperial ethic."

Part II looks at films made from novels. In "Inventing from Knowledge: Notes toward a Remake of *For Whom the Bell Tolls*" (pp. 41–
53), John Garrick makes suggestions for a better film of this novel, including improved translation of Hemingway's pseudo-Spanish, more
probable casting, and greater fidelity to the work's intention. Linda
Dittmar's "Larding the Text: Problems in Filming *The Old Man and
the Sea*" (pp. 54–63) chronicles this film's failure to find verbal equivalents for Santiago's internal musings and visual equivalents for the
novella's marine wonders. Thomas Hemmeter and Kevin W. Sweeney,
in "Marriage as Moral Community: Cinematic Critiques of *To Have
and Have Not*" (pp. 64–75), show how three film adaptations challenge the novel's alienation from moral community with an expanded
and positive view of Harry's relationship with his wife. John Garrick's
"Hemingway and *The Spanish Earth*" (pp. 76–90) scrutinizes Hemingway's collaboration on Joris Ivens's propaganda film, its contemporary reception, and the effectiveness of its narration. In "*The Sun Also
Rises*: The NBC Version" (pp. 91–113), Frank Laurence considers an
unfaithful and unpopular interaction of television production values
with Hemingway's novel, while in "Hemingway's Hollywood Paris"

(pp. 114–21) Hugh Ford deplores the infidelities of Darryl Zanuck's *The Sun Also Rises*.

A final section ponders films made from short stories. Stuart Kaminsky's "Literary Adaptation: 'The Killers'—Hemingway, Film Noir, and Daylight" (pp. 125–34) discusses how 1946 and 1964 film versions each made significant cultural and historical changes in the plot of this 1927 short story. Robert E. Morsberger's " 'That Hemingway Kind of Love': Macomber in the Movies" (pp. 135–40) examines film adaptations of the "Short, Happy Life" by Zoltan Korda and Casey Robinson, while Marianne Knowlton in " 'Soldier's Home': A Space Between" (pp. 141–47) contemplates changes wrought in a Hemingway short story for a public television production. In the volume's final essay, "Hemingway, Film, and U.S. Culture: *In Our Time* and *The Birth of a Nation*" (pp. 148–61), Stanley Corkin finds common values in Hemingway's short story cycle and D. W. Griffith's famous film and asks how each posits reality and perpetuates cultural conservatism. An extensive film bibliography compiled by Bruce Crawford and Lisa Middents (pp. 163–78) concludes *A Moving Picture Feast*.

Approximately half of Hemingway's short stories have received scant critical attention, and in an effort to help correct this problem I have put together an anthology of 25 new essays treating 30 little-discussed stories—*Hemingway's Neglected Short Fiction: New Perspectives* (UMI Research Press). In the introduction (pp. 1–18) I argue that many fine Hemingway short stories remain neglected today because their experimental techniques resist conventional critical methods, because their plots defy the ethical paradigms we use to justify canonization, or because their subject matter—androgyny, homosexuality, perversion—is disturbing. Essays in the volume are arranged in the order of composition of the stories.

Mimi Reisel Gladstein's " 'The Mercenaries': A Harbinger of Vintage Hemingway" (pp. 19–30) explores characteristic themes, character types, plot lines, and stylistic devices in a piece of juvenilia. "Uncle Charles in Michigan" by Susan Swartzlander (pp. 31–41) covers the indebtedness of "Up in Michigan" to Joyce's combination of multiple subjective and objective narrative elements in a single, third-person omniscient voice. In "Ethical Narration in 'My Old Man' " (pp. 43–60), Phillip Sipiora uses Aristotle and Quintilian's theories of rhetoric to elucidate how the story's narration shapes our response to the jockey Butler's ambiguous morality. James Steinke in " 'Out of

Season' and Hemingway's Neglected Discovery: Ordinary Actuality"
(pp. 61–73) discounts psychobiographical, theory-of-omission readings to view the story as a comedy of everyday errors. By contrast,
Bickford Sylvester's "Hemingway's Italian *Waste Land*: The Complex
Unity of 'Out of Season' " (pp. 75–98) sees the same story as heavily
indebted to Eliot in its treatment of modern spiritual alienation.

In " 'A Very Short Story' as Therapy" (pp. 99–105), biographer
Scott Donaldson reveals the story's three successive drafts moving
toward a more impersonal yet more bitter version of Hemingway's
1919 jilting by Agnes von Kurowsky. "The Bullfight Story and Critical
Theory" (pp. 107–21) by Bruce Henricksen subjects the bullfighting
interchapters of *In Our Time* to a Bakhtinian analysis and describes
how this polyphonic text gives full expression to the self's dialogic
nature. Paul Smith's "From the Wasteland to the Garden with the
Elliots" (pp. 123–29) shows Hemingway in "Mr. and Mrs. Elliot" com-
bating T. S. Eliot's powerful literary influence with sexual and artistic
insults, and explores the tortuous relationship between an artist's
sexual and creative impulses. A fragment omitted from "Big Two-
Hearted River" illuminates the artist's formative process in Lawrence
Broer's "Hemingway's 'On Writing': A Portrait of the Artist as Nick
Adams" (pp. 131–49), and in "The Writer on Vocation in Hemingway's 'Banal Story' " (pp. 141–47) George Monteiro researches back
numbers of *The Forum* to describe the story's satire and self-conscious
reflection upon its own artifice.

Robert Coltrane's "Hemingway and Turgenev: *The Torrents of
Spring*" (pp. 149–61) connects Hemingway's most extended satire
with the novella from which it took its name, demonstrating how
Hemingway used allusions to Turgenev to attack his own critics and
disguise his own sexual and artistic frustrations. In " 'An Alpine Idyll':
The Sun-Struck Mountain Vision and the Necessary Valley Journey"
(pp. 163–83), Robert Gajdusek reads this grotesque tale as a parable
of abstraction from the cycles of nature. "Waiting for the End in Hemingway's 'A Pursuit Race' " (pp. 185–94), by Ann Putnam, views the
short story as a masterpiece of *nada*, a short story blending humor and
terror in the gothic tradition. Gerry Brenner's "A Semiotic Inquiry into
Hemingway's 'A Simple Enquiry' " (pp. 195–207) groups this often-
overlooked work with puzzle stories like "Hills Like White Elephants"
and "The Sea Change," whose interpretation pivots on an unarticu-
lated word and on readers' responses to sign-laden dialogue. In " 'Mais
Je Reste Catholique': Communion, Betrayal, and Aridity in 'Wine of

Wyoming'" (pp. 209–24), H. R. Stoneback urges critics to consider the important influence of Catholic thought on Hemingway's fiction.

Warren Bennett's "'That's Not Very Polite': Sexual Identity in Hemingway's 'The Sea Change'" (pp. 225–45) discusses why Phil's relationship with a lesbian shatters his masculine identity. Charles Stetler and Gerald Locklin admire the postmodern qualities of Hemingway's experimental short fiction and read "'A Natural History of the Dead' as Metafiction" (pp. 247–53), while Michael Reynolds, in "'Homage to Switzerland': Einstein's Train Stops at Hemingway's Station" (pp. 255–62), explores this cryptic short story's striking experimentation with time and space. Erik Nakjavani tackles the same problem story in "Repetition as Design and Intention: Hemingway's 'Homage to Switzerland'" (pp. 263–82), inquiring minutely into how its tripartite structure and numerous repetitions conspire to produce intention.

Robert E. Fleming's "Myth or Reality: 'The Light of the World' as Initiation Story" (pp. 283–90) uses recent evidence to read "Light" as "an ironic tale of how initiations go wrong in a world where the loss of youthful illusions may be too painful to bear." Linda Gajdusek's "Up and Down: Making Connections in 'A Day's Wait'" (pp. 291–302) uncovers a story about "the need to reconcile opposites, the danger of unbridged schism, and the hero-father engaged in the healing task of establishing vital connections." In "Illusion and Reality: 'The Capital of the World'" (pp. 303–11), Stephen Cooper discusses how this Spanish short story treats Hemingway's characteristic subjects in uncharacteristic ways. Allen Josephs's "Hemingway's Spanish Civil War Stories, or the Spanish Civil War as Reality" (pp. 313–27) groups five stories that acted as "a kind of cathartic fictional memoir" to prepare Hemingway for writing *For Whom the Bell Tolls.* "The Hunting Story in *The Garden of Eden*" (pp. 329–38) by James Nagel explores how David Bourne creates significant art by "using present emotions to capture the feelings of the past." Howard Hannum's "Hemingway's Tales of 'The Real Dark'" (pp. 339–50) concludes *Hemingway's Neglected Short Fiction* with an examination of two late stories of darkness within and without.

e. **General Essays: Fitzgerald.** It seems ironic that an excellent feminist essay by Alice Hall Petry, "Women's Work: The Case of Zelda Fitzgerald" (*LIT* 1:69–83), should appear under the heading "F. Scott Fitzgerald," since Petry criticizes biographers for failure to emphasize that various career frustrations, including Scott's usurpation of her writing, helped precipitate Zelda's mental illness. The essay then surveys Zelda's attitudes toward "women's work" as exemplified in the "Girl Stories" she wrote for *College Humor* and in her novel *Save Me the Waltz*.

f. **General Essays: Hemingway.** One of this year's finest Hemingway essays, Thomas Strychacz's "Dramatizations of Manhood in Hemingway's *In Our Time* and *The Sun Also Rises*" (*AL* 61:245–60), explores "the extent to which the act of performance before an audience constitutes male identity" in Hemingway's work and how "such performances of manhood imply a radical lack of self that must be constantly filled and refashioned." Strychacz's work suggests how gender-based studies can invigorate appreciation of Hemingway's ambiguities. My favorite essay, however, is James C. McKelly's "From Whom the Bull Flows: Hemingway in Parody" (*AL* 61:547–62). By studying innumerable parodies of Hemingway's work, McKelly identifies the most characteristic aspects of the author's style and thematic concerns and provides an explanation of Hemingway's vulnerability to parody—his exaggeration and perversion of the characteristics that had elevated him to mythic cultural status. Like parody itself, McKelly's essay is refreshingly funny, and as insightful as it is entertaining.

Two general essays visit the Spanish Civil War. In "The Francoist Censorship of Hemingway's Works About Spain" (*JILS* 1:277–90), Douglas LaPrade records how Franco's censors viewed Hemingway alternately as a "pro-Communist, irreligious nihilist who reduced Spain to a bullfight," and as a "skillful writer of action and adventure who was enamored of Spain and expressed a humanitarian point of view," with lingering effects on Spanish editions of Hemingway's work. Allen Josephs's "Hemingway and the Spanish Civil War or The Volatile Mixture of Politics and Art" (*Rewriting the Good Fight*, pp. 175–83) argues that Hemingway's distaste for politics turned *For Whom the Bell Tolls* into an "unintentional literary distortion" of an intensely political civil war.

From Jackson Benson, we have "Criticism of the Short Stories: The Neglected and the Oversaturated—An Editorial" (*HN* 8, ii:30–35), surveying the last 10 years of Hemingway short story criticism, chiding critics for continually repeating one another, and suggesting new directions for future work. Other general essays of note include "American Nightmare: Hemingway and the West" (*MQ* 30:361–71) by Robert Fleming, arguing that Hemingway avoided writing about the American West because it was difficult to integrate a heroic myth of brave men and pristine wilderness with a grim reality of senseless violence and despoiled nature. Using concepts of thinking drawn from psychiatry and philosophy, Erik Nakjavani in "Hemingway on Non-Thinking" (*NDQ* 57, iii:173–98) defines how and why various Hemingway characters alter their minds to achieve the state of grace Hemingway called "not thinking."

g. Essays on Specific Works: Fitzgerald.

The Great Gatsby is Fitzgerald's most-criticized single work this year. Two essays bounce particularly high. Tony Magistrale and Mary Jane Dickerson's "The Language of Time in *The Great Gatsby*" (*CollL* 16:117–28) uses the Bakhtinean concept of the chronotope to demonstrate how Fitzgerald's handling of time reflects "our own personal and national anxieties about the complex ambiguities of history." In "Aquinas vs. Weber: Ideological Esthetics in *The Great Gatsby*" (*Mosaic* 22, iv: 1–12), Paul Giles finds the novel's aesthetics shaped by conflict between the traditional Catholic ideology of work solely for the support of self and community, and the Protestant insistence on money-making as "an ethical imperative in itself." Less weighty, but still valuable, Hilton Anderson's "Synedoche in *The Great Gatsby*" (*NDQ* 57, iv: 162–68) discusses how Gatsby's disarming smile and Daisy's thrilling voice come to represent the superficial and illusory aspects of their characters.

h. Essays on Specific Works: Hemingway.

This year's writing about *The Garden of Eden* has a freshness not vouchsafed to criticism of canonical works. In a fine piece titled "The Endings of Hemingway's *Garden of Eden*" (*AL* 61:261–70), Robert Fleming gently upbraids editor Tom Jenks for giving *Garden of Eden* an upbeat conclusion and argues that the novel should conclude with a still unpublished fragment Hemingway labeled "Provisional Ending." That ending reveals Bourne living out his life as a kind of psychiatric nurse to Catherine, with whom he makes a pact to commit suicide should her madness require her return to a hospital. H. R. Stoneback, in "Memorable Eggs 'in Danger of Getting Cold' and Mackerel 'Perilous with Edge-Level Juice': Eating in Hemingway's Garden" (*HN* 8, ii: 22–29), uses the novel's food imagery to create a readable and sensitive interpretation. Quotation-rich and wittily written, Roy S. Simmonds's "The British Critical Reception of *The Garden of Eden*" (*HN* 8, ii:14–21) reviews the difficulties of British readers with this ruthlessly edited text and its controversial subject matter.

The 60th anniversary of the publication of *A Farewell to Arms* generated an unusual number of essays about that novel. Pick of the crop is James Phelan's "Narrative Discourse, Literary Character, and Ideology," pp. 132–46 in his anthology *Reading Narrative*. Engaging the novel's feminist critics, Phelan tackles the controversy-fraught question of whether Hemingway's portrayal of Catherine Barkley is sexist. Phelan's dispassionate assessment of how various narrative elements in *Farewell* legitimate both positive and negative evaluations of Catherine while promulgating an essentially sexist vision is both wise and light-handed. By contrast, Robert Solatoroff's "Sexual Identity in *A Farewell to Arms*" (*HN* 9, i:2–17) and John Beverluis's "Dispelling the Romantic Myth: A Study of *A Farewell to Arms*" (*HN* 9, i: 18–25) adopt Fiedleresque "the only good woman is a dead woman" readings without responding to challenges posed by recent constructive feminist criticism.

David Williams's "The Poetics of Impersonality in *A Farewell to Arms*" (*UTQ* 59:310–33) argues a "real aesthetic problem" with Hemingway's use of the first person singular, narration by a subject that "only pretends to objectify itself in an attempt to avoid self-knowledge." Robert Gajdusek's "*A Farewell to Arms*: The Psychodynamics of Integrity" (*HN* 9, i:26–32) takes a more sympathetic approach to the same problem, detailing the shifting referents of personal pronouns in the novel to show how both love and war erode identity.

H. R. Stoneback's " 'Lovers' Sonnets Turn'd to Holy Psalms': The Soul's Song of Providence, the Scandal of Suffering, and Love in *A Farewell to Arms*" (*HN* 9, i:33–76) provides a comprehensive guidebook to the novel's religious allusions, one that reads *Farewell* as a "neo-Catholic novel" of "secular spiritual epiphany or Theophany." Other essays on the novel include "Hemingway's Experiment in *A Farewell to Arms*" (*LHY* 30, ii:37–51), where A. Banerjee views the work as a *Romeo and Juliet* botched by Hemingway's bitterness about his own failed relationships, and Robert W. Lewis's "The Inception and Reception of *A Farewell to Arms*" (*HN* 9, i:91–95), providing a brief overview for the uninitiated.

The Sun Also Rises accounted for two essays. Wolfgang Rudat's pseudo-Freudian study, "Sexual Dilemmas in *The Sun Also Rises*: Hemingway's Count and the Education of Jacob Barnes" (*HN* 8, ii: 2–13), views Brett's sitting close to Jake in the final taxi scene as attempted "psychological emasculation," and Jake's "Isn't it pretty to think so?" as an effort to defend himself against female sexual aggression by using homosexual language. In "Hunting Ritual in *The Sun Also Rises*" (*HN* 8, ii:46–48), Peter L. Hays places the bullfight in the context of primitive hunting rituals and sees it as "an attenuated form of religious worship culminating in live sacrifice."

Elizabeth D. Vaughn's "*In Our Time* as Self-Begetting Fiction" (*MFS* 35:707–16) stands out as one of the savviest essays on a specific Hemingway work this year. Using the deleted coda of "Big Two-Hearted River" published by Philip Young as "On Writing," Vaughn reads *In Our Time* as metafiction, arguing persuasively that Nick Adams is the volume's sole narrator and that voices identifying themselves as someone other than Nick constitute his experimentation with "the convention of the narrator's status as a disembodied voice." Other worthwhile essays include Stephen Mathewson's on *Islands in the Stream*—"Against the Stream: Thomas Hudson and Painting" (*NDQ* 57, iv:140–45)—which argues that Hudson suffers from "the anxiety of influence," his realistic paintings opposing the currents of contemporary art. Paul Smith, in "A Note on a New Manuscript of 'A Clean, Well-Lighted Place' " (*HN* 8, ii:36–39), examines a corrected typescript and carbon recently acquired by the University of Delaware Library and concludes that even new evidence cannot resolve the continuing problem of attributing the speeches of the two waiters. Another note by Smith, "An Open Letter to Mike Reynolds" (*HN* 9, i:100–101), offers the most extended treatment received to date by Hemingway's bizarre allegorical short story, "A Divine Gesture." And George Monteiro's "The Hit in Summit: Ernest Hemingway's 'The Killers' " (*HN* 8, ii:40–42) draws analogies between bullfighting and events in the short story. Anthony Palmieri's "The Function of an Era in 'The Short Happy Life of Francis Macomber' " (*Piedmont Literary Review* [Spring]:36–40) judges Margot's blowing her husband's brains out as the act of a pre-liberated wife striving to maintain dominance.

v. Miscellaneous

A handful of Hemingway items defy classification. John Leland's *A Guide to Hemingway's Paris* (Algonquin) describes numerous Parisian sites with Hemingway associations and includes walking tours for the tourist. Carefully researched, the book could serve as a useful reference for critics seeking to understand the Parisian settings of works like *A Moveable Feast* and *The Sun Also Rises*. An Ernest Hemingway Commemorative issue of *The Lost Generation Journal* (22, i) is chockful of poems, tributes, notes, and travelogues, while *Hemingway's Spain* (Chronicle Books) offers a few pages of text by Barnaby Conrad and lots of luscious color photographs by Loomis Dean, the latter captioned with quotations by and about Hemingway. *The Best of Bad Hemingway* (Harcourt) collects choice parodies submitted to the now defunct Harry's Bar Imitation Hemingway contest.

Let's conclude with *Papa and Fidel* (St. Martin's), a science-fiction novel by Karl Alexander. In the novel a 60-year-old Hemingway, armed only with a knife, saves Fidel Castro's life after underwater combat with two CIA frogmen and a great white shark. Would that Hemingway criticism could so easily vanquish its subject's reputation as a monster of machismo. And if Fitzgerald scholars regret that their man received less attention than Hemingway this year, at least they may rejoice that he was spared *such* attention.

Part II

11. Literature to 1800

William J. Scheick

This year a number of useful editions appeared: a Dutch narrative of wilderness exploration, the complete poetry of Michael Wigglesworth, the sermons of Edward Taylor on biblical types, biographies by Increase Mather and Cotton Mather, verse and a funeral sermon by Cotton Mather, ethical writings and a history of redemption by Jonathan Edwards, a commonplace book and letters by Thomas Jefferson, essays by Benjamin Rush, prose by Noah Webster, poetry by Phillis Wheatley, and periodical fiction by various hands. The year was also characterized by an attempt to identify what is American about the literature of the colonial period, an effort that urged an expansion of the conventional sense of the canonization of this literature and suggested that the question of a truly American literature may be spurious and inconsequential.

i. Native Americans and the Colonial Imagination

Whereas in *Albion's Seed: Four British Folkways in America* (Oxford) David Hackett Fischer controversially concludes from his study of New World settlements that American culture never developed a distinct identity and remains to this day a mere extension of its British heritage, in *A Mirror for Americanists: Reflections on the Idea of American Literature* (New England) William C. Spengemann argues for a broader definition of American writing, one that would include works about the New World in languages other than English. One such document is identified in "Voices of Resistance: The Epic Curse and Camões's Adamastor" (*Representations* 27:111–41), in which David Quint stresses the curse and suicide of two Native Americans at the end of Gaspar Perez de Villagrá's epic about 16th-century New Mexican conquistadors; both acts are ideological signs challenging conventional epic closure and its usual implication of victory by the conquerors. Summaries of the most recent historical and archaeological research on early Spanish contact with New World peoples is reported in the extraordinarily handsome *First Encounters: Spanish Explorations in the Caribbean and the United States, 1492–1570*, Jerald T. Milanich and Susan Milbrath, eds. (Florida).

A Dutch rather than Spanish encounter with Native Americans is documented in *A Journey into Mohawk and Oneida Country, 1634–1635*, Charles T. Gehring and William A. Starna, trans. and eds. (Syracuse, 1988), a handsome edition, with a Mohawk word list, of a journal by a 23-year-old in search of beaver pelts in Iroquois country. Other 17th-century documentary evidence, according to Alfred A. Cave in "The Pequot Invasion of Southern New England: A Reassessment of the Evidence" (*NEQ* 62:27–44), discredits Puritan historian William Hubbard's propagandistic claim that the Pequots invaded colonized territory.

Conflicting cultural claims inform the thesis of Arnold Krupat's *The Voice in the Margin: Native American Literature and the Canon* (Calif.), which emphasizes how Native American oral literature varies from Euro-American textual literature. Native American autobiographies embody a dialogism characteristic of the frontier itself, Krupat explains, and they valorize a collective self and a pluralism of narrative voice alien to the expectations of text-based cultures. The respect of one Puritan minister for Native American oral ability and spiritual sensibility is observed by Robert James Naeher in "Dialogue in the Wilderness: John Eliot and the Indian Exploration of Puritanism as a Source of Meaning, Comfort, and Ethnic Survival" (*NEQ* 62:346–68); Native Americans responded to Eliot's religion because it provided them with an explanation of their experience of declension as well as offered them an opportunity to voice, through the language of Puritan devotional practices, their new need for an alternative self-definition. A similar reformation of self-identity is studied by William G. McLoughlin and Walter H. Conser, Jr., whose " 'The First Man Was Red'—Cherokee Responses to the Debate over Indian Origins, 1760–1860" (*AQ* 41:243–64) discloses that the Cherokee honored their own myth of racial origins until 1794, when covenants with Euro-Americans forced them to confront other interpretations of their difference from the colonists.

A general review of British influence on a fictional portrait (1769) of the New World by a woman who lived in Quebec for five years and who apparently viewed the Hurons' social structure with objectivity appears in Anna Jakabfi's "Colonial Life in the First American Novel:

Frances Brooke's *The History of Emily Montague"* (*Americana & Hungarica*, pp. 29–34).

ii. Early Colonial Poetry

The differences the colonists perceived between themselves and their country of origin interest Patricia Caldwell, whose excellent "Why Our First Poet Was a Woman: Bradstreet and the Birth of an American Poetic Voice" (*Prospects* 13[1988]:1–35) defines the coincidence of the condition of New World settlers in general and women writers in particular; in a community marginalized and to some extent feminized by the home country, Bradstreet's gender-sensitive struggle to achieve an authentic voice within a traditionally patriarchal poetic tradition is representative of general early American artistic problems of self-definition. How this poet's English contemporaries renegotiated the boundaries of the framework established by male literary authority, specifically how women argued on the basis of virtue for their involvement in Commonwealth society and how they later argued on the same basis for their withdrawal from Restoration affairs of state, are the concerns of Elaine Hobby's *Virtue of Necessity: English Women's Writing 1649–88* (Michigan), which mentions Bradstreet. And several excerpts of the poet's verse appear in *Kissing the Rod: An Anthology of Seventeenth-Century Women's Verse*, Germaine Greer et al., eds. (Noonday).

In my "The Theme, Structure, and Symbolism of Anne Bradstreet's 'Contemplations'" (*Américana* 4:147–56), I detect in this poem an underlying emblem of the Christian cross which unites theme and imagery around the vectors of verticality (trees, birds, eternity, pride) and horizontality (rivers, fish, time, humility); this emblem also informs the peculiar fragmentation of the structure of this poem, ruptures designed to level (make horizontal and humble) from within the potentially Babel-like (vertical and prideful) exterior shape of the poem as a sinful monument to the poet's ability. Bradstreet's humility in the poetic guise of rhetorical techniques, supplicating voice, thematic patterns, diction, and imagery adapted from the Davidic model is identified in Beth M. Doriani's " 'Then Have I . . . Said With David': Anne Bradstreet's Andover Manuscript Poems and the Influence of the Psalm Tradition" (*EAL* 24:52–69).

The correlation of humility and women surfaces in "Night Pollution and the Floods of Confession in Michael Wigglesworth's Diary"

(*ArQ* 45, ii:15–33), in which Eva Cherniavsky precariously interprets the poet's dream of a stable door; this portal symbolizes not his renunciation of temptation but his indulgence in self-abasement, an indulgence in a female helplessness that paradoxically becomes an enjoyment of forbidden sensuality. A valuable first complete collection of this poet's verse, with a chronology of the significant events in his life, appears in *The Poems of Michael Wigglesworth*, Ronald A. Bosco, ed. (Univ. Press), which should become the edition from which to cite.

Another worthy editorial undertaking is evident in the two-volume *Upon the Types of the Old Testament*, Charles W. Mignon, ed. (Nebraska). Mignon suggests that these 16 doctrinal, 13 disciplinary, and 7 confirmatory sermons reveal Edward Taylor's endorsement of the Alexandrian typological tradition, with moral meaning following allegorical interpretation, as well as his distinctive homiletic application of Old Testament types to the individual. *Early New England Meditative Poetry: Anne Bradstreet and Edward Taylor*, Charles E. Hambrick-Stowe, ed. (Paulist, 1988), provides an introduction to the devotional concerns of these poets; and *The Poems of Edward Taylor* (No. Car.) presents an abbreviated version of Donald E. Stanford's superb earlier complete edition (1960) with the same title.

Quibbles with Stanford's editing surface in two observations by J. Daniel Patterson. "Notes on Emending Edward Taylor's *Gods Determinations*" (*AN&Q* 2:13–15) recommends the restoration of three words from the manuscript version of the poem in order to honor the poet's intention; and "Edward Taylor's 'Christs Reply,' Stanza Eight" (*AN&Q* 2:132–33) refers to the manuscript to clarify a syntactic crux resulting from the poet's negligence while revising. A crux of another sort, the predicament of a poet who is obliged to praise a deity beyond praise, interests Jerome D. DeNuccio, whose "Linguistic Dilemma in Edward Taylor's 'Meditation 1.22' " (*ELN* 26:19–24) indicates that the poet arrives at a resolution of this problem by means of a mystical vision of the final judgment.

The prospect of this eschatological joy sanctioned by the New Testament, together with the jubilant celebration of the "comic incongruity" of the Incarnation and an awareness of the place of grace in creation, defined the margins of safety for Taylor's ambivalent use of wit, which otherwise might readily have implicated him in damning prideful ambition. This is the thesis of *Gracious Laughter: The Meditative Wit of Edward Taylor* (Missouri), John Gatta's assess-

ment of wit as a playful yet earnest management of language whereby
the poet conducted his search for salvation. Gatta's insistence on our
appreciation of Taylor's humor is an important reminder, but his book
unfortunately remains a curiously belated preliminary report; it un-
derestimates the range and nature of Taylor's comic art, prefers surface generalities to in-depth closure, often asserts rather than demonstrates its claims, and uses terminology in need of clarity, consistency,
and critical definition.

Several references, allusions, and patterns pertaining to the influence of earlier writings upon Taylor and other authors are noted in
Harrison T. Meserole's " 'By Chaucer's Boots': Some Medieval Strains
in Colonial American Literature," in *Medievalism in American Culture*, Bernard Rosenthal and Paul E. Szarmach, eds. (SUNY at Bing-
hamton: Center for Medieval and Early Renaissance Studies, pp. 113–
28). And in "Colonial Poets and the Magazine Trade, 1741–1775"
(*EAL* 24:112–19), Pattie Cowell urges a consideration of the impact
of verse published in magazines, which were more influential than
their short runs might superficially suggest.

iii. Early Colonial Prose

The impact of the confessional narrative on Puritan culture cannot be
underestimated, as Daniel B. Shea's revised *Spiritual Autobiography
in America* and Joseph Fichtelberg's *The Complex Image* both demonstrate. Fichtelberg (pp. 70–82) emphasizes the ways John Woolman's heavily edited journal reveals the divided sensibility of a man
who wished to remove himself from earthly corruption and at the
same time wished actively to reform the world. A conflict occurs as
well in Shepard's autobiography, in which Fichtelberg (pp. 53–70)
sees the spiritual inconclusiveness and doubt expressed in the early
private English part become transformed as revisionary tropes cur-
tailing similar tensions in the later politically public and more resolute
American part of the narrative. A related conflict between affirmation
and renunciation in Shepard's sense of self is remarked by Mary Cap-
pello, whose "The Authority of Self-Definition in Thomas Shepard's
Autobiography and *Journal*" (*EAL* 24:35–51) argues that this tension
is a product of the fact that conversion is an unfixed continual process
in time (which is distant from eternity) and, in turn, results in an ill-
defined style evidencing Shepard's discomfort in framing his voice.
And disputes over the spiritual relation itself are identified by Baird

Tipson, whose "Samuel Stone's 'Discourse' against Requiring Church Relations" (*WMQ* 46:786–99) reports on a first-generation divine's protest against the practice as both unscriptural and too sectarian.

Such explicit and implicit conflicts, according to Andrew Delbanco's *The Puritan Ordeal* (Harvard), were critical to Puritan self-definition. Puritan immigrants required a psychological dependency on persecution, a sense of oppositional forces that aided them in maintaining a tenuous identity comprised of numerous tensions or incipient divisions within their self-conception: for example, the simultaneous defense of individual piety and communal discipline, of sin as subjective privation and as objective reality, of the human capacity for moral renovation and incapacity to overcome innate depravity, of aspirations toward and revulsion over the future of Protestantism in England, of the sense of potentiality in the New World and sense of loss toward the Old World. Especially fine are Delbanco's expositions on John Winthrop's failed vision, Edward Johnson's perception of the elusiveness of Puritan culture, John Cotton's notion of the unsayable, and Roger Williams's wish to make sin abstract.

The ambivalence of these first-generation divines toward nature in the New World is explored in J. R. Rougé's "Puritanisme et *Wilderness*" (*Américana* 4:131–46). In reaction to this wilderness, explains A. Carl Bredahl, Jr., in *New Ground* (pp. 8–28), Puritan authors tended to enclose their experience within a protective imaginative framework composed of Old World rational paradigms, definitions, traditions, and rhetorical patterns; occasionally, however, as in Bradford's account, experience (wilderness) breaks through this intellectual enclosure and ruptures form when history becomes chronicle. First-generation uncertainty over the attainment of material wealth through nature, especially land, is noted by J. Beranger, whose "A L'ombre de Calvin: Argent et biens matériels dans les écrits de William Bradford et John Winthrop" (*Américana* 4:61–73) indicates that whereas Bradford cited Calvin to condemn the accumulation of earthly riches, Winthrop cited Calvin to defend the value of personal riches as a means of doing God's work.

Other early New World spokesmen figure in Lehel Vadon's "John Smith in Hungary" (*Americana & Hungarica*, pp. 13–17), which urges scholars to pay more attention to the fact that Smith visited Hungary; in Sargent Bush, Jr.'s "John Cotton's Correspondence: A Census" (*EAL* 24:91–111), which usefully suggests the importance of Cotton's 100 extant letters; and in L. Raymond Camp's *Roger Williams*,

God's Apostle of Advocacy: Biography and Rhetoric (Mellen), which carefully considers the background of Williams's life, beliefs, and language, especially his skillful eclectic methods in discourse. How John Cotton's grandson tried to manage his own method of discourse is the topic of "Cotton Mather and 'Criolian Degeneracy' " (*EAL* 24:20–34), in which John Canup reveals Mather's sensitivity to the notion that English culture degenerated in the New World, his personal ambivalence concerning the inferiority of the colonies in comparison with the Old World, and his attempt to provide a compromise position.

Compromise through displacement is featured in my edition of *Two Mather Biographies: "Life and Death" and "Parentator"* (Lehigh), which includes nearly 400 annotations. Whereas Increase early in his life, in his biography of his father, could locate his identity in terms of a continuity of divine will expressed through his succession as an agental ministerial father, Cotton late in his life could not achieve the same self-image, in his biography of his father, because of his sense of diminishment and his uncertainty over the place of the Matherian heritage in the providential scheme. Consequently, Cotton displaced Increase's anonymous emphasis on the image of the father with a heavily "signatured" hope that in the instance of his own seemingly less successful ministry the continuity of divine will is expressed through the agency of ministerial books, Cotton's as well as Increase's. *Cotton Mather's Verse in English*, Denise D. Knight, ed. (Delaware), records both Mather's fears about poetry and his uneven achievement in the genre; the editor's annotations are helpful, but unfortunately her bibliography of Mather's poems attributes the Latin epitaph on Increase in *Parentator* to Cotton instead of to Samuel Mather. A facsimile of a funeral sermon written by Cotton in 1718 is included in "Providence Asserted and Adored: A Cotton Mather Text Rediscovered" (*EIHC* 125:201–38), introduced by David Levin, who warns against exaggerating how much Puritan doctrine changed during Mather's lifetime.

A historian who resisted all signs of change and who valorized an image of New England as a divinely elected liminal preserve from all such human contingencies and institutions interests Ormond Seavey, whose "Edward Johnson and the American Puritan Sense of History" (*Prospects* 14:1–29) carefully details how this resistance expressed a response to both Independent and Presbyterian criticism of the Puritan undertaking. One way in which an old pattern survived in Mather's time emerges in "Of Providence and Pirates: Philip Ashton's Narrative Struggle for Salvation" (*EAL* 24:169–95), Daniel E. Williams's report on how John Barnard managed a story of captivity by pirates and isolation on an island so that it parallels the pattern of conversion narratives; both dramatize a sudden awareness of divine presence and a self undergoing purification. The date of the birth in England of a woman who wrote another captivity narrative, which was also rhetorically managed as a spiritual relation, is identified as probably 1637 in Kathryn Zabelle Derounian's "A Note on Mary (White) Rowlandson's English Origins" (*EAL* 24: 70–72).

Whether New World women could read such works concerns E. Jennifer Monaghan, whose "Literacy Instruction and Gender in Colonial New England" (*Reading in America*, pp. 53–80) concludes that Puritan women could read but not write, and that these women taught their children to read, whereas men taught boys to write. One "text" which New England men and women were reading was the symbolic medium of dress; Leigh Eric Schmidt's " 'A Church-going People are a Dress-loving People': Clothes, Communication, and Religious Culture in Early America" (*Church History* 58:36–51) discusses how colonial dress expressed ideas about hierarchy, equality, gender, clerical authority, and communal ritual.

iv. Edwards, the Great Awakening, and the New Divinity

The degree to which the heritage of the Enlightenment impoverished ideas about religion, society, and politics is assessed by Robert W. Jenson, whose polemical *America's Theologian: A Recommendation of Jonathan Edwards* (Oxford, 1988) argues that Edwards's radical Christian vision exposes how the infection of Arminianism and Pelagianism weakened the American social fabric. According to San Hyun Lee in *The Philosophical Theology of Jonathan Edwards* (Princeton, 1988), Edwards was more modern than even Perry Miller suspected; Edwards reconceived the nature of reality by replacing the traditional Western belief in substance and form with a belief in a metaphysics of dynamic dispositional forces and habits, which mediate between permanence and process.

Edwards's apocalyptic vision is evident in two new meticulous contributions to *The Works of Jonathan Edwards*. In *A History of the Work of Redemption* (Yale), editor John F. Wilson explores the ideas, reception, and anonymous 18th-century revisions made in this posthumously published document. Wilson also insists that this work is theological rather than historical, evidences rhetorical patterns of sub-ordination of parts within a logical framework, and contains imagery and repeated episodes designed to combine diversity and unity. How the plurality of virtues resolves into divine unity is a concern in *Ethical Writings* (Yale), in which editor Paul Ramsey also provides a sys-tematic reading of Edwards's concepts of self-love, secondary beauty, conscience, and affections.

That Edwards increasingly looked to practice in assessing religious affections as he became more skeptical of interiority is remarked by Wayne Proudfoot, whose "From Theology to a Science of Religions: Jonathan Edwards and William James on Religious Affections" (*HTR* 82:49–68) notes the oddity of this development given Edwards's initial emphasis on the primacy of a biblically defined divine provi-dence only secondarily confirmed by temporal experience. The direct involvement in the temporal concern of revolutionary politics by the Edwardseans interests Mark Valeri in "The New Divinity and the American Revolution" (*WMQ* 46:741–69), which draws upon manu-script evidence to show how concepts of virtue, benevolence, and justice were applied to the Anglo-American crisis. The amalgamation of 18th-century rationalism, voluntarism, and moralism with Re-formed theology by one leader of the New Divinity is featured in An-nabelle S. Wenzke's detailed *Timothy Dwight (1752–1817)* (Mellen), which also closely scrutinizes Dwight's reliance upon the New En-gland village as the divinely sanctioned model for America.

v. Franklin, Jefferson, and the Revolutionary Period

How an emergent Whig politics during this Anglo-American crisis would find support through the management of a sense of the sublime (including natural, social, and political terror) is remarked in "Wil-liam Livingstone's *Philosophic Solitude* and the Ideology of the Natu-ral Sublime" (*EAL* 24:217–36), Rob Wilson's reading of the contra-dictory modes of the pastoral and the sublime in a poem (1747) that adumbrates this emergent ideology of liberation. Another poet is ob-served by David S. Shields, whose "Nathaniel Gardner, Jr., and the Literary Culture of Boston in the 1750s" (*EAL* 24:196–216) empha-sizes the backward-looking neoclassical disposition and the forward-looking aesthetics of participation in the manuscript verse of this poet, who probably published under the pseudonym "Philo Muses."

A casual reminder of the importance of almanacs to pre-Revolutionary readers is provided by Benjamin Franklin V and Karen L. Rood in *American Literary Almanac: From 1608 to the Present*, Karen L. Rood, ed. (Facts on File, 1988). That cheap, ephemeral booklets printed in the colonies were scarce in the pre-Revolution years but much more prevalent later is Victor Neuburg's finding in "Chapbooks in America: Reconstructing the Popular Reading of Early America" (*Reading in America*, pp. 81–113). By the middle of the 18th century treatises on rhetoric were being sold extensively in Philadelphia, Dennis Barone observes in "Hostility and Rapprochement: Formal Rhetoric in Philadelphia Before 1775" (*Pennsylvania History* 56:15–32), which contrasts this practice with the Quaker distrust of formal rhetoric and preference for a plain style that had prevailed.

Management of rhetoric receives attention in "Exposing the 'Sacred Juggle': Revolutionary Rhetoric in Robert Rogers' *Ponteach*" (*EAL* 24:4–19), in which Laura E. Tanner and James N. Krasner reveal how a verse drama presents the same discursive strategies as were employed by Loyalists who critiqued the revolutionary language of the Whigs. Rhetoric is also at issue in James M. Farrell's "John Adams's *Autobiography*: The Ciceronian Paradigm and the Quest for Fame" (*NEQ* 62:505–28), which accuses Adams of shaping language to achieve fame and immortality by presenting himself as a great Ciceronian statesman and orator of American independence. Adams's deliberate self-inscription of himself in history as the first voice of independence in the new republic parallels that of Benjamin Rush and Thomas Jefferson, explains Elizabeth M. Renker in " 'Declaration-Men' and the Rhetoric of Self-Preservation" (*EAL* 24:120–34). The personal, political, and social implications of Rush's ideas are evident in *Benjamin Rush's Essays: Literary, Moral and Philosophical*, Michael Meranze, ed. (Union, 1988).

Another essayist is found wanting by A. J. Ayer in *Thomas Paine* (Atheneum, 1988), which provides a decontextualized assessment of Paine as a journalist with a gift for language but whose sayings are dated political philosophy not contributive to the present and his arguments unfair to his opponents. Gary Kates concludes in "From Liberalism to Radicalism: Tom Paine's *Rights of Man*" (*JHI* 50:569–87) that the two separately published parts of this book reveal that Paine's radicalism, which is evident in Part II as an acceptance of violence in the abolition of monarchies, represents a genuine transformation of his views on pacifist progress in Part I. Paine's interest in the "new rationalism" and his differences from contemporary European thinkers, particularly in his arguments concerning republicanism, are featured in *Thomas Paine: Updated Edition* (TUSAS 301) by Jerome D. Wilson and William F. Ricketson. And a useful overview of specific books, besides Paine's, purchased by Philadelphians is available in *The Book Culture of a Colonial City: Philadelphia Books, Bookmen, and Booksellers* (Clarendon, 1988) by Edwin Wolf II.

Jefferson's Literary Commonplace Book (Princeton) has been edited and annotated by Douglas L. Wilson, and *The Adams-Jefferson Letters: The Complete Correspondence between Thomas Jefferson and Abigail and John Adams*, ed. Lester J. Cappon (No. Car.), has been reissued. Another glimpse at Jefferson's personal thoughts emerges in Frank Shuffelton's "Travelling in the Republic of Letters" (*Voyage et tourisme en Bourgogne à l'époque de Jefferson*, Michel Baridon and Bernard Chevignard, eds. [Éditions universitaires de Dijon, 1988], pp. 1–16), which reviews Jefferson's notes and letters written while he was touring southern France and concludes that as a representative of the republic of letters he combined the language of sentiment and of science; for him, any fact simultaneously possessed scientific, historical, political, and aesthetic significance. The significance of Jefferson's behavior with five women is explained by Gisela Tauber, whose "Thomas Jefferson: Relationships with Women" (*AI* 45[1988]:431–47) claims that he was a masochist motivated by his inability to find in these women a substitute for the mother who left him in his youth. Jefferson's management of self-representation concerns James M. Cox in *Recovering Literature's Lost Ground* (pp. 33–54), which reads his autobiography as a death mask; only the outer lineaments of an impersonal self are autobiographically presented to the world in a portrait of an author knowable only through a public history paradoxically authored by the unseen private self he does not reveal.

If Jefferson interprets his life in terms of his contribution to a public government generated by his authorship, in Cox's opinion Benjamin Franklin openly represents himself as succeeding through self-government (*Recovering Literature's Lost Ground*, pp. 15–19); in Franklin's autobiography there are no turning points, but rather a sense of the essential equality of events that allows the narrator a maximum of detached freedom to explore a wide range of possibilities and to present himself to others as a historical and cultural model of self-determination. This self-portrait is designed to manage his audience, Cynthia S. Jordan instructively observes in *Second Stories* (pp.

27–57); in his narrative Franklin discloses his youthful acts of forgery and counterfeiting to improve on patriarchal political authority, and in the process he inadvertently gives a glimpse of another, opposite story: an underlying dissent from the suspect, merely fabricated authority he seems to valorize both as the author of his text and as the representative of his culture. On a related point, Joseph Fichtelberg (*The Complex Image* pp. 83–115) observes in this work a reduction of the self characteristic of the old spiritual relation into a cipher of representation that can, like any text, be subject to ongoing compositional revision; as a result, Franklin's voice mutates, from ruminative to hortative to documentary, in response to his sense of changing audiences.

Another reading of Franklin's awareness of audience is provided by R. Jackson Wilson's *Figures of Speech* (pp. 21–65), which argues that the *Autobiography* implies readers who are personally collaborative rather than anonymously remote; Franklin did not encounter the sort of alienation that would characterize the experience of later writers who sensed only an uncertain commercial link to an undefined mass public and who, as a result, emphasized the gap between words and actions, ideas and things. One of Franklin's commercial ventures is scrutinized by Charles E. Clark and Charles Wetherell in "The Measure of Maturity: The *Pennsylvania Gazette*, 1728–1765" (*WMQ* 46:279–303), which identifies the essentially English viewpoint of this periodical, including its emphasis on economic matters and the conduct of local affairs. And the ways in which this publication reveals the ever-present threat of enslavement for runaway and emancipated African-Americans are detailed by Billy G. Smith and Richard Wojtowicz in "The Precarious Freedom of Blacks in the Mid-Atlantic Region: Excerpts from the *Pennsylvania Gazette*, 1728–1776" (*PMHB* 113:237–64).

The freedom occasioned by irrelevant analogies, according to Wayne Glowka's "Franklin's Perfumed Proposer" (*StAH* 4[1985–86]: 229–41), permits the insulting virtuoso in "To the Royal Academy" to advance his inconsistent interests. Franklin's belief that the spreading of oil on water might reveal important facts about "ultimate particles" and the forces between them is assessed in the context of 18th-century science as related to later experiments in Charles Tanford's well-written *Ben Franklin Stilled the Waves* (Duke). Franklin's confrontation with Franz Mesmer is reviewed in Stephen Jay Gould's "The Chain of Reason vs. the Chain of Thumbs" (*Natural History* 98, vii:

12–21), and Franklin's entries in his early journals are contrasted with his later morally directed memoirs in P. M. Zall's *Franklin's Autobiography: A Model Life* (Twayne). In a letter to the editor (*EAL* 24: 164), A. Owen Aldridge retracts his previous claim that "Letter from China" has been falsely attributed to Franklin (*ALS 1988*).

The writings of a contemporary of Franklin appear in two editions: *The Collected Works of Phillis Wheatley*, John C. Shields, ed. (Oxford, 1988), which provides variant texts and revisions with remarks concerning the poet's awareness of restraints on her work; and *The Poems of Phillis Wheatley*, Julian D. Mason, Jr., ed. (No. Car.), which provides a handsome, expanded version of an earlier publication of this volume. Wheatley is included in *Afro-American Women Writers* and is the subject of Samuel J. Rogal's "Phillis Wheatley's Methodist Connection" (*BALF* 23:85–95).

vi. The Early National Period

A Quaker woman is featured in Kathryn Zabelle Derounian's edition of *The Journal and Occasional Writings of Sarah Wister* (Fairleigh Dickinson, 1987), which provides fully annotated journals, letters, and poetry. Spiritual relations interest Susan Juster, whose " 'In a Different Voice': Male and Female Narratives of Religious Conversion in Post-Revolutionary America" (*AQ* 41:34–62) reports that while early national men were ministerially encouraged to renounce a sense of self that interferes with their search for salvation, women were encouraged to enlarge their sense of self by reducing their dependence on others and by assuming a more active role as moral agents. One woman who expressed a longing for independence for herself and broad social influence for women in general emerges in "Sarah Pierce and the Poetic Origins of Utopian Feminism in America" (*Prospects* 14:45–63), in which Albert J. von Frank reads a late 18th-century poem as a virtually unprecedented expression of the basic features of the later feminist perspective.

More studies of this kind are called for by Linda K. Kerber and five other historians in "Beyond Roles, Beyond Spheres: Thinking about Gender in the Early Republic" (*WMQ* 46:565–85), which urges further attention to the function of gender in the early republic, especially in terms of the Bakhtinian concept of dialogism (i.e., social heterogeneity produces heteroglossia, or conflicting cultural dialects). Such a Bakhtinian perspective informs Cynthia S. Jordan's "Old

Worlds in 'New Circumstances': Language and Leadership in Post-Revolutionary America" (*AQ* 40[1988]:491–513), an excerpt from Jordan's *Second Stories* that specifically remarks Hugh Henry Brackenridge's argument in *Modern Chivalry* for governmental control by an educated patriarchal elite. Nevertheless, various traces of disintegration in the book undermine this thematic aim, especially as dissident voices increasingly manifest themselves, until in the last volume the author seems to have lost aesthetic control over his work.

A work hardly under control of its collaborators, but designed to undermine the authority of those who opposed the formation of the Constitution, is reviewed in "The Design of Anarchy: *The Anarchiad*, 1786–1787" (*EAL* 24:237–47) by J. K. Van Dover. One of these authors receives attention from John Seelye, whose "Flashing Eyes and Floating Hair: The Visionary Mode in Early American Poetry" (*VQR* 65:191–214) suggests that Joel Barlow's *Vision of Columbus* and *The Columbiad* should not be read as examples of classical epic form; on the contrary they represent stages in the emergence of a uniquely American genre—the Vision Poem—applying both English optimism and Puritan millennialism even to the territories beyond the Ohio River. Yet Barlow's valiant effort to revise the epic tradition especially by rejecting warfare and individual renown as primary subjects, faltered, explains John P. McWilliams, Jr., in *The American Epic*. McWilliams maps out in valuable detail the struggle of New Republic authors with epic panegyric, which remained less tractable as a form than did mock-epic satire in accommodating post-Revolutionary experience and artistic imagination.

An account of one man's 18th-century contribution to and assistance in the study of the historical matter within this vision is provided by George Pilcher in "Ebenezer Hazard and the Promotion of Historical Scholarship in the Early Republic" (*Pennsylvania History* 56:3–14). An account of the private, public, and idealized self-conception of a contemporary of Hazard appears in *The Autobiographies of Noah Webster: From the Letters, and Essays, Memoir, and Diary*, Richard M. Rollins, ed. (So. Car.). And an account of how another contemporary perceived North Africa is given in Marwam M. Obeidat's "Royall Tyler's *The Algerine Captive* and the Barbary Orient: An Example of America's Early Literary Awareness of the Muslim Near East" (*American Journal of Islamic Social Sciences* 5 [1988]:255–61).

vii. Brown and Contemporaries

A reflection of instability at the center of early national history, culture, and politics defines the paralysis of will of the female protagonist assessed in "An Assault on the Will: Republican Virtue and the City in Hannah Webster Foster's *The Coquette*" (*EAL* 24:135–51), in which Kristie Hamilton reveals how vacillating Eliza Wharton is vulnerable to seduction because of her experience of a conflict between an inadequate republican ideology and attractive urban materialism; this conflict is also reflected in the epistolary mode of the book, replete with contradictory messages and multiple voices. A similar weakness in the traits of an American struggling to be a federal citizen emerges in "Narrative Irony and National Character in Royall Tyler's *The Algerine Captive*" (*SAF* 17:19–32), John Engell's discussion of Tyler's management of ironic distance from his naive narrator, who never discerns human villainy and is a lure for the equally naive reader.

Early national instability and narrative uncertainty are correlated by Robert S. Levine, whose *Conspiracy and Romance* (pp. 15–57) studies the relationship between the villainy of insidious foreign influence and the vulnerability of the virtuous American identity in Brown's fiction of the 1790s; this relationship exposes not only the countersubversive mentality of the precarious new republic, but Brown's dual role as a concerned citizen unmasking conspiracy and also as an imagined villain-like subversive whenever he destabilizes authority or weakens cause-and-effect reasoning. The function of Brown's destabilized narrative endings, specifically the way they raise questions about narrative credibility, is featured in Cynthia S. Jordan's *Second Stories* (pp. 78–97), which suggests that for Brown the fiction-making processes of the mind are necessary for human survival; storytelling represses the anarchistic impulses of human nature and provides a means for negotiating the need for ongoing revision in an ambiguous world. Revision is at issue in David M. Larson's "*Arthur Mervyn, Edgar Huntly* and the Critics" (*ELWIU* 15[1988]:207–19), which argues that the second part of *Mervyn* was written in reaction to *Huntly* and anticipates Brown's subordination of imagination to moral instruction in his subsequent fiction.

Some of the tales printed in the regional publications of Brown's time are edited by Keith J. Fennimore in *Short Stories from Another*

Day: Eighteenth Century Periodical Fiction (Mich. State). Some of the readers of these works are identified in David Paul Nord's "A Republican Literature: Magazine Reading and Readers in Late Eighteenth-Century New York" (*Reading in America*, pp. 114–39), which concludes that the *New-York Magazine*'s working-class audience possessed a sense of its participation in a political elite culture that was once closed to it. This culture remained exclusive to white audiences, according to Dana Nelson Salvino's "The Word in Black and White: Ideologies of Race and Literacy in Antebellum America" (*Reading in America*, pp. 140–56), which indicates that white institutional efforts to improve black literacy were based on white concepts of literacy and resulted in no change in the economic deprivation of blacks.

That Olaudah Equiano's autobiography evidences a correspondence between evolving abolitionist thought in England and his own developing racial and political consciousness interests Keith A. Sandiford in *Measuring the Moment* (pp. 118–48); besides emphasizing only certain features of his experience in response to his awareness of the areas of tolerance in his audience, Equiano alternates between a naive voice that seems artless and a self-affirming voice that advances his politics of abolition.

viii. Miscellaneous Studies

In "Early Histories of American Literature: A Chapter in the Institution of New England" (*AmLH* 1:459–88), Nina Baym discusses a curious paradox in American literary history: that colonial American literature has been principally defined in terms of its exemplary New England didactic and moralistic content but denigrated as belles lettres because of this same content. *Books about Early America: 2001 Titles* (Institute of Early American History and Culture) is a handy selective bibliography compiled by David L. Ammerman and Philip R. Morgan that includes such topics as magic, painting, science, medicine, and literature. New journals this year include *Studies in Puritan American Spirituality* (Michael Schuldiner, ed.), which prints essays on all aspects of Puritan literature and culture; *The Edwardean* (Richard Hall, ed.), which prints articles on all aspects of Jonathan Edwards's thought and influence; and *American Colonial Authors Society Newsletter* (William J. Scheick, ed.), which prints queries, announcements, bibliographic data, and abstracts of recent publications in American colonial studies.

Perhaps apt at this point are some words penned in 1643 by the French Jesuit Isaac Jogues concluding an account of his captivity by the Mohawks: "But I am now weary of so long and so prolix a letter. I therefore earnestly beg Your Reverence ever to recognize me, though unworthy, as one of yours ... though [I am] savage in dress and manner, and almost without God in so tossed a life."

University of Texas at Austin

12. 19th-Century Literature

Alice Hall Petry

It was an eclectic year for 19th-century American literature. Some canonical writers, such as the Fireside Poets, continued dramatically to lose ground; others, notably Cooper and Howells, have rarely had better years. Excellent books were written about Lucy Larcom and William Gilmore Simms; disappointing ones were accorded Stephen Crane and John W. De Forest. Western humorists and Southern novelists enjoyed considerable notice; poets from every region were largely ignored. Theoretical studies were rare; feminist concerns were evident even in studies of male writers by male scholars. If anything, the scholarly work on the 19th century produced in 1989 suggests that the field is in flux, as traditional and revisionist scholars continue to explore a literary landscape whose boundaries and features had seemed so clear, so fixed, just a few years ago.

i. General Studies

The uncertainty over the precise nature of 19th-century American literature renders particularly valuable an essay such as Nina Baym's "Early Histories of American Literature: A Chapter in the Institution of New England" (*AmLH* 1:459–88), which surveys the formal literary histories that began to be published after the Civil War—histories that sought to "Americanize" their often foreign-born readers and to instill in them a preference for spiritual (as opposed to commercial) values. Though much of this will sound familiar to readers of Richard Brodhead (see *ALS 1986*, pp. 26–27) and Kermit Vanderbilt (see *ALS 1986*, pp. 385–86), Baym expands their work by focusing on the historical narrative presented collectively in these histories and by offering a timely caveat: "If we practice American literature in the classroom for the ultimate aims of forming students' characters and making them better citizens, we find ourselves—to our surprise—carrying on Whig goals, no matter how radical our claims." A good companion study to Baym's is Lawrence J. Oliver's "Theodore Roosevelt, Brander Matthews, and the Campaign for Literary Americanism" (*AQ* 41:93–111), which examines the conscious efforts of the president and the professor to establish a stridently conservative American literary canon.

Particular movements within that canon continued to be studied and evaluated in 1989. One of the best studies is Robert S. Levine's *Conspiracy and Romance*. Levine argues that the American romance of the 19th century was "historically situated, ideological, and interested—a text that attempted to re-create community by calling attention to conspiratorial threats against it," including those of the Freemasons and the Catholic church. Levine's readings are more level-headed and persuasive than one might expect. Conspiracy of a different sort is detected by William Ellis in *The Theory of the American Romance*. Ellis sees the concept of the American romance as a construct of 20th-century literary historians (such as Trilling), who in their insistence on the uniqueness of the American experience made inflated claims for the uniqueness—and the excellence—of the romance mode. Few will find this interpretation tenable, especially since Hawthorne himself spoke of the special nature of American romance; but Ellis's approach should remind us nonetheless of the capacity of politically oriented critics to shape our responses to literature. More theoretical than political is Emily Miller Budick's *Fiction and Historical Consciousness*, which examines the historical romance from Brockden Brown to E. L. Doctorow. Budick maintains that the historical romance involves a "double consciousness of interpretive processes. Its symbols and allegories enforce an awareness of the unknowability of material reality. Simultaneously, the historical romance presents a world that . . . is still intensely recognizable." In so doing, it forces the imagination "to consider something outside itself," namely, a feeling of responsibility in "the national venture." At times a bit wordy and abstract, Budick's book nevertheless offers an original approach to the American romance. Her analysis of Cooper's *The Spy* will be considered below.

Realism is the topic of one of the best books of the year, Daniel H. Borus's *Writing Realism*. But don't let the subtitle, "Howells, James, and Norris in the Mass Market," mislead you; this is not a tripartite study of those writers, and in fact there are only scattered references to them. Borus's primary interests are, first, the socioeconomic conditions which made American readers impatient with romance and responsive to the realists' more concrete world peopled with anti-heroes; and, second, the extraliterary changes—the advent of stenography, new copyright laws, more vigorous marketing techniques, the rise of the agent as a professional—which made possible a generation of novelists who saw writing less as an imaginative endeavor than as a business grounded in hard work and careful research. Borus's is an engaging, enlightening book that students of realism will find invaluable.

Two movements closely aligned with realism also were accorded book-length studies in 1989. In *Determined Fictions: American Literary Naturalism* (Columbia), Lee Clark Mitchell focuses on just four texts—including Norris's *Vandover and the Brute* and Crane's *The Red Badge of Courage*—to argue that what critics have regarded as the "bad writing" of the naturalists may be attributed to the deterministic philosophy underlying the texts. The repetitious, flat syntax, the "narrative gaps and omissions," the often personality-less characters—these are not flaws but "narrative strengths" in texts designed to express a deterministic worldview. This approach seems valid, though it would hardly make most readers suddenly regard, say, *Moran of the Lady Letty* as brilliant. In contrast to the four books examined by Mitchell, Robert Glenn Wright studies 145 examples of *The Social Christian Novel* (Greenwood), a once-popular mode of fiction which sought to apply Christian (especially American Protestant) principles to those social problems attributable to inequities in labor and capital. Wright wisely makes no claims of literary excellence for these forgotten novels, which cornered much of the marketplace from 1865 to 1900; unfortunately he also avoids placing them within the context of other movements. (Might not the naturalists have been reacting consciously against this brand of fiction?) Likewise unfortunate, the book is mechanical in organization and dry in presentation. On the other hand, it also is comprehensive, authoritative, and astute, with an excellent Bibliography of Interpretive Works and an annotated list of all 145 novels. This is an important contribution to the scholarship of American reformist literature of the 19th century. Social fiction of a different sort is examined in a less rewarding book, Laura Hapke's *Girls Who Went Wrong*. Focusing on just six writers (including Joaquin Miller, Edgar Fawcett, Stephen Crane, and Harold Frederic), Hapke explores the ambivalent fictional renderings of the "fallen woman": was she a victim? a victimizer? a resourceful capitalist? Hapke's study would be stronger if she included some women writers of the period (who tended to use prostitutes only as minor characters in subplots) and examined the pornography and erotica. Even so, some may find useful the readings of the lesser-known novels and the extensive bibliography.

Ladies of a different sort are the focus of three studies which reflect the revisionist interest in the nexus of women and race. Glenn Cannon Arbery in "Victims of Likeness: Quadroons and Octoroons in Southern Fiction" (*SoR* 25:52–71) argues that Stowe, Cable, and Longfellow ("The Quadroon Girl") unwittingly encouraged readers to participate vicariously in the exploitation of women of mixed race. That seems true; what is less convincing is Arbery's argument that the whiter the women looked, the more obvious it was that they were "already damned" as the products of multi-generational sexual transgression—and hence "more powerfully subject to victimization." In a related study, Anna Shannon Elfenbein in *Women on the Color Line* uses selected texts by Cable, Grace King, and Kate Chopin to argue that they were using their fictional examinations of the plight of mixed-race women to illuminate the plight of white women. This is an old argument (critics have been saying it for years about Stowe), and Elfenbein breathes no new life into it. Much more incisive is Helen Taylor's *Gender, Race, and Region*. British critic Taylor is more willing to explore the biographical bases of the ambivalences of King, Chopin, and Ruth McEnery Stuart, who were not so naive as to think that shared gender could override differences in race and social class. Taylor's analysis is insightful and mature, though one wishes she had looked at more than just three women, all of them from Louisiana.

Other books devoted to Southern literature evinced less interest in gender and race. Louis D. Rubin, Jr., in *The Edge of the Swamp* focuses on Simms, Poe, and Henry Timrod to determine why the antebellum South produced so few writers of permanent reputation during the American Renaissance. The key may well have been slavery, which effectively cut the South off from "the larger world of letters"—a world into which Poe, by divorcing his work from Southern politics and history, was able to enter freely. His book's title notwithstanding, Rubin has little interest in the Southern swamp as reality or metaphor; but it is the primary focus of David C. Miller's *Dark Eden*. Miller examines the ways in which the romantic ideals of landscape gave way at mid-century to a nationwide fascination with swamps and jungles, wild terrains which defied conventional ideas of the picturesque and challenged the belief that landscapes imparted moral lessons. Chockablock with illustrations and even color plates, this book offers sharp observations on the painters, illustrators, and writers—including Stowe, Simms, and Sidney Lanier—who used these exotic terrains to comment on American society. A more limited study in a similar vein is Jan Bakker's *Pastoral in Antebellum Southern Romance* (LSU), which looks at the traditions of the pastoral and the "inverted pastoral" in works by such authors as John Pendleton Kennedy, William Alexander Caruthers, and John Esten Cooke. Though it seems true that these antithetical responses to landscape underlie their writings, Bakker's concentration on the antebellum period precludes the possibility of seeing how these antitheses affected later Southern writers who had seen their landscape literally destroyed by war. A good study to be considered in conjunction with Bakker's is Lawrence Buell's "American Pastoral Ideology Reappraised" (*AmLH* 1:1–29), which argues that the motifs underlying this ideology are "too complex to permit monolithic categorization of most texts either as consensual or anticonsensual documents."

Landscape also figured prominently in other studies. Robert Thacker's *The Great Prairie Fact and Literary Imagination* is an uneven multicentury look at the prairies and at the writers, historians, and painters who attempted to convey the prairie scene. Except for Cooper, most 19th-century writers unfortunately receive scant coverage, and much of that is plot-heavy. Scholars with a broader interest in "frontier" as both a physical and cultural entity may wish to look at *The Frontier Experience and the American Dream*. Depending on one's tastes, the book is either compromised lamentably or enriched significantly by the protean nature of "frontier," as the many essayists commenting on it invoke figures as varied as Anne Bradstreet and Sam Peckinpah. Nineteenth-century specialists will probably want to read this collection selectively, focusing on such essays as James K. Folsom's "Imaginative Safety Valves: Frontier Themes in the Literature of the Gilded Age" (pp. 87–94). Folsom argues that the West during this period was perceived as embodying quintessentially American values that had been abandoned by the East.

Two quite different books round out the year's work. Allan Gardner Lloyd-Smith in *Uncanny American Fiction* takes a psychoanalytical approach to supernaturalism in American literature, beginning with Brockden Brown. Though his primary focus is on such recognized authors of the uncanny as Poe, Hawthorne, Wharton, and James,

Lloyd-Smith does provide some commentary on William Dean Howells ("A Sleep and a Forgetting"), Charlotte Perkins Gilman ("The Yellow Wallpaper"), and Ambrose Bierce ("The Death of Halpin Frayser"), plus scattered references to Emma Dawson, Frank Norris, and the like. Lloyd-Smith's readings of individual texts, though occasionally suggestive, have less value than his broader effort to define the uncanny by exploring its myriad manifestations (gothic, romantic, transcendental, psychological, symbolic). For those with a particular interest in writers of the haunted dusk, *Uncanny American Fiction* is a valuable study. Even more impressive is a book which seems destined to become a classic: David Leverenz's *Manhood and the American Renaissance*. A deft examination of what it took to be a "man"—or a "woman," for that matter—in the minds of 19th-century writers, it offers a sensible, sensitive study of gender issues as they affected writers of both sexes.

ii. Cooper, Simms, Irving, and Contemporaries

Inasmuch as 1989 marked the bicentennial of his birth, Cooper received an unusually large amount of scholarly attention, much of it quite good. The entire Winter issue (20, iii) of the *Canadian Review of American Studies* is given over to him, seven of the 10 essays having been presented originally at the 1989 Cooper Seminar at Oneonta. Not all are worthwhile, but a few stand out. Donald Darnell in "Cooper's Problematic Pilot: 'Unrighteous Ambition' in a Patriotic Cause" (pp. 47–55) argues that Cooper's ambivalent rendering of John Paul Jones in *The Pilot* reflects his personal mistrust of ambition in men of less-than-genteel birth. Donald A. Ringe in "Cooper Today: A Partisan View" (pp. 21–34) traces how the responses of critics and literary historians to Cooper have reflected different historical and intellectual biases. In the 1930s and 1940s, for example, he was perceived primarily as a social commentator. And Richard Morton in "The Double Chronology of Leatherstocking" (pp. 77–95) puts a few new spins on the old chestnut of whether the tales should be read in their order of publication or according to the age of Natty Bumppo. Maybe, says Morton, there is a third way of reading them, one that seeks out "large, informing patterns" in the two possible chronologies. Morton's ideas regarding intertextuality and prequels are especially valuable.

The other studies devoted to the Leatherstocking tales were wide-ranging in approach and quality. Thomas Hill Schaub in " 'Cut in

Plain Marble': The Language of the Tomb in *The Pioneers*" (*The Green American Tradition,* pp. 58–74) considers the implications of Natty's inability to read the inscriptions on the tombstones of Major Effingham and Chingachgook in the last scene of the novel. He argues that Cooper felt ours had become "a nation of words alienated from the original meanings of the New World's possibilities." Schaub's is a thoughtful, sobering reading of the novel. Also attentive to words is Cynthia S. Jordan in "Two Sides to Every Story: Cooper's *The Last of the Mohicans*" (*Second Stories,* pp. 110–32). Jordan feels that Cooper explores power and gender by playing off "feminine" Indian speech against "patriarchal" white man's speech. Even the fundamentally honest Natty responds to politicized language, declining to translate Indian statements that white men could never understand. It is a provocative analysis which qualifies the more sentimental readings of Natty. Also worth noting is Leland S. Person, Jr.'s "Cooper's Queen of the Woods: Judith Hutter in *The Deerslayer*" (*SNNTS* 21:253–67). Person feels critics have "overemphasized Judith's adversarial role as part of an Adam-Eve dichotomy." Not really a coquettish would-be despoiler of Natty, Judith seeks to marry him so as to identify herself positively with the land. Cooper's women also are a prime concern of Alide Cagidemetrio in "A Plea for Fictional Histories and Old-Time 'Jewesses,'" pp. 14–43 in Werner Sollors, ed., *The Invention of Ethnicity* (Oxford). Unfortunately, there is little new in Cagidemetrio's look at the Walter Scott/Cooper connection or the sexual/racial issues underlying Cooper's treatment of Alice and Cora Munro. A final discussion of the Leatherstocking tales appears in Thacker's *The Great Prairie Fact and Literary Imagination.* Alas, his observation that Cooper took liberties with his sources in creating *The Prairie* has long been known.

The bicentennial Cooper explosion also generated studies of his less-known writings. Ernest H. Redekop in "Real versus Imagined History: Cooper's European Novels" (*Mosaic* 22, iv:81–97) looks at *The Bravo, The Headsman, The Wing-and-Wing,* and *The Heidenmauer* in relation to theories of historical fiction expounded by Henry James and Frank Kermode on the one hand, and by Alessandro Manzoni on the other. It's an engaging analysis which raises good points about Cooper and about historical fiction as a genre. Likewise provocative is Robert S. Levine's reading of *The Bravo* in chapter 2 of his *Conspiracy and Romance.* Levine argues that Cooper perceived himself as a "Republican Jeremiah" charged with warning Americans of the British government's conspiracy "to divide the Union so as to regain control over its former colony." This stance, according to Levine, even affected Cooper's writing style in the novel, most notably the use of an "authoritative omniscient narrator" who, like Cooper, "knows all and reveals all." Less convincing is Emily Miller Budick's reading of *The Spy* in her *Fiction and Historical Consciousness*. That novel, argues Budick, shows Cooper swerving away from "the real world" of the British novel in favor of the "neutral ground of exaggerated melodrama." Perhaps. Meanwhile, Louis S. Gross in *Redefining the American Gothic* argues that *Lionel Lincoln* integrates elements of the Gothic and the historical romance in a parable of a young man coming to grips with the burden of the past.

A final 1989 study involving Cooper is Thomas S. Gladsky's "Jerzy Kosinski: The Polish Cooper" (*NConL* 19, ii:11–12). Gladsky points out that the many references to Cooper in Kosinski's *The Hermit of 69th Street* are meant to reflect his sense of himself as a patriotic but misunderstood critic of Poland, much as Cooper in the late 1830s was a patriotic but misunderstood critic of changes in American life.

Compared to Cooper, William Gilmore Simms received scant attention in 1989, but it was uniformly good. Mary Ann Wimsatt's *The Major Fiction of William Gilmore Simms: Cultural Traditions and Literary Form* (LSU) offers a judicious blend of biography, history, economics, and literary criticism in a sympathetic study of a man whose career was a microcosm of the literary life in the antebellum South. His personal knowledge of the Tidewater, Piedmont, and Gulf South, his ambivalent relationships with Northerners, and his desperate response to the Panic of 1837 (including the abandonment of long novels in favor of more marketable histories and magazine pieces) render him an ideal figure for understanding the plight of the man of letters in the South. An essential book for Simmsians, Wimsatt's study also is a model of how best to approach the career of an admittedly secondary writer whose output was voluminous—and shockingly uneven. Rubin covers some of the same ground, albeit necessarily much more sketchily, in his *The Edge of the Swamp*, which complements Wimsatt's book in his extended discussion of Simms's relationship with disgraced politician James Henry Hammond and in his sensitive reading of Simms's novel *The Yemassee* vis-à-vis Cooper's novels. Rubin argues that *The Yemassee* embodies Simms's conviction that demonstrated ability, and not just high birth, should be the entrée into respectable society.

Scholarship devoted to Washington Irving was less impressive. The one outstanding item is Edwin T. Bowden's *Washington Irving: Bibliography* (Twayne). At more than 760 pages it significantly builds on comparable efforts by Langfeld and Blackburn (1933), Williams and Edge (1936), and Blanck's *Bibliography of American Literature* (1969); the section on *Salmagundi* alone takes 83 pages. A comprehensive record of both Irving's "Original Works" and "Contributions to Other Books," it is essential for any Irving scholar. The charms of the other Irving studies in 1989 are not always so visible. Charles E. May in "Metaphoric Motivation in Short Fiction: 'In the Beginning Was the Story,'" pp. 62–73 in *Short Story Theory at a Crossroads*, argues that "The Legend of Sleepy Hollow," although "realistically motivated to embody a social theme, is really about the triumph of the story world over that of the practical." In a similar fashion, R. Jackson Wilson in his *Figures of Speech* reads this story as a parable of Irving's decision to pursue a career as a writer, an occupation traditionally perceived as "marginalizing, almost feminizing." Wilson is more convincing when he focuses on biography instead of literature, tracing the myriad poses ("youthful dandy," "grief-stricken artist," etc.) assumed by Irving while he pursued—or pretended not to pursue—his literary career. It's an overlong but interesting study of one writer's search for a sense of authorization.

The scholarly work devoted to other writers of this period may be noted briefly. Ronald J. Zboray's "The Book Peddler and Literary Dissemination: The Case of Parson Weems" (*PubHist* 25:27–44) has as much to say about the transformation of book peddlers from distributors to subscription agents as it does about Weems. David Leverenz, meanwhile, looks at both Richard Henry Dana, Jr., and Francis Parkman in the "Hard, Isolate, Ruthless, and Patrician" chapter of his *Manhood and the American Renaissance*. Leverenz sees both writers as having appropriated "the entrepreneurial ideology of competitive dominance, along with a more general manly code of self-control, to stifle feelings of humiliation associated with their [sickly] bodies and their depressed patrician fathers." Leverenz sees Dana in particular as a twit, a heartless and friendless soul capable of having feelings only for those (such as a puppy) clearly inferior to him. Parkman, in contrast, admitted his weaknesses while pursuing a sense of manliness in the most self-destructive ways possible (such as hunting buffalo). Less lively but no less astute are two essays on Parkman as a historian. Daniel James Sundahl in "Cunning Corridors: Parkman's *LaSalle* as

Quest-Romance" (*CLQ* 25:109–24) argues that the book is extrinsi-
cally a history but intrinsically an "archetypal drama of self-identifi-
cation" set against the backdrop of "an American literary landscape."
Ellen Donovan in "Narrative Voices in Francis Parkman's *Montcalm
and Wolfe*" (*ClioI* 18:275–90) points out that Parkman as histori-
ographer tends to summarize official documents while quoting heavily
from individuals' personal responses to events.

Those interested in the Kentucky Tragedy will appreciate William
Goldhurst's "The New Revenge Tragedy: Comparative Treatments of
the Beauchamp Case" (*SLJ* 22:117–27). Goldhurst examines the literary renderings of the case by Poe, Simms, George Lippard, Thomas
Holley Chivers, and C. Fenno Hoffman. A good study within its limits,
it would be stronger if Goldhurst explored why—beyond matters of
writing style and temperament—these male authors reacted so differently to Ann Cooke, who had compelled her lover to murder her husband and then committed suicide as he awaited execution.

Finally, work continues to be done on Charles Sealsfield, the
Moravian-born monk who wrote so eloquently of the American frontier. In "Charles Sealsfield's *Images of Life from Both Hemispheres*: A
New Acquisition" (*YULG* 64, i–ii:66–72), Jeffrey L. Sammons describes the six-volume set at Yale, provides a brief sketch of the author's life, and concludes that Sealsfield was "a peculiar and rambunc-
tious" sort of author who knew well "just how offensive his writing
could be."

iii. Popular Writers of Mid-century: Women and Men, Prose and Poetry

Continuing the trend of recent years, the lion's share of interest in this
period still goes to women fiction writers, particularly Harriet Beecher
Stowe and Louisa May Alcott. Unfortunately, much Stowe scholarship of 1989 either covered familiar ground or failed to develop fully
some interesting new approaches. Steven Sarson in "Harriet Beecher
Stowe and American Slavery" (*NewComp* 7:33–45) questions why
Uncle Tom's Cabin, a book instrumental in achieving emancipation,
is anathema to slaves' descendants a century later. Sarson urges us to
consider the novel against the backdrop of cultural relativism: modern
blacks resent the Christlike passivity of slaves depicted by Stowe. This
is hardly a breakthrough. Meanwhile, Hortense J. Spillers does a comparison study (a comparison meditation, actually) of *Uncle Tom's*

Cabin and Ishmael Reed's *Flight to Canada* (1976) in "Changing the
Letter: The Yokes, The Jokes of Discourse; Or, Mrs. Stowe, Mr.
Reed" (*Slavery and the Literary Imagination*, pp. 25–61). Spillers
feels that "slavery" as a concept is *"primarily* discursive"; somehow
this leads to a Fiedleresque analysis of the sly sexuality of Little Eva
(Eva to Daddy re Tom: "I want him") and of Tom himself ("a potentially 'dirty old man'"). Spillers's ideas may have some validity,
but they are difficult to locate in all the verbiage.

But there was also some excellent work on Stowe in 1989. In his
double chapter on *Uncle Tom's Cabin* and Susan Warner's *The Wide,
Wide World,* David Leverenz in *Manhood and the American Renaissance* examines how Stowe's text offers a "matriarchal solution" to
slavery: if white men "can be brought to feel what any mother feels,"
they will end that peculiar institution. As Leverenz points out, this is
a "simplistic . . . fantasy" which chooses to ignore the reality of economics. Also interesting is Christina Zwarg's "Fathering and Blackface
in *Uncle Tom's Cabin*" (*Novel* 22:274–87), which examines the "feminist subversion inherent in [Stowe's] treatment of fatherhood and its
effects upon the 'home.'" Zwarg offers a sharp examination of Tom's
shifting paternal roles and the implications of what are essentially
blackface renderings of America's two white fathers, Washington and
Emerson. In a similar vein, Myra Jehlen in "The Family Militant:
Domesticity versus Slavery in *Uncle Tom's Cabin*" (*Criticism* 31:383–
400) argues that Stowe used the rhetoric of domesticity to urge men
to reaffirm the "right" conduct of society—one that readily accommo-
dates both sexism and racism within the social hierarchy of power and
property envisioned by the Founding Fathers. Such irony is bound
to make this a controversial addition to Stowe scholarship. More conservative is Lora Romero's "Bio-Political Resistance in Domestic
Ideology and *Uncle Tom's Cabin*" (*AmLH* 1:715–34). Romero feels
that Stowe was indeed criticizing patriarchal power, but doing so
through an insistence on spiritual health. Her thesis gains much from
the observation that Stowe's hysteria-induced eye problems in the
1840s rendered her unable to see details: the larger picture was all,
and the larger picture was what America needed to see as well.

Two books on Stowe also warrant notice. Theodore R. Hovet's
*The Master Narrative: Harriet Beecher Stowe's Subversive Story of
Master and Slave in* Uncle Tom's Cabin *and* Dred (Univ. Press) avers
that Stowe in both novels was working in accordance with a "master
narrative" recounting humanity's fall and redemption. The narrative

probably became familiar to Stowe via the 19th-century mystics, while its insistence on duality (black/white, slave/master) did much to explain "the endless cycle of oppression and revolution" which characterized slavery in the United States. The other book on Stowe is John R. Adams's updating of his 1963 Twayne volume (TUSAS 42). Always one of the better Twayne volumes, it now reflects more recent scholarship involving feminist concerns, racial issues, and "high-level literary theory that staggers the imagination."

In contrast to Stowe, most of the scholarly work devoted to Alcott in 1989 did not focus on one work. The essay that concentrated most squarely on *Little Women* is Angela M. Estes and Kathleen Margaret Lant, "Dismembering the Text: The Horror of Louisa May Alcott's *Little Women*" (*ChildL* 17:98–123), which argues that Alcott had to repress images of self-reliant female characters to ensure publication; hence Jo March, so independent and strong-willed for much of the novel, had to be "destroyed" and replaced by the dead Beth. The analysis, unfortunately, is undercut by repetition and melodramatic writing. Beverly Lyon Clark's "A Portrait of the Artist as a Little Woman" (*ChildL* 17:81–97) is a less-inspired essay which argues that "little women" may write for self-therapy or income, but never for anything so crass as self-expression. And James D. Wallace's "Where the Absent Father Went: Alcott's *Work*," pp. 259–74 in *Refiguring the Father*, posits *Work* as Alcott's "provocative analysis of the disappearance of the father into linguistic abstraction."

The year's two outstanding studies of Alcott are an essay and a book. Jean Pfaelzer's "The Sentimental Promise and the Utopian Myth: Rebecca Harding Davis's 'The Harmonists' and Louisa May Alcott's 'Transcendental Wild Oats'" (*ATQ* n.s. 3:85–99) argues that Alcott and Davis used these texts to challenge "male hegemony as a utopian alternative. When radical men presume to define domestic needs, the results are at best absurd and, in the end, dangerous." It is practical, hard-working women who enable utopian communities to function at all—a fact which suggests the dire consequences of women's exclusion from 19th-century business and politics. Alcott scholars will want to look at Pfaelzer's essay, but they will want to buy the sensibly priced *Journals of Louisa May Alcott*, judiciously edited by Joel Myerson and Daniel Shealy (Little, Brown). Alcott kept diaries from August 1843 (age 10) until the month she died; at various junctures she summarized the entries in journals, and still later revised the summaries. The *Journals* volume reproduces all extant materials, restoring what Ednah Dow Cheney had deleted from her 1889 memoir of Alcott, and occasionally conflating entries from the daily diaries and the journals "to show a continuous chronological record of Alcott's life and career." In a thoughtful 36-page introduction, associate editor Madeleine B. Stern maintains that Alcott baldly saw her writings as both cathartic and remunerative.

Work devoted to other mid-century women writers is notable for both quality and diversity. Stridently different readings of *The Wide, Wide World* are offered by David Leverenz and Nancy Schnog. Leverenz, in the previously mentioned chapter on Stowe and Warner, argues that the latter's novel "preaches patriarchal submission and dramatizes solitude." Its subtext is that a woman must have the strength to break her own will, and that Christianity provides that strength: the goal is "masochism, not spiritual empowerment." In contrast, Schnog in "Inside the Sentimental: The Psychological Work of *The Wide Wide World*" (*Genders* 4:11–25) avers that the stylistic excesses of Warner's novel, including artesian weeping, are less a wallowing in sentimentality than an acknowledgment of the intense emotional bonds that existed between women in the 19th century—plus a strategy (albeit more emotional than rational) for dealing with life crises. Women therefore were not "the duped buyers of a system of belief that exacted their submission or obedience."

No such controversy reigns in scholarship devoted to other women writers of the period. Lydia Maria Child is among many authors accorded chapters in Jean Fagan Yellin's *Women and Sisters: The Anti-Slavery Feminists in American Culture* (Yale). Though there are no searing insights in Yellin's analysis of Child, it does provide an appreciative look at the Tragic Mulatto figure in her writings. Carolyn L. Karcher offers two studies of Child. In "From Pacifism to Armed Struggle: L. M. Child's 'The Kansas Emigrants' and Antislavery Ideology in the 1850's" (*ESQ* 34[1988]:141–58), she analyzes Child's short story as a call for violent action in the cause of abolition. It is an astute if mechanical study of the political crises that impelled Child to return to active abolitionism after a decade "on the sidelines." Karcher's "Lydia Maria Child's *A Romance of the Republic*: An Abolitionist Vision of America's Racial Destiny," pp. 81–103 in *Slavery and the Literary Imagination*, examines that novel's advocacy of interracial marriage as a means of ultimately eliminating racial categories—and injustice. Child, believes Karcher, endorsed the idea intellectually but could not quite free herself imaginatively from "the genteel canons of white middle-class culture."

Two writers less known than Child were accorded book-length studies in 1989. Patricia D. Maida's *Mother of Detective Fiction: The Life and Works of Anna Katharine Green* (Bowling Green) is a slim book about the writer whose novel *The Leavenworth Case* established her as the first important American practitioner of the detective story since Poe. Though Maida makes some effort to place Green's achievement within the contexts of feminism (including her unconventional marriage) and the European tradition of detective literature, this book is essentially a sketchy introduction to a very complex writer. Far more impressive is Shirley Marchalonis's sensitive, mature, gracefully written biography *The Worlds of Lucy Larcom, 1824–1893* (Georgia). Based on extensive original research (including some 2,000 letters), it makes no extravagant claims for Larcom as writer or editor. Rather, Marchalonis is concerned with the complexities of Larcom's situation as a talented 19th-century woman afflicted by psychosomatic illness, torn between the financial security of teaching and the need to write, and ambivalent about her (strictly platonic) relationship with her mentor Whittier.

Work devoted to other women writers may be noted briefly. Mary Suzanne Schriber in "Julia Ward Howe and the Travel Book" (*NEQ* 62:264–79) considers the difficulties Howe faced in pursuing a career as a travel writer, not only because the market was glutted, but because both her husband and her father opposed her career. Alfred Bendixen brings together 10 tales by Harriet Prescott Spofford in *The Amber Gods and Other Stories* (Rutgers). Bendixen's introductory essay is especially valuable for suggesting Spofford's capacity to work within traditionally male literary forms, such as the symbolic romance. Helena Michie in " 'Dying Between Two Laws': Girl Heroines, Their Gods, and Their Fathers in *Uncle Tom's Cabin* and the *Elsie Dinsmore* Series," pp. 188–206 in *Refiguring the Father*, is a Lacanian study which offers more insights into Martha Finley's "Elsie" books than it does into Stowe. Unlike Eva, Elsie survives because she can create a "private world into which the world only intrudes to be absorbed." David Leverenz looks at both Sarah Hale and Caroline Kirkland in chapter 5 of his *Manhood and the American Renaissance*. Hale, argues Leverenz, used the *Godey's Lady's Book* to send a double message to her female readers: "I am utterly done to [by men],

I am utterly superior [to men]." And Kirkland's "pervasive self-consciousness about writing to sophisticated people about a low subject" (i.e., pioneer life) renders her "more the Erma Bombeck than the Willa Cather of the frontier."

A handful of male literary figures received scholarly attention. That poet Frederick Goddard Tuckerman was more concerned with literary success than is usually recognized is evident from a newly discovered 1864 letter; see Jeffrey D. Groves, "A Letter from Frederick Goddard Tuckerman to James T. Fields" (*HLQ* 52:403–08). The impact of Charles Dickens's death on Fields—and, less dramatically, on his wife Annie—is examined in Jerome Meckier's " 'A World without Dickens!': James T. to Annie Fields, 10 June 1870" (*HLQ* 52:409–14.) And devotees of Horatio Alger will appreciate the new bibliographical entries provided by Victor A. Berch in "Further Additions and Corrections to Horatio Alger's Short Stories and Poetry" (*DNR* 58:54–62).

Just three of the Fireside Poets maintained interest in 1989. Albert F. McLean updated his Twayne volume on Bryant (TUSAS 59), adding a chapter on the travel literature and incorporating references to studies which appeared since it was first published in 1964. Gary Scharnhorst published two minor Longfellow letters ("Longfellow and Europe: Two Uncollected Letters," *ANQ* n.s. 2:53–54), and Edward J. Piacentino reprinted an anonymous 1845 rejoinder to charges that Longfellow had committed plagiarism in *The Waif* ("The Poe-Longfellow Plagiarism Controversy: A New Critical Notice in *The Southern Chronicle*," *MissQ* 42:173–82). Oliver Wendell Holmes, meanwhile, is one of the authors Louis S. Gross examines in *Redefining the American Gothic*. Gross's usually perceptive reading of *Elsie Venner* is limited by his disinclination to consider the meaning of Holmes's killing off the female protagonist in this "startlingly feminist text."

iv. Humorists and Southern Writers

Humorists of the South and West had a good year in 1989. David C. Estes edited *A New Collection of Thomas Bangs Thorpe's Sketches of the Old Southwest* (LSU), which brings together 38 items by Thorpe arranged in order of publication. Estes also offers a lengthy biocritical essay on Thorpe and the checkered publishing history of his writings, plus an extensive "Textual Apparatus" section which compiles, for example, post-copy-text substantive variants. This is destined to be the definitive text for Thorpe scholars.

Davy Crockett is the subject of a rich and unusually wide-ranging collection of essays, *Crockett at Two Hundred: New Perspectives on the Man and the Myth*, edited by Michael A. Lofaro and Joe Cummings (Tennessee). In "Crockett and Nineteenth-Century Music" (pp. 83–96), Charles K. Wolfe examines how the Crockett mystique has been presented musically in everything from the 1830s minstrel tune "Pompey Smash" to Bing Crosby's 1955 recording of "Farewell to the Mountains." In "Cats, Coons, Crocketts, and Other Furry Critters: Or, Why Davy Wears an Animal for a Hat" (pp. 153–78), John Seelye traces the popular image of Crockett to the Wild Man of European tradition. Crockett, notes Seelye, embodies both aspects of the Wild Man, the chivalric child of nature and the "bodaciously bad-mannered" yahoo. For lagniappe, there are plenty of illustrations in this book, plus an excellent bibliography of Crockett letters, legal documents, songs, poems, etc.

Another figure who is enjoying critical attention, albeit due largely to the efforts of one pioneering scholar, is Western humorist Dan De Quille (born William Wright). A former roommate and probable mentor of Mark Twain, De Quille was the chronicler of the Comstock era (*The Big Bonanza*), a respected Nevada journalist—and a shameless perpetrator of hoaxes. Lawrence I. Berkove has been diligently examining De Quille's achievement and reprinting his tales and sketches in such articles as "Dan De Quille's Narratives of Ohio: 'Lorenzo Dow's Miracle' " (*NOQ* 60[1988]:47–56); "Dan De Quille's Narratives of Ohio: Four Sketches" (*NOQ* 61:3–12); "De Quille Sells a Christmas Story" (*Palimpsest* 69[1988]:186–90); and "Iowa Pioneers Find a Lost Child: A Dan De Quille Memoir" (*Palimpsest* 69 [1988]:120–31). Berkove also looks at De Quille's rising anti-Semitism during the depression of 1893 in "Free Silver and Jews: The Change in Dan De Quille" (*American Jewish Archives* 41:43–51) and reprints a cache of letters exchanged between De Quille and Twain in the belatedly published " 'Nobody Writes to Anybody Except to Ask a Favor': New Correspondence Between Mark Twain and Dan De Quille" (*MTJ* 26, i[1988]:2–21). Berkove brings together his extensive knowledge of De Quille in his excellent "Biographical and Critical Introduction" to the De Quille novella *Dives and Lazarus* (Ardis [1988]). De Quille's stock appears to be rising. Richard A. Dwyer and Richard E. Lingenfelter have collected his Nevada sketches in *Dan De Quille, The Washoe Giant: A Biography and Anthology* (Nevada). Scholars with a general interest in hoaxes and tall tales will want to look at Henry B. Wonham's "In the Name of Wonder: The Emergence of Tall Narrative in American Writing" (*AQ* 41: 284–307).

Southern nonhumorists were particularly well served in 1989. As noted, Louis D. Rubin, Jr., devotes much of his *The Edge of the Swamp* to a consideration of Henry Timrod, the "Great Might Have Been in the literary history of the Old South." Under the pressure of the Civil War, argues Rubin, Timrod changed suddenly from a self-consciously "elevated" and unmoving writer into a powerful poet capable of devising brilliant imagery (often couched in bluntly economic terms) to transmute his private sensibility into a deeply meaningful public one. That Timrod is not better known is explained readily: he was the poet laureate of "the losing side." Sidney Lanier, meanwhile, is the subject of R. S. Gwynn's "Looking for Sidney" (*Shenandoah* 39:57–67). Though his point is well-taken that even as a former Union prisoner Lanier never mentions the Civil War in his poems, Gwynn is primarily interested not in him but in Andrew Hudgins, who used Lanier as his persona in the 1988 dramatic monologue *After the Lost War.*

Southern fiction writers receiving more extensive attention included George W. Cable, Grace King, and Ruth McEnery Stuart. Anna Shannon Elfenbein in *Women on the Color Line* is a good explicator, but she strains to prove that, for example, Cable's interest in female characters of mixed race was somehow indicative of his personal commitment to women's rights. His erotic response to dark ladies would suggest the situation was far more problematic. Equally unconvincing is Philip A. Tapley's " 'Dropped Upon a Strange Planet': Racial Identity Crises in *Madame Delphine* and *Pudd'nhead Wilson*" (*UMSE* n.s. 7:168–79), which argues that Cable's "influence upon Twain's mind and work can be seen quite strikingly in *Pudd'nhead Wilson.*" Much of Tapley's essay is little more than plot rehash and the usual statements regarding uncertain racial identity in both men's writings. Cable and several others in his circle are mentioned in passing in Judith H. Bonner's "*Arts and Letters*: An Illustrated Periodical of Nineteenth-Century New Orleans" (*SoQ* 27, ii:58–76).

Grace King received lengthy analyses in Elfenbein's *Women on the Color Line* and Taylor's *Gender, Race, and Region.* Elfenbein argues that in King's fictional world of the defeated South, black and white

males are inept or absent, leaving women of both races to struggle together to survive. Taylor is more sensitive to the nuances of King's
temperament, which had been molded by her superior social status.
Taylor also offers astute commentary on a much less-known writer,
Ruth McEnery Stuart, who is remembered (if at all) for "charming"
stories peopled with blacks and whites living harmoniously in a care-
free antebellum world. But Taylor rightly detects an edge to Stuart's
writings in which, for example, "feminized" black men are depicted
in positions of powerlessness. The complexities of Stuart's case suggest she is a writer who warrants further attention by feminist revisionist scholars.

Finally, John Pendleton Kennedy (*Horse-Shoe Robinson*) and
William Alexander Caruthers (*The Knights of the Golden Horse-shoe*)
are the focus of Ritchie D. Watson's "Frontier Yeoman versus Cavalier: The Dilemma of Antebellum Southern Fiction," pp. 107–19 in
The Frontier Experience. Watson uses these two novels to make a
case that running counter to the South's Walter Scott-spawned self-
image as a courtly aristocracy was an image grounded in the tradition
of the yeoman farmer. This is a solid analysis which indicates that the
cavalier mentality of the antebellum South was not as monolithic as
commentators would have us believe.

v. Post-Civil War Women Writers

Sarah Orne Jewett, Mary E. Wilkins Freeman, Kate Chopin, and
Charlotte Perkins Gilman continue to be the dominant figures,
though the quality of work devoted to them was uneven. One of
the best studies is Sarah Way Sherman's *Sarah Orne Jewett: An
American Persephone* (New England). It actually is a helical study:
one strand examines the rise of interest in alternative (especially
matriarchal) religions in the late 19th century, while the other is a
solid critical biography of Jewett set against that theological background. Sherman's book does much to rescue Jewett from the nether-
world of local-color sentimentality, while confirming the need to approach women writers of this period from a firmer grounding in their
cultural milieu. Sherman's ideas would have enhanced the thinking
of Diane D'Amico in "The Significance of the Dunnet Shepherdess to
Jewett's Matriarchal Christianity" (*UDR* 20:33–38). D'Amico feels
that Esther Hight of *The Country of the Pointed Firs* is "a type of
female Good Shepherd" who replaces the late Mrs. Blackett as the

"Christ-Mother" of Jewett's matriarchal world. A more theoretical approach to the novel is offered by Sivagami Subbaraman in "Rites of Passage: Narratorial Plurality as Structure in Jewett's *The Country of the Pointed Firs*" (*CentR* 33:60–74). Subbaraman avers that there are "interlacings" between the embedded narratives and the main narrative," as opposed to the more rigid web model advocated by Elizabeth Ammons. Jewettites with more interest in biography would glean little from Judith Fryer's "What Goes on in the Ladies Room? Sarah Orne Jewett, Annie Fields, and Their Community of Women" (*MR* 30:610–28), primarily a study of the "Boston marriage" as a social institution.

Freeman, meanwhile, was the subject of two interesting essays. Lorne Fienberg in "Mary E. Wilkins Freeman's 'Soft Diurnal Commotion': Women's Work and Strategies of Containment" (*NEQ* 62: 483–504) examines several of Freeman's less-known stories so as to codify her characters' disparate responses to housework. Though attention to minor stories is welcome, Fienberg's study is too brief to generate many fresh insights into either Freeman or 19th-century domestic economy. On the other hand, Robert M. Luscher offers a fine study of a late, little-known story collection in "Seeing the Forest for the Trees: The 'Intimate Connection' of Mary Wilkins Freeman's *Six Trees*" (*ATQ* n.s. 3:363–81). Deeply symbolic and mystical, these six experimental stories "constitute a small Emersonian forest amid the seemingly barren terrain of Freeman's spiritual landscape." They suggest that Freeman was less a protorealist than a mystic akin to Jewett— a mind-set she felt she had to repress earlier in her career when " 'I was forced to consider selling qualities.' "

Studies devoted to Chopin were more numerous but less rewarding. One of the best is Virginia M. Kouidis's "Prison into Prism: Emerson's 'Many-Colored Lenses' and the Woman Writer of Early Modernism," pp. 115–34 in *The Green American Tradition*. Though the bulk of the essay deals with other writers, it begins with a consideration of the implications of Edna Pontellier of *The Awakening* falling asleep over a volume of Emerson. Kouidis feels that Emerson would have been a double-edged guide for a would-be liberated woman, since most of his writings are grounded in an androcentric value system that advocated passivity and marriage for women. One of the few Emerson texts that could have helped her is "Experience," which confirms the need to find one's true self. Perhaps, muses Kouidis, Edna chose the wrong text—a choice that may indirectly have led her to suicide. Far less convincing is Dorothy Goldman's "Kate Chopin's *The*

Awakening: 'Casting Aside That Fictitious Self,' " pp. 48–65 in *The Modern American Novella*. The first half looks at the technical importance of the story's being presented as a novella; the second half muses on Edna's death, which Goldman reads as a suicidal response to her inability to remove the "scars" of her past history. More upbeat but no more persuasive is the reading of Sandra M. Gilbert and Susan Gubar in *Sexchanges*, volume II of their *No Man's Land*. They see Chopin's story as a parable of how one New Orleans matron chose to dedicate her life to the prototypical New Woman, Venus/Aphrodite, and joined her in her oceanic realm. That's a lot to hang on the technicality that Chopin never really *says* Edna dies. Meanwhile, Margit Stange in "Personal Property: Exchange Value and the Female Self in *The Awakening*" (*Genders* 5:106–19) uses the description of Edna's hands and rings in the opening scene to argue that the story examines the "sexual exchange value" of women. That sounds right; but Stange mars her analysis by claiming that Edna's husband "obediently" drops her rings into her hand. Obviously, Edna is "obediently" putting out her hand to receive what her husband compels her to accept.

Studies that went beyond *The Awakening* were more rewarding. As noted, *Gender, Race, and Region* and *Women on the Color Line* deal at length with Chopin, with the former especially valuable for shedding light on how Chopin could create strong female characters while declining to participate in organized feminist movements. A final study of Chopin is Susan Lohafer's "Preclosure and Story Processing," pp. 249–75 in *Short Story Theory at a Crossroads*. Lohafer surveyed 180 readers, from high school students to graduate students, to see which sentences could serve as the final one in Chopin's story "Aunt Lympy's Interference." Though the study has more to say about fictional theory and pedagogy than it does about the story, it does suggest the technical complexity of Chopin's writing.

An increased attention to technical complexity, narrative discourse, and reader response is likewise the hallmark of studies devoted to Gilman, although too often they fail to range much beyond these matters. Jeannette King and Pam Morris in "On Not Reading between the Lines: Models of Reading in 'The Yellow Wallpaper' " (*SSF* 26: 23–32) argue that "the narrative discourse does not create a unified, autonomous subject. . . . There is therefore everything to be gained from an espousal of openness." In a similar vein, Richard Feldstein proposes that Gilman chose to write a story resistant to clear interpretation ("Reader, Text, and Ambiguous Referentiality in 'The Yellow

Wall Paper,' " pp. 269–79 in *Feminism and Psychoanalysis*). According to Feldstein, the text is "an ambiguous, doubled referent, cast in the interrogative mode, a gestalt of changing patterns." That's a lot to build on the observation that the text spells "wall paper" three different ways. Doubleness is also at issue in Barbara Johnson's contribution to the collection, "Is Female to Male as Ground Is to Figure?" (pp. 255–68). Observes Johnson, "in the end we don't know which side of the paper she is on, and hence, we no longer know quite where to locate *ourselves*." Less abstract is Catherine Golden's "The Writing of 'The Yellow Wallpaper': A Double Palimpsest" (*SAF* 17:193–201), which makes the case that various elements in the story (including Gilman's use of pronouns) betoken "a positive change in self-presentation precisely at the point when [the narrator's] actions dramatically compromise her sanity and condemn her to madness." That's a nice ironic touch, but what are the implications—for her, for Gilman, for society—of this "dubious victory"? All this attention to "The Yellow Wallpaper" leads Susan S. Lanser to observe that there is a "profound unity in white, American feminist criticism across apparent diversity," a monolithic response which has reduced "the text's complexity to what we need most: our image reflected back to us" as white middle-class academics unable to respond to the racial implications of "yellow" (as in "yellow peril") wallpaper ("Feminist Criticism, 'The Yellow Wall Paper,' and the Politics of Color in America," *FSt* 15:415–41).

Some scholars have attempted to go beyond that text in their studies of Gilman, albeit not appreciably further than her utopian novels. Marsha A. Smith in "The Disoriented Male Narrator and Societal Conversion: Charlotte Perkins Gilman's Feminist Utopian Vision" (*ATQ* n.s. 3:123–33) points out that males narrate Gilman's utopian novels. This manipulation of perspective confirms that a reformed society requires New Men as well as New Women. In the same issue of *ATQ*, David Bleich in "Sexism and the Discourse of Perfection" (pp. 11–25) bemoans Gilman's brand of "utopian discourse," including maudlin speeches, sentimentality, and "tired bucolic images" of young girls skipping through forests. No doubt Bleich is correct that this style renders the text of *Herland* "unconsciously conciliatory with the values it opposes," but that doesn't explain why Gilman chose to use it. Part of the answer may be found in *Sexchanges*, wherein Gilbert and Gubar examine *Herland* against the backdrop of shifting male/female roles (pp. 71–82).

The broad range of Gilman scholarship is evident in the essay collection *Charlotte Perkins Gilman: The Woman and Her Work* (UMI Research Press), edited by Sheryl L. Meyering. Caveat emptor: 10 of the 14 essays are reprints, with only one from before 1979. The four original essays vary greatly. Linda Wagner-Martin's "Gilman's 'The Yellow Wallpaper': A Centenary" (pp. 51–64) offers a sensitive reading of the story's narrator as a "wife-mother" who regresses to the status of a child. K. Graehme Hall in "Mothers and Children: 'Rising with the Resistless Tide' in *Herland*" (pp. 161–71) discusses the sex—or lack thereof—in that novel. Sharon M. Rambo in "*What Diantha Did*: The Authority of Experience" (pp. 151–60) discusses that novel of "visionary housewifery" which sought to remove women from the drudgery of food preparation. And Maria Bruno in "Teaching 'Women in America': Some Notes on Pedagogy and Charlotte Perkins Gilman" (pp. 109–15) reports how she introduced women authors into a writing course.

Other female writers of the post-Civil War period clearly were over-shadowed by the Big Four, though some good work was done on them. Cheri L. Ross offers an engaging introduction to Marietta Holley in "Nineteenth-Century American Feminist Humor: Marietta Holley's 'Samantha Novels'" (*JMMLA* 22:12–25). Ross shows how the 21 novels ostensibly written by "Josiah Allen's wife" pioneered new dimensions "in both humor and feminist discourse." Susan Goodman's "Ella Rhoads Higginson (c. 1862–1940)" (*Legacy* 6, i:59–68) is a competent introduction to this forgotten writer of the Pacific Northwest and ardent activist. Rebecca Harding Davis receives intelligent scrutiny by Sharon M. Harris in "Rebecca Harding Davis: From Romanticism to Realism" (*ALR* 21, ii:4–20). Harris attempts to reconcile the conflicting critical appraisals of "Life in the Iron Mills"—grimly realistic, romantically hyperbolic, deterministic, sentimental—by examining its complex narrative structure and multiple levels of irony. It is an important contribution to studies of Davis, realism, and romanticism.

Work on four other women writers may be reviewed quickly. Cheryl B. Torsney provides a thoughtful critical biography of a once-popular novelist in *Constance Fenimore Woolson: The Grief of Artistry* (Georgia). Cynthia Griffin Wolff's "Emily Dickinson, Elizabeth Cady Stanton, and the Task of Discovering a Usable Past" (*MR* 30: 629–44) is largely an overview of women's lack of legal status in the 19th century, and has little to offer about Stanton or *The Woman's*

Bible. Anita T. Sullivan's "The Secret Garden" (*KR* 11:99–160) is a plodding meditation on how real memories tend to blur with details and events from literature—a problem which particularly affects "us bookish folks" who read Frances Hodgson Burnett. On the other hand, readers of Helen Hunt Jackson will treasure *Helen Hunt Jackson's Colorado*, edited by Joseph T. Gordon and Judith A. Pickle (published by the Hulbert Center for Southwestern Studies at Colorado College), which reprints six sketches from *Bits of Travel at Home* and features charming pen-and-ink drawings, plus an appreciative introduction by Gordon.

vi. The Howells Generation: Realism and Utopianism

The work devoted to William Dean Howells in 1989 was, for the most part, varied and lively. Particularly engaging is Martin Bucco's "*The Rise of Silas Lapham*: The Western Dimension" (*WAL* 23:291–310), which probes the "implied West" in the background of Howells's best-known "Boston novel." Bucco argues that its three Western loci—the Middle West, the Southwest (Texas), and Vermont (once the Wild Frontier, let us remember)—all impart amplitude to the novel while presenting "social and moral 'reality' on the grand and mutable American scale." Brenda Murphy looks at the same book in the esoterically titled "Howells and the Popular Story Paradigm: Reading *Silas Lapham*'s Proairetic Code" (*ALR* 21, ii:21–33). Murphy sees this novel as rejecting two popular 19th-century modes of literature, the rags-to-riches myth and the sentimental tale of self-sacrifice. Although there's nothing new in her argument that Howells was challenging the unrealistic conventions of popular literature, Murphy does reveal much about his methods of challenging them, including the use of four discrete levels of discourse. In contrast to Bucco and Murphy, Axel Knoenagel unimaginatively applies Howells's ideas about realism (as expressed in *Criticism and Fiction*) to *Silas Lapham* and *A Hazard of New Fortunes* in "The Artist as Critic as Artist: Howells's Realism in Criticism and Fiction" (*DR* 69:64–79).

Much stronger is John E. Bassett's "'A Heart of Ideality in My Realism': Howells's Early Criticism" (*PLL* 25:67–82). Bassett considers how Howells used the reviews and articles he wrote for the *Atlantic Monthly* to work through his positions on realism and the future of American literature; he seems to have felt that the "new" American novel would be a boy's life or a picaresque adventure.

Lawrence J. Oliver in "Brander Matthews and the Dean" (*ALR* 21, iii:25–40) examines Howells's long relationship with the professor, confirming that despite being sharply divided on U.S. imperialism and Ibsen, the two men ardently supported each other's work and mutually defended the rise of realism.

Finally, John W. Crowley's *The Mask of Fiction: Essays on W. D. Howells* (Mass.) brings together nine of Crowley's scholarly articles on Howells, eight of which appeared previously in books or journals. Heavily revised and grouped loosely within "gender issues" or "self-analysis," they are excellent pieces which work well together as a book. Several stand out. "Howells's Obscure Hurt" (pp. 17–34) probes his guilt over his failure to serve in the Civil War and his attempts to use his writings to assuage it. "Howells: The Ever-Womanly" (pp. 35–55) details his impulse to create admirable women characters— and his counterimpulse to denigrate women authors, whom he perceived as his competition. With a father like that, it is no surprise that his daughter Winny succumbed to "nervous prostration" (read "anorexia"): see "Winifred Howells and the Economy of Pain" (pp. 83–114).

Edward Bellamy also continues to generate thoughtful commentary. Virtual companion pieces are Merritt Abrash's "*Looking Backward*: Marxism Americanized" (*Extrapolation* 30:237–42) and Stephen Coleman's "The Economics of Utopia: Morris and Bellamy Contrasted" (*JWMS* 8, ii:2–6). While the ideas of both Marx and William Morris were vehemently rejected by Americans, the similar ones of Bellamy were embraced precisely because they had been "domesticated" to accommodate such familiar American activities as buying and selling (albeit with credit cards in lieu of cash). Similarly, Walter Benn Michaels in "An American Tragedy; Or, The Promise of American Life" (*Representations* 25:71–98) points out that the concept of the industrial army was designed to cater to the Yankee sense of individuality by offering ranks, rewards for outstanding service, and so on.

The special issue on American utopias in *ATQ* (n.s. 3, i) includes several fine essays on Bellamy. William J. Scheick in "The Letter Killeth: Edward Bellamy's 'To Whom This May Come'" (pp. 55–67) argues that in this late story Bellamy used language to "refute the cogency of language itself." He seems to have arrived at the conviction that language was inherently deceitful—and that his readers were focusing too readily on the words themselves rather than on the ideas

behind them. Less accessible is Richard Toby Widdicombe's " 'Dyna-
mite in Disguise': A Deconstructive Reading of Bellamy's Utopian
Novels" (pp. 69–84), which uses an "eclectic blend of American deconstruction and Gallic post-structuralism" to prove that *Looking
Backward* "fails as didactic literature." Maybe so, but it sure was
popular—as popular in the early 1890s as *The Wide, Wide World*,
which leads Kenneth M. Roemer to conclude that it succeeded precisely because it embodies features of sentimental literature ("The
Literary Domestication of Utopia," pp. 101–22). Between the sepa-
rated-lovers motif and a narrative voice which sounds suspiciously
like that of "hysterical female heroines" (remember Julian's unmanly
swooning?), Bellamy had produced a novel very familiar to America's
readers of sentimental fiction. Roemer's reading is sharp, as is that of
Susan M. Matarese in "Foreign Policy and the American Self-Image:
Looking Back at *Looking Backward*" (pp. 45–54). Matarese explores
the ambivalence underlying Bellamy's thought, which wobbled between a faith in America's messianic destiny to convert the world to
socioeconomic bliss—and a conviction that a nation as unique as ours
should be isolationist.

Work devoted to other writers of the period was less consistently
rewarding. Albion Tourgée was the subject of two fine essays. Brook
Thomas in "Tragedies of Race, Training, Birth, and Communities of
Competent Pudd'nheads" (*AmLH* 1:754–85) looks at Tourgée's novel
Pactolus Prime in relation to both Twain's novel and *Plessy* v. *Ferguson* (1896). Thomas makes a good case that Tourgée and Twain had
quite different attitudes toward racial inequality and the separate-
but-equal paradigm. Robert O. Stephens in "Tourgée's *Bricks without
Straw*: History, Fiction and Irony" (*SoQ* 27, iv:101–10) argues persuasively that Tourgée's ostensible lack of "art" in this novel reflects
a conscious subjection of art to the requirements of history: better to
use character types capable of conveying concrete ideas than fully
fleshed Howellsian individuals. Finally, *The Invisible Empire* has
been reissued in a facsimile reprint of the 1880 edition (LSU), with
an excellent introduction by Otto H. Olsen.

Hamlin Garland scholarship continues to be modest but steady.
Mark William Rocha published two interesting essays. In "The Bibliographer as Biographer: Accounting for the Unpublished Endings of
Hamlin Garland's Early Works" (*UMSE* n.s. 7:193–200), he offers
thoughtful commentary on the role of the bibliographer in understanding a writer's mind and career. His own research involving

Under the Wheel revealed two endings, including a happy wedding scene which suggests that optimistic humanism had always been a part of Garland's temperament, and not just late in his life. In "Hamlin Garland's Temperance Play" (*ALR* 21, iii:67–71), Rocha looks at *The Rise of Boomtown* as an attack not on alcoholics but on profiteering saloonkeepers. Other work on Garland includes Gary Scharnhorst's "Hamlin Garland and Feminism: An Early Essay Recovered" (*ANQ* n.s. 2, i:15–18), which reprints an 1889 essay confirming Garland's belief that single-tax reform would benefit women; and Thacker's discussion of *The Moccasin Ranch* in *The Great Prairie Fact and Literary Imagination*. Though his reading is not profound, it is refreshing to see interest in a forgotten novel. Thacker also provides a slight reading of Joseph Kirkland's *Zury: The Meanest Man in Spring County*. Much better served is Edgar Watson Howe in Steve Wiegenstein's "Naturalism, Literary History, and *The Story of a Country Town*" (*UMSE* n.s. 7:161–67). Taking his cue from Howe, who preferred the sentimental subplot of his novel to the "deterministic" main plot, Wiegenstein argues that *The Story of a Country Town* has been misread, and hence misclassified, as primarily a "pre-naturalistic" novel. Read aright, it is a more impressive book.

T. W. Higginson also was the subject of several essays. Sam Worley in "*Army Life in a Black Regiment* and Reconstruction" (*ESQ* 34 [1988]:159–79) sees the book as a "critical puzzle" which draws upon three different genres—the transcendental essay, the "Orientalist" travel book, and the war memoir—to pose the question of whether blacks were capable of functioning in a free labor economy. Mary Kemp Davis in "Arna Bontemps' *Black Thunder*: The Creation of an Authoritative Text of 'Gabriel's Defeat' " (*BALF* 23:17–36) examines how the story of Gabriel Prosser is told differently by Bontemps and Higginson. Davis feels that Bontemps, "in effect, overthrows Higginson, the benevolent retriever and keeper of the Gabriel Prosser tradition, just as the slaves sought to overthrow their masters." Though such political rhetoric is distracting, Davis actually offers a good analysis of how writers of different races treat the same racially charged material.

Work on other authors of the period may be reviewed quickly. Leslie Katz in "Flesh of His Flesh: Amputation in *Moby Dick* and S. W. Mitchell's Medical Papers" (*Genders* 4:1–10) would have us believe that the phantom limbs of S. Weir Mitchell's war-amputee patients "materialize[d] in the body of the female hysteric." As for another minor author, John W. De Forest, James A. Hijiya's *J. W. De Forest and the Rise of American Gentility* (New England) essentially replicates Frank Bergmann's 1971 book *The Worthy Gentleman of Democracy* (see *ALS* 1972, p. 199). Hijiya's reading of *Miss Ravenel's Conversion* offers no new insights. More worthwhile is chapter 5 of William K. Buckley's *Senses' Tender: Recovering the Novel for the Reader* (Peter Lang). Buckley sees *Miss Ravenel's Conversion* as having been written within the tradition of English Victorian literature, including the "double-think" of apparent hypocrisy or pruriency regarding sexual matters; but he also feels that De Forest occasionally undermined those expectations "in an effort to free his art." It is a sound analysis, but too brief to probe fully the complexities of De Forest's achievement.

vii. Crane, Norris, and Fin-de-siècle Writers

Crane scholarship in 1989 was uneven, with the old critical problems generating few convincing new insights. The two books published on Crane reflect the situation well. David Halliburton's *The Color of the Sky: A Study of Stephen Crane* (Cambridge) is a disappointing meditation which probes such familiar matters as the meaning of Henry Fleming's red badge and the death of Maggie Johnson. Chester L. Wolford's *Stephen Crane: A Study of the Short Fiction* (Twayne) is just what it was intended to be: a competent survey of Crane's ideas and techniques, aimed primarily at mature undergraduates. Wolford discusses some neglected stories in addition to the most-anthologized ones, and he reprints a Crane interview, some 40 letters, and six critical essays. Crane's relationship with an early editor receives extensive notice in Bruce A. White's *Elbert Hubbard's The Philistine: A Periodical of Protest (1895–1915)* (Univ. Press). White argues convincingly that Joseph Katz and R. W. Stallman had downplayed Crane's relationship with Hubbard, who was vital for Crane's development as a writer.

Individual essays devoted to Crane were stronger. In "*The Red Badge of Courage:* Form and Function," pp. 28–38 in *Modern American Fiction*, John Conder maintains that Henry is not an individualized person but a "psychological type called adolescence" and a "social type" called farm boy "meeting the congeries of conditions called war." He argues further that *Red Badge* turns on a "would-have-been axis." It is a wordy but suggestive essay which might be read in tandem with A. Robert Lee's "Stephen Crane's *The Red Badge of Courage*: The Novella as 'Moving Box,'" pp. 30–47 in his *The Modern American Novella*. Lee sees the text as a series of physical and lexiconical enclosures, including "boxes-within-boxes" which check impulses toward individual action. It is a sharp reading. This novella is also one of the texts discussed by Fredson Bowers in "Regularization and Normalization in Modern Critical Texts" (*SB* 42:79–102). That printers, editors, and Crane himself worked at crosspurposes helps explain the unexpected shifts between dialect and standard English in *Red Badge*. Much less worthwhile is Jean R. Halladay's "*Sartor Resartus* Revisited: Carlylean Echoes in Crane's *The Red Badge of Courage*" (*NCP* 16:23–33). Halladay seems justified in seeing clear parallels (she is reluctant to insist on direct influence) between Carlyle's "Everlasting No"/"Everlasting Yea" chapters and Crane's story, but she makes no effort to explain how an awareness of those parallels would help us understand *Red Badge*. Her reading is further weakened by her assertion that Henry Fleming at the end of the novella "behaves, as he had always hoped he would, like a hero."

"The Open Boat" was the subject of two essays. In "Two Tales 'Intended to be After the Fact': 'Stephen Crane's Own Story' and 'The Open Boat,'" pp. 125–51 in Chris Anderson, ed., *Literary Nonfiction: Theory, Criticism, Pedagogy* (So. Ill.), Phyllis Frus uses the two accounts of Crane's shipwreck to confirm the arbitrariness of such categories as "fiction" and "journalism." "Stephen Crane's Own Story," for example, "subverts the reader's expectations of journalism's 'five W's.'" Far more energetic is Bill Brown's "Interlude: The Agony of Play in 'The Open Boat'" (*ArQ* 45, iii:23–46). Brown sets the story against the backdrop of postbellum interest in leisure, play, and amusement, including the staging of real disasters (e.g., "The Defeat of the Spanish Armada," a Coney Island attraction). This mind-set explains why would-be rescuers on shore simply wave at the survivors in the open boat—a misreading of reality that "becomes a psychological burden." This is a vivid, important analysis.

The same cannot be said for Joseph Petite's "Expressionism and Stephen Crane's 'The Blue Hotel'" (*JEP* 10, iii–iv:322–27). Petite feels that the story makes sense only if read "expressionistically," with the Swede "symbolizing the irrational in man." More, the story is "not deterministic," for it "clearly focuses on choice, on blame." Not very convincing. Finally, John Blair in "The Posture of a Bohemian in the

Poetry of Stephen Crane" (*AL* 61:215–29) argues that Crane's early poems are those of a self-absorbed young man unduly influenced by his artsy colleagues in the Needham Building. As a result of his "facade of rebellion," young Crane wrote poems that are "more than just bad, they are insincere." The poems of the older Crane, however, show him more honestly rejecting not God but the Church. Repetitious but authoritative, this is a good essay. But one wishes Blair had examined more fully a point he raises at its end: the part played by war-weariness and impending death—not just "greater maturity"—in causing this change of heart.

Frank Norris, meanwhile, was the subject of a series of brief and usually insightful essays. Craig S. Abbott's "Reflexive Revision in Frank Norris's *McTeague* and *A Man's Woman*" (*FNS* 8:9–10) is a clever study of Norris's efforts to revise both novels in ways that accommodated the existing plates; that is, "the fit had to be not only thematic but physical." More, Norris intentionally devised substitute passages that refer to characters who, like him, were working in limited spaces. In a similar vein, Joseph R. McElrath, Jr., and Jesse S. Crisler propose that Norris replaced the scene of Owgooste wetting his pants with one of McTeague searching for his hat not because of the outrage of U.S. critics or Mrs. Frank Doubleday, but because he wished to facilitate publication of the novel in Britain ("The Bowdlerization of *McTeague*" [*AL* 61:97–101]). *McTeague* as a "funny" story— i.e., "peculiar as well as laughable"—is the subject of James E. Caron's "Grotesque Naturalism: The Significance of the Comic in *McTeague*" (*TSLL* 31:288–317). Caron makes a strong case that the novel shows links to the comic tradition of the American frontier, including the comparison of people to animals. Less original but still worth a look is Winifred Farrant Bevilacqua's "From the Ideal to Its Reverse: Key Sociocultural Concepts in *McTeague*" (*CentR* 33:75–88), which considers McTeague's life as a reverse Horatio Alger story and Trina's as a pursuit of True Womanhood to the point of masochism. Of more peripheral interest to Norris scholars is Richard Allan Davison's "*Of Mice and Men* and *McTeague*: Steinbeck, Fitzgerald, and Frank Norris" (*SAF* 17:219–26). Working from marginalia in a copy of *McTeague* given by F. Scott Fitzgerald to Edmund Wilson, Davison reviews the parallels between Norris's novel and *Of Mice and Men*. It is a sensitive essay, but says more about Fitzgerald's professional insecurities than it does about Norris. And Mary Lawlor's "Naturalism in the Cinema: Erich von Stroheim's Reading of *McTeague*" (*FNS* 8:6–8) is a centerless but absorbing analysis of von Stroheim and *Greed*.

The remaining work on Norris warrants an overview. Jesse S. Crisler in "Norris in South Africa" (*FNS* 7:4–7) reprints a series of items which appeared in the San Francisco *Chronicle* in late 1895 and early 1896 regarding Norris's apparent disappearance while a journalist in South Africa. James Stronks in "Frank Norris and the Eighth Grade" (*FNS* 7:2–4) surmises what the 13-year-old Norris might have studied at Chicago's preppy Harvard School. Two more chapters are added to the continuing soap opera of the divorce of Norris's parents in Stronks' "The Norris Divorce Suit: Another Newspaper Account" (*FNS* 8: 8–9) and Davison's "The Marriage, Divorce, and Demise of a Father of Novelists: B. F. Norris" (*FNS* 8:2–5). And Mary R. Ryder argues convincingly that Norris's influence on Willa Cather "may have been considerable, particularly in setting the pastoral tone of her early stories and in shaping the character of her female heroic figures." See " 'All Wheat and No Chaff': Frank Norris' *Blix* and Willa Cather's Literary Vision" (*ALR* 22, i:17–30).

Unlike the wide range of Norris studies, work on Henry Adams concentrated on his attitudes toward history and toward women. Robert F. Sommer in "*Mont-Saint-Michel and Chartres*: Henry Adams's Pilgrimage into History" (*CentR* 33:32–51) argues that the later Adams assumed the pose of pilgrim (as opposed to tourist) as part of an effort to redefine "history" as a spiritual rather than political entity. Such a stance enabled him to use nonliterary records of history (glasswork, architecture) and to sidestep events whose written records were in disagreement. Though all this sounds correct, it does not explain why Adams's vision of history shifted so dramatically. Surely, it is not enough to say that he was reacting to a negative review of his *History of the United States during the Administrations of Jefferson and Madison* in the New York *Tribune*. Keith R. Burich, meanwhile, maintains that Adams's "The Rule of Phase Applied to History" is predicated on a theory of history as the record of unpredictable cataclysms (" 'Our Power Is Always Running Ahead of Our Mind': Henry Adams's Phases of History," *NEQ* 62:163–86).

Adams's attitudes toward women are investigated by Nancy Comley and Kim Moreland. Comley in "Henry Adams' Feminine Fictions: The Economics of Maternity" (*ALR* 22, i:3–16) draws on *Democracy*, *Esther*, and the *Chartres* to argue that Adams was sympathetic toward some aspects of women's lives, but felt nonetheless that all they could do at the turn of the century was choose their method of victimization, i.e., by " 'a man, a church or a machine.' " Moreland maintains that while critics "point to Adams's celebration of medieval women as evidence for his feminism," that very nostalgia "came to justify his distaste for the 'New Woman' of the nineteenth century" ("Henry Adams, The Medieval Lady, and the 'New Woman,' " *ClioI* 18:291–305). The essays by Comley and Moreland are provocative and readable. Not so Susan Manning's " 'The Plots of God are Perfect': Poe's *Eureka* and American Creative Nihilism" (*JAmS* 23:235–51). Manning feels that the writing of Adams, Poe, and Thomas Pynchon is "its own self-consuming entropy, leveling distinctions, destroying categories and flattening nuances of response in a kind of literary heat-death." Overblown in style and substance.

Two more accessible essays on Harold Frederic appear in the Spring issue of *ALR* (21, iii). Jean S. Filetti in "*Seth's Brother's Wife*: The Triumph of the Political Machine" (pp. 41–51) makes a strong case that this novel is not "an affirmation of public morality and an expression of its author's political optimism," but an attack on rural politics which "denies the healing power of grassroots politics and the agrarian myth." Healing of another sort is examined by Susan Albertine in " 'With Their Tongues Doom Men to Death': Christian Science and the Case of Harold Frederic" (pp. 52–66). Albertine reviews the sensational circumstances surrounding the death of Frederic while under the care of his mistress and Mrs. Athalie Mills, both ardent Christian Scientists. Though particularly strong in its exploration of the antifeminist underpinnings of popular opposition to Christian Science at the turn of the century, Albertine's essay is more reportorial than insightful.

Ambrose Bierce garnered one note: William Conlogue's "Bierce's 'An Occurrence at Owl Creek Bridge' " (*Expl* 48:37–38), part of it a study of Bierce's hemp/rope wordplay and part an attempt to show that Farquhar ("no vulgar assassin") is "an addict ["assassin" is derived from "hashish-eater"] hooked on . . . war romanticizing." Neither part works well. Finally, Daniel Stempel in "Lafcadio Hearn's Translations and the Origins of Imagist Aesthetics," pp. 31–37 in Cornelia N. Moore and Raymond A. Moody, eds., *Comparative Literature East and West: Traditions and Trends* (Hawaii), makes a solid case that the Imagist movement owed much to the Japanese poems collected, translated, and explicated by Lafcadio Hearn beginning in

1894. Stempel seems justified in arguing that Hearn's modification of haiku to include introductory lines for the benefit of Western readers had a particular impact on Ezra Pound, who mistakenly believed he was following Japanese practice in providing explanatory passages such as "The apparition of these faces in the crowd." That he wasn't should lead us to reevaluate Pound, the Imagist movement, and Hearn's impact upon both.

Rhode Island School of Design

13. Fiction: The 1930s to the 1960s

Gary Scharnhorst

While 1989 was marked, on a somber note, by the deaths of such prominent writers of this period as Mary McCarthy, Malcolm Cowley, Edward Abbey, and Robert Penn Warren, the year also occasioned the publication of new fiction by Saul Bellow and Frederick Manfred; a new best smeller by Mickey Spillane; collections of letters by Manfred, Henry Miller, Vladimir Nabokov, Cowley, and Kenneth Burke; and even Robert B. Parker's completion of Raymond Chandler's last novel. While some Southern writers attract a disproportionate share of critical comment, others such as Flannery O'Connor and Eudora Welty, along with non-Southerners Nabokov, Saul Bellow, and John Steinbeck, continue to command the most individual attention. In fact, the Steinbeck industry operated at near-capacity this year, the semicentennial of the publication of *The Grapes of Wrath*. But these trends should not obscure the rich diversity—yea, even the proliferation—of the scholarship surveyed in these pages.

i. Proletarians

a. **John Steinbeck.** The Viking Press celebrated the semicentennial of Steinbeck's classic with the "fiftieth anniversary edition" of *The Grapes of Wrath*. The publisher spared most expense, however, by merely reproducing the pages of the original edition with a new 15-page introduction by the peripatetic Studs Terkel—a marketing gambit worthy of Chum Frink. Terkel quotes generously from *Working Days: The Journals of* The Grapes of Wrath (Viking), admirably edited and annotated by Robert DeMott. This volume, a far more valuable commemoration of the novel than the anniversary edition, documents the "complicated foreground" which shaped the story during its composition in the summer and fall of 1938 and the controversies which erupted after its publication. DeMott describes this journal, fairly enough, as "the truest story of the making of *The Grapes* *of Wrath.*" Steinbeck was beset by recurring doubts about his ability to write the "big book" he planned, and he failed to gauge accurately either the power of the story or its potential popularity even as he was writing it. DeMott also recommends in passing that Warren French's "invaluable little book" *A Companion to* The Grapes of Wrath (1963) "be updated and reprinted," and Viking Penguin has complied with at least the second of these suggestions.

Louis Owens, the author of *John Steinbeck's Re-Vision of America* (*ALS 1985*, p. 255), has scored a hat trick of sorts by publishing a book and two new essays this year devoted to Steinbeck's novel. In The Grapes of Wrath: *Trouble in the Promised Land* (Twayne), Owens admirably reviews the book's historical context and critical reception, then provides a perceptive and straightforward reading of the story as a "human tragedy on a national" or "epic scale," a jeremiad replete with biblical parallels and sociopolitical implications. Owens's study takes its cue from Steinbeck's own claim that there are several "layers" in the novel, and it concludes with a useful chapter on John Ford's 1940 film adaptation, a more sentimental than angry treatment of the plight of the migrants. Owens also collaborates with Hector Torres on "Dialogic Structure and Levels of Discourse in Steinbeck's *The Grapes of Wrath*" (*ArQ* 45, iv:75–94), a brilliant exposition of the dialectic between the Joad and the intercalary chapters of the novel, with particular reference to chapters 1, 25, and 29. Owens and Torres conclude from their Bakhtinian analysis that "no single voice speaks with final authority" in the text, that "the endings of neither the Joad chapters, nor the interchapters, nor the novel as a whole can be taken as final narrative closures." Owens also contributes "The Culpable Joads: Desentimentalizing *The Grapes of Wrath*" to *Critical Essays on Steinbeck's* The Grapes of Wrath (Hall), ed. John Ditsky. Here Owens argues (pp. 108–15) that, comments by such critics as Edmund Wilson and R. W. B. Lewis notwithstanding, Steinbeck tried "to unsentimentalize" the story of the Joads' displacement through the device of the interchapters.

On the whole, Ditsky's anthology is an invaluable resource, worthy of a place on the shelf beside the Viking critical edition of the novel. It collects a sheaf of contemporary reviews and previously published analyses by such Steinbeck scholars as French, Jackson Benson, and Peter Lisca, as well as three original essays in addition to Owens's. Roy Simmonds surveys transatlantic reviews of the novel in "The Reception of *The Grapes of Wrath* in Britain" (pp. 74–86). In "From

Heroine to Supporting Player: The Diminution of Ma Joad" (pp. 124–37), Mimi Reisel Gladstein examines Ford's "reduction and devitalization of the role of woman," particularly Ma, in his film version of the novel. Whereas Steinbeck portrayed Ma as a "citadel" of strength, the character played by Jane Darwell—she received an Oscar for Best Supporting Actress—is "weaker" and "more conciliatory." Carroll Britch and Cliff Lewis tack upwind against prevailing readings of the novel in "Growth of the Family in *The Grapes of Wrath*" (pp. 97–108). Britch and Lewis contend that "the Joad family does not break up so much as grow up." They assert, for example, that after Noah and Connie disappear "the essential family is still intact, and stronger without them." This essay perfectly illustrates a central tenet of the reader-response school: I obviously read a different text. John H. Timmerman elaborates a more conventional view of the disintegration of the Joad family in "The Squatter's Circle in *The Grapes of Wrath*" (*SAF* 17:203–11). As Timmerman explains, "Steinbeck very carefully directs the reversal of leadership roles" as Ma displaces Pa from his position at the center of the concentric circles of authority. Jim Sanderson echoes Frederic I. Carpenter's essay "The Philosophical Joads," published nearly a half-century ago, in his "American Romanticism in John Ford's *The Grapes of Wrath*: Horizontalness, Darkness, Christ, and F.D.R." (*LFQ* 17:231:44), yet another article on the film version of the novel. According to Sanderson, Ford offers an "Emersonian" solution for Tom Joad and "the dispossessed American poor." Finally, James N. Gregory updates the fate of the croppers in "Dust Bowl Legacies: The Okie Impact on California, 1939–1989" (*California History* 78:74–85). Gregory should beware of the subjunctive mood, however: Steinbeck "would have been quite surprised," he opines, to learn that the migrants and their descendants have enjoyed "considerable improvements" in their "social position and standard of living" over the past century.

Nor did the novel monopolize critical attention to Steinbeck's career this year. Jackson Benson, the author of *The True Adventures of John Steinbeck, Writer* (*ALS 1983*, p. 260) and last year's *Looking for Steinbeck's Ghost* (*ALS 1988*, pp. 259–60) eloquently champions the work of the literary biographer and scolds the theorists in "Steinbeck—A Defense of Biographical Criticism" (*CollL* 16:107–16). R. S. Hughes's *John Steinbeck: A Study of the Short Fiction* (Twayne) is a splendid introduction to the author's 50-plus tales, including a page or two on each of the 15 in *The Long Valley*, the several uncollected stories of the 1940s and 1950s, and an entire chapter on the short-story cycle *The Pastures of Heaven*. For the most part, however, Hughes's volume contains more synopsis than analysis. In "Profiles of the Scientific Personality: John Steinbeck's 'The Snake' " (*Mosaic* 22, i:87–99), Cheryl Weston and John V. Knapp rightly insist on the centrality to the story of the marine biologist, a figure who silhouettes "several of the emerging paradigms of scientific personality." In their view, the failure to appreciate this puzzling tale demonstrates how hostile literary critics may be toward science or, in their jargon, how inadequate are the current "modes of explanation in a provincial world of emotional and cognitive estrangement between humanists and scientists." I would be more convinced if their rococo prose were more lucid. In "The Devil Quotes Scripture: Biblical Misattribution and *The Winter of Our Discontent*" (*SJS* 15:19–28), John Ditsky explains how Steinbeck deliberately misquotes the Gospel of Matthew to warn his readers of imminent moral collapse. Richard Allan Davison's "*Of Mice and Men* and *McTeague*: Steinbeck, Fitzgerald, and Frank Norris" (*SAF* 17: 219–26) is, in effect, two distinct note-length essays joined at the hip: one on Norris's alleged influence on Steinbeck, the other on Fitzgerald's frustration with Steinbeck's success as his own career was in decline.

The scholarship published under the aegis of the Steinbeck Society is, as usual, a credit to the indefatigable Tetsumaro Hayashi, director of its bibliography and monograph series and editor of the *Steinbeck Quarterly*. *Steinbeck's Posthumous Work: Essays in Criticism*, ed. Hayashi and Thomas J. Moore, contains four original and substantial selections: Nancy Zane's "The Romantic Impulse in Steinbeck's *Journal of a Novel*: The *East of Eden* Letters" (pp. 1–12); John H. Timmerman's "*Steinbeck: A Life in Letters*" (pp. 12–22), which assesses the author's place in the modern epistolary tradition; Clifford Lewis's "Outfoxed: Writing *Viva Zapata!*" (pp. 22–34), on the backstage political maneuvers which influenced Steinbeck's work on this screenplay; and Michael Sundermeier's "Why Steinbeck Didn't Finish His *Arthur—The Acts of King Arthur and His Noble Knights*" (pp. 34–42), on the author's aborted translation and modernization of Malory's legend. In the current volume of *StQ*, Roy S. Simmonds concludes from "Steinbeck's *The Pearl*: A Preliminary Textual Study" (22: 16–34) that "the possibility exists either that Steinbeck did not read" the proofs of the novel or that he read them rather carelessly before its publication in 1947. C. Kenneth Pellow offers a "radically feministic" reading of another of Steinbeck's chestnuts in " 'The Chry-santhemums' Revisited" (22:8–16). Both John Ditsky ("Steinbeck's 'Slav Girl' and the Role of the Narrator in 'The Murder,' " 22:68–76) and Charlotte Hadella ("Point of View in John Steinbeck's 'The Murder,' " 22:77–82) reach remarkably similar conclusions about the intentionally "elusive" narrator of this gothic tale and the violence he describes. Finally, Harbour Winn's "The Unity of Steinbeck's *Pastures* Community" (22:91–103) traces some of the motifs and thematic ties that bind together this story cycle.

b. **Edmund Wilson and Others.** Ironically, the social novelists of the 1930s and 1940s—excepting Steinbeck—seem to have fallen on hard times recently, even while such leftist critics of the same period as Wilson and F. O. Matthiessen continue to fascinate scholars. In *Edmund Wilson: A Critic for Our Time* (Ohio), Janet Groth discusses Wilson's literary criticism with sympathy and insight, but deliberately omits extended reference to his fiction, poetry, and social commentary. James Guimond discusses Wilson's two novels and three of his stories in light of his disappointed hopes for the fusion of high art and mass culture in "The Green Tradition: Found and Lost in Edmund Wilson's *I Thought of Daisy* and *Memoirs of Hecate County*" (*The Green American Tradition*, pp. 171–92). Daniel O'Hara's *Lionel Trilling and the Work of Liberation* (Wisconsin) regards Trilling's career "as a single comprehensive work" of self-definition and notes his flirtation with the Trotskyites in the 1930s, though it contains only about 15 pages on his subsequent novel of political ideas *The Middle of the Journey*. Similarly, in his *F. O. Matthiessen and the Politics of Criticism* (Wisconsin), William E. Cain reviews Matthiessen's career by way of proposing that critics and scholars "acknowledge the primacy of their political commitments" as they "shape literary and critical choices" vis-à-vis the canon. Matthiessen's criticism, Cain concludes, "reveals the dangers, both intellectual and political, that result when the teacher/critic seeks to distinguish between art and politics, literary criticism and criticism of other kinds." David S. Reynolds calls and raises Cain in "What Do We Do with F. O. Matthiessen?" (*Review* 11:319–23) by accusing him of merely posing as an "avant-garde rebel," of being in fact "a joiner of the firmly established Marginal Literature Club—that group of faddish academics who foreground once-marginal writers for political reasons." And so it goes. Despite the obvious differences in their subjects and approaches, the books by Groth, O'Hara, and Cain address a common problem: each of them is a self-reflexive study of the plight of the modern scholar-critic. *The Selected Correspondence of Kenneth Burke and Malcolm Cowley 1915–1981* (Viking), ed. Paul Jay, publishes several hundred of the more than 1,700 letters which passed between these two distinguished men of letters. It is a remarkable and unique exchange which documents "the literary life of twentieth-century America from consistent and quite different perspectives," detailing in particular Cowley's fling in the 1930s with what David E. Shi calls in "A Critical Friendship: Kenneth Burke and Malcolm Cowley" (*AmLH* 1:920–31) a "cosmopolitan Stalinism." The new journal *Horns of Plenty* continues to fill its niche in the scholarly arena with special issues on Burke (2, i) and Lewis Mumford (2, iii) and general issues containing both original and reprinted essays about Cowley's life and career.

The minor writers on the left receive scant attention this year, as though their relevance has waned after a decade of Reaganomics and the revolutions in Eastern Europe. James R. Giles's *Confronting the Horror: The Novels of Nelson Algren* (Kent State) is a notable exception to this trend. According to Giles, Algren reinvented the naturalism of Norris, Crane, and Dreiser, combining a commitment to the lumpen proletariat with a belief in "existential absurdity." Giles perceptively analyzes each of Algren's novels and, in all, his volume should serve to refocus critical attention on an undeservedly neglected writer. Bob Perlongo also transcribes his 1957 interview with Algren for the *Arizona Quarterly* (45:101–06). Moreover, two essays in the journals this year dispute the conventional proletarian reading of Henry Roth's only novel. Stephen J. Adams elaborates Walter Allen's 1964 remark that the novel evokes "the terrors of childhood" in " 'The Noisiest Novel Ever Written': The Soundscape of Henry Roth's *Call It Sleep*" (*TCL* 35:43–64). David Schearl's cultural assimilation and personal maturation are marked by a progression of "sound symbols," Adams explains, and the novel as a whole derives its power from "Roth's ability to create the sensory world of the child, particularly the sense of sound." In "An American Messiah: Myth in Henry Roth's *Call It Sleep*" (*MFS* 35:673–87), Lynn Altenbernd develops Leslie Fiedler's suggestion some 30 years ago that the novel is "finally and astonishingly a religious book," arguing that it "depicts the birth and childhood of a New World messiah whose story conflates elements of the Jewish and Christian traditions" in order "to develop a myth for a democratic society."

ii. Southerners

a. **Flannery O'Connor.** O'Connor's critical stock continues to rise, though the conflicting interpretations of her achievement seem in no way to converge. As usual, much of the scholarship devoted to her work—this year, no less than four books and a dozen or so major articles—explores her "incarnational" theory of writing; that is, these readers insist on reading O'Connor's fiction as crypto-theology. As a result, this (un)orthodox brand of scholarship is more biblical exegesis than critical analysis. As its very title may indicate, Brian Abel Ragan's *A Wreck on the Road to Damascus: Ignorance, Guilt, and Conversion in Flannery O'Connor* (Loyola) explains how "Parker's Back," "The Life You Save May Be Your Own," and *Wise Blood* are "animated" by the "essential Christian doctrines" of original sin, redemption, and the Incarnation. Ragan's study connects the dots in all the predictable ways, though his remarks on O'Connor's use of the automobile "as an image of complete personal freedom" are fresh and reasonably interesting. In "Knowledge and Innocence in Flannery O'Connor's 'The River' " (*SAF* 17:143–55), Stephen C. Behrendt discusses the spiritual knowledge gleaned by little Harry Ashfield which culminates in his innocent death by immersion. Mark S. Sexton offers only a slightly less dogmatical reading of this story in "Flannery O'Connor's Presentation of Vernacular Religion in 'The River' " (*FCB* 18:1–12). Richard Giannone protests in *Flannery O'Connor and the Mystery of Love* (Illinois) that his "interest in the theology of O'Connor's fiction remains subordinate to [his] interest in the poetry of her ideas" and that he treats "the biblical material from the point of view of a literary critic." He doth protest too much, methinks: as in the other cases, Giannone's perspective is fundamentally theological. He claims, for example, that "Read by the light of salvific possibilities O'Connor's fiction can be seen as not only clarifying the idea of God for the unbelieving modern mind, but also as modifying our image of the human person." Only in that final, infelicitous phrase does Giannone begin to qualify his near-exclusive concern with the "spiritual" in O'Connor's work. The "love" he mentions in his title is, of course, divine love. His reading of individual stories, particularly *The Violent Bear It Away*, is perfectly respectable within the parameters he has drawn—I merely object to the parochial parameters. Similarly, Tony Magistrale traces O'Connor's ostensible use of food imagery "to mirror the spiritual condition of the characters" in his note on "The Lame

Shall Enter First" (*Expl* 47:58–60); and Ronald L. Grimes underscores the putative importance to her fiction of another sacrament in "Anagogy and Ritualization: Baptism in Flannery O'Connor's *The Violent Bear It Away*" (*R&L* 21, i:9–26). This council of critics regards Saint Flannery as a canonical writer in the synodal sense of the term.

Fortunately, O'Connor criticism is not the domain only of her doctrinaire defenders. With the publication of *The Manuscripts of Flannery O'Connor at Georgia College* (Georgia), a catalog of several hundred files deposited in the Ina Dillard Russell Library by Regina O'Connor in 1970, Stephen G. Driggers has completed a project Robert J. Dunn began in 1972. Robert H. Brinkmeyer, Jr.'s *The Art and Vision of Flannery O'Connor* (LSU) is the most valuable new book on O'Connor to appear in years, a groundbreaking and breathtaking study of the conflicting "dialogic forces" at work in her writing. In Brinkmeyer's view, O'Connor is something more than a religious writer—she is a writer, thank God, who "resisted the temptation to isolate herself either in a valorized conception of self or in a vapid Catholicism." Not only did she usually write in the mode of Middle Georgia humor, she refracted her Catholicism "through a narrative frame essentially un-Catholic in vision." Similarly, in "The Rhetoric of Heteroglossia in Flannery O'Connor's *Wise Blood*" (*QJS* 75:198–211), Mary Frances HopKins analyzes O'Connor's first novel in Bakhtinian terms. Like Brinkmeyer, HopKins emphasizes the "dialogic relationship" between the "conscious parodic heteroglossia of the narrator" and the "unconscious heteroglossia of characters" in the novel. Ben Satterfield launches a frontal assault on the standard anagogical reading of the same work in "*Wise Blood*, Artistic Anemia, and the Hemorrhaging of O'Connor Criticism" (*SAF* 17:33–50). "From a literary point of view," Satterfield contends, with conviction, this novel "is an ironic study in pathology" rather than an allegory of redemption, and Hazel Motes's death at the end is a meaningless event rather than an act of sacrificial atonement. Sectarian readers have mistakenly "superimpose[d] a pattern of redemption on O'Connor's work that is not warranted by the fiction itself," he concludes. He disparages the classroom proselytizers who "use her fiction for a dive into mystical speculation." Hear, hear. In "Flannery O'Connor's *Others*: Freud, Lacan, and the Unconscious" (*AL* 61:625–43), James M. Mellard theorizes that the novelist feared psychoanalysis because it threatened to "displace her theology as a mode of spiritual orientation" and that Freud is "her other in the Imaginary." David Leon Higdon weighs the implications of O'Connor's tendency to use philosophical propositions as story titles and identifies several of their sources in "Flannery O'Connor's Sentence Titles" (*SAF* 17:227–34). In "Hawthorne and Flannery O'Connor: A Literary Kinship" (*FCB* 18:46–54), Ronald Emerick plots some of the vectors which influenced O'Connor's romantic tales. Bruce Bawer also compares Hawthorne to O'Connor in "Under the aspect of eternity" (*NewC* 7, v: 35–41). Like Bawer's essay, Benjamin Griffith's "After the Canonization: Flannery O'Connor Revisited" (*SR* 97:575–80) is an appreciative review of O'Connor's *Collected Works*, a volume edited by Sally Fitzgerald and published last year by the Library of America. Griffith is one of three essayists this year who address the question of O'Connor's racism. Her "attitudes about race were complex," Griffith allows, fairly enough, by way of discussing "The Artificial Nigger" and "Everything That Rises Must Converge." In "The Black Outsider in O'Connor's Fiction" (*FCB* 18:79–90), D. Dean Shackelford defends O'Connor's racial attitudes as she expressed them in these same two stories, though the analysis is complicated by the spirit of Christian apology in which it is written. Finally, Alice Hall Petry, a prolific and ever-perceptive critic, notes in "Miss O'Connor and Mrs. Mitchell" (*SoQ* 27, iv:5–15) several echoes of *Gone With the Wind* in "Everything That Rises Must Converge," a series of parallels and ironic reversals which together "underscore the story's thesis that Julian's and his mother's responses to life in the South of the civil rights movement are unreasonable and, ultimately, self-destructive."

b. **Eudora Welty.** As in O'Connor's case, Welty's fiction has become the raw material for a burgeoning critical industry replete with subcontractors, foreign investors, and even an industry bulletin. The *Eudora Welty Newsletter* serves its readers as a clearinghouse of tidbits about the author and lists of textual variants among published versions of such stories as "A Curtain of Green," "Keela," and "Petrified Man." Lauren Berlant claims the latter story illustrates sexual difference in "Re-writing the Medusa: Welty's 'Petrified Man'" (*SSF* 26:59–70). Berlant asserts that the story with its evocation of the Perseus-Medusa myth "is designed strategically to expose the grotesque, the inelegant level of women's desires." In "'When Our Separate Journeys Converge': Notes on *The Optimist's Daughter*" (*MissQ* 42:147–60), Margaret W. Pepperdene contends that "every

part" (i.e., "language, image, character, theme") of Welty's novel "co-
inheres." Louise Westling, author of *Sacred Groves and Ravaged
Gardens: The Fiction of Eudora Welty, Carson McCullers, and Flannery O'Connor* (*ALS 1985*, p. 259), has returned this year to the first
of these writers in *Eudora Welty*, a volume in the Barnes and Noble
Women Writers Series. Given the limitations of the format within
which she writes, it is not surprising that Westling dismisses some
novels in scarcely a paragraph or two, though she devotes considerably more attention to the mythic overtones and feminist implications
of *Delta Wedding, The Golden Apples,* and *The Optimist's Daughter*.

   Two anthologies of Welty essays which also appeared in 1989 are
far more ambitious in scope. Dawn Trouard edits *Eudora Welty: Eye
of the Storyteller* (Kent State), a collection of 16 papers delivered at
a Welty symposium hosted by the University of Akron in September
1987 and which by design open "new approaches to familiar texts" or
consider "heretofore-neglected texts." The publication of these essays
is the year's most important event in Welty studies, and at least eight
of them command special interest. Ruth D. Weston in "American Folk
Art, Fine Art, and Eudora Welty" (pp. 3–13) proposes "aesthetic
precedents" for the stories, particularly "Lily Daw and the Three
Ladies," that are akin to "abstract visual artifacts." In " 'Contradictors,
Interferers, and Prevaricators' " (pp. 32–43), Susan V. Donaldson offers a Bakhtinian analysis of the "opposing modes of discourse" in
Losing Battles. Ann Romines discusses the deliberately flawed first-
person narrators of "Why I Live at the P.O." and "Circe" in "How Not
to Tell a Story" (pp. 94–104). Cheryll Burgess remarks on metaphors
of storytelling in the collection *A Curtain of Green* in "From Metaphor to Metafiction" (pp. 133–41). Noel Polk's "Going to Naples and
Other Places in Eudora Welty's Fiction" (pp. 154–64) revises the
commonplace assumptions about the meaning and significance of
Welty's settings, challenging the notion that Welty fits comfortably
into the "Southern writer" pigeonhole. Nancy K. Butterworth insists
upon Phoenix Jackson's role as a black avatar in "From Civil War to
Civil Rights: Race Relations in 'A Worn Path' " (pp. 165–72). Ruth
M. Vande Kieft, author of both the original and revised Welty volumes
in the TUSAS program (*ALS 1987*, p. 265), recounts her success at
teaching Welty's fiction and offers a few pedagogical hints in " 'Where
Is the Voice Coming From?' " (pp. 190–204). And Marilyn Arnold
comments on the rhetorical subtleties of *The Ponder Heart* in "The
Strategy of Edna Earle Ponder" (pp. 69–77). Arnold completes a

critical hat trick of her own by contributing two other original essays on Welty to journals this year. In " 'The Magical Percussion': Eudora Welty's Human Recital on Art and Time" (*SHR* 23:101–18), she analyzes "June Recital," arguably the author's "most important story," in light of Welty's 1973 essay "Some Notes on Time in Fiction." Arnold speculates in "Somnambulism in San Francisco: Eudora Welty's Western Story" (*SoQ* 27, iv:16–24) that Welty was indebted to the silent film *The Cabinet of Dr. Caligari* for the dreamlike quality and "shifting, almost surrealistic detail" of "Music from Spain," another of the tales in *The Golden Apples*. Two earlier essays by Arnold, on *The Robber Bridegroom* and *The Optimist's Daughter*, are reprinted in *Critical Essays on Eudora Welty* (Hall), ed. W. Craig Turner and Lee Emling Harding, the other collection of Welty scholarship to appear this year. This volume reprints vintage essays by such noted critics as Vande Kieft, Michael Kreyling, Louis D. Rubin, Jr., Larry J. Reynolds, and Granville Hicks; and it contains four original pieces written specifically for its pages. Of particular value: Pearl Aurelia McHaney's "Historical Perspectives in 'A Still Moment'" (pp. 52–69), on the sources of this story in works by and/or about Lorenzo Dow, John J. Audubon, and the outlaw John Murrell; and Merrill Maguire Skaggs's "Eudora Welty's 'I' of Memory" (pp. 153–65), on several parallels between Welty's and Katherine Anne Porter's fiction.

c. Katherine Anne Porter, Caroline Gordon, and Others. Porter and Gordon have become obvious beneficiaries of the growing interest in Southern women writers and the critical campaign to expand the canon. In "Death and Repetition in Porter's Miranda Stories" (*AL* 61: 610–24), George Cheatham suggests the tales "Old Morality" and "Pale Horse, Pale Rider" undermine the "perhaps too-pat" or reassuring conclusion to "The Grave," the climactic story in Porter's *The Old Order*. Cheatham thus modifies the perhaps too-pat Christian interpretation of "The Grave" he published last year (*ALS 1988*, pp. 270–71). In "Continuity and Change in the Southern Novella" (*The Modern American Novella*, pp. 113–38), Peter Messent analyzes the "movement from the historical to the personal" in an honorable tradition of Southern writers that includes Porter, Welty, Andrew Lytle, Truman Capote, Robert Penn Warren, William Styron, and Carson McCullers. Veronica A. Makowsky's *Caroline Gordon: A Biography* (Oxford) labors under a peculiar disadvantage: though authorized by Gordon, it covers much the same field, albeit with a looser weave, as

Ann Waldron's *Close Connections: Caroline Gordon and the Southern Renaissance* (*ALS 1987*, p. 260), which Tennessee reissues this year in a paperback edition. Both of these biographies are, unfortunately, litanies of dates and undigested detail—they cite many of the same unpublished letters and relate some of the very same anecdotes in virtually identical language. Neither is a genuine literary life of Gordon, though Makowsky at least summarizes and briefly evaluates each of the novels and several of the stories in her volume. Whereas Waldron "tends to be slavishly reportorial," as Lauren Weiner suggests in "Looking Back at Caroline Gordon" (*NewC* 8, ii:80–84), Makowsky "errs in the other direction" with "impressions, hunches, and literary theorizing." For the record, Donald E. Stanford recommends Makowsky's "solidly written and thoroughly researched" biography in his "Caroline Gordon: An Uprooted Agrarian" (*SR* 97:572–75). Porter, Gordon, O'Connor, Welty, Warren, and other Southern writers such as Allen Tate, Peter Taylor, and John Crowe Ransom also figure prominently in Marian Janssen's first-rate critical history *The Kenyon Review 1939–1970* (LSU).

As it happens, Gordon, who was working on a Civil War novel in the mid-1930s, scorned *Gone with the Wind*, Margaret Mitchell's tear-jerking panegyric to the Old South. (Both Waldron and Makowsky quote a letter Gordon wrote her friend Sally Wood in 1936 to the effect that Mitchell took "ten years to write that novel. Why couldn't it have taken her twelve?") Ironically, Rutgers this year commemorates the fiftieth anniversary of the release of the movie adaptation of Mitchell's book by issuing Helen Taylor's *Scarlett's Women: Gone with the Wind and Its Female Fans*. Taylor explores "the multiple meanings and associations" both the novel and film have inspired through the years—their reception history, especially the racial and sexual subtexts, the ambiguous ending—from what might best be described as a conflicted feminist perspective ("offended as I was by the political argument, I enjoyed virtually every minute of it"). Similarly, Amy Levin in "Matters of Canon: Reappraising *Gone With the Wind*" (*Proteus* 6:32–36) argues that Mitchell's novel "is significant precisely because it provokes" critical scrutiny, though in the end Levin merely questions the applicability of conventional standards of literary merit to the novel. She nowhere explicitly calls for its canonization, her title notwithstanding.

Among the essays devoted this year to other Southern women

writers, the fiction of Elizabeth Spencer, hitherto obscured in a critical blind spot, earns a few well-deserved kudos in Mark Royden
Winchell's "A Golden Ball of Thread: The Achievement of Elizabeth
Spencer" (*SR* 97:580–86). Similarly, two journal essays address Lillian Smith's writings. Hugh Murray summarizes the case for their
revival in an amicus curiae brief, "Lillian Smith: A Neglected Southern Heroine" (*JEthS* 17:136–40). In "Reflections on Lillian Smith and
the Guilt of the Betrayer" (*SoQ* 27, iv:71–78), Margaret Jones
Bolsterli contends that Smith's autobiographical volume *Killers of
the Dream* and her novel *Strange Fruit* "present a textbook example"
of the way racial guilt "can operate in a white southerner's consciousness." Mary Ann Brennas has also compiled a checklist to works by
and about Harriette Simpson Arnow (*BB* 46:46–52).

d. Thomas Wolfe, Erskine Caldwell, and Others.

Scholars stalked
Wolfe into tall grass this year, the 60th anniversary of the publication
of *Look Homeward, Angel*. In "Autobiography and Ideology in the
South: Thomas Wolfe and the Vanderbilt Agrarians" (*AL* 61:31–45),
Thomas A. Underwood chronicles the checkered relations between
the novelist and the members of the Fugitive/Agrarian group. According to such critics as Tate, Ransom, and Donald Davidson, Wolfe was
a self-indulgent egomaniac who failed "to structure his novels in any
traditional manner." On his part, Wolfe failed to appreciate the Agrarians' social critique, particularly their belief, which he shared, in the
"evils of mass production and the myth of industrial progress." Louis
D. Rubin, Jr., reminisces about his own introduction to Wolfe's fiction
during his stint in the army and probes the sources of the novelist's
appeal to young readers in "Thomas Wolfe: Homage Renewed" (*SR*
97:261–76). His debt to Wolfe "goes too deep for dispassionate critical
analysis," Rubin allows—a remarkable compliment from one of the
most admired critics of Southern fiction. At the other extreme, Seymour Rosenberg reduces Wolfe's roman à clef to a mere data base in
"A Study of Personality in Literary Autobiography: An Analysis of
Thomas Wolfe's *Look Homeward, Angel*" (*JPSP* 56:416–30). Wolfe
expressly cautioned against reading the novel from such a "local
angle," declaring it was "a writer's creation and vision of life." Not
only does Rosenberg ignore the obvious—that the novel is not "literary
autobiography" as that phrase is normally understood—but his conclusions (e.g., "Family members are less stereotyped than nonfamily

members") will seem self-evident to literary scholars who rarely need graphs and charts to prove their points.

The *Thomas Wolfe Review* exceeds its usual high standards for criticism this year. Suzanne Stutman compares Wolfe's correspondence with Aline Bernstein and the fiction each of them wrote about their love affair in "'Esther' Bernstein and 'Eugene' Wolfe: Fact versus Fiction" (13, i:1–10). In "Allegory as Subterfuge in Wolfe's 'Fame and the Poet'" (13, i:11–14), James D. Boyer demonstrates that this fantastic little story "is really an examination of sexual fidelity" based on Wolfe's affair with Bernstein. Reid Huntley discusses in "Wolfe's Obsession with Time" (13, i:33–45) a philosophical issue implicit in the fiction which has been treated more thoroughly by such critics as Rubin, C. Hugh Holman, and Margaret Church; and Carol Johnston recounts in "Thomas Wolfe's First Triumph" (13, ii:53–61) the publication history of Wolfe's early story "An Angel on the Porch." The *Review* commemorates the diamond anniversary of Wolfe's first novel with a special Fall issue that contains three noteworthy essays: Richard Walser's "Concerning the Form of *Look Homeward, Angel*" (13, ii:2–9), on the epic devices which structure the work; Terry Roberts's "Narrative Distance in *Look Homeward, Angel*" (13, ii:13–19), on Wolfe's use of "irony and experience" to "manipulate the distance between the narrative voice and Eugene Gant"; and Constance Pedoto's "A Deconstructive Approach to Thomas Wolfe's *Look Homeward, Angel*" (13, ii:23–30), which argues, however presumptuously, that the novel exhibits its "true literary merit" only when the guns of post-structuralism are turned on it. The *Review* also prints three brief intertextual studies this year: on the novelist's debt to the American Bard in David K. Perelman-Hall's "Wolfe and Whitman" (13, i:15–25); on "Wolfe's fascination with Joycean themes, leitmotifs, and characters" in Vernon Hyles's "Ben, Ruby and the Fantastic" (13, ii:44–48); and on particular parallels between chapter 10 of *Ulysses* and chapter 14 of *Look Homeward, Angel* in Claire A. Culleton's "Joycean Synchronicity in Wolfe's *Look Homeward, Angel*" (13, ii:49–52).

The *Southern Quarterly* devotes its Spring issue to Erskine Caldwell, who died in April 1987. Guest-edited by Edwin T. Arnold, this number contains a tribute to Caldwell by John Hersey, interviews with two of Caldwell's former wives, and four substantial essays on aspects of his career. Harvey L. Klevar, a sociologist, speculates, rather too neatly for my taste, in "Caldwell's Women" (27, iii:15–35), that Caldwell's "essential dependence upon women" was "the catalyst which first fueled [his] creative surge and later compromised it." Sylvia J. Cook in "Caldwell's Fiction: Growing Towards Trash?" (27, iii: 49–58) offers a more plausible though no less simple explanation for the novelist's decline: he abandoned the Georgia crackers, the subject of his most successful novels, "for new subjects and topicality" in the 1940s. Ronald Wesley Hoag pleads the case for resurrecting Caldwell's 1943 story cycle from that academic hell, the footnote, in "Canonize Caldwell's *Georgia Boy*" (27, iii:73–85). William L. Howard concludes in "Caldwell on Stage and Screen" (27, iii:59–72) that each of the popular adaptations of Caldwell's stories "distorted to some extent [his] artistic and social vision" of life in the South during the Great Depression.

Among the miscellaneous scholarship on other Southern writers: *Conversations with Shelby Foote* (Miss.), ed. William C. Carter for the Literary Conversations Series, collects a total of 18 interviews with Foote, two of them transcripts of unpublished television programs, conducted between 1950 and 1987.

iii. Expatriates and Émigrés

a. **Vladimir Nabokov.** The vault beneath the castle yields a few more secrets this year with the publication of *Vladimir Nabokov: Selected Letters 1940–1977* (Harcourt), ed. Dmitri Nabokov and Matthew J. Bruccoli. This charming collection of several hundred personal letters to such correspondents as Philip Rahv, Allen Tate, Stanley Kubrick, Alfred Appel, Jr., and Andrew Field proves once again that Nabokov was no cold and aloof aesthete: he liked to watch soccer on television, fired off many a letter to newspaper editors, and was not above occasionally threatening a biographer with a lawsuit. Leona Toker officiates at the wedding of two traditions of Nabokov scholarship in *Nabokov: The Mystery of Literary Structures* (Cornell). Toker proposes to demonstrate the "close connection" between Nabokov's mastery of form and structure and the ideological or moral attitudes expressed in 10 of his 17 novels, among them *Pnin, Lolita,* and the critically neglected *Glory.* These texts "provide the best examples of the mutual adjustment of Nabokov's virtuoso techniques and humanistic concerns." No doubt, as Toker concludes, the "aesthetic in Nabokov is inseparable from the ethical"—he should not be read as somehow approving murder or child molestation in *Lolita,* for example—but this study mostly ignores such late, intricate riddles from his pen as *Ada, Pale Fire,* and *Transparent Things.* Toker applies her thesis to another of Nabokov's overlooked works in "Fact and Fiction in Nabokov's Biography of Abram Gannibal" (*Mosaic* 22, iii:43–56). This sketch of the life of Pushkin's great-grandfather anticipates the "heteroglot procedures" of *Pnin,* Toker explains. Ellen Pifer reaches conclusions similar to Toker's in "Shades of Love: Nabokov's Intimations of Immortality" (*KR* 11, ii:75–86). Focusing on *Lolita* and *Transparent Things,* Pifer argues that the ghosts or "emissaries of 'the hereafter' " in Nabokov's fiction "express and indeed celebrate the most generous forms of human love." In " 'Lo' and Behold: Solving the *Lolita* Riddle" (*SNNTS* 21:182–99), Trevor McNeely takes a position diametrically opposed to that of Toker and Pifer (and, for that matter, all other Nabokovians). According to McNeely, whose essay exudes a heady air of self-congratulation, Nabokov wrote *Lolita* as a sort of elaborate practical joke on the professoriate, whom he expected (correctly) "to find meaning where none exists." The "only possible escape" from the intellectual trap Nabokov set is "to reject totally both book and author for the frauds they are."

Like O'Connor, Nabokov scorned psychotherapy and "the Viennese quack," though his fiction has scarcely been immune to Freudian analysis. *Russian Literature and Psychoanalysis* (Benjamins), ed. Daniel Rancour-Laferriere, prints three papers on Nabokov originally delivered at the University of California at Davis in February 1987. Peter Welsen's "Charles Kinbote's Psychosis—A Key to Vladimir Nabokov's *Pale Fire*" (pp. 381–400) is by far the most pedantic of these, presuming to trace the clinical etiology of symptoms exhibited by fictional figures (e.g., "Gradus's psychosexual development is also determined by an Oedipal wish to sleep with his mother and to kill his father"). Welsen concludes that the paranoid Kinbote has repressed his latent homosexuality and thus disguises his tale of the homosexual King Charles, his alter ego, in the confused commentary on Shade's poem. Alan C. Elms in "Cloud, Castle, Claustrum: Nabokov as a Freudian in Spite of Himself" (pp. 353–68) explores the "apparently unintentional fetal and birth imagery" in the 1937 story "Cloud, Castle, Lake"—a pattern which seems "to have been stimulated in part" by the dangers the Nazis posed for the Nabokovs during their residence in Berlin. To his credit, Elms allows that the novelist "would have been outraged" by this brand of armchair psychoanalysis. Geoffrey Green, the author of last year's *Freud and Nabokov* (*ALS 1988*, p. 273), reappears with "Splitting of the Ego: Freudian Doubles, Nabokovian Doubles" (pp. 369–79). Green relates Freud's theory of defensive ego-splitting to Nabokov's recurring theme of the double.

Despite the growing interest in the novelist's life, most Nabokov criticism continues to emphasize formal qualities of his fiction. The Nabokov chapter in Elizabeth Klosty Beaujour's *Alien Tongues* (pp. 81–117) is a case in point. Beaujour summarizes the circumstances which led Nabokov to abandon Russian for English prose, to be sure, but only by way of concluding that his "plexed artistry" epitomizes those "characteristics that neurolinguistics has shown to be associated" with bilingualism. Brenda K. Marshall examines "some of the postmodern impulses" which shape Nabokov's 1941 novel in "Sebastian Speaks: Nabokov's Narrative Authority in *The Real Life of Sebastian Knight*" (*Style* 23:213–24). Not only do his narrative strategies "undermine Nabokov's own insistence on absolute control" of his characters, Marshall asserts, but his "awareness about the impossibility of recapturing the past" disrupts the closed "modernist" reading of the novel and opens the text to other interpretive possibilities. Nabokov's fiction also attracts its usual share of attention from the source- and symbol-hunting school of critics this year. Three intertextual studies in the Spring number of the *Slavic and East European Journal* are particularly provocative: Katherine Tiernan O'Connor's "Rereading *Lolita*, Reconsidering Nabokov's Relationship with Dostoevskij" (33: 64–77), on *Lolita* and *Crime and Punishment*; John Burt Foster, Jr.'s "Nabokov Before Proust: The Paradox of Anticipatory Memory" (33: 78–94), on Proustian analogues in such work as *Glory, The Gift*, and *Speak, Memory*; and Dale E. Peterson's "Nabokov and the Poeetics of Composition" (33:95–107), on Poe's influence on *Transparent Things* and the novelist's aesthetic of play. Liza M. Kozlowski also glosses Nabokov's allusion in *Lolita* to Browning's "Soliloquy of the Spanish Cloister" in "Tracking McSwine's Fiendish Spoor" (*Nabokovian* 23:28–35).

b. Henry Miller, Anaïs Nin, and Others.

The letters Miller sent his friend and mentor Emil Schnellock between 1922 and 1934, edited by the eminent Miller scholar George Wickes, appear this year under the title *Letters to Emil* (New Directions). These several dozen letters are a unique record of Miller's literary apprenticeship and are distinguished, as Wickes explains in his introduction, by "the evidence they provide of his work in progress" even before he first broke into print. As Miller struggled to find his voice, Schnellock was the correspondent "to whom he could express himself most freely in his bawdiest vein." The works of Miller and Nin are also featured in Richard Pine's *The Dandy and the Herald* (St. Martin's), an ambitious "genealogy of modern aesthetics" which traces the demise of the fin de siècle dandy and the emergence of a savage and rebellious "herald" in Anglo-American fiction of the 1930s. The current volume of *Anaïs*, the journal of the Anaïs Nin Foundation, contains a hitherto withheld section of Nin's novel *The Winter of Artifice* and at least two essays of note: Patricia M. Lawlor's "Beyond Gender and Genre" (7:23–31), on the significance of the labyrinth symbol in Nin's fiction and diaries; and Patricia-Pia Célérier's "The Vision of Dr. René Allendy" (7:78–94), on the influence of Nin's first psychotherapist on her "intellectual and artistic growth."

Several minor expatriate and émigré writers also attract attention in a variety of forums this year. The composer and novelist Paul Bowles was, in Anatole Broyard's memorable phrase, "the grand panjandrum of paranoid expatriation" ("The Man Who Discovered Alienation," *NYTBR* 6 Aug.:3). Christopher Sawyer-Lauçanno's *An Invisible Spectator* (Weidenfeld & Nicholson) adequately covers the first 55 years of Bowles's melancholy life in some 400 pages, though it abstracts the events of the next 20 years in barely 20 more. Despite its stylistic infelicities, the volume is a more reliable biographical source than Bowles's 1972 autobiography *Without Stopping* (which William Burroughs thought should be entitled *Without Telling*). Nathaniel Branden, the founder of something called the Branden Institute for Self-Esteem, assumes in *Judgment Day: My Years with Ayn Rand* (Houghton Mifflin) the truth of a central tenet of Objectivism: inquiring minds want to know. Branden's book is a perfect gag gift for an M.B.A., a kiss-and-sell memoir of his 18-year relationship with the author of *The Fountainhead*, a novel he read as an adolescent "with the dedication and passion of a student of the Talmud." Beverly Rizzon's *Pearl S. Buck: The Final Chapter* (ETC) is a sophomoric if no less self-serving account of Buck's last years in Vermont by her personal secretary. Finally, Yiorgos D. Kalogeras offers an intriguing poststructural analysis of the competing "New World" and "Old World" discourses in Theano Papazoglou-Margaris's immigration stories in "Suspended Souls, Ensnaring Discourses" (*JMGS* 8:85–96).

iv. Westerners

This year, as usual, the volume of scholarship devoted to Western writers of the period is relatively slight, especially compared to the attention paid the Southerners, though it is of consistently high quality. Frederick Manfred, who nearly won a National Book Award in 1955 for his novel *Lord Grizzly*, enjoys a modest, albeit long-overdue critical revival. The University of Nebraska Press has published *The Selected Letters of Frederick Manfred 1932–1954*, ed. Arthur R. Huseboe and Nancy Owen Nelson. This collection of 161 letters, including several to such prominent literary figures of the period as Sinclair Lewis, Peter De Vries, Wallace Stegner, William Carlos Williams, and Nelson Algren, silhouettes the salient events in the life of the author from his student days at Calvin College at the nadir of the Depression through his literary successes of the late 1940s and early 1950s. Manfred, at the age of 78 a fixture in the Western Literature Association, also has two new novels in press. The Dancing Badger Press issues *Flowers of Desire*, his first novel since 1980, and the University of Oklahoma Press is scheduled to publish his baseball story *No Fun on Sunday* in the spring of 1990. Les Whipp also contributes two fine essays on Manfred's earlier work to the *South Dakota Review*. In "Frederick Manfred's *The Golden Bowl*—The Novel and The Novelist Emerging" (27, iii:54–73), Whipp examines Manfred's 1944 novel as it evolved through its several extant drafts in order to demonstrate the writer's "decreasing responsiveness to the immediate and the local in favor of the timeless and universal" and his "increasing exploitation of Biblical and epic tradition." Whipp's companion piece "Frederick Manfred's *The Wind Blows Free*: Autobiographical Mythology" (27, ii:100–128) reviews Manfred's memoir of the experience on which he based that first novel. *The Wind Blows Free*, as he explains, is "autobiographical reminiscence imaginatively shaped as artistic explanation and creed" and is undergirded by a mythology of female figures "rendered correlative with a sense of response to sexuality, unity, nature, and the transcendent."

Frank Waters and Edward Abbey are each the subject of two major essays in 1989. According to Alexander Blackburn in "Frank Waters's *The Lizard Woman* and the Emergence of the Dawn Man" (*WAL* 24:121–36), Waters's first novel develops the "motif of a nightmare journey into desolation and its paradoxical illumination." Similarly, Frances M. Malpezzi argues in "Meru, the Voice of the Mountain" (*SDR* 27, ii:27–35) that the character of Meru in Waters's novel *The Woman at Otowi Crossing* is "the *axis mundi* through which fictional inhabitants and literary sojourners of Waters' world might find the divine." James I. McClintock in "Edward Abbey's 'Antidotes to Despair' " (*Crit* 31:41–54) places Abbey in the tradition, not of Thoreauvian nature lovers, but of such Western writers as Jack London and Robinson Jeffers "who angrily call attention to self-inflicted social deterioration and advocate radical political solutions." On the other hand, Paul T. Bryant contends in "Edward Abbey and Environmental Quixoticism" (*WAL* 24:37–43) that Abbey was not so much the yeast as the leaven in the loaf of radical activism: the views he expressed in his essays were those of "a balanced, eminently rational environmental moderate." Two other nature essayists are subjects of excellent pamphlets published this year in the Western Writers Series (Boise State): *Joseph Wood Krutch* by Paul N. Pavich and *John Graves* by Dorys Crow Grover. Elisabeth C. Foard also compiles *William Saroyan: A Reference Guide* (Hall), an annotated listing of over a thousand items published between 1934 and 1986. The single most significant contribution to Western literary studies to appear this year, however, is Forrest G. Robinson's revisionist "Heroism, Home, and the Telling of *Shane*" (*ArQ* 45, i:72–100). Whereas earlier criticism of Jack Schaefer's novel is "dominated by attention to broad historical and mythic considerations," Robinson underscores the "subversive strain that runs through the novel." Deliberately or not, Schaefer "gave life in *Shane* to an extremely subtle and complicated triangular struggle" among the hero, Joe, and Marian; that is, "Shane's heroic sacrifices in the service of the all-American family have the effect of undermining that institution by drawing out the weaknesses in the adult members." The narrator cannot "fully grasp the significance" of his own story, which in turn allows readers to ignore the "painful revelations" at its center.

Two Western minority writers also inspire a pair of first-rate essays this year. In "The Red Road to Nowhere: D'Arcy McNickle's *The Surrounded* and 'The Hungry Generations' " (*AIQ* 13:239–48), Louis Owens compares an early manuscript version of McNickle's first novel with the published version—the former something of "a conventional romance" and the latter "a naturalistic novel." Owens concludes that in revising the story, McNickle "chose to underscore the predicament of the mixed-blood trapped irretrievably between worlds and identities." And in "Legacies Revealed: Uncovering Buried Plots in the

Stories of Hisaye Yamamoto" (*SAF* 17:169–81), Stan Yogi perceptively discusses Yamamoto's proficient use of limited narrators in her tales "Seventeen Syllables" and "Yoneko's Earthquake."

v. Easterners

a. **Saul Bellow and Bernard Malamud.** Like a monument or a mountain, the Nobel laureate continues to attract critical, even reverent admirers and more than a few awkward gawks and stares. His novella *A Theft* was published in 1989 as a Penguin paperback original to mostly favorable if mixed reviews. For example, Joyce Carol Oates praised the "parable-like brevity" of the story in the *NYTBR*, though she admitted it is "far from major Bellow" (5 March: 3); and John Updike commended the tale in the *New Yorker*, though he questioned its "curious" and "gossipy" tone (1 May:111–14). Robert F. Kiernan contributes *Saul Bellow*, the only new book-length study on the novelist to appear this year, to Ungar's Literature and Life Series. Kiernan's volume is a splendid introduction to the oeuvre of "America's most obviously intellectual novelist," with a biographical sketch and a separate chapter devoted to each of Bellow's 10 novels and two story collections published through 1987. Gloria L. Cronin and L. H. Goldman edited the critical retrospective *Saul Bellow in the 1980s* (Mich. State), a collection of 18 previously published essays on various aspects of Bellow's work by such scholars as Cronin, Allan Chavkin, Jo Brans, and Gerhard Bach. Only one of these items appeared earlier in 1989: Bach's "The Dean Who Came in From the Cold: Saul Bellow's America of the 1980s" (*SAJL* 8:104–14), an incisive analysis of *The Dean's December* as "parafictional" commentary "on the present state of America, its cultural disorientation and tortured, smug pharisaical *Selbstbild*." Two other contributors to the Cronin/Goldman anthology also publish original essays on Bellow this year. In "Bellow's Dire Prophecy" (*CentR* 33:93–107), Allan and Nancy Feyl Chavkin place *The Dean's December* in the tradition of the jeremiad. In "Holy War Against the Moderns: Saul Bellow's Antimodernist Critique of Contemporary American Society" (*SAJL* 8:77–94), Cronin traces the novelist's "profound dissatisfaction with modern estimates of man" expressed in each of his novels since *The Adventures of Augie March*. Over the past 40 years, according to Cronin, "Bellow has quarreled powerfully" with such modern thinkers as Freud, Nietzsche, and Heidegger. Michael K. Glenday's "Some Versions of Real: The Novellas of Saul Bellow," another essay in *The Modern American Novella* (pp. 162–77), isolates a recurring theme in Bellow's social critique, particularly as it surfaces in *Seize the Day* and *What Kind of Day Did You Have?*: his indictment of "the escapism of Americans, their refusal to face [reality] squarely." And in her chapter on Bellow in *Witness Through the Imagination* (pp. 36–62), S. Lillian Kremer demonstrates that in *The Victim* and *Mr. Sammler's Planet* "Bellow turns to substantive Holocaust exploration." While the Holocaust "is rarely at the dramatic center" of his fiction, its specter haunts his work.

The *Saul Bellow Review* this year features two essays each on *Herzog* and *Humboldt's Gift*. M. Gilbert Porter expertly analyzes "the actual functioning of narrative technique" in the former work in " 'Weirdly Tranquil' Vision: The Point of View of Moses Herzog" (8, i:3–11); and Dan Vogel asserts the novel is nothing less than a Bellovian animadversion on T. S. Eliot's best-known poem in "Bellow, Herzog, and *The Waste Land*" (8, i:44–50). In "Rip Van Citrine: Failure of Love and Marriage vs. Sanctity of Male Relationships in *Humboldt's Gift*" (8, i:12–23), William G. Coleman contends, not altogether convincingly, that Bellow's 1975 novel "seems almost written according to [Leslie] Fiedler's theory of American male fiction" promulgated in *Love and Death in the American Novel*; and in the ponderously prolix "Gender and Self-Deception in *Humboldt's Gift*" (8, ii:14–23), David L. Cowles opines that Charlie Citrine must learn "to jettison his socialized masculine roles" and "listen to the inner voice of his own deepest, most real self." Karl F. Knight also examines in "The Rhetoric of Bellow's Woody Selbst: Religion and Irony" (8, i:35–43) the verbal strategies the writer used in "A Silver Dish" to depict the ironic struggle between "feminized Christianity" and "a hearty Jewish masculinity." Among the other essays in *SBN* are three fine comparative studies: M. A. Quayum's "Finding the Middle Ground: Bellow's Philosophical Affinity with Emerson in *Mr. Sammler's Planet*" (8, ii:24–38); David D. Anderson's "Hemingway and Henderson on the High Savannas" (8, ii:59–75); and David H. Hirsch's "Jewish Identity and Jewish Suffering in Bellow, Malamud and Philip Roth" (8, ii:47–58).

Despite his lesser celebrity, Malamud inspires three excellent articles this year in his own right. Kremer devotes another chapter of *Witness Through the Imagination* (pp. 81–102) to the "Holocaust consciousness" that permeates Malamud's postwar tales of Jewish life, particularly such stories as "The Lady of the Lake," "The German Refugee," and, of course, *The Fixer.* Kremer determines that, like Bellow, "Malamud appears reticent to treat the Holocaust directly," though its impact informs much of his fiction. In "Malamud's Revisions to 'The Magic Barrel'" (*Crit* 30:252–60), Lawrence Dessner concludes on the basis of the "small-scale refinements" made in this story after its initial publication in 1954 that its "real subject is the ambiguous evidence of the presence of the supernatural." Also, James M. Mellard assays Malamud's ironic treatment of pastoral conventions in his college novel in "Academia and the Wasteland: Bernard Malamud's *A New Life* and His Views of the University," an essay in *The American Writer and the University* (pp. 54–67).

b. **J. D. Salinger and Others.** Like magnets in a bucket of metal filings, a menagerie of minor writers attracts a glut of interest this year. For example, the former host of "Ralph Gardner's Bookshelf" on local New York radio publishes transcripts of his on-air chats with such figures germane to this chapter as Isaac Asimov, Budd Schulberg, and Evan Hunter in *Writers Talk to Ralph D. Gardner* (Scarecrow). Gardner proves he is definitely no master of the talk radio format, asking such banal questions as (to Asimov) "How do you find time to write all those books?" Rod McKuen contributes an introduction. Despite her scholarly credentials, Elizabeth Evans has written a remarkably poor book in *May Sarton, Revisited* (TUSAS 551), with its pedantic style and defensive tone; e.g., "There will always be the academic critic who finds [Sarton's] appeal unacceptable for scholarly response." Certainly Sarton deserves better. Not only does Evans ignore Sarton's short stories, but she covers her 21 novels in a single chapter of only 35 pages.

Fortunately, some of the other minor Eastern writers of the period receive more creditable consideration. David Seed undertakes the critical reclamation of the Glass family saga in "Keeping It in the Family: The Novellas of J. D. Salinger," yet another chapter in *The Modern American Novella* (pp. 139–61). Whereas most reviewers agree Salinger "lost the critical detachment necessary to view his characters" more or less objectively, Seed suggests that the opacity of the Glasses enabled Salinger "to use a variety of narrative methods" otherwise unavailable to him. James Finn Cotter speculates in "A Source for Seymour's Suicide: Rilke's *Voices* and Salinger's *Nine Stories*" (*PLL* 25:83–98) that Salinger borrowed the "scaffolding" for his col-

lection from the German poet and asserts, more problematically, that
reading the stories "in the light of Rilke's *Voices* enriches our appreciation of Salinger's intention."

Three other members of the *New Yorker* coterie are subjects of
recent biographical and bibliographical projects. Arthur F. Kinney
edits "Dorothy Parker's Letters to Alexander Woollcott" (*MR* 30:
487–515). Thomas Fensch, who last year compiled *Conversations with
John Steinbeck* for the Literary Conversations Series (*ALS 1988*, p.
260), returns in 1989 with *Conversations with James Thurber* (Miss.),
a selection of 23 interviews with the humorist conducted between
1939 and 1961. Judy Oppenheimer's *Private Demons: The Life of
Shirley Jackson*, first issued in 1988, appears in a paperback edition
this year. It is a literate and literary biography of the writer which
should bring the simmering revival of interest in Jackson's work to
full boil. Judie Newman also fuels the revival with "Shirley Jackson
and the Reproduction of Mothering: *The Haunting of Hill House*"
(*American Horror Fiction*, pp. 120–34). Newman discusses the dynamics of the mother-daughter relation in Jackson's gothic novel from
a feminist-psychoanalytical perspective. Casey Herrick also has compiled a supplemental checklist to criticism of Jackson's "The Lottery"
(*BB* 46:120–21). Two additional volumes merit brief mention in this
category. Edwin W. Gaston, Jr., has revised and updated his TUSAS
book on Conrad Richter in light of recent scholarship and biographical data available only since Richter's death in 1968 (TUSAS 81). And
Jack Bales publishes *Kenneth Roberts: The Man and His Works*
(Scarecrow), a pioneering biobibliographical study which includes a
first-rate sketch of Roberts's life based on interviews and extant correspondence as well as an annotated listing of about a thousand reviews
and other published comment about his work. Bales is currently writing a book on Roberts for the Twayne series.

vi. Iconoclasts and Detectives

Critical interest in the "iconoclasts," as in the leftists, seems to be on
the decline nowadays. Ted Morgan's *Literary Outlaw* (Holt, 1988),
a biography of William Burroughs received too late for inclusion last
year, is irreverent if not "gonzo" journalism—chatty and impression-
istic, occasionally even wrong (as when Ring Lardner, Jr., is described
as "the author of M*A*S*H"), but thoroughly entertaining withal.
For better or worse, Nathanael West's novels enjoy little more than a

cult following, at least to judge from the frequency with which they are mentioned in the journals. Only two articles appear on West this year. In "*Miss Lonelyhearts* and the Rhetoric of Disintegration" (*CollL* 16:219–31), Robert Wexelblatt argues that in its very clichéd and parodic style the novel is designed to illustrate the breakdown of civilized order. As Wexelblatt explains, "*Miss Lonelyhearts* demonstrates how the disease of disintegration may be said to provide the language of its own diagnosis." Similarly, Harold Beaver's "Nathanael West's 'Chamber of American Horrors'" (*The Modern American Novella*, pp. 85–96) emphasizes the comic-strip quality of West's fiction: He "wrote not 'novellas' so much as Menippean farces to shock America out of its mass-produced and mass-consumed formulaic expectations."

The horror- and science-fiction writers of the period fare little better. The major exception to the wholesale neglect of these figures is *American Horror Fiction*, a first-rate collection of critical essays which not only includes Newman's piece on Shirley Jackson but Clive Bloom's "This Revolting Graveyard of the Universe: The Horror Fiction of H. P. Lovecraft" (pp. 59–72), an excellent introduction to Lovecraft's enigmatical corpus and his xenophobic "materialistic belief system"; David Punter's "Robert Bloch's *Psycho*" (pp. 92–106), on the "pathological contexts" of Norman Bates's psychodrama; and Odette L'Henry Evans's "A Feminist Approach to Patricia Highsmith's Fiction" (pp. 107–19), a rather superficial linguistic analysis of such stories as *High Water* and *The Glass Cell*.

Old gumshoes never die; they just charge more for their stories. Mickey Spillane's Mike Hammer and Raymond Chandler's Marlowe polish the rust off their guns and come out of retirement this year. At 18 bucks a book, who can blame them? Spillane's *The Killing Man* (Dutton) has the grace of a jackhammer and all the subtlety of smeared lipstick. Robert B. Parker, author of the Spenser novels, completes the fragment of "The Poodle Springs Story" Chandler left at his death in 1959. (In fact, the four chapters that are bona fide Chandler were published in 1962 in *Raymond Chandler Speaking*. Do I smell an expiring copyright?) *Poodle Springs* (Putnam) thus is a sidekick of sorts to last year's *Raymond Chandler's Philip Marlowe: A Centennial Celebration* (Knopf), ed. Byron Preiss, a collection of 23 new Marlowe stories by contemporary mystery writers. Obviously, the heirs are trying to generate a little cash flow. The works of Chandler and Dashiell Hammett are discussed sympathetically this year in T. J.

Binyon's taxonomic 'Murder Will Out': The Detective in Fiction (Oxford); and each of them receives a fair hearing at the bar of critical journals. In "Raymond Chandler and the Business of Literature" (TSLL 31:592–609), Johanna M. Smith suggests that Chandler expressed a conflicted view of his own writing as both business transaction and art in the "ambivalent professionalism" of Marlowe, who was likewise "a broker in an exchange economy." According to Charles Wasserburg in "Raymond Chandler's Great Wrong Place" (SWR 74: 534–45), Chandler depicted Los Angeles as both seedy city and dream machine so as to represent the cultural as well as criminal deceptions which occur there. G. Michael Doogan summarizes the available data on Hammett's wartime service in the Aleutians in "Dash-ing Through the Snow" (ArmD 22:82–91). William Marling, the author of the TUSAS volume on Hammett (ALS 1983, pp. 281–82), resurfaces this year with "The Style and Ideology of The Maltese Falcon" (Proteus 6:42–50), on the modern architectonics of the novel. And, finally, James F. Maxfield sensibly summarizes the naturalistic implications of Hammett's story and John Huston's adaptation of it in "La Belle Dame Sans Merci and the Neurotic Knight: Characterization in The Maltese Falcon" (LFQ 17:253–60). Rather than an avenging angel in a trench coat, it seems, Sam Spade is an amoral, compulsive neurotic. Little wonder his hands shake and he thinks the cops are on his case.

University of New Mexico

14. Fiction: The 1960s to the Present

Jerome Klinkowitz

Unlike earlier periods where styles of interpretation may have held sway for a generation or longer, contemporary studies provide the level playing ground where opposing forces choose to test their finest skills. Major fiction written in the 1970s and 1980s postdates by as much as a decade the introduction of new critical issues from deconstruction and feminism to revived interest in literary history and the authority of canonical selection. Indeed, when one of this year's most challenging works of scholarship includes the words "mastery" and "masterwork," bells ring and signals flash, because by his employment of these terms the critic is engaging not just the work at hand but the very language that another school of analysis would disallow. Questions to keep in mind: is the secondary business of interpretational style displacing the literary work itself, and are those literary works being shaped, in their contemporaneous inception and execution, by such extraliterary concerns?

i. General Studies

With their sights set, respectively, on the past, the present, and the future, Stacey Olster, Tom LeClair, and Ihab Hassan cover the range of interpretations available to contemporary critics facing the fiction of their own age. Olster's *Reminiscence and Re-Creation in Contemporary American Fiction* (Cambridge) rescues history for an era that has striven to deny its authority. Five significant authors reaching across recent decades "portray history in terms of various spiral processes" that deny time any notion of stasis, prevent the past from being repeatable, and effectively close off simultaneity of direction, thereby contradicting three tenets of literary postmodernism. For Olster, Norman Mailer's career is an encapsulation of withdrawal and reemergence in terms of an author's relationship to his or her subject. Loving or hating it, Mailer cannot exist without such represented material, which in his recent work is "engaged in making the destiny of Western man." Yet if a scientific relationship to such subjects protects the artist from ambiguity, Thomas Pynchon's fiction restores ambiguity to both science and art, a career development that takes the author from the sacred to the secular, "from a religious to an entropic vision of history." John Barth's early novels establish how fictive tools are needed to convey historical knowledge, while his later works "consider what occurs when those tools no longer prove adequate to the task," an interesting situation in which the novel's form is deliberately strained as it struggles to represent itself without repeating itself. Much like Linda Hutcheon in *A Poetics of Postmodernism* (*ALS 1988*, pp. 288–89), Olster finds a contemporary solution to these struggles in the "subjective historicism" favored by Robert Coover and E. L. Doctorow, a disposition in which authors "do not feel compelled to limit themselves to facts alone when re-creating the past in their works."

Coover's *The Public Burning* is the "hot center" of Tom LeClair's *The Art of Excess: Mastery in Contemporary American Fiction* (Illinois), and within what LeClair describes as a "syntext" knit together from the era's most important novels Coover's work serves a vastly different function. What Olster delights in as historically relevant but clearly imaginative play, LeClair sternly professes as an essentially political lesson of how primitive cultural and religious forms underlie our supposed rational progress in governance. Moreover, *The Public Burning* is a warning about the ghastliness of future politics, something LeClair fears cannot be reversed unless scholars of the contemporary cease "amusing themselves to death." "Signs are taken for wonders," he complains, quoting T. S. Eliot as a corrective to the present age in which "small minds and small books are taken for cultural achievements." Like Olster, LeClair would return a consciousness of history to contemporary fiction, but argues from a posture of moral empowerment that a definite style of "mastery" is needed for survival. His vehicle for such authority is systems theory, and within its paradigms he reads Pynchon's *Gravity's Rainbow* as the philosophy of a new earthly model (replacing fragmentation with a transformed sense of wholeness), Joseph Heller's *Something Happened* as a sociology of effaced identity, William Gaddis's *JR* as a critique of current economics, Joseph McElroy's *Women and Men* (described as the decade's best novel and most important since *Gravity's Rainbow*) as his syntext's central reformulation, John Barth's *LETTERS* as a re-examination of how far the godly authority of paternal authorship can be carried, and Ursula Le Guin's *Always Coming Home* (a prognosis for the best fiction of the 1990s and a prescription to save our next millenium) as a reversal of patriarchal structures with an emphasis on reconstructing notions of home, family, and future. The urgency of LeClair's mission reflects the apocalyptic tenor of *The Public Burning*, a text the critic finds uncomfortably close to the America in which he lives. Admittedly more of an argument with other interpretations than a studied treatment of the fiction itself, *The Art of Excess* nevertheless proves what can be accomplished by a dedicated reader who has found personal meaning in a philosophy of communications that may or may not prove as useful for understanding current fiction as have the contending theories of humanism and deconstructive postmodernism employed by his colleagues.

As Olster argues for a fiction that engages history, and LeClair debates our present literary ways of facing present-day life and their implications for survival, Ihab Hassan addresses himself to a style of writing that by definition "cohabits with belief" in a way both Olster and LeClair desire in their own models. *Selves at Risk* (Wisconsin) argues that history alone cannot always provide a useful example, for it is at times regressive (certainly in our own age, when the popular historical imperative is represented by *Rambo I*, *Rambo II*, and *Rambo III*); nor can any theory, whether humanistic, systemic, or deconstructive, solve problems of survival, because facing the future is ultimately a test of self. Although Hassan's study ranges broadly through American thought and literature, his view of recent fiction is especially pertinent to the issues Olster and LeClair raise. The genuine quest novel "puts all pieties of belief or disbelief in question" because its very being places itself at risk, yielding the seriousness of purpose LeClair requires while providing a subject at once more compelling and less complicated than Olster's "subjective historicism." A hybrid mode "that conveys both the perplexities of the postmodern condition and the ancient, visionary powers of myth," Hassan's quest literature encompasses a development in fiction that runs from Harriet Doerr's *Stones for Ibarra* (overcoming the challenge of cultural misapprehension) and Joan Didion's *A Book of Common Prayer* (moral regeneration at the cost of erasures, evasions, and deferrals) through Eleanor Clark's *Camping Out* (memory and atonement) and James

Dickey's *Deliverance* (deliverance from the ordeal of otherness). At
Hassan's fictive pinnacle are Norman Mailer's *Why Are We in Vietnam?* (individual fulfillment in a landscape of defeat) and Saul Bellow's *Henderson the Rain King* (Emersonian *whim* helping the hero
transcend social limitations while maintaining human allegiance, with
identity found in communion with all life); significantly, each is a
work of language, relying on a preeminence of fictively narrative
voice rather than on reference. Anticipating both Olster's and Le-
Clair's needs, Hassan reminds us that even fiction has its limits; for
narratives to become truly exemplary in the way both of these younger
critics require, the writer must turn to actual experiences in life, as
the experiential quest narratives of Paul Bowles, Paul Theroux, and
Peter Matthiessen show.

Can fiction ever be sufficiently real to satisfy the deep concern
that resides, however paradoxically, in each of us? To amplify and extend her position on matters of representation, Linda Hutcheon turns
from the poetics of postmodern to its politics. The historiographic
metafiction celebrated in her earlier work avoids both the "pre-
sentism" and "nostalgia" that characterize the two major contending
views by denaturalizing the temporal relationship between fiction
and any possible subject, historical or otherwise. In *The Politics of
Postmodernism* (Routledge) she demonstrates how novelists such as
Doctorow and Coover "juxtapose what we think we know of the past
(from official archival sources and personal memory) with an alternate
representation that foregrounds the postmodern epistemological questioning of the nature of historical knowledge." The questions *Ragtime*
and *The Public Burning* ask are not whether fact outweighs fantasy
(or vice versa) or whether something like systems theory is the solution to planetary survival, but "Which 'facts' make it into history?
And *whose* facts?" From that inquiry comes a style of fiction that is
both reflective and reflexive, examining not the world but our examination of it. Hutcheon's argument becomes especially convincing
when she allies it not with notions of authority and mastery but with
the reconsiderations feminism has urged regarding even larger challenges, including "that humanist universal called 'Man' " and the de-
naturalization of inhibiting mythologies.

A more traditionally informed study of alternatives to realism mo-
tivates John Kuehl's *Alternate Worlds* (NYU). His worry is that departures from realism have found an audience only among academics,
and a minority of academics at that. Wishing to broaden the perti-

nence of such work, Kuehl employs his editor, James W. Tuttleton, to write a 20,000-word introduction placing contemporary innovative fiction within the great American traditions of romance and unbounded imagination. Tuttleton's view of irrealism, however, is one used by neoconservatives such as Gerald Graff (*Literature Against Itself*) and Christopher Lasch (*The Culture of Narcissism*): that discarding reality "exemplifies the human spirit's break with political oppression and psychic repression." Such freedoms may play a role in innovative fiction's form, but when their terms of definition remain realistic in themselves the invitation to refutation by tautology remains open (as both *Literature Against Itself* and *The Culture of Narcissism* prove). As Hutcheon has shown, postmodern fiction has its own commitment to both the political and the psychic, but by following Tuttleton's lead, Kuehl struggles with his task of justifying what is too easily dismissed as a nihilistic surrender to nightmare existence. The basis for this interpretation is in modernism, and it is no surprise that for each of Kuehl's typologies he can match a current model with an older one. For the ludic style of metafiction favored by Gilbert Sorrentino and William H. Gass, he compares the work of Flann O'Brien and Vladimir Nabokov; the irrational grotesqueries practiced by John Hawkes find their analogue in those of Flannery O'Connor, just as John Barth's absurd quests are prefigured by Nathanael West's. Only for Kuehl's last category, the apocalypse, do his comparisons stay within current bounds, but even here Kurt Vonnegut's idiosyncrasies get lumped together with Norman Mailer's involvements with history, while Thomas Pynchon's use of entropy collapses into the simpler Christian viewpoints operative in the novels of William Gaddis. Because Kuehl reads all of his types as variants of the first, work such as Walter Abish's—a fiction that strips language of its referentiality so that matters of surface and generative system can be sufficiently narrational in themselves—is treated as metafiction that replays the same realistic terms instead of shooting beyond them into a genuinely postmodern realm.

Similar limitations detract from Peter Conn's *Literature in America: An Illustrated History* (Cambridge). By interpreting techniques in terms of their effect on theme, Conn is able to follow Josephine Hendin's lead (established 11 years ago in *Vulnerable People*) and reduce Vonnegut's fiction to psychosis, Hawkes's to nightmare, Barth's to simple storytelling, and Barthelme's to an evaporation of the authorial self into nebulous fragments and formulae. Yet flanking these reductive readings of the major innovationists are solid appreciations of the ethical and political concerns in Philip Roth's increasing reliance on Kafka and of how Henry Miller's ideals for the self in art are central to the work of Ronald Sukenick.

Sukenick himself demonstrates this point in his "Introduction: The Dirty Secret" (*Witness* 3, ii–iii:7–9). Amplifying Miller's aesthetic and adapting it to postmodern times, Sukenick (as guest editor of a double issue devoted to his type of fiction) argues that "experimental writing is just writing that breaks out of the modes of literature into something resembling the freaky uniqueness of individual experience beyond the usual brainwash of official culture." Such goals are shared by Ihab Hassan's questers in *Selves at Risk*, though Sukenick sees "the literary" as an additional piece of received authority that needs to be eclipsed to reach a different level of reality—what Sukenick calls in another introduction, "Not for Everyone" (*Black Ice* No. 5: v–vi), "an unusual kind of verisimilitude" that can "reproduce the cryptic, complex and bewilderingly various textures of contemporary experience. In so doing they implicitly subvert the numbing monotony that a prefab version of reality promotes."

A plea for the moral verities of art is lodged by another guest editor, James Carroll, whose "The Virtue of Writing" (*Ploughshares* 15, ii–iii:1–10) reminds readers that there is a core of meaning at the heart of every good work of fiction: "Writers . . . dig down to the world's secret—their own version of it—having already committed themselves to reveal its truth without knowing in advance what it is. They are like the first nuclear scientists in that sense and unlike farmers and miners who always know what the earth holds for them." Without John Gardner's moral fiction, readers would be "in the dark hole . . . cut off from one another and from any real sense of themselves. Moral fiction enables readers to identify with—become one with—someone else's experience." It is not this sense of sharing that Sukenick eschews, but the style of authority behind such claims that the grounding for it is as scientific as nuclear physics (if not of agronomy or geology).

The insularity of such assumptions prompts the revolution described by Robert Siegle in *Suburban Ambush: Downtown Writing and the Fiction of Absurdity* (Hopkins). Siegle derives the label from the lower New York City neighborhoods where these writers live, in touch with a more vibrant energy than is available to "the tunnel and bridge set" who flee the city's vitality for the sterile suburbs where they read the academically polite midlist fiction published by equally cloistered editors working in midtown Manhattan (for a defense of such self-described "midfiction," see Alan Wilde's *Middle Grounds*, *ALS 1987*, pp. 284–85). The downtown writers include Kathy Acker, Lynne Tillman, Catherine Texier, Theresa Cha, Ron Kolm, and Constance DeJong. Several qualities set their work apart from that school of neorealism: an aggressive pursuit of the issues of language and representation (born of postmodern theory rather than moral piety), a retention of fictive form's reflexive edge, an ability to be "savvy about the role of institutions and discourses," a willingness to play "the double agent's game" (occupying institutions and subverting them from within, such as Kathy Acker's "violent appropriations and rewriting of literary classics"), a commitment to practice no exclusionary rules, a "hunger for spirit without theology and the church," and a privileging of feminist elements. It is this last element that insures the significance of downtown writing, since it faces directly the major cultural transformation of our times.

ii. Women

For the first time since topics and techniques of special pertinence to women's issues became a focus of this chapter, they correspond directly with theses developed and debated in the best of 1989's general studies. Setting this trend is Patricia Waugh's *Feminine Fictions: Revisiting the Postmodern* (Routledge) and editors Ellen G. Friedman and Miriam Fuchs's *Breaking the Sequence: Women's Experimental Fiction* (Princeton). Both volumes recognize that fiction by women writers has been largely excluded from the canon of innovative novels and short stories established in the 1960s and 1970s, and each argues that several women merit treatment in the terms customarily reserved for the work of Barthelme, Gass, and Sukenick.

Waugh's case for exclusion is based not on stereotyping or overt sexism but rather on the fact that as postmodernism deconstructed character, feminism constructed it with an aim toward expressing women's "need to discover . . . and fight for . . . a sense of unified selfhood, a rational, coherent, effective identity." What is deconstructed is "the myth of woman as absolute Other and its exposure as a position within masculine discourse." Such subjectivity foregrounds "the construction of identity *in relationship*," a much more savvy political plan for attaining subjecthood than allowed by conventionally postmodern dispersal. Waugh's readings similarly enlarge our understanding of the truly contemporary aspects of a fully gendered postmodernism: Sylvia Plath's *The Bell Jar* allows opposing demands to coexist in a state "where the need for resolution no longer makes its conflicting claims on body and mind"; Anne Tyler eschews radical experiment in favor of deploying the conventions of family sagas and gothic novels in new ways; Grace Paley refuses totalization in both form and content. An apparently more conventional group of writers that includes Joanna Russ, Alice Walker, and Marge Piercy writes in a manner that "reveals fictional structures in which the forms of desire, only superficially if at all modified by a realist consensus and a liberal ethos, are closer to the surface of the text" than traditional form allows. Between these examinations of literary theory and practical readings are helpful chapters that sort out the various psychological approaches to gender in fiction and a discussion of the misinterpretations that led to the exclusion of women from discussions of innovative fiction in the first place.

The most convincing arguments in *Breaking the Sequence* are made for British authors who have received their most sustained attention in France: Ann Quinn and Christine Brooke-Rose. It is interesting to recall that Brooke-Rose, a fictionist championed by Ronald Sukenick, was dismissed by the same academicians who in the 1970s derided Sukenick's theories, while the style of preference in America remained what Josephine Hendin termed the psychological realism of Joyce Carol Oates. There is an attempt here to recover Oates for the innovative fiction tradition by claiming that in *Bellefleur* she makes topical reference to ideas that are structurally innovative among the recognized literary disruptionists. But the collection's most convincing argument is made by Larry McCaffery ("The Artists of Hell: Kathy Acker and 'Punk' Aesthetics," pp. 215–30) on behalf of Acker's use of performance, process, and the self's energy in the service of art, which extends rather than simply reflects the major innovations of 1960s fiction—an approach shared with Siegle's *Suburban Ambush* (considered above).

Mickey Pearlman is the editor of two similarly useful collections: *Mother Puzzles: Daughters and Mothers in Contemporary American Literature* (Greenwood) and *American Women Writing Fiction* (Kentucky). In the first, she and her contributors suggest that current writers treat mothers not as sainted or overwhelming, blessed or blamed, but as characters more integrally artistic to the literary work. Where mothers are absent, they are often maintained as ghostly presences, a function that relates to memory as a creative force—something particularly strong in mother-daughter relationships. *American Women Writing Fiction* seizes a more political issue, asking what happens to the standards of American literature when it is written by women and not by men (whose work has established those standards). Here, the most convincing essays are Pearlman's "Susan Fromberg Schaeffer: The Power of Memory, Family, and Space" (pp. 137–47), which treats enclosed space as a woman might experience it, together with the negative powers of memory and the tension between family and outsiders, and Phyllis Lassner's "Jayne Anne Phillips: Women's Narrative and the Recreation of History" (pp. 193–206), which explores Phillips's complex definition of space as home and probes the need for escape from it even though it is the locus for a woman's identity.

Joining the generalists in their trend toward studying fiction in relation to language theory and poetics are Nancy Walker in "Language, Irony, and Fantasy in the Contemporary Novel by Women" (*LIT* 1:37–57) and Marilee Lindemann in " 'This Woman Can Cross Any Line': Power and Authority in Contemporary Women's Fiction" (*Engendering the Word*, pp. 105–24). Wallace relates irony and fantasy to language, remarking that in Marge Piercy's fiction "the perception that language is arbitrary and mutable can be the first step toward liberation." Though male-dominated conceptualization tends to silence women's language, Maxine Hong Kingston's work transposes that condition into a new form of articulation by taking advantage of the situation's irony: the very thing that is denied woman, her freedom to speak up and be heard, becomes the medium through which she expresses herself. Lindemann's essay outlines further strategies that fictionists have used to gain access to linguistic power and cultural authority, emphasizing how the reader is implicated in what becomes both a spiritualized and politicized act. Gayle Jones, Annie Dillard, and Leslie Marmon Silko are especially effective in recasting reading as an initiation into the female process.

How science fiction as a subgenre offers further opportunities for women's expression is explained by Sarah Lenfanu in *Feminism and Science Fiction* (Indiana). Like feminism itself, science fiction benefits from the latitude established by the gothic novels of the nineteenth century. When the socially radical politics of the 1960s and

1970s are added, science fiction can offer women genuinely new ways
of writing and of viewing feminist issues in various social constructs.
Joanna Russ, Ursula Le Guin, James Tiptree, Jr., and Marge Piercy
take advantage of science fiction as a natural vehicle for critiquing
ideas otherwise accepted without question as "innate."

Single-author studies proliferate, but among the most significant
is Sau-ling Cynthia Wong's refutation of certain Asian-American objections to the text now considered central to feminist minority concerns. Her "Necessity and Extravagance in Maxine Hong Kingston's
The Woman Warrior: Art and the Ethnic Experience" (*MELUS* 15,
i[1988]:3–26) recounts how the work has been considered "ideologi-
cally suspect" and passed off as autobiography by its publisher, who
declined to recognize its obviously fictive nature. These charges,
Wong believes, reflect the way ethnic literature is received in an
America that considers "unique" depictions reprehensible because
they "threaten to 'distort' " accepted definitions of specific minority
groups. A new biography, *Bitter Fame: A Life of Sylvia Plath*
(Houghton Mifflin) by Anne Stevenson, attempts to sort out the
self-constructed icons in Plath's life by balancing the recriminations
of *The Bell Jar* and various journals against a more generous account
of Ted Hughes's role as husband and mentor (as established in materials provided by Hughes's sister, Olwyn Hughes, the literary agent
to Plath's estate). Welcome attention to a less studied author is provided by Martha Ravits in "Extending the American Range: Mari-
lynne Robinson's *Housekeeping*" (*AL* 61:644–66) and by Anne-Marie
Mallon in "Sojourning Women: Homelessness and Transcendence in
Housekeeping" (*Crit* 30:95–105). Set consciously against the great
texts of the American tradition, Robinson's novel engages both that
tradition and the countertradition established among newer interests
of more recent years. "By shaping a plot about a young woman's discovery of solace and self-realization in solitude with nature," Ravits
indicates, "Robinson lifts herself upon the shoulders of literary ancestors to demonstrate that the empowering attribute of self-reliance
can be claimed by female as well as male protagonists." Mallon prefers to read the novel in terms of traditional expectations being broken,
a structural ploy that reinforces the theme that "Robinson's women
will not be contained within customary frames nor distracted by conventional stories of feminine valor." Crucial to the author's modification of our literary canon is the belief expressed in *Housekeeping* that

"the order of the world is informed by mystery and should be received with awe."

iii. Cynthia Ozick, Philip Roth, and other Jewish-Americans

"It would be hard to think of two writers who differ more sharply about Jewishness than Roth and Ozick," Sanford Pinsker admits in his "Jewish-American Literature's Lost-and-Found Department: How Philip Roth and Cynthia Ozick Reimagine Their Significant Dead" (*MFS* 35:223–35). Drawing on Saul Bellow's experimentation with the responsibilities of the dead to the living, Roth uses Kafka as a model for having a character live what otherwise might just be imagined (not just in *The Breast* but throughout *The Ghost Writer*), while Ozick's *The Messiah of Stockholm* plays off the Kafka-like author Bruno Schulz as a way of incorporating the history of literature into her literature of history. A second major Roth critic, Stanley Trachtenberg, also studies *The Ghost Writer*, and to similar effect. "In the Egosphere: Philip Roth's Anti-Bildungsroman" (*PLL* 25:326–41), he proposes that by privileging the imagination over reality, the hero's education becomes more a matter of invention than experience (even Lonoff influences Zuckerman more as an author than as an interactive character). Rounding out the key essayists on Roth is Mark Schechner, whose "Zuckerman's Travels" (*AmLH* 1:219–30) praises *The Counterlife* for its counterpointing of the inertia of history with the agility of imagination, a strategy that yields not only startling paradoxes but outright contradictions that sustain themselves in narrative suspension. Roth's career since *My Life as a Man* "has been an exercise in getting beyond the platitudes of the Freudian system and finding resonances and amplitudes that expand and enrich the character rather than, as psychoanalysis finally does, infantilize and deplete it," Schechner believes, finding that *The Counterlife* turns away from analysis and "toward synthesis, toward putting the self back together through history and culture."

An important overview is provided by S. Lillian Kremer in *Witness Through the Imagination*. Her question is a good one: why, in the 1960s, did so many writers address the Holocaust of 20 years before? The apprehension and trial of Adolf Eichmann may have been a stimulant, just as the Seven Day War empowered a more aggressive sense of articulating Jewish concerns. Yet the Holocaust has always

been a subject that exceeds words, and so it is the newer era's innovative aesthetics that returns to that event as a challenge for the
literary imagination. The range of Kremer's examples is noteworthy,
from the documentary testimony in Leslie Epstein's *The King of the
Jews*, the openness of Richard Elman's Holocaust trilogy, and the
historical dimension treated almost theologically by Isaac Bashevis
Singer (where the emphasis is not on the ghetto itself but on its loss)
to Cynthia Ozick's fusing of Jewish and Western sensibilities, Arthur
A. Cohen's success at posing all Jews as survivors, and Chaim Potok's
vision of restoration in Israel.

iv. Walker Percy, Mary Lee Settle, and other Southerners

As usual, Walker Percy dominates the field of literary study when it
comes to the contemporary American South. Lois Parkinson Zamora,
who chooses Percy together with Pynchon and Barth as her chief
American exemplars in *Writing the Apocalypse: Historical Vision in
Contemporary U.S. and Latin American Fiction* (Cambridge), suggests why his fiction is so attractive to those with a cause to be championed. Percy's Christian eschatology offers a real physical end of the
line, as opposed to Pynchon's metaphorical repository of historical
consciousness as an impetus for apocalyptic renewal and Barth's reflexive aesthetic (a posture shared with the Latin American writers in
Zamora's study). Pynchon overcomes the apocalypse by substituting
entropy as a metaphor; Barth survives it by draining apocalyptic
forms of their historical significance; only Percy, in her view, finds a
solution within a more traditional orientation. The skeptical side of
this equation is explored by Kieran Quinlan in *"The Moviegoer*: The
Dilemma of Walker Percy's Scholastic Existentialism" (*Modern American Fiction*, pp. 213–34). In this initial novel, form fails to achieve
the function Percy intends because it is not textually apparent that
Binx leaps from the aesthetic to the religious, skipping over the ethical
(hard as it is to convey the supernatural, Binx's change of heart is
nevertheless unprepared). "Walker Percy's Comedy and *The Thanatos Syndrome*" (*SLJ* 22:3–16) finds Robert Hughes making a convincing case that the author's supposedly dour philosophy in truth
serves a comic function: "the absurd is no mere abstraction in his
work, but something funny," which provides "an essential aspect of
his art and the key element in his liberating moral view."

"Mary Lee Settle and the Critics" (*VQR* 65:401–17) is more than just a reputation study, for in it Brian C. Rosenberg traces Settle's uneven reception to academia's prejudice against historical fiction as a Victorian form and as a style of writing that demands a closer correspondence between subject and the world than is currently fashionable. Settle's own nonchronological completion of her canon is another complicating factor. Rosenberg explores these issues and others in "The Price of Freedom: An Interview with Mary Lee Settle" (*SoR* 25:351–65); Settle's goal of combining the breadth of Tolstoy with the intimacies of Proust reveals her dislike for strategies that limit one to the "either/or."

Gail Godwin's sixth novel, though set in upstate New York, is "a testament to the endurance of the Southern sense of place," according to Anne Cheney's "A Hut and Three Houses: Gail Godwin, Carl Jung, and *The Finishing School*" (*SLJ* 22:64–71), the key being a Jungian reference to the meaning of the crumbling stone hut that "resembles the Southern cabins of slaves, whom Justin's grandfather respected for their moral and spiritual strength." The South is also a key factor in Joseph C. Voelker's thesis for *Art and the Accidental in Anne Tyler* (Missouri); by resisting Flannery O'Connor's violence and inexorability, Tyler is able to avoid John Updike's hellfire and sinful consciousness while sharing the more tolerant side of his Quaker quietism. Tyler prefers a "gentle decency" that invites a "shuttling of the imagination between inner and outer worlds, a series of impossible or at least impermanent choices," all of which yields a dynamic that generates her narratives.

Tolstoy and Proust, frequent allusions in Rosenberg's treatment of Mary Lee Settle, are cited time and again by William C. Carter in "Seeking the Truth in Narrative: An Interview with Shelby Foote" (pp. 241–69) from Carter's edition of otherwise previously published dialogues, *Conversations with Shelby Foote* (Miss.), and also in Jefferson Humphries's "Taking Things Seriously: Reynolds Price as Teacher and Writer" (*SWR* 74:10–24). Carter's approach emphasizes how Foote works from character rather than from situation, certainly a method shared with Proust, Flaubert, and Browning; Humphries's references to Stendhal, Flaubert, and Tolstoy are meant to show how Price's "vision of humanity *and* of the English language is grander, more complicated, more *serious*, and (risking redundancy) less trivial, less parochial in time in space" than conventionally best-selling authors might rate.

A Southern writer often faulted for stretching the boundaries of his work is defended by Rhoda Sirlin in *William Styron's* Sophie's Choice: *Crime and Self-Punishment* (UMI Research Press). At the heart of this novel is a critique of presumed American innocence, finding the potency of evil to be a force worthy of Melvillean study. Sirlin's best defense is an aggressive engagement with the reams of critical objections to the novel; by the conclusion of her volume, in which Styron himself is given space to answer the critics, *Sophie's Choice* has been elevated from distracting concerns of the moment and treated in the more seriously engaged manner current critics too often reserve for only foreign writers (a tradition dating from the American reception of Camus to the present-day respect for Kundera).

Battles of another type, perhaps equally extraneous but affecting the state of fiction nevertheless, are detailed by Pat Carr in "John Kennedy Toole, *The Neon Bible*, and a 'Confederacy' of Friends and Relatives" (*MFS* 35:716–18), a record of the legal struggles within and against Toole's estate associated with this novel's publication.

v. The Mannerists: John Updike and John Cheever

For Updike scholars, the Rabbit trilogy continues to draw the lion's share of attention, but other studies help broaden this mannerist's appeal. The finest of recent work is by Brooke Horvath, whose "The Failure of Erotic Questing in John Updike's Rabbit Novels" (*DQ* 23, ii[1988]:70–89) appreciates how "our present erotic crisis" can be traced to "the debasement of love" in "the economic and technological myths informing life in America," a route followed by Updike's protagonist in the trilogy. Raymond A. Mazurek's more sociologically based study, " 'Bringing the Corners Forward': Ideology and Representation in Updike's Rabbit Trilogy" (*Politics and the Muse*, pp. 142–60) interprets it all as "an illness narrative" which by definition tends to be nonanalytical, thus "presenting a way of seeing dominant in middle-class America without the critical distancing that would reveal its own limitations as a narrative rooted in the ideology of post-1950s U.S. society." Victor K. Lasseter prefers locating Updike's third installment within a literary rather than strictly social tradition; his "*Rabbit Is Rich* as a Naturalistic Novel" (*AL* 61:429–45) sees Updike creating as grim a world as Dreiser does in *Sister Carrie* and restricting his hero's freedom as severely (and as ironically) as does Frank Norris in *McTeague*. Emily Miller Budick mediates the issue in *Fiction and Historical Consciousness* by showing how *Rabbit Is Rich* is "deeply vested in historicity" both outwardly to the real world and inwardly to Updike's earlier novels in the cycle. Most significant is what Budick calls the narrative's "absent history": Rabbit's dangerous fantasies that control the novel's action and ultimately give him a historical self. Budick's thesis also covers E. L. Doctorow's *Ragtime*, a work that begins with absent history and prompts an escape into fantasy, a style which makes literary meaning undecidable and thus places indeterminacy within the claims of history. In each case fantasy is historically valid when it opens space for moral and social change.

More familiar but interesting studies are provided by Susan Garland Mann in "John Updike's *Too Far to Go*: The Maples Stories" (*The Short Story Cycle*, pp. 173–83) and by John F. Fleischauer in "John Updike's Prose Style: Definition at the Periphery of Meaning" (*Crit* 30:277–90). Mann is impressed by how patterns in the Maples stories create a unified effect, even though nearly all were written with no thought of being published together; it is the strength of Richard and Joan's own relationship, even in its being sundered, that holds this cycle together. Fleischauer is more closely analytical, noting such techniques as Updike's flamboyant adjectives interrupting his narrative while metaphors "concentrate the flow." The actual in Updike's work is magnified by his soft focus, supported by "a syntax that moves tangentially, through subordinate structures, often by association from noun to noun rather than in a forward logical sweep."

Emerging from letters and biographies, John Cheever seems an even more important writer than when he was alive. Foremost in sorting out critical insights from stereotypes and simplifications has been Robert A. Morace, whose "From Parallels to Paradise: The Lyrical Structure of Cheever's Fiction" (*TCL* 35:502–28) corrects the misunderstanding that the author's novels struggle to hold themselves together within a genre he could never master. It is true that the short story form feels natural for Cheever's treatments of contemporary life, but his novels are in fact "unobtrusive disruptions" of traditionally expected shapes; much like John Hawkes, he felt uneasy with determined plot, preferring "intuition, apprehension, dreams, concepts"—characters and event came to him simultaneously. What unifies *Bullet Park* is the writer's control of rhythm, imagistic repetition, echo, and the accretion of incidents: "Essentially, Cheever plays the same scene or situation over and over with slight but cumulatively significant changes, gradually transforming the real into the fantastic, time into dream."

vi. Realists Old and New: Norman Mailer, Ann Beattie, and Others

A fresh agenda for realism is proposed by Robert J. Begiebing in *Toward a New Synthesis: John Fowles, John Gardner, Norman Mailer* (UMI Research Press). *The Sunlight Dialogues* involves a magical transformation much like Fowles's magus, allowing the novel to propose a philosophy that can be tested in the real world. From the dialectical exchange among Gardner's characters derives a new synthesis of "fully presented yet representative characters." Through imaginative power the aesthetic is connected to the historical, renewing the mystery and vitality of life in the face of the machine age and life's own worst potential. Mailer's *Ancient Evenings* reveals a desire to express all: courage and power, magic and power, sex and power. The constancy of Egyptian civilization is compared to epochs of change, an arrangement which lets the pharaoh's power be examined in the context of competing authorities (notably those of ethics and magic). In the end it becomes a problem of judging one's motives, base or noble—a common Mailer theme. A more theoretical view is taken by Ronald Schleifer in "American Violence: Dreiser, Mailer, and the Nature of Intertextuality" (*Intertextuality and Contemporary American Fiction*, pp. 121–43), building on Mailer's intertextual reading of American literature. In these terms *The Executioner's Song* stands opposed to the novel of manners, thanks to its "violent understanding of literature and experience altogether." By presenting a valid American tragedy as a media event, Mailer provides a vision of our country in a way Dreiser hoped to do but was unable to achieve, given the limitations imposed by a culture pledged to the novelistic values of James and Wharton.

Current issues also show up in this year's work on Joyce Carol Oates. The materials from 1969–89 reprinted in *Conversations with Joyce Carol Oates*, ed. Lee Milazzo (Miss.), often show the hand of a daily newspaper's book critic, an approach that works well when the critic in the trenches is a well-informed theorist such as George Myers, Jr., who senses that it is male rather than female reviewers who keep pressing Oates on her "prodigious" literary production. Myers also raises questions about male as opposed to female veracity and the role of feminist criticism in Oates's work, concerns that more academic and literary reviewers seldom probe. Victor Strandberg, however, is fascinated by the spectacle of "a middle-aged ectomorphic lady with gentle eyes and a soft voice" involving herself with boxing; his "Sex, Violence, and Philosophy in *You Must Remember This*" (*SAF* 17:3–17) sees Schopenhauer and Spinoza as "the two opposing heavy-weights in this ideological match" that is noteworthy for revealing how "violence, that male preserve of power so purely rendered in the boxing ring, exerts a subversive appeal upon this author's feminist sensibility." Yet it is conventional humanism, expressed as "the re-demptive power of memory," that Strandberg sees as finally over-coming such violence.

Although Brooks Landon's *Thomas Berger* (TUSAS 550) buries itself in a surfeit of hagiography and orphic prose (with a dose of television language as an excuse for *Neighbors*), his "The Measure of *Little Big Man*" (*SAF* 17:131–42) provides a valuable reading of this work not in terms of history or anthropology but "as a Thomas Berger novel" that displays "the distinguishing aspect of Berger's style as a novelist," specifically "a thorough-going tendency toward dialectic and paratactic structures." Such structures create multiple levels of meaning, which is where anthropological notions become important, as the protagonist's sense of himself "always looks beyond the concrete satisfaction of his very real accomplishments to the impossibly ab-stract ideal of civilization." How language challenges the world with similar limits is Jon Wallace's concern in "A Murderous Clarity: A Reading of Thomas Berger's *Killing Time*" (*PQ* 68:101–14). Here, the protagonist believes that "spiritual reality is the only reality worth bothering about, and that language is of little value since it partakes of, or can only describe, the material value of ordinary experience," while his antagonists label him according to just one aspect of his personality, thus distracting from his total concrete reality.

Postmodern concerns make their impact on literary realism by just such attention to language and especially the contrasting philos-ophies that structure it. The architect Robert Venturi expresses this idea by substituting "both/and" for "either/or," which is the same formulation Matthew J. Morris finds indicative in "Murdering Words: Language in Action in Don DeLillo's *The Names*" (*ConL* 30:113–27). "Instead of talking about the opposition between linguistic structures and worldly action in this novel," Morris insists, "we should be talking about how different kinds of language permeate and motivate the novel's action," a practice "which opens up the possibility of inclusion, perhaps *and*rogyny" as a way to avoid "murdering words." In "The Revision of the Western in E. L. Doctorow's *Welcome to Hard Times*"

(*AL* 61:78–95), Winifred Farrant Bevilacqua notes another postmodern phenomenon, "the impulse to revitalize the novel by recourse to noncanonical genres as the vehicle of a new vision, style, and content," and reads Doctorow's second novel in these terms, emphasizing how variation of traditional patterns readjusts readers' ways of "seeing, interpreting, and responding to the western story."

Conversely, Joan Didion has followed a course back to closer engagement with politics and social landscape, at least according to this year's leading critics. In the revised edition of *Joan Didion* (*TUSAS* 370), Mark Royden Winchell complements his 1980 reading of Didion's "prismatic" vision and "uncommon ear for speech" with an interpretation of *Salvador, Democracy*, and *Miami* that sees her shifting her critique of the left to a critique of the right in a way that makes politics much more central to her fiction. It is "passionlessness" that poisons the politics Didion critiques in *Miami*, Sharon Felton suggests in her nicely synthetic overview, "Joan Didion: A Writer of Scope and Substance" (*HC* 26, iv:1–10), while Merritt Mosley's "Joan Didion's Symbolic Landscapes" (*SCR* 21, ii:55–64) finds that in her essays fictive devices take the place of exposition, serving as "objective correlatives for intense emotional reaction to things as they are." Meanwhile, two interviews with William Kennedy show him as the consumately engaged author, shifting from journalism to fiction as a way of "really trying to write history," as he tells Douglas R. Allen and Mona Simpson in "The Art of Fiction CXI: William Kennedy" (*Paris Review* No. 112, pp. 34–59) and relates his Albany essays to his novel cycle on that city for Edward C. Reilly in "On an Averill Park Afternoon with William Kennedy" (*SCR* 21, ii:11–24).

The "minimalists," that group of realists that includes Raymond Carver, Bobbie Ann Mason, and Ann Beattie, continue to attract some of the brightest new scholarship. Arthur M. Saltzman, who has distinguished himself as the foremost scholar of innovator William H. Gass (*ALS 1985*, pp. 295–96), takes special care in *Understanding Raymond Carver* (So. Car., 1988) to locate his subject within the contrary streams of innovative and moral fiction. Critics who object to postmodern concerns have used Carver's success as smug revenge, but readings such as these yield an arid minimalism too easily dismissed by theorical-based commentators. Instead, Saltzman urges a study of craft, believing that Carver's work shows the same suspicion of referentiality (especially the expansive sort) that stimulates the innovationists to their more extreme efforts. Innovative fiction broadens what a story can be "about," and Carver takes advantage of this broadness to challenge "received notions of what constitutes significant delivery of information." Like Donald Barthelme, Carver trusts honest fragments more than synthesized wholes; like Ihab Hassan, he avers silence; and like most other innovative fictionists, he strives to defamiliarize the quotidian aspects of life. A similar but more specific analysis informs Adam Meyer's "Now You See Him, Now You Don't, Now You Do Again: The Evolution of Raymond Carver's Minimalism" (*Crit* 30:239–51), establishing from textual evidence that stark minimalism was only a passing phase in the development of Carver's work.

Positive virtues of the harshest minimalism are established by Barbara Henning in "Minimalism and the American Dream: 'Shiloh' by Bobbie Ann Mason and 'Preservation' by Raymond Carver" (*MFS* 35:689–98). Henning's appraisal of intent may be the finest encapsulation of this trend and its effect: "In order to better appreciate the potential implications of Carver's and Mason's flat prose, the reader must be willing to suspend the interpretive moment, following the particular narrator's lead. By concentrating on the literal detail, the narrators rely upon the metonymic pole of language for narrative movement and hesitation. The reader is required to read first syntactically, literally, witnessing and sharing the consciousness and experiences of the narrator and character until the scene or story is finished; then the prose offers the reader a way to resolve the robotic dilemma presented: a metaphoric frame for comparison and reflection, an afterthought for grappling with meaning, a hope for resolution." The scheme, Henning recalls, is Roman Jakobson's, but the key fact is that in *The Modes of Modern Writing* (1977) David Lodge used this same distinction to clarify the achievement of the 1960s' boldest innovators. Ann Beattie's ability to extend and exploit a central image—certainly a conventional technique—is demonstrated by Deborah Dezure in "Images of Void in Beattie's 'Shifting'" (*SSF* 26:11–15), an essay that also indicates Beattie's understanding and employment of contemporary art.

vii. Experimental Realists: Grace Paley, Kathy Acker, Russell Banks

Grace Paley's commitments to feminism and peace activism are not impeded by her allegiance to the more innovative forms of fiction, and by studying her narratives' definitions of love and community Barbara Eckstein elucidates the author's politics and her strategies of plot-making. "Grace Paley's Community: Gradual Epiphanies in the Meantime" (*Politics and the Muse*, pp. 124–41) thus locates Paley's work within a larger tradition that advances women from passive to active roles in tandem with a more activist stance toward disrupting literary conventions, a progression especially evident between *The Little Disturbances of Man* and *Enormous Changes at the Last Minute; Later the Same Day* then resolves the needs of characters "who explicitly seek understanding of time and space beyond the details of their own lives."

The most emphatic disrupter of both conventions and traditional attitudes has been Kathy Acker, whose work is central to Robert Siegle's *Suburban Ambush* (discussed in section *i.*) and receives diverse critical attention in a special number of *RCF* (18, iii), guest-edited by Ellen G. Friedman and Miriam Fuchs. The editors introduce their subject with the advice that "women's experimentalism, though in some ways parallel to its male counterpart tradition, generally has a different political agenda—to search for a language and a form that allow what has been repressed in the patriarchal construction of woman to surface, or if not to surface, at least to recognize the pressures that the repressed exerts on conventional narrative." For this agenda Acker's fiction is a natural, having conspired to define its author as a self-professed outlaw and pariah from which posture she can deconstruct virtually all of Western culture. In *RCF* Acker is allowed the first words—in an interview with Friedman, with a short story, and in a commentary on her own work. Important essays by Naomi Jacobs, Douglas Shields Dix, Martina Sciolino, Lynne Tillman, and Robert Siegle follow, the most helpful of which is Jacobs's "Kathy Acker and the Plagiarized Self" (pp. 50–55), a brilliant justification not just of Acker's work but of how postmodern fiction in general abolishes distinctions "between the real and the imaginary, between the conscious and the subconscious, between the past and the present, between truth and untruth"—a cornerstone of innovative fiction laid by Raymond Federman that now supports the radically new world of feminist literary art. Similar resources support Kathleen Hulley's reading in "Transgressing Genre: Kathy Acker's Intertext" (*Intertextuality and Contemporary American Fiction*, pp. 171–90), a challenging essay that shows how Acker "explicitly transforms current conventions of feminist and political content by articulating the ways in which sexuality and the contradictory liberation movements of our time are predicated on a social construction whose political unconscious is embedded in textually sanctioned father/daughter incest."

The importance of a more subtle work of experimental realism, *Continental Drift*, is weighed by Charles Vandersee in his two-part study in *Cresset*, "Drifting Toward Greatness" (52, ix:9–13) and "Russell Banks and the Great American Reader" (53, ii:13–17). Unlike strictly historical novelists, Banks writes in a way that shows how "the past works upon the present and aspects of the present become the significant (or 'usable') past." Ostensibly a part of the writer's "knowledge" informing the content of his book, Banks's appreciation of Haitian religion in fact provides structural elements that rescue the "young white sensitive male" story line from exhaustion and banality.

viii. Early Innovators: Barth, Heller, Vonnegut, Brautigan, and Pynchon

"The Ideology of Parody in John Barth," John T. Matthews's contribution to *Intertextuality and Contemporary American Fiction*, pp. 35–57, at once narrows Barth's achievement and expands its impact by tracing his method to a Bakhtinian use of parody that lets him not just "thoroughly rearrange source material" but personally reappropriate it in a way that rewrites literary history. As for real history, Barth's same parody keeps it on the margins, a "context denied by content" (such as the women's movement in *Chimera* and the Vietnam War in *Lost in the Funhouse*). Coincidentally, Julius Rowan Raper studies a similar topic in "John Barth's *Chimera*: Men and Women Under the Myth" (*SLJ* 22:17–31) but concludes that the steady movement in Barth's work toward a contrast of protean characters with those of fixed destinies implies a critique of male psychosexual anxieties. Mark Winchell's "Beyond Existentialism: or, The American Novel at the End of the Road" (*Modern American Fiction*, pp. 225–36) describes Barth's first two novels as installments in a series on nihilism that quickly exhausted realism as a technique and nihilism as a subject. That *Lost in the Funhouse* could be not just a collection of stories but the new form of novel Barth was seeking is indicated by Carolyn Norman Slaughter in "Who Gets Lost in the Funhouse" (*ArQ* 44, iv: 80–97), a well-argued case for how postmodern views on the nature and significance of signs affects fiction and how the emphasis has turned "from events themselves to interpretations of them." The strictly metafictional aspects of *Lost in the Funhouse* and *LETTERS* are stressed by Silvio Gaggi as part of his larger thesis in *Modern/ Postmodern* (Penn.); the stories "describe an ironic impasse in which language struggles to escape from itself," while *LETTERS* faces the impasse of metafiction itself, something Gaggi sees as "a huge personal intertextuality" that functions as an even larger "prisonhouse of language" which can be escaped only by projecting "a humanistic content for the novel."

The finest synthesis yet of a sometimes uneven canon is provided by David Seed in *The Fiction of Joseph Heller: Against the Grain* (St. Martin's). Against his earlier attempts at emulating the literary authority of the moderns, Heller learned how to mix the comic and tragic for a grotesque effect that characterized an era: "catch-22." The key to this first novel is its use of circles, repetitions, and flat characters as a way of countering tradition. Public images are given a similar treatment, albeit more thematically, in *Something Happened*, while Heller's subsequent works exploit the ambivalence of political ambition (*Good as Gold*), subvert the ultimate authority (*God Knows*), show how comedy can survive almost anything, even the author's illness (*No Laughing Matter*), and build a narrative from the cynicism behind accepted ideals (*Picture This*). An especially helpful outline of what will probably stand as Heller's greatest novel is found in Stephen W. Potts's *Catch-22: Antiheroic Antinovel* (Twayne). Here, Yossarian is related to the long tradition of absurd heroes, something previous criticism assumes but does not demonstrate (especially in terms of the affinities and distinctions crucial to a postmodern work); Potts also spends time sorting out the novel's chronology rather than surrendering to what earlier commentators have praised or dismissed as "absurdist prose."

Twenty years after the first critical essays on Kurt Vonnegut appeared, a new generation of scholars (who in 1969 were just learning to read) has begun to make key reappraisals of his fictive art. In "The Machine Within: Mechanization, Human Discontent, and the Genre of Vonnegut's *Player Piano*" (*PLL* 25:99–113), Leonard Mustazza refutes arguments that this first novel qualifies as dystopian science fiction by showing how Vonnegut in fact repudiates Huxley's and Orwell's "observations about freedom, bondage, politics, the future, and the human condition." It is not machines but people who cause the novel's problems, specifically "the human romantic urge to envision and create utopias"; *Player Piano* exposes as "simplistic" the belief that "happiness and justice depend upon outward forms alone." A Derridean reading of *Breakfast of Champions, Jailbird,* and Philip José Farmer's *Venus on the Half-Shell* is undertaken by Creed Greer in "Kurt Vonnegut and the Character of Words" (*JNT* 19:312–30), based on the narrator's assertion of his power to "invent" Kilgore Trout. In *Breakfast of Champions,* the schizophrenic narrator cannot establish himself independently of the text, a condition Farmer alleviates by toying with pseudonymity ("The covers of *Breakfast of Champions* cannot contain Kilgore Trout, but neither can the covers of *Venus on the Half-Shell* keep Vonnegut out"). *Jailbird* explores the boundaries between author and text "and between one text and another" so that readers "can see and participate in the boundaries' crossing over."

For Richard Brautigan "the imagination works as both a curse and a blessing," according to Keith Abbott, whose *Downstream from Trout Fishing in America: A Memoir of Richard Brautigan* (Capra) combines biography, critical interpretation, and scholarship to present the most complete picture available of the writer's life and work. What was initially an uncontrollable force in Brautigan's fiction becomes, near the end, a "runaway battle with reality." Although commentators have celebrated his lyrical powers, the truth is that "Brautigan showed how the imagination burgeons inside the mundane, widening what can be admitted as a possibility, until it sometimes parasitically grows to a point where the surrounding host structure (society, friendship, whatever) collapses, explodes or is consumed."

Thomas Pynchon continues to engage the imaginations of critics and scholars, the best of whom publish in *PNotes*. Although two years behind schedule with its 1987 issue carrying a 1989 copyright, the combined nos. 20–21 is nevertheless ahead of other journals and university presses in charting new directions. Chief among these is Alex McHoul's clarification of how the rocket and phallus relate textually (and not just thematically) in "*Gravity's Rainbow*'s Golden Sections" (pp. 31–38). Other essays read Pynchon in the light of Walter Benjamin, realistic materialism, the theories of Lukács and Bakhtin, quantum physics as interpreted by Werner Heisenberg, the rendered forms of popular illustration, narrative voice, Wilfred Owen's war poetry, acoustic collage, industrial history, and a piece of juvenilia surviving from his high school newspaper. But also noteworthy is "Thomas

Pynchon's Intrusion in the Enchanter's Domain" (*TCL* 35:131–46)
in which Michael W. Vella looks into the affinities between *v.* and
surrealistic practice and aesthetics.

ix. Innovative Extremes: Gins, Federman, Abish, Coover, and Gaddis

Much of the debate over truly innovative fiction centers on asking
what it is "about." Saying that it is about itself (metafiction) has become less satisfactory than saying it is about nothing at all (nihilism),
but with Mary Ann Caws's treatment of Madeline Gins in *The Art of
Interference: Stressed Readings in Verbal and Visual Texts* (Princeton) one finds an answer that clarifies how such work is meant to be
received. Using Shushaku Arakawa's paintings as an analogue, Caws
shows how Gins's fiction explores the matrix of consciousness as a
thinking field with mental moves all its own; what is committed to the
page and shared with the reader is a dimensionalizing of consciousness, and so if there is to be a subject for such a work it would be not
simply the process of Gins's writing but of the possibilities it enter-
tains. "Fictions are made by acts of perception," Caws remarks, acts
that arise "from the most minimal source"; it is from this minimum
that maximum energy is produced, which is the possibility Gins's fiction exploits. That concretely referential subject matter can be introduced into this process is shown by David Dowling's analysis in "Raymond Federman's America: Take It or Leave It" (*ConL* 30:348–69);
here, the writer's fictional reverberations "enact an archetypal American experience" not by representing the country but by liberating
rather than locating the self in relation to it. Science fiction also provides the chance for displacement, an opportunity Federman takes in
The Twofold Vibration, but here—as Paula Bryant proves in "Extending the Fabulative Continuum; DeLillo, Mooney, and Federman"
(*Extrapolation* 30:156–65)—the exercise is more properly metafictive.

A more theoretically based yet readable approach to innovative
fiction's subject matter is studied by Paul Wotipka in "Walter Abish's
How German Is It: Representing the Postmodern" (*ConL* 30:503–
17). There is an obviously recognizable Germany in Abish's novel,
but the author focuses on it not as a social, political, geographical, or
historical entity, but as a sign. As such, "the novel itself moves well
beyond the question of national identity to the broader problems of
a multinational culture that characteristically suppresses or erases

the terror of specific historical events." Therefore Abish, while not participating in Fredric Jameson's notion of history as pastiche, portrays that attitude as it is practiced among his novel's subjects as they try to bury history while worrying that the smooth surface of their new world might be disrupted by terrorists. "An analogy between the historical event and terror is explicit: the sudden appearance of each threatens to rupture the familiar present, to defamiliarize a world that is based on assimilation, repetition, and predictability; each inserts a moment of uncertainty into a stable system of signs."

Rescuing another writer from the metafictionist label and reestablishing his work as a type "that assiduously attempts to extract all [of the] false, mythic content" that language holds is Wayne B. Stengel's task in "Robert Coover's 'Writing Degree Zero': 'The Magic Poker'" (*ArQ* 45, ii:101–10). Taking Roland Barthes's perspective on this story reveals how Coover attacks "one of the most dubious myths of literature: the literary mythos itself, the belief that literature must exclusively concern itself with the dissemination of ideas or feeling, that it should contain an explicitly defined subject-object relationship, or take the goal of instructing an audience how to think, act, or respond."

This literary mythos, however, is one that William Gaddis's critics strive to recover for his work. Steven Moore's *William Gaddis* (*TUSAS* 546) leans heavily on the social criticism perceived in his fiction and emphasizes the satiric. The author of *Carpenter's Gothic* may well be one of D. H. Lawrence's "great American grouches," and beyond such pessimism Moore counsels the benefits of art; yet the Gaddis offered here is mostly an artist with a sword. Other critics cite M. M. Bakhtin and use theories of intertextuality to update Gaddis with varying success. "Double-Voicing, Intertextuality and the Proliferation of Simulacra in William Gaddis's *The Recognitions*" (*Genre* 22:41–67) is John Johnson's attempt to harmonize this novel's "concern both to represent a world and at the same time to register prior wordings of textualizations of it." Bahktin's replacement of mimesis with dialogy justifies such "double-voicing," while adding the theory of simulacra lets *The Recognitions* "fully maintain the novel's outward conventions and compositional strategies." A more direct consideration of how Gaddis's second novel recovers "meaning and value" is found in Gregory Comnes's "Fragments of Redemption: William Gaddis' *JR*" (*TCL* 35:161–81), where the informing theorists are George Steiner and Walter Benjamin. That the novel may be a figure of the author's own self-consciously artistic experience is propounded by Joseph Tabbi's "The Compositional Self in William Gaddis' *JR*" (*MFS* 35:655–71). The best of these efforts is Alan Singer's "The Ventriloquism of History: Voice, Parody, Dialogue" (*Intertextuality and Contemporary American Fiction*, pp. 72–99) in which *Carpenter's Gothic* becomes "a proliferation of contingencies within an apparent resemblance," a parodic impulse borrowed from Bakhtin and genuinely helpful in showing "how contradiction can be the motor of a dialectic that does not elude historical particulars."

x. Fiction of the Vietnam War

In novels and short stories generated by the war in Vietnam (and by its debate at home), matters of conventional subjects and postmodern theories meet head-on. As Walter W. Höbling notes in "The Impact of the Vietnam War on U.S. Fiction: 1960s to 1980s" (*Literature and War*, pp. 193–209), the whole range of previously assumed descriptions of order, cultural paradigms, and "explanatory symbol systems" no longer applied to this war in which the high-tech modernism of Western civilization was forced "right into the heart of an agrarian culture in Asia," with the result that warfare itself and the ways of perceiving it had to be radically revised. In his concise yet complete essay Höbling relates the breakthroughs of Barth, Pynchon, Brautigan, and others to novels more directly responsive to the war, principally Mailer's *Why Are We in Vietnam?* and Tim O'Brien's *Going After Cacciato*, reading the former in comparison to Heller's *Catch-22* and the latter with one eye on O'Brien's use of the "westward" tradition in American literature and the other on how his methods anticipate efforts by Joan Didion, Toni Morrison, and John Irving to write novels "where the unbridled flight of imaginative discourse had to come to terms with pragmatic realities."

A special issue of *Genre* (21[1988]) edited by Gordon O. Taylor begins with Taylor's sensitive reading, "Cacciato's Grassy Hill" (pp. 393–407), in which several of the finest novels from the war are shown to record "the obliteration . . . of all [conventional] assumptions of traceable or manipulatable relation between the actual and the imaginary." Thomas Myers adds to the expertise he displayed with this literature in *Walking Point* (*ALS 1988*: pp. 287–88) by contributing "Dispatches from Ghost Country: The Vietnam Veteran in Recent American Fiction" (pp. 409–28), a study directed toward the conflict's special nature as an undeclared war and as a memory that not even high school history teachers are certain should be preserved. Other essays focus on film and nonfiction prose, but most critics here and elsewhere agree with Myers's point that "how we live is also how we remember," making aesthetic responses to Vietnam a subject that should remain pertinent as long as veterans survive.

A new edition of William Eastlake's *The Bamboo Bed* (New Mexico) contains a preface by the author that clarifies his own role in writing in response to Vietnam. "An objective nonfiction version of war does not make sense," Eastlake suggests, not only because warfare is irrational in intent and chaotic in its practice but because "the terror of war is a liberator" that frees the subconscious to act in ways that only imaginative art can hope to equal. "In *The Bamboo Bed*," therefore, "I am attempting to accomplish what a painter attempts to see beyond what a photograph shows."

xi. Popular Subgenres

Like war, aggressive behavior in general fascinates certain readers and prompts certain writers to direct themselves to that market. In *Murder Off the Rack: Critical Studies of Ten Paperback Masters* (Scarecrow), Jon L. Breen and Martin Harry Greenberg assemble a phalanx of essays; some, like the worst of science-fiction criticism, spend their time tolling out profundities on golden ages and editorial epochs as if they are the doings of Persian armies and Greek philosophical schools, but the best—which in this book is Donald Westlake's treatment of Peter Rabe's fiction (pp. 113–33)—looks beyond subgeneric literary history to examine the roots of an author's success in his or her manner of writing instead of simply the topics such writing engages. That there is something to be learned from such work is evident from David Richter, the brilliant Chicago-trained critic of postmodern fiction, whose "Murder in Jest: Serial Killing in the Post-Modern Detective Story" (*JNT* 19:106–15) notes that because current theory asks readers to be aware of characters as literary constructs there are limits "to which we can respond to them as representations of real persons who act and suffer and whose suffering evokes a response in us." Similarly, Richter cites Umberto Eco's axiom that "a narrative that belongs to a series develops different expectations in its audience than one that stands alone."

In Dennis Massey's *Doing Time in American Prisons* (Greenwood), the scene shifts to one of aggression's consequences. Here,

Malcolm Braly's fiction takes the perspective of a hard insider—which becomes a multiform one in response to the complex nature of prison life. Edward Bunker's work finds its complexity in the full criminal justice system and looks to the social turbulence of late 1960s and early 1970s for the social substructures that can generate such fiction. Prison's larger effect on society becomes the focus for Nathan C. Heard.

If the professors and teaching assistants who read this chapter ask their classes who is being read outside the curriculum, the most frequent answer might be "Stephen King." Those who would place this writer's work inside the canon will benefit from reading James B. Twitchell's *Preposterous Violence: Fables of Aggression in Modern Culture* (Oxford), especially Twitchell's third chapter, "Preposterous Violence in Prose Fiction: The Coronation of Stephen King" (pp. 90–128). King himself testifies that terror is "the finest emotion" and therefore counsels that the writer "go for it" wherever possible; if all else fails, then just "gross out" the reader and collect one's reward. Twitchell ascribes King's success to knowing exactly what his readers want to experience and being willing to sacrifice all else, including his own pride and self-respect, to deliver it. His narratives boast the primitive effect of flip-card images, and even their plots are secondary to "gathering and exploding" moments of violence, all of which results in the "unmediated frantic action" untutored readers demand.

xii. Chicano, Native American, and Western Fiction

Editors Francisco A. Lomeli and Carl R. Shirley make great headway in *Chicano Writers, First Series* (DLB 82) and are to be commended for their balance between younger and more established writers (a total of 52 are covered). Yet too often the structural depths of novels and short stories are neglected for matters of social surface, an approach that makes Oscar Zeta Acosta little more than a foil for the shenanigans of Hunter S. Thompson instead of the sensitively complex author he was. *The Autobiography of a Brown Buffalo* merits treatment as a delicate interface of both textual and autobiographical concerns, but it has yet to receive the aesthetic (as opposed to strictly sociological and political) attention routinely accorded to similar transgeneric works by Norman Mailer, Tom Wolfe, and even Thompson.

Such concerns come more readily to Elizabeth I. Hansen, whose

*Forever There: Race and Gender in Contemporary Native American
Fiction* (Peter Lang) appreciates how because of their otherness and
difference, Native Americans have been written out of the country's
mainstream. The white impulse to tribalize has led to a loss of individual tradition that a visionary world strives to restore (as in the
fiction of James Welch), yet there often remains an alienated individual within (as the works of Paula Gunn Allen express). Even
newer writers find a less terrifying and more welcoming personal
vision that touches the complexity of the Native American experience, especially women's experience. Here, the writings of Louise
Erdrich and Michael Dorris find their place in Hansen's thesis. There
are major dislocations but also "translocations" of the self as fiction
mediates the demands of majority and minority worlds; structural
lessons can be learned from the inversions made by Ken Kesey and
Thomas Berger, novelists who say more about white American than
Native American concerns but who nevertheless form part of a larger
picture Hansen paints. Her treatment of the field is complemented by
editor Gerald Vizenor's *Narrative Chance: Postmodern Discourse on
Native American Indian Literature* (New Mexico)—a caution that
the traditionally realistic novel (as canonized by Ian Watt) is just
one bourgeois way of looking at the world. The essays Vizenor collects are mostly familiar treatment of Momaday, Silko, and Erdrich,
but thanks to their new style of engagement they tell us as much about
postmodernism as about Native American concerns.

Louise Erdrich's ability to look on tribal life in a less than optimistic light fascinates Louise Flavin, whose "Louise Erdrich's *Love
Medicine*: Loving Over Time and Distance" (*Crit* 31:55–64) shows
how this newer writer discards not just traditional themes but traditional techniques as well (including a central conflict and protagonist, both of which are set aside in favor of fragmenting the reader's
attention over a broad worldscape that has lost its ceremonies, rituals, and cultural identity). Such previously unifying elements, of
course, may have been shams all along. Nora Barry and Mary Prescott take a different approach, their "The Triumph of the Brave: *Love
Medicine*'s Holistic Vision" (*Crit* 30:123–38) selecting one character,
Nestor Kashpaw, as pivotal (something Flavin's reading would dis-
courage) and therefore redemptive. Mary Slowik has more success by
applying the axioms of magical realism (in the manner of Gabriel
García Márquez) to an otherwise familiar text in "Henry James,
Meet Spider Woman: A Study of Narrative Form in Leslie Silko's

Ceremony" (*NDQ* 57, ii:104–16); Márquez shows a "good-humored tolerance for the unverifiable event" while maintaining a realistic base, and Silko's novel benefits from a similar ability to hold two narrative modes, magical and real, in suspension "without one dominating the other." Magical realism plays a role in James Welch's "Long Time Ago" (pp. 2–8), a critically important section introduction to editors William Kittredge and Annick Smith's *The Last Best Place: A Montana Anthology* (Helena: Montana Historical Society, 1988, distributed by the University of Washington Press). Welch reminds readers that Márquez's term refers to narratives that for both Native and Latin Americans are rather common fare; in them material beyond conventional relations of cause and effect and time and space are treated matter-of-factly, a style appropriate to a worldview "shaped by the explanations contained in our stories, our histories, our religions." Kittredge's own "Montana Renaissance" (pp. 760–65) praises *Winter in the Blood* as one of the region's best advertisements for writers "seeking a good place in which to conduct a good life," an interest that becomes "the most evident pattern in Montana narratives."

How technique grows out of an engrossing interest in one's materials characterizes Fred Erisman's interpretation in *Tony Hillerman* (BSWWS 87), while the almost apocalyptic transformation of a midwesterner into an intimate of the Pacific Northwest rivets Ron Mc-Farland's attention in *David Wagoner* (BSWWS 88); interestingly, Wagoner lightens up considerably in his comic Westerns, while Hillerman's journalistic training often keeps him on the reportorial rather than interpretive side of "the facts." Nature writing interests two critics who relate their subject to Jack London and to environmental concerns, respectively: James I. McClintock ("Edward Abbey's 'Antidotes to Despair,'" *Crit* 31:41–54) and Paul T. Bryant ("Edward Abbey and Environmental Quixoticism," *WAL* 24:37–43). A more familiar view of the American West appears in Larry McMurtry's novels of the early 1980s—*Cadillac Jack, The Desert Rose,* and *Lonesome Dove*—and tracking such interests as "the cowboy Western, masculine self-testing, female consciousness, and contemporary urban rootlessness" keeps Janis P. Stout busy in "Cadillac Larry Rides Again: McMurtry and the Song of the Open Road" (*WAL* 24:243–51). Within the American tradition of the "road novel" McMurtry is motivated by "a principle of restlessness and an omnivorous curiosity" that takes his work into less certain structures than this tradition usually contains. Although the author himself disavows any interest in structures, his novels invoke conventional patterns and therefore raise readerly expectations that are fulfilled not by structural integrity but by "sheer storytelling and keen observation."

University of Northern Iowa

15. Poetry: 1900 to the 1940s

Melody M. Zajdel

i. General

The book to read this year is Cary Nelson's *Repression and Recovery: Modern American Poetry and the Politics of Cultural Memory, 1910–1945* (Wisconsin). Nelson's study is a fascinating meditation on how and why the modernist canon was shaped and how poetry, as a result, has been limited in its role within American culture. Canonization and literary history are, as Nelson vividly demonstrates, "deeply implicated in the ideological formulation and obliteration of cultural memory and in the process of establishing our current rhetorical and political options." Using a Marxist and post-structuralist critical base, Nelson looks at the marginalization of diverse poets, particularly women, blacks, and members of the political left, who were directly engaged in critiques of American society, politics, and art. Current literary historians have deemed their works political, not aesthetic. What Nelson challenges is not just this evaluation but the assumption that such an evaluation is not itself profoundly political. As he elucidates, what is at stake in the formation and maintenance of literary history is not just subject matter, but whose experiences and voices will be heard, what audience will be valued, what function literature will have in a culture, what criteria will be used to determine literariness, and what defines art as a category.

Nelson starts by noting the loss of diversity and the exclusivity of current notions of modern poetry. He "recovers" or brings back to our attention a plethora of artists and journals interacting and flourishing in the poetic enterprise of the century's first four decades. His discussions of authors such as Angelina Weld Grimke, Sterling A. Brown, Mike Gold, Genevieve Taggard, Mina Loy, and the writers of the Rebel Poet booklets show that poetry served multiple functions and audiences, now discredited. Their exclusion denotes the profound sexism, racism, and conservatism of our current literary history. The depoliticizing of literary history achieved by their exclusion has "valorized political passivity and impotence" and defined poetry in America as "apolitical and historically irrelevant." Women, minorities, and proletarian poets used poetry to articulate their position toward understanding of the government, the historical events of their day, and other classes; it was not isolated from other discourse of the period. What most concerns Nelson, however, is not the recovery (however worthy) of individual writers; he is critiquing the ongoing construction and/or deconstruction of the cultural meaning of poetry, the definition of modernism, and the process of literary history itself. He argues that we must begin our recovery by disregarding current definitions of poetry, literariness, and literary history and return to reading and studying the period's actual publications. He recommends that original forms of writing (rather than collected or edited works) be studied, that works be examined chronologically (to recover context), that illustrations and design elements be included in literary studies, and that we read the journals and little magazines of the time as referential to one another. By challenging choices made by critics and teachers regarding canonization, Nelson deconstructs our received notion of literary history and invites us to engage with him in the act of examining our own critical assumptions.

Nelson presents his argument as an uninterrupted essay, using his form to emphasize the connectedness of literary history, canonization, and politics. While this achieves his goals of resisting false segmentation, it unfortunately relegates an enormous amount of excellent information to his endnotes. The notes are a gold mine of information regarding individual writers and poems; readers need to read them, not skim them. Nelson's essay is stimulating and his documentation meticulous. *Repression and Recovery* should be required reading.

A more typical and less provocative literary history is Alan Shucard, Fred Moramarco, and William Sullivan's *Modern American Poetry, 1865–1950* (Twayne). This second in a three-volume set on American poetry sets out to chronicle the evolution of modernism from Emily Dickinson to the Objectivists. While useful for survey purposes (particularly with undergraduate students), it does little to discuss problems of interpretation or new critical trends on any of its subjects. The editors divide the writing roughly into thirds: Shucard does the early chapters on Dickinson, Stephen Crane, late 19th-century poets, Robinson, Frost, and the Midwestern and Harlem renaissances; Moramarco does Imagism, Eliot, Pound, Williams, and

Stevens; and Sullivan does Cummings, Jeffers, Hart Crane, the Fugitives, and the Objectivists. Perhaps the strongest point of the text is the delineation of how cross-fertilization between European and American ideas has always been fruitful for modern poetry. Still, without (and particularly after) the self-reflexiveness and challenging nature of Nelson's book, this literary history is pretty bland.

The third general work to note this year is Jeffrey Walker's *Bardic Ethos*. Taking Whitman as the model for the American bard struggling to write an American epic, Walker examines how Pound, Hart Crane, Williams, and Olson either fulfill, fail to fulfill, or transform Whitman's vision and expectations for the genre. Walker defines a bardic epic as an extended lyric aiming at "moral education and transformation, leading to cultural revolution." His chapters on the second wave of bardic poets (Pound, Hart Crane, and Williams) will interest this chapter's readers. In *The Cantos* Pound succeeds in establishing a sacerdotal class of writer and a privileged, initiated audience. He retains the Whitmanesque function of moral conscience for the culture but has difficulty achieving a rhetorical strategy adequate to his desire. He is, however, more successful in creating an epic than is Crane in *The Bridge*. According to Walker, Crane's poem is severely flawed. While announcing his intent to create a Pindaric epic, one which praises the world rather than bespeaks loss, Crane thwarts the expectations of the genre and loses both his audience and his moral persuasiveness. However, Walker is most interested and most interesting in his discussion of William Carlos Williams, whom he sees as transforming the rhetoric of the bardic epic while posing a thematic counterstatement to Pound. Williams's determination in *Paterson* to use the actual, albeit vulgar, speech and world he knows leaves open the possibility of direct dialogue with, and real transformation of, his audience. Rather than a single voice, Williams's poetic center is polyphonous *and* paradoxical, which produces his principal distinction from Pound and Crane. Walker's careful individual readings of the three modernist poems are good ones, and the book provides a useful new way of defining and discussing the modernist long poem in America.

ii. Stevens

Two volumes edited by Milton J. Bates were added to our Stevens resources this year, *Sur Plusieurs Beaux Sujects: Wallace Stevens'*

Commonplace Book (Stanford) and a revised *Opus Posthumous* (Knopf). *Sur Plusieurs Beaux Sujects*, the last major hitherto unpublished Stevens material in the Huntington collection, provides a facsimile and transcription of two commonplace books Stevens kept on his readings from 1932 through 1953; it clearly demonstrates the interplay between his reading, thinking, and writing. Bates notes in his introduction that approximately a fifth of the entries are directly quoted or paraphrased in Stevens's poetry, while many others are referentially important. He provides detailed notes on the sources of the quotations, as well as English translations where necessary. The new edition of *Opus Posthumous* has been enlarged to include primary and biographical material made available since Samuel French Morse's 1957 edition. More than 20 poems either have been corrected or newly added, while sequencing and dating have been revised. Publication of these two volumes should make almost all Stevens material at the Huntington available to the public.

The second volume of Joan Richardson's Stevens biography, *Wallace Stevens: The Later Years, 1923–1955* (Morrow, 1988), studies Stevens after the publication of *Harmonium* and after the birth of his daughter, using both as pivots to show that "the posture he assumed toward life, changed fundamentally" in the second half of his life. Richardson makes abundant use of letters, journals, and notebooks to chart the evolution of Stevens's sensibility. Throughout the volume she reads Stevens's life and poems as the attempt to resolve his crisis of faith, his crisis of *how* to believe. The volume is pleasurable reading, well-written, and effective at integrating biographical facts with Stevens's poetry and aesthetics.

The epistemological problems of whether reality is empirically knowable and whether language can adequately represent it are the topics of several studies of Stevens this year. *What I Cannot Say: Self, Word, and World in Whitman, Stevens, and Merwin,* by Thomas B. Byers (Illinois) places Stevens in a tradition of Romantic epistemological struggle. Byers situates Stevens's "An Ordinary Evening in New Haven" between Whitman's "Song of Myself" and Merwin's "The Lice" in his exploration of this tradition. Byers shows that, unlike Whitman, Stevens cannot transcend the dualism of speaker and subject—cannot make himself, his poem, and the world one, and that one holy—so he chooses to foreground his consciousness of reality as always fictive. As a result, he engages via his language in endless cycles of imaginative constructions. Byers skillfully shows how self-undermining thus becomes essential to Stevens's poetics. Stevens's power, says Byers, resides in his humanity, not his divinity. His choice to believe in language is the only pleasure and transcendence possible in his aesthetic. Although the close reading of "An Ordinary Evening in New Haven" is not terribly original, it is solid, and the links made between Whitman and Stevens are interesting and well-made. An additional plus is Byers's use of Stevens's essays and journals to explore the productive tension between his criticism and his poetry. Less positively, Burt Kimmelman, in "Centrality in a Discrete Universe: William Bronk and Wallace Stevens" (*Sagetrieb* 7, iii:119–29), compares the two writers' views of the phenomenal world, then contrasts their resultant different relationships to language. Kimmelman shows that Stevens "retreats to the comfort of the subjective experience," while Bronk rejects subjectivity; Bronk requires autonomy for the universe, even if it must remain incomprehensible. Kimmelman judges Stevens's Supreme Fiction to be empty ontologically, preferring Bronk's direct presentation of emptiness as central to any knowledge of reality.

Frank Doggett and Dorothy Emerson, in "A Primer of Possibility for 'The Auroras of Autumn'" (*WSJour* 13:53–66), examine how Stevens establishes a continuous discourse of intimation as the basis of his poetry. They propose that "descriptive elements of the given attach with symbolic effect to the possible" and, in doing so, create the tension that sustains the act of reading. All ideas in Stevens are a result of the reader's willingness to play with his evasive language in the hope of discovering significance. Ultimately, the reader "must surmise import for the symbols and tropes that speak a language that is evasive within a language that progresses in a course that is recognizably readable." This is the continuous discourse at the heart of reading Stevens.

A tangential view of Stevens's use of image and language in discourse appears in "Wallace Stevens: Non-Rational Discourse," a chapter in Stephen-Paul Martin's *Open Forms and the Feminine Imagination: The Politics of Reading in Twentieth-Century Innovative Writing* (Maisonneuve, 1988). Martin notes that in Stevens's longer poems images "consistently pull the ideas that surround them into a meditative depth that interrupts what logical motion might have been creating." Martin identifies this as a feminine mode of perception and discourse and cites it as underexplored and underacknowledged in studies of modern innovative writing.

A similar use of the feminine/masculine dichotomy is a part of
" 'Sepulchres of the Fathers': 'Notes Toward a Supreme Fiction' and
the Ideology of Origins" (*WSJour* 13:15–26), by Paul Morrison. Morrison reads "Notes" as a new ideology of beginnings, one which rejects the old script gendering the female as sensible and the male as
intellect. According to Morrison, in "Notes" Stevens rejects this false
binary opposition and establishes his intention and ability to devalue
neither.

William W. Bevis's *Mind of Winter: Wallace Stevens, Meditation,
and Literature* (Pittsburgh) looks at a relatively unstudied area: Stevens's experimentation with a meditative consciousness in some of his
poems. In doing so, Bevis locates "the aesthetic and impersonal aspects
of his work not so much in a language artifact removed from a speaker,
as in a speaker oddly removed from himself." Bevis does not claim influence, but rather illustrates how references to Buddhism and brain
physiology can help a reader-critic to understand Stevens's mind-
frame in his meditative poems. Meditation offers a complement to
imagination, working in Stevens's poetry via images rather than metaphors. The book is divided into four parts. Part I explains Buddhist
meditation and suggests how poems like "The Snow Man" or "The
Course of a Particular" might be profitably read as re-creations of the
speaker's meditative perception and experience. Part II looks at the
physiological aspects of the meditative experience and further explores how the Mahayana (or Middle Way) tradition of meditation
can be paralleled to the experiences in "A Clear Day and No Memories" and "The Latest Freed Man." Bevis includes in this section a
useful table showing meditative stages of experience identifiable in a
number of Stevens's poems. He does a particularly interesting gloss of
"Not Ideas about the Thing but the Thing Itself," showing that escape
from the Romantic ego is "not more self, but not-self." A meditative
stance allows Stevens to avoid both the tragedy of desire and an ironic
point of view, as Bevis shows in his reading of "Esthétique du Mal."
Part III looks at Stevens's contemporaries and potential influences,
such as Pound, Yeats, and Santayana, to show that his meditative consciousness was not learned from them, but rather constituted a personal evolution. Finally, Bevis examines the fragmented structure of
Stevens's longer late poems, seeing them as manifestations of the
rhetoric of the meditative point of view and experience. What Stevens
develops in them is a special form that Bevis calls the comedy of consciousness. The second half of this section, however, is extremely

problematic. Bevis adds Emerson and Beethoven to his shaping paradigm of meditative consciousness and form. The analogy with Beethoven in particular is difficult to follow and weakens the ideas in the first half of this concluding section. Nonetheless, Bevis makes a good case that meditation or detachment "may offer the *only* true collage—collage with no subtext of desire or thought," an idea with interesting implications for the study of modernist forms. The book provides a new way to see Stevens and does so, given the unfamiliarity of most Westerners with the topic and terminology of meditation, quite well. As a distinctly new approach to Stevens, the book is well worth reading.

The final volume on Stevens is *Critical Essays on Wallace Stevens* (Hall, 1988), ed. Steven Gould Axelrod and Helen Deese. In addition to the editors' useful and comprehensive introduction to the history of Stevens criticism, the volume contains 14 reviews spanning his career, 11 reprinted articles from 1963–85 (most notably by Frye, Miller, Bloom, Lentricchia, Riddel, Cook, and Jameson), and two newly commissioned articles by Claudia Yukman and Paul Douglass. Yukman's "An American Poet's Idea of Language" (pp. 230–45) sees Stevens's syntactical repetition as directly related to Whitman and reads both as expressive of a distinctly American view of language. According to Yukman, both Whitman and Stevens view "the word as Creator rather than absence," and their repetitive structures are indicators of "the generative structures of language . . . an image of meaning inside rather than outside language." Stevens is thus a poet for whom language is reality. This essay might be usefully read in conjunction with Byers's book. Douglass, in " 'The Theory of Poetry Is the Theory of Life': Bergson and the Later Stevens" (pp. 245–60), also looks at Stevens's affinity and indebtedness to Henri Bergson, who like Whitman would see the artist as "a secularized version of the Creator" and proposes that the "Bergsonian tension between form and fluidity lies at the heart of Stevens' work." Bergson provides not only philosophical theory, but techniques for the creationist poet—humor and indirection. The tension in form and language advocated by both Stevens and Bergson is what gives meaning, says Douglass, for "to become engaged, through literature, in the unending process of invention and revelation is really to confront the nature of our own being."

The exploration of influences on Stevens continues in two additional articles: "Wallace Stevens' 'Esthétique du Mal' and the Evils of Aestheticism," by Henry Weinfield (*WSJour* 13:27–37), and "Stasis Versus Continuity: Mallarmé and Wallace Stevens," by Du-Hyoung Kang (*WSJour* 13:38–52). Weinfield argues that in "Esthétique du Mal" Stevens conducts dialogues with three literary progenitors: Baudelaire (in the poem's title), Nietzsche (in the body of the poem), and Wordsworth (in his conclusion). Weinfield sees the poem as a descent into the underworld, for which both pain and art are necessary. Stevens's seemingly bleak version of the human condition, which Weinfield links to Baudelaire and Nietzsche, is, he argues, mitigated by a return to Wordsworthian values in the poem's final 10 lines. Humanism and an ethical (not amoral) Nature triumph there. Kang's article contrasts Stevens and Mallarmé to show that Stevens is not fundamentally connected to Symbolist poetics. Reading "The Auroras of Autumn," Kang shows that Stevens does not dichotomize the Ideal and the Real, that he rejects stasis (and hence the Ideal) as neither achievable nor desirable, and that he refuses to see nothingness as a nihilistic fact but as "a stage that his poetic imagination must pass through in its journey of constant decreation and recreation."

The remaining articles of interest this year apply new historical critiques to the reading of Stevens. Michael O. Stegman, "Variations on a Theme in 'Peter Quince at the Clavier' " (*WSJour* 13:3–14), shows how the contemporary art scene of the winter and spring of 1915 may have been a source of Stevens's poem. He cites Granville-Barker's production of *A Midsummer Night's Dream*, a performance of a Scriabin symphony, and the ongoing aesthetic debates in *Poetry* as possible influences on the "comic cadence" of the poem. Stegman effectively suggests that a study of this milieu will "serve to remind us of the redefinition of art that changed this era and of Stevens' comic contribution to this milieu."

New historical readings of Stevens dominate a special issue of *Wallace Stevens Journal* (13, ii), "Stevens and Politics." The essays are uniformly good. Harvey Tere's "Notes Toward the Supreme Soviet: Stevens and Doctrinaire Marxism" (pp. 150–67) is a well-argued reading of the poems of the 1930s, particularly "Owl's Clover," as attempts to "revise leftist political discourse through [a] trenchant but patient and relatively sympathetic critique of orthodox Marxism." The crux of the critique hinges on Stevens's desire to find within the social and political world of the period a place for poetry and the imaginative artist. Tere sees Stevens's argument revolving around the question of human subjectivity and the refusal of Marxism to take the unconscious into account either politically or aesthetically. Robert Emmett Moore looks at how form rather than content may reveal Stevens's politics ("Figuration and Society in 'Owl's Clover,'" pp. 127–49). Moore proposes that Stevens uses mock-heroic figuration to show political struggle; in effect, the clash between the levels of style in the mock-heroic epic parallels the clash of political ideologies. Like Tere, Moore sees Stevens as critiquing Marxist doctrine by developing the point that "a fully effective work of art cannot spring from inhumane ideology, and a political system which cannot produce a convincing artistic representation lacks vital force." Melita Schaum's "Lyric Resistance: Views of the Political in the Poetics of Wallace Stevens and H.D." (pp. 191–205) looks at gender asymmetry in criticism differently than we normally see it. After noting discrepancies in the critical response and analyses given Stevens's "Notes Toward a Supreme Fiction" and H.D.'s "Trilogy," Schaum suggests that the feminist redefinition of the political which has been applied to H.D. could be fruitful if also applied to Stevens. Feminist revision of the political "sets the lyric voice centrally in the sphere of political relevance"; hence, lyrics such as Stevens's may be read as having new political potency. Stevens's focus on subjective imagination becomes "not escape but resistance . . . not solipsism but rebellion." By foregrounding a personal reality in his poetry, one which especially considers language, imagination, and human desire, Stevens becomes a political writer.

Two articles in this issue look at the impact of the world wars on Stevens. Jacqueline Vaught Brogan's "Stevens in History and Not in History: The Poet and the Second World War" (pp. 168–90) interprets the frequent references to war in Stevens's postwar poetry as showing his preoccupation with the historical event and its implications. She makes the case that the war changed Stevens's aesthetic "from that of a relatively private poet to one with a public voice and conscience." Similarly, James Longenbach, in "The 'Fellowship of Men that Perish': Wallace Stevens and the First World War" (pp. 85–108), reads *Harmonium* as a poem of that war. In particular, Longenbach gives a strong reading of "Sunday Morning" as a product of Stevens's war anxiety and fear of mortality. As he explains, "to find the unknown new in the mundane is Stevens' way of surviving the shadow of death." Finally, Paul Bauer, in "The Politics of Reality, 1948: Wallace Stevens, Delmore Schwartz, and the New Criticism" (pp. 206–25), explains Stevens's preference for Delmore Schwartz and the *Partisan Review* over John Crowe Ransom and the New Critical method. Bauer employs "Effects of Analogy" to show why Schwartz's rejection of totalizing order and formalism would be more attractive to Stevens, with his emphasis on imagination versus logic. All in all, it was a good year for Stevens criticism.

iii. Williams

New primary material and editions of Williams appeared this year. Most noteworthy is *The Collected Poems of William Carlos Williams: Volume II, 1939–1962* (New Directions, 1988), ed. Christopher Mac-Gowan, which contains the seven books of poetry (excluding *Paterson*) published after 1930 and a number of previously uncollected poems. MacGowan has been a scrupulous editor, providing comprehensive notes. With its first volume counterpart, this edition is the definitive collected Williams. *William Carlos Williams Review* also continues to print new material. MacGowan and A. Walton Litz present a high school poem, "Peter Kipp to the High School" (*WCWR* 15, i:1–3), which appeared too late for inclusion in *The Collected Poems*. Likewise, David Frail, in "Citizen Williams: Thirty New Items from the Rutherford Newspapers. Part Four" (*WCWR* 15, i:4–21), provides a compilation of and commentary on Williams's writings in that forum. Finally, Hugh Witemeyer has edited *William Carlos Williams and James Laughlin: Selected Letters* (Norton), a collection of 149 letters (123 by Williams or by Mrs. Williams on her husband's behalf) written from 1934–62. The letters provide some new and informal glimpses into Williams's view of his contemporaries (particularly Pound and Eliot), his concern regarding his own work and public reception, and his interest in the enterprise (publishing, reviewing, marketing, writing) of literature in America.

Other biographical notes confirm what is apparent in some of Williams's letters. Williams was neither objective nor always kind in his evaluations of other writers. As Barry Ahearn shows in "Williams and H.D., or Sour Grapes" (*TCL* 35:299–309), Williams's belittlement of H.D. in his *Autobiography* is unwarrantedly malicious. Ahearn notes that Williams omits mentioning his early unrequited infatuation with her, his testiness at her critical comments on his early poems, and his positive review of her 1925 *Collected Poems*; instead, he presents only the spiteful anecdote regarding the Bryher-

McAlmon marriage. Not so malicious, but perhaps more ambivalent, were his feelings toward James Joyce, as Marion W. Cumpiano explains in "The Impact of Joyce on William Carlos Williams: An Uneasy Ambivalence" (*WCWR* 15, i:48–58). Cumpiano chronicles Williams's personal and critical engagement with Joyce, highlighting his attraction and resistance to this iconoclast of language. The relationship was one-sided. Joyce was a significant figure for Williams, but there is no evidence that Williams served a similar role for Joyce. Indeed, as Cumpiano suggests, Williams grew to resent the attention and acclaim given Joyce, which increased his ambivalent feelings: "His wish to occupy the master's authoritative position constituted a guilt that he projected onto the rival father figure."

Williams's interest in experimenting with language is the focus of several articles. J. D. Scrimgeour provides a good discussion of Williams's reasons for including prose in *Paterson* in "Coarse, Irregular Features: Prose in William Carlos Williams' *Paterson*" (*Connecticut Review* 11, ii:64–77). In *Paterson*, prose provides the shifting tempo and voice that allow the poet to sustain a poem for more than 200 pages, provides a link between theme and language, and "serves as the poetry of the non-poet." The inclusion of prose changes the definition of poetry and deconstructs the hierarchical superiority of poetry to prose. Because prose addresses, engages, and represents the language of a broader group, "*Paterson* seems as much a product of the community as a product of the poet." Bryce Conrad, in "The Deceptive Ground of History: The Sources of William Carlos Williams' *In the American Grain*" (*WCWR* 15, i:22–40), sees language as a central theme in *In the American Grain*, for "a history of America must be, in part, a history of *language* in America, a study of the tropes and verbal configurations which have historically defined the place." Since history is a matter of texts, history is a matter of language, not events. Williams provides a model for how to read history; his editing and his editorializing show how it is shaped. In the end, "Williams renders the past open to aesthetic repossession in the present by cancelling out the myth of historical verisimilitude."

In the American Grain generated two other strong essays: Bryce Conrad's "Engendering History: The Sexual Structure of William Carlos Williams' *In the American Grain*" (*TCL* 35:254–78) and Stephen Fredman's "Williams, Eliot, and American Tradition" (*TCL* 35:235–53). Conrad effectively argues that, for Williams, America (as literal landscape and literary ideal) is "the necessary bride for an

American poet." Using the metaphors of marriage and rape, Williams creates an America, a landscape, which "as a woman . . . can castrate the determining power of an invading Old World patriarchy . . . She will marry . . . but she will not be raped." But the image of woman in *In the American Grain* is consistently that of victim or ideal. While Williams may claim to desire a marriage between the poet and the New World, "his poetics actually celebrate a ritualized violation of the female, forcing an inscription upon the woman, writing upon the body of the mother." Fredman's essay looks at the similarity in attitude regarding the lack of an American tradition in Williams's *In the American Grain* and Eliot's "Tradition and the Individual Talent." Each is anxious to create a history, however idiosyncratic, to authorize his own poetry. Both use the principle of collage to construct such a history; both also acknowledge "the provisional nature of our acts of grounding." The result is the uniquely American creation: "the tradition of the new."

Williams's concern for form and experimentation is clearly documented elsewhere as well. Eleanor Berry provides a prosodic analysis of Williams's triadic-line verse and its variable foot meter ("William Carlos Williams' Triadic-Line Verse: An Analysis of Its Prosody," *TCL* 35:364–88). Among the significant points she makes is how well the theme of temporality is visually represented in triadic lines and how the rhythm of the triadic line allows for a sustained poem with an inherently elegiac and meditative tone. Christopher MacGowan looks at what prompted Williams to depart from triadic-line verse in the late 1950s, in "Williams' Last Decade: Bridging the Impasse" (*TCL* 35:389–405). Williams's desire to focus again on concrete, immediate experience required a looser line and shape than the reflective rhythm and structure embodied in the triadic line. MacGowan examines "The High Bridge Above the Tagus River at Toledo" and "Tapiola" to show the strategies with which Williams sought to replace the triadic line.

The influence of the visual on Williams is discussed in two different, albeit fine, articles. Henry M. Sayre, in "American Vernacular: Objectivism, Precisionism, and the Aesthetics of the Machine" (*TCL* 35:310–42), explores why Williams suffered a decline in poetic output from 1927 through 1946. He suggests that the answer rests with Williams's solution to the problem of finding a controllable form for lengthy poems, a solution linked to Williams's analogy of poetry as a machine. Sayre traces the machine aesthetic through various avant-garde adaptations. Rejecting the formalism implicit in objectivism and precisionism, Williams "rejects the aesthetics of the machine for the aesthetics of collage, the rhetoric of precision for the rhetoric of inclusion." This in turn led him to study "the American idiom." Charles Sheeler's work in the American visual vernacular struck a chord in Williams; his recognition that he needed a new unit of measure for his vernacular speech led to his developing the variable foot and creating the longer poems of his final two decades. William Marling looks at the spatial template Williams constructs to represent a basic tension in his writings—the relation between sexuality and vision (in " 'Corridor to a Clarity': Sensuality and Sight in Williams' Poems," (*TCL* 35:285–98). Williams argues, according to Marling, that sex provides "a corridor to a clarity," but it also interrupts vision; he constructs a visual pattern of triangulation in poems like "Postlude" and "January Morning" to represent this tension, and this form becomes his stay against formlessness.

Williams's relationship to music was the topic of a special issue of *William Carlos Williams Review* (15, ii). In "Whose Blues?" (pp. 1–8), Aldon L. Nielsen justly accuses Williams of a "white misreading of blackness" and documents how he appropriates jazz as a symbol, divorced from its social and historical reality. As Nielsen makes clear, Williams uses jazz and blackness thematically to represent "an uninhibited libidinal flow." Still, what is most significant to Nielsen is the recognition that the colonization of black culture is matched by its power to transform the white culture that envelopes it. Both are affected and changed by the contact. Steven C. Tracy, in "William Carlos Williams and *Blues: A Magazine of New Rhythms*" (pp. 17–29), agrees with Nielsen that jazz is "more co-opted than understood in its socio-economic complexity." For Williams, the blues represents characteristics associated with freedom: sexual taboos, vulgarity in language and subject, and a spirit of revolt. He "associated blues, in an abstract way, with the kind of revolt he felt was necessary for American poetry." His "For a New Magazine" (1929), a manifesto for *Blues*, reveals his limited understanding of the blues as a separate genre as well as his sincere interest in what the blues represented to him. Carol Donley recovers some of the historical context Williams scantily knew by providing information on Bunk Johnson and his relation to Williams's "Ol' Bunk's Band" ("William Carlos Williams and 'Ol' Bunk's Band,' " pp. 9–16). Donley does not sketch influences, but notes kinship between jazz innovations and innovations in poetic form.

Philip Furia (" 'Halving Man/hattan:' Lorenz Hart, Popular Song, and Modernist Poetry," pp. 300–35) also forgoes a search for influences, but suggests parallels between the visual breaks in the phrasing of modern poetry and the musical breaks in phrasing in Lorenz Hart's lyrics. Both disrupt the semantic sense and syntax of their lines in a distinctively modern way. Joseph A. Coroniti, Jr., examines a different musical link with Williams: composer Steve Reich's setting to music of *The Desert Music* ("Scoring the 'Absolute Rhythm' of William Carlos Williams: Steve Reich's *The Desert Music*," pp. 36–48). Coroniti goes over the score to show that Reich's setting is faithful to the meaning of the poems without being dominated by them. As he explains, "rather than create a music that simply imitates Williams' reference to music, the signified, Reich creates what Williams is referring to, the principle of music itself, the signified."

Two final critical pieces should be noted: Ann W. Fisher-Wirth's *William Carlos Williams and Autobiography: The Woods of His Own Nature* (Penn. State) and Nancy K. Barry's "The Fading Beautiful Thing of *Paterson*" (*TCL* 35:343–63). Fisher-Wirth shows that "the self inheres not in any one work but in the pattern which evolves over a lifetime of creation"; hence, she reads a variety of Williams's works as autobiography. Moving from most to least obvious biography, she explores Williams's creation and presentation of his self in *The Autobiography of William Carlos Williams, A Dream of Love*, "Philip and Oradie" (an early, incomplete long poem), and "Asphodel, That Greeny Flower." Reading the works as private as well as public autobiographical statements, she further argues that Williams effectively creates a new definition of autobiography: "the self does not exist apart from its enactment." I found particularly thought-provoking Fisher-Wirth's tracing of how Williams uses the metaphor of marriage; she posits that "marriage creates identity because it creates 'the first wife,' the initial and essential acknowledgment of the other." Hence, the tension between marriage and adultery in so much of Williams becomes simultaneously symbolic and concrete. Barry explores the genesis of *Paterson* and why it took Williams so long to move from idea to result. Williams was stymied by what structure to give the poem. Barry says that "*Paterson* was so 'fully formed' in Williams' imagination that the process of writing and publishing the poem seemed like an act of 'dismembering.'" She effectively delineates Williams's frustration in transforming the ideal into the poem's text, a frustration thematically central to both *Paterson* and to Williams's role as writer.

iv. Moore and H.D.

Though there were slightly fewer critical works this year than last on these two feminist modernists, the material remains of consistently high quality.

The most interesting book on Moore this year is Celeste Goodridge's *Hints and Disguises: Marianne Moore and Her Contemporaries* (Iowa). Goodridge examines Moore's public and private criticism of four of her contemporaries, arguing that her aesthetic allegiance is with Stevens and Pound, not Williams and Eliot. Moore's public criticism, unlike her private correspondence and notes, champions all four in the attempt to instruct readers on how to read modernist texts. Her imitative appreciations and her use of extensive, interpolated quotations in her reviews force her readers to question the fundamental definitions of poetry and text. Moore sees criticism as directly shaping the reception and understanding of a poem, feeling that "the launching of a text becomes inseparable from the critical commentary that accompanies it, or surrounds it." For Moore, therefore, the critic is equal in significance to the poet. In fact, Goodridge argues that it is as a critic that Moore most values Eliot and, sometimes, herself. Moore's focus on "the aesthetic or sensibility behind the text," her preference for the fragmentary rather than a totalizing whole, her use of shifting and self-concealing voices, lead to her artistic alignment with Pound and Stevens. Williams's content and linguistic vulgarity, as well as Eliot's excessive directness and overly romantic quest for self-meaning, make them less appealing to Moore than Pound, with his constant creation and rupture of form, and Stevens, with his conscious creation of dissonance between "his disguises and his disclosures." Goodridge's examination of private writings illuminates the reservations Moore has regarding each poet, reservations she approaches only through "hints and disguises" in her published criticism. Stevens's disregard for his readers and his aloofness, Pound's excessive unpredictability and associative leaps, Eliot's self-conscious questing, and Williams's vulgar content all are more clearly identified as problems in her correspondence and notebooks. Goodridge's juxtaposition of public and private criticism informs us anew about how literary criticism is shaped. The book requires us to reconsider both Moore as a critic and the function of artists' criticism of one another in the creation of literary movements and history.

"The Odd Couple: The Correspondence between Marianne Moore and Ezra Pound, 1918–1939" (*TCL* 34:507–27), by Lois Bar-Yaacov, also looks at the unpublished critical and personal exchanges between Moore and Pound. Bar-Yaacov, from a slightly different perspective, reinforces Goodridge's point that although Moore and Pound seem to have multiple superficial differences, they are linked by "mutual admiration and laser-sharp aesthetic integrity." To demonstrate, she examines the first three parts of their four-part correspondence. She denotes 1918–23 as their introduction to each other, 1925–29 as the period they worked as editor (Moore at *The Dial*) and entrepreneur-critic, and 1929–39 as the time when as part of a growing personal attachment Pound looked to Moore as a "cultural attaché for him in the United States." Taken together, the Goodridge and Bar-Yaacov essays clarify Moore's centrality to the shaping of the modernist enterprise.

Three essays look at Moore in light of current feminist and postmodernist interest in Lacan, Kristeva, and *l'écriture féminine*. Leigh Gilmore, in "The Gaze of the Other Woman: Beholding and Begetting in Dickinson, Moore, and Rich" (*Engendering the Word*, pp. 81–102), examines Moore's "Marriage" as part of a feminist poetic tradition that "resists patriarchal and heterosexist assumptions projected through the oedipal tale onto women's literary affiliations." Gilman explores how women (particularly Eve in "Marriage") function as the Muse for Moore. Looking at Eve and perceiving her as having equal access with Adam to language, Moore is able to see herself as a writer outside patriarchal restraints. By looking not to man's definition of woman, but at another woman, writers like Moore, Dickinson, and Rich are able to write as women outside the narrative form and script that culture provides for them. Carolyn A. Durham, in "Linguistic and Sexual Engendering in Marianne Moore's Poetry" (*Engendering the Word*, pp. 224–43), argues that Moore's "linguistic and formal experimentation conceals the subversive rejection of male language" in her poetry. Opposing other critics who assert that Moore's poetry is gender-free in content and voice, Durham shows how the feminine takes three forms in Moore: she critiques male sexual oppression covertly, she inscribes women's experience and language, and she challenges dualist thinking and presentation. Durham gives a particularly good reading of "Nevertheless," with its metaphors for female genitalia, to make her point that Moore connects woman's body directly to woman's language. Marilyn L. Brownstein, in "The Archaic Mother and Mother and Mother: The Postmodern Poetry of Marianne Moore" (*ConL* 30:13–32), compares Moore and Williams in their use of linguistic strategies to convey the "sensational memory . . . [and] the preverbal mind." Brownstein shows how Moore subverts expected syntax and lexical categories to create non–hierarchical structures and how Moore is wilder and more ambivalent in her strategies than Williams. Like Durham, Brownstein sees Moore undermining binary opposition, the source of culture's "symbolization of difference." Like Gilmore, she sees Moore's use of mirror images as central to her sexual poetics.

Last, Bernard Engel provides two offerings on Moore, "A Disjointed Distrust: Marianne Moore's World War II" (*ConL* 30:434–43) and a revised edition of his 1964 *Marianne Moore* (TUSAS 54). In the essay Engel examines why Moore's work after World War II is less intense, albeit more public, than her earlier poems. He focuses on "In Distrust of Merit" to show that the war raised the fundamental question of whether a moralistic philosophy was any longer possible. Engel notes that Wallace Stevens's "Notes Toward a Supreme Fiction," which equated literal soldiers to the individual struggle within each conscience, also may have prompted Moore's growing disillusionment. His revised *Marianne Moore* reads all of Moore's poems, making use of primary material unavailable 25 years ago. It is a useful text for a general reading of Moore but, like many TUSAS volumes, it lacks a sharp critical bite.

Essays on H.D. this year also consider her in terms of feminist questions and continue to explore in various ways her rejection of traditional gender ideology. In "Orpheus and Eurydice in the Twentieth Century: Lawrence, H.D., and the Poetics of the Turn" (*TCL* 35:407–28), Helen Sword notes how profoundly gender-inflected Lawrence's and H.D.'s use of the Orpheus and Eurydice myths becomes. Lawrence acknowledges the significance of the Eurydice figure as Other, but claims that "only the male can claim real credit for creativity, artistic power, and utterance"; he not only accepts, he propounds the traditional, hierarchical inscription of gender. As Lawrence's cosmology becomes increasingly misogynistic after World War I, H.D.'s revision of Eurydice becomes more insistent. In "The Poet" and *Bid Me To Live*, she denies the supremacy of Orpheus, gives Eurydice a strong and independent voice, and attempts to pose the powers of Eurydice and Orpheus as complementary, not hierarchical.

Jeanne Larsen, "Text and Matrix: Dickinson, H.D., and Women's Voice" (*Engendering the Word*, pp. 244–61), sees H.D. in "The Flowering of the Rod" as celebrating the feminine by focusing on the multiple manifestations of Mary Magdalene rather than Christ; thus, she locates the poem's self-generative power as a function of the mother. Larsen claims that H.D. refuses the false dichotomy and power struggle of male-female opposition and manages to valorize the female without proscribing the male. She reads the accepted duality in the text as the product of a bisexual poet who "does not blur the two elements of her inward duality, but also does not deny the speech and power of either one."

Susan Stanford Friedman, "The Writing Cure: Transference and Resistance in a Dialogic Analysis" (*HDN* 2:25–35), examines the process of H.D.'s analysis with Freud to demonstrate that their exchange was dialogic and that it can serve as a potent paradigm for women on how to resist being a victim to patriarchal authority or discourse. H.D.'s refusal to talk only to Freud and her continuing writing established a secondary analysis, one whose terms she, not Freud, controlled. Friedman follows H.D.'s reconstruction and interpretation of her analysis in eight writings: her letters to Bryher, her journal, *Advent*, "The Master," *Tribute to Freud*, "Trilogy," "Helen in Egypt," and *The Gift*. H.D.'s questioning of process, not just product, is presented as a model for all women writers. Friedman warns that critics—and poets—need to be careful in engaging with "the discourse of male masters—Father-Freud, and all the other Father-theorists on the contemporary critical scene." Her caveat is timely in this period of post-structuralist criticisms.

The most provocative work on H.D. this year is *The Unspeakable Mother: Forbidden Discourse in Jean Rhys and H.D.* (Cornell), by Deborah Kelly Kloepfer. Kloepfer explores the idea that the expression or repression of the mother-child dyad may be "one of the elusive specificities of women's work." Based on Lacanian and Kristevan theory, Kloepfer's book shows that the image of the archaic mother (and in her, access to the pre-Oedipal imaginary) is not absent, but "occupying a 'blind spot' " in many of H.D.'s and Rhys's texts, a spot that identifies the space and scripts they need to speak. She cogently argues that in the fiction of the 1920s H.D. reworks the Oedipal journey to find her identity as a woman and artist, coming to associate both "within the body, specifically the maternal body." In fiction and poetry alike (and particularly in *Palimpsest*, "Trilogy," and "Helen in Egypt"), H.D.'s determination to revise and reinscribe the place of the mother in the Oedipal plot is the basis of her work. What Freud saw as a mother fixation "becomes to H.D. a kind of liberating center to be cultivated, much like the *chora* Kristeva describes, opening a gap in language." Kloepfer's original and illuminating readings of "Trilogy" and "Helen in Egypt" reveal how H.D. finds the mother, or a pre-Oedipal voice, in cadence more than token: "What H.D. and Rhys teach us is that the passage from the semiotic to the symbolic is perhaps *not* necessary, at least not textually." If you have time to read only one critical piece on H.D. this year, this is the one.

Angela DiPace Fritz, *Thought and Vision: A Critical Reading of H.D.'s Poetry* (Catholic, 1987), argues that H.D.'s lifelong poetic quest is not merely personal, but mythic and communal in form and intent. She chronologically examines H.D.'s poems, tracing her progressive identification with mythic figures, to her move from object to subject (by her shattering of old myths), to her transcendence via internalization of the mythic into the personal psyche. At the heart of H.D.'s spiritual quest is the recognition that "human experience is epiphanous and sacred." One of Fritz's more interesting points is that H.D.'s works become increasingly meditative; hence, her use of incantational language and her creation of ritual (such as the spiritual calendar in "Hermetic Definition") are the tools by which the meditative mystic achieves prayerful transcendence.

v. Frost, Aiken, Crane, Ransom, Jeffers

Two biographies may be of use to Frost scholars this year. Sandra L. Katz's *Elinor Frost: A Poet's Wife* (Mass. Studies, 1988) highlights the part Elinor Frost played in the creation of her husband's poetry and interprets many of Frost's poems as directly based on their relationship. She makes the case that "ambiguous religious and political views in several poems derive not so much from an inner conflict as from Frost's wrestling with the contrary ideas of his wife." Katz offers fresh anecdotal material from conversations and correspondence with Elinor's daughter-in-law, Lillian LaBatt Frost. One problem: although Katz justly accuses Lawrance Thompson's biography of being slanted and stereotypic in its treatment of Elinor Frost, she still relies upon it as her final authority. The other biography, John Evangelist Walsh's *Into My Own: The English Years of Robert Frost, 1912–1915* (Grove, 1988), sees itself as a corrective to Thompson's interpretation. Walsh emphasizes how crucial this entire period was for Frost: he published his first two books, he developed and decided upon his mature poetic techniques and voice, and he realized that "the stimulus of literary companionship, professional encouragement, was not what he needed or wanted." Walsh uses letters, recorded anecdotes, and versions of poems to establish that Frost's creativity in Beaconsfield (he wrote "Birches" and "Mending Wall" while there, for example) was less a new direction than "a continuation of work he had started while still engaged at the Normal School in Plymouth." One of Walsh's strengths is his rereading of incidents also treated in Thompson; for example, his explanation of one of Frost's fights with his sister, regarding a pistol, is fascinating, and much more believable than Thompson's.

Harry Marten's *The Art of Knowing: The Poetry and Prose of Conrad Aiken* (Missouri) is aimed at a general audience. Marten selectively surveys Aiken's writings to show his "vision of the stages of human consciousness." The range and diversity of Aiken's poetic endeavor are made clear, and "Senlin," "Preludes for Memnon," *A Heart for the Gods of Mexico*, and "The Crystal" are provided with helpful readings. *Hart Crane: A Re-Introduction* (Minnesota), by Warner Berthoff, is similarly intended. Berthoff forgoes extensive critical apparatus and jargon to read Crane freshly. Both critics see the multiplicity of forms and the technical flexibility of their poets as being integral to each one's aesthetic and deserving of the admiration of readers. Berthoff argues that for Crane the process of poetic creation is dialectical: "the appetite for a richer language opens up new possibilities of form; in turn the idea of an 'absolute' synthesis of form becomes an important imaginative and expressive heuristic." His strong readings of the "Voyages" section of *White Buildings* and *The Bridge* illustrate this dialectic in action.

Kieran Quinlan, in *John Crowe Ransom's Secular Faith* (LSU), finds the key to Ransom's philosophic development in his struggle to "replace a shattered Christian cosmology." Quinlan argues that Ransom wrote poetry only so long as it served a function in his philosophic quest (by giving him a space to explore emotions), then focused his attention on prose. He makes the case that in the search for how to live, how to find something to believe in, Ransom is more like the Wallace Stevens of "Sunday Morning" than the Eliot of *Four Quartets*: his secular faith is ultimately an aesthetic faith.

Finally, in "A Voice in Nature: Jeffers' *Tamar and Other Poems*" (*AL* 61:230–44), Tim Hunt presents an interesting argument that Robinson Jeffers's aesthetic evolved as "a more subtle and involved process than we have realized." Noting that many critics cite Jeffers's abandonment of rhyme as the "climactic step" in developing his mature poetic voice, Hunt shows that equally significant was his much slower evolution of the role of nature. He traces a four-phase movement in which from 1920 through 1923 Jeffers explored the possible relationship between nature and the human world. The article is informative and reaffirms that Hunt is one of our strongest Jeffers critics.

Montana State University

16. Poetry: The 1940s to the Present

Richard J. Calhoun

The year 1989 narrowly missed being a considerable one for criticism on contemporary poetry. Two significant biographies, William Pritchard's of Randall Jarrell and Paul Mariani's of John Berryman, were early 1990 publications. Charles Altieri's *Painterly Abstraction in Modernist American Poetry* (Cambridge) was listed in the PMLA bibliography as a 1989 item but in *Books in Print* as early 1990. This (reinforced by the publisher's not sending the book for review) means that a report on a study by a critic who has always believed that modernism has extended well into postmodernism must wait till next year. Consequently, there was no essential critical study. Nevertheless, there was a very serviceable biography of Allen Ginsberg and a needed demythologizing one on Sylvia Plath. Demythologizing comes early these days. This was not a major year for establishment favorites, for criticism on John Ashbery, James Merrill, A. R. Ammons. It was somewhat better for W. S. Merwin. There was, surprisingly, a sign of interest in old antiestablishment rebels, now nearly forgotten, Lawrence Ferlinghetti and Gregory Corso. Revision of the canon is still under way, and I shall begin with mention of a new anthology of American literature as possibly the most significant criticism of that canon. There is a sameness this year about feminist criticism, additional reports on how women writers have needed the catharsis of engaging in "dialogic relations" with parental and literary "fathers," although there are also efforts to establish that the feminist cause effectively serves the purpose of the poetry. It was once more not a prosperous year for Robert Lowell; in contrast, the upgrading of John Berryman continues with a further demonstration of how he made his neurosis, his illness, the meaningful subject of poetry. The current reevaluation of Anne Sexton, furthering her reputation from minor confessionalist to an accomplished woman poet, progresses. There is a discernible interest in the long poem, leading inevitably to reexamination of the impact of Walt Whitman. Contemporary poets have difficulty embracing the world as willingly as he did. More, but not enough, is being said about recent and younger contemporaries, with interest especially in the language poets and in the new formalists.

i. Overview

It might seem strange to begin with notice of an anthology, but The *Heath Anthology of American Literature*, ed. Paul Lauter et al., was touted at the 1989 MLA American Literature Section meeting as one of the most significant books published since 1950. I have even found great interest in Europe in the revisionist ideas represented here. It speaks for feminist and revisionist criticism that American literature should mirror the full variety of American cultural heritage and respect "difference" as a central principle in American literature. Authors are included because they represent "different cultural voices" and disclose the nature of the difference through entertaining issues and subjects that "have often been downplayed, even avoided." This is the theory; actual practice does not substantially affect the major writers, though there is a substantial addition to the minor writers. Women, Afro-American, Hispanic, Native American poets receive greater representation than in other anthologies, but not by a large margin. The introduction to "The Contemporary Period: 1945 to the Present" is written by Linda Wagner-Martin, who finds a loss after the 1950s of "a unified vision of American culture." The civil rights movement in the 1960s and a new feminism, combined with the presence of women poets, changed the direction of American poetry during the 1960s. The new frontiers of literature had to do with the exploration of "difference," and the development of difference produced new centers of culture away from the traditional Eastern cultural establishment. In all these movements the poetry is clearly influenced by the prose. Adrienne Rich's *The Will to Change* and *Diving into the Wreck*, Anne Sexton's "wonderfully satiric" and feminist *Transformations*, and Denise Levertov's *To Stay Alive* are singled out as especially decisive. The introduction concludes with a credo: literature can no longer be divided into mainstream and marginal. But it always has been, and many teachers may decide that much that has been added to represent "difference" may be, in itself, "marginal."

Thanks to Earl G. Ingersoll, Judith Kitchen, and Stan Sanvel

Rubin, 19 very contemporary poets have their say in *The Post-Confessionals* (Fairleigh Dickinson). This collection of interviews from the Brockport Writers Forum Videotape Library makes no claims to "being all inclusive," but it permits us to listen to poets who seldom make these pages. Among the better-known writers are Charles Wright, Stanley Plumly, Gregory Orr, Nancy Willard, Edward Hirsch, Linda Pastan, Jonathan Holden, and Paul Zimmer. They are presented as a "generation" of writers, what James E. B. Breslin has called "the fourth generation—born around 1940 and starting to write around 1960." The editors buy Charles Altieri's "burn-out" theory that poets in the '70s and after were aware that they must come to terms with "failed expectations" and the guilt arising from realization that poets in the prior decade had held dreams that were too ambitious. The "fourth generation" has a new freedom because all the "received dogmas" concerning poetry have been thrown open once more. Poetry wars among factions may seem to have ended, but they have simply turned more inward. Above all, these poets are seriously concerned with language and form, aware that how they perceive their past and their present is dependent on perception through words.

Walter Kalaidjian's *Languages of Liberation: The Social Text in Contemporary American Poetry* (Columbia) is a good example of what we used to call sociological criticism, concerned with demonstrating how contemporary American poetry has been at the same time influenced by and resistant to the commercial, institutional, and social pressures of our milieu. Kalaidjian gives readings of James Wright, W. S. Merwin, Charles Olson, James Merrill, Robert Bly, and Gwendolyn Brooks, finding their ideas of "poetry" to be radical in that they disrupt the reigning ideologies and resist being incorporated into the narratives of ruling critical theories. Kalaidjian disclaims the value of introspection in much contemporary verse. In his judgment poetry should generate debate about social change. His critical approach is "indebted to and critical of the Frankfurt School, based on the work of Max Weber, George Lukács, and Herbert Marcuse," and especially to the criticism of Theodore W. Adorno. His formal concern is with "lyric verse, long verse forms, and social modes of poetry." I commend his account of the lyric endeavors of James Wright and Merwin perceived as minimalist verse forms. He sees Merwin as a significant poet in the lyric mode who has dethroned "author, voice, and reference in favor of language, textuality, and writing." I also recommend his analysis of Olson's *The Maximus Poems* and Merrill's *The Changing Light at Sandover*. Olson undermines poetry's conventional remove from worldly involvement; Merrill "fuses high modernism with contemporary pop culture in an operatic pastiche." If Merwin debunks the introspective private lyricism of contemporary poetry, Robert Bly, Adrienne Rich, and Gwendolyn Brooks "open special lines of dialogue between poetic language and America's wider discoursive scene," reflecting, resisting, and even remolding history. As the number of my extracts illustrate, I believe this to be an interesting book, even a provocative study, that has the merit of finding value in what has been undervalued in contemporary poetry. It displays knowledge of post-structural and deconstructive criticisms, with especially intelligent use of the work of Michel Foucault. The jargon is sometimes, but not too often, bothersome. It is the perceptions that matter.

The Whitman tradition is alive and well in postmodernist poetry. Thomas Gardner's *Discovering Ourselves in Whitman* focuses on how Walt Whitman's "Song of Myself" has influenced self-portraits by John Berryman in *The Dream Songs*, Galway Kinnell in *The Book of Nightmares*, Theodore Roethke in "North American Sequence," Robert Duncan in "Passages," John Ashbery in "Self-Portrait in a Convex Mirror," and James Merrill in *The Changing Light at Sandover*. Gardner's thesis is based on Duncan's description of his turning, as a follower of Ezra Pound, back to Whitman and "the lonely, isolate melodic singer pouring forth from its utter individuality and the power en masse of the ensemble in which he sings." What Gardner hopes to find is how the contemporary poets he examines "have also discovered in the 'two co-inherent figures' of Whitman's work ways of framing and finding generative the tensions implicit in singing oneself." Gardner reads "Song of Myself" as meditation on what "is in me" through an embrace of all creation. He sees contemporary poets as concerned with what blocks such an embrace. Berryman and Kinnell locate the obstructions in the perceiver, in the poet himself. For Roethke and Duncan the problems lie in using the medium. The two poets who have the greatest difficulty embracing the world, Ashbery and Merrill, paradoxically "most forcefully discover Whitman for the present" because they see the issue as a "language problem." This vision is also reflected in the shorter poems of such "language centered poets as Jorie Graham, Louise Glück, Robert Hass, Michael

Palmer, and, preeminently, Elizabeth Bishop," poets who seem to be reserved for future investigation. Gardner's attention to significant poets will receive more detailed consideration later, since his chapters read very well as separate essays on contemporary authors of the poem.

Frederick Feirstein's collection, *Expansive Poetry* (Story Line), is a manifesto of the turn away from the open forms favored by some postmodernist poets back to the use of closed forms in poetry while sustaining an accent on narrative. The poets included prefer the longer narrative poems, while most postmodernists have had a penchant for shorter. Some even take a retrospective look back at the good things in the modernist poetry and criticism of T. S. Eliot and voice their rejection of the rival tenets and practice of William Carlos Williams. The argument they have with the poets of the '50s is that that generation regarded artistic form as confining, whereas today's new formalists see form as liberating. They accept much of the movement toward a diction more like speech but add that it should be written in rhyme and in meter. Form should be "wedded" to the diction of Williams. They have sought an alternative to the "short, free verse, imagistic lyrics" that have become the new establishment in all the proper literary magazines. There is an unconvincing editorial disclaimer of espousing any kind of new ideology, but the essays clearly extol the long poem, especially Dana Gioia's "The Dilemma of the Long Poem" (pp. 3–8) and Feirstein's "The Other Long Poem" (pp. 9–15). They also implicitly advocate a new formalism—Gioia, once more, on "Notes on the New Formalism" (pp. 158–75), Robert McPhillips, "What's New About the New Formalism?" (pp. 195–208), and Christopher Clausen, "Explorations of America" (pp. 55–76). They share a new narrative poetry, explained in Mark Jarman's "Robinson, Frost, and Jeffers and the New Narrative Poetry" (pp. 85–99). The most succinct account of the poetics of the movement is Paul Lake's "Toward a Liberal Poetics" (pp. 113–23). Wyatt Prunty ("Emaciated Poetry," pp. 176–94), spells out specific things these poets have not liked about contemporary poetry written since the late '50s. Timothy Steele's "Tradition and Revolution: The Modern Movement and Free Verse" (pp. 124–57) is an account of why the expected new forms failed to come from the revolution started by Eliot, Ford Madox Ford, and Ezra Pound. It is this failure that the new formalists are trying to emend. All the essays are reprints of not widely dispersed recent articles. A hyperbole of statement and a rigidity of position in this volume have irritated some reviewers who have gone on to question the accuracy and objectivity of the account of the rival poetries these poets have opposed.

On the subject of poets speaking, I should mention that George Plimpton has edited, with an introduction by Donald Hall, a selection, *Poets at Work* (Penguin), from 25 years of *Paris Review*. Poets relevant to this chapter are Robert Penn Warren, Allen Ginsberg, Anne Sexton, James Dickey, Elizabeth Bishop, and Robert Fitzgerald. In his introductory comments Hall reports a surprising sense of community among contemporary poets.

Ronald Wallace's *Vital Signs: Contemporary American Poetry from the University* (Wisconsin) is of little critical interest since it is an anthology, not a history. But the introduction and reprinting of poems effectively illustrate how many important contemporary poets have been published by university presses, revealed as the major support of the entire poetic enterprise; the contribution of the small commercial press seems by comparison mostly mythic exaggeration.

Cary Nelson's *Modern American Poetry and Cultural Memory 1910–1945* (Wisconsin) ends where my period begins, concluding with scant mention of the first books "by 1946" of Roethke, Berryman, Lowell, Bishop, and Levertov. Their diverse work is simply verification that modern poetry is no "single coherent development, but . . . a shifting mixture of alliances and rejections, innovations and counterreactions, with new poets frequently discovering what had already been anticipated in the careers of others." Nelson's special interest is in poets who are forgotten in the cultural memory.

I shall make use of James McCorkle's *The Still Performance* in later discussions of the five postmodern American poets he examines—Ashbery, Bishop, Merwin, Rich, and Charles Wright. His title is intended to call attention to his metaphor for what it means to write poetry for a contemporary audience. It is a "still performance, with a pull of contrarieties—public and private performance, rhetorical surface but poetic depth, durational and yet enduring." The uncertainty these poets display is a symptom of their times but also essential to their vision. McCorkle sees modern poets from a different perspective from that he attributes to Charles Altieri and Mary Kinzie, that contemporary poetry is self-reflexive, a "self-indulgent expressive mode generated from the romantics." He finds instead attention to poetry itself and to culture, "with the hope that the process of transformation will be initiated." The poets he admires insist on "the writing, the recovery, and the revision of interconnection in a poem or book. . . . By moving into the space of writing . . . relations are reinvented and redefined." One of the problems of the book is that McCorkle's critical aims are not sufficiently stated in the introduction or appreciably recounted in his conclusion. Its value depends on the individual treatment of the poets.

Contemporary poets (Pound and Robert Creeley come readily to mind) who have come to acknowledge their debt to Whitman have pointed out their resistance to confessing his influence. Thomas B. Byers in *What I Cannot Say: Self, Word and World in Whitman, Stevens, and Merwin* (Illinois) begins with Wallace Stevens's pronouncement that poetry is "the statement of a relation between a man and the world." Whitman is the starting point for a scrutiny of this relation because the energy of the fusion between German and English romantic philosophy, hermeneutics, and poetics "burst into full flower with *Leaves of Grass*." Byers's Whitman is a poet "of radical language theory, the poet who finds solutions to personal problems and responses to his desires in the transcendentalist system his poem embodies." For later poets Whitman was "too radical" in his mission of asserting "the recentering of being around the self as voice and the poem as holy word." His recentering has, however, provoked responses by other poets. Stevens and Merwin have each produced "a major work that has been identified as an overall rewriting of "Song of Myself."

Jeffrey Walker's *Bardic Ethos* focuses on only one contemporary epic bard, Charles Olson. American bards write rhetorical poems, with an act of persuasion in mind, and produce "a rhetoric of ethos" with the ultimate aim of altering and directing "the national will." These ambitious intentions lead to rhetorical power but also to an ultimate frustration of their desires. Olson's Maximus Poems are viewed as signifying the collapse of this bardic tradition in American poetry.

I cite Irvin Ehrenpreis's *Poetries of America: Essays on the Relation of Character to Style* (Virginia) even though it is a posthumous collection mostly of book reviews featuring his usual emphasis on the relationship of life and poetry. The collection includes review essays on Robert Penn Warren, Elizabeth Bishop, John Berryman, James Merrill, John Ashbery (with the memorable condescending opening sentence: "There is room in our literature for John Ashbery"), Donald Justice, Sylvia Plath, A. R. Ammons, Mark Strand, and Gary Snyder. The essays on Bishop and Lowell are of special value because of the intimate acquaintance of Ehrenpreis with the poets and their work. The accounts of Ashbery, Strand, and Snyder are censorious, written by an antiromantic who believed that poets must have something to say and that style must be either appropriate or ironically inappropriate to what they have to say.

J. D. McClatchy's *White Paper: On Contemporary Poetry* (Columbia) focuses on the problem of the blank page, the problem of making something of nothing, or, alternately, "how to make something new out of something else." His title implies a position paper, though McClatchy claims that he bears "no ideological grudges." He does build a brief against attempts to make over American poetry "into images of any narrow critical orthodoxy." He reads contemporary poetry "in the light of American and English romanticism," and he values the use of autobiography in contemporary poetry, under critical attack recently, as a dominant influence on the poetry of the last three decades. He also appreciates poets like Ashbery and John Hollander, who avoid autobiography but are concerned with figuring out the self amid a play of voices and parables. This is a book more valuable for its essays on individual poets than for any new theories about modern poetry or arguments for one view of contemporary poetry over another. Poets included are Warren, Lowell, Bishop, Berryman, Plath, W. D. Snodgrass, Merrill, Richard Howard, Hollander, Amy Clampitt, Anthony Hecht, all rather establishment.

For a regional overview we have Lee Bartlett's exemplary *The Sun Is a Morning Star: Studies in West Coast Poetry and Poetics* (New Mexico), a collection of essays on "West Coast poets who have come into prominence since 1940." Included are several writers relevant to my chapter, Kenneth Rexroth, William Everson, Duncan, Snyder, and Michael McClure, plus an essay on two émigré writers, Thom Gunn and Nathaniel Tarn. Most of these essays have been published in "an earlier form," which implies rewriting for this volume. The essay on the émigré poets is interesting because it clearly documents the attraction of "the western ethos" for foreign as well as native poets. Also informative is "Theory of the Flower: Michael Palmer, Ron Silliman, and Language Poetry," an examination of two poets who are identified with San Francisco Bay poetry and with language poetry. The opening essay, on Rexroth, highlights his importance as a senior figure in poetry of the West and identifies him as a neoromantic consistently doing battle with the prevailing formalism represented to poets of his generation by the early poetry of Robert Lowell. Characteristic of Rexroth and many of these Western poets is "a poetry of direct communication and sacramental community." The other senior figure or "primary presence" is William Everson, whom Bartlett appears to overvalue. He regards Everson's Catholic poetry as his best, even "the most powerful achievement of any religious writer since the war, certainly ranking with Eliot's later work." Of value in spite of its structure as merely "notes" is "The Sun Is But a Morning Star: Notes on Gary Snyder," an attempt to specify definite Buddhist influences on Snyder's poetics. The collection concludes with an interesting interview with Everson on Robert Duncan.

It would be helpful to have an in-depth study not just of the long poem but of the long line in contemporary American poetry. So there is promise in the title of Daniel McGuiness's essay, "The Long Line in Contemporary American Poetry" (*AR* 12:269–86), and he does raise some interesting questions. Has the long line been used traditionally for more public poetry and more rarely for private lyric poetry? Does the long line lose some of its significance when the poet ignores meter? Unfortunately, his examples of the use of the long line as "a straight shot of interiority" are limited to Charles Wright's *Zone Journals* and Jorie Graham's *The End of Beauty*. The value of his essay is thereby largely limited to the few insights he has into Charles Wright's poetry.

Sherman Paul's *Hewing to Experience: Essays and Reviews on Recent American Poetry and Poetics, Nature and Culture* (Iowa) is a collection, heavily burdened with the influence of Olson, on the positive aspects of modern American poetry—specified as *descendentalism, ambulation, wordling*—made known through their polar opposites—*transcendentalism, saltation, world alienation*. To Paul, the task of postmodern poets is to "bring poetry back (and down) to life and make it once again, as Tristan Tzara said in thinking of 'primitive peoples,' 'a way of life rather than a subsidiary manifestation of intelligence and will.'" The New Criticism of his own student days is a "road no longer taken." His work on Emerson in his previous collection of essays, "*Repossessing and Renewing: Essays in the Green American Tradition* (1976), is now extended to Emerson's presence in William Carlos Williams, Snyder, and, of course, Olson. The tradition that Paul has been concerned with in previous books, including Williams, Crane, Olson, Creeley, Edward Dorn, Duncan, David

Antin, Jerome Rothenberg, Snyder, Armand Schwerner, continues
in this book with Olson, Creeley, and Snyder, and adds Wendell Berry
and Barry Lopez. With its highlights, the best account of the correspondence of Creeley and Olson, the best appreciative reading of
recent work by Snyder and Berry, and an appreciation of Lopez's
Crossing Open Ground, the book as a whole makes for an easy and
pleasant contrast to most poststructuralist criticism.

ii. The Middle Generation and Contemporaries

a. **Roethke.** Peter Balakian's *Theodore Roethke's Far Fields*
(LSU) is not a big book; it is merely a good, clearly written, well-
thought-out comprehensive survey of Roethke's work. I cannot even
claim that it offers anything new; it simply covers Roethke's intellectual, religious, psychological, and poetic development with concision. There is a valuable brief discussion of his relationship with
and the influence of William Carlos Williams. The shift Balakian
detects in Roethke's poetry from individuality and self-absorption
to otherness and union with the other is persuasively documented. If
I have an adverse comment, it would be that although this book deals
suitably with the development of Roethke as a poet, it does not mean-
ingfully associate him with modernism or with postmodernism or
sufficiently declare his stature as a major, or near major, poet. But that
is not—contrary to the promise of the publisher's blurb—Balakian's
intention. It is not an imperative to make a case today for Roethke
as a major poet. Recent critics seem agreed: he is.

Henry Hart's "Crossing Divisions and Differences, Seamus
Heaney's Prose Poems" (*SoR* 24:803–21) makes brief mention of
the influence of "deep image poets"—Bly, Snyder, and James Wright—
on the Irish poet's assumptions about the prose poem and treats in
greater depth the influence of Roethke on Heaney's preoccupation
with organicism—further evidence that Roethke has also been one of
the most influential of recent poets.

Thomas Gardner's chapter on Roethke's North American Sequence, "Far from the Crash of the Long Swell" (*Discovering Ourselves in Whitman*, pp. 78–98), deserves mention for its resolutely
close reading of the text of this long poetic sequence. The conflict
divulged is that Roethke desires something outside himself but fears
that he will be lured out of the confines of the self to court death—
"the fearful unadulterated loss of the self." Roethke becomes fright-

eningly aware of a force of violent expansion which may be a corresponding rush toward reduction and annihilation. He is able to counterbalance his fear of annihilation by recounting a long, circuitous journey that delivers him from self-absorption to union with the external.

b. **Lowell.** My only excuse for mentioning Michael Hoffman's review essay on recent books on Robert Lowell, "Guides and Assassins" (*TLS* 26 May:578), is that it is a declaration of war in one of the most public of critical places against "Lowell bashing." Hoffman censures Katharine Wallingford's *Robert Lowell's Language of Self* (No. Car.) for being "patronizing" and Jeffrey Myers's *Manic Power: Robert Lowell and His Circle* (Macmillan) for outright "treachery," a volume only for those who love to hate Lowell. I read Myers as more sympathetic with the troubled writers he specializes in than Hoffman gives him credit for. Still, as one who grew tired of Frost bashing and of James Dickey bashing, I have to be sympathetic to a protest against Lowell bashing.

Cushing Strout's "Reflections of History: Lowell's Revision of Hawthorne and Melville" (*SoR* 25:549–62) turns attention to Lowell's three plays, formal "imitations" of stories of these two great writers, published in "The Old Glory," neglected either because the poetry is forgotten or not taken seriously as "imitations," something a few poets seemed to think important in the '6os. Strout's rather minor point is that it was Lowell's own personal crises, brought about by his recurring mental illness, that led him to reconnoiter periods of crisis in American history. He points out that the time was close to his study of another crisis, his only Civil War poem, and one of his greatest compositions, "For the Union Dead."

c. **Berryman.** The most useful reference work is Harold Bloom's collection of previously published essays in another of his edited volumes on contemporary poets, *John Berryman* (Chelsea). I always consider Bloom's appreciative introductions as well worth reading. He is especially sensitive to a writer like Berryman. Bruce Bawer's "Dispossession, Crams, Delusions: The Poetry of John Berryman" (*NewC* 8, iv:19–28) gets valuable mileage out of the failure of a father, in this case the childhood tragedy of Berryman's father's suicide, on his search for identity through his poems. Bawer's approach is reasonable in that he detects an important theme but does not overemphasize it to the detriment of other influences. He also demonstrates that the event did not always lead to great poetry: Berryman could be bothered with this obsession in his doggerel as well as in his major poetry.

Thomas Gardner's "In Ill Health" (*Discovering Ourselves in Whitman*, pp. 29–58) sees the suicide as the primary limitation for Berryman in imparting a Whitman embrace to the world.

d. **Wilbur.** John Gery in "The Sensible Emptiness in Three Poems by Richard Wilbur" (*Essays in Literature* 16:113–26) offers a defense of Richard Wilbur from a charge as old as Jarrell's criticism that Wilbur ignores "the serious dangers of the modern condition." Gery examines three of Wilbur's best-known poems, "A World Without Objects Is a Sensible Emptiness," "Advice to a Prophet," and "In the Field," and argues that Wilbur has a concept of "annihilation, of nothingness evolved to a darker vision over the years" that reflects "if not a loss of faith in nature as a vial for the spirit, [at least] a profound skepticism." Gery strikes out against current critical opinion by maintaining that Wilbur's art possesses an increasing relevance to his time.

iii. The Poetry of Women

a. **Theory and History.** One of the leading feminist critics, Catharine R. Stimpson, has brought together her essays on women's topics written over the last two decades in *Where the Meanings Are: Feminism and Cultural Spaces* (Routledge). Feminism is for her "a space where the meanings are." Matthew Arnold in "On the Modern Element in Literature" called for "intellectual deliverance" from "the spectacle of vast multitude of facts awaiting and inviting . . . comprehension." As a "self-named step-daughter," Stimpson also seeks "intellectual deliverance" and finds that feminism provides "a hearing room and a reading room in which to realize how energetic women's engagements with language have been." It is evident that her engagement has rarely been with poetry. The only essay on a contemporary woman poet is her 1985 essay "Adrienne Rich and Lesbian/ Feminist Poetry," reprinted from *Parnassus* and reviewed in *ALS* for that year.

Sandra M. Gilbert and Susan Gubar now offer a sequel, *No Man's Land: The Place of the Woman Writer in the Twentieth Century*, vol.

2, *Sexchanges*. This study of the sex roles in the midst of war between men and women covers the period between the turn of the century and the high modernism of the '20s and '30s. Nevertheless, two poems by Adrienne Rich, "Diving into the Wreck" and "The Images," Sylvia Plath's splendid "Fever 103" and "Getting There," Anne Sexton's "To Like, to Love," and Elizabeth Bishop's "Exchanging Hats" earn brief mention. For further word we must await volume 3 and direct concern with contemporary poetry.

b. **Plath.** Anne Stevenson's biography of Sylvia Plath, *Bitter Fame: The Life of Sylvia Plath* (Houghton Mifflin), has been anticipated, and the wait has been worth it. Not a literary biography, such as William Pritchard's on Frost, it is rather in the tradition of psychological biography, disclosing "warts and all," as Lawrance Thompson on Frost. Stevenson does a good job of catching the fever of Plath's life. This is unmistakably not a feminist biography that makes the male, husband Ted Hughes, the villain. Stevenson writes rather to demythologize what has been constructed about the victimization of Sylvia. She has had the aid of the Hughes family, particularly Hughes's sister Olwyn, and friends like Lucas Myers (who could see what in Sylvia threatened to victimize Ted), Dido Merwin, and Richard Murphy, who feared that Sylvia was trying to move in with him as she and Ted were separating. The accounts of all three friends are included in the appendices of the book. Auriel Plath was not consulted on the grounds that her version has been given before. This may be true, but a certain balance is sacrificed.

Stevenson depicts Sylvia's life as exhausting for anyone to live with her and for her to live out herself. Her view of Sylvia is concisely stated in her comments on the poem "Medusa": "Her raw-edged response to personal sorrows and joys, her apprehension of the world's horrors and injustices, as well as its beauty, were excessive to an unusual degree. To counter this great vulnerability she devised complex defense systems in both her life and art." Any account of Plath's life is inherently interesting, but it is hard to kill a myth; and a reader might wish *Bitter Fame* were more of a literary biography with insights into the poetry from a reading of the life.

Lucas Myers's separately published account, "Ah, Youth . . . Ted Hughes and Sylvia Plath at Cambridge and Afterwards" (*GrandS* 8,iv:86–103), offers first-hand impressions of the developing love affair between Ted and Sylvia at Cambridge and the course of the relationship. Myers's few encounters with Sylvia during the last years lead to a series of observations on the demands in life-style of some American women, including a feeling that Sylvia was trying "to swallow Ted whole." Myers was on the scene two days after Sylvia's suicide. He testifies that Ted was sure Sylvia thought she would be rescued and that they would have been together again soon. In his judgment it was all inevitable: the same fuel that impelled her poetry propelled her life. This a well-written account partial to Ted but without blaming Sylvia. That may be about right, but other opinions will undoubtedly be heard. Worth a final mention is Nancy D. Hargrove's "Christian Imagery in the Poetry of Sylvia Plath (*MQ* 31:9–28). The young Sylvia said she would never speak to God again after her father's death. She does use more Christian imagery than one might suspect, though mostly of God as an authoritarian and harsh father figure and of Christ as sufferer.

Elizabeth Butler Cullingford's "A Father's Prayer, A Daughter's Anger: W. B. Yeats and Sylvia Plath" (pp. 233–55) is the only study of a contemporary poet in Lynda E. Boose and Betty S. Flowers, *Daughters and Fathers* (Johns Hopkins). The book proposes to break the critical silence on daughter and father as a paired topic with the intention of seeing the relationship as a "paradigm of women's relations to male culture" and of challenging the patriarchal nuclear family concept which, sociologically, has already broken down. Cullingford's chapter is principally a comparison of Yeats's poem "A Prayer for My Daughter" and Plath's "Daddy," beginning with the recognition that the "two poems are an ocean apart," literally and figuratively. The emotion in Yeats's poem is controlled by form: Plath's is "vividly angry," even "a nursery rhyme tantrum." But as Yeats's poetic daughter, Sylvia felt "the weight of his paternalistic prescriptions for femininity." The two poems provide "a model in miniature of the father-daughter dialectic," resolved only by a bridegroom who "legitimately replaces the father." In "Daddy," Sylvia determines that her marriage was false because her husband was "merely a projection of her fantasy of the absent father." Since her own ego is identified with the lost object, an attack on the father figure is a suicidal attack on herself. Cullingford effectively uses Freudian and other psychological symbolism, but strangely fails to make anything out of Plath's likely final symbolic act of choosing to die in Yeats's London house. More crucial, her approach precludes any possibility of tension from any love-hate ambiguity toward the father.

c. Rich. The most informative essay on Adrienne Rich's poetry is James McCorkle's " 'Fiery Iconography': Language and Interconnection in the Poetry of Adrienne Rich" (*The Still Performance*, pp. 87–129). McCorkle readily departs from his concern with the self-reflexivity of writing to an account of how Rich "redirects our responses in order to foreground the issues of power, tradition, and the institution of language as a medium of exclusion." Her feminism had led her to seek a "passionate" and "lucid" ideological dissent as well as "reflective and critical self-definition." Her meditations on language have always been, however, part and parcel with the issues she considers. McCorkle defends Rich against the charge of narrowness since Rich's concerns are those of her culture. Her "occasional poems" in her role as public poet, he argues, should not be viewed as "propaganda" or as violations of her stated belief that "a poet is the voice of the community, a voice for the voiceless" but rather as a product of a convergence of political and personal commitments. Her poetry seeks to move us from aesthetic response to ethical consideration. She must break both poetic decorum and "the poetic code by defining herself as a woman writer with a woman's consciousness." McCorkle's conclusion is that Rich proposes a new poetics not only for definitions of self but for "lucid" and "passionate" confrontations.

Mary S. Strine in "The Politics of Asking Women's Questions: Voice and Value in the Poetry of Adrienne Rich" (*TPQ* 9:14–41) attempts to relate the feminist revisionist approach taken to her poetry to Rich's expanding self-consciousness as a woman. The question raised is how a politics of asking women's questions has affected the value of the poetry. The answer owes much to the theories of Mikhail Bakhtin and his critical circle. Rich's poetry is revitalized by a contest of values—her women's questions which challenge patriarchy, "the value system that represents repressive regulation of women's lives." Through writing feminist poetry in open forms Rich seeks to use her own experiences to represent "suppressed and silent conflicts and contradictions within women's lives" and to make "an alternative culture enlightened by feminist principles" seem in her poetry an imaginative possibility. A change in voice, which to Bakhtin includes worldview, is also a change from an apolitical formalist poet to an intensely politicized feminist poet writing in open forms, who uses her poetry as an instrument for "interrogating and countering the stifling effects of patriarchal language." She is able with her women's questions to create art and to promote cultural dialogue. It is obviously now considered important to make a case for Rich's contributions to poetry along with her contributions to feminist literature. The case is being made.

Suzanne Matson in "Talking to Our Father: The Political and Mythical Appropriations of Adrienne Rich and Sharon Olds" (*APR* 18, vi:35–41) offers another examination of a "dialogic relation" between women poets and "a controlling male force." The force is "the father principle." These two poets do not seek to kill the father but rather to talk to him in order to vent their rage and their sense of "separation from the personal, cultural, and literary parent as necessary for them to develop an independent voice and become a maker of their own myths." The focal points are Rich's *Your Native Land* and Olds's *The Gold Cell*. The works are recent, but the approach and the findings are not new; Matson does not discover the kind of rhetoric in these books that Alicia Ostriker identifies in *Stealing the Language* as necessary to communicate to their audiences as feminist poets.

d. **Bishop.** The best contribution this year on Elizabeth Bishop is the chapter in McCorkle's *The Still Performance*, "Concordances and Travels: The Poetry of Elizabeth Bishop" (pp. 7–45), a good overview of the poetry. McCorkle stresses Bishop's sensitivity as observer, the preciseness in the minute details of her descriptions and in her recordings of "acute changes of perception and interrelation." It is hardly news that Bishop uses the figure of the traveler in her poetry, but McCorkle sees this figure as also "an emblem of her own character and that of the poet," of the state of the self in flux. There are good corroborative readings of several poems, including the ubiquitous "The Fish," "The Map," "Questions of Travel," "The Moose," "Crusoe in England," and "Poem."

Brett Candish Millier in "Modesty and Morality: George Herbert, Gerard Manley Hopkins, and Elizabeth Bishop" (*KR* 11,ii:47–56) begins with customary praise for Bishop's economy in use of words and her precise language, reaffirms her unhappiness with the practice of centering on personal experience and on the self, and identifies Herbert and Hopkins as the sources of the modest, self-criticism, and projection of a moral voice of Christian humility. What begins promisingly ends as an influence study without much revelation. S. R. Murthy's "Bishop's 'The Man Moth,'" (*Expl* 47:52–53) explains the origin of the title as Bishop's reaction to a misprint of the word "mammoth" in a New York *Times* article and sees the poem as an extended metaphor depicting man's inner being as a moth attracted to the magic and danger of the moon's light without regard to the consequences of such a dangerous flight. Yet the flight is also an important reprieve from an existence weighted by the "cloak of reality that hangs about him."

e. Levertov. Terrell Couch prints an interview with Denise Levertov recorded on 11 November 1986, "Interview with Denise Levertov" (*Sagetrieb* 8,iii:99–113). The focal point is Levertov's own description of her metamorphosis from an English neoromantic into "a more American, W. C. Williams-style poet." Of major concern is the influence of Williams toward the more specific, the line break in her poetry, the triadic line. Also discussed are topics such as whether she would call herself a "mystic" (she would not); process writing; and political action groups she would support in 1986.

Catherine Georgoudaki is the author of "The Human Body as Poetic Tool and Subject Matter in Denise Levertov's Poems" (*ArAA* 14:57–72). Body language and women's anatomy are important concerns of contemporary feminists and poets, and Levertov in her concern with women's self-concepts and social-sexual roles uses the human body as both poetic tool and subject, to celebrate love and life as well as to show the physical and psychological vulnerability and mortality of all human beings.

f. Sexton. Caroline King Barnard Hall has followed up the reevaluation of Anne Sexton's reputation as far more than just a confessional poet follower of her master Robert Lowell with an appreciative, detailed, and well-crafted survey, *Anne Sexton* (TUSAS 548), a welcome addition to this series. The best way to estimate Sexton's station is through an examination of all her work, especially the last poems, for signs of development; Hall does this admirably. There may not yet be the excitement about Sexton that there is about her friend Sylvia Plath, but it is gathering. Catherine Georgoudaki's "Kitchen Imagery in Anne Sexton's Poetry" (*Yearbook of English Studies*, Thessaloniki 1, 323–49) may not be a major contribution, but it is another demonstration of how effectively Sexton can use domestic materials, even from the woman's kitchen, to dramatize her conflicts and to express her themes. The roles recent critics specify—daughter, wife-mother, poet, spiritual seeker—are all acknowledged, as is her entire range of themes—loneliness, exploitation, unhappiness, madness, death, acceptance and affirmation of life, the importance of communication, the nature and function of poetry, the duality of the poet and the religious seeker. Karen Alkalay-Gut's "Sexton's 'House-wife'" (*Expl* 47,ii:52–54) also demonstrates how Sexton can move a humorous and trivial subject to some profound conclusion.

iv. Beats, Open Form, Deep Image Poets

a. **Ginsberg, Ferlinghetti, Corso, Snyder.** I suppose I would have thought that if there is a poet about whom I would have little to learn from his biography it would be that most public of poets, Allen Ginsberg. In poetry and in prose he has been a public figure. But Barry Miles's *Allen Ginsberg: A Biography* (Simon & Schuster) shows that there is a good deal still worth knowing. The outline is familiar; still, some of the details, the nuances of that life as lived, are interesting as presented here. On the negative side, Miles is so conscious of writing about a celebrity, a man who early in his career "became famous for being famous," that he somehow fails to reveal the private man or to discuss adequately what he should be attentive to—the poetry. He makes apparent the influence of the man who "single-handedly willed the Beat Generation into being," but he fails to exhibit the influence of Ginsberg's radical poetics on a rebellious movement in poetry.

It is good to see a book on Lawrence Ferlinghetti, at one time considered indispensable to the Beat Movement back when it was remembered by critics and readers. Michael Skau's *"Constantly Risking Absurdity": The Writings of Lawrence Ferlinghetti* (Whitston) is actually a short study restricted to examining Ferlinghetti as the most politically committed of the Beats but, with a dual ironic perspective, compelled to respond politically while fully conscious of the "futility in politically motivated artistic endeavors." He believed that political satirical poems are effective only at the time they are written and that they are destined to be forgotten. Skau's evaluation of the political poems runs contrary to Ferlinghetti's pessimism: "the best of his satirical tirades hold up remarkably well as affecting and complex statements of enduring values." His appraisal is based on his belief that Ferlinghetti's most successful poems are personal. Yet he admits that Ferlinghetti also intends his voice to be "la voce delpopolo," that of an enraged populace. His target is not limited to individuals who hold power, but also directed against capitalism, which he indicts as a mindless depleter of natural resources and irresponsible begetter of social and economic inequities. A chapter is devoted to Ferlinghetti's plays; another to his prose volume *Her*; only two short chapters are given to the poetry. The first, "The Poet as Poem," examines Ferlinghetti's Beat poetry as "an intentional rebuke" to the sterility of academic poetry expressed in poems that demand the reader's engagement. *"Constantly Risking Absurdity"* also reconsiders the experiments in jazz-accompanied poetry, which Ferlinghetti himself came to see as a failure. All of this is good enough, but Skau fails to prove the value of Ferlinghetti's political stance to the worth of his poetry.

John O'Kane's "Lawrence Ferlinghetti: Anarchism and the Poetry Revolution" (*Enclitic* 11,ii:47–58), based on an interview, pictures Ferlinghetti as an "admitted populist" who believes that poetry should "be an emotionally-charged public event cementing personal will into social bond." In everything he has done, Ferlinghetti has sought to create an impact. He has mocked all his poetic masters—Eliot, Pound, Yeats, Whitman, Dylan Thomas. He has always objected to writing that dramatizes the "alienation of the subjective from the objective." Since poetic revolution no longer seems possible, "Ferlinghetti's mission as a populist poet is to keep railing against the blights that prevent a rebirth of wonder, raging against 'the dying of the light.'" The difficulty with this essay is that it is more attentive to the man than to his poetry.

Michael Skau is back at work on another lately neglected Beat poet in "'To Dream, Perchance to Be': Gregory Corso and Imagination" (*UDR* 20:69–88). And no wonder Corso is not for today. As Skau makes clear, in an age in which the industrial criterion of maximum efficiency predominates, Corso deliberately extols the "idiosyncratic imperfection of man." Even the mad and the criminal element have appeal for him if they "disturb the smooth functioning of society." His most popular poems, like "Hair" and "Marriage," focus on conflicts between individual integrity and social conventions. But also there is more complexity: many of Corso's poems dramatize the ambiguities of choice. Corso's choices actually lean in the direction of his imagination at work in rejoinders to a society that would eliminate individuality and with it imagination and fantasy. His faith is not in the mass-induced false dream but in the visionary capability of the poet. In this creativity lies the hope for rising above conventional limitations. "Only a poet can renew hope."

Tom Lavazzi, "Pattern of Flux: The 'Torsion Form' in Gary Snyder's Poetry" (*APR* 18,iv:41–47), turns to a principle of "looping— from present to past and back again, from self to other and back again," evident in a touchstone image in Snyder's poetry, the "spiral, whorl or knot." This "torsion form" comes from Snyder's whirling together of Buddhist, ecological, and primitive poetic perspectives as expressions "of the density and diversity of consciousness" and to provide a sense of an exploding, expanding consciousness. Snyder is clearly not a moralist in conventional Judeo-Christian terms, but he is a poet who feels the ethical responsibility to delve "into personal depths for nutrients there" to give back "to the community."

b. **Olson.**   Burton Hatlen in "Kinesis and Meaning: Charles Olson's 'The Kingfishers' and the Critics" (*ConL* 30:546–73) points out the critical disagreement on the meaning of one of Olson's most frequently explicated poems. He suggests that disagreements come from the approaches used, specifically from not applying the appropriate approach to the kind of poem Olson was writing. Olson regarded his mission as "the liberation of mythos from logos, art from discourse." His type of poem was intended to do something more than "be"; it must, if at all possible, "act." "The Kingfishers" must be read "not as a sequence of images or symbols which "body forth a meaning that the poem wishes to communicate" but be regarded as "a kinetic event." This much-explicated poem is visited again in George Butterick's major reexamination of "Charles Olson's 'The Kingfishers' and the Poetics of Change," (*AmerP* 6, ii:28–59). Butterick's long article is not only a careful reading of key lines but a careful placement of the poem in the context of Olson's work. If a reading can be called definitive, this one (among Butterick's last articles) is so as formalist criticism and as background/context study.

c. **Bly, Wright.**   Paul Lake, "Return to Metaphor: From Deep Imagist to New Formalist" (*SWR* 74:515–29), engages in comparing the Deep Imagists (Charles Wright and Robert Bly in particular) and the new formalists in their use of metaphor. Lake believes that next to their restoration of formal verse, their notions about the importance and function of metaphor are significant. To demonstrate this difference, he compares Wright's "At Zero," Bly's "Waking from Sleep,"

Gjertrud Schnackenberg's "The Paperweight," Charles Martin's "Metaphor of Grass in California," and Timothy Steele's "Last Tango."

v. Nature: Surrealism, Realism, Metaphysics

a. **Ammons and other Landscape Poets.** Bonnie Costello in "The Soil and Man's Intelligence: Three Contemporary Landscape Poets" (*ConL* 30:412–33) returns to one of the traditional concerns of American poetry, an attachment to the land, a desire of poets to make portraiture of the American landscape. Costello believes that contemporary American poets have revealed a desire to find a way to an "earth bound" poetry, while "preserving the authority, or at least autonomy of the imagination and language." Three poets who have taken separate stances toward American landscape are Snyder, Ammons, and Charles Wright. Snyder is characterized as an "immanentist," a term Costello borrows from Charles Altieri to designate a poet who seeks an unmediated presentation of the plenitude he finds in the landscape. Ammons is the analogist, the poet who pursues the parallels between landscape and mind. Charles Wright is the transcendentalist who "attends to the landscape for the traces of an inorganic ideal." The modes these three poets represent could alternatively be called pantheistic, contemplative, and mystic. Costello's argument is that the vitality of our poetry depends on the coexistence of these three modes. Her major interest among the three is Wright, who in his later works has become more immersed in landscape and "in developing the theme of death as the source of creative energies, another major solicitude of American poets like Whitman, Dickinson, and Stevens." This is an article that manages to say something of tangible interest.

b. **Kinnell, Dickey.** Two of our most interviewed poets, Galway Kinnell and James Dickey, are interviewed once more. Cynthia Atkins and Jeanne Beaumont recorded "Being with Reality: An Interview with Galway Kinnell" (*Columbia* 14:169–82). In this conversation Kinnell touches on whether a poet has "mind censors" that keep him from revealing parts of himself, on whether it is still harder for him to write a short poem than a longer one, on his interest in resurrecting words, on the disappearance of religion and his own disbelief in Christianity, on the role of the past in his poetry, on his views of the myth of the muse in poetry, and on his perspective of the new formalists and language poets. Since most of these topics are being re-visited, I shall report only that Kinnell feels free verse has become "rather prosaic" and that the new formalists may be valuable not for a return to forms but in "helping to restore some of the formal charac-ter to free verse."

To match Dickey's earlier volume, *Self-Interviews*, Ron Baugh-man has brought together a complete collection of previously pub-lished actual interviews, *The Voiced Connections of James Dickey* (So. Car). I agree that Dickey sometimes says too much and is often opinionated, but I also believe that he is often one of our best poet-critics. It is good to have the collection, and it cannot hurt, and may help, a reputation that has unfortunately been at low ebb.

In the Dickey *Newsletter* the factory output continues. Spiros Papleacos, "James Dickey's Use of the Heraclitean Oracle in 'The Shark's Parlor'" (*JDN* 5,ii:27–30), turns to one of the truly comic poems in recent American poetry, "Shark's Parlor." His subject is not humor but Dickey's use of myth, employing here "a variation of the Heraclitean Oracle to give the poem a dimension of mythos." Gor-don Van Ness is also concerned with Dickey's use of myth in " 'Stand-waiting, my love, where are you?'" (*JDN* 6,i:21–24). He explores Dickey's concern with mythic archetypes drawn from what Joseph Campbell identifies as "the Queen Goddess of the World." For Dickey, women are ideal figures who serve as a means of actualization since "without women men remain unfulfilled and for whom they seek because as ideal figures they offer larger possibilities." Since Dickey is known for his macho image, sometimes unfairly, it is useful to be reminded that women have a role in his poetry. John Blair in "The Question of Race in James Dickey's 'Cherrylog Road'" (*NConL* 19,i:2) seeks to modify the usual view of the typical Dickey protago-nist as "Southern White Anglo-Saxon" by the unpersuasive suggestion that the speaker may be black. He notes the "nihilistic abandon" and the "impetus toward self-destruction" in the speaker's attitude. Of course, anyone who ever heard Dickey read the poem cannot forget it as a comic tour-de-force and Dickey's hints, perhaps to further the performance, that the poem was—in part at least—autobiographical.

My essay in *MissQ* (42:83–88), "James Dickey: A Poet of Repu-tation," is an attempt to review recent books that may assess Dickey's true stature, if not help him back up to his reputation in the mid-1960s at least adjust it higher than it is today. Recent books have contributed but not shown the total picture of Dickey as poet, novelist, and critic right. Each tends to ride a particular thesis, which in the end makes him less than he may merit. Negative views of the man or legend and a critical consensus about his poetry from the mid-1970s on thwart a reassessment of the many fine poems he wrote earlier. Their considerable lyric and narrative skill merits a more extensive reassessment than recent studies are providing. In " 'The Big Wink': Essay Review" (*JDN* 5,ii:27–30), the poet David Smith concludes that Dickey's reputation needs a study that invites the real James Dickey to stand and declare his value. Smith's annoyance with what has been published recently on Dickey is a reminder that Dickey's fellow poets still tend to appreciate his poetry.

c. Berry, Stafford. There is a single item on Wendell Berry, the most agrarian of poets writing today, by Jerry Alan Twiggs, "A Kinship of the Fields: Farming in the Poetry of R. S. Thomas and Wendell Berry" (*NQD* 57,ii:92–102). We are reminded of Berry's sincerity in that he is the only poet who left academic life for a career in farming. The Welsh poet, R. S. Thomas, who influenced Berry, by contrast always looked at being a farmer from the outside; Berry takes the inside view, and his poetry has profited from farming as a rich source of metaphors. He might, however, Twiggs admits, be criticized for romanticizing it. This is a valuable essay documenting some of the distinctive qualities of Berry's poetry.

Judith Kitchen's *Understanding William Stafford* (So. Car.) is a competent introduction to a good poet who falls outside the mainstream of the establishment. Kitchen sees Stafford's poems as about more complex relationships between the public and the private person, between people and land, than some readers have observed. The strongest argument made for that complexity is the presence of dualisms in Stafford's perceptions and in the apparent simplicity of his poems: "Stafford is best read by looking for the countless opposites that his poems contain. His basic concerns are doubled and redoubled as he explores the dual nature of language life." It is this approach that Kitchen takes to explications that adequately argue that Stafford is no ordinary poet.

vi. Poets, Men of Letters

a. Warren. Hugh Ruppersburg's *Robert Penn Warren and the American Imagination* (Georgia) precedes what will undoubtedly be a number of articles in the aftermath of Warren's death. We think of Warren as a Southern writer, but this book demonstrates that his concern with the South was an instance of his belief in the importance of using regional materials to help reveal America. Warren was pre-occupied with modern America and with its sometimes tenuous rela-tionship to the ideals laid down by the Founding Fathers. Few of our' writers have used American place more effectively to dramatize the search for the American dream. I have always admired Warren's *Brother to Dragons*. So does Cleanth Brooks. His "Robert Penn War-ren and American Idealism" (*SR* 97:566–91) makes corrections to John Burt's *Robert Penn Warren and American Idealism* (Yale) reviewed here last year. Brooks feels, as I did, that Burt does not do full justice to the importance of *Brother to Dragons* and that theoriz-ing gets in the way of a real confrontation with Warren's essential themes and situations.

b. **Ciardi.**   Burton Raffel, "John Ciardi: A Man of Much Reason" (*LitR*, 32:273–77), discusses the recent collection of essays, *John Ciardi: Measure of the Man*, reviewed here last year. He focuses on the survival of Ciardi's reputation despite the fact he did not fit into the modernist or postmodernist picture "as either a recognized peg or hole," and yet was able to be a successful poet and man of letters and subsist outside the academy.

vii. Eastern and New Establishment

a. **Ashbery.**   The contribution on John Ashbery this year is James McCorkle's "John Ashbery's *Artes Poeticae* of Self and Text" (*The Still Performance*, pp. 46–86). Ashbery is viewed as "tellingly self-reflexive," a poet whose poetry is "of engaged and continuous specu-lation" and who suggests "that the music of the poem can never be contained within the frame of the word." McCorkle explores beyond the few poems that Ashbery's critics usually focus on. The *artes poeticae* he finds in them are "openings where each poem acknowl-edges its beginnings as "something / Nobody can translate." Ashbery's subject is "always death and its supplement—life." This is a better essay on Ashbery than it is illustration of the theme of McCorkle's book. It is also refreshingly less abstruse than some items on Ashbery have been.

b. **Merrill.** It was a lean year for critical commentary on a major poet, but I do recommend James Baird's "James Merrill's Sound of Feeling: Language and Music" (*SWR* 74:361–77). Baird argues that Merrill is "unique" among contemporary American poets in that his poetry is directed by his return to the Greek principle of *mousike*, or the naming of poetry and music as one. He traces Merrill's fascination with "the sound of feeling," with "the doublevoiced poetry of feeling," over a 30-year period from the late 1950s to the present, and contends that "no other Major American poet . . . has so clearly assumed the important double role of song maker, mythmaker."

c. **Merwin.** The principal article on W. S. Merwin is James Mc-Corkle's "W. S. Merwin's 'Poetics of Memory'" (*The Still Performance*, pp. 130–70). An essay that begins as arrestingly and as accurately as this one I would have to recommend: "In W. S. Merwin's poetry, we are always on the threshold of some disquieting revelation." McCorkle evokes from Merwin's poetry a strong sense of impending extinction and response to a poetic grammar, which "corresponds with a vanishing natural world." He discusses the silence that comes from the lack of discourse between the self and others or from reaching the abyss where language and memory end any journey or pilgrimage. He detects Merwin's *ars poetica* in "Learning a Dead Language," where he locates memory in the word, and in "Daybreak," where he recognizes the limits of poetic language and his own language. What Merwin seeks is the moment of equilibrium between the epiphanic and failing, public and private communication, silence and continuance in the "still performance." His poetry is like Pound's—one work, "one vast intertext."

Brian Daldorph's "'the pulse/ Of a stone was my flag/ And the Stone's in pieces': Merwin's Breaking Voice in *The Moving Target*" (*AmerP* 6,iii:3–54) is an argument that the early poems (those written January–October 1960) in *The Moving Target* are radically different from the poems in Merwin's first four volumes while still retaining elements of those earlier poems. Not only is *The Moving Target* a pivotal volume, but "Departure's Girlfriend" (written January 1961) is a pivotal poem. It is analyzed in detail, as are other poems that mark Merwin's transformation of his poetry to achieve the quality of "transparency."

In a note, "Influence Without Anxiety: Dylan Thomas and W. S.

Merwin" (*NConL* 19, v:6–7), William V. Davis locates in Merwin's early essay on Thomas the source of one of Merwin's important themes and celebrated poems. The poem, another apocalyptic one, is "For the Anniversary of My Death," published in *The Lice*; the source is Thomas's "I dreamed my genesis," where Thomas finds the knowledge of his death in his genesis. Davis, interested in defining how Merwin is a "religious poet," concludes: "In the celebration in this inexorably coming but unknown moment of death, in linking it, as anniversary, to birth, Merwin defines and identifies himself as a 'religious poet.' " Davis offers a second note, " 'The Light Again of Beginning': W. S. Merwin's Little Apocalypse" (*NConL* 20,iv:8–9) on Merwin's "The First Darkness." In this seven-line poem he finds "the essence of Merwin's contribution to the apocalyptic mode so important to the history of recent American poetry." Merwin reverses the myth of genesis by arguing the existence of God not through presence at the creation but by his absence. The only thing left for the religious poet is a ritual of celebration of "the same mysterious blessing."

viii. Others

***a*. Wright.**   Charles Wright gets the briefest treatment in James McCorkle's " 'Things That Lock Our Wrists to the Past': Self-Portraiture and Autobiography in Charles Wright's Poetry" (*The Still Performance*, pp. 171–211). McCorkle compares Wright with Hopkins in that for both the "self's writing extends and collaborates with the natural world's writing." This idea informs Wright's concept of language and of the poem. He is autobiographical not in the sense that he is purely personal or confessional but in that he translates his experiences into "meditations on mutability, memory, and degeneration." To Wright, the moment in which the poet's self is mirrored in a poem is analogous to a painter's self-portrait. Central in that poetry are the confrontation with death, the recognition of difference, and a concern with place and relationship to a particular place.

***b*. Hecht.**   There are two books out this year on Anthony Hecht, a series of essays edited by Sydney Lea, *The Burdens of Formality: Essays on the Poetry of Anthony Hecht* (Georgia), and Norman German's *Anthony Hecht* (Peter Lang). German's book is a rigid survey of Hecht's poetry limited to the four volumes published from 1967 to 1979—*A Summoning of Stones, The Hard Hours, Millions of*

Strange Shadows, The Venetian Vespers—with the briefest of introductions and an afterword. There are extensive quotations from
poems, followed by brief paraphrases and comments. The emphasis
is not on Hecht's place in contemporary poetry but on influences—
his "indebtedness to Auden, Yeats, Ransom, the Metaphysicals." Only
in the miniscule afterword does German turn to assessment. Hecht's
major concerns are with a "philosophical quarrel with the-world-as-
it-is and a corrective reveling in nature's splendor." But his stances
in getting his themes across are limited to "aesthetic stances" primarily from John Crowe Ransom. Of greater value and definitely
needed for a poet of Hecht's importance is Lea's collection of essays.
Alicia Ostriker, "*Millions of Strange Shadows*: Anthony Hecht as
Gentile and Jew" (pp. 97–105), makes a case for the formal excellence
and mastery evident in many of Hecht's poems. J. D. McClatchy in
"Anatomies of Melancholy" (pp. 186–203) looks at the effect of
Hecht's often bleak pessimism on his poetry. Joseph Brodsky in
"Anthony Hecht and the Art of Poetry" (pp. 49–50) delivers the
pronouncement that Hecht is the "best poet writing in English today."
Peter Sacks in "Anthony Hecht's 'Rites and Ceremonies': Reading
The Hard Hours" (pp. 62–96) tries to demonstrate through focus on
one book how Hecht's poetry should be read overall. Linda Orr dis-
cusses Hecht as translator through concentration on the Voltaire in
"Pastiche and Pain: After Anthony Hecht's Translation of Voltaire"
(pp. 106–19). John Frederick Nims gives a reading of another book in
" 'The Venetian Vespers': Drenched in Fire" (pp. 120–41). So much is
said about the dark in Hecht that I liked William Matthews's "Horatian Hecht" (pp. 145–58), attempting to find Horatian serenity in
Hecht's work, and the slight twist of Kenneth Gross's "Anthony Hecht
and the Imagination of Rage" (pp. 159–85) from the formal eloquence
usually stressed by the critics as characteristic of Hecht's verse.

c. Donald Hall. Liam Rector, "Donald Hall, An Interview" (*APR*
18,i:39–45), elicits the usual biographical information about Hall's
adolescence, his education, his own views of his poetic development,
but directs major attention to Hall's most recent book, *The One Day*.
Hall sharply declares himself against elitism, against separating creative writing departments from English departments because readers
of poetry should not be disconnected from writers. He denies any
role as a leader of an Eastern establishment in poetry though he resides in the East. Hall also defends the diversity of his writing—

poetry, criticism, anthologies, children's books. This diversity provides
a means for the poet to remain financially solvent.

d. **Levine.** Richard Jackson, "The Long Embrace: Philip Levine's
Longer Poems" (*KR* 11,iv:160–69), further manifests the current interest in the long poem. Jackson shows Poe wrong in his belief that
the "long poem" is an oxymoron because a poem should express an
intense, brief emotion by discussing three Levine poems, "Letters for
the Dead," "A Poem with No Ending," and "A Walk with Tom
Jefferson."

e. **Eshleman.** Paul Christensen's "Clayton Eshleman: The American Background" (*AmerP* 6, iii:66–81) is wider-ranging than the title
would designate, perhaps wider than the organization can sanction.
It begins with Charles Olson and his choice of Ishmael as the embodiment of postmodernist sensibility. What Christensen tries to substanti-
ate is that American poetry "in the twentieth century has evolved
steadily toward a vision of unified sensibility, but its irregular progress
has been by discontinuous jumps of theory and execution." Olson's
"The Kingfishers," Duncan's "Poetry, a Natural Thing," Donald Allen's "The New American Poetry," Creeley's "The Awakening," Levertov's "The Goddess," Snyder's "Statement on Poetics" are discussed
as background for Eshleman's *Indiana* (1969) and his key question:
"how to change one's self by one's own effort and will." What Olson
had formulated in the abstract, Eshleman brought down to the level
of a personal desire for freedom and renewal. Christensen centers on
Eshleman's plot of retrogression to a prior stage of selfhood, even all
the way back to the memory of conception, the ultimate retrogression
in his recent poetry. This is a very ambitious essay that never accomplishes quite what it sets out to do.

Clemson University

17. Drama

Peter A. Davis

It is curious that the most interesting contributions to dramatic scholarship continue to be reference works. There are notable exceptions,
of course, especially in African-American theater and feminist theory.
But the lack of substantial, groundbreaking writing, either critical or
historical, remains a fundamental weakness in dramatic studies. Indicative of the problem is the proliferation of author-subsidized publishing, which appears to be increasing every year; modestly revised
doctoral dissertations in hardcover are generally poor substitutes for
original monographic research or larger integrated studies. Yet the
pressure—particularly among junior faculty—to produce published
tomes for promotion and tenure has become more important than the
need to genuinely contribute to the field. Publishers, recognizing a
profit potential, have provided cheap and easy outlets by offering
"camera-ready" contracts for those who are willing to invest in their
own future and pay for the honor of a published book.

One cause for optimism, however, was the arrival of *The Journal
of American Drama and Theatre*, ed. Vera Mowry Roberts and Walter
Meserve and published by the Center for Advanced Study of Theatre
Arts at CUNY-Graduate School. Implied in its inaugural issue is an
integrated approach to American theater and drama that is long overdue. Judging from the first two editions, the project is off to a good
start. As with most theater journals the entries are uneven, but a sufficient number of good to excellent pieces make a subscription worthwhile. Once the editors work out some annoying glitches, including an
appalling lack of proofreading, the journal should become a major dis-
seminator of new research. On the whole, however, the field is still
dominated by traditional literary criticism and shows only modest efforts to incorporate new historiography and performance studies. The
quantity of publication seems to have declined slightly. Perhaps it
is premature to say, but we may be seeing the first signs of the pro-

jected shortage of professors manifested in fewer offerings and waning quality.

i. Reference Works

Greenwood Press maintains its dominance of reference materials by producing four major volumes that are already standard sources for American scholars. *American Playwrights Since 1945: A Guide to Scholarship, Criticism, and Performance,* ed. Philip C. Kolin, contains 40 chapters each dealing separately with a recent American playwright. The uniformly organized chapters concentrate on six principal areas: Achievements and Reputation, Primary Bibliography, Production History, Survey of Secondary Sources, Future Research Opportunities, and Alphabetical Checklist of Secondary Sources. The research appears to be quite complete and expertly edited. If a weakness is to be found, it may be in the brief introductory sections on reputation; they tend to be a bit too glib for my taste, although they may be helpful to undergraduates looking for a critical handle. Most important, the work provides the first anthologized collection of bibliographic reference materials on most of the important and influential playwrights since World War II. This alone should make it an invaluable addition to any theater scholar's library.

Another fine collection, long overdue, is *Notable Women in the American Theatre: A Biographical Dictionary,* ed. Alice Robinson et al. (Greenwood). With over 300 entries ranging from America's first known professional actress, Mrs. Lewis Hallam, to women in recent theater, the book is the most comprehensive biographical encyclopedia of its kind yet published. The quality and accuracy of the entries varies, of course, but some are distinctive not only for their insight but for the depth of information on long-forgotten or lesser-known artists. While the work tends to focus on actresses, playwrights, and managers, it refreshingly gives attention to agents, critics, educators, and even patrons. Two appendices list women by place of birth and by profession. The index is thorough and capably cross-referenced. Like Kolin's volume, this too should be of great use.

Robert A. Schanke's *Eva Le Gallienne, A Bio-Bibliography* offers a detailed bibliographic account of this remarkable woman's career. The book is divided into seven sections, including a biography, chronology, list of productions, and annotated bibliography of her writings. The biographical chapter is helpful to those unfamiliar with Le Gallienne, providing a brief summary of her life. Much of this information is repeated in the chronology, but the list of productions is very detailed and helpful. Another important bibliographical source in this general area is Don B. Wilmeth's "Tentative Checklist of Indian Plays" (*JADT* 1, ii:34–54). The list covers more than 600 plays from 1606 to 1987 and is the most comprehensive on the topic to date. The plays, many of them accessible in one form or another, are listed according to date of publication or first production and include author's name and occasionally location of performance or type of production.

In theater history, the principal work this year was *American Theatre Companies: 1931–1986*, ed. Weldon B. Durham (Greenwood), completing a series that includes *American Theatre Companies, 1749–1887* (1986) and *American Theatre Companies, 1888–1930* (1987). The series represents a monumental undertaking, and few would argue its standing as a major contribution. The final volume follows the organization and format of the previous two—alphabetical order with each entry composed of an introductory essay followed by lists of personnel and repertory and concluding with brief bibliographies. My only quibble is with the index, which does not include names of the theater companies themselves (presumably because they are presented in alphabetical order in the text). But the oversight makes for awkward scanning, particularly for companies that may be cross-listed under different names.

Although it was published in 1988, I would be remiss in failing to mention a resource that was not covered last year. *The Cambridge Guide to World Theatre*, ed. Martin Banham, clearly goes beyond the scope of *ALS*, but it does contain a healthy amount in American theater and drama. In contrast to the established *Oxford Companion to the Theatre*, the Cambridge guide is more suited to American tastes and interests. Indeed, the editorial board is dominated by American scholars and this bias is reflected in the contents.

ii. Anthologies

A number of significant anthologies emerged this year, but again none offer that ideal combination long sought by professors of American theater and drama. Instead, they are specific in their foci and in most cases contain works usually excluded from the traditional canon. Errol Hill has assembled an important anthology of seven plays dealing with *Black Heroes* (Applause); included are Langston Hughes, *Emperor of Haiti*; Randolph Edmonds, *Nat Turner*; May Miller, *Harriet Tubman*; William Branch, *In Splendid Error*; Edgar White, *I. Marcus Garvey*; Phillip Hayes Dean, *Paul Robeson*; and Ron Miller, *Roads of the Mountaintop*. Introductions of the heroes portrayed precede each play, and short biographies of the authors follow. *Black Female Playwrights*, ed. Kathy A. Perkins (Indiana), is equally noteworthy. The book contains a rare collection of 19 plays by seven black women (Georgia Douglas Johnson, Mary P. Burrill, Zora Neale Hurston, Eulalie Spence, May Miller, Marita Bonner, and Shirley Graham) who were writing before 1950 and thus influential in laying the foundation for such writers as Alice Childress, Lorraine Hansberry, and Elaine Jackson. For the benefit of those largely unfamiliar with these playwrights, Perkins has thoughtfully included brief biographies that are every bit as interesting as the plays. Rounding out the anthologies in African-American theater is *New Plays for the Black Theatre*, ed. Woodie King, Jr. (Third World), containing 15 recent one-acts by such leading black playwrights as Amiri Baraka, Pearl Cleage, and Oyamo.

Jorge Huerta has produced a volume of Chicano plays appropriately entitled *Necessary Theatre* (Arte Público). With well-written introductions and production histories preceding the plays, Huerta defines the historical significance of each work and describes the development of the Chicano theater movement since its inception in 1965 by Luis Valdez and the Teatro Campesino. Although the plays count among the most influential in Chicano theater, none apart from *Soldierboy* by Judith and Severo Pérez have been previously published. The other plays include *Latina*, Milcha Sánchez-Scott and Jeremy Blahnik; *The Shrunken Head of Pancho Villa*, Luis Valdez; *Guadalupe*, El Teatro de la Esperanza; *Money*, Arthur Girón; *La víctima*, El Teatro de la Esperanza. *Womenswork* (Applause) collects five recent plays by writers of the Women's Project: *Abingdon Square*, Maria Irene Fornes; *Ma Rose*, Cassandra Medley; *Etta Jenks*, Marlane Meyer; *Five in the Killing Zone*, Lavonne Mueller; *Mill Fire*, Sally Nemeth. Julia Miles, founder of the Women's Project and editor of the anthology, provides a brief introduction, describing the playwrights as women who "take chances with difficult subjects and often break the perimeters of the strict realistic form."

iii. History of Theater and Drama

Substantial histories of American theater and drama remain scarce. Of the handful of new works reviewed this year, half are hardbound doctoral dissertations with little or no substantive revision. The dearth of original work in theater history is a dilemma that reaches back many years. More significantly, few histories of the theater demonstrate a functional knowledge of current historiography. The sad fact is that theater historians are still not trained as historians. Thus the field is dominated by largely positivistic, descriptive studies that focus on performance re-creation and chronology.

Nevertheless, a few highlights should be mentioned. Perhaps the best publication in this area is the collection edited by Judith L. Fisher and Stephen Watt, *When They Weren't Doing Shakespeare: Essays on Nineteenth-Century British and American Theatre* (Georgia). As the title implies, the essays are a mixture of American and British topics, written by a respectable group of authors, designed to highlight non-Shakespearean influences in the 19th-century theater. The book is divided into three sections, dealing with "Actors and Their Roles," "Playwrights and Genres," and "Comedy and Social Drama." Of the 18 essays, seven are devoted to American topics. Especially worth consideration: Bruce A. McConachie's "The Theatre of Edwin Forrest and Jacksonian Hero Worship" (pp. 3–18) places Forrest's commissioned melodramas in the context of Jacksonian democracy and liberal idealism. McConachie provides a credible summary of Forrest's liberalism and Jacksonian manifestation in his plays and offers an important view of innate American drama. Edwin Booth's second most famous non-Shakespearean character is the focus of Lorraine Commeret's piece, "Edwin Booth's Bertuccio: Tom Taylor's Fool Revised" (pp. 64–83). The study attempts to elevate Booth's portrayal of Bertuccio to the level of his Richelieu and succeeds in attracting our attention to this neglected role. Myron Matlaw retells the story of "James O'Neill's Launching of *Monte Cristo*" (pp. 88–105), and Joy Harriman Reilly recalls "A Forgotten Fallen Woman: Olga Nethersole's *Sapho*" (pp. 106–20). Gary A. Richardson's "In the Shadow of the Bard: James Nelson Barker's Republican Drama and the Shakespearean Legacy" (pp. 123–36) presents the popular thesis that Barker was one of the primary proponents of an American drama distinct from its English traditions. In a brief essay Tice L. Miller explores "The Image of Fashionable Society in American Comedy, 1840–

1870" (pp. 243–52). Miller demonstrates how New York high society is lampooned by the popular comedies of the day, and the traditional American display of "rural innocence and purity [is] pitted against urban corruption." And James Hurt in "Dion Boucicault's Comic Myths" (pp. 253–65), examines Boucicault's melodramatic comedies and the influence of the shaughraun characters on later American drama. On the whole, the collection offers a valuable perspective on England and American theater of the last century.

The other side of the issue is nicely presented by Helene Wickham Koon in *How Shakespeare Won the West: Players and Performances in America's Gold Rush, 1849–1865* (McFarland). This short but skillfully focused and well-researched volume presents the rich and colorful history of Shakespeare in early California. From the earliest performances by amateurs and U.S. Army soldiers during the Mexican War to the traveling companies headed by such notable families as the Starks, Chapmans, Bakers, and Booths, the book is more than a recounting of Shakespeare in the West—it is one of the best production histories of theater in California.

This year's crop of published doctoral dissertations is a typically mixed lot; they are distinguished from each other largely by the production values of the respective presses. Robert W. Snyder's *The Voice of the City: Vaudeville and Popular Culture in New York* (Oxford) traces the rise of vaudeville from its early 19th-century origins in the Bowery to its dominant position in the 1920s. Largely chronological, the history does not shy away from pointing out both the good and the bad. While vaudeville did much to bring the working class to the theater and offered middle-class women of the '20s an unprecedented opportunity for urban adventure, it nonetheless was notoriously racist and sexist. Snyder does a good job in presenting a balanced view, and despite occasional florid lapses, the book is well-written and an excellent addition to the study of popular theater in New York.

John S. Gentile's *Cast of One: One-Person Shows from the Chautauqua Platform to the Broadway Stage* (Illinois), in its quest to cover the entire history of the one-person show from Dickens and Poe to Whoopi Goldberg and Eric Bogosian, confronts the usual problem of representative selection encountered by most historians attempting to assimilate broad historical vistas. The book makes a noble effort in presenting a varied lot of solo performers. Gentile's work on the founding of the Chautauqua and its development into the 20th century is refreshing and important. But the book is flawed by the author's conceptual limitations. In his passion to cover the topic, Gentile has resorted to a textbook account of various solo performances in chronological order. Although he sets himself the task of answering such crucial questions as "Why have certain periods been more receptive to the one-person show? Which cultural forces hinder it?"— he never thoroughly answers them. Significant political, economic, and social influences are largely ignored in favor of cultural generalizations and critical assessments based on newspaper reviews. As a narrative list of solo performances over the last century, this book may have some scholarly merit—if only as a reference. Its insubstantial thesis and lack of historiographical acumen, however, make it an awkward history.

One of America's most important Off-Broadway theater groups is detailed in Mary S. Ryzuk's *The Circle Repertory Company: The First Fifteen Years* (Iowa State). Most of the work is concerned with the four founder-members (Lanford Wilson, Marshall W. Mason, Rob Thirkeild, and Tanya Berezin) and their evolution as major theatrical artists through the company's growth. The writing is interesting and the research solid, relying mostly on the author's personal correspondence and interviews with principal characters. Its traditional chronological structure is a predictable aspect of such studies and serves to document the company's history without historiographical fanfare.

The Federal Theatre Project remains a constant source of fascination for doctoral students, if dissertation topics are any indication. It seems increasingly unlikely that anything new can be dredged up, assessed, or codified. But the effort continues. George Kazacoff has managed to find another suitable niche that has somehow gone unnoticed. This time the development of new plays by the FTP is the focus, and indeed it appears that we have still much to learn about this relatively brief but increasingly researched period. Kazacoff divides *Dangerous Theatre: The Federal Theatre Project as a Forum for New Plays* (Peter Lang) into New York City and regional units. The work's comprehensiveness must be admired; most of the major FTP programs are discussed, and the regional attention is unusual among similar studies. But the book fails to draw major conclusions persuasively. In some ways it reads like a compendium of plays, a valuable resource but offering little insight and theory. In contrast, Barry B. Witham writes about the particular effect of an individual FTP production in "The Living Newspaper's *Power* in Seattle" (*THStud* 9: 23–35). Witham shows how the play, originally produced in New

York, took on new significance in Seattle, where a crucial battle was developing between competing power companies for electric rights in the city.

Richard Traubner's 1983 *Operetta: A Theatrical History* (Oxford) has been reissued in paperback and is worth mentioning not only for its two chapters on American musicals, but because it is an excellent history of the form. Perhaps in its new format it will find its way into more class syllabuses. Mary C. Henderson has produced a pleasant collection cheerfully entitled *Broadway Ballyhoo: The American Theater seen in Posters, Photographs, Magazines, Caricatures, and Programs* (Abrams). Organized precisely as the title states, the book is filled with illustrations in each venue. Henderson's comments are little more than annotation and adequately explain the contents. It is not history in a formal sense and may be better suited to the coffee table than the scholar's bookshelf, but it is a nice reference emphasizing New York theater over the past century.

Examining the European perspective of "Edwin Booth's Tour of Germany and Austria in 1883: A Perspective on the Critical Responses" (*THStud* 9:41–53), Lorraine Commeret presents a summary of reviews that have been largely overlooked. Her study of the German critics reveals that Booth's tour was not the overwhelming success that some have contended. It is refreshing to view American theater history from a European perspective.

Walter Meserve reassesses the state of American drama during the third quarter of the 19th century in "Our English-American Playwrights of the Mid-Nineteenth Century" (*JADT* 1, i:5–18). He observes that American playwriting begins to supplant the traditional dominance of English drama, and he highlights several key writers in this movement. The development and changes in the portrayal of American Indians on stage is brilliantly presented by Don B. Wilmeth in "Noble or Ruthless Savage?: The America [*sic*] Indian on Stage and in the Drama" (*JADT* 1, i:39–78). The existence of a hitherto unknown play from the colonial period is discussed and analyzed by me in " 'Copy Play Wrote at Boston 1732' and the Extension of Theatrical Satire in Colonial America" (*JADT* 1, ii:73–87).

iv. Criticism and Theory

Judging by the meager output, 1989 was not the best year for critical studies. I can offer no explanation other than to speculate that scholars may have momentarily exhausted themselves by unintentionally creating the "post-Foucault era."

Two books deserve attention for their nontraditional interdisciplinary approach. *By Means of Performance: Intercultural Studies of Theatre and Ritual* (Cambridge), ed. Richard Schechner and Willa Appel, is a collection of essays culled from three conferences on ritual and the theater held in 1981 and 1982. Not all the essays deal with American theater, but the work represents an excellent summary of the state of performance theory in this country. The essayists include Victor Turner, Richard Schechner, Colin Turnbull, Edith Turner, Barbara Kirshenblatt-Gimblett, James L. Peacock, Miles Richardson, Barbara Myerhoff, and Herbert Blau. Natalie Crohn Schmitt reevaluates the "anti-reality" of postmodern theater in *Actors and Onlookers: Theater and Twentieth-Century Scientific Views of Nature* (Northwestern). Schmitt begins her analysis by examining the fundamental distinction between "new theatre" and "earlier theatre," contrasting Aristotelian aesthetics with the aesthetics of John Cage. She then uses this new aesthetic to compare the Wooster Group's *Rumstick Road* and O'Neill's *Long Day's Journey into Night*. After finding similar theoretical reflections in *A Chorus Line*, Schmitt turns to acting techniques, contrasting Stanislavsky with several contemporary theorists.

Philip Auslander looks at "the most neglected portion of a generally underexplored literary corpus," *The New York School Poets as Playwrights: O'Hara, Ashbery, Koch, Schuyler and the Visual Arts* (Peter Lang). The book is straightforward in approach and organization. After providing a useful historical context, Auslander examines each poet individually and includes an appendix that provides brief chronologies. It is an important study of an often overlooked aspect of the American avant-garde. But like many Peter Lang publications, the book lacks an index and generally has a cheap feel. Another interesting work is Patricia R. Schroeder's *The Presence of the Past in Modern American Drama* (Fairleigh Dickinson). Taking a traditional focus, Schroeder finds commonality in the use and perspective of the past as an element of the present in the plays of O'Neill, Wilder, Miller, and Williams. Another book worth noting is Michael D. Bristol's *Shakespeare's America, America's Shakespeare* (Routledge), which argues "that the interpretation of Shakespeare and the interpretation of American political culture are mutually determining practices." The study is a fine example of cultural theory and reveals both the institutionalization of Shakespeare and the adaptation of Shakespeare to American ideology.

Tiny Alice, *The Cocktail Party*, and the Wooster Group's 1978 production of *Nayatt School* are the subjects of Ruby Cohn's "Explosive Cocktails: Albee, Eliot, Wooster" (*JADT* 1, ii:5–16). This comparative work draws together the literary and conceptual foundations of each play. Noting that "American theatre of the 1930s rarely touched on frontier western themes," Richard Wattenberg looks at how "Sherwood and Saroyan attempt to come to terms with the frontierless modern West" in his " 'Old West'/'New West': The New Frontier in Sherwood's *The Petrified Forest* (1934) and Saroyan's *The Time of Your Life* (1939)" (*JADT* 1, ii:17–33). A typical example of dramatic criticism on a traditional theme, it should please the more orthodox.

v. Feminist Studies

One area of theater scholarship that has grown rapidly in recent years is feminist theory and history. My decision to set it apart is not meant to distance it from the "traditional" venues, but to highlight its current status and direction. One of the most intriguing aspects of the field is how quickly it has changed and how diverse its critical voice has become. Three major publications in 1989 confirm this assessment: all are edited collections of essays with topics ranging from traditional literary criticism to avant-garde performance theory.

Feminine Focus: The New Women Playwrights (Oxford), ed. Enoch Brater, includes essays on English, American, and French topics, and many of the pieces take a truly intercultural look. The American essays make up the final eight in the collection and begin with Sue-Ellen Case's Euro-American perspective "From Split Subject to Split Britches" (pp. 126–46). Linda Ben-Zvi writes on Susan Glaspell, W. B. Worthen on Maria Irene Fornes, Deborah R. Geis on Ntozake Shange, Judith E. Barlow on Tina Howe, and Leslie Kane concludes with Marsha Norman. Mixed in are Timothy Murray's piece on *Chucky's Hunch* and Helene Keyssar's assessment of the drama of black American women.

A similar view is found in *Making a Spectacle: Feminist Essays on Contemporary Women's Theatre* (Michigan), ed. Lynda Hart. The collection takes a largely Anglo-American perspective, though there are exceptions. Stephanie Arnold examines Japanese-American women playwrights, while Yolanda Broyles Gonzales exposes the sexism inherent in El Teatro Campesino. Again, much of the focus is on specific playwrights and plays, with essays on Norman, Howe, Wendy Kesselman, Joan Schenkar, and Fornes. Margaret Wilkerson, however, evaluates the importance of music in the works of black women playwrights, and Janelle Reinelt covers the breadth of plays and reviews by Michelene Wandor.

Taking feminist theory to the center of the mainstream is the apparent concern of *Feminist Rereadings of Modern American Drama* (Fairleigh Dickinson). Editor June Schlueter has put together 13 essays in five sections covering the playwrights under scrutiny—O'Neill, Miller, Williams, Albee, and Shepard. Anne Flèche's " 'A Monster of Perfection': O'Neill's 'Stella' " (pp. 35–36) concludes that "she is indeed, in the seventeenth-century phrase" quoted in the title, one whose "presence is uncongenial to the very form that produces and requires her." Within the Oedipal terms Flèche uses, Mary becomes whore, betrayer, and prophet. Suzanne Burr challenges the notion of O'Neill's women as misogynic expressions and argues that he expressed a greater sympathy than is generally recognized ("O'Neill's Ghostly Women," pp. 37–47). Her essay is intriguing but not entirely convincing. O'Neill's controversial *All God's Chillun Got Wings* receives a revisionist analysis by Bette Mandl ("Theatricality and Otherness in *All God's Chillun Got Wings*," pp. 48–56) who explains why the work unintentionally became an uncomfortable portrayal of racial issues.

Four essays focus on Arthur Miller's early works, from *Death of a Salesman* to *After the Fall*. Drawing from the theories of Gayle Rubin and Eve Kosofsky Sedgwick, Gayle Austin discusses "The Exchange of Women and Male Homosocial Desire in Arthur Miller's *Death of a Salesman* and Lillian Hellman's *Another Part of the Forest*" (pp. 59–66) to see the different manner in which women are treated as objects of exchange. Her point is well-developed and the distinctions clear. Equally effective is Kay Stanton's "Women and the American Dream of *Death of a Salesman*" (pp. 67–102), which examines in detail the male-oriented nature of the American Dream in the play and its "unacknowledged dependence upon women as well as women's subjugation and exploitation." How Miller uses "the methods and espouses the sexual politics of melodrama" is the subject of Jeffrey D. Mason's essay, "Paper Dolls: Melodrama and Sexual Politics in Arthur Miller's Early Plays" (pp. 103–15). Typical of Mason's work, the article is concise and convincing. Complementing this article is Iska Alter's "Betrayal and Blessedness: Explorations of Feminine Power in *The Crucible, A View from the Bridge,* and *After the Fall*" (pp. 116–45).

Two essays deal in different ways with popular misconceptions about Tennessee Williams's perception and use of female characters. Anca Vlasopolos's "Authorizing History: Victimization in *A Streetcar Named Desire*" (pp. 149–70) is a reprint from *Theatre Journal* (October 1986) and is most appropriate for the collection. John Timpane questions Williams's sympathetic identification with women through a case analysis of his major female characters " 'Weak and Divided People': Tennessee Williams and the Written Woman," pp. 171–80). Edward Albee is given short shrift. Mickey Pearlman offers a brief feminist rereading of *Zoo Story* and *The American Dream* (pp. 183–91), while Naomi Conn Liebler gives a more thorough analysis of *Tiny Alice* (pp. 192–210). *Fool for Love* is the overwhelming favorite of the two authors in the last section, on Sam Shepard. In "Sam Shepard's Spectacle of Impossible Heterosexuality: *Fool for Love*" (pp. 213–26), Lynda Hart proposes that Shepard offers heterosexual love in the play as "only his male characters' encounters with their imaginary others." She maintains that his inability "to create female subjectivity in his plays" is the result of his "maintenance of the patriarchy [as] the collective vision of our culture's majority." Rosemarie Bank's "Self as Other: Sam Shepard's *Fool for Love* and *A Lie of the Mind*" (pp. 227–40) explores "the doubling and transformation of gender . . . and the space of representation thereby created."

Judith L. Stephens has found a new source for feminist reflection in the socially progressive plays at the turn of the century. "Gender Ideology and Dramatic Convention in Progressive Era Plays, 1890–1920" (*TJ* 41, i:45–55) deconstructs five representative plays following Michele Barrett's "compensation" and "recuperation" processes to examine the dichotomous expression of conventional female moral superiority and iconoclastic social change. J. Ellen Gainor writes about one of the more controversial pieces produced by the Provincetown Players in "A Stage of Her Own: Susan Glaspell's *The Verge* and Women's Dramaturgy" (*JADT* 1, i:79–99). The play was produced during the 1921–22 season in New York, the same season that saw the premiere of *The Hairy Ape* and the departure of Glaspell and her husband, George Cram Cook, from the Provincetown Players. Gainor provides the play's historical background and properly connects it to

Charlotte Perkins Gilman's classic and chilling story of female hysteria, "The Yellow Wallpaper." This is a solid piece of literary feminist history.

vi. African-American Theater

Perhaps the finest critical study of the year is Femi Euba's *Archetypes, Imprecators, and Victims of Fate: Origins and Developments of Satire in Black Drama* (Greenwood). Expanding upon Wole Soyinka's *Myth, Literature and the African World,* in which tragedy is identified with Ogun, the Yoruba god of metallurgy, Euba conceptualizes the essence of black theater through the Yoruba culture and specifically in the god of fate, Esu-Elegbara, as an instrument of satire in African culture. Although seen mainly from an American perspective, the study is cross-cultural and international in scope and methodology.

Two books focus on the history of black musical theater. Allen Woll's *Black Musical Theatre: From Coontown to* Dreamgirls (LSU) is a broad survey, covering the development of black entertainment forms over the last century. Chapters cover the earliest musicals in the 1890s, Bob Cole and the Johnson Brothers, Bert Williams and George Walker, the attempted moves to Broadway, the black revues of the '20s and '30s, and Langston Hughes. Along the way, Woll fills in crucial information on economic influences and employment practices, making the study among the best of its kind and certainly required reading for any course in American theater history. Taking a more focused view, Thomas L. Riis's *Just Before Jazz: Black Musical Theatre in New York, 1890 to 1915* (Smithsonian) is a study of music history with numerous musical notations and a methodological approach suited for exploring the origins of jazz. There is much overlap in these two books, of course, but Riis is more concerned with the construction of musical performance and its influence on subsequent music than the sociological issues surrounding the rise of black theater. Still, his is a good study, well-researched and documented.

The University Press of Mississippi has issued two new volumes in its Literary Conversation Series that should be of interest: Fred L. Standley and Louis H. Pratt's *Conversations with James Baldwin* and Jeffery Elliot's *Conversations with Maya Angelou.* Both texts are organized in the usual manner of the parent series, beginning with brief introductions and chronologies, followed by an assortment of the most important published interviews with each artist. Standley and Pratt start with Studs Terkel's famous radio interview in 1961 and conclude with Quincy Troup's final interview less than a month before Baldwin's death. Similarly, Elliot begins with Susan Berman's 1971 article on Angelou in the *Oregonian*, traces various live and written encounters, including one with Bill Moyers, and finishes with Rosa Guy's 1988 interview excerpted from *Writing Lives: Conversations Between Women Writers*, ed. Mary Chamberlain. Neither book provides any surprises, but both are vital resources, containing rare transcriptions of television and radio interviews in addition to previously published work.

vii. Hispanic Drama and Theater

Arte Público Press, one of the more prolific publishers of Hispanic material, has finally reprinted the 1983 issue of *Revista Chicano-Riquena* containing material from "Two Centuries of Hispanic Theatre in the Southwest," an exhibit that toured the country in the spring and summer of 1982. Edited by Nicolás Kanellos, *Mexican Theatre: Then and Now* is a digest of recent scholarship and research material. Articles include a survey of Hispanic theater history by Kanellos, a biography of the vaudeville star La Chata Noloesca by Tomás Ybarra-Frausto, a history of El Teatro Carmen by Armando Miguélez, an assessment of Latin American influences on Teatro Chicano by Jorge Huerta, and an evaluation of the use and popularity of *teatropoesía*, a lyric theater popular among Hispanic women, by Yvonne Yarbro-Bejarano. There are also four short vaudeville sketches in Spanish and interviews with Luis Valdez and Roderigo Duarte. As a compendium of an exhibition, it is far too brief and incomplete to be satisfying, but it is an important publication nonetheless, helping to define a critical and historical voice for Hispanic theater and drama.

Elizabeth C. Ramírez writes on "Spanish-Language Combination Companies on the American Stage: Organization & Practice in Texas, 1915–1935" (*THStud* 9:77–91). She takes a traditional approach, focusing on chronology, repertory, costs, and major performances and performers. It is clearly a rich and largely unexplored subject, which Ramírez does her best to cover as thoroughly as possible in a short article. One hopes she will follow with more detailed studies. Kanellos and Jorge A. Huerta have edited a collection of recent Chicano and Puerto Rican plays, *Nuevos Pasos* (Arte Público). Among the contents are plays by Ron Arias, Estela Portillo-Trambley, Rúben Sierra, Jaime Carrero, and Miguel Pinero.

viii. Notes on American Musical Theater

The proliferation of studies on the great American musical theater continues unabated. This year's entries to the ever-expanding canon begin with an updated second edition of Craig Zadan's illustrated survey of Stephen Sondheim's musicals, *Sondheim & Co.* (Harper). Lacking documentation, analysis, and objectivity, this piece has little to commend it as scholarship. It falls into the genre of glitzy gossip books, a published paean, filled with anecdote and production photos.

In contrast, the two studies of Harold Prince are more promising. Carol Ilson's *Harold Prince: From* Pajama Game *to* Phantom of the Opera (UMI Research Press) is another doctoral-dissertation-turned-published-book. One must be cautious of a study that begins "Harold Smith Prince was born in New York City on 30 January 1928. . . ." Although the book improves, it is still a chronological history, moving from production to production without much critical insight or analytical revelation. Foster Hirsch's *Harold Prince and the American Musical Theatre* (Cambridge) attempts to place Prince within a broader frame. But ultimately this is a shorter version of Ilson's book, tracing Prince from his early days to his work on *Phantom of the Opera.*

ix. Remnants of O'Neill

Published celebrations of the O'Neill centennial are still coming and may continue for several years. While no monographs were published, several collections of essays and journals warrant review. Marc Maufort is editor of "Eugene O'Neill and the Emergence of American Drama," volume 75 of *Costerus* (New Series). Primarily consisting of papers from the May 1988 international O'Neill conference held in Han-sur-Lesse, Belgium, the book is an illustrious selection of American and European critical approaches. It would be a disservice to reduce this volume to a handful of glib observations, but a few of the more interesting studies ought to be mentioned. O'Neill's early years are expertly covered by Frederick C. Wilkins's "'Arriving with a Bang:' O'Neill's Literary Debut" (pp. 5–13) and Paul Voelker's "Success and Frustration at Harvard: Eugene O'Neill's Relationship with

George Pierce Baker (1914–1915)" (pp. 15–29). John Henry Raleigh renders a penetrating comparison in "Strindberg and O'Neill as Historical Dramatists" (pp. 59–75), as does Marc Maufort in his splendid analysis "*Typee* Revisited: O'Neill's *Mourning Becomes Electra* and Melville" (pp. 85–95). Other commendable pieces include Marie-Claire Pasquier's "You Are One of Us, You Are a Russian" (pp. 77–83), Jean Chothia's "Theatre Language: Word and Image in *The Hairy Ape*" (pp. 31–45), and Ulrich Halfmann's "'With Clenched Fist...:' Observations on a Recurrent Motif in the Drama of Eugene O'Neill" (pp. 107–21).

Volume 76 in the same series, "New Essays on American Drama," ed. Gilbert Debusscher and Henry I. Schvey, also published Marc Maufort's "American Flowers of Evil: *Long Day's Journey into Night* and Baudelaire" (pp. 13–28) and "The Legacy of Eugene O'Neill" (pp. 29–40) by Herbert Grabes. O'Neill fanatics may want to discover Michael Hinden's "Missing Lines in *Long Day's Journey into Night*" (*MD* 32:177–82). Additionally, the *Eugene O'Neill Review* continues to produce its usual assortment of essays. Between the two issues there are several valuable pieces, including Frank R. Cunningham's "'Authentic Tidings of Invisible Things': Beyond James Robinson's *Eugene O'Neill and Oriental Thought*" (13, i:29–39), James A. Robinson's "O'Neill's Indian *Elms*" (13, i:40–46), Egil Tornqvist's "O'Neill's Firstborn" (13, ii:5–11), and Kelli A. Larson's "O'Neill's Tragic Quest for Belonging: Psychological Determinism in the *S.S. Glencairn* Quartet" (13, ii:12–22).

x. Recent Dramatists (Hellman, Inge, Odets, Saroyan, Williams, etc.)

With a title like *The Cold War Romance of Lillian Hellman and John Melby* (No. Car.), Robert P. Newman's history of this curious couple was not high on my priority list. I was pleasantly surprised. In a book reading as much like a novel as a history, Newman has painstakingly researched this odd affair between Hellman and Melby, a senior State Department official. It is a compelling piece of work with much new information about Hellman's political views and personal life during the McCarthy era, a combination of theater history and political intrigue. Equally good, though for very different reasons, is *Critical Essays on Lillian Hellman* (Hall), ed. Mark W. Estrin. This collection brings together an illustrious group of Hellman scholars and is divided into three sections dealing with the plays, her memoirs, and something titled "The Hellman Persona." With articles by Jacob H. Adler, Marvin Felheim, Henry W. Knepler, Mary Lynn Broe, Pamela S. Bromberg, Sidney Hook, Martha Gelhorn, Timothy Dow Adams, Pauline Kael, and Robert Brustein (to name a few), it is an impressive collection. Certainly some of the pieces in the last section are of disputable distinction, but they are more than compensated for by the rest.

R. Baird Shuman has revised his 1965 overview of *William Inge* (TUSAS 95). The major distinction of this edition is the assessments of plays produced after 1965. It is a good scholarly treatment of Inge and his works, especially apt for undergraduate studies. A more complex work is Ralph F. Voss's *A Life of William Inge: The Strains of Triumph* (Kansas). Focusing less on play analysis and more on the complexities of Inge's life, Voss has written a grand traditional biography. Chronologically arranged and thoroughly documented, it should appeal to both the theater scholar and the popular reader.

Avery Hopwood was once America's most popular playwright. When O'Neill was still honing his early skills, Hopwood was at the top of the commercial theater. All but forgotten by most theater students, he has been revived by Jack F. Sharrar in the published version of his doctoral dissertation, *Avery Hopwood: His Life and Plays* (McFarland). The book covers Hopwood's life from beginning to end, assigning two final chapters to a recently discovered unpublished novel and the Hopwood awards at the University of Michigan. Along the way, Hopwood's plays are assessed and the major events in his life are presented in the usual fashion. Unfortunately, my copy suffered from a number of blurred pages and serious printing errors, a problem not uncommon among the academic vanity presses. Gabriel Miller's study of *Clifford Odets* (Continuum) has a similar feel. In eight chapters and an afterword, Odets is dissected chronologically according to his major works, as if his life and plays naturally fell into eight neat piles complete with chapter titles. Admittedly, it surpasses Gerald Weales's *Odets: The Playwright* as a literary history and does a good job evaluating the plays. William Saroyan fans will be pleased with Elisabeth C. Foard's *William Saroyan: A Reference Guide* (Hall). It is well-annotated and appears to be thorough, with a good introduction and index.

Work on Tennessee Williams seems to have slowed in comparison to previous years. The one published text is a 42-page paperback reference piece, part of the "Authoritative Studies in World Literature" Series (York) entitled *Tennessee Williams: Life, Work, and Criticism*, ed. Felicia Londré. The five sections contain a biographical essay, a chronology of works, a summary of themes, a summary of achievements, and an annotated bibliography. A fascinating comparison of performance interpretations is found in Susan Spector's "Alternative Visions of Blanche DuBois: Uta Hagen and Jessica Tandy in *A Streetcar Named Desire*" (*MD* 32:545–60). And Gerald Weales offers a brief critical assessment of Williams's *Period of Adjustment* in "High Comedy Over a Cavern," (*JADT* 1, i:25–38).

xi. Current Dramatists (Albee, Gray, Miller, and Shepard)

Work on Sam Shepard proliferates unabated with the only significant distinction being an emphasis on primary data and reference materials—the sign of genuine respectability. *Joseph Chaikin and Sam Shepard: Letters and Texts, 1972–1984* (NAL), ed. Barry Daniels, is precisely what the title states, a collection of correspondence between these two men organized into six chronological chapters. Daniels has given each section a focus by prefacing the material with introductions explaining the significance and relationship of the letters to plays and productions. It is a rich collection, well-edited and appropriately introduced, and offers new insights. *File on Shepard* (Methuen), compiled by John Dugdale, is the most recent addition to the neatly succinct Writer-Files series. Like the rest of the series, this compact paperback contains a chronology of the playwright's life, checklist of plays and other published work, excerpted reviews, and personal comments taken from diaries, letters, and interviews. The bibliography is useful, though somewhat brief for serious scholarship, while the short play synopses should appeal to the undergraduate crowd. Kimball King has assembled a dozen articles by an assortment of scholars into *Sam Shepard: A Casebook* (Garland). Along with an introduction and chronology, King has added a brief bibliography. Among the contents are articles by Patrick J. Fennell, Albert E. Wilhelm, Elizabeth Proctor, Doris Auerbach, Christopher Brookhouse, Jane Ann Crum, Bruce J. Mann, Ron Mottram, Leonard Wilcox, Phyllis R. Randall, Ann Wilson, and Tommy Thompson. They represent a wide range of critical approaches and add significantly to the body of critical work on Shepard.

Claiming that in Shepard's plays "Artaud's notion of theatrical violence as it pertains to audience response or 'theoria' is realized to a greater extent than in any other major American playwright," Peter L. Podol writes about the "Dimensions of Violence in the Theatre of Sam Shepard: *True West* and *Fool for Love*" (*EiT* 7:149–58). Luther S. Luedtke's "From Fission to Fusion: Sam Shepard's Nuclear Families" (*Costerus* 76:143–66) traces the playwright's "'chronicle' of self" in nine family dramas from *The Rock Garden* (1964) through *A Lie of the Mind* (1985). In trying to explain the title of the piece, Luedtke observes that "the challenge one faces in writing about Shepard's theater is to grasp the organic wholeness in this crackling and eruptive career where life, culture, and imagination meet."

Surprisingly little was produced this year on the other major dramatists. Liliane Kerjan gives a short account of Albee's playwriting in "Pure and Simple: The Recent Plays of Edward Albee" (*Costerus* 76:99–109). Kerjan looks at *Counting the Ways*, *Listening*, and *The Lady from Dubuque* to explain why Albee has apparently disappeared from the scene. C. Bordewijk's "Simultaneity or Separation: Edward Albee's *Who's Afraid of Virginia Woolf?*, on Stage and Screen" (*Costerus* 76:111–26) provides a brief comparison of a Dutch theatrical performance and Mike Nichols's film to find out how they each "shape the structure of tension and meaning underlying Albee's text." Neither article is especially insightful, and both suffer from dated sources.

William W. Demastes reevaluates Spalding Gray's recent work in a well-presented essay, "Spalding Gray's *Swimming to Cambodia* and the Evolution of an Ironic Presence" (*TJ* 41:75–94). Although Demastes looks at the playwright's background with Schechner and the Wooster Group, his real purpose is to find the experimental roots and political agenda in Gray's most commercially popular play. Henry I. Schvey considers Miller's maturing themes and changing perspectives in "Arthur Miller: Songs of Innocence and Experience" (*Costerus* 76:75–97). After examining Miller's early career, Schvey concentrates on the last 20 years and concludes that "while [Miller] has bravely sought new intellectual and emotional challenges with each new work, these challenges have on the whole not met with outstanding success." It is a kind perception.

Tufts University

18. Themes, Topics, Criticism

Michael J. Hoffman

Enormous productivity continued in 1989 in all the areas of literary scholarship relevant to this chapter. We continue to drown in seas of paper. While a number of good overviews of American literature were published, the most distinguished work was done in the areas of modernism and gender studies. I have tried to represent that excellence in my selections. The chapter is slightly shorter than some of its predecessors, a reflection of time and space limitations. Selectivity has therefore been an especially high priority for me, and the result is most noticeable in the section on literary theory.

i. American Literature

Renewed interest in R. P. Blackmur's work continues with *Outsider at the Heart of Things: Essays by R. P. Blackmur* (Illinois), ed. and introd. James T. Jones, containing uncollected essays written between 1928 and 1964. In an excellent introduction the editor, who previously wrote a good book on Blackmur, explains his principles of selection and presents a good overview of Blackmur's theories of criticism and American literature. He states that a few long pieces are still uncollected, including five on Henry Adams and four "catalogue" essays in each of which Blackmur reviews nine to 12 volumes of new poetry. There are also more than 100 short reviews and essays as well as some unpublished manuscript plays and fiction that Jones believes need not be collected. Most items in this volume are about American topics, although a few are concerned with more general critical issues. Of special interest is an essay on T. S. Eliot that *Hound and Horn* published in two parts in 1928.

Since Yiddish is a major linguistic subculture in American literature, scholars will find useful and charming a new reference work compiled by Gene Bluestein, *Anglish/Yinglish: Yiddish in American Life and Literature* (Georgia), a dictionary of Yiddish words and phrases that have been incorporated into American literature and culture. I find the entries useful, straightforward, and often funny. If you want to know what a *kluhts* really is or the meaning of *SHMOOes* (vulgarly spelled schmooz), a word that has become popular among academics, you can find the entry in *Anglish/Yinglish*. Where possible, Bluestein gives a contemporary literary source for the word.

A. Carl Bredahl, Jr.'s *New Ground* is as much a discussion of canonicity as it is of Western narrative. Starting with some comments Henry James made in his notebooks during his return trip to the United States (1904), Bredahl contrasts Eastern and Southern notions of space with those of the West. In the former he finds the trope of enclosure to be strong, while Western literature constantly asks the individual to confront vastness, or a space that is limitless and not amenable to enclosure. Bredahl believes that it is Eastern writers who have the power to establish the canon. Aside from writers of conventional "Western" novels and movies, Bredahl also discusses Hemingway and Sherwood Anderson. I was disappointed, however, that he did not have more to say about Willa Cather.

I shall make only brief mention of *Fiction and Historical Consciousness* by Emily Miller Budick, because almost all of Budick's readings of well-known American novels are covered in other *ALS* chapters. I am puzzled, however, that a book so thoroughly documented and apparently scholarly does not even mention some of the best-known treatments of the American romance, such as those by D. H. Lawrence, Richard Chase, Edwin Eigner, and Nicolaus Mills. Why didn't one of the press's outside readers insist on it?

Peter Conn's *Literature in America: An Illustrated History* (Cambridge) is a handsomely produced book that contains many interesting photographs and reproductions of paintings, including some in color. Intended for a general reading public, it will be used by high school students or placed on coffee tables. The book is written as a fairly simple historical narrative, but the unwary reader should take care to check its factual accuracy. On looking at the material on Gertrude Stein I discovered the following errors: Stein "completed two years of medical school at Johns Hopkins"—she actually completed four years, but left without taking a degree; *Three Lives* was published in 1905—the actual date was 1909. Perhaps these are anomalies.

James M. Cox's *Recovering Literature's Lost Ground* collects essays written over a quarter-century. It is a solid, well-written book that is reflective on the matter of autobiography, but it does not attempt to develop a theory of the genre. Cox's subjects include many classic American autobiographers, including Richard Henry Dana, Jr., Ulysses S. Grant, Henry James, and Henry Adams. Cox has fresh things to say about all of these writers, and he writes in a highly personal way that befits his subject. My favorite essay deals with Shelby Foote, creator of an epic history of the Civil War that Cox claims should rank with Thucydides and Gibbon. I'm not sure how Cox can justify Foote's work as an autobiography, but I do share his somewhat extravagant admiration of its author.

Another angle on the study of autobiography appears in Joseph Fichtelberg's *The Complex Image*. Starting from Nietzsche's *Ecce Homo*, Fichtelberg posits the autobiographer's continuous revision of self as a model for the autobiographical process. It is in the meeting of subject and language that autobiography constructs the self. The matter of revision is used primarily as a metaphor in some of the earlier chapters, such as those on Thomas Shepard and John Woolman, but with other authors the process of revision as we know it—as in the various versions of Benjamin Franklin's *Autobiography* or in Gertrude Stein's changes in the manuscript of *The Autobiography of Alice B. Toklas*—becomes the focus of analysis.

In *The Thirsty Muse*, Tom Dardis has written primarily for a popular audience a book that is solid and scholarly. It discusses with great frankness the phenomenon of alcoholism among major American writers of this century, pointing out that five of the eight American Nobel Prize winners were alcoholics. Dardis focuses on Fitzgerald and three Nobel winners—Faulkner, Hemingway, and O'Neill—skipping over Sinclair Lewis and Steinbeck. This is a narrative about how "manly" drinking became a disease, destroying talents rather than enhancing them as the authors themselves liked to claim was the case. Most of us have some familiarity with the lives of these authors, but Dardis discusses their careers through the lens of alcoholism, producing a relentless inventory of hospitalization, accident, and loss of control. Dardis knows a lot about the subject, and he is rarely tempted to romanticize his authors. His presentation of alcoholism as a disease corresponds to our current understanding of addiction.

Reading in America is a collection of 12 essays that study the history of the book in the United States and explore the connections that social historians make among books, social institutions, culture, and literature. The essays cover a wide range of topics, from bibliographical studies, to examinations of how books reflect ideologies, to treatments of books as popular icons and of how the other mass media are beginning to replace the book. It is always interesting to know who is reading what, who is buying books, who controls the publishing houses, and what happened to a particular book over a long period of time. Because this is a developing scholarly field, the range of topics in this collection will provide scholars with an agenda for the next few years.

In *Regression and Apocalypse: Studies in North American Literary Expressionism* (Toronto), Sherrill E. Grace places within an international artistic movement writings in fiction and theater by U.S. and Canadian authors. Grace focuses primarily on German Expressionist painting, and the book reproduces many examples in black and white and a few in color. Aside from general chapters on Expressionism and German Expressionism, there are interesting discussions of theater in New York and Toronto, "Eugene O'Neill: The American Georg Kaiser," Djuna Barnes's *Nightwood*, and Ralph Ellison's *Invisible Man*. This is a good piece of literary history.

The Origins of Literary Studies in America: A Documentary Anthology (Routledge), ed. Gerald Graff and Michael Warner, is a fascinating collection of documents that in themselves outline the major issues in the early study of English in the United States. Almost all of the essays were written during the late 19th and early 20th centuries, with many taken from early issues of *PMLA*, and many themes that are struck in them are still timely. They include the claim that English studies occupy a marginal place in a curriculum dominated by science, that we need to establish a methodological rigor like that which exists in linguistics, and that we must become more professional. Authors include Richard G. Moulton, Woodrow Wilson, Bliss Perry, Irving Babbitt, and Frank Norris. I found it hard to interrupt my reading. Being required to study ourselves as a profession might reduce a certain amount of silliness in department meetings.

I found another reference work to be surprisingly captivating: Karen Hinckley and Barbara Hinckley's *American Best Sellers: A Reader's Guide to Popular Fiction* (Indiana). The subject of the book is best-selling fiction from about 1964 to 1989. The opening section lists all authors of best-selling fictional works during that period, gives brief biographical sketches, and presents one-paragraph descriptions of the best-selling books. Further chapters analyze the types of people who write best-sellers, including their educational backgrounds and ages, the categories that have become popular, and types of characters as well as themes. A concluding chapter discusses current trends in popular fiction. The authors clearly delight in their subject. They obviously enjoy reading these books, and they write about them with wit and seriousness, and without any patronizing tone.

Brief mention goes to another book that is concerned with popular fiction, this one from a series, Reading Popular Fiction, *Gender, Genre and Narrative Pleasure* (Unwin Hyman), ed. Derek Longhurst, a collection of essays written mostly by British scholars but heavily concerned with American subjects. There are interesting essays on the thriller, detective fiction, science fiction, horror fiction (Stephen King), and "women's" fiction, as well as a really perceptive essay by Jane Tompkins on the Western. All the essays deal in some way with matters of gender and/or genre, and the modes of criticism range from the deconstructive to the sociological.

Steven Mailloux's *Rhetorical Power* (Cornell) interprets American texts, primarily *Huckleberry Finn*, through issues that are basic to any theory of interpretation. The paradox is that Mailloux labels himself, with some irony, as part of the "anti-theory" movement, following the now well-known essay, "Against Theory," by Steven Knapp and Walter Benn Michaels. Mailloux uses the realist/idealist debate in interpretation as a prime example of how theory is unable to provide a foundationalist account of interpretation, but he also knows that coming to such an understanding requires us to theorize. "Rhetorical hermeneutics, then, gives up the goals of Theory and continues to theorize about interpretation only therapeutically, exposing the problems with foundationalism and explaining the attractions of realist and idealist positions. But a rhetorical hermeneutics has more to do: it should also provide histories of how particular theoretical and critical discourses have evolved. . . . Rhetorical hermeneutics always leads to rhetorical histories. . . . Such attempts place theory, criticism, and literature itself within a cultural conversation, the dramatic, unending conversation of history which is the 'primal scene of rhetoric'" (pp. 17–18).

Consistent with this methodology, Mailloux writes a series of rhetorical histories. These include the rhetoric of recent theory from the New Criticism to reader-response criticism, the rhetorical context in which *Huckleberry Finn* was written and reader response to that novel since then, and a devastating analysis of the congressional discussions surrounding the Reagan administration's abrogation of the ABM Treaty. That such discussion can take place in three distinctive areas suggests the wide-ranging utility of rhetorical hermeneutics.

Jean Méral's *Paris in American Literature* (No. Car.) is a narrative history of American writers in Paris and the effect that city had on their work. It covers the period since the mid-19th century when American writers began to write about Paris and go there to live. Méral divides the history into two distinct parts separated by World War I. The first is the age of Henry James, the American writer most profoundly affected by Paris; the second is the Lost Generation of expatriates following the Great War. In presenting Paris, Méral quotes from the literary texts themselves, although he sets the context by references to historical event and cultural material. This is traditional literary history, not New Historicism. The major authors covered include James, Wharton, Stein, Hemingway, and Henry Miller. The main problem I have is that Méral does not remain long enough with most of the writers to establish a sufficient thematic richness. As a result, the book is more useful as a reference work than as a book one might wish to read through.

I am not normally a fan of such thematic studies as are represented by David C. Miller's *Dark Eden,* but this work manages to transcend that genre's frequently mechanical shortcomings quite well. In the 19th century a fresh focus of interest began to draw Americans to the imagery of new landscapes. "Whether faraway places—tropical forests, ice-bound vistas, desert islands—or the swamps, marshes, and uninhabited beaches closer to home, landscapes previously neglected were seized upon." Miller shows how the American interest in this new imagery manifested itself in writing and painting, and how both art forms represent a corresponding impulse. Major authors covered include William Gilmore Simms, Harriet Beecher Stowe, Emerson, and Thoreau; the painters include Frederic Church, Thomas Cole, Thomas Moran, and Winslow Homer. There are a great many good reproductions in black and white and some striking ones in color. Miller's analysis is informed by an impressive knowledge of Jungian psychology and the 19th-century interest in myth, as represented, for instance, by Nietzsche.

One of the year's more ambitious works is *The Real Thing: Imitation and Authenticity in American Culture, 1880–1940* (No. Car.), by Miles Orvell. Orvell's basic argument is that with the rise of sophisticated technology a culture of imitation developed in the 19th century in which the machine could increasingly produce accurate reproductions of original objects. Americans became acclimated to the simulacrum and even began to value it. And yet the culture "had not fully absorbed the methods of the machine, and in the end it was a culture of types, of stylizations, of rounded generalities. The culture of authenticity that developed at the end of the century and that gradually established the aesthetic vocabulary that we have called 'modernist' was a reaction against the earlier aesthetic, an effort to get beyond mere imitation, beyond the manufacturing of illusions, to the creation of more 'authentic' works that were themselves real things" (p. xv).

Orvell's concept of authenticity clearly derives from Lionel Trilling's *Sincerity and Authenticity* and is represented by the romantic/modernist attempt to get beyond the second-rate and imitative to the "real thing." Orvell begins with a meditation on Whitman, based particularly on that poet's response to photography, but his emphasis throughout the book is on all forms of reproductive culture, including furniture, design, the various crafts, photography, and the graphic arts. The book is, in effect, a well-written, witty essay on American cultural modernism. It concludes with a delightful chapter on "junk," entitled "The Dump Is Full of Images."

I should briefly mention a collection of Sherman Paul's essays and reviews, *Hewing to Experience: Essays & Reviews on Recent American Poetry & Poetics, Nature & Culture* (Iowa). Most of these were previously published in periodicals, and they reflect the long-standing interests that lie behind Paul's many books and articles. Each section contains a number of essays on William Carlos Williams, Hart Crane, Charles Olson, Robert Creeley, Gary Snyder, and Wendell Berry. They represent an admirable consistency of vision and an intellectual rigor. Paul writes reviews as seriously as he writes a book.

Lewis P. Simpson's *Mind and the American Civil War: A Meditation on Lost Causes* (LSU) was given originally as the Walter Lynwood Fleming Lectures in Southern History at Louisiana State University. A brief book, it posits North and South as binary opposites and yet as reflections of one another. In describing Quentin Compson's going to Harvard, for instance, Simpson suggests that "like most educated southerners, the Compsons—in spite of their resentment of New England and New England's resentment of them—are spiritual New Englanders." He establishes the grounds for this thesis by writing about the friendship that developed between the young Boston scholar George Ticknor and the venerable Thomas Jefferson, pointing out the similarities in their types of regionalism and parochialism.

Simpson goes on to write a somewhat scathing study of Emerson, pointing out the ambivalences he felt toward the South and what he calls Emerson's Negrophobia. While there is nothing in this book that most of us don't know, Simpson's presentation of the information and his interpretations are disquieting and thought-provoking, particularly during a period that has seen a strong renewal of interest in the Civil War.

A Mirror for Americanists: Reflections of the Idea of American Literature (New England) is a collection of essays by William C. Spengemann that attempts to do what Howard Mumford Jones did many years ago in *The Theory of American Literature*. While a number of the essays are quite stimulating, they all attempt to define American literature by posing much the same problem and expressing a similar paradox: "that Anglo-America and England have always constituted a single, complex, English-speaking culture; that Americans have written in many languages other than English; and that, both historically and geographically, the boundaries of the United States embrace only part of Anglo-American culture." When, however, "scholars of American literature aspire to be literary critics, they cannot freely employ two of the principal contexts in which any literary work is normally described and explained: the language in which the work is written and other works written in the same language" (p. 122). This conflict between the historical and linguistic dimensions of literary study replicates discussions that are going on throughout the profession, and they have to do with not only the works we choose to study but with whether we allow the past or our contemporary critical standards to determine those choices. Spengemann would probably admit that his proposed solutions are not as interesting as his trenchant formulations of the problem.

The final work in this section is Cornel West's *The American Evasion of Philosophy: A Genealogy of Pragmatism* (Wisconsin), a timely book given the current interest in pragmatism among American literary theorists and "anti-theorists." West establishes the pragmatic tradition by claiming that Emerson embodies the pre-history of American pragmatism, most particularly in its tendency to "swerve from mainstream European philosophy." West moves from there to Charles Sanders Peirce and William James and then to the book's long central chapter on John Dewey. After that he deals with such apparently disparate figures as Sidney Hook, W. E. B. Dubois, Reinhold Niebuhr, Lionel Trilling, W. V. Quine, and Richard Rorty. This clearly and passionately written book is motivated by a belief that pragmatism is the most important American form of cultural criticism and that it is more likely to change contemporary society than any more conventional form of philosophy.

ii. Modernism and Postmodernism

Each year the number of books I must consider for this section grows, and each year I'm forced into greater selectivity. My apologies for those books not discussed. Although Charles Altieri's *Painterly Abstraction* is discussed in detail elsewhere in this volume, I want to briefly commend that impressive book to students of modernism. Altieri asks an important question about how modernist poets responded to the innovations of abstract painters. This book is not so much an influence study as a thoughtful argument about how innovations in both art forms reflect similar ontological situations and philosophical justifications. Although a bit wordy, it is well-argued and contains comprehensive treatments of such figures as Eliot, Stevens, and Stein. I was particularly impressed with Altieri's discussion of cubism in relation to Williams and Stein.

Debate about postmodernism continues. The first book I'll consider is Steven Connor, *Postmodernist Culture: An Introduction to Theories of the Contemporary* (Blackwell), both a summary of theories about postmodernism and an original synthesis of them in something of a postmodern manner. Much of the argument consists in contrasting modernism and postmodernism, as in the following distinction: "If modernism is a name that we can give to the movement of thought that attempts to expel the improper from the domain of art, postmodernism is the deconstructive intensification of that logic of modernism to the point where the two binary extremes are seen to include and imply each other" (p. 93). The work of art begins to engage more and more in what modernist aesthetics had forbidden, namely commentary upon itself. The work of art is no longer self-sufficient, no longer defined by its boundaries. "Postmodernist art is characterized increasingly by means of the critical accounts that it can give of itself, or the forms of rapprochement that it can make with advanced art theory." Connor considers not only theories of postmodernism, but such topics as the academy, architecture and the visual arts, literature, performance, TV, video and film, popular culture, and cultural politics.

One of the most impressive historical studies I have ever read about the impact of modernism on this century's events is Modris Eksteins, *Rites of Spring: The Great War and the Birth of the Modern Age* (Houghton Mifflin). Throughout, Eksteins contrasts German and British attitudes, using them as central metaphors for opposing perspective on modernism and modernization. Another central metaphor is Stravinsky's *Le Sacre du Printemps*, which illustrates the energies that were accumulating in the years just before the war and were released during the events of the summer of 1914, a year after the ballet's premiere in Paris.

Eksteins calls the so-called aestheticism of the Russian ballet profoundly political because "it displayed a basic sympathy with progressive and even revolutionary tendencies, because aestheticism was founded squarely on the rejection of existing social codes and values." The forces that were aligned against one another were represented by the two great European industrial economies. "For the Germans this was a war to change the world: for the British this was a war to preserve a world. The Germans were propelled by a vision, the British by a legacy." The apocalyptic German vision was the one we have come to associate with modernism. "What was important above all for Germans was the overthrow of the old structures. That was the whole point of the war. Once that had been achieved, the revolutionary dynamic would proceed to erect new structures valid for the new situation." However, as individual artists experienced the horrors of the war as soldiers, "they connected the sights and sounds of war with art. Art became, in fact, the only available correlative of this war; naturally not an art following previous rules, but an art in which the rules of composition were abandoned, in which provocation became the goal, and in which art became an event, an experience." Eksteins sees this cultural shift as having causal importance for the next war's cataclysmic events. "The Great War was the psychological turning point, for Germany and for modernism as a whole. The urge to create and the urge to destroy changed places. The urge to destroy was intensified; the urge to create became increasingly abstract." In isolating what I see as the book's thesis, I have had to leave out Eksteins's remarkable evocations of historical event and cultural frame of mind. This is an excellent, beautifully written cultural history, one that all students of modernism will want to read.

Silvio Gaggi treats the issue of postmodernism from a perspective similar to Connor's in *Modern/Postmodern: A Study in Twentieth-*

Century Arts and Ideas (Penn.). Gaggi sees self-referentiality as a key term in the discussion, and he contrasts modern and postmodern art on the following axes: "the contrast between overt stylization and the frame-tale, between art that openly declares its artifice and art that confuses the realms of art and life, between works of art that implicitly deal with their own style and processes and works of art that explicitly deal with works of art." Gaggi opens the book with a discussion of Velázquez's great painting, *Las meninas*, which Foucault also discusses at the start of *The Order of Things*. What follows is concerned with theater (Genet, Brecht, Pirandello), painting (Escher, Warhol, Lichtenstein), film (Godard, Bergman), and fiction (Fowles, Barth). The concluding chapter, "Postmodernism, Posthumanism, and Politics," contains the book's most interesting generalizations. It should probably have come first.

Sexchanges is the second volume of Sandra M. Gilbert and Susan Gubar's trilogy, *No Man's Land: The Place of the Woman Writer in the Twentieth Century*. This brilliant, controversial book continues the argument first presented in *The War of the Words* that literary modernism is essentially defined by the battle over the accepted social roles created for the two genders. Here the argument is explored from three distinct perspectives: (1) feminism and fantasy in late–19th– and early 20th–century literature, in which both male and female authors (Rider Haggard, Charlotte Perkins Gilman, Kate Chopin) explore in fantasy the possibility of new sex roles amid male fears of women; (2) astringent criticism of sex roles, particularly the created concept of femininity, by such writers as Edith Wharton and Willa Cather; (3) works written primarily by lesbians, such as Gertrude Stein and Renée Vivien, in which an encoded language masks deep sexual anxieties and hostilities. The book's final section explores the phenomenon of cross-dressing as manifesting a belief that sexual roles can be transcended by asserting that either sex can wear whatever clothing it wants. The authors focus on women who "transgressively appropriated male costumes or oscillated between parodically female and sardonically male outfits, as if to declare that, as Woolf said, we can be anyone." A great many books have begun to appear that focus on gender and modernism, but none that I have yet seen seems so comprehensive, witty, and profound.

David Harvey's *The Condition of Postmodernity* (Blackwell) approaches postmodernism from the perspective of the history of ideas. It focuses on a variety of disciplines, including architecture, literature, politics, cultural movements, city planning, economics, and popular culture. Harvey's analysis is informed by a rich knowledge of history and philosophical thought since the Enlightenment. He is primarily concerned with the connection "between the rise of postmodernist cultural forms, the emergence of more flexible modes of capital accumulation, and a new round of 'time-space compression' in the organization of capitalism." Harvey wonders, however, whether "these changes, when set against the basic rules of capitalistic accumulation, appear more as shifts in surface appearance rather than as signs of the emergence of some entirely new postcapitalist or even postindustrial society." The argument includes some astute observations about modernism's manifestation in a number of cultural forms. This is a well-written, well-argued book with an amazing range of reference.

A more poetic and playful approach to these issues appears in a book by a political scientist, Henry S. Kariel: *The Desperate Politics of Postmodernism* (Massachusetts). Kariel sees postmodernist art as a reaction to forces in our lives that are out of control, to "the extremities of experience." The classic modernist authors "could still assume the existence of some wholesome reality beyond the process of modernization, some stable transhistorical ground on which to take one's stand." For postmodernists, on the other hand, "appeals to a fixed order of natural rights or transcultural values ring hollow." The book is informed by wide reading in most areas of 20th-century ideas and culture. Its tone is harder to describe: it is, in turn, interactive, playful, transactional, sardonic, desperate; we must always keep moving, avoiding fixed positions. This is a lively, unsettling work.

A more positive assessment of postmodern culture occurs in Jerome Klinkowitz's *Rosenberg/Barthes/Hassan* (Georgia), which uses these three thinkers to define the nature of contemporary culture. For Klinkowitz, the essence of postmodernism lies in movement: "Arising out of movement, the work is received as movement, and for once the essence of art can be located in an identity of production and reception." Because of this emphasis on action, postmodern writers and artists can avoid the kind of nihilism to which some have objected in the major modernists. "Instead, the motive is affirmative: by declining to represent a sign, the postmodern maker gives us the ultimate sign, which is that of his or her presence at work in the activity of creation. What is created is the artist's self, and the emphasis on action above order means the self can be remade at will." This emphasis on the active creation of self suggests the ways in which the postmodern has gone beyond its predecessor. "Opposed to modernism's exhaustion is the postmodern sense that since life is action and reality is system, there need be no end to creative play." Klinkowitz's summaries of each of his subjects are elegant and thoughtful, written in a non-postmodern style but with postmodern energy and movement.

Brief mention goes to a rather extraordinary book that will not appeal to everyone: Greil Marcus's *Lipstick Traces: A Secret History of the 20th Century* (Harvard). This work can best be described as a history of the "dada" impulse in 20th-century art, literature, and music. It is initially concerned with the punk rock group, the Sex Pistols. It moves from there into a historical meditation on various apparently nihilistic impulses and actions, which suggest a greater continuity in 20th-century artistic culture than critics such as Klinkowitz imply. The book is filled with reproductions of photographs, paintings, posters, and manifestos, all of which suggest a spirit of both rebellion and *blague*. The book is a lot of fun to read, but it leaves one with a distinctly uneasy feeling—precisely, I'm sure, what the author intended.

Postmodern Genres (Okla.)—the final book in this section—is a collection of essays edited by Marjorie Perloff that attempts to define artistic forms in a cultural setting that defies traditional categories. Perloff speaks to her title's paradox in the introduction, quoting from many writers, including Maurice Blanchot, Roland Barthes, and Jacques Derrida, on the ineffability of genre. This is precisely the kind of paradox on which postmodernism thrives. The essays are almost all on such topics as music, opera, photography, and literature. I can especially recommend Michael Davidson, "Palmtexts: Postmodern Poetry and the Material Text"; Herbert Lindenberger, "From Opera to Postmodernity: On Genre, Style, Institutions"; Renée Riese Hubert, "Gertrude Stein, Cubism, and the Postmodern Book"; and Perloff, "Music for Words Perhaps: Reading/Hearing/Seeing John Cage's *Roaratorio*."

iii. Gender Studies

Most books appropriate to this section are collections of essays by many hands. In *Discontented Discourses: Feminism/Textual Intervention/Psychoanalysis* (Illinois), ed. Marleen S. Barr and Richard Feldstein, a number of critics deal with the vexed issue of feminism and psychoanalysis. After much early anti-Freudian rhetoric, recent feminist critics have examined gender issues through such neo-Freudians as Jacques Lacan and his French feminist disciples. The essays in *Discontented Discourse* are organized as "Family: The Other Woman," "Rhetoric: The Referential Woman," "Humor: The Displaced Woman," "Influence: The Vital Woman." Included are excellent essays on "Virginia Woolf's Double Discourse" (Pamela L. Caughie), "Displaced Feminine Representation in Woody Allen's Cinema" (Richard Feldstein), "Imaginary Images: 'H.D.,' Modernism, and the Psychoanalysis of Seeing" (Elizabeth A. Hirsh), and "Dora and the Name-of-the-Father: The Structure of Hysteria" (Ellie Ragland-Sullivan).

Women's Writing in Exile (No. Car.), ed. Mary Lynn Broe and Angela Ingram, treats the concept of exile both literally and metaphorically, with essays on expatriate writers as well as on those who felt themselves exiled on the margins of their own societies. Several essays focus on classic expatriate women authors, others deal with women exiled by their sexual preference, still others concentrate on women who write about the colonial experience. Especially recommended are essays by Mary Lynn Broe on Djuna Barnes, Sonia Saldívar-Hull on Gertrude Stein, Celeste M. Schenck on "Exiled by Genre: Modernism, Canonicity, and the Politics of Exclusion," and Jane Marcus on "Alibis and Legends: The Ethics of Elsewhereness, Gender and Estrangement."

Arms and the Woman: War, Gender, and Literary Representation (No. Car.), ed. Helen M. Cooper et al., is another interesting collection made coherent by being carefully structured around a central theme. The essays deal with how women relate to war as both complicit with its activities and also resistant to them. What role has gender played not only in the acts of war but in their representation? The book's historical scope is broad, ranging from how Shakespeare represents the Trojan War in *Troilus and Cressida*, to images of nuclear war, to recent Arab-Israeli conflicts. Among many fine essays, the following are representative: James Longenbach, "The Women and Men of 1914"; Jane Marcus, "Corpus/Corps/ Corpse: Writing the Body in/at War"; and Gillian Brown, "Nuclear Domesticity: Sequence and Survival."

Rita Felski's *Beyond Feminist Aesthetics: Feminist Literature and Social Change* (Harvard) contains both summary and critique of recent feminist theory as well as readings of a number of women writers to illustrate Felski's own critical position. The author opposes such universal categories as masculine and feminine. She believes these terms have no meaning outside the contexts in which the works to which they relate were produced. She does not believe we can use such terms as forms of validation, for they have no function outside a specific sphere of activities. This revisionary work is carefully argued and erudite. Following a theoretical introduction, the chapter titles give a good sense of the book's focus: "Against Feminist Aesthetics," "Subjectivity and Feminism," "On Confession," "The Novel of Self-Discovery: Integration and Quest," "Politics, Aesthetics, and the Feminist Public Sphere." I found the earlier, more theoretical sections more interesting than the readings.

Another collection of essays, *Breaking the Sequence: Women's Experimental Fiction* (Princeton), ed. Ellen G. Friedman and Miriam Fuchs, quite comprehensively covers the experimental literature written by 20th-century female authors, mostly in English. The editors' introduction provides an excellent overview of the field and the period. A few essays on authors from the "First Generation: Before 1930" include a really clever one called "Woolfenstein" by Rachel Blau Du-Plessis. The rest of the book is divided about equally between "Second Generation: 1930–60" and "Third Generation: After 1960." A final section, "Literature in Translation," contains two essays about recent French writers. Authors covered include Djuna Barnes, Jean Rhys, H.D., Marguerite Young, Kathy Acker, and Joyce Carol Oates.

Marianne Hirsch, in *The Mother/Daughter Plot: Narrative, Psychoanalysis, Feminism* (Indiana), takes a different tack on Freud's family romance by focusing on the relation of mother and daughter. Hirsch believes that the 19th-century novel largely avoided dealing with the roles of mothers, a situation that corresponds to Freud's avoidance of theorizing about the mother/daughter relationship the way he did about either mothers and sons or fathers and sons. The book "concentrates on novels by nineteenth- and twentieth-century women writers from the Western European and the North American traditions, reading them with psychoanalytic theories of subject-formation in the context of the narrative conventions of realism, modernism, and post-modernism." Hirsch alternates throughout between psychoanalytic theorists and novelists, covering most of the important British, French, and American women writers, as well as Sigmund Freud and Karen Horney, and such neo-Freudians as Luce Irigaray, Julia Kristeva, and Nancy Chodorow. This is a densely textured, well-argued book.

Seduction and Theory: Readings of Gender, Representation, and
Rhetoric (Illinois), ed. Dianne Hunter, contains essays that discuss
one of the important concepts in contemporary theory. They focus on
the woman as a fetish, subject to the "male gaze" in patriarchal culture. Seduction is a concept much used in French feminist theory,
and it has been important to deconstruction. The book's four sections
give some sense of how the text is organized: "The Politics of the
Gaze: The Visible and the Invisible," "Seduction at the Origins of
Psychoanalysis," "Seduction of the Reader," and "Lacan, Baudrillard,
Irigaray: 'Masculine' and 'Feminine' in the Rhetoric of French Theory." I found the essays on psychoanalysis particularly interesting,
especially those that deal with the controversy surrounding Freud's
apparent repression of his early theories about the sexual abuse of
children.

Linda Kauffman, ed., Gender and Theory: Dialogues on Feminist
Criticism (Blackwell), includes pairs of essays by both male and
female critics discussing the role of gender in theory and intellectual
analysis. The focus is mostly on the political impact of feminism, and
the essays are paired to give the sense that a male-female dialogue is
taking place. The book makes no attempt to achieve consensus; rather,
the essays explore the major issues and give a sense of their variety.
The organization makes use of the following sections: "Representing
Philosophy," "The Body Writing/Writing the Body," "Transforming
Texts and Subjects." The authors include a number who are well
known in the fields of gender and literary theory such as Timothy J.
Reiss, Frances Ferguson, Jane Tompkins, Toril Moi, and David
Shumway.

The final work in this section is Speaking of Gender (Routledge),
ed. Elaine Showalter. It too consists of essays written by both men
and women, although there is less attempt to make them seem as if
they are in dialogue. Showalter's introduction clearly outlines the
history of the discussion of gender, and it lays out the central issues,
particularly the roles played by men and women in defining them.
Some of the essays are already well known, and a number have been
reproduced elsewhere, including Patrocinio P. Schweickart's "Reading Ourselves: Toward a Feminist Theory of Reading," Barbara
Johnson's "Gender Theory and the Yale School," and Eve Kosofsky
Sedgwick's notorious (but lively) "The Beast in the Closet: James and
the Writing of Homosexual Panic." This is a good introduction to the
field.

iv. Literary Theory

The books in this section represent only a handful of those I might have discussed. Thus limited, I have attempted to represent the field of theory in some of its variety and contradictory positions. Critics have, of course, a professional stake in disagreeing with one another, but some of the most prominent live in such different worlds that they find it difficult to talk back and forth, let alone disagree.

Ruin the Sacred Truths: Poetry and Belief from the Bible to the Present (Harvard), by Harold Bloom, was first presented to a Harvard audience in 1987–88 as the Charles Eliot Norton Lectures. In this book Bloom calls for a return to a literature of excess, or what he calls the High Sublime. "Poetry and belief, as I understand them, are antithetical modes of knowledge, but they share the peculiarity of taking place *between* truth and meaning, while being somewhat alienated both from truth and from meaning. Meaning gets started only by or from an excess, an overflow or emanation, that we call originality." Bloom applies the theories with which we are by now familiar, particularly emphasizing the power of the "strong" writer from the time of J (the writer of the Old Testament) to Kafka, along the way touching on such as Homer, Dante, Milton, Wordsworth, Freud, Kafka, and Beckett. This is the opinionated, aphoristic, brilliant work of a modern Gnostic.

The essays in Jonathan Culler's *Framing the Sign: Criticism and Its Institutions* (Cornell) are organized around the current contextualization of critical theory. Culler chooses the term "frame" rather than context, because it is an active verb as well as a noun, reminding us that we actively frame things even though the frame itself may be something intangible. "Two important movements," Culler writes, "have marked literary criticism and theory in recent years. First, there has been an expansion of the domain in which critics work, attention to new sorts of objects, new kinds of texts." Examples of the latter include texts from "law, anthropology, art history, even psychoanalysis." "The second trend in recent literary studies springs from a desire to make criticism political. This involves, on the one hand, an interest in the political dimensions of literary works themselves, their role in promoting change, in subverting authority, or in containing social energies. . . . On the other hand, the desire to make criticism political has produced an interest in the institutional and ideological dimensions of criticism itself: in the implications of its theoretical orientations and in its relations with the institutions which empower and contain it" (pp. xii–xiii). A learned weather vane, Culler is extremely sensitive to new trends, and he explains them very well. The book contains interesting discussions of "Deconstruction and the Law," "The Semiotics of Tourism," and "Rubbish Theory." It also contains a nicely balanced discussion of Paul de Man and the scandal surrounding his World War II writings.

In *Against Deconstruction* (Princeton) John M. Ellis mounts a closely reasoned critique of deconstruction, pointing out what he considers to be its exaggerated claims, inflated rhetoric, and pompous trivialities. Ellis criticizes deconstruction's reliance on a critique of logocentrism. "The recurring tendency to think of all criticisms of deconstructionist ideas on language as logocentric . . . the resistance to any awareness of other critiques of logocentrism means that all criticism of the deconstructive critique must be regarded as a return to logocentrism. There is no room in this framework of thought for the possibility that such criticism might come from the other direction." Ellis is also critical of a peculiar conservative tendency in deconstructive critics. "Old views," he says, "are not to be allowed to die and be replaced; they are to retain stage center in order to be debunked for all time. It is as if they are to be left in eternal purgatory instead of being laid to rest to make way for the next generation of ideas." Ellis feels that it is easier to understand how deconstruction could have arisen from a French context. In that country there really is a tendency toward centrally authoritative opinion, within an intellectual life that has been traditionally more repressive than in the United States. Given the pluralistic traditions of this country, Ellis therefore finds the American interest in deconstruction more puzzling. While *Against Deconstruction* contains many telling criticisms, it is weakened by a tendency to turn deconstruction into a caricature, becoming guilty on occasion of the kind of action for which Ellis criticizes Derrida and company.

Stanley Fish's new book, *Doing What Comes Naturally: Change, Rhetoric, and the Practice of Theory in Literary and Legal Studies* (Duke), collects essays written throughout the 1980s, most of which have been previously published. Fish, who is an extremely skillful reader and debater, shows much range in this collection, with essays on rhetoric, hermeneutics, and law, as well as a number on the profession of literary study. One of my favorite examples of the latter is "Profession Despise Thyself: Fear and Self-Loathing in Literary

Studies." Many of the essays were given as talks, and they retain an informal character. Fish would classify himself to some extent as an anti-theoretical theorist, much like Steven Mailloux. In another guise he is a reader-response critic. But whichever hat he wears, he is pragmatic, erudite, and witty, and a fearsome adversary. These essays, like Culler's, are a good barometer of what has concerned the profession during the past decade.

Brief mention goes to an authoritative collection of essays by another distinguished theorist-critic, Wolfgang Iser, *Prospecting: From Reader Response to Literary Anthropology* (Hopkins). This book basically consists of two kinds of essays: summaries of and statements about reader-response theory and applications of that theory to specific texts. In a third section the essays look forward to the potential for new directions in Iser's particular school of criticism in such essays as "Toward a Literary Anthropology."

Towards a Literature of Knowledge (Chicago) is the fifth in a series of books written by Jerome J. McGann that attempt to establish new grounds for a literary historiography. McGann believes that "poetry is a form of action rather than a form of representation." He enunciates three principles early on to establish his argument. "The first is that the mind is not an abstract or abstracting power, though of course the power of abstraction is one of its functions. . . . In poetry, therefore, knowledge will appear as a form of activity rather than as a content, a possession, or an idea. . . . Finally, to understand the thought-activity of poetic discourse means that we have to grasp the social character of human thinking. The truth-experience of poetry is always transactional—what Habermas, in a different context, spoke of as 'communicative action' " (p. 7). McGann explores these ideas chronologically through analyses of William Blake, Lord Byron, Dante Gabriel Rossetti, and *The Cantos* of Ezra Pound. I found his readings quite compelling, particularly his analysis of Pound. Because poetry is an *act* of representation, McGann states, it "can only be read when the entire facticity of those acts is raised into consciousness." He concludes by claiming that "the cognitive dynamic played out through poetic discourse . . . involves real, objective knowledge because the poetic field remains, finally, under the dominion of experience and not of consciousness." McGann's five books are an impressive, cumulative achievement.

Robert Scholes takes the title of his new book, *Protocols of Reading* (Yale), from a phrase of Jacques Derrida's. Scholes claims the latter says that "we need them but he has never found any that satisfy him. This book is *not*, let me hasten to say, an attempt to provide a set that would please him." This book is, in fact, a kind of anti-Derridean exercise that starts from a few Derridean principles. Scholes says, "I have accepted the Derridean principle that there is no outside to textuality, but I have also said that the reader is always outside the text. This looks like confusion at worst and paradox at best, but it is neither. We are always outside any particular text we may attempt to read. This is why interpretation is a problem for us. But we are never outside the whole web of textuality in which we hold our cultural being and in which every text awakens echoes and harmonies" (p. 6). Scholes divides the book into three sections—reading, interpretation, and criticism—and he treats all of them from a semiotic perspective. His texts include not only those composed of language, but photographs, works of art, and pieces of advertising. We stand outside all of them, but we live inescapably within the context in which they find their being. My only criticism is that this wise book tends to ramble a bit.

George Steiner's *Real Presences* (Chicago) definitely moves against the grain of contemporary literary theory, but not without a good understanding of it. Steiner believes in the immanence of great art, an argument that is at least quasi-theological. He believes "that any coherent account of the capacity of human speech to communicate meaning and feeling is, in the final analysis, underwritten by the assumption of God's presence. This study," he says, "will contend that the wager on the meaning of meaning . . . is a wager on transcendence." Steiner's argument ranges widely, as one might expect, given his legendary erudition, and he stands firm against various kinds of relativist positions. He certainly believes, for instance, in the importance of having a canon of recognizably great works of art, although he also certainly believes that we should choose the elements of that canon carefully and consciously and not fall into them blindly and coercively. I felt a certain regret in watching a thinker I have always respected trying desperately to hold on to a set of old beliefs.

Finally, *Work Time: English Departments and the Circulation of Cultural Value* (Stanford), by Evan Watkins, analyzes the nature of work done in English departments from the perspective of "concrete" and "abstract" labor, terms that derive from Marx's *Capital*. " 'Concrete labor' names the actual effort of work, the physical/intellectual process whereby a particular material is transformed by work into something else. 'Abstract labor' in contrast points to the social organization of work, the relations among people at the work location." As a point of comparison for what circulates throughout the general society as cultural value, Watkins proposes advertising. His analysis of how knowledge circulates from the two institutional sources is the basis for his extended discussion. Unfortunately, these discussions often go on at too tedious a pace, and even though his use of Antonio Gramsci's analysis of intellectual life is often quite enlightening, the point of his telling juxtaposition of English departments and advertising frequently gets lost.

University of California, Davis

19. Foreign Scholarship

i. East European Contributions

F. Lyra

Access to scholarly publications on American literature in 1989 was limited to two countries, the Soviet Union and Poland. While Polish contributions were readily available, some Soviet work, for reasons embedded in the deficient distribution system, continues to defy the internationally acclaimed postulate of the free flow of information. Even the prestige and authority of the Library of Congress do not generate sufficient inducement for Soviet distributors or publishers to meet orders of all Soviet materials devoted to things American. Thanks to *Knizhnaya letopis* and *Letopis zhurnal'nykh statei*, we are at least aware of which Soviet books and periodicals are prevented from making it beyond the boundaries of the Soviet Union. Now the deteriorating economic situation seems to have affected the efficient publication even of these two *Letopises*: for the first time in decades there was a delay in their availability. Consequently, in the present survey, I cannot claim to be comprehensive.

a. **General Studies.** In this category two Soviet books, one of them published in 1987, are known to me only by titles. *Traditsii i novatorstvo v literaturakh stran Zapadnoi Evropy i Ameriki XIX–XX v.* [Tradition and Innovation in the Literatures of Western Europe and America] (Gorki) announces the treatment of weighty matters. Experience, however, prompts us not to expect full correspondence between the title of the collection and its contents. The other book deals with the history of American poetry, a subject that in the past enjoyed far less interest in the Soviet Union than other literary genres, especially the novel and short fiction. It is T. D. Venediktova's *Poeticheskoe iskusstvo SSHA. Sovrmennost' i traditsiya* [Poetic Art of the U.S.A.: Contemporaneity and Tradition] (Moscow, 1988).

The American short story was the subject of yet another lengthy study by Valentina Oleneva (see *ALS 1979*, p. 464, and *ALS 1985*, pp. 450–51), "Novella SSHA. Mnogoobrazie form" [The American Short

Story: Formal Diversity], pp. 192–299 in *Zhanrovoe raznoobrazie sovremennoi prozy Zapada* [Genre Diversity of Contemporary Western Prose] (Kiev: Naukova Dumka). The work is thoroughly grounded in Marxist literary theory as modified by B. Suchkov and D. Markov, propagators of the thesis of the openness of socialist realism "recognized by scholars in our country and in the countries of socialist friendship." (How anachronistic such words sound today.) Valentina Oleneva distinguishes between the realistic and the modernist short story, but surveys only the former, relegating the latter to a separate study. Hers is basically a history of linear evolution from Washington Irving to Truman Capote's *Music for Chameleons* (1980). In her opinion, during its history the short story has emerged as "a synthesis of literary genres (the novel, tale, poetry) and other art forms, such as the theater, painting, and music"—a provocative thought echoed after Capote, who suggested it in his preface to *Music*, which she, alas, does not develop. By concentrating only on the realistic short story tradition descending from Poe and Maupassant, she forfeits a rich vein originated by Chekhov, Joyce, and D. H. Lawrence. The limitations of her book notwithstanding, Oleneva demonstrates a fresh (by Soviet Marxist standards) approach to some American writers of short fiction, whose work is infused with thought alien to Marxist ideology. For instance, not only does she accept Flannery O'Connor's Catholicism but emphasizes its value: it enriches the short story with new content. Oleneva reads O'Connor's work not as that of a Southerner but as that of an American writer.

The South has attracted K. Yurgaitene, "Ku istorii ponyatiya Yuzhnoi shkoly' v literature SSHA XX v." [Toward a History of the Idea of the "Southern School" in 20th-Century American Literature] (*Darbai lietuvos TSR Mokslu Akademijas* 4:138–49), who offers a synthesis of the "school." The Lithuanian scholar provides good historical background to the Southern Renaissance, starting with the 17th century. He discusses its crucial literary events, movements, and representative authors of the post-World War I era, emphasizing their characters' strong sense of community, which lives on even with those Southern characters who have chosen to leave the South and "cannot go home again." Yurgaitene is less interested in the Southern authors' ambiguous vision of their native region than in their attempts at demythicizing the South, discrediting "the legend of its past perfection," and relying on the grotesque as the most appropriate device for achieving their artistic goal.

b. **Pre-20th-Century Studies.** In accord with the latest historio-graphical proposition, now realized in the *Columbia Literary History of the United States* and the *Heath Anthology of American Literature*, that the story of American writing begins with prehistoric oral and pictographic texts of American Indians, it is fitting to begin this section with Aleksandr V. Vashchenko's *Istoriko-epicheskii fol'klor severo-amerikanskikh indeitsev. Tipologia i poetika* [The Historic-Epic Folklore of the North American Indians: Typology and Poetics] (Moscow: Nauka). With this book and two earlier shorter studies, Vashchenko has emerged as the foremost Soviet authority on Native American literature. Assuming that the historical epics of North American Indians have not been studied adequately, he devotes his first chapter to a survey of scholarship on the subject. I am not pre-pared to pass judgment on his claim that the material has not been fully analyzed as either folklore or epic. A glimpse into Alan R. Velie's *American Indian Literature* (1979) supports his claim, for indeed "Walam Olum," Vashchenko's primary text, is treated there as a "song." Vashchenko admits that the number of Indian historical epics is not great. Apart from the "Walam Olum" and its continuation, "Fragment of the History of the Leni-Lenape," he examines the legend of the origin of the Iroquois League, "The National Legends of the Chahta-Muskokee (Creek) Tribes," and the Osage "Wi-gi-e" epics originally described by F. La Flesche. The highly diversified texts constitute—according to Vashchenko—"variations of the same epic model." He discusses the works and then brings them together in a typological framework, derived mainly from studies of Russian epic literature. In his opinion, the peculiarity of the Indian historical epic lies in its ethnocentrism; the customary epic hero is replaced by the "ethnos," the Leni-Lenape. Vashchenko accounts for the mixed nature of the "Walam Olum" chronicle by pointing to the gradual tran-sition of the epic from mythical time to legendary historical time. With the transition, the mythological heroes make room for the 87 chiefs of the Lenape. Furthermore, Vashchenko traces European influences on the epic folklore of the Algonquians and the Iroquois. He examines the various stages and ways of the epic-forming process brought about by evolving political and social circumstances.

Whereas the book's four chapters devoted to Indian material are remarkable for in-depth scholarship, the final chapter on "The His-toric-Epic Folklore and Literature" disappoints because of its shallow-ness. Vashchenko hinges the originality of American works on the

degree of their organic relationship with Indian literature and claims
that the originality and national character of American writing has
been determined by Indian folklore. He exaggerates many prominent
Americans' interest in Indian culture. While it is true, for example,
that Jefferson as a scholar regretted the extinction of the Indians, his
interest in their culture was limited to collecting vocabularies of as
many tribes as possible to find out whether they had any common
parentage with those of Asia. As a politician, he was determined to
attain peace with them by giving them "a thorough drubbing" and
then to maintain that peace "by eternal bribes." By claiming so much
Indian influence on American writers, Vashchenko contradicts himself in the second subchapter on "The Indian Historic-Epic and the
Literature of the Native Americans," in which he says that Indian epic
tradition became assimilated into American literature thanks only to
the work of contemporary Indian writers; he presents eight of them
and introduces discussion of their work with a lengthy reference to
Daniel Hoffman's poetry, thus suggesting that the poet-scholar is of
Indian origin. He singles out Hoffman's *Brotherly Love* as a work that
"sinks into the atmosphere of "Walam Olum." But "Brotherly Love"
is steeped in the atmosphere of Philadelphia, not Indianness. Despite
these objections, Vashchenko's book is a valuable contribution to the
study of Native American literature and the most important Soviet
book this year. For the Russian reader it possesses additional value:
it includes a reproduction of both the original text and pictograms
of "Walam Olum" and its Russian translation, as well as Russian
renditions of other Indian texts enriched with numerous extensive
commentaries.

Chronology now requires that we pay attention to Zofia Sinko's
contribution, "Polska recepcja tworczosci Washington Irvinga.
Miedzy oswieceniem a romantyzmem" [The Polish Reception of
Washington Irving: Between Enlightenment and Romanticism]
(*Pamietnik Literacki* [1988] zesz. 4:141–73), a penetrating study,
though she confines it to only the third decade of the 19th century,
the peak of Irving's reception in Poland, when *The Sketch Book*, the
first volume of *Bracebridge Hall*, and selected pieces from *Tales of a
Traveller* appeared in Polish translation. Sinko presents the translated
works in the context of Irving's literary life; she traces the origins from
which they were translated (French, German, and English); and she
analyzes the translations. Thus her long article turns into an erudite
historical study that should inspire and renew Polish interest in Irv-

ing. I might add that only nine of his tales have appeared in modern Polish translation (*Rip van Winkle i inne opowiadania* [Rip Van Winkle and Other Tales], 1966; 2nd ed., 1970).

In the Soviet Union, American romanticism elicited a number of contributions. Following two articles on Emerson during the last two years (cf. *ALS 1987*, p. 425; *ALS 1988*, pp. 469–70), E. F. Osipova's "Osobennosti romanticheskogo mirovospriyatiya Ral'fa Emersona (dva esse Emersona 'Priroda')" [Peculiarities of Ralph Emerson's Romantic Worldview (Emerson's Two Essays "Nature")] (*Vestnik Leningradskogo Universiteta* ser. 2 vyp. 3:26–33) seems to corroborate the impression that the long neglect of Emerson in the Soviet Union is over. Osipova reads both "Nature" essays as a "diptych" unifying Emerson's concept of "the romantic and the real." In her interpretation, by 1844, when his second essay appeared, he had developed under the influence of science an evolutionary concept of nature without however giving up his idealistic view of nature. "Emerson unified things which appeared to be incompatible: the dialectic principles of neoplatonism and scientific approach toward the world." It is interesting that Osipova finds it necessary to correct the earlier Russian translation of *Nature* published in *Estetika amerikanskogo romantizma* [The Aesthetics of American Romanticism] (1977).

My opportunity to work in the Library of Congress for this year's review offered access to Osipova's book on Henry Thoreau, published several years ago, *Genri Toro* (Leningrad: Izdatel'stvo Leningradskogo Universiteta, 1985), which deserves notice in *ALS*, belated though it is. The book is a well-balanced study, free of Marxist jargon, though the trinity of Marxism is referred to several times unobtrusively. Osipova presents Thoreau's thought in the context of the intellectual, social, and religious movements of the time. In her discussion of "Civil Disobedience" she comes close to eulogizing his principles in a way that even the staunchest conservative Soviet ideologue of the early '80s could not quarrel with. Like many misguided readers, however, Osipova interprets Thoreau's view of the state as being anarchistic. At the same time she stresses the social values of his thought, his endeavor to improve society, for he "lived for society."

Especially illuminating is Osipova's chapter on Thoreau and Tolstoy. The Russian writer did not like *Walden*, not so much because of its content as because of its unconventional style and the poor Russian translation. Tolstoy "took Thoreau's utopia literally and not in its metaphorical meaning, and thus proved to be in this regard a greater utopian than Thoreau." She documents Tolstoy's spiritual affiliation with the American Transcendentalists, their common critical attitude toward institutionalized religion; discusses at length Tolstoy's understanding of love, which was different from Emerson's and Thoreau's; and points out that Thoreau's " 'puritanism' was consonant with Tolstoy's disposition." She traces Thoreau's ideas expressed in "Civil Disobedience" in Tolstoy's writings and asserts that the American's were not unique in contemporary America. She describes Tolstoy's adherence to the idea of nonviolence and the criticism it exposed him to, recalling the campaign against him at home and abroad (Theodore Roosevelt protested against Tolstoy's meddling in American affairs). Regrettably, Osipova does not elaborate on Lenin's criticism of his countryman's adherence to nonviolent principles.

Unfortunately, I have not had access to S. D. Pavlychko's *Filosofskaya poeziya amerikanskogo romantizma: Emerson, Uitman, Dikinson* [The Philosophic Poetry of American Romanticism: Emerson, Whitman, Dickinson] (Kiev: Naukova Dumka, 1988), which seems to be one of the more interesting Soviet contributions on 19th-century American literature in recent years. Equally futile was my search for the collection *Natsional'naya spetsifika proizvodenii zarubeshnoi literatury XIX–XX vekov. Problemy khudozhestvennosti* [The National Characteristics of Foreign Literature of the 19th and 20th Centuries: Artistic Problems] (Ivanovo, 1988), which contains an article by V. N. Sheinker, "Gotorn i Uells (O vliyanii tvorchestva amerikanskogo pisatelya N. Gotorna na tvorchestvo G. Uellsa" [Hawthorne and Wells (Hawthorne's Influence on H. G. Wells] (pp. 32–41).

To end this section, I should note V. E. Barykin's "Edgar Po i ego izdateli" [Edgar Allan Poe and His Publishers] (*Kniga* 58:149–67), which supplies a well-informed survey of how Poe's works were issued during his lifetime and the story behind the first posthumous edition of his collected works. Parenthetically, Barykin provides a fascinating literary tidbit for Poe enthusiasts. It is known among specialists that the original edition of *Tales of the Grotesque and Arabesque* numbered 750 copies; its Russian edition in 1980 had a tirage of 1,500,000.

c. 20th-Century Literature. For rather obvious reasons, scholarly interest in 20th-century American literature continues to dominate. In Poland one monograph study was produced, in the Soviet Union several books, some of which remained out of reach even of the Library of Congress, as did several items published in 1988, notably V. A. Kostyakov's *Amerikanskii roman serediny XX veka. Konteptual'-nost' zhanra* [The American Mid-century Novel: The Concept of the Genre] (Saratov: Izd-vo Sarat. Un-ta) and A. N. Lyuksemburg's *Anglo-amerikanskaya universitetskaya proza* [Anglo-American College Prose] (Rostov: Izd-vo Rost. Un-ta). Among this year's Soviet contributions, V. K. Shpak's *Istoriya amerikanskoi poezii XX v.* [A History of 20th-Century American Poetry] (Kiev: UMKVO) and the collection *Problemy poetiki v. zarubezhnoi literature XIX–XX vekov* [Problems of Poetics in Foreign Literature of the 19th and 20th Centuries] (Moscow) might have generated interest among *ALS* readers had the publications been available for comment. At least I was able to learn the contents of *Problemy poetiki*, which includes 12 articles by as many authors: A. O. Boyarskaya, T. V. Vorochenko, A. F. Golovenchenko, N. B. Kolesnikova, N. N. Nartyev, V. L. Nechesov, O. N. Oleinikova, O. E. Osovskii, O. V. Polukhin, V. G. Prozorov, V. A. Fedchenko, and I. V. Fedchenko, whose contributions are mostly on individual authors—Carson McCullers, Hawthorne, S. Levitt(?), Robert Penn Warren, Harry Crosby, Kurt Vonnegut, and Thornton Wilder.

A leftover from 1988 by Aleksandr A. Mulyarchik manifests the endurance of reading ideological presuppositions into literature. In his *Sovremennyi realisticheskii roman SSHA 1945–1980* [The Contemporary Realistic Novel of the U.S.A., 1945–1980] (Moscow: Vys-shaya Shkola, 1988) he platitudinizes on realism as the most valid and aesthetically satisfying method of storytelling. Literary history is for Mulyarchik a cyclical process energized by the struggle of realism against nonrealistic movements such as naturalism, modernism, "black humorism." In his view, the years under survey form an era, which he divides into three periods that circumscribe his book's structure. It consists of three chapters, each divided into three subchapters. The social-critical novel of the '40s, war novels, and the novel of socialist ideas and anti-McCarthy protest make up the first period. They constitute, he says, "a living legacy" of the "angry '30s." The second period is distinguished for "the centripetal novel in which the realistic novel is dominated and modified by the conformism of the '50s," the realism of subjective prose, and "existential motives." In the final period Mulyarchik shifts thematic focus. First, he discerns an ascension of social-critical fiction; he continues with a discussion of "the realistic novel and conventional forms"; and finally he directs attention to "the historical fortunes of the U.S. in the novel of the '70s," noting a return to "actualization of social-political and ethical problems." One wishes the neatly schematic structure of the book concealed rich content. Instead, Mulyarchik treats the material in a highly selective manner. As a book addressed to university students, it is woefully deficient in scholarly apparatus, having no bibliography and few footnotes; and it discusses works that are not available in Russian translation, though the reader is not told this. As a result, the student is deprived of the possibility of verifying the author's interpretative pronouncements.

In a sweeping study of the historical novel, *Sovremennyi istoricheskii roman* [The Contemporary Historical Novel] (Kiev: Vysshaya Shkola), A. G. Bakanov discusses at length the works of Gore Vidal and Thornton Wilder, and in passing he looks at several American historical works, such as those by John Gardner, John Hersey, and John Barth. By examining the works in an international context of historical fiction, he provides a new perspective. For instance, Vidal's *Burr* is brought into relief with Bertolt Brecht's *The Affairs of Mr. Julius Caesar* and the Bulgarian novelist V. Mutafchiev's *Delo sultana Dzhema* as an example of the creative link between the historical-documentary novel and history as a science. Bakanov devotes several pages to Wilder's *The Ides of March*, which he reads in the context of the work of Herman Hesse and others as "an original specimen of the conventional historical novel," but he does not have any new insights.

Tamara N. Denisova does not display such reticence in "Noveishaya gotika (O zhanrovykh modifikatsiyakh sovremennogo amerikanskogo romana" [The Newest Gothic (On Genre Modifications of the Contemporary American Novel)], pp. 59–127, in *Zhanrovoe raznoobrazie sovremennoi prozy Zapada* [Genre Diversity of Contemporary Western Prose] (Kiev: Naukova Dumka). Hers is a forceful justification of the new Gothic novel as one "means of sublimation of social consciousness"—a stance that breaks with the conventional Soviet literary scholars' view of American practitioners of the genre. Her unconventional (by Soviet standards) position is complemented by her opinion "that there is no wall between 'high' and 'mass culture' "—a distinction her fellow scholar Ol'ga Tuganova (see below) still preserves. Denisova discusses several authors, among them Barth and Walker Percy.

The same theme, though in a much narrower scope, is explored by

Anna Machinek in "William Faulkner and the Gothic Tradition" (*Kwartalnik Neofilologiczny* zesz. 2:105–14), where she says that "the initiation into evil, an indispensable part of a Gothic story, becomes the pivotal point of Faulkner's novels." She recalls the basic assumptions of and objections to the Gothic novel and applies them to *Sanctuary* and *Absalom, Absalom!*

The year abounds in studies of individual authors, among whom Nabokov was the subject of the most comprehensive treatment by the Polish critic Leszek Engelking in his *Vladimir Nabokov* (Warsaw: Czytelnik). Nabokov has enjoyed wide popularity in Poland, shown by the translations of several of his novels, poems, and tales. Engelking enhances his monograph by including Nabokov's comments about himself and literature and a collection of various writers' and critics' comments—all too brief sections, unfortunately. This deficiency is largely made up for by an extensive bibliography of secondary sources, which assures continued inquiry into Nabokov's work.

While not a scholarly contribution, R. Orlova's long article "Russkaya sud'ba Khemingueya" [The Russian Fate of Hemingway] (*Voprosy Literatury* 6:77–107) is this year's most "newsworthy" literary piece. Orlova has bequeathed (her article was published posthumously) an insider's glimpse into Soviet literary life under Stalin and later, a fascinating insight into the background of the ups and downs of Hemingway's Soviet reception, especially the ominous silence in 1939–55 following American publication of *For Whom the Bell Tolls*, which was translated into Russian in secret by E. Lalashnikov and N. Volzhin. It is said that Stalin himself suppressed the novel's publication. Be that as it may, the Russian version was circulating among readers in manuscript for years before it was finally made available in the third volume of Hemingway's collected works in 1968, albeit not without the censor's interference, especially in chapter 18. In Poland Andrzej Weselinski presents "F. Scott Fitzgerald: The Novelist Looks at Hollywood" (*Kwartalnik Neofilologiczny* zesz. 2:89–103), a thoroughly researched article describing the writer's ambivalent attitude toward film in both his life and his work. Ewa Chrzanowska-Karpinska offers "John Barth's *Lost in the Funhouse* as a Comic Metafiction," pp. 209–22, in Anna Zagorska and Grazyna Bystydzienska, eds., *Literatura angielska i amerykanska: Problemy recepcji* [English and American Literature: Problems in Reception] (Lublin: Uniwersytet Marii Curie-Sklodowskiej). She reveals that "the stories in *Lost in the Funhouse* can be seen to be dealing with the problems of artistic cul-de-sac. Taken together, they are all about a failure to write a story." In the same volume Jerzy Kutnik presents "The Readers' Plight in Raymond Federman's Fiction" (pp. 223–34), a sort of synopsis of chapters 9 and 15 of his book *The Novel as Performance: The Fiction of Ronald Sukenik and Raymond Federman* (see *ALS 1986*, p. 298); and in "Toward a History of American Literature in Poland" (pp. 194–208), I test the extent and quality of the Polish reception of American literature from the beginning (the end of the 18th century), asking provocatively whether a scholar could write a comprehensive history of American literature on the basis of the translated writings and their critical reception in Poland so far. My answer is negative.

The growing significance of "minority" authors in American literary culture has yet to be fully recognized in Eastern Europe. Occasional articles on works of individual hyphenated writers often express unqualified acclaim verging on encomium. A. Vashchenko opens his "Realism i magiya Rudol'fo Anaii" [Rudolfo Anaya's Realism and Magic] (*Literaturnaya Ucheba* 4:185–88) thus: "Delightful recognition! One still encounters a rare type of writer with whom acquaintance is like love on first sight—it takes one's breath." Having "discovered" Anaya's novel *Bless Me, Ultima* in 1972, the year of its publication, Vashchenko, assuming to speak for all readers, declares that through it "a reader discovers not only one writer, but a whole literature—that of Mexican Americans, or Chicanos." He proceeds to describe in detail Anaya's first three novels. In emphasizing the confluence of Anaya's magic symbolism and realism, Vashchenko follows the critical mainstream. But unlike other critics he differentiates the novels by their social messages rather than their artistry: *Bless Me, Ultima* contains various parallel conflicts; *Heart of Aztlán* is a "revolutionary etude" of the American masses in the late '60s and early '70s; and *Tortuga*—a variant of Thomas Mann's *Magic Mountain*—is "a book about people's responsibility for the surrounding world."

An increasing number of American works are being subjected to a variety of linguistic, semantic, and semiotic examinations, with the results published sometimes under excruciating titles. Most of these efforts are hard to come by, as is the case with A. B. Murza's "Vliyanie soderzhaniya na sochetanie form povestvovaniya i struktury dialoga v romanakh E. Khemingueya" [The Influence of Content on the Combination of Narrative Form and Dialogue Structure in Hemingway's Novels], pp. 29–37, in *Funktsionalnaya stilistika i lingvodidaktika*

[Functional Stylistics and Language Teaching] (Moscow, 1988). I was able, however, to see S. A. Panchuk and A. A. Kaldushina's "Strukturno-semanticheskaya korrelyatsiya yazykogo tematicheskogo polya i tematicheskoi setki khudozhestvennogo teksta (na materiale romana I. Stouna Zhazhda zhizni)" [The Structural-Semantic Correlation of the Language-Thematic Field and the Thematic Net of an Artistic Text (On the Material of Irving Stone's Novel *Lust for Life*)], pp. 150–60, in *Kontekstual'no obuslovlennaia variatnost' edinits yazyka* [Contextual Conditionality of a Language Unit Variant] (Riga). The authors apply the methodology announced in the article's title to analyze the artistic deployment of the opposition "Good/Evil" in demonstrating the "indissolubility" of ethical and aesthetic qualities in Stone's novel.

d. **Miscellaneous.** Nearly half of Ol'ga E. Tuganova's *Sovremennaya kul'tura SSHA: Struktura. Mirovozzrencheskii aspekt. Khudozhestvennoe tvorchestvo* [Contemporary American Culture: The Ideological Aspect: Artistic Creation] (Moscow: Nauka) is devoted to literature, which the author views in the panoramic context of Amercan culture presented with ideological restraint, though the works of Marx, Engels, and Lenin head the bibliography of primary sources. She begins by enumerating the ideological currents which, in her opinion, have determined in various configurations the works of individual artists and authors: "The liberal humanistic; the social-critical (democratic); leftist-democratic; anarchic-radical; conservative; liberal-conservative; reactionary-conservative; nihilistic." Tuganova substantiates the currents with readings of a wide range of American and foreign works. In the treatment of American literature, however, she is less concerned with such ideological orientations than with "characteristic themes and images." The book's broad subject matter compels her to treat the numerous authors' writings in a highly selective fashion and in nonanalytical terms. In the context of traditional Soviet literary criticism, Tuganova's readings are rather unconventional. Unlike other Soviet critics, she is not particularly interested in bringing all writers into the realistic fold. She treats Mailer, the Beats, and Henry Miller with the same fairness as she does Barrie Stavis, Meridel Le Sueur, Phillip Bonosky, and the Black Humorists. She perceives positive values in the counterculture and avant-garde movements, which have been favorite subjects of negative criticism on the part of traditionalists. Tuganova devotes an entire chapter to American black culture, including a comprehensive survey of black authors' writings, on the whole treating them with discriminating understanding, though I cannot accept her putting Toni Morrison's *Song of Solomon* and Alex Haley's *Roots* on a par. She is, surprisingly, also critical of the African-American nationalist movement.

Yu. I. Sokhryakov's *Russkaya klassika v literaturnom protsesse SSHA XX veka* [Russian Classics in the American Twentieth Century Literary Process] (Moscow: Vysshaya Shkola, 1988) is disappointing for its flat application of Marxist principles and its defective documentation; the sources of numerous quotations and references go unacknowledged. Sokhryakov's book consists of four monograph chapters, each dealing with one Russian writer and his influence on American authors: "Tolstoy and the American Prose Writers Between 1910 and the '30s"; "Dostoevsky and American Realistic Prose"; "Chekhov and American Realistic Art"; and "Gorky and American Writers Between 1910 and the '30s." No question that the works of these writers exerted a considerable impact on many American authors, but Sokhryakov exaggerates the influence. Thus we learn that "Tolstoy helped [Thomas] Wolfe (as he did his contemporary Hemingway) to avoid James Joyce's modernist extremes." Ignoring forces that began to shape American culture after the Civil War, he asserts that "Russian classical literature became for American writers a powerful support in the struggle for overcoming the complex of 'cultural provincialism,' in search for their own artistic forms," contributing to the defeat of the genteel tradition; and, of course, the Russians shaped American realism. Sokhryakov does not admit, however, that American non-realistic writers also may have been influenced by Russian authors. Lest my criticism of the book be too severe, I would emphasize that it contains excellent passages: the characterizations of Dostoevsky and Wolfe, of Truman Capote, of Chekhov and Eudora Welty, among others.

I should end with an appreciative note on Anna D. Jaroszynska's "Krytyka retoryczna w Stanach Zjednoczonych" [Rhetorical Criticism in the United States] (*Pamietnik Literacki* zesz. 3:97–119), a concise historical survey of the field. Her observation, however, that Americans' preoccupation with rhetoric began in the mid-19th century is off the mark, as Harry S. Stout's *The New England Soul* (1986) testifies.

Central Missouri State University

ii. French Contributions

Michel Gresset

a. **General.** As last year, I would like to begin with two preliminary remarks, the first of which has to do with translation and poetry. Poetry in general has always been a blind spot toward American literature in France, and the work of Wallace Stevens in particular: hardly anything by him (as opposed to William Carlos Williams) was available in book form until recently. Now there are four published titles. The first, *Poèmes*, was published in 1988 by Delta (Montpellier), in a translation by an American, Nancy Blake, and Hedi Kaddour. It is by far the most comprehensive collection, since it excerpts seven titles published from 1931 (*Harmonium*) to 1957 (*Opus Posthumous*). But it is also the least felicitous translation, as the renderings are often flat and stale for being far too passively literal. The second is a very fine version of the one-act play *Three Travelers Watch a Sunrise* by Leslie Kaplan and Claude Régy (Actes Sud-Papiers, 1988). The third is the collection *The Man with the Blue Guitar*, well-translated by Olivier Amiel (Michel Chandeigne, 1989). And the fourth is a much less extensive anthology, *Description sans domicile* (from the poem "Description Without Place"), translated—with some inexplicable mistakes but a good deal of felicity, too—by the well-known poet Bernard Noël (Paris: Editions Unes). The latest triumphs elsewhere in translation from American literature also had to do with poetry. A selection of 250 of Emily Dickinson's poems have been beautifully translated into French by Claire Malroux, who also exquisitely rendered Edith Wharton's *Old New York*, and thus got the M. E. Coindreau Prize for 1989. Even more arresting though less even in quality was Jacques Darras's new translation of the complete *Leaves of Grass*. To someone used to any of the former, rather prosaic translations, this is almost the first time Whitman can be read in French: at last, there is rhythm in *Feuilles d'herbe*!

The second preliminary remark has to do with current trends in France, where the long-favorite authors of the post-World War II period (particularly the "big five" of Claude Edmonde-Magny's 1948 book, *L'Age du roman américain*: Faulkner, Hemingway, Caldwell, Dos Passos, and Steinbeck), are changing as fast as the postwar period itself, with the first two names now well-established in the classics' niche, the next two almost forgotten, and the fifth still somehow popular only because *Of Mice and Men* and *The Pearl* are read in translation in secondary schools. As for the following generation, no writer (even those who are dead: Carson McCullers, Flannery O'Connor, Truman Capote) has ever reached the same magnitude as the elders. This is even truer of the next generation—particularly the so-called postmodern writers. It is evident that America's "culture" at large (including movies, painting, music, clothing, soft drinks, and the like) is now more widespread than its literature, strictly speaking. In the academic world, however, one has lately seemed to witness a renewal of interest in the 19th century and in poetry, as well as a sustained interest in the most contemporary fringe of fiction; the United States has always been associated with what is live—both living and lively.

b. **Colonial.** The title of Jean Béranger's "A l'ombre de Calvin: argents et biens matériels dans less écrits de William Bradford et de John Winthrop" is self-explanatory. It appears in "Le Puritanisme en Amérique, 1630–1692" (*Americana* 4:61–73), an interesting issue also containing an essay on Anne Bradstreet (see under Poetry, below). In "Beauté et vertus de l'altérité: Thomas Roderick Dew et les différences caractéristiques entre les sexes," published in "De la normalité," a special issue of *Cycnos* (4 [1988]:3–16), Anne-Marie Bonifas shows at length how the concept of otherness applied to woman embarrasses the author of the *Pro-Slavery Argument*. Ideally brief and useful in spite of its somewhat muddled title is Bernard Chevignard's "Confusion, fusion, diffusion: les variations révolutionnaires de Saint-John de Crèvecoeur" (*RFEA* 40:141–48), in which is set right (and in a far less idyllic perspective) the image of the utopian American farm bequeathed by the author to Europeans in 1782, and much later (1904, in fact) to Americans. Crèvecoeur was no Irving, nor was his James, Rip van Winkle. In "Cinq inédits de Thomas Paine" (*RFEA* 40:213–23), Bernard Vincent has most unexpectedly exhumed, and reproduces with facsimiles, five letters, all of some interest, dated between 1787 and 1795—three in English, two in a French translation.

c. **19th-Century Literature.** It is fitting to begin with Poe for several reasons, the least of which is that, in spite of William Carlos Williams, Allen Tate, and Richard Wilbur, he is very much a French writer. The better reason (two years after my predecessor's brief tribute to him as he reviewed his book *Lettres américaines* in *ALS*

1987, pp. 435–36) is to honor once more the work of Claude Richard. The 1,600-page volume, *Edgar Allan Poe: Contes, Essais, Poèmes*, published by Laffont, however impressive it may be, especially with 300 pages of notes, is only the latest avatar of the Pléiade edition once undertaken by Richard. With 73 and 58 items, respectively, this is the first chronological edition of the complete tales and poems in French. *Arthur Gordon Pym* is not there, but a little over 200 pages are devoted to nonfiction prose: 10 of the essays, half of *Marginalia*, and the whole of *Eureka*. The book opens with a 15-page introduction, "Le mythe de Poe," in which Richard repeats his theses in laconic terms: "Poe's literary reputation in France rests essentially on three successive appropriations by Rufus W. Griswold, by Charles Baudelaire, and by Marie Bonaparte. These appropriations have given birth to three myths: the myth of morals, the myth of revolt and the myth of madness." Each section is also preceded by an introduction: the tales are introduced by Richard's self-explanatory "Poe's Tales or the Modes of Contamination," the essays by Richard's "Poe critique," and the poems by a brief "Poète, irrévocablement?" by Robert Kopp, who completed the edition after Richard's death. In spite of many misprints, this is by far the best edition of Poe that we have had. The irony is that at the same time it was published, Gallimard brought out a collection of the 25 tales left untranslated by Baudelaire, edited by Alain Jaubert, an "amateur éclairé" if not a scholar, under the title *Ne pariez jamais votre tête au diable* ("Never Bet the Devil Your Head"), with a long preface and a substantial critical apparatus in which the editor's debt to Richard conspicuously appears.

Four critical articles on Poe have been published by Christian La Cassagnère in *Visages du l'angoisse* (Centre du romantisme anglais, Clermont-Ferrand). The first is only a reprint of Richard's well-known "Poe et l'esthétique du double" (1984). Next is "Poe et la femme aux yeux vides," in which Henri Justin studies the changes wrought by Poe in the motif of the vacant gaze of the "Life-in-Death" character of the mother or of the muse by comparison with Coleridge's "Ancient Mariner" and Keats's "The Fall of Hyperion." La Cassagnère himself writes at length on "Angoisse et écriture dans *The House of Usher*," finding it somewhat difficult to communicate his conviction that there is such a thing as "un texte d'angoisse"—a phrase which I find impossible even to translate, unless as a Freudian concept, which supposes the German rather than the English language. Last is a long contribution by Bertrand Rougé called "*Lingua ex Machina*: angoisse de la mécanique et mécanique de l'angoisse dans l'oeuvre d'Edgar Allan Poe"—an ambitious title, both in scope and in definition, in which machines and mechanisms are said to be what fill the void of an absence—metaphors of the text, in fact. Ultimately, only language eludes the reign of mechanisms; only language eludes the nothingness of death—because only language is not a machine. Bonaparte, Cabau, Pinto are quoted for support, but the conclusion is unquestionably Poesque: what is at stake is "the power of words." As for the purpose of Denis Gauer's "*The Tell-Tale Heart* de Poe: angoisse et stratégie littéraire" (*RFEA* 42:395–406), I fail to see where it lies, as it seems to enter doors long opened in other publications (*Delta* 1 in particular) that the essay does not even mention.

Number 26 of *Caliban* is devoted to the South before Faulkner, "Le Sud avant Faulkner." It is aptly introduced with an essay devoted by Paul Carmignani (who wrote his dissertation on Shelby Foote) to "Sud historique, Sud mythique, Sud diégétique" (pp. 5–14): the South is less geography or even history than it is legend, i.e., literally "what is to be read." Carmignani is followed by Cassilde Tournebize, who writes briefly on "Représentation du Sud dans *Tales of Soldiers* d'Ambrose Bierce" (pp. 15–20). The core of the number is aptly devoted to pieces on half a dozen Southern writers (the two poets are dealt with under "Poetry" below) whose works are known only to specialists in France. Yet these writers belong to a literary canon. Yvette Salvati writes on "La fascination d'un sudiste pour la frontière: *The Knights of the Golden Horse-Shoe* de William Alexander Caruthers" (pp. 47–56). Four contributions are then devoted to better-known writers whose works, although quite well-known in the United States, have had little success in this country—often simply for lack of a timely and adequate translation. Daniel Royot writes on "A nat'ral born durn'd fool: l'irrésistible déchéance de Sut Lovingood" (pp. 57–64), Etienne de Planchard on "Entre fleuve et marais ou les 'bayous-conteurs' dans *The Grandissimes* de G. W. Cable" (pp. 81–90), and Danièle Pitavy-Souques on "Paysage langage ou l'impossible accès à la parole: une relecture de *The Awakening* de Kate Chopin" (pp. 91–104)—perhaps the best-known of these Southern books in France (could it be because of the parallel to be made between *The Awakening* and *Madame Bovary*?). The last contribution is devoted by Jean Rouberol to "De Falkner à Faulkner: *La rose blanche de Memphis* [*The White Rose of Memphis*]" (pp. 105–13); this best-seller went through 35 editions between 1881 and 1909, 20 years after its author's death. Rouberol supplements the excellent, informative preface Maurice Edgar Coindreau wrote for the French translation in 1970. He lays stress on the particular structure of the novel, which he says can also be found in the great-grandson's works.

In a publication devoted to a not too literary theme, "L'éthique du loisir dans *Norwood* de Henry Ward Beecher" (*Les Etats-Unis: Images du travail et des loisirs*, Université de Provence, pp. 111–26), Yves Lemeunier shows that the author's views on leisure had changed completely from the strictly Puritan ones expounded in his *Seven Lectures to Young Men* published 23 years before, in 1844. In *Norwood*, under the mixed influences of Rousseau, Thoreau, Hawthorne, Whitman, and Jefferson, one is surprised to read a plea for culture as the perfect complement of leisure. But the thrust of research in 19th-century American literature lay in a workshop on literature and revolution headed by Maurice Gonnaud (who introduces the subject in *RFEA* 40:135–39) and André Muraire. Most of the six articles in this number are discussed elsewhere in this report, but at least one has its place here: Yves Carlet's "Révolution, révélation, résolution: Boston et l'image révolutionnaire" (*RFEA* 40:187–200), whose modest aim is to show how "spontaneous metaphors" such as the objective correlatives of order and disorder (on which side is the guillotine?), of tyranny (Jehovah), and of emancipation (Jesus) always pop up to "crystallize ideology." In "Washington Irving et le pittoresque post-romantique" (*RFEA* 42:439–53), Bruno Montfort sets out to (re)-locate Irving in the history of an important category, that of the picturesque. Unfortunately, his article, clogged by at least two dozen critical authorities, is so allusively and/or clumsily written as to annihilate one's hope of better understanding the selected passage, "London Antiques," from *The Sketch Book*. The same author's even longer search of "a few Melvillean episodes" (chosen from "Benito Cereno" and *Pierre*) for "La Figure du méridien" (*Delta* 27:1–31) is scrupulous and exacting in its method. As far as "Benito Cereno" is concerned, the method consists in comparing the chronological and the horological setups of the action and in finding a "factor of identity" in the 12-hour hiatus between the two. This is expressed in a 13-line sentence which is immediately "translated" into a much more readable sentence beginning "In other words . . . ." Apparently more readable, too, though no less recondite on another level—that of the concepts used—is Line Koïs's "Henry D. Thoreau, *Walden:*

transaction et translation, le ravissement de la lettre" (*Delta* 27:33–43), in which ambiguity is carefully kept hovering over the main concepts, that of "ravissement" (the rape of the letter or the fact of being charmed by it?), of the letter (whether a type or a message), and of the epistemological nature of the subject (whether grammatical or Lacanian). The consequence is a carefully written article, with some quite accessible propositions—such as "Only by exposing himself to nature is the subject exposed to himself"—in which, however, one is surprised to find that all the key concepts are loose ends.

For reasons that have nothing to do with popularity, but with the three American books set on the syllabus of the Agrégation d'Anglais for 1989 (*Moby-Dick, The Education of Henry Adams,* and Ginsberg's *Poems*), by far the most plentiful critical crop was a set of no less than seven articles on *Moby-Dick* published after an introduction by Jeanne-Marie Santraud in *Americana* 3. With "La Dimension tragique de *Moby-Dick*" (pp. 15–25), Claude Coulon reverts to an aesthetic preoccupation shared by such excellent critics of a former generation as Jean-Jacques Mayoux and Henry A. Murray. Only in his appreciation of Philippe Jaworski's judgments on Ahab and Ishmael in his *Melville: le Désert et l'empire* (1986), however, can he be considered as bringing anything new. More useful is the slightly misnamed "*Moby-Dick* ou les métamorphoses d'Ismael" (pp. 27–36), in which F.–X. Mioche seeks to explain what he calls "the illusion of a symmetrical relationship between Ahab and Ishmael" by distinguishing between two Ishmaels, the narrator and the protagonist, whose originals in the Bible are the son of Abraham and Agar in Genesis, and the gang leader in Kings and in Jeremiah—or the founding father and the rebel i.e., the American par excellence. As action recedes before narration, the first Ishmael gradually takes over the latter, only to yield in his turn before the author—hence the title, which could have been "Melville and the quest for the sublime of a 'democratic diction,'" since there—albeit much too briefly—is seen to lie the insoluble problem raised by the novel. In "*Thar She Blows in the Wind*: Quelques Obiter Dicta Post Mortem sur Moby dit le Dick" (pp. 37–46), an article whose title and constantly parodic style convey the choice of a learned, grotesque humor à la Melville, Pierre-Yves Pétillon begins by asserting that the origins of the monster book go back to the year 1536 because of the conjunction of Rabelais, Cabeza de Vaca, and Jean Calvin: he goes on by briefly mentioning some of what he calls the "loomings" of *Moby-Dick* in post-World War II American literature: *The Naked and the Dead, On the Road, Trout Fishing in America,* and Robert Lowell's *The Quaker Graveyard at Nantucket.* More recently, however, *Moby-Dick* has been revived in the motif of the Great American Novel. The "loomings" of Melville's book can be seen in Philip Roth, of course, but also in *Humboldt's Gift* and in *Gravity's Rainbow.* Somewhat expectedly, Pétillon's conclusion is that the true "great American novel" of our time is Thomas Pynchon's third. The next three articles can hardly be called critical essays, as they seem to be geared essentially toward the Agrégation students. Nothing is wrong with these articles, only that they do not seek to uncover anything new. In "Before Ahab: The Function of the Opening Chapters of *Moby-Dick*" (pp. 47–52), Thomas Philbrick assumes, F.-X. Mioche notwithstanding, that "the distinction between the youthful actor and the mature narrator is virtually erased" in Ishmael after "the tale of maturation" is over in the early chapters and leaves room for the adventure of consciousness, and that "the image of stillness at the center . . . is the signal of Melville's most profound passages of affirmation." In "*Moby-Dick*: Enjeux et transgressions d'un langage romanesque" (pp. 53–60), Catherine Pouzoulet, after quoting Emily Dickinson's remarkable "Tell the Truth but tell it slant," travels from one critical commonplace to another before concluding, somewhat surprisingly, with the idea that in Ishmael "the visionary is saved from the symbolist vision by the ironist." Jeanne-Marie Santraud's "Creating What Creates, or *Moby-Dick* the Dynamic Vision" (pp. 61–70) is perfectly reassuring, as it deals only with what is hardly questionable in the book. As for "Les Stratégies narratives de Melville dans *Moby-Dick* (pp. 71–82), it expounds Marc Saporta's unsophisticated and somewhat arbitrary distinction (what cannot be called a "strategy" if viewed as a means to an end?) between eight such "strategies" in *Moby-Dick*, the latest of which, here called "objectal," is the relationship curiously found between Melville and the French "new novelists" on the ground of their treatment of objects.

d. 20th-Century Fiction to the Fifties.   The same *Americana* 3 has three articles on *The Education of Henry Adams.* Under the title "The Unwritten Education of Henry Adams" (pp. 83–89), Pierre Lagavette has written a terse reminder that Adams was acutely aware that, although he privileged style over fact as all artists must, "true education, the process of identifying and controlling the shaping forces of the universe, had yet to be told." In "Les Antimémoires de Henry

Adams" (pp. 91–94), Jean Rouberol has even more briefly sought a fittingly "negative" inspiration in André Malraux's unconventional memoirs. His insistence on the key value of the statue in the church-yard at Rock Creek, which he calls "the apotheosis of the un-said," is thoroughly convincing. Robert F. Sayre's *"The Education*: Henry Adams's Epistolary Last Hurrah" (pp. 95–106) is a useful, though a perhaps unnecessarily long demonstration that the book can be considered as the longest among the letters written to accompany or to follow the 40 plus 60 copies sent to the select between 1907 and 1909; "The *Education* was the old Boston pol's greatest letter, his obituary, and his last hurrah!"

Not far from Henry Adams, at least in time, is Henry James, on whose relationship with a photographer for the New York edition of his works Catherine Vieilledent has brought her indefatigable intellectual curiosity to bear in "Texte et image: la collaboration de Henry James et Alvin Langdon Coburn" (*RFEA* 39:29–43). Another tireless Americanist in France is Nancy Blake, who wrote what is perhaps one of her best articles as a contribution to *CCV* 11: "Psychoanalyse et littérature." In "Les ombres et *Lumière d'août* de Faulkner: le retour du refoulé" ["Shades and *Light in August*: The Return of the Suppressed"] (pp. 131–45), she shows forcefully that death, the central shade, is at the core of the book, associated with the feminine element. Marielle Rigaud's *"The Violent Bear It Away*: la Quête du Père" (*Delta* 27:45–54) is an impeccable analysis of how Flannery O'Connor's novel is built on Marion Tarwater's useless revolt against the father among too many, including God.

e. 20th-Century Fiction: Contemporary. No less than 18 articles and one book were devoted to contemporary (all living, in fact) American writers of fiction in 1989—about one fifth of this year's production. Chief among the posse of academics running after the "post-moderns" is Marc Chénetier, whose long-brewing book was published by Le Seuil in Paris in the first days of the year, an event which deserves some space in this review. Although somewhat mistakenly called *Au-delà du soupçon* (this seems to place all the writers examined under the aegis of *L'Age du soupçon* [*The Age of Suspicion*], Nathalie Sarraute's epoch-making essay of 1956), the book is charitably subtitled *La nouvelle fiction américaine de 1960 à nos jours.* The subtitle is both ambitious (it assumes, with some provocation, that whatever is left out can hardly be considered "new") and wry ("today" is an endless time reference). However, the book, as full of juice as a ripe fruit, is fine, and important to boot (were it only because it is the first in France on this subject.) Chénetier has organized it rather cleverly, in fragments as of a puzzle rather than in chapters, from "New Directions" (neatly subdivided into "Traditions," "Transitions," "Revisions," "Evolutions") through the nine central sections of "Beyond Suspicion" to the final essay, "The Age of American Fiction," whose title clearly refers to Claude-Edmonde Magny's memorable *L'Age du roman américain* (1948). He has sought to avoid a catalog, handbook, or rambling commentary. The book's very structure reflects the old, perhaps inevitable, compromise between the extremes of scope and depth. This shows perhaps most after p. 238, when, first with a chapter entitled "Images/Bruits," then with two longish chapters on "the cultural tradition and the present," the discourse, instead of gushing forth with a good deal of gusto (and not a few witticisms), albeit with praiseworthy economy and a minimum of repetition, purports to cover the valley of culture rather than follow the ridges of literature, strictly speaking. The 40-page bibliography lists 385 writers, which is 85 more than even the "Three Hundred American Novels" in which, a few years ago in the *New York Review of Books*, Robert Coover argued against the distinction between the so-called avant-garde and the mainstream of fiction—and it is true that most of today's mainstream is made up of yesterday's "avant-garde," if not of the day before (think only of the part played by *Moby-Dick* in the history of the American novel). Out of these 385 writers, however, fewer than 20—all white and male, if not all Anglo-Saxon—are dealt with most repeatedly. Without exception, these writers are dubbed "post-modern" because, to put it briefly, their writings illustrate Chénetier's key concept, metafiction. The danger, negotiated rather than confronted by Chénetier (who dutifully bows to Sterne and to Nabokov), is to assume that metafiction did not exist before postmodernism, when of course there has always been such a reflexive quality in the greatest books of fiction—from, say, *Don Quixote* to *Absalom, Absalom!*. To assume that metafiction is absent from the work of Eudora Welty (the greatest living American writer?), for example, would blind oneself to one of the most permanent ingredients in literature. Indeed, like subversion, metafiction might even turn into a standard of literary evaluation. This book clearly was written not to please the many, but to be a (somewhat difficult, and admittedly personal) companion-guide to contemporary American fiction aimed at the happy few who are already in the know. As such, and even though one may not share all of Chénetier's enthusiasms (or react with a strong sense of reservation toward the idea of "progress" in literature, which is implicit here), the book is nothing less than remarkable—as will be made clear to Americans when the English translation is published.

Also bravely (as well as briefly, simply, and usefully) devoted to postmodern fiction in general is "Ecritures américaines des années 1980, L'héritage de la métafiction: liberté et contraintes" (*TLE* 7: 111–16), in which Noelle Batt seeks to take her bearings and assess what it is that has changed in fiction from the time of positivistic realism, and what the prospects are—whether in the '90s "scientists and writers will be able to combine their models and metaphors, their metaphors and their models, in order to produce discursive systems capable of endowing with form and figure our new way of being-in-the-world." Her attempt at generalization is preceded by a remarkably competent and intelligent study of the technique of Grace Paley in *Enormous Changes at the Last Minute*. In "Raconter à voix nue" ["Telling with a Naked Voice"] (*TLE* 7:99–110), Chantal Delourme proposes that Paley's unmistakable originality may lie in withdrawing "her narratives from specular appropriations in order to return them to listening." It is significant that a study of another writer who, like Paley, can be considered as one of the direct parents of American postmodernism should also be centered on voice. In " 'Building the Clutter': Conversation, dialogue, voix dans *JR* et *Carpenter's Gothic* de William Gaddis" (*RANAM* 21[1988]:29–39), Brigitte Félix demonstrates in almost everyday language that the *JR* and *Carpenter's Gothic* are really "music scores for voices." Another pioneer (*The Floating Opera* was published in 1956, one year after *The Recognitions*, two before *The Little Disturbances of Man*, three before *The Naked Lunch*) is John Barth, whose *Lost in the Funhouse* is the subject of two articles, " 'Glossolalia' de John Barth: variations sur un air secret," in *Les Cahiers de Fontenay* ("Mémoire et création": 61–72), in which Chénetier delivers what might be a rather discouraging message when he tells us that in the end the story signifies "Run, there is nothing to be seen"; and a no less difficult (nor less facetious—see the title, a reference to Einstein's reported question: "Do you really believe that the moon exists only when you look at it?") longer article by Marie Blaise, "De l'existence de la lune: post-modernisme et rédemption" (*Delta* 27:65–80), a fine meditation on the part played by the gaze in postmodern fiction, which (she says) should be looked at like a painting. Also fine and less difficult are two articles on William Gass. "La liberté de l'artiste dans la prison du langage" (*TLE* 7:129–36), by Claire Maniez, concludes that to Gass the aim of language is more than just "consolation," as implied in the title of Arthur Saltzman's book; it is "the capture of consciousness" (a statement Poe would not deny). And in "Les métamorphoses des stalactites: 'Icicles' de W. H. Gass" (*Delta* 27:55–64), Isabelle Bastrenta uses Heidegger as a convincing guide to a literature restored to its true "ontological" function. In "Metaphors of Reading and Writing in William H. Gass's Short Stories" (*NLA* 5:81–89), Maniez examines two stories from *In the Heart of the Heart of the Country*, "Order of Insects" and "Mrs. Mean." Next by date of birth is Guy Davenport, perhaps the one writer who most conspicuously resorts to "mélange des genres" or, as Laurence Zachar puts it more fashionably in her mostly descriptive "Guy Davenport: une mosaïque de genres. Emprunts à l'universal et écriture personnelle" (*RANAM* 21:51–63), to "generic hybridation." Under the same heading can be placed Chénetier's "Plaisirs coupables [Guilty Pleasures]: graphisme et langage dans l'oeuvre de Donald Barthelme," published in *La Lettre et la figure: la littérature et les arts visuels à l'époque moderne*, ed. Wolfgang Dröst and Géraldi Leroy (Winter), pp. 158–76, which self-explanatorily studies the relationship between text and illustrations in "At the Tolstoi Museum," a story in *Come Back, Dr. Caligari.* (But why aren't quotations always given in the original language, especially when dealing with such verbal writers as the postmodernists?) Chénetier again, in two articles in English and on the same subject—"Why William S. Wilson doesn't write like Franz Kafka: The Story as Operation" (*NLA* 5:255–65) and "Paul Cézanne & William S. Wilson vs. Franz Kafka" (*TLE* 7:117–28), the second a more systematic and more leisurely version of the first—argues that Wilson is an important writer in spite of his minimal production because his works are, like Cézanne's, "reports on his rapport with the world"; they can be called epistemological fictions. The youngest of the postmodern writers is Annie Dillard, whose *Teaching a Stone to Talk: Expeditions and Encounters* was published in 1982. In "Constructing the Artificial Obvious" (*RANAM* 21[1988]:41–49), Ruth Torrent rather inconclusively develops the argument that "Dillard's constructions . . . pose special critical problems." In particular, it is difficult to understand why a sophisticated critic of postmodernism should still use with such innocence the category of realism. One who was a major agent in the shattering of modernist tradition in 1959 was William Burroughs, on whose main novel a student, Pascal Michelucci, has written a simple but endearing essay, "Esprits de corps: *The Naked Lunch* de William Burroughs," in *Métaphore* (18: 99–117), a number devoted to "S[cience] F[iction] et surréalisme" (Centre d'Etude de la Métaphore, Nice).

No less than four studies have been devoted to a whale among minnows—Thomas Pynchon's *Gravity's Rainbow*. One, probably drawn from her doctoral dissertation, is fairly long and general and clear and useful. Bénédicte Chorier's "Thomas Pynchon ou la subversion de l'ordre de la mort" (*Delta* 27:81–126) begins by picking up on the writer's question: "Is it O.K. to be a Luddite?" in order to take the "preterite"—in Pynchon's vocabulary the Badass—as her guide into the novel, particularly into Tyrone Slothrop's itinerary in a world in which death is ever-present ("When we speak of 'seriousness' in fiction, ultimately we are talking about an attitude toward death," Pynchon writes in *Slow Learner*). In the end it appears that the preterite are paranoiacs terrified by the "They-system," that the Luddite subversion is a gross, collective refusal of rationality, and that death itself is ambivalent, as it is "pitted against death in a reversal in which decadence operates as a brake to the fall." What Chorier says in passing on Pynchon's borrowings from Rilke's Orpheus sonnets as well as on his use of Henry Adams's predicament seems excellent to me. Much lesser in scope is her "Arc-en-ciel, arc-en-terre: une métaphore chez Thomas Pynchon" (*TLE* 7:91–97), in which she tries to do justice to the double metaphor in the title of Pynchon's third novel, comparing it with the central metaphor in *V.* Next is an article by Regine Rosenthal, "*Gravity's Rainbow*" (*RFEA* 42:407–26), designed "to place Slothrop in the picaresque tradition" and to show "how he relates to the problem of identity." As one can imagine, not only is it found that "Slothrop's redemption does not materialize," but that "by his identity diffusion [he] has reached an entropic state of the highest possible disorder. . . . The postmodern picaro does not survive in his identity but in a diversification and a fragmentation of the self." The last article, Ann Battesti's " 'And It All Goes Along to the Same Jolly Song': Chansons et poèmes dans *Gravity's Rainbow*" (*RANAM* 21:5–12), is a study of the 68 songs or song fragments scattered somewhat disconcertingly through the novel, the conclusion of which, "Orpheus [is] dismembered" (without as much as a reference to Ihab Hassan), is a bit of a showdown.

f. **Poetry.** By distinguishing four parts and two dimensions (the verticality of nature in trees and the horizontality of time in the river) in the poem, William J. Scheick in "The Theme, Structure, and Symbolism of Anne Bradstreet's 'Contemplations' " (*Americana* 4:147–56) can make out the presence of "an emblem of the cross" informing all three categories of the title. Two articles are devoted to Philip Freneau in the same number. In "Héroïsation et révolution dans la poésie de Freneau" (*Americana* 4:161–74), Jean Béranger accomplishes what his title announces; he also shows how changing, to say the least, was the light in which the American poet considered Louis XVI, for example. Robert Sayre's title, however (" 'Romantisme anticapitaliste' et révolution chez Freneau," pp. 175–86), does not exactly describe his argument; there are *two* visions in Freneau's work (both prose and poetry). One is commanded by the Erklärung, and the other is the romantic, anticapitalist vision, whose social radicalism might explain why Freneau is more or less neglected in the United States. The next two poets under consideration were writing before and after the Civil War. Nathalie Hind seeks the success of William Grayson's "*The Hireling and the Slave*: la littérature au service de l'idéologie" (*Caliban* 26:21–29) not only in the fact that, as Rouberol put it in his book *Les Sudistes* (1971), it was to upholders of slavery what *Uncle Tom's Cabin* was to abolitionists, but in the choice of a neoclassic poetic form. Is this not precisely, however, what makes it unreadable nowadays—even more so than Freneau's poetry?

Sidney Lanier sounds much nearer to us. With *The Marshes of Glynn*, according to Michel Barrucand in "Sidney Lanier: Les Hymnes aux marais" (*Caliban* 26:65–80), he wrote a description of nature marked not only by a decided transcendental strain, but with a highly elaborate pattern of sounds. About the same time, Emily Dickinson was building what has become a monument of American poetry. In "Le Style oral d'Emily Dickinson" (*RFEA* 42:385–94), Antoine Cazé, finding support no less in linguists such as Roland Barthes and Claude Hagège than in scholars such as Robert Weisbuch, Claude Richard, and Philippe Jaworski, makes the point that the oral style was for Dickinson "a means of efficiently turning her mystical crises into so many 'crises du vers' (Mallarmé)." Dickinson is also present in Massimo Bacigalupo's sweeping review of what is perhaps the most pregnant tradition in American literature—Transcendentalism, or "Romanticism in a Puritan setting." In " 'Life Is an Ecstasy': A Transcendentalist Theme in Whitman, Pound, and Other American Poets" (*Interspace* 3[1987]:107–20), he traces both the preoccupation with "the nature of consciousness" and a consistent concern with ecstasy from Emerson to Whitman to Dickinson, and then, perhaps most originally, even though "Pound has not been usually aligned with the Transcendentalist cluster," to *The Cantos*, especially the Pisan Cantos.

Written in impeccable French, "Wallace Stevens: la violence du dedans contre la violence du dehors" (*Visages de l'angoisse*, pp. 101–12) proves Nancy Blake to be a much better critic than she is a translator (but again, as with Chénetier, why should all the quotations be translated?). Alain Suberchicot has written a fitting introduction to a body of poetry almost unknown in France in "Lieux de plénitude et de vacuité dans l'oeuvre poétique de William Bronk" (*RFEA* 42: 373–83). Finally, in two remarkably spare articles, Antoine Cazé has described two poetic experiences that can equally be placed on the limit: one, in which he studies the prose of *Three Poems*, is entitled "Positions de John Ashbery" (*TLE* 7:83–90); the other, "Poésie, texte métisse: une lecture de David Antin" (*RANAM* 21:21–28), explains Antin's performances as interfaces (between the provisional and the naming), and the poet's activity as "talking at the boundaries." The two studies on Ginsberg published in *Americana* 3 are strictly designed for the Agrégation students: Colette Gerbaud's "L'un et le multiple, ou unité et multiplicité dans *Howl, Kaddish*, et autres poèmes d'Allen Ginsberg" (pp. 107–22) is a review of the main themes of the poetry, and Michèle Wolf's "Kaddish: A Socio-religious Enquiry" (pp. 123–34) is one more interpretation of the poem through biography and the history of Jewish immigration to New York. It is better to fall back on the poet himself, as he can be candid as well as wry, in Yves Le Pellec's (third) interview with Allen Ginsberg published as "A Collage of Voices" in *RFEA* (39:91–110).

g. Theatre. Apart from a study (mostly in genetic terms, as blueprints for the novels) by Patricia Bleu-Schwenninger of the three plays written by John Dos Passos in the late '20s and early '30s as "Dos Passos et le théâtre de la révolte" (*RFEA* 40:201–12), all that was written on the theater in the United States was published by the

"Groupe de recherches sur les arts dramatiques anglophones contemporains" (Dijon) in *Coup de théâtre* 9. In "Rêve et réalité dans *Ah, Wilderness!* d'Eugene O'Neill, ou l' 'intermède' comique" (pp. 55–67), Colette Gerbaud analyzes the status of the play in the playwright's career; her article is well-informed. Liliane Kerjan offers a slight but lively review of Cynthia Heimel's 1986–87 success off-Broadway with *A Girl's Guide to Chaos*, here called "Les Joyeuses commères de New York [*The Merry Wives of New York*]" (pp. 69–75). And Claude Coulon begins with some analysis, but ends with a mere review of the highlights in the history of the musical comedy: "Cavalcade ou notes pour l'histoire de la comédie musicale américaine" (pp. 77–84).

h. **Ethnic Literature.** Michel Fabre provides the usual wealth of information, reports, abstracts, and reviews on both Afro-American and "new" (i.e., former Commonwealth) literatures in his hastily printed but useful *AFRAM Newsletter.* Number 30 (November) has a long review of James Coleman's 1989 book on John Edgar Wideman (pp. 20–28) by Jacqueline Berben, also the author of "Towards a Black Realization of the Hegelian Ideal: John Edgar Wideman's *Homewood*" (*Cycnos* 4:43–48). Although she admits she cannot prove it, Berben is convinced of the identity of "the lament for the lost ideal community" in both writers. There are two contributions on the American black woman in *Les Etats-Unis: images du travail et des loisirs [Work and Leisure in the United States]* (GRENA, Aix-en-Provence). One, Wolfgang Binder's " 'O, ye daughters of Africa, awake! awake! arise . . .': The Functions of Work and Leisure in Female Slave Narratives" (pp. 127–44), is well-informed (see the bibliography), though perhaps more interesting through the problem of sources raised than through its conclusion: "Any way and anywhere we look in these slave narratives by black women . . . work occupies a central position, as a curse or as a source for dignity . . . ." The other is Hélène Christol's " 'The Black Woman's Burden': Black Women and Work in *The Street* (Ann Petry) and *Brown Girl, Brownstones* (Paule Marshall)" (pp. 145–58).

   The second of two successive issues of *Annales du CRAA,* number 14, this time subtitled "Temps, Mythe et Histoire," is again entitled *Multilinguisme et multiculturalisme en Amérique du Nord,* since it chooses to juxtapose the study of cultures and languages in the U.S. other than WASP and English. In the programmatic words of Yves-

Charles Granjeat (who, oddly enough, introduces the volume on pp. 185–89), "interculturality is at work in literature." This is shown in 14 articles—the same number as last year, and by the same authors, albeit on different writers (except for Serge Ricard, who writes on Villareal). The same remark must be made about the end and means of such a publication; since it is aimed primarily at information, its authors are too often content with plot summaries, without caring too much for a problematic.

No less than six of these essays are devoted to Chicano (or Latin American) literature. Suzanne Durruty writes on *"Nambe Year One* d'Orlando Romero"* (pp. 7–17), an autobiographical novel written by a New Mexican (with Indian blood, however) about the relationship between a New Mexico village and the narrator growing into adulthood. Christian Lerat has chosen to write about the first three stories of a collection published in Spanish in 1964 and in translation in 1971: "Le Retour aux sources de Sabine Ulibarri dans *Tierra Amarilla*" (pp. 33–43). Again, the subject is the young narrator's adventures. In "Tradition et révolution dans *The Fifth Horseman* de José Antonio Villareal" (pp. 59–71), Serge Ricard writes of the book that it is "as of today the only book devoted by a Chicano writer to the revolution of 1910," only to point out immediately that the writer was born in the United States of Mexican-born parents, went to Berkeley and to UCLA, is now a Mexican citizen living in Mexico— but insists on writing in English. As its subtitle indicates, the article is a study of the "odyssey of Heraclio Ines," a peon who becomes a hero by joining Pancho Villa. The trouble with the novel—as with so many Chicano writings, according to the author—is style. In "Palimpseste sur un inceste: *Graveyard of the Angels* de Reinaldo Arenas" (pp. 157–69), Jean Cazemajou describes the novel as a parody of *Cecilia Valdès* (1882) by Cirilo Villaverde and sees in it "a modernist achievement as concise and abrasive as a black humor comic strip." The other two articles are more theoretical, bearing on the *Plan Espiritual de Aztlan,* or "the manifesto in which the Chicano cultural nationalism originates," as Yves-Charles Grandjeat writes in his "Idéologie, Mythe et Histoire: les masques d'Aztlan" (pp. 85–94). As the only possible mediator, the Chicano intellectual attempted to deliver a narrative "capable of symbolically producing the Chicano nation," and Aztlan became a key symbol to usher in a revival of indigenous cultures. The article briefly analyzes how Luis

Valdez and the Teatro Campesino have shown that the myth in fact acts "as a bridge towards the dominant society it had formally excluded." In "Les Vicissitudes d'Aztlan" (pp. 73–84), Elyette Andouard-Labarthe chimes in with the idea that Alurista's Aztlan is a creation of the intellectual Chicano elite and concludes that "Aztlan can only endure since it exists in spite of the fighting, the difference, the absence of Aztlan."

There are also four essays on Italian culture. Robert Rougé writes on "Louis Forgione and *The River Between*: A Story of Water and Fire" (pp. 45–57); Nicole Bensoussan on "La Femme, creuset du temps [Woman as the Crucible of Time] dans *The Fortunate Pilgrim* de Mario Puzo" (pp. 135–42); Jean-Michel Lacroix on "L'itinéraire des Italo-Québecois dans l'espace montréalais: L'aventure des Editions Guernica" (pp. 143–56); and Jean Béranger on "John Fante: refus et acceptation du passé dans le cycle Molise" (pp. 171–84). Also self-explanatory are the titles of two articles devoted to Native American writing, "Naanabozho contre Chronos ou les ambiguités de l'histoire chez [Gerald] Vizenor" (pp. 19–31), in which Bernadette Rigal-Cellard concentrates on the "narrative histories" of *The People Named the Chippewa* (1984), and "Louise Erdrich recueille les miettes de son héritage [picks up the crumbs of her heritage] dans *Love Medicine*," by Elisabeth Béranger (pp. 121–33), in which both *Huckleberry Finn* and *As I Lay Dying* are evoked. The last two minorities to be the subjects of articles are the Greeks, with Nicole Ollier's "*Eleni* [1983] de Nicholas Gage [Nikola Gatzoviannis]: Antigone ou Hécube? *Orestie* ou *Odyssée?*" (pp. 95–108), and—unexpectedly—the Jews, with Ginette Castro's "*Anya* de Susan Fromberg Schaeffer ou le rachat du temps [or Buying Back Time]" (pp. 109–20).

i. **The Short Story.** There are two "centres de recherche," two journals, and two parallel tendencies to organize symposia with mostly Anglo-American participants and publish the proceedings almost exclusively in English. One of the two has precedence in time. *JSSE* has been published at the University of Angers by founding editors Ben Forkner and C. Pamela Valette in the spring and autumn of each year since 1983. Not only are the three numbers at hand (10, 11, and 12) all in English, but only three of 22 articles in them are by non-Americans. I am not necessarily thinking of French scholars, since the magazine should clearly invite as many European contributors as possible.

However, has it not simply become one more American journal, with
the former French title "Les Cahiers de la nouvelle" now a mere
subtitle, and with the only difference that it is published abroad?
The problems with the periodical *La Nouvelle de langue anglaise*
(*NLA*), published (with the English subtitle "The Short Story")
somewhat irregularly by Claire Larrière and the "Centre de Recherches sur la nouvelle de langue anglaise" at the University of
Paris III, are the same (only four of the nine French out of 29
participants in the 1988 symposium offer their essays in French)
and different (the interest is less with America than with England
and the former Commonwealth). In no. 4 (1988), "L'Illusion" and all
in French, only Danièle Pitavy-Souques has written on an American
topic. In "Du Tulle Illusion [A Gauze Named Illusion]: 'Old Mr.
Marblehall' de Eudora Welty" (*NLA* 4:83–99), she uses the tools
offered by structuralism (especially by Gérard Genette) to analyze
the paradigmatic nature of this "variation upon the art of writing
about nothing"—by which she may well be forcing poor Eudora
Welty into the role of pre-postmodern. No. 5 (also 1988), "Rencontres
internationales," is almost entirely in English, and the expected summary is not always in the other language (even worse, some titles
are in French in the table of contents, when they and the essays are
in English in the text!). Apart from Claire Maniez's already reviewed
article on Gass's stories, there are three contributions on American literature, all by Americans. In "Richard Wright's 'Long Black Song':
A Moral Dilemma" (*NLA* 5:71–77), Joyce Ann Joyce vindicates the
character of Sarah: she, not Silas her husband, is "our center of consciousness." In "Worlds Spinning Within Worlds: *Unanimism* in
Waldo Frank's *City Block* and Jean Toomer's *Cane*" (*NLA* 5:129–35),
Charles Scruggs starts from both the evidence of the influence of
Jules Romains's *unanimisme* on *City Block* and from Robert Bone's
remark that the "French connection" exists in both *City Block* and
Cane and that Frank was responsible for the presence of *unanimisme*
in *Cane*. However, he shows that the key to understanding *Cane*'s
connection with *City Block* and to Toomer's conception of *unanimisme* lies in the image of the circle. Douglas D. Hesse devotes his
essay to "Defining the Short Story: A Demonstration Using William
Carlos Williams' *Doctor Stories*" (*NLA* 5:275–85)) and finds that
the medium was chosen for the "translucence" it allows.

   In the Spring 1988 issue of the other "French" journal on the
short story in English, one finds the same Charles Scruggs writing,

though at much greater length, on "Textuality and Vision in Jean Toomer's *Cane*" (*JSSE* 10:93–114), with the same conclusion that, as he wrote to Sherwood Anderson (whose rather obvious part in the genesis of *Cane* is dealt with here), art to Toomer had "a sort of religious function." The other contribution to be noted is Peter E. Firchow's "The Americanness of the American Short Story" (*JSSE* 100:45–66). The author bravely attempts what at least 28 authors he cites have done before him; needless to say, he ends up with the somewhat disappointing suggestion that only by teaching the American short story in China did he teach himself how American was the short story he was teaching. The next number was a special issue devoted to "Short Story Cycles," under the "quest" (a delightful misprint!) editorship of J. Gerald Kennedy, who wrote the introduction. Richard Dilworth Rust contributes a slight, rather obvious article on the motif of liminality in Hawthorne: "*Twice-Told Tales* at the Threshold" (*JSSE* 11:27–36). John Lowe, who has read Bakhtin, Barthes, Genet, Lukács, and Ricoeur, writes at length on "Wright Writing Reading: Narrative Strategies in *Uncle Tom's Children*" (*JSSE* 11:49–74). Susan V. Donaldson, who has read Derrida as well as the best American and French critics of her author, offers her "Meditations on Nonpresence: Re-visioning the Short Story Cycle in Eudora Welty's *The Wide Net*" (*JSSE* 11:75–91). On the occasion of a reissue of the French translation (one of the last works done by Maurice Edgar Coindreau), Paul Carmignani has written a brief review of Shelby Foote's "*Jordan County*: Going Back to the Roots" (*JSSE* 11:93–98) as an exploration (and merciless exposition) of the sources of evil, which he thinks the author sees, like Paul Ricoeur, not in being but in doing. The number closes on Robert M. Luscher's examination of "John Updike's *Olinger Stories*: New Light Among the Shadows" (*JSSE* 11:99–117). The collection is seen as "a progressive ceremony of farewell." The next issue of the journal has only one title for us. In "The Idea of an Audience in the Short Stories of Zora Neale Hurston and Alice Walker" (*JSSE* 12:33–44), Mary Jarrett traces the presence of an implied audience (black or white).

Université Paris VII

iii. German Contributions

Rolf Meyn

Nineteen eighty-nine was a good year for German scholars. A number of monographs, joint ventures, dissertations, and some interesting articles cover American literature from colonial times to the present, although, as usual, 20th-century studies predominate. Bi-national and comparative studies were more frequent than in past years.

a. **Literary Criticism and Theory: Comparative Studies.** A good illustration of a truly multinational endeavor is Franz Link, ed., *Paradeigmata. Literarische Typologie des Alten Testaments* (Berlin: Duncker & Humblot). The 45 contributions to this two-volume enterprise are concerned, as Link explains in his introduction, with basic patterns and types of the Old Testament as they have reappeared in Christian-Occidental literature since its beginnings. The essays in volume I cover examples from early Christian literature to the end of the 19th century, and volume II is entirely devoted to the 20th. Of the essays dealing with American literature, Ursula Brumm's "Der Typ des Moses in den Meditationen von Edward Taylor" (pp. 299–308) focuses on Moses as a prefiguration of Christ in Edward Taylor's meditations. Hans Galinsky follows suit with his "Typologisches Deuten zwischen kolonialem Puritanismus und Frühaufklärung. Drei Proben aus dem Lebenswerk Benjamin Tompsons (1642–1714)" (pp. 309–22), using typology to illustrate Tompson's mediating position between Puritanism and Enlightenment. Uwe Baumann's "Herman Melvilles *Moby-Dick* und das Alte Testament" (pp. 411–29) is a courageous venture, given that so much has been written on Melville's religious typology. Yet this essay really succeeds in incorporating most of that criticism; by concentrating on "Job's Whale" and Ahab as an inverted Christ figure of satanic dimensions, Baumann contributes something substantial to this realm.

Discussions of religious typology in 20th-century American literature begin with Bernd Engler's "Der 'doppelte' Sündenfall ins menschliche Selbstbewusst-Sein: Alttestamentliche Typologie in Dramen Archibald MacLeishs, Howard Nemerovs, Arthur Millers und Jean-Claude van Itallies" (pp. 591–609). Engler assumes that these dramatists created antitypes of Old Testament figures and by showing typological relations added new dimensions to understanding the archetypes. The biblical Fall and the dramatized Fall are seen as a myth containing the fall into self-consciousness. Helen Hagenbüchle reexamines John Steinbeck's most ambitious novel in "Die Kainsgeschichte in *East of Eden*: John Steinbecks Plädoyer für Selbstverantwortung und Selbstverwirklichung" (pp. 629–50). She holds that *East of Eden* is the last great 20th-century novel using the Bible as a metatext that structures and interprets the fictional text and is in turn interpreted by it. Paul Goetsch's "Die Sintfluterzählung in der modernen englischsprachigen Literatur" (pp. 651–705) is a bi-national essay that discusses recent versions of the Flood theme in English and American drama, poetry, and prose. Manfred Siebald scrutinizes "Archibald MacLeish's *J.B.* und das Buch Hiob" (pp. 759–74). For Siebald, the affinities between *J.B.* and the Book of Job are far more intricate and complicated than hitherto seen. Link turns to Thornton Wilder in "Thornton Wilders Adam und Messias" (pp. 789–801). According to Link, Wilder was drawn to biblical typology because he wanted to put religious questions in modern forms, that is, by fusing biblical and Greek myths and creating antitypes to the already existing ones he intended to explain modern man's existential situation. The book ends with a series of overviews. Konrad Gross in "Die Deutung des Alten Testaments in der afro-amerikanischen Literatur" (pp. 817–30) discusses examples of black literature from Phillis Wheatley to Toni Morrison, thereby illustrating a development that extends from assimilative acquirement and transformation of the Bible (into spirituals, etc.) to rejection as a meaningful frame (since Richard Wright). Kurt Müller singles out E. L. Doctorow's *The Book of Daniel* and Bernard Malamud's *God's Grace* in "Biblische Typologie im zeitgenössischen jüdisch-amerikanischen Roman" (pp. 831–51) to show that in contrast to the self-reflexive, playful texts of many of their postmodern contemporaries, these authors cling to a moral vision in spite of epistemological uncertainty and skepticism. An excellent summary ends the book, which will be the most comprehensive study of literary Old Testament typology for some years to come.

Quite a different undertaking is Jens-Peter Becker's *Das Automobil und die amerikanische Kultur* (Trier: Wissenschaftlicher Verlag). It is certainly not surprising that Becker had to be extremely selective. His examples range from highbrow literature to road movies, popular songs, and pop art. His main focus, however, is on literature. His book deals with the automobile in poetry and popular songs, in fiction (with a special emphasis on Fitzgerald's *The Great Gatsby*), in road movies from the 1950s on, and in painting, photography, and advertisements from 1900 to the 1980s. Movie stills, rare car designs, and reproductions of funny ads complete a highly individualistic study, which is a valuable contribution and offers ample opportunity for further research in American studies. For Fitzgerald scholars, Becker's comments on the role of the automobile in *The Great Gatsby* should be of special interest.

Another bi-national and comparative study I did not mention last year is Konrad Weiss's *Der anglo-amerikanische Universitätsroman. Eine historische Studie* (Darmstadt: Wissenschaftliche Buchgesellschaft, 1988). It is a condensed but exhaustive overview of the history of the college novel both in England and in America. Weiss begins with medieval works such as Nigel de Longchamp's *Speculum Speculorum* (ca. 1180) and Chaucer's *Canterbury Tales*, but his main interest is the 19th and 20th centuries. For him, Hawthorne's *Fanshawe* (1828) is the first American college novel. Until the end of the century, Harvard and, to a lesser degree, Yale and Princeton provided the settings. Then, more provincial colleges of the West were often favorably compared to the decadent East Coast universities. As Weiss shows, in contrast to England university education in the United States had to compete with two other powerful educational ideals, namely, the mystic experience of life in nature (as in Emerson's "The American Scholar") or the active work life in a democratic society. After 1900, college novels often became Bildungsromane, as in Owen M. Johnson's *Stover at Yale* (1912), whose protagonist had to reconcile society with university. This tradition ended in the 1940s, only to make room for financial, psychological, and, most important, sexual problems of campus life, presented realistically, comically, or satirically. Weiss's thesis is that democratization on both sides of the Atlantic was responsible for the discovery of the professor as a literary figure: if he worked in the humanities, he often appeared as a problematic character, since he constantly had to justify his work in a materialistic world or was in danger of falling prey to ideology. His position was even more precarious when he became the prime target of a rebellious student generation in the late 1960s. The college novels of the 1970s frequently depicted the university as a utopian experiment where "revolutionary" scientists like Malcolm Bradbury's Howard Kirk in *The History Man* (1975) saw themselves in the vanguard of anti–bourgeois changes in society. According to Weiss, a new type of professor appears in more recent college novels. It is the world traveler who like the figures in David Lodge's *Small World* (1984) belongs to what is commonly known as "the academic jet set." Weiss's concise study concludes with an appendix in which he briefly touches on the role of women, the academic detective novel, and elements of fantasy and science fiction in college fiction. Further research on the Anglo-American college novel, wherever it is done, will be incomplete without considering this stimulating book.

Klaus Lanzinger's *Jason's Voyage* is a different kind of comparative study. Lanzinger explores the effect of the Grand Tour on Melville, Hawthorne, James, and Wolfe. He starts from the familiar assumption that the intellectual foundations of the American writers' ambivalent encounters with Europe were "the two antithetical concepts of (1) the democratic bias and (2) the cultural myth of the Old World." In Lanzinger's opinion, Melville kept a critical distance from the Old World until the very end of his writing career. Hawthorne was the first American to fully develop the Old Home theme, the search for the ancestral home in the old country. Lanzinger also thinks that in the end Hawthorne included Italy and Rome in his idea of the Old Home in Europe. Hawthorne also prepared the way for the international novel that James and the following generation of American writers were to write. James created the figure of the "Passionate Pilgrim," who came to Europe full of illusions of the Old World and with a thirst for aesthetic indulgence. But it was Wolfe who in Lanzinger's eyes created international novels that excelled all previous works of this kind because Wolfe was able to endow the American pilgrim in Europe with a new poetic voice. Lanzinger, however, does not deal with Wolfe's *You Can't Go Home Again*, in which the protagonist returns as a disillusioned pilgrim from a Europe that is threatened by a barbaric totalitarianism.

A book I should have reviewed last year is Alfred Weber and Bettina Friedl, eds., *Film und Literatur in Amerika* (Darmstadt: Wissenschaftliche Buchgesellschaft, 1988). All 11 of the essays in this collection start from the assumption that a film is a special kind of narrative or that it is related to drama. Literature adapted to movies is discussed in most of the essays. In his general remarks on this theme (pp. 21–44), Johann N. Schmidt points to the tendency to break down the barriers between high and popular culture in films. He also reminds us that the pioneers of the modern cinema—Chaplin, Keaton, Fairbanks, among others—received their training as actors in the circus and vaudeville, where emotions grow out of body gestures. Thus, the modes of perception and illusion in film are situated somewhere between the theater and narrative fiction. Any adaptation of literary works to film, however, is embedded in a structure that reflects the historical dimensions of the genre or is subjected to a director's predilections, as in the case of Visconti, who in all his adaptations of James M. Cain, di Lampedusa, or D'Annunzio emphasizes the theme of family decay. Ultimately, a film is an art form in its own right, which should not be judged against the foil of a literary work but only compared to it. This is what Paul Goetsch does in his essay (pp. 45–64). He selects a few well-known examples—Michael Anderson's *1984*, Edward Dmytryk's *The Caine Mutiny*, Fred Zinnemann's *From Here to Eternity*, and Miloš Forman's *One Flew Over the Cuckoo's Nest*—to show that it is impossible for a director to follow a literary work step-by-step and imitate it truthfully. Instead, he has to destroy the novel, the short story, or the drama to produce his film, using the literary work simultaneously as model, inspiration, and material. Christine N. Brinckmann turns to a special comparison—that between a first-person singular narrative and its counterpart in film (pp. 65–95). She chooses Jim McBride's *David Holzman's Diary* (1967) to demonstrate how a first-person singular point of view can be successfully employed in a film. She then turns to more popular examples in which a subjective camera dominates—Robert Montgomery's adaptation of Chandler's *Lady in the Lake* (1947), Alfred Hitchcock's version of Daphne du Maurier's *Rebecca* (1940), and Orson Welles's *Lady from Shanghai* (1947).

No book dealing with American film should be without a discussion of Welles's *Citizen Kane*. Here it is provided most competently by Winfried Fluck (pp. 96–118), who interprets the film as a cultural text. He emphasizes that the plot is comparable to Fitzgerald's *The Great Gatsby*, and like it is not just the story of a tycoon, but, as the film's original title, *The American*, hints, another attempt at cultural self-exploration. As a film, *Citizen Kane* proves that forms of popular culture do not exist as contradictions to highbrow literature, but as supplements in a cultural nexus of communication. This view is supported by Jan-Christopher Horak's essay on the silent film (pp. 119–34), which is also a plea for the study of silent film adaptations of literature. Horak especially praises Cooper's *The Last of the Mohicans* as "one of the greatest literature/film adaptations of the silent era." In contrast to Horak, Klaus W. Vowe's contribution (pp. 135–51) is limited to a short-lived phenomenon of the '30s, the "Contemporary Historians, Inc.," a group of left-wing writers and directors including

Joris Ivens, Lillian Hellman, and Dorothy Parker. Vowe analyzes their best-known product, Ivens and Hemingway's propaganda documentary film *Spanish Earth*. However, Vowe's Marxist conclusion that the Contemporary Historians "partly gave up their petty-bourgeois artist mentality and so changed themselves and the world" is, in light of the Hitler-Stalin Pack of 1939, rather one-eyed and optimistic. Marc L. Ratner's exploration of George Stevens's translation of Theodore Dreiser's *An American Tragedy* into the movie *A Place in the Sun* (1951) (pp. 152–70) is full of admiration for Stevens, because, Ratner maintains, it probably took a great deal of courage to make a social tragedy of American life at the high tide of American domestic anticommunism.

Peter Bauland's reflections on the popular hero in American drama and film (pp. 171–88) culminate in the thesis that although a Gary Cooper, John Wayne, or Humphrey Bogart, all endowed with Anglo-Saxon backgrounds and a keen sense of justice, have been replaced by Western heroes and detectives of various ethnic origins, they share fierce independence, self-reliance, and a strict code of conduct. Bettina Friedl (pp. 189–212) focuses on Hollywood novels of the '30s—Fitzgerald's *The Last Tycoon* and the Pat Hobby stories, Nathanael West's *The Day of the Locust*, and Budd Schulberg's *What Makes Sammy Run?* She discovers in all of them the "basic assumption of a cultural degeneration through a cheap popularization of literature and the arts." This fine collection is concluded by an exhaustive bibliography and Alfred Weber's astute observations on the forms and functions of film scripts and their usefulness for students.

b. **Literary History.** A book of which I became aware belatedly is Franz Link's *Geschichte der amerikanischen Verskunst bis 1900* (Stuttgart: Kohlhammer, 1988). It contains the customary canon—from Anne Bradstreet, Edward Taylor, and Phillis Wheatley to the Genteel poets (Longfellow, Lowell, Holmes, Whittier) and the Transcendentalists (Emerson, Thoreau) as well as the "classic" poets Poe, Whitman, and Dickinson. A few lesser contemporaries conclude the book. Link provides the reader with concise introductions and illustrations of the literary and philosophical traditions underlying the works under consideration, but what makes this history really valuable are the many sensitive and thorough interpretations of the poems he selects. In contrast to Link's history, Wolfgang Karrer and Eberhard Kreutzer's *Werke der englischen und amerikanischen Literatur von*

1890 bis zur Gegenwart (Munich: Deutscher Taschenbuchverlag), the fourth and revised edition of a project first published in 1973, is far more comprehensive, containing brief discussions of the main works of British and American poetry, drama, and fiction. For students and readers in need of quick information, this comparative literary history will certainly be helpful; all the more so, since the book begins with brief, but by no means superficial, outlines of the main literary trends in both national literatures.

Definitely the most extensive recent discussion of American poetry of the 1960s is Ingrid Kerkhoff's *Poetiken und lyrischer Diskurs im Kontext gesellschaftlicher Dynamik—USA: "The Sixties"* (Frankfurt: Peter Lang). Kerkhoff begins by mapping the decade's socioeconomic, cultural, and ideological background. She believes the '60s were shaped by the "qualitatively new experience of a threatening holocaust," the result of a huge military-industrial complex Eisenhower had warned against. Equally important, she says, was the intellectual atmosphere of the '50s, which also affected the arts. She thinks the rejection of Marxism and the development of Stalinism, as well as the insecurity of the cold war, were responsible for creative impotence among poets in the 1950s. Although holding the cold war climate responsible for many cultural changes in the 1960s, she is aware of other phenomena, e.g., the blurring of boundaries between high culture and popular art, the emergence of alternative media, the nascent renaissance of feminism, and growing self-awareness of ethnic groups—all of them rooted in the repressive '50s. Kerkhoff then examines the decade's poetry as "suicidal art" (Robert Lowell, John Berryman, Sylvia Plath), as the poetry of the Black Mountain poets (Charles Olson, Robert Creeley, Robert Duncan, Denise Levertov), and as the New York school, which includes such diverse figures as Frank O'Hara, John Ashbery, Kenneth Koch, Barbara Guest, and James Schuyler. The Minnesota poets Robert Bly, James Wright, and William Duffy are treated in the next chapter, which includes the neosurrealists Robert Kelly and Jerome Rothenburg. James Dickey enjoys a chapter of his own, "The Poet as Convalescent: Animalism and Revitalization in the Poetry of the White Southerner James Dickey." Even more space is given to West Coast authors from Ginsberg and Ferlinghetti to Gary Snyder and Michael McClure. She turns to the "lyrical underground" as exemplified in the works of Charles Bukowski and D. E. Levy. One might argue that black, Chicano, Puerto Rican, Native American, and feminist poetry of this turbulent decade are too significant to be squeezed into the concluding four comparatively short chapters. I think, however, that on the whole Kerkhoff does an admirable job of presenting '6os' poetry in all its diversity as a product of historical and sociocultural influences.

The swan song of East German interpretations of American literature is probably Robert Weimann, ed., *Der nordamerikanische Roman 1880–1940. Repräsentation und Autorisation in der Moderne* (Berlin: Aufbauverlag). In three bulky chapters, Weimann outlines the traditional Marxist concept of modernism, enriched by some critical approaches (Lotman, Baudrillard) and Alfred Kazin's evergreen *On Native Grounds*. According to Weimann, the march into modernism began in the age of Emerson, born in a spirit of protest, criticism, and renewal. Yet the poetic discourse of Emerson's and Whitman's day, which still expressed a boundless trust in authors' ability to make the world their own, was deeply shaken by developments of the 1880s. National moral norms that had sustained American Romantics and Transcendentalists from Irving to Hawthorne disappeared under the onslaught of industrialization, commercialized culture, and imperialism. But even before the Civil War, Weimann asserts, American artists were outsiders who had to compete with the increasing trivialization of culture, a growing ideologization, and the pressures of conformity. More than artistic alienation, however, monopoly capitalism, the rise of Darwinism shattering the foundations of a theocratically ordered life, the catastrophe of World War I, and finally the Great Depression destroyed traditional authorities and middle-class consensus.

The other contributors to this collection remain within the editor's theoretical framework. Frederike Hajek's "Theodore Dreiser" (pp. 143–82) focuses on *Sister Carrie* and *An American Tragedy*. Carrie Meeber is seen as a creature of advertising and desire, while the strength of *An American Tragedy*, Hajek holds, is Dreiser's fictive discourse: in the end Clyde Griffiths is neither able to confess his guilt nor can he be sure of his salvation; thus, the reconciliation between individual and society is made impossible. Doris Dziwas and Utz Riese follow with a chapter on proletarian literature (pp. 183–238). But I doubt that their readings of Mike Gold's *Jews Without Money*, Jack Conroy's *The Disinherited*, Robert Cantwell's *The Land of Plenty*, William Rollins's *The Shadow Before*, and Henry Roth's *Call It Sleep* add insight to our understanding of American left literature. The same holds true for Günther Klotz's chapter on Dos Passos (pp. 239–84). Again, the focus is on the two most important works, *Manhattan Transfer* and *U.S.A.* Klotz, like most Marxist critics, is not interested in showing how in *U.S.A.* Dos Passos voiced his dissatisfaction with a dogmatic radicalism that was trying to impose new ideological restrictions on intellectuals and artists, who first and foremost wanted to escape from the conforming pressures of mass culture.

Riese's chapter on Hemingway (pp. 285–323) also reflects the Marxist view of him as a writer who always "tried to keep his tools clean." Riese celebrates the Hemingway of *A Farewell To Arms* and *For Whom the Bell Tolls* as a writer who despised the role of man of letters and aspired to the mass-culture image of a movie star or sports hero, but who above all became a committed antifascist in the later 1930s. Klotz's essay on Fitzgerald deals with the fascination and erosion of the American Dream in *The Great Gatsby*. In Klotz's opinion, no other American writer of the '20s and '30s sensitized his readers to the artificiality of that dream, the widening gap between sign and meaning, and the discrepancy between cliché and reality. It comes as quite a surprise to find a chapter on Faulkner by Riese (pp. 364–400) after that on Fitzgerald. But Riese plausibly explains why Faulkner cannot be left out of a volume concerned with the realist-naturalist tradition as a vital part of modernism. Faulkner's concept of literature, Riese argues, was also a concept of history, a "vision of history without alienation." Riese proceeds to Wolfe (pp. 401–28), who, though too young to belong to the Lost Generation, by temperament turned the language of being lost into the discourse of individual fulfillment. In his last work, *You Can't Go Home Again*, Wolfe moved away from this individualistic stance. The obvious failure of laissez-faire capitalism and the threat of fascism turned his eyes to the future of his country, which he envisioned as a socially and morally better America.

Hajek ends the book with an essay on the black novel between 1900 and 1940 (pp. 429–87). She briefly discusses novels by Paul Laurence Dunbar, Charles W. Chesnutt, W. E. B. DuBois, and Sutton E. Griggs before moving on to writers of the Harlem Renaissance, notably Jean Toomer and Claude McKay. The 1930s are tackled in part through Wright's *Native Son*. It is understandable that Hajek picks out special works to illustrate the three stages of modernism. But I think any Marxist interpretation of American literature that is concerned with a writer's attitude toward social or political crises should ponder why so many authors bitterly criticized their country, yet sooner or later came to reject any Marxist vision of a better society. So long as this question is avoided, as the contributors to this book so often do, there will not be any honest ideological discussion of the modernist phase in American literature.

c. **Colonial Literature.** Since I have already mentioned essays on colonial literature in connection with Link's *Paradeigmata*, there is only one more left to be briefly discussed. As every year, Hans Galinsky shows up with a contribution. His essay "Kolonialer Autor und 'geteilte' Leserschaft: Anfänge sprachlich-kulturell bearbeiteter amerikanischer Dichtung in zwei Londoner Ausgaben von Benjamin Tompsons Indianerkriegsepik" (*Wege amerikanischer Kultur*, pp. 1–45) deals with the differences in British and American editing and the different reception of an epic poem on the Indian Wars in England and the United States. Galinsky meticulously demonstrates how the description of a crisis situation in New England was linguistically adapted to the expectations and cultural conditions of the mother country as early as 1676.

d. **19th-Century Literature.** This chapter should fittingly start with Klaus Lubbers's "The Status of the Native American in Fourth of July Orations" (*Wege amerikanischer Kultur*, pp. 97–110). Lubbers points out that from the beginning "the native functioned not only as a stumbling block for Canaanites and Columbians," but sometimes even provided the orators with other models, e.g., Indian life as a state of freedom or the Indian as part of local history. The same volume contains an essay by Link (pp. 159–73) on the biblical image of "face to face" (as in Exod. 32:30 and elsewhere) as it was adapted by Emerson, Thoreau, Whitman, Dickinson, Stephen Crane, and various 20th-century writers.

Since the publisher refuses to send me review copies, I was not able to discuss Thomas Krusche's excellent *R. W. Emersons Naturauffassung und ihre philosophischen Ursprünge. Eine Interpretation des Emersonschen Denkens aus dem Blickwinkel des deutschen Idealismus* (Gunter Narr, 1987) earlier. Krusche begins with Emerson's Puritan roots and his indebtedness to the philosophy of John Locke and the Scottish school, then goes on to Transcendentalism in the context of the momentous changes in religion and philosophy of the early 19th century. The best part of the study is Krusche's evaluation of the influence of Carlyle, Coleridge, Jacobi, Kant, and Goethe on Emerson. Yet his analyses of Emerson's concept of nature and some of his most important essays are by no means inferior. Krusche ends with a chapter on Hegel's philosophy as a metaphysical system corresponding to the doctrine of evolution. Brief comments on Emerson's influence on Nietzsche, followed by a discussion of Harold Bloom's view of Emerson, conclude what I find one of the best Emerson studies of the past few years. Gudrun Grabher's "Adding to the Myths of *Moby-Dick*: The Question of Being as Shared by Existential and Oriental Philosophy" (*ArAA* 14:167–78) is an attempt to present a new mythological approach after summarizing various mythological interpretations. Grabher discovers in Ahab's hunt a quest for the nature of being that is based on a philosophy built on Far Eastern and modern existentialist worldviews. What Ahab fears is the indefiniteness of whiteness as a mystery, although not an evil one.

In recent years German scholars have been busy resurrecting Charles Sealsfield as a binational writer whose works are an indispensable part of American literature in the Jacksonian era. It is about time that American scholars rediscover a writer who was by no means only a minor disciple of Cooper, but an independent observer of the European and American scene and an ardent Jacksonian Democrat. An instructive achievement—and a solid basis for American scholars— is Alexander Ritter and Günter Schnitzler, eds., *Schriftenreihe der Charles-Sealsfield-Gesellschaft, Band IV* (Freiburg: Rombach). Of the seven essays contained in this book, four deal with Sealsfield as an American writer. Karl J. R. Arndt in his "Sealsfield-Postl als amerikanischer Dichter" (pp. 49–69) discloses that it was partly Sealsfield's own fault that he is almost unknown in the United States even today. He did not allow a reprint of his works because as a former Catholic priest he repented his defection and was afraid of the Church's attacks. Yet even Mencken paid tribute to Sealsfield's linguistic achievements. I wholeheartedly agree with Arndt that a reconsideration of Sealsfield as a worthy rival of Irving and Cooper is overdue in the United States. Franz Schüppen's essay on the moral and didactic dimensions of Sealsfield's view of the American (pp. 71–126) successfully brings out Sealsfield's qualities as an American writer compared with his German contemporaries Novalis, Mörike, Gotthelf, and Stifter. Alexander Ritter in his "Geschichten aus Geschichte. Charles Sealsfield's erzählerischer Umgang mit dem Historischen am Beispiel des Romans *Das Kajütenbuch*" (pp. 127–45) scrutinizes Sealsfield's best novel, *The Cabin Book*. Ritter holds that, though conceived as a Texan-American epic, *The Cabin Book* offers advice for the political future of Germany and Europe in general. Quite a different theme is taken up by Walter Grünzweig and Viviana N'Diaye in their "Vodoo im Biedermeier. Charles Sealsfields *Pflanzerleben* aus afroamerikanischer Sicht" (pp. 147–66). The authors interpret Sealsfield not as a defender of slavery but as a writer who skillfully undermines the Southern viewpoint. They think he did not openly take the abolitionist side because he had planned to return to Louisiana and so wanted to hide his aversion to slavery. Besides, he realized that a seemingly racist attitude would help him get a better reception in Germany.

Stephen Crane, Frank Norris, and Theodore Dreiser are dealt with in Jan Vester's stimulating essay *Wirklichkeit und Text/Wirklichkeit als Text. Exemplarische Studien zum amerikanischen Naturalismus* (Frankfurt: Peter Lang). Vester rejects the view that understands naturalism as an attempt to reflect reality and man as a bioteleologically determined being. Aside from the fact that no one ever deals with reality as such, but only with its historically (and hence, religiously, politically, economically, and aesthetically) conveyed forms, there is the problem that the representation of reality is always textual. In addition, there is the structure of "vertical socialization": man is no *homo sociologus*, but an individual on whom society imposes a role. Making use of Derrida's comments on textuality, Vester develops a model of social roles, which he applies to Crane's *Maggie, A Girl of the Streets*, Frank Norris's *McTeague*, and Dreiser's *Sister Carrie*. Although I am unable to see any of the characters in these novels as inner-directed types in David Riesman's sense, I agree with Vester's thesis that naturalism proves not the reality of a text but the textuality of reality.

e. **20th-Century Literature.** Udo J. Hebel's *Romaninterpretation als Textarchäologie. Untersuchungen zur Intertextualität am Beispiel von F. Scott Fitzgeralds* This Side of Paradise (Frankfurt: Peter Lang) attempts to exhaustively analyze Fitzgerald's novel with the help of intertextuality, allusions, and quotations. Hebel's book is a pioneering work. He begins with a long methodological discussion developing a comprehensive paradigm of allusion, based on the intertextuality theories of Barthes, Kristeva, and others. He then succinctly points out how a novel—or any literary text—becomes a point of intersection in the net of its textual and cultural-historical setting, whose textual manifestation can be the starting point of its reconstruction. It goes without saying that any textual analysis that follows Barthes and

focuses on lexical items as microelements of "intertextual allusions" is
a positivistic endeavor that largely consists of gathering quotations
and allusions. All these details help us see a writer's indebtedness to
tradition, other writers, or products of popular culture. But Hebel's
bulky volume proves how extensive we have to be, if we want to
properly place a novel-length text into the net of allusions. The book
ends with a 300-page appendix of 447 intertextual allusion paradigms!

Women's studies have resulted in two books. Irene Neher in *The
Female Hero's Quest for Identity in Novels by Modern American
Women Writers* (Frankfurt: Peter Lang) analyzes Wharton's *Summer*, Chopin's *The Awakening*, Cather's *O Pioneers!*, Glasgow's *Barren Ground*, and Hurston's *Their Eyes Were Watching God*. Her aim
is to show the complex interrelation of two themes, "the heroes' quest
for identity and their development of a relationship with nature."
Neher cogently shows that over the sequence of novels under discussion, female protagonists are gathering in strength, changing from
passive to active roles, and taking, with the exception of the orphan
Charity in Wharton's *Summer*, their freely chosen place in society. Yet
in spite of their social recognition, all of them suffer from an inner,
psychological isolation, expressed in what Neher calls "naturistic
images of their visions and dreams."

Quite different is Birgit Erika Kretzer's *Idealität und Realität der
Frauenfiguren im modernen amerikanischen Roman—Saul Bellow—
Herbert Gold—John Hawkes* (Frankfurt: Peter Lang), a 900-page
monster published in two parts. The first is entirely devoted to Bellow,
except for a brief introduction. Kretzer maintains that the three
writers complain of society's suppression of Eros in favor of Thanatos.
Their reactions, however, are different. Bellow uses mythology as a
basis for his female types of the Madonna, the prophetess, or the sex
goddess. In Hawkes's fiction, women are reduced to sexual objects and
at times resemble animals. For Gold, there is still hope that after the
breakdown of traditional norms a self-realization of his female characters is possible.

Hawkes is also the theme of Elisabeth Kraus's *Erwartungs-Angst
als Modus kognitiver Ästhetik in John Hawkes Werk* (Munich: Fink).
The author begins with a competent discussion of the many attempts
to classify Hawkes either as modern or postmodern. She refuses to
treat him under any specific label, but shows instead that his fiction
contains elements of a Wildean aestheticism as well as a postmodern
predilection for self-reflexive prose and parody. Kraus concentrates

on Hawkes's protagonists, who always look at the world through an "innocent eye" that excludes practical life, reason, and morality. Kraus tends to see Hawkes as a phenomenologist who incessantly creates new settings and exposes his figures to intense stimuli. Most of them, even when not threatened by a hostile environment, soon retreat into their world of mysterious, alogical, timeless daydreams and nightmares with their acoustic, visual, and kinetic paradoxes, of which Kraus presents a few striking examples. Outer and inner worlds fuse into a symbolistic soulscape. Man is either incapable of establishing human relations and contents himself with autoeroticism, or he manipulates his fellow beings like inanimate objects according to aesthetic categories, thereby dehumanizing them. Kraus argues that Hawkes's call for detachment, i.e., for human relationships free of emotions, is a dehumanizing and dehumanized worldview, but in artistic terms it is also a declaration of artistic autonomy and ethical disengagement. Whether Hawkes is as close to Wilde's aestheticism as Kraus wants us to believe is open to debate. What I am sure of is that Kraus's book is an excellent discussion of John Hawkes and should soon be translated into English.

Another remarkable publication on modernism and postmodernism is Gerhard Hoffmann, ed., *Making Sense: The Role of the Reader in Contemporary American Fiction* (Munich: Fink), a collection of extensively revised essays delivered at a 1985 symposium on the text/reader relationship. The title may be misleading because the "reader" in most cases is not representative of a reading community but is someone akin to the article's own author. Since my space is limited, I can mention only that *Making Sense* contains interesting contributions by Maurice Couturier, Barbara Herrnstein Smith, Steven Mailloux, Frank Lentricchia, Charles Caramello, Douwe W. Fokkema, Marc Chénetier, and Ihab Hassan. Of the German contributors, Lothar Bredalla in "Making Sense of Literary Texts: A Meaningful Activity?" (pp. 15–34) admits that any attempt at making sense of a literary text, especially a postmodern one, is an ambivalent undertaking because it can end in constructing a solipsistic universe. Yet we have to take that risk "to do justice to the particular and see it in its otherness." Herbert Grabes's "Texts or Processes?" (pp. 35–50) reminds us that the past unfolds to us only in a continual process of rewriting. Similarly, literary criticism over the past two decades has increasingly resorted to process-oriented approaches, e.g., to metalinguistic and communication theories of writing. Gerhard Hoffmann in "Play, Irony, and Comedy as Constituents of the Postmodern Aesthetic Imagination" (pp. 120–68) sees a preference for possibility thinking in postmodern aesthetics. Notions like limitlessness, immanence, and indeterminacy replace traditional concepts like mimesis, interpretation, and meaning. Postmodern imagination favors play, irony, and comedy because they share a combination of deconstruction and reconstruction. The disjuncture of meaning and history is the theme of Rüdiger Kunow's chapter "Making Sense of History: The Sense of the Past in Postmodern Times" (pp. 169–97). This disjuncture is by no means new, as the author emphasizes, but one harking back to the epistemological crisis of the 19th century. Yet as the historical metafiction of postmodern writers proves, no escape from history is possible, even for them. Alfred Hornung turns to quite a different topic in "Art Over Life: Henry James's Autobiography" (pp. 198–219). He holds that James's autobiography represents "the final triumph of his art over the inevitable failure of his life," thus proving that the autobiographical structure with its resolution of crisis is a vital part of modern literature. Gabriele Schwab's "Creative Paranoia and Frost Patterns of White Words: Making Sense in and of Thomas Pynchon's *Gravity's Rainbow*" (pp. 198–219) interprets Pynchon's novel as the story of the great refusal: it refuses to make sense in the way conventional historical novels do, although it makes full use of war mythologies and turns them into obscure war stories. Ultimately, however, Pynchon even refuses to let the text be about World War II, deliberately ending with unresolved ambiguities.

Also concerned with postmodern writing, though in only a brief space, is the booklet *Die Postmoderne—Ende der Avantgarde oder Neubeginn?* (Eggingen: Edition Klaus Isele). Joseph C. Schöpp's "Die Er-Schöpfung des Romans in der Postmoderne" (pp. 31–48) is devoted to the "deconstruction and reconstruction of a genre" as exemplified in Raymond Federman's *Take It Or Leave It* (1976) and *The Voice in the Closet* (1979). Schöpp demonstrates that Federman's writing no means fools around with outworn narrative devices but is filled with reverberations of past terrors, of which the Holocaust is the most pervasive.

Twentieth-century American drama still attracts German scholars. Martina Wächter's *Darstellung und Deutung der Vergangenheit in den Dramen Arthur Millers* (Frankfurt: Peter Lang) is based on Miller's admission that presentation of the past in drama was his "biggest single dramatic problem." Wächter differentiates among three types of plays: the analytical (*All My Sons, The Price*), the limited point of view (*Death of a Salesman, After the Fall*), and the epic of the past (*A View from the Bridge, The American Clock*). All of Miller's other plays are touched on under one of these categories. Wächter believes several recurrent experiences constitute Miller's interpretation of the past—critical private experiences, alienation in or growing up without a family, failure of the father as a leader in society, and traumatic historical experiences such as the Great Depression, the McCarthy era, or the Holocaust. Another chapter deals with Ibsen and his concept of the past, which Wächter believes considerably influenced Miller.

Sam Shepard is rapidly becoming for many German scholars a dramatist to be ranked with Williams and Miller. Ulrich Adolphs's *Die Tyrannei der Bilder—Sam Shepards Dramen* (Frankfurt: Peter Lang) is, as the title "tyranny of the pictures" tells us, a comprehensive study of Shepard's reality patterns, which are always modeled after earlier forms in other media. Adolphs is aware of Shepard's affinity to the theater of the absurd, but argues cogently that he makes use only of absurd elements, which he incorporates in one form or another into what can be called "metatheater," as plays such as *Action* or *Cowboys No. 2* clearly illustrate. Adolphs also denies any influence exerted on Shepard by the experimental or political theater of the 1960s. Shepard, Adolphs holds, is a postmodern playwright in his own right. His plays are marked by self-reflection and playful but critical use of conventions and traditional modes of presentation.

A few articles cover American drama of the 1920s. Kurt Müller in "Aspekte des Modernen in den frühen See-Einaktern Eugene O'Neills" (*Amst* 34:391–402) reads *Where the Cross Is Made* as an allegory of O'Neill's own Oedipal conflicts. *The Moon of the Caribees* is to him a self-critical reflection on the impact of the romantic-melodramatic imagination on the individual consciousness. Margit Sichert, in "Die Moderne, das Unbewusste und der Traum: O'Neills *The Emperor Jones*" (*Amst* 34:403–12), sees the triumph of the irrational in this play in the context of Jones's metaphysical destruction since Jones betrays two religions and loses all ethical orientation. The third article turns to O'Neill's colleague Susan Glaspell, who in Germany has rarely been noticed. In "Die dramatischen Experimente Susan Glaspells: *The Outside* und *The Verge*" (*Amst* 34:413–21), Klaus Schwank analyzes a one-act play and a full-length play and surmises that Glaspell not only adapted techniques of European Ex-

pressionism, but some of its themes. In addition, the female protagonist's struggle for identity makes Glaspell a forerunner of women
writers of the 1980s.

The old guard of modern writers—above all Hemingway and
Faulkner—will probably never cease to fascinate German scholars.
Karl-Heinz Stoll looks at Hemingway's Catholicism in his "Heming-
ways Haltung zum Katholizismus" (*Wege amerikanischer Kultur*, pp.
199–211) and decides that neither the author's propensity for existentialism, embodied in his "nada" concept, nor his sympathy for the
church and its tradition ever became for him full-fledged creeds. They
remained masks, which were often unable to hide anxiety and despair.
Sabine Matter's "Change and Continuity in Faulkner's Snopes Trilogy" (*Wege amerikanischer Kultur*, pp. 229–50) interprets these
works as a chronicle of changes and continuities.

My overview ends with a study of William Styron. Heike Krome's
Das Vaterbild in ausgewählten Werken William Styrons (Frankfurt:
Peter Lang) is not a psychoanalytical book on Styron, as the title
might suggest. Krome's thesis is that history in Styron's novels appears
as a conflict between the protagonists and concrete father figures. She
dissects *Lie Down in Darkness*, *The Confessions of Nat Turner*, and
Sophie's Choice. In her opinion, the father image can have many hidden meanings—Southern traditions, the dominance of society's norms,
and religious alternatives.

Universität Hamburg

iv. Italian Contributions

Massimo Bacigalupo

At the beginning of my 1988 survey I noticed that the present dearth
in Italy of new university openings in American literature "may mean
that only books inevitable to their authors will get written, rather
than the usual academic run-of-the-mill, but on the whole can only
have baneful effects." As printed in *ALS 1988*, this statement has
been shortened, and its meaning somewhat altered by the substitution
of "which" for "but." Clearly, in a perfect world only "inevitable"
scholarship would be written, but it would be disingenuous to pretend
that this can ever be so. Like most writing, scholarly work is either
commissioned or occasional. In Italy some of the most distinguished

criticism appears in the form of introductions and afterwords to commercial editions of writers old and new, for publishers like to have an
authoritative and informative essay in every book (with the exception
of contemporary novels, and pulp). So it turns out that much scholarship is commissioned by the publishing industry, and often follows
publishing trends. The same may be said of reviews, which, though
not properly scholarship, often contain some of the most lively writing
in the field. The reviewer follows the publisher at second remove, by
way of his editor. Given this state of things, there seems little chance
for neglected figures to receive attention from reputed scholars, and
the "canon," for good or for ill, perpetuates itself through the decades.

This scenario is confirmed by the 1989 work that has come to
my attention. There is a prodigious quantity of conference papers and
forewords and afterwords, but of book-length studies and academic
editions there is only a handful.

a. **General Work, Theory, and Criticism.** *Letteratura inglese e
americana,* a bibliographical guide edited by Giuseppe Sertoli and
Giovanni Cianci (Milan: Garzanti), devotes 68 of its 437 pages to a
survey of American literary scholarship (by the editors and Claudio
Gorlier), with capsule bibliographical discussions of 35 major authors,
alphabetically deployed, from Saul Bellow to William Carlos Williams. Though perforce highly selective, the book is useful and notable
for accuracy and judiciousness. It is also fully indexed. Critical questions are likewise addressed by the contributors to *L'ansia dell'interpretazione: saggi su ermeneutica, semiotica e deconstruzione,* ed. Vita
Fortunati and Giovanna Franci (Modena: Mucchi). Stefano Rosso
("Aspetti del dibattito sul postmoderno nella critica statunitense,"
pp. 229–61) develops his discussion of Ihab Hassan and William V.
Spanos (see *ALS 1988,* pp. 517–18). Gino Scatasta ("Umanesimo e
nichilismo," pp. 263–80) reports the Hillis Miller vs. M. H. Abrams
debate centering on the latter's humanistic account of Romanticism,
Natural Supernaturalism, and finds that opposites meet within the
groves of academe: the central role he believes to have now passed
"to a historically oriented criticism, and Foucault appears to have
taken Derrida's place as lodestar of American intellectuals" (p. 277).
Giovanna Franci (Oltre la decostruzione?" pp. 281–313) is more sympathetic to the Derridas than to the Foucaults of the Republic. The
American critical debate on Romanticism contributes significantly
to Francesco Rognoni's annotated translation of the two *Hyperions*:

John Keats, *Iperione, La caduta di Iperione* (Florence: La Nuova Italia, 1990), while Harold Bloom is taken apart and put together again in a brilliant piece of work by Luisa Villa, "Tra Harold Bloom e Narciso: note sul narcisismo, la lettura e la critica" (*Nuova Corrente* 35[1988]:85–120). Villa finds that "the central conceptual instrument of Bloom's theoretic universe [Freud's theory of narcissism] is . . . obsolete," for he ignores the fundamental contributions of Bela Grunberger and Heinz Kohut, "chief contemporary theorist of Narcissism." Bloom would also do well, "if he hasn't done so yet," to read Viktor Tausk's 1919 essay on schizophrenia as "influencing machine." Villa notes Bloom's problematic return to the concept of a "literal meaning," and closes with praise for the "intellectual adventure" that Bloom has afforded his readers. (By the way, "Literal Interpretation" was the subject of a 1990 conference organized by Guido Fink, on which see my review in *Unità*, 11 June 1990.) An earlier version of a philosophical approach to literature can be found in Enzo Paci (1911–76), *Il mito di Moby Dick e altri saggi americani*, ed. Agostino Lombardo (Rome: Editori Riuniti, 1988), an attractive booklet containing suggestive phenomenological readings of Melville, John Dewey, George Santayana, and T. S. Eliot: "Great American literature (Hawthorne, Melville, and Poe) demands an attitude that is not only contemplative, and in this is similar to American thought, which is substantially characterized by pragmatism." Villa's account of Bloom's "star wars" shows that this idea of literature as something that should change life is still active.

For Northrop Frye, on the other hand, works of literature reflect a timeless pattern or cycle reminiscent of Yeats's phases of the moon. Caterina Ricciardi's essay, "Frye, l'America e le finzioni supreme," pp. 245–80 in Agostino Lombardo, ed., *Ritratto di Northrop Frye* (Rome: Bulzoni), is a careful review of how American literature is fitted into Frye's supreme fiction, with particular reference to Hawthorne's *The Marble Faun*, Dickinson, Poe, Whitman, Eliot, and Stevens. As usual, Frye is more convincing as a close reader than as a compulsive systematizer, but Ricciardi does not allow herself to question the lesson of the master which she so competently expounds.

The proceedings of a big conference on poetry translation (Bergamo, March 1988) are collected in *La traduzione del testo poetico*, ed. Franco Buffoni (Milan: Edizione Angelo Guerini et Associati). Six of the 62 essays have American subjects. The poet Giovanni Giudici tells of his work on Ezra Pound and Robert Frost, among others.

Tommaso Pisanti ("Traduzione come interpretazione," pp. 313–22) discusses Poe's poetry and his own translation of it (Rome: Newton Compton, 1982). I provide a survey of modernist practices of translation (pp. 323–29) as an ongoing process which sometimes becomes the subject of a text, as in Pound's Cantos 20 and 23 and in Leopold Bloom's reflections in *Ulysses*: *"—A cenar teco.* What does that *teco* mean? Tonight perhaps." *Teco,* however, means "with you." I also point out a connection between a fine line in *The Pisan Cantos* ("Cythera, in the moon's barge whither?") and Marlowe's translation of Ovid's *Heroides* as quoted by Pound in a 1917 essay: "Aurora whither slidest thou down againe. / And byrdes from Memnon yearly shall be slaine." Nadia Fusini has several portentous things to say on "The Enigmas of Translation" and Wallace Stevens (pp. 331–35), and comes to this conclusion: "Translation is passion of the word, but it is love at a distance, passion of exile, adventure of exodus. It is not a pronouncing of one's own words, but of the words of the other." (Incidentally, the recent Italian translations of Stevens's poetry, by Fusini and me, are carefully appraised in Stefano Maria Casella's review-essay, "La poesia di Wallace Stevens," *Lingua e letteratura* 12:175–81.) A veteran translator and poet, Margherita Guidacci, contributes a note on Jessica Powers and Elizabeth Bishop (pp. 337–419). Guidacci is also responsible for one of the better-known translations of Dickinson's poems and letters, recently reprinted: *Poesie e lettere* (Florence: R.C.S. Sansoni). Buffoni's volume closes with the transcription of a panel, chaired by me, on "Untranslatability and Emily Dickinson" (pp. 477–92), with the participation of Guidacci, Fusini, and Barbara Lanati. I note that, as with jokes, the witty and compact kind of poetry that Dickinson wrote makes for misunderstandings and untranslatability. As an example of the first, I suggest that, in "The Soul selects her own Society," most Italian translators have taken "Majority" to mean "a number greater than half of the total" (an error suggested by a modern misreading of "Society") rather than "the status of one who has attained majority of age," which is of course what the proto-feminist Dickinson meant. The discussion was lively. Two other general books that have interest for Americanists are Claudia Corti's treatment of gothic romance, *Sul discorso fantastico* (Pisa: ETS), and Anna Dolfi's collection of essays by various hands, *"Journal intime" e letteratura moderna* (Rome: Bulzoni).

Andrea Mariani devotes an article, "Arcadia perennis: un topos della letteratura americana dall'Ottocento al Novecento" (*Itinerari*

1988:141–54), to literary and sculptural fauns. Part of this article appears in expanded form as "Sleeping and Waking Fauns: Harriet Goodhouse Hosmer's Experience in Italy, 1852–1870," a contribution to Irma B. Jaffe, ed., *The Italian Presence in American Art, 1760–1860* (New York: Fordham), pp. 66–81. A new look at an old theme is my article "Da Huck a Lolita: i terribili bambini americani" (*Paragone* 468:33–51), the first part of which is a sequential reading of chapters 21–22 of *The Adventures of Huckleberry Finn* for repeated patterns of feigning, befuddling, and send-up. The Duke soliloquizes after Shakespeare, taking in Huck; Boggs plays the madman but is shot in the real by Sherburn; the Bricksville audience at once mimics the killing and attempts to put on another show, the lynching of Sherburn, which fails miserably, giving Sherburn the chance for his own soliloquy. Finally, Huck goes to the circus and is wonderfully taken in by the drunk in the audience who gets on the horse and then reveals himself as one of the acrobats. A pattern emerges from the sequence, a questioning of fact and fiction, and perhaps a praise of the artist—Duke, Boggs, Sherburn, acrobat, even Huck, for if we believe *him* we are as naive as he is when he takes the ringmaster to be genuinely surprised. The rest of the article provides related comments on other classical instances of the child theme—*The Turn of the Screw*, *The Catcher in the Rye*, and *Lolita*—where the parody becomes more and more involuted. The relation of the Duke and King to Huck repeats itself with variations in the Governess vs. Miles and Flora, the phonies vs. Holden Caulfield, and Humbert vs. Lolita, and it is possible to see it as a projection of the relationship of the artist to his work. Of course, the four novels present extremely different accounts of the one situation from different points of view, more or less fictitious. The common moral is that the child, the world of art and creativity, should be left his or her freedom.

b. **19th Century.** *RSA 7* collects 22 papers given at a 1987 conference in Perugia on "Birth of *Which* Nation? America's Self-Images: 1865–1929," arranged in four seminars with introductory talks by the chairpersons. The result is a lively survey of themes and individual writers, by older and younger scholars, among them Vito Amoruso on the twilight of the American Renaissance, Marisa Bulgheroni on Dickinson, Gigliola Nocera on Rebecca Harding Davis, Marilla Battilana on art and society, 1865–77, Cristina Giorcelli on *The Bostonians*, Agostino Lombardo on *The American Scene*, Biancamaria Tedeschini Lalli on *McTeague*, Guido Carboni on the 1915 San Francisco Exhibition, Mario Maffi on Buffalo Bill and Coney Island, and Stefania Piccinato on Afro-American identity. Several foreign scholars participate, including Emory Elliott ("Representation of Race in the Gilded Age," pp. 11–27) and Werner Sollors ("Intermarriage and Mulattoes in the 1920s," pp. 269–85). For a contrast to so much painstaking scholarship one may turn to Ivan Arnaldi's fictional account of the birth of the West, *Il bisonte bianco* (Turin: Giulio Einaudi), nothing less than a rewriting of *Moby-Dick* (with profuse excuses to Melville's ghost). It is interesting to compare these recent Italian views of the character of the United States with those, often unfavorable, of the '30s, discussed by Michela Nacci in *L'antiamericanismo in Italia negli anni 30* (Turin: Bollati Boringhieri).

An unusual collection of 19th- and early 20th-century American science fiction, concisely but competently introduced, is Carlo Pagetti's *Il laboratorio dei sogni* (Rome: Editori Riuniti, 1988). It includes stories by Irving, Poe, Melville ("The Bell Tower"), Hawthorne, T. W. Higginson ("The Monarch of Dreams"), Edward Everett Hale ("Hands Off"), Mark Twain, Ambrose Bierce, Frank Lillie Pollack ("Finis"), Edward Bellamy ("The Blindman's World"), Percival Lowell ("Evidence"), Jack London ("The Dream of Debs"), and Charlotte Perkins Gilman ("The Yellow Wallpaper"). "The Dream of Debs" is also included, with another 25 stories of the North, the Pacific, class warfare, boxing, and fantasy, in Mario Maffi's two-volume collection, *Racconti dello Yukon e dei Mari del Sud* (Milan: Arnoldo Mondadori). Another, partially overlapping Jack London volume, *Racconti del Pacifico*, appeared in 1990 (Parma: Guanda), with an enthusiastic introduction by Beniamino Placido. This elicited a sobering response from Claudio Gorlier in his review for *Stampa*, 3 March 1990 ("Dear Placido, this is not the fabled Great American Novel").

A curiosity by one of the inventors of SF is a new translation of Poe's *Eureka* (Genoa: ECIG), by a physicist, Maria Rosa Marin, who in an appendix explains how the universe really began, and how Mr. Poe more or less got it right. Meanwhile, Carlo Izzo's 1953 edition of Poe's stories and poems, *Tutti i racconti e le poesie*, has been reprinted (Florence: Casa Editrice Le Lettere, 1990), with 24 fine plates (1907) by Alberto Martini, and a sparkling foreword by Guido Fink, who also provides a full, updated bibliography (pp. 1191–1210). Another scholarly edition of Poe, by Gabriele Baldini (1972), was reissued in revised form: *Racconti* (Garzanti, 1988.) Fink's bibliography is silent about one Giorgio Ghidetti's ominously titled *Poe, l'eresia di un americano maledetto* (Florence: Arnaud), of the existence of which I know only through a review in *Il Messaggero Veneto* for 14 December. Given the subject, let us allow the mystery to remain unsolved. Fink also wrote the introduction to Nathaniel Hawthorne, *La casa dei sette abbaini*, trans. Marcella Bonsanti (Florence: R. C. S. Sansoni), using Melville's "Pittsfield Secret Review" letter as a guide to the intricacies of the novel and to its critical reception. Meanwhile, Poe's and Hawthorne's forerunner Charles Brockden Brown is well-served by Alessandro Ceni's fine translation (with introduction), *Wieland, o la trasformazione* (Pordenone: Studio Tesi, 1988).

An attractive booklet is Henry David Thoreau, *Camminare* (Milan: SE)—a translation, by Maria Antonietta Prina, of "Walking," with an appreciative afterword by editor Franco Meli. The format is just right for taking it into any remaining woods. This would be difficult to do with the third volume of Ruggero Bianchi's complete edition of Melville, *Redburn—Giacca Bianca*, trans. Oriana Palusci and Stefano Manferlotti (Milan: Mursia), with its 86-page introduction by the editor (on "Small everyday abysses"), and its 592-page text. A seagoing passenger, however, would do well to take it along, for these are the first satisfactory translations of the two novels to appear in Italy, and Manferlotti's rendering of *White-Jacket* is particularly praiseworthy. A careful review of the new Melville edition and of previous ones, by Alberto Lehmann, appeared in *Indice* (8:16). Some of Melville's poetic remains are capably edited from the manuscripts and critically assessed by Gordon Poole in *At the Hostelry and Naples in the Time of Bomba* (I.U.O.). Poole offers much accurate information and comparative lists of emendations, and is particularly strong on the Neapolitan and Italian historical and geographical background. References in *Clarel* to Giacomo Leopardi are discussed by Giuseppe Lombardo in a well-researched article, "La fortuna del Leopardi in America, 1852–1887" (*Nuovi Annali della Facoltà di Magistero dell'Università di Messina* 5[1987]:167–218), with bibliography; other sections are devoted to Henry T. Tuckerman (whose 1852 Leopardi article is reprinted in Appendix 1), Thomas W. Parsons, W. D. Howells, and H. W. Longfellow. Lombardo's knowledgeability about the Boston Brahmins is again in evidence in his discussion of " 'My Hunt After the Captain' di Oliver Wendell Holmes" (*Nuovi Annali* 6 [1988]:495–522)—a familiarity that does not make him less aware of the Autocrat's lapses, for example, when, surveying the bloody field at Antietam just after the battle, he comments: "It was a great pity that we had no intelligent guide to explain to us the position of that portion of the two armies which fought over this ground" (p. 521). Another contribution from Messina, Mario Corona's "Testo e para-testo: *Leaves of Grass* . . . 1855" (*Nuovi Annali* 5[1987]:421–29), takes a look at the physical aspect of the 1855 *Leaves of Grass* and what it tells us.

Cooper has been somewhat neglected by Italian scholars, if not by readers: new translations have recently appeared of *The Spy* (Florence: R. C. S. Sansoni, 1988) and *The Prairie* (Milan: Arnoldo Mondadori, 1990), the latter with a brief but informative introduction by Mario Maffi (who, with Bruno Maffi, is the translator). Algerina Neri has published a fine scholarly translation of *Excursions in Italy* (1838): *Viaggio in Italia, 1828–1830* (Pisa: Nistri-Lischi), with an ample and cogent 42-page introduction, followed by a chronology and a bibliography. Cooper's travel notes are fascinating both for the fresh view they offer of his beloved Italy as it was 160 years ago and for their glimpses of social life at the Tuscan court and elsewhere. Neri, born in Livorno, offers precise notes, especially on the Tuscan part of the journal. I in turn was fascinated by the animated descriptions of Genoa, which Cooper was much taken with, and of the coast toward Nice, which dazzled him.

Viaggio e scrittura: le straniere nell'Italia dell'Ottocento, ed. Liana Borghi et al. (Florence: Libreria delle Donne, 1988), includes brief articles on two other American travelers in Italy: Martha Carey Thomas (1882), by Bianca Tarozzi (pp. 149–56), and Margaret Fuller, by Rosella Mamoli Zorzi (pp. 119–26). Zorzi also produced one of the most attractive of this year's many editions: Henry James, *Lettere da Palazzo Barbaro* (Milan: Rosellina Archinto), with a foreword by Leon Edel. This is a selection, in Italian, of 28 James letters (1869–1907) from and about Venice (nine of them heretofore unpublished), followed by 11 letters of Ariana, Daniel, and Ralph Curtis, owners from 1885 of Palazzo Barbaro on the Grand Canal—the original of Palazzo Leporelli of *The Wings of the Dove*. Another view of James's Venetian set is offered by Zorzi in the abundantly illustrated yet compact catalog of a centenary exhibition she organized, *Robert Browning e Venezia* (Venice: Fondazione Querini Stampalia).

In a letter of 20 November 1889 Ralph Curtis gives us a glimpse of "Henry James driven to death by the printers devil (what a pity he knows no other)." This was the James who a decade later was to set quite a few readers' and scholars' devils loose with *The Turn of the Screw*, the subject of a usefully didactic account by Eliana Elia, "*Il giro di vite*" *di Henry James: strutture e immagini* (Lecce: Franco Milella), an inventory of structures and images which shows sensitivity. A more ambitious contribution to James scholarship is Luisa Villa's *Esperienza a memoria: saggio su Henry James* (Genoa: Il Melangolo), a doctoral thesis of 180 large-format pages that has few, if any, of the defects of the genre (in fact, an index and bibliography would have been a welcome addition). After a somewhat intimidating "Prologue" on "Images of the City," Villa gets down to business and in seven chapters offers cogent and subtle accounts of (1) James's ghosts (see *ALS 1986*, pp. 465–66—by the way, Einaudi of Turin brought out in 1988 a handsome volume of James's *Racconti di fantasmi*), (2) "The Shrines of Memory" (*The Sense of the Past, The Beast in the Jungle*), (3) "The Gold of the Dove," (4) "The Language of Entropy" (largely on Georg Simmel's *Philosophy of Money* [1900], one of Villa's chief theoretical sources), (5) *The Ambassadors* ("Travel, Objects, Renunciation"), (6) "Experience and Form" (Villiers de l'Isle-Adam, Arthur Symons, the *Prefaces*), (7) *The Sacred Fount* and *The Golden Bowl*. Villa practices a form of New Historicism, concentrating on the contradictions of James's "great consciousness": what is presented as detachment and victory over material things may also be seen as a reduction of the spirit to an object and the world to a commodity. Palazzo Leporelli is not only Palazzo Barbaro-Curtis, but also "poor little patient [Palazzo] Dario . . . one of the most flourishing booths at the fair" (from "The Grand Canal").

More recently, Villa's writing has become increasingly dependent on psychoanalysis, as appears from her extensive but tightly reasoned eight-part article, "L'incendio di Poynton: su Henry James, la merce, il feticcio e l'amore per i morti" (*Nuova Corrente* 35[1988]:239–82). In her book she had already noticed the contradiction between Fleda Vetch's faintness at the loss by fire of Poynton and the wholly positive reading James offered of his heroine's experience in his Preface. Here, things get much more involved and dramatic, with poor Owen Gereth being reduced in the process to the "fecal stick" of the psychology of narcissism: "he had a higher hat and light gloves with black seams and an umbrella as fine as a lance." So Fleda is a collector more perverse for her ethics of renunciation, converting things and people

(Owen) into "anal objects, rigid mannequins in which the false phallus (the fetish) of a supposed virile resolution punctually conceals the true castration." *The Spoils of Poynton* is included, with eight other short novels (1888–1910), in Henry James, *Romanzi brevi*, vol. 2, ed. Sergio Perosa (Milan: Arnoldo Mondadori, 1990)—vol. 1 appeared in 1985. The editor's helpful and compact introduction and notes extract, needless to say, a less devastating moral from the master's late writings. (There is also a bibliography.) Surely, it is wonderful to think of what James would have said to Villa's relentless investigation (is he, like Owen, also being reduced to a "fecal stick"?).

c. **20th-Century Prose.** A cogent discussion of the modern English novel is Leonardo Terzo, *Una letteratura per bene: tre saggi sul romanzo inglese* (Milan: Marcos y Marcos). Its reflections on "Mrs Woolf, Mr Bradbury e Mr Derrida" (pp. 107–93) will interest Italian Americanists. What treatment American writing receives at the hands of Italian publishers is instead the subject of two informed and persuasive review-essays by Franco La Polla: "Letteratura americana: la riscoperta del passato," and "Letteratura americana: una panoramica a 360" (*L'informazione bibliografica* 3[1988]:443–50; and 1 [1990]:42–49). La Polla is disappointed by the publishing industry that blindly follows trends like minimalism (a mere generic name for bad and predictable books, in his opinion) and neglects "some of the most advanced and exciting writing of all contemporary Western literature." What this writing is La Polla does not say, but a conference on postmodernism he organized early in 1990 in Macerata, with the participation of Stanley Elkin, William Gass, Ishmael Reed, and others, suggests his preferences. He also writes that *Portnoy's Complaint* is decidedly inferior to John Hawkes's *Second Skin* (the two novels have recently been reissued in Italy). And he singles out for praise a translation of Gertrude Stein's *Tender Buttons* (*Teneri bottoni*) by Marina Morbiducci and Edward G. Lynch (Macerata: Liberalibri) and the reissue of Claudio Gorlier's anthology *Gli umoristi della frontiera*, first published in 1967 (Rome: Editori Riuniti, 1988): "With these men, and with their humor, the national culture of America was born." Talking of "literary phenomena," La Polla is generally unsympathetic to William Least Heat Moon ("failed"), Erica Jong ("inferior"), and John Fante ("invented," i.e., by the industry; cf. *ALS 1988*, p. 530).

Fernanda Pivano, a staunch supporter of Bret Easton Ellis and company and therefore a bête noire of La Polla's, tells of how it was in the '6os in *C'era una volta un beat: l'avventura degli anni '6o* (Rome: Arcana, 1988). Though we may deplore it, it is a fact that the postwar American writers most popular abroad, perhaps even at home, are those with a recognizable public image: first the Beats, now the minimalists. The postmodernists never made it onto the front pages. So it is no surprise that Milan's *Corriere della Sera* should choose for the main feature of its literary insert on Sunday, 15 October, a reconsideration of Jack Kerouac 20 years after his death (21 Oct. 1969), with articles by Pivano, Enzo Siciliano, Antonio Troiano, and Massimo Piattelli Palmarini, and a map for those who want to follow in the wake (or exhaust) of *On the Road.*

Unlike Kerouac, the more fastidious Richard Brautigan has only recently been published in Italy: *La pesca alla trota in America*, trans. Riccardo Duranti, came out in 1989; *Zucchero di cocomero*, trans. Andrea Pellizzari, in 1990 (Milan: Serra e Riva). The former was sensitively reviewed by Michele Neri (*La Stampa*, 16 Sept.). I reviewed it for *Il Secolo XIX* (1 Feb. 1990), together with the translation of Raymond Carver's *Fires*, *Voi non sapete cos'è l'amore* (Naples: Pironti), noting a similar despair in the two writers, born only four years apart, one of them associated with the spaced-out '6os, the other with the grim '8os. One should be able to look beyond the cultural mood to the actual writing, though it is difficult. Barbara Lanati writes appreciatively of Carver in her introduction to the reissue of *Cattedrale* (Milan: Arnoldo Mondadori), with a biobibliographical note. A brief survey of some recent novelists (Jay Gummerman, Ethan Canin, Richard Ford, Jay McInerney, Jonathan Franzen, Allan Gurganus), is volunteered by Claudio Gorlier (*La Stampa*, 18 Nov.), who is more sympathetic than La Polla to recent publishing trends. In particular, McInerney's *The Story of My Life* (*Tanto per cambiare*), trans. Marisa Caramella (Bompiani), was the occasion of many reviews and interviews, more and less favorable, by Fernanda Pivano (*CdS*, 12 Nov.), Anna Detheridge (*Il Sole-24 Ore*, 3 Dec.), Giuseppe Venostra (*Il Secolo XIX*, 15 Dec.), and others. This is what happens when a major publisher brings out a hardcore book and the author is available for interviews. Instead, when a quasi-private publisher issues a softcore lesbian novel like *Un posto per noi* (*A Place for Us*) by Isabel Miller (Alma Routsong), with an afterword by Liana Borghi (Florence: Estro), the fact is scarcely noticed in the literary supplements, though one book may be as good as the other.

***d*. Ethnic Literature.** Male homosexuality in a Nazi concentration camp is the subject of *Bent*, a 1979 play by Martin Sherman. Dario Calimani's pithy article, "*Bent*: il testo come memoria" (*Miscellanea* [Univ. di Trieste, Facoltà di Magistero] 21[1988]:209–14), persuasively places Sherman's work in the context of Jewish memory. This is also the subject of Leslie A. Fiedler's moving and witty story *L'ultimo ebreo in America*, trans. Daniela Fink, intro. Guido Fink (Florence: Editrice La Giuntina). It is surely one of the recurrent motifs in Mario Materassi's valuable two-volume collection of *Scrittori ebrei americani* (Bompiani), which brings together 40 short stories, from Abraham Cahan (b. 1860) to Lynne Sharon Schwartz (b. 1939), and comments in the introduction on the vanishing hyphenated writer. The immigrant's loss of the Language of origin in the (American) Babel is equally central a motif to *Call It Sleep* (1934) and *The Imported Bridegroom* (1898), as Rocco Coronato points out in his brilliant (though somewhat esoteric) article "Il libro sigillato: sulla nominazione in Cahan e Henry Roth" (*Paragone* 472:27–40). Philip Roth's construction of alternative pasts in *The Counterlife* is analyzed and clarified in Giordano De Biasio's reading, "Philip Roth tra *facts* e *fictions*" (*Lingua e letteratura* 13:144–59), where we find that Zuckerman, like Sherman's Max, cannot but accept his Jewish heritage (he has his son circumcised).

Roth's indispensable novel is thoughtfully assessed by Alessandra Contenti in "Herzog e Portnoy: lo 'Schlemiel' come eroe positivo," in Marino Freschi, ed., *Ebraismo e modelli di romanzo* (I.U.O.), pp. 7–35. Contenti notes the best-seller status of the two novels and the small difference in the '60s between the highbrow and the commercial. She goes on to show how essentially traditional in construction and ideology the two novels are, and how they could interest a middlebrow public: *Portnoy's Complaint*, for example, would appeal to Roth enthusiasts, and to readers with ethnic, humor, and pornography orientations. Similarly, the softcore *Herzog* is not lacking in glamour and sex. Finally, Contenti agrees with Mary McCarthy that the two novels are weakened by "soliloquacious" self-indulgence—the authors are too fond of the characters; Herzog and Portnoy know too much about themselves for a satisfactory critical stance to emerge (Henry James noted he had made this mistake with Hyacinth Robinson in *The Princess Casamassima*).

What is to be the first issue of a new forum on *Native American Literatures*, ed. Laura Coltelli, includes 17 contributions from U.S.,

German, Danish, and Italian scholars and authors. The editor writes
of Leslie Marmon Silko's *Ceremony* ("Re-Enacting Myths and Stories," pp. 173–81), finding that in the novel "contemporary events flow
like an eternal repetition of mythical happenings." Fedora Giordano
closes the issue with a useful survey (with bibliography for 1976–88)
of "Italian Images of the American Indians" (pp. 197–210), from the
frescoes (1770) in the Indian Room of Palazzo Barberini, Rome, to
recent translations and studies. Clara Bertocci collects some interesting information in "Puritans Versus Pequots: Four Eye-Witness
Reports of the First War in Colonial New England" (*Storia Nord-
americana* 4[1987]:71–91)—the reporters being John Underhill, Lion
Gardiner, John Mason, and Philip Vincent. Bertocci devotes another
essay to a sympathetic early approach to Indian culture: "Roger Williams e la sua 'chiave' del nuovo mondo," in Lidia Curti et al., eds., *Il
muro del linguaggio* (I.U.O.), pp. 263–77—a discussion of *A Key into
the Language of America* (1643).

In "La poetica della trasformazione nei romanzi di Tony Morrison"
(*Il ponte* 3–4:144–64), Giulia Scarpa applies Gérard Genette's con-
cept of "hypertext" (*Palimpsestes* [1981]) to *The Bluest Eye, Song of
Solomon,* and *Tar Baby,* showing the dependence of the three novels
on *Uncle Tom's Cabin,* the Flying Africans myth, and the tale of the
Tar Baby, respectively. The approach is rewarding and sensitive.

e. 20th-Century Poetry. Two essays by Italians are included in
Interspace 4, ed. Alain Suberchicot and Jacqueline Ollier, an issue
entirely devoted to U.S. poetry. "W. C. Williams and the American
Language" (pp. 77–97) by Maria Anita Stefanelli is a cogent and
well-researched essay that uses sophisticated linguistic theories and
much material from Williams's unpublished papers at Yale to throw
light on two parallel poems, "Proletarian Portrait" (1934) and "A
Negro Woman" (1955). In "Compound Ghosts: The Modernists'
Canon in the Thirties and Forties" (pp. 35–42), I give a brief account
of the "shift to the historical and the social" in the later work of Stevens, Eliot, and Pound, by way of adjustments in their chosen canon.
So, for Pound, Dante, first perceived as poet of vision and clear
images, becomes the prophetic denouncer of usury, the two models
coalescing in *The Pisan Cantos* and Eliot's *Little Gidding.* Fourteen
Cantos are included by Mary de Rachewiltz in her paperback anthology *Per conoscere Pound* (Mondadori), pp. 290–443: 1, 4, 13, 38,
47, 51, 53, 67, 81, 85, 90, 93 (in which she figures), 106, 115, 116. This

is a praiseworthy attempt to call attention to the often neglected historical parts of the poem, but the reader of this introductory anthology will be nonetheless disappointed by the exclusion of all but one of the Pisan Cantos, and by the absence of notes. The choice of earlier poems is more balanced, whereas the prose section (pp. 79–245) shows the same preference for the prophetic over the literary, and includes new translations of, among other works, *Confucian Analects* and "I Gather the Limbs of Osiris" (the latter marred by many mistakes). This handy but erratic volume includes a chronology and bibliography, reprinted from *I Cantos* (1985).

A smaller personal Ezra Pound anthology, *La muraglia infinita*, ed. Andrea Molesini (Montebelluna: Amadeus), includes a selection of poems from "A Girl" to Cantos 13, 45, and 53, the main offering being a full translation of *Cathay* (pp. 62–117). The editor's introductory essay (pp. 9–42) enthusiastically sketches a theory of Poundian translation in 18 points, among them, "Do not obscure the text out of deference to so-called 'erudite accuracy.'" Molesini follows his precept, rendering "the five-score nightingales" as "gli usignoli dalle cinque ugole," but his poet's approach to Pound is a pleasant relief. The howlers in Maria Luisa Ardizzone's translation of "Gli Ur-Cantos"—i.e., the canceled "Three Cantos" of 1917 (*Almanacco dello Specchio* 13:63–109)—are less excusable as well as more frequent (for example, "the rose . . . winds in" becomes "la rosa . . . venti sopra"). Molesini also wrote the introduction to the first Italian translation (by Charlotte Whigham) of *Gaudier-Brzeska* (Milan: Edizione Angelo Guerini). Pound's relation to Vorticism is touched on in my essay, "Art and Artists in Ezra Pound's *Mauberley*" (*Poetry and the Fine Arts*, pp. 14–20), which offers a reading of "Envoi" and defends the view that Pound is the speaker throughout *Hugh Selwyn Mauberley*, a view which finally seems to be gaining acceptance (see Ronald Bush in *AmLH* 2 [1990]:60–65). In a long article in French, "L'écriture des *Cantos*," which is collected in an anthology of writings by and on Pound, *Je rassemble les membres d'Osiris*, intro. Jean-Michel Rabaté (Auch: Tristram), pp. 243–96, I report on the poetry drafts of the '30s and '40s, and print much heretofore unpublished material. Section 1 retraces the variant versions of "Seven-Lakes" Canto 49, unearthing two prologues that Pound scrapped. The second of these is particularly telling because, by mentioning Byron, Swinburne, and Henry James in connection with a sea grotto, it traces a sort of lineage of the expatriate poet-traveler-swimmer which leads directly to the opening line of the final version of the canto, here first drafted: "For the Seven Lakes, and by no man these verses." The explication of this draft involved some amusing field research, of which I write in "Con Byron, a Portovenere" (*Il Secolo XIX*, 30 Aug.). Section 2 reconstructs the history of Pound's seminal essay "European Paideuma" (1939), never published in its entirety, which sketches much of the background for the Pisan Cantos. Section 3 prints and discusses Pound's notes of 1940–45 for the "Paradiso" of *The Cantos*, the most exciting of which are drafts in Italian for two cantos tentatively numbered 74 and 75, probably from early 1945, passages of which turn up, again in Italian, in Cantos 74–80. This accounts for some of the most tantalizing lines of the Pisan Cantos, those involving the "Triedro," Cunizza, "the sun in his great periplum," and the figure who says "I am the moon."

A final Poundian contribution of mine is the publication, with Italian translation, of the canceled passages of Canto 84, in "Un inedito pisano" (*Poesia* 11 [Nov.]:2–5), followed by a commentary and an article ("Ezra Pound e i fichi di Rolando Monti," pp. 7–8), which has biographical interest and quotes a possible source of Canto 116. In response to this, Enrico I. Rambaldi reminisces on his meeting with Pound and his defense of the poet when he was invited in 1961 to talk at the University of Milan and Rambaldi's young fellow Communists were planning to disrupt the proceedings ("Un incontro con Ezra Pound," *Poesia* 27 [March 1990]:21–25).

Passages from H.D.'s *Trilogy* are excerpted and introduced (with bibliography) by Marina Camboni (*Galleria* 38:437–58). Camboni also edited and wrote the biographical introduction to a selection of Anne Sexton's poems, *La doppia immagine e altre poesie* (Caltanissetta-Rome: Salvatore Sciascia), and did further feminist-oriented work in the introductory essay to Myriam Díaz-Diocaretz, *Per una poetica della differenza* (Florence: Estro), a booklet which offers views on Sexton, Rich, Woolf, and others. *La poesia indifesa*, ed. Paola Bono and Emanuela Dal Fabbro (Rome: Carucci), has notes on Lowell and Leopardi by Annalisa Goldoni, Dickinson's "Safe in their Alabaster Chambers" by Biancamaria Tedeschini Lalli, and Rich and John Donne by Camboni.

Besides Camboni's Sexton anthology, 1989 saw the reprint of an Adrienne Rich volume, *Segreti, silenzi, bugie*, trans. Roberta Mazzoni (Milan: Tartaruga) and of the long-delayed selection of over 100

Robert Lowell sonnets (from *For Lizzie and Harriet* and *The Dolphin*) by Rolando Anzilotti, *Il delfino e altre poesie* (Milan: Arnoldo Mondadori), with a fine introduction by the editor. Unfortunately, Anzilotti did not live to supervise publication of this, his fifth Lowell volume, and the publisher has done badly: sometimes the English text is at variance with the translation, for it is well-known that Lowell printed numerous versions of the same poem; the editors at Mondadori apparently didn't bother to check, or ask someone who knew (see Francesco Rognoni's careful notes in *Testo a fronte* 2[1990]:182–87). No wonder that Anna Detheridge in her review (*Il Sole-24 Ore,* 8 Oct.) complained that the translation "doesn't always help to understand the original"! (There were other reviews, by Claudio Gorlier, *La Stampa,* 21 Oct., and me, *Il Secolo XIX,* 25 Oct.) In Italy as elsewhere, poetry is often not taken very seriously by large publishers, for it represents a negligible part of their business, and in fact loses them money.

A more optimistic view of the profession is taken by Robert Creeley in an interview (*Il Secolo XIX,* 12 April), recording his happy return to Genoa and Rapallo nearly 40 years after an earlier Poundian pilgrimage. Asked about his New York State laureateship, he thought such honors called attention to the relevance of poetry: "Making poetry is important. You can love it or hate it but it is important." In Creeley's happy world there is, apparently, no place for indifference.

Università di Genova

v. Japanese Contributions

Keiko Beppu

Japanese scholarship on American literature for 1989 mirrors some of the significant critical vicissitudes witnessed in the United States for the past decade or so. The impact of new critical theories (deconstructionist, feminist, or New Historicist) on American literary studies is one; the subsequent reassessment of the so-called literary canon is another; a third is the question of literary history as a unified story, such as was attempted in *Literary History of the United States* (1948).

Since its publication in 1988, *The Columbia Literary History of the United States* has challenged literary historians and scholars on both sides of the Pacific, inviting them to redefine and reconstruct America's literary past; the awesome volume is a stone, as it were, thrown into a pond called Academe, whose ripples go on and on. The question of the canon is further challenged by the compilation of *The Heath Anthology of American Literature* (1990). As expected, Japanese scholars are sensitive to this critical climate.

Somewhat belatedly, a considerable number of applications of contemporary critical theories, successful or otherwise, to American writers have been attempted by our scholars. Noteworthy was a book on the American Renaissance writers, *Bungaku suru Wakaki America: Poe, Hawthorne, Melville* [*American Renaissance Re-presented: Poe, Hawthorne, and Melville*] (Nan'undo), by Takayuki Tatsumi et al. At the same time, traditional interpretative studies of individual American authors continue unabated. Ironically, Japanese scholarly achievements for 1989 indicate that the controversy over the American literary canon goes no more than skin-deep. Long-time literary favorites such as Poe, Hawthorne, Thoreau, James, and Faulkner receive unflagging critical attention; of special import amid such scholarly ventures is the completion of *Jack London: Essays on the Man and the Work* (Sanyusha Shuppan) compiled by the Jack London Society, an acknowledgment of the impact New Historicism has made on American literary studies in Japan.

Articles here surveyed are restricted, as is the custom in this section, to those published in the major Japanese academic journals: *SALit, SELit,* and *EigoS.* Unless otherwise indicated, all books were published in Tokyo.

a. **Literary History and General Studies.** In response to the publication of *The Columbia Literary History,* 1989 saw two literary histories of a different scope and kind: *America Bungaku-Shi* [*A Literary History of the United States*], ed. Keiko Beppu and Kazuko Watanabe (Kyoto: Minerva-shobo), and *America Bungaku to Jidai Hembo* [*American Literature and Its Historical Changes*], ed. Shigeo Hamano (Kenkyusha). The first is a modest proposal to ongoing debates among our academic circle. Primarily intended as a text for college students, it presents American literature up to 1987 from colonial writings to postmodernist. In only some 300 pages, it covers the ground fairly well, with discussions of literary works in relation to their historical backgrounds, as well as with literary maps, diagrams, and a detailed chronology. No drastic revision of the canon is proposed; *A Literary History of the United States* is written for "this" generation, which "redefine[s] the past in its own terms."

More ambitious and pretentious is *American Literature and Its Historical Changes*; it is meant, the editor says, to be "interdisciplinary" studies on literary currents since the mid-19th century. Its objective appears to be an exploration of possibilities for a new literary history. Hence, the book does not concern itself with literary periods in chronological progression.

The book consists of five chapters: The Disappearing Pastoral America; The Structure of the City Novel; The Destructive Paradigm—Jazz, Automobile, Alcohol, and Depression; The Southern Temper; From the Traditional America to Modern/Postmodern Society. The chapters are further divided into a half dozen sections which examine "major" and "minor" American writers and their relations to their times. Many of the essays, contributed by 19 scholars, are good discussions on the given themes and subjects. To mention a few: Naoto Hatano's "Henry David Thoreau Speaks to Our Time" (pp. 84–97) clarifies the meaning of the ideological and cultural heritage of this unique American thinker; Tateo Imamura's "Tropism of 'Crack-up' " (pp. 221–38) is a succinct representation of the '20s and the '30s through an examination of Hemingway, Dos Passos, and Steinbeck; Shoji Goto's "In a Strange Civilization: Sherwood Anderson's Small Town" (pp. 204–20) discusses the virtue of a small town in America—still a living ideal, as exemplified in the recent movie *A Field of Dreams*. Yet the book as a whole falls short of its original plan; it is a bric-a-brac of literary criticism, out of which emerges no clear historical perspective.

As for other general studies on American literature, Masao Shimura's series in *EigoS*, "American Literature and Mysticism," needs a few comments. Started in mid-1988, the series was completed with its 22nd installment in *EigoS* (135:596–98). Shimura enters a territory, as he says, "where angels fear to tread" and comes out with an interesting cross-cultural speculation in Oriental and Western mystic experiences observed in the works of diverse American (and Japanese) writers (by no means all-inclusive): Charles Brockden Brown, Jonathan Edwards, Hawthorne, Emerson, Thoreau, Clemens, Sherwood Anderson, Hemingway, William Goyen, poets of the Beat generation, and the Japanese poet Kenji Miyazawa.

b. **19th-Century Fiction and Poetry.** As has been noted, despite the controversy over the canon of American literature, Japanese scholarly activities center on the writers of the American Renaissance and other "major" 19th-century authors. The books in this group published in 1989: the aforementioned *American Renaissance Re-presented*; Eiichi Fujita's *America Dentoshosetsu to Sogai [Alienation in the Traditional American Novel]* (Sogensha); Chitoshi Motoyama's *Poe wa Doracula Daroka [Is Poe Dracula?]* (Keiso-shobo); Ichiro Tsujimoto's *Poe no Tampen-ron Kenkyu [Studies in Poe's Theory of Short Fiction]* (Kazama-shobo); Joichi Okuda's *Kesshoka suru Thoreau: Fuyu no Shikaku Kara [Henry David Thoreau and Crystallization]* (Kirihara-shoten); Satoru Shimpo's *Thoreau—Sono Ikikata [Thoreau— His Way of Life]* (Hokuju Shuppan); Toshikazu Niikura's *Emily Dickinson: Fuzai no Shozo [Emily Dickinson: A Portrait of the Absentee]* (Taishukan); and Yuko Adegawa's *Henry James Kenkyu: Inkutsubo to Cho [Henry James: A Man Catching Butterflies in an Inkwell]* (Kirihara-shoten).

American Renaissance Re-presented is a successful collaboration by three rising scholars, Takayuki Tatsumi, Hiroko Washizu, and Michiko Shimokobe. The project has been stimulated by numerous attempts by American scholars to deconstruct and reconstruct/ redefine what is called "the American Renaissance." Widely read in recent scholarship on the subject—to name only a few, Evan Carton's *The Rhetoric of American Romance* (1985), *The American Renaissance Reconsidered*, ed. Walter Benn Michaels et al. (1985), and Jeffrey Steele's *The Representation of the Self in the American Renaissance* (1987)—and well-equipped with recent critical tools, the threesome do what they will with Poe, Hawthorne, and Melville.

Tatsumi's Poe is first and foremost "Poe the Rhetorician," obsessed with the effects of words, letters, and signs. Tugged between the "telling" and the "writing," *The Narrative of Arthur Gordon Pym of Nantucket* is reduced at the end to the white blank page that confronts the reader; torn apart between a masque and a detective story, the form of "The Man of the Crowd" remains undetermined; the narrator of "The Black Cat" transforms from "the hunter" into "the hunted," and Poe's story changes into a metaphor for the witch. Most intriguing is the chapter on "The Man of the Crowd" (pp. 61–87).

Washizu's chapters in the section "Nathaniel Hawthorne—Fictionalism in America" have appeared previously in *SELit* and elsewhere. Her utmost concern in reading *The Scarlet Letter, The House of the Seven Gables,* and "Wakefield" is, as the subtitle for her section indicates, fictionalism itself. In that context the heroine of *The Scarlet Letter* is no other than the letter *A;* Hawthorne's romance completes itself when the letter gets textualized in the last line of the romance: "On a field, sable, the letter A, gules" (p. 128). Most convincing is her chapter on "Wakefield" (pp. 146–62); Washizu plays with the idea that there is no definitive "Wakefield" but many "Wakefields" who defy characterization/textualization.

The most readable of Shimokobe's chapters on Melville is a Lacanian rendering of *Pierre* (pp. 207–33). The discussions of *Moby-Dick,* "Benito Cereno," and *Pierre* clearly reflect her maturity as a critic. If the title of the book is to be taken seriously, surely Shimokobe's chapter on *Pierre,* which concludes the book, is rightly placed; here, Tatsumi's highfalutin' rhetoric in the "Introduction—Why American Renaissance, Now?" (pp. 9–31) makes for a happy landing. The chapter is plainly written, the prose flows smoothly, and the Lacanian formula is logically developed, all of which makes Shimokobe's sensitive diagnosis of the novel a fine exercise in Lacanian psychoanalysis. The variations played on the theme "Young America in Literature"— the book's Japanese title is taken from that of chapter 17 of *Pierre*—are Pierre, Pierre/Melville, American writers, the American Republic. While Pierre fails because of his immaturity as a writer who cannot distinguish "signifier" from "signified" (that is, his inability to sever himself from his mother), Melville survives because he was aware of the "différance" between the two. So does Young America interpreted as American Renaissance weather repeated deconstructions and representations through its critical history.

Radically different in approach to the three re-presented writers is Eiichi Fujita's *Alienation in the Traditional American Novel,* which adds Henry James to the list. Fujita's thesis that the pursuit of the modern self to its extremes leads to various forms of alienation in American society is examined in what he terms "traditional American novels": *Arthur Gordon Pym, The Scarlet Letter, Moby-Dick,* and *The Turn of the Screw.* The use of "traditional American novel" is arbitrary; the inclusion of James's potboiler in particular is suspect. With extensive excerpts, *Alienation,* like the author's *The Ambiguity of Henry James* (see *ALS 1985*), is no more than a well-prepared reader for college students.

In addition to the chapters just surveyed, two book-length studies of Poe came out. Chitoshi Motoyama's *Is Poe Dracula?* is an interesting reader-response reading of Poe as text. Motoyama's fascination with Poe the writer/text-reader, like Tatsumi's, centers on Poe's obsession with the power of language. Motoyama considers most of Poe's stories under the headings Civilization, Nature, False Nature/Artifice, Transformation of the Negative Self, Conclusion—Is Poe Dracula? The concluding chronology (pp. 237–40), a summary of and annotations to his discussions, is also a biography in disguise—Motoyama's own chronology as a reader of Poe's corpse/text laid in the coffin/text. Naturally, Poe/text wants to be read/reborn. Hence, the book's title. Though well-versed in recent and relevant scholarship on Poe, Motoyama is not always judicious in his use of that expertise. Sometimes sensitive and insightful in reading Poe/text, as in the case of "The Fall of the House of Usher" (pp. 31–39) or "William Wilson" (pp. 40–62), he often verges on self-contradiction; the frequent use of apologetic phrases—"If I may say so" and "I'd like to think so"—mars his argument.

On the other hand, Ichiro Tsujimoto's *Studies in Poe's Theory of Short Fiction* is a solid scholarly exploration of Poe's strength as a theoretician and the development of American short fiction; it is a culmination of the late Professor Tsujimoto's lifelong research in Poe and American short fiction, on which he published extensively.

In the introductory chapters Tsujimoto gives a good summary of theories of short fiction before Poe, touching on Aristotle's *Poetics* and Schlegel's *Vorlesungen über dramatische Kunst und Literatur*; then he explains how Poe assimilated their theories as his own, how literary and journalistic situations in early 19th-century America led to the publication in 1842 of what is now known as Poe's theory of creating "a single effect" or "the unity of effect" in a story. The book's real objective, however, is to closely examine critical receptions of Poe's theory and its impact on American writers since 1842 through seven periods to the present. Well-documented and informative, Tsujimoto's survey of the stages covering 1885, 1886–1919, and the '30s is of special interest. A few observations worthy of note: the publication of Brander Matthews's "Philosophy" (1885) helped to stabilize the influence of Poe's theory on American writers; ironically, the very popularity of "The Philosophy of Composition" led to its abuse in college creative-writing courses; in the '20s and '30s Poe's theory and the practice of modern American writers such as Hemingway, Anderson, and Porter became mutually exclusive. Tsujimoto concludes by reaffirming the validity of Poe's theory of short fiction today, citing in support John Gerlach's *Toward the End: Closure and Structure in the American Fiction* (1985). Tsujimoto's painstaking research and avid reading in relevant sources and scholarship, evident in a thorough concluding checklist, makes his *Studies in Poe's Theory of Short Fiction* an authentic critical history of American short fiction, the unanimously acknowledged American genre. Indeed, *Studies in Poe's Theory of Short Fiction* is the significant scholarly achievement of the year.

Tunemasa Yamamoto's "Edgar Poe: 'Eureka' Revisited" (*EigoS* 135:62–64) is a readable essay on "The Fall of the House of Usher" examined in the context of Poe's theory of the universe, though somewhat reminiscent of a chapter in Maurice Beebe's *Ivory Towers and Sacred Founts* (1964). The prodigious corpus of Japanese scholarship on Poe this year seems more than enough to vindicate Tatsumi's effort in *American Renaissance Re-presented* to restore Poe's stature as a major American Renaissance writer.

Thoreau also receives a fair amount of critical attention. Hatano's essay in *American Literature and Its Historical Changes* aptly illustrates Thoreau's favorable critical reception among Japanese scholars and writers. Thoreauvian "economy" has always appealed to the Japanese temperament, contradictory as it may seem in this age of plenty. Joichi Okuda's *H. D. Thoreau and Crystallization* is a welcome addition which contends that Thoreau's writings, especially *The Journal*, abound in the images of "a crystal" and of "crystallization," used to describe scenes of winter, the dawning of day, and the moment of poetic contemplation, which becomes the very image of Walden Pond, "the crystal well." According to Okuda's tally, the frequency with which Thoreau employs the four seasons and their cognate words in *The Journal*—spring, 722 times; summer, 1,033; autumn, 347; and winter, 957—reveals his strong preference for winter, which, Okuda contends, is expressed in the images of "crystal" and "crystallization," and the "fresh and unmelted" crystal becomes the very vehicle for Thoreau's idea of "concentration"—"atonement with the spirit." This is a slim volume; yet it clarifies the close-knit relation between Thoreau's ideal mode of living and a crucial set of images—a point unnoticed in previous scholarship.

Satoru Shimpo's *Thoreau—His Way of Life*, also a slim book, tries to compare Thoreau with Donne, Blake, Goethe, Schopenhauer, and the Japanese writer Tokutomi Roka. Unfortunately, Shimpo's discussion is muddled; no feasible relationship is established between Thoreau and these poets and philosophers. The book is poorly written and leaves much to be desired, because it contains some interesting topics that deserve fuller treatment. Shoko Itoh's article, "A Study of *Cape Cod*: From Wilderness to Wasteland" (*SELit* 65: 209–27), is an intelligent and clearly written essay which makes a good case for the structural/formal art of Thoreau's critically slighted work. The seemingly fragmentary structure and the digressions in *Cape Cod* are "innately connected with the theme of 'wreck'," which anticipates, Itoh argues, a similar leitmotif in Eliot's *The Waste Land.*

Emily Dickinson has enjoyed, perhaps more than any other 19th-century American writer, concentrated critical attention in recent years. She receives fully deserved treatment in Toshikazu Niikura's *Emily Dickinson: A Portrait of the Absentee*. A noted scholar of American poetry, with books on Dickinson and more modern poets, Niikura tries his hand at a portrait (not a sketch) of the poet, who is strangely "absent" in her poetry and letters. The book concerns, first, the poetry and, second, the letters. Niikura's curiosity about his subject is, however, not so much that of a biographer as of a reader-critic whose interest is in the problem of *ecriture*. Of special interest is his exploration in "Intertextuality of Women's Poetry" (pp. 134–67), a readable and timely discussion of the intertextuality in Dickinson and Sylvia Plath through comparatively examining the father-daughter relationships hidden in their texts. In her tribute to the 19th-century poet, Adrienne Rich writes, "you in your variorum monument/ equivocal to the end—/ who are you? . . ." Similarly, Niikura's book asks the same question in coming as close to the poet as any study has done. One of the year's few newly written books, this work is a much appreciated scholarly accomplishment.

Among the articles written on Dickinson, Hiroyuki Koguchi's "Emily Dickinson and Dream" (*SALit* 26:1–15) deserves mention. Koguchi discusses the use of dream in Dickinson's poetry, comparing it with the vision of dream in other American poets—notably Thoreau and Emerson—and observes that Dickinson has tried to integrate "conflicts, discords, paradoxes, and dilemmas into a tolerable unity by the vision of dream." Regrettably, the comparison is only partially successful.

Recent critical theories have found Henry James convenient to prove their validity; but so far no Japanese book-length study on James has been done which employs new critical strategies. Yuko Adegawa's *Henry James: A Man Catching Butterflies in an Inkwell* is no icebreaker. Hers is an old-fashioned interpretative study of the

Jamesian world which she says is composed of eight different aspects: the first three chapters discuss James's relations to France, Germany, and Italy; the remaining five consider money, children, women, marriage, and religion as components of James's world. Adegawa simply lists examples and passages from James's stories and novels in which references are made to these elements. Unfortunately, no sufficient discussion of any of them is provided. For example, she offers an interesting suggestion that the child in James's writings is a metaphor for one's inadequacy, helplessness, or pain; but she leaves the suggestion as such, and concludes the chapter on children in James without making any mention of Muriel G. Shine's *The Fictional Children of Henry James* (1968). The only exception is her consideration of Jamesian women in chapter 6 (pp. 127–44); her analyses of Mrs. Touchett in *The Portrait of a Lady* as a typical "new woman" and her reading of *The Bostonians* are convincing enough. Like many of the books surveyed, Adegawa's is a collection of essays published in academic journals. It suffers from a flaw common to such works—undue repetition: discussions overlap, and the same excerpts are used in different chapters, which revision and editing could easily redeem.

In contrast, Hideo Masuda's article on James's *The Wings of the Dove* (*SALit* 26:17–30) presents an interesting reading of "The Shepherd," "St. Luke," and "The Dove." Masuda's thesis that Mrs. Stringham, Sir Luke, and Milly herself participate in a drama of deception is fully articulated, well-supported by his judicious reading of James's text.

c. **20th-Century Fiction and Poetry.** Compared with the impressive scholarship on 19th-century fiction and poetry, Japanese academic work this year on 20th-century writers is meager in volume. Significant achievements are *Jack London: Essays on the Man and the Work*; Kiyoshi Nakayama's *Steinbeck no Kenkyu: California Jidai* [*John Steinbeck: California Years*] (Osaka: Kansai University Press); and Yoshio Hasegawa's *William Faulkner no Bungaku: Jisaku e no Akunaki Chosen* [*William Faulkner: His Persistent Challenge to His Own Work*] (Kirihara-shoten).

The first book in this list has been long in coming, having been launched as a joint research project with the establishment of the Jack London Society in 1982; its completion is an achievement worthy of celebration. Interestingly enough, most of London's major writings, fiction and nonfiction, have been translated into Japanese and widely

read among scholars in fields other than literature, it seems, long before his writings received any significant literary criticism. Many titles
are available in more than one edition.

Jack London: Essays consists of three parts. The first is devoted to
individual introductions to his major novels: *The Call of the Wild*
(Jinichi Kofuruma), *The Sea-Wolf* (Kazuhiro Kobayashi), *White Fang*
(Kiyoshi Okazaki), *The Iron Heel* (Nobuyuki Uchino), *Martin Eden*
(Takaharu Mori); the most readable is Mori's discussion of *Eden*,
which is repeatedly referred to in the book's other essays. The second
part consists of essays on the stories and critical writings: "Love of
Life" (Ryota Iijima); "Stories of Socialist Ideas" (Tadashi Saito);
"*The People of the Abyss*" (Kiyoshi Takatori); "*War of the Classes*
and *Revolution and Other Essays*" (Kiyohiko Murayama). This last
essay places London in the tradition of "American writers in action"
who embody the Emersonian "American Scholar," with whom action
is essential if subordinate; Murayama includes in the group Thoreau,
Twain, John Reed, Hemingway, and Mailer. His essay exposes the
limitations of London the man and the writer as a socialist, an evaluation shared by other contributors. The last part contains essays on
London the writer: "The Heroes and 'the logic of whiteness'" (Fu-
miko Goto); "Realism and Romanticism" (Takafumi Saito); "The
Critical Reception of Jack London Today" (Hisao Fukushi); "A Review of London's Biographies" (Akio Oura). Fukushi's reception
study (pp. 219–33) is a succinct summary and a judicious review-
essay of London scholarship. Oura's survey (pp. 234–57) of various
London biographies shows us the dramatic life this American writer
in action lived.

Discussions in all the essays are well-coordinated, a model for
scholarly collaboration. An interesting chronology of the writer in
cross-cultural context and a thorough bibliography, which includes all
the translated works, make *Jack London: Essays* a well-informed
and comprehensive contribution to London scholarship here and
abroad.

Another California writer, John Steinbeck, is perhaps a good example of "critical paradox": despite the long-term popularity he has
enjoyed in Japan—there is no English reader for Japanese high school
or college students that does not include either *Red Pony* or *The
Pearl*—his critical reception has never been enthusiastic. In this respect, Nakayama's book, like the Jack London volume, is an important

scholarly achievement for 1989. A collection of articles published in academic journals over some 20 years, the book is the culmination of Nakayama's long involvement with Steinbeck. In his modesty he admits that his critical work lacks in methodology—that is, he does not wield any of the recent critical tools. His is traditional textual analysis based on close readings of Steinbeck's works and biographical materials—manuscripts and letters—where all scholarly investigations begin. In his introductory chapter Nakayama offers a survey of Steinbeck's literary world; "the Phalanx Theory" and "Non-Teleological Thinking" Steinbeck shared with Edward Ricketts are explained as central to our understanding of Steinbeck the man and the writer. The novels and stories published during the California years are then discussed in the frame of reference defined in the introductory chapter. Taken in chronological order, they are *The Cup of Gold, The Pastures of Heaven, To a God Unknown, The Red Pony, Tortilla Flat, In Dubious Battle, Of Mice and Men, The Long Valley*, and *The Grapes of Wrath*. A concluding "Steinbeck Chronology" (pp. 334–413) with 28 beautiful new photographs (with one exception, all taken by the author) speaks for itself, old-fashioned as it may seem: to Nakayama, the writer's life (another text) is intrinsically interwoven into his literary creations.

William Faulkner is still the most frequently discussed 20th-century American writer in Japanese academe. In recent years Japanese scholars have made a few significant contributions to Faulkner scholarship. Kenzaburo Ohashi with his three-volume *Studies* and as co-editor of the international collaboration of essays (see *ALS 1987*) is now a familiar name to readers of *ALS*. The most recent book-length study in Japan on Faulkner is Yoshio Hasegawa's *William Faulkner: His Persistent Challenge to His Own Work*, a modest contribution. Hasegawa's volume is a collection of his articles written and published over 15 years. His intention, he explains, is to see the intertextuality among Faulkner's own writings. Discussion of the works is unevenly divided: 105 of 239 pages are given to the theme of love and death—"the front and the back door of the world"—in Faulkner's early stories and novels. Hasegawa contends that Faulkner's personal preference for epicene women led him to create the romantic heroes of the early stories and novels: Sir Gawain in *Mayday* and Donald Mahon in *Soldier's Pay*. And Quentin Compson in *The Sound and the Fury* and *Absalom, Absalom!* shares with Sir Gawain, his prototype, a similar preference for and attitude toward women. They are distant lovers, and their fear of sexuality or a peculiar stoicism concerning sex and women, Hasegawa argues, is Faulkner's own. His examination of erotic images in the immature and heavily romantic stories—"The Hill" and "Nympholepsy"—in relation to this theme is informative and useful for an understanding of Faulkner's more mature work—*The Sound and the Fury* and *Absalom, Absalom!* Yet, as might be expected, Hasegawa's discussions are repetitious. Further, quotations from the texts, accompanied by Japanese translations, make the book unnecessarily long and cumbersome. More careful revision might have prevented much of the awkwardness. In this, Hasegawa could have learned a lesson from Faulkner himself. Yet despite such technical snags, *William Faulkner* is a moderately significant contribution to Faulkner studies in Japan. The book fairly well accomplishes what it proposes to do—examine the intertextuality within Faulkner's early works.

Among the articles on 20th-century writers and poets, the following deserve brief comment: Hirotsugu Inoue's " 'The Snake' Centering on the Figure of Dr. Phillips" (*SALit* 26:31–41); Takashi Morita's "The Model Southern Gentleman—Faulkner's *The Reivers*" (*EigoS* 135:386–88); and Yoichiro Miyamoto's "On Ecriture and Cubist Painting in *In Our Time*" (*EigoS* 135:106–10). Inoue's essay on Steinbeck's unusual story in *The Long Valley* considers Dr. Phillips "as an image of modern man who lost his sense of God," a substantial complement to his *John Steinbeck: California Years*. In his article on *The Reivers*, Morita argues that Faulkner's idea of the Southern Gentleman culminates in the ideal gentleman's world realized in the final novels. And Miyamoto focuses on how through the process of "ecriture"/cubist painting, Nick Adams translates the landscape onto a blank page which eventually becomes the text we read—"The Big Two-Hearted River."

Although no book-length study of 20th-century American poetry appeared this year, two articles on Eliot are worth mentioning: Shunichi Murata's "Landscape in T. S. Eliot's Poetry" (*SELit* 65:17–32) and Yasuo Moriyama's "The Making of Eliot's 'Love Song of J. Alfred Prufrock' " (*EigoS* 135:648–50). The first discusses how Eliot creates "landscape in his poetry," using Dante's sense of "visual imagination" and his own memory of "a particular place in time." The second examines such ingredients that went into the making of "Love Song" as the rhythm of Ecclesiastes and the language of Henry James's "Crapy Cornelia."

d. **Contemporary Literature.** Japanese scholarly accomplishment on contemporary writers and poets is even slighter in volume than for the earlier 20th century. It seems that the endeavor to redefine the literary past, either the American Renaissance or the period of American Realism and Naturalism, has turned our attention from the contemporary scene. There was a single book-length study, Iwao Iwamoto's *Henyo suru American Fiction: Henka o Yomu* [*The Changing American Fiction: Reading the Changes in Style and Expression*] (Nan'undo). This also is a collection of essays, this time by a seasoned scholar who has published in various journals for two decades. Iwamoto's essays succinctly describe developments of Realism in American fiction going back to Henry James and "The Art of Fiction." Indeed, James constitutes the frame of reference for Iwamoto's discussions of writers after 1945. The book provides a good survey of changes in the American literary climate from modernism through postmodernism, concentrating on Mailer, Salinger, Capote, Malamud, Updike, Barth, Vonnegut, and Gass. The list is not all-inclusive; yet it serves Iwamoto's purpose.

The following articles on contemporary writers published in 1989 deserve mention: Sumiko Niimi's "Picaro and Circus: An Interpretation of *The Adventures of Augie March* as a Comedy of Survival" (*SALit* 26:45–56); Akiko Nakata's "A Questionable Quester—V in *The Real Life of Sebastian Night*" (*SALit* 26:59–71); Yoichiro Miyamoto's "*Gravity's Rainbow* and the Question of Postmodernism" (*SELit* 65:209–27); Tsutomu Yamasaki's "Collage, Rhythm, Parody— A Study of Donald Barthelme" (*EigoS* 135:391–93); Kiseko Mizuguchi's "Eudora Welty As She Is" (*EigoS* 135:644–50); Jun'ichiro Takachi's interview in "Something Different and New—Questions to John Ashbery" (*EigoS* 135:271–74); and Ifumi Yaguchi's "John Ashbery in Japan" (*EigoS* 135:275–76).

e. **American Culture.** A few words on our scholarly achievement in the field of American culture are necessary. Shunsuke Kamei's new collection of essays and articles, *Sei Kakumei no America: Utopia wa Dokoni* [*Sex Revolution in America: Will Utopia Ever Come?*] (Kodansha), is, like its companion piece, *Huckleberry Finn Now* (see *ALS 1985*), an entertaining and insightful critique. The reader is best advised to read the book in tandem with Kamei's earlier examination of sex and its expression, *The Descendants of the Puritans* (see *ALS 1987*). Kamei's critical vitality remains unabated, and his love affair with American cultural heroes and their antagonists (Marilyn Monroes and Anthony Comstocks) will endure, it is hoped. American literary studies in Japan are best conducted in such a sociocultural context.

Kobe College

vi. Scandinavian Contributions

Jan Nordby Gretlund, Elisabeth Herion-Sarafidis, Hans Skei

The activity in American literary scholarship in Scandinavia this year was not high. Most contributions were of a traditional nature, although some contemporary writers were studied (Hass, Tyler, Ashbery). Nineteenth-century writers Mary Boykin Chesnut and Grace King were examined from a feminist point of view, and Emily Dickinson was analyzed as "the poet of the moment" on the basis of Søren Kierkegaard's philosophy of "the moment." Also, an attempt at revisionist O'Neill scholarship can be found, together with an intertextual reading of *A Moon for the Misbegotten*. Inevitably, James, Faulkner, Hemingway, and Eliot figure on the list of American writers discussed by Scandinavian critics and scholars, and it is only fair that the most central authors play such a prominent role in the study of a foreign literature in small countries. A book in Danish on Eliot as a critic and poet and an essay on the legacy of Henry James as found in Hemingway and Fitzgerald, reissues with new afterwords (in Norwegian) of *Sanctuary* and *A Farewell to Arms*, and an essay on style in Faulkner's short fiction also indicate that most of the work in 1989 concentrated on 20th-century writers. The interesting work on Flannery O'Connor and Eudora Welty only strengthens this tendency. The great activity in literary criticism and theory in American literary scholarship has also been clearly felt in the 1980s in the Scandinavian countries, and a general introduction to the Yale school appeared in Danish in 1988. Perhaps the effects of the theoretical debates have been more strongly felt among literary scholars in general and comparative literature than among Americanists, who seem to continue in a fairly conventional and solid tradition of "scholarship."

a. **19th-Century Fiction.** Monica Papazu has dealt with Poe's thoughts on man and life in two essays. In "Man, a Thought of God: An Essay on Poe's Tales" (see *ALS 1988*, pp. 552–53), she maintains that Poe believed in the "meaning" of the world and in "a vision of the meaning that permeates all things." He was "always in search of man's identity," and his preoccupation with "the terrible evil of crime" was really a sign of his awareness of alienation. Papazu claims that Poe thought man unable to escape the terror of his own soul except in the act of creation. He held, with Erasmus and Swift, that analytical thought and abstraction are the true enemies of rationality and unity. His tales can be read as a warning against the lack of respect for the individual which parades as abstract "love of mankind." The continuation of this argument is Papazu's "The Search for Life and Truth in Edgar Allan Poe's Tales" (*Atlantis* [Spain], 11:125–36). For Poe, the essence of knowledge lies in the continuous movement toward it in the act of searching. As an uncompromising antireductionist, Poe was always imagining "the possibility of a truth entirely different from the received one." Death was one of the established truths that Poe questioned. He returned to this subject again and again, Papazu argues convincingly, because he could *not* imagine the reality of nothingness; and in his stories Poe showed that death is *impossible*.

In her essay "Writing Herstory: Mary Chesnut's Civil War" (*SoSt* 26:18–27), Clara Juncker has described Chesnut's diary as a feminist document written by a "veteran of the battlefields of Confederate drawing-rooms." The diary is seen as "a statement on Woman-as-Artist," in which Chesnut saw Confederate society as a storybook "written by and writing herself." In recording her observations, Chesnut also redefined the notion of history, as the form of the diary is in itself "a rebellion against male conceptions of genre and gender." Juncker's feminism has also found expression in several essays on Grace King, the late 19th-century New Orleans novelist. In her "Grace King: Woman-as-Artist" (*see ALS 1987*, p. 210), Juncker first described King's feminism as expressed in stories such as "One Woman's Story" and "Madriléne; Or, The Festival of the Dead." She continues her study of King as a paradigm of woman-as-writer in "The Mother's Balcony: Grace King's Discourse of Femininity" (*NOR* 15:39–46), claiming that King's true subject was the lives of women occupying a position of marginality. Her literary reputation has suffered from her lack of interest in plot, as in *Balcony Stories*, but since she saw reality as basically plotless, this practice can be defended. What Juncker finds more damaging to her fiction was King's failure to reconcile her emancipatory stance on gender with her conservative position on region, race, and class. Juncker's recent essay "Grace King: Feminist, Southern Style" (*SoQ* 26, iii:15–30) is less partisan in its feminism. King is still seen as a feminist, but now "perhaps inadvertently," and her feminism is viewed as subtle and discreet. In a consideration of King's life and art, particularly of her last novel *La Dame de Sainte Hermine*, Juncker celebrates the renewed interest in King by showing that "a woman in the world of Grace King is like a jewel in a museum case."

b. 19th-Century Poetry. Brita Lindberg-Seyersted, whose *The Voice of the Poet: Aspects of Style in the Poetry of Emily Dickinson* (1968) remains one of the most important books in the field, published "An Analysis of Emily Dickinson's 'Further in Summer than the Birds'" (pp. 260–68 in *Nineteenth-Century Literature Criticism* 21, Gale), which is basically a reprint of the concluding chapter from *The Voice of the Poet*, with minor revisions. In this chapter the poem is discussed to bring together the various aspects of Dickinson's style in an analysis which can "account for the greatest quantity of data in the words of the poem." The conclusion, that Dickinson has "successfully made her raid on the inarticulate," is well-warranted on the basis of this careful explication.

In his monograph *Søren Kierkegaard og Emily Dickinson:En sammenlignende studie* [*A Comparative Study*] (Faaborg, Denmark) Niels Kjær argues that Dickinson was "the poet of the moment" in exactly the sense that Kierkegaard was "the philosopher of the moment." As his point of departure, Kjær looks at some resemblances in their lives: their early years were dominated by puritanical fathers, and they always remained obsessed with their fathers. Both were able to transform the father-opposition into a radical distrust of all ideologies and of all religious systems that attempt to explain human life; but they were unable to form lasting relationships with the other sex and became solitary and strange figures in Amherst and Copenhagen. They chose to remain unknown to the public, she using various voices in her poems and not wanting to publish, he publishing his essays under pseudonyms; therefore, his existentialism and her poetry did not become subjects for discussion until this century. Kjær claims that they selected their own roles and acted them perfectly, sublimating private losses into art and immortality. The parallels between their lives are, however, less interesting than similarities between their attitudes to official Christendom. Their passionate relationship with God brought them into conflict with established denominations. Kierkegaard was perhaps the most religious man in Denmark in the 19th century; nevertheless, he wrote a series of essays undermining the very idea of a respectable official Christianity. Dickinson was also very religious, but she stopped going to church. Kjær maintains that "she rebelled against the puritanical god her father had created in his own image." A shared feature of Kierkegaard's theology and Dickinson's poetry is the emphasis on the paradoxical nature of Christianity. Both identified with the absolute paradox as represented in the suffering Christ: God in human form. Kjær points out that the greatest difference between them is that Dickinson had no sense of guilt, whereas Kierkegaard was constantly conscious of his guilt. He never questioned God's ways, unlike Dickinson whose unsent "private letters to the world" reveal much doubt. The most original idea in this monograph focuses on Kierkegaard's idea of the moment: "A man can lose himself in the past, in the present, and in the future. But a man can as well choose to assume his own existence in the present moment—and then he is. The moment is the only occasion on which time touches upon eternity—and God reveals himself to man!" Kjaer is convincing in showing that Dickinson in her poetry used the moment in the same manner to focus on existential despair. Each of her poems contains the divine moment, and only the experience of that moment was able to inspire her.

c. **20th-Century Fiction.**   Ernest Hemingway's *A Farewell to Arms* was reissued in a Norwegian translation (*Farvel til våpnene*, Bokklubben) with an afterword by Hans Skei. Stating that the borders between life and fiction in Hemingway's case are more difficult to establish than for most writers, Skei outlines what helped to create the Hemingway *myth*; he also gives a survey of Hemingway's career and critical reception. In the same critic's afterword to William Faulkner's *Sanctuary* (in Norwegian: *Det aller helligste*, Bokklubben, 1988), he concentrates on the genesis of this novel, which Faulkner revised considerably in galleys. The afterword includes comments on style and language and attempts to give *Sanctuary* the place it deserves in the development of the American novel in this century.

Hans Skei's "Inadequacies of Style in Some of William Faulkner's Short Stories" (*Faulkner's Discourse*, pp. 234–41) investigates the relationship between the rhetorical force of Faulkner's language and his choice of subject matter, characters, and theme, and finds that in some cases one is tempted to use the term "inadequate" to describe his style. To show Faulkner's stylistic peculiarities and preferences in the short fiction, Skei discusses four stories, each from a different period: "Moonlight," "Uncle Willy," "Shall Not Perish," and "Sepulture South: Gaslight," finding "Moonlight" and the overwritten World War II story "Shall Not Perish" inadequate as to style. Skei argues, finally, that "stylistics" has an important role to play in evaluation, a position so many critics today find problematic.

Jan Nordby Gretlund's "The Terrible and the Marvelous: Eudora Welty's Chekhov" (*Eudora Welty: Eye of the Storyteller*, ed. Dawn Trouard [Kent State], pp. 107–18) argues that Welty has been able to combine more essentially Chekhovian elements in her fiction than anybody else writing in English. There *are* obvious differences between the two writers, but in her use of the convincing detail, in her psychological realism and humorous vision of people and their illusions, in her subtle development of social issues, in her emphasis on imagination, sensibility, and compassion, and in her cautious optimism, Welty combines several essential Chekhovian elements and deserves the epithet "the Chekhov of the South." Bo Green Jensen's "En vej i vildnisset" [A Road in the Wilderness] (*Revue* [Aarhus] 1: 20–21) is an introduction to Larry McMurtry's fiction. Green Jensen claims that McMurtry has done for the West what Faulkner did for the South. In *Lonesome Dove* and in *Anything for Billy*, he has written novels in the tradition of the peculiar mythology associated with the Wild West, as if he were trying to fix the Old West in his mind one last time in an attempt to fully comprehend it before it disappears. The novels are described as equal parts anecdote and conscientious authentic chronicling, and Green Jensen sees the mixture of "pathos, humor, action, tragedy, lyrical moments and coarse jokes" as an irresistible narrative method.

Erik Nielsen's "Om Detaljen" [On Detail] (*Fantasi og fiktion*, ed. Erik Svejgaard and John Thobo-Carlsen [Odense], pp. 99–135) was written in defense of a literary element often neglected in criticism. With examples from Flannery O'Connor's *Wise Blood*, Faulkner's *Sanctuary*, and Norris's *McTeague*, Nielsen demonstrates that detail is far from uninteresting for us in experiencing fiction and analyzing it.

Detail is often vital for our ability to flesh out the text with our own images; as an example, Nielsen uses Temple Drake's shoe and Tommy's handling of it. It is demonstrated that a detail does not have to be integrated into the life of the character, nor does it have to be necessary or symbolic to add substantially to our experience of fiction. Except for some misconceptions about Faulkner's racial attitude, this is a very convincing demonstration of the importance of detail. In the second part of the essay the point of departure is Georg Lukács's total rejection of emphasis on details and Georg Brandes's acceptance of the importance of apparently peripheral details. Nielsen's own contribution to the discussion is his discovery that often the detail *is* the whole, in fragment. As an example, he mentions the description of the Old Frenchman's Place in *Sanctuary*, a detail at the opening of the novel; the short description of the ruin is important as an image of a lost tradition, and if this detail is missed, the necessary counterimage to the degenerate South of the whole novel is overlooked as well. Other examples of the function of detail in structuring a novel are the position of Aunt Emily's three fingers in Walker Percy's *The Moviegoer* and the baptism of the dead Rose Aster in Pat Conroy's *The Prince of Tides*. The detail makes concrete, it vitalizes, and it characterizes, according to Nielsen. In "Ligbegængelse- Et byproblem i urbanitetens hjørne" [The Handling of Bodies: A City Problem in the Corner of Urbanity] (*Moderne bykultur: A Newsletter* [Odense] 9: 16–23), Erik Nielsen elaborates further on Flannery O'Connor's use of detail. He asks: why is it so important for Mason Tarwater to be buried in the ground rather than cremated? A part of the answer is that it is a heathen custom to burn bodies. But young Tarwater's refusal to carry out the old man's burial instructions is, Nielsen claims, more than just stubborn flirting with heathenism, and it is more than anti-Christian pragmatism; it is also a violation of the old-fashioned Southern ways of burying. The issue reflects on O'Connor: although she was a Catholic, her faith was also very much of her region.

In "Arven fra Henry James" [The Legacy of Henry James] (*Passage* [Aarhus] 6:105–18), Helle Porsdam sees Ernest Hemingway and F. Scott Fitzgerald as the inheritors of James's international theme. James used this theme to express his own mental conflicts, in particular the conflict between the American and the European in his split personality; the international theme was thus an element in his discussion of self-definition, and it was this aspect that appealed to Hemingway and Fitzgerald, according to Porsdam. It is in the meeting with Europe that their protagonists live through an existential crisis. In the Old World the expatriates of *The Sun Also Rises* and of *Tender Is the Night* are forced to reevaluate and perhaps re-create their native country and its ideals. For both Hemingway and Fitzgerald any true appreciation of James would have been experienced as a surrender to their own more feminine characteristics, according to Porsdam, and therefore it occurred only in spite of their conscious selves. It is interesting that in this essay James is seen exclusively as a novelist of a feminine sensibility. The portrait of Hemingway's "struggles" with the Master is more successful than the passages postulating Fitzgerald's interest in James. The truth seems to be that Fitzgerald did not think much about James one way or the other. But it is, of course, true that the stay in Europe for all three meant an increased awareness and understanding of their Americanness. Morten Brask's "Manden der græd om natten" [The Man Who Cried at Night] (*Standart* [Aarhus] 3/4:22–23) also reflects the continued Scandinavian interest in Hemingway. It is mainly a biographical sketch which perpetuates misconceptions about his supposedly chauvinistic male characters, overemphasizes the effect of the lacy girl's dresses of Ernest's first years, and yet never even mentions *The Garden of Eden*.

The novelist Anne Tyler has so far met with very little interest in the scholarly community as a whole, despite her critical acclaim and large readership. With *The Temporal Horizon: A Study of the Theme of Time in Anne Tyler's Major Novels* (Almquist and Wiksell), Karin Linton seeks to redress this situation, choosing as her approach to the fictional world of Tyler the temporal psychology of the main characters in four of her 11 novels, *Celestial Navigation*, *Searching for Caleb*, *Dinner at the Homesick Restaurant* and *The Accidental Tourist*. Linton takes as her point of departure Tyler's avowed interest in character, sees her as a novelist whose overall purpose it is "to populate a town," who is preoccupied with day-to-day change and endurance. Time is not viewed as an abstraction but rather as a "succession of changes to which man has to adapt." It is the novelist's task to describe such temporal losses and the characters' reactions to them, their varying ability to adapt and respond to changes. The terminology Linton uses in her discussion is taken from the psychologist Fraisse, notably the concept of "temporal horizon," which consists of the interrelated perspectives of the past, the present, and the future.

Each human action is, somewhat self-evidently, said to take place "in a temporal perspective; it depends on our temporal horizon at the precise moment of occurrence." Linton focuses on moments of dramatic change in the lives of the protagonists of these four novels (adding in a conclusion a survey of Tyler's remaining work), outlining their different temporal attitudes, establishing to what extent their existence is dominated by a perspective of the past, the present, or the future, or whether they have taken refuge in the intemporal. It is not an investigation overburdened by theoretical argument; its strength lies rather in perceptive and sensitive readings.

Lars Ole Sauerberg's "The Novel in Transition: Documentary Realism" (*OL* 44:80–92) deals with the many attempts to create alternatives to traditional realism. Sauerberg focuses on what he calls "documentary realism," which he sees as "an intermediary category" between mainstream realism and the nonfiction novel. The experimentation that takes place in E. L. Doctorow's novels, for example, it is argued, does not really challenge the conventions of the traditional realistic novel. Unlike Mailer's and Capote's experiments with the nonfiction novel, documentary realism as in *Ragtime* is easily categorized as fiction by its readers, and therefore the "mental processing" of facts happens according to the conventions of fiction. The author's vision, which is so important in the realistic novel, is also the essence of documentary realism, and perhaps even of the nonfiction novel. Sauerberg concludes that the realistic novel is simply adapting to modern times; its instruments are not obsolete, they just need adjusting and sharpening.

När Nick Carter drevs på flykten [*When Nick Carter Was Driven Off*] (Sweden: Gidlunds) deals with popular literature and is a most interesting study of reception. Ulf Boëthius writes the story of the campaign, really something of a moral crusade, against "the literature of filth," occasioned by the first wave of multinational mass-produced literature to hit Sweden shortly after the turn of the century. It was the first real equivalent of the popular paperbacks of today and was modeled on the American dime novels and nickel weeklies. "The Nick Carter literature" was the name disparagingly given to this whole genre, consisting of all kinds of detective and adventure stories, by those who saw Nick Carter as embodying the potentially dangerous American mentality. They feared the disintegration of the existing social order, seeing that Sweden at the time was a society facing

rapid, great, and, for some, drastic change. Nick Carter became the
scapegoat for what was generally perceived as "threats to our spiritual
life" when the campaign against this extremely popular and widely
read literature was at its most intense. Boëthius's aim in this study is
threefold: to determine the nature of "these abhorrent books," why
youth found them so attractive; second, to throw light on what really
happened when they were banned; and, third, to determine the underlying causes for the moral panic and violent campaign against them.

d. 20th-Century Poetry. Viggo Hjørnager Pedersen's *Fra T. S.
Eliots verden: Eliot som kritiker, samfundsdebatør og digter* [*From
T. S. Eliot's World: Eliot as Critic, Social Critic, and Poet*] (Copenhagen: POET) sets out to correct misleading impressions left in debates by indiscriminate quoting from Eliot's works without reference
to his changing points of view. Pedersen is good at summarizing
Eliot's opinions of any given period. He argues that Eliot did not
become the critics' critic by establishing a system once and for all. He
was, in fact, never satisfied with his own critical definitions and always sought new ways of defining the poetic sublime. Pedersen traces
the slow change in Eliot's interests from the purely aesthetic to questions about the function of poetry, and he sees the development as
being from "cleverness" to "wisdom," an expression frequently used
by Eliot himself. The development in his critical point of view, it is
argued, can be fully understood only in relation to his views on society and religion: Eliot's cultivation of the past and of tradition was
balanced by his pessimistic view of the role of art in his own time.

Throughout the book it is implied that Eliot's critical declarations
on poetry are of particular importance because he wrote successful
poetry. Pedersen is, however, unimpressed with Eliot's critical view
of the personal in art. He argues that, whatever metaphysical justification he offered, Eliot's frequent play with the word "personality"
had the sole purpose of showing that the individual is of inferior importance in the creation of art. Pedersen argues that if art is to be
created and received in an impersonal way, it would finally be not
only an impersonal but an inhuman and dispassionate exchange, as if
two computers exchanged already defined bits of information. He
points out that Eliot never observed his own impersonality theory;
even in "Ash Wednesday" the first person of the poem is far from being impersonal. And in his essay "The Frontiers of Criticism" (1956),

Eliot's view on the necessity of the impersonal in the creation and reception of art had developed to the point where he encouraged personal positions and attitudes.

It was his personal view of Christianity that brought Eliot into opposition to Romanticism. Eliot did not use the words "classic" and "romantic" in the usual vague way; instead, he stressed certain aspects of these concepts to help his argument against the latter. Pedersen argues that Eliot's attitude to Romanticism was based not on aesthetic principles but on personal emotions: what Eliot hated about Romanticism, i.e., the literary period, was its belief in the possibility of a happy life, a belief founded on the conviction that man is good. One of the ideas that strongly appealed to Eliot about Christianity was the doctrine of Original Sin, which supported his view of man as being essentially bad. Pedersen finally looks at Eliot's poems and concludes that they are classical in that they demonstrate a sense of the past and strive to be impersonal, but the poems are not traditional in form or content. The form is mostly new and provocative; the content argues that life is insufferable—in particular the relations between the sexes— and this attitude is far from being classical or resigned. There was, especially in the early years, a marked difference between Eliot's poetic ideals and poetic practice. Fortunately, the poet was unable to control his feelings in the manner of Dr. Johnson and Alexander Pope.

The relation of three major contemporary poets to their region, the American Northwest, is the subject of Lars Nordström's *Theodore Roethke, William Stafford, and Gary Snyder: The Ecological Metaphor as Transformed Regionalism* (Almquist and Wiksell). It is Nordström's contention that a change can be observed to have taken place in Northwestern regionalism since World War II, an evolution "into some kind of Northwestern sense of place." The theme he pursues in this study is the development in poetry of an environmental ethic. He sees the ecological metaphor as an expression of place, arguing that it must be understood as a general poetic strategy selected by the three poets in question, representing a transformed regional impulse, resulting in "a poetry of place with an ethical stance." Through close readings of the works of the three poets, Nordström establishes direct links between these poems in their attempt to formulate "a broad ethic which defines a more general, noncombative relationship between man and nature." There is a strong sense of being present in an American geography, often articulated in the Native American context, ranging from Roethke's vision of unity with divine nature, to Stafford's more explicit advocacy of reverence toward nature, to Snyder's philosophy of re-inhabitation, of truly being attuned to the American continent and its environment.

Niels Frank's "Doubletalk" (*Revue* [Aarhus], 1:16–19) is an interesting interview with John Ashbery. Several collections of Ashbery's poetry have appeared in Scandinavia in translation. Frank, who has done some of that translation, describes the poetry as encyclopedically positioned in the space between the poet and the world around him. In this position Ashbery's poems can examine the limits of and the transitions between his two existential poles. He admits to using bits of street conversation in his poetry in an attempt to make the form as open as possible. He writes every day, as poetry first and foremost is practice and experience. He has stopped writing art criticism, since it is a demanding job, whereas "the poems write themselves." He has become aware of Ashberyisms in work by others, and now he tries not to imitate himself. He has no use for political poetry, would not recognize "a basic value" if he stumbled upon one, and is not aware of having any. At present he tries to depersonalize himself in his poems, but not to the point of confusing the reader, which he does not see as the purpose of poetry. Ashbery thinks the critic Harold Bloom misinterprets his poetry in order to prove the influence of Wallace Stevens, whereas Ashbery believes himself to be more influenced by W. H. Auden.

In his essay "The Discursive Muse: Robert Hass's 'Songs to Survive the Summer'" (*SN* 61:193–201), Bo Gustavsson introduces a group of poets, not much known in Scandinavia, who appeared in the 1970s. They had in common their rejection of the aesthetics of modernist lyric poetry and attempted "a new discursive poetry." The discussion of Robert Hass's work culminates in an analysis of the poet's longest and most successful poem, "Songs to Survive the Summer," which appeared in *Praise* in 1979. Hass sees discourse as a "form of time," using it as a means to meditate on the human condition, staying close to the essentials of life, always firmly rooted in the here and now, sensually alert to the wonder of being alive. Gustavsson finds "Songs" to be a poem concerned with different facts of death, with the necessity of recognizing and confronting one's fears, ultimately the fear of death, but also concerned with death as intensifier of life, life-enhancer.

e. 20th-Century Drama.   Eugene O'Neill has been of special interest to Scandinavian scholars for a long time. This year two contributions are devoted to him. Seeking to deepen our understanding of the characters Jim Tyrone and Josie Hogan and their interaction, Sven-Johan Spånberg in "*A Moon for the Misbegotten* as Elegy: An Intertextual Reading" (*SN*, 61:23–36) focuses on the many quotations and poetical allusions in the play. He demonstrates that in these can be found the intertextual answer to the "ungrammaticality" of Josie as well as "an understanding of loss, mourning and consolation as the central themes of the play, themes which constitute its elegiac matrix." The character of Jim is approached through the endlessly echoing allusions to Ernest C. Dowson's poem "Cynara," while the origin of Josie, an earth-mother figure, is traced to the dual source of Baudelaire's "La Géante" and Swinburne's elegy on the dead brother poet Baudelaire, "Ave Atque Vale." Spånberg demonstrates persuasively how O'Neill retained the symbolic allusions of these poems, how the weblike structure of echoes of "Cynara" aids in the shaping of the despairing, sorrowful character of Jim Tyrone, how the play absorbs the poem and moves beyond it, and how the poems by Baudelaire and Swinburne, "with the mythic, pagan visions of a giant woman with an adult man-child," can be seen as an intertext, symbolically incorporated and re-created in this naturalist drama.

Of minor interest, except for information contained in the footnotes, is Pat M. Ryan's "*Long Day's Journey* Was the 'Wrong' Play" (*ThS* 29,i[1988]:103–12), a translation of a 1973 newspaper article by Karl Ragnar Gierow, manager of The Royal Dramatic Theatre in Stockholm and responsible for the many O'Neill world premieres there. In a brief introduction and in the notes, Ryan gives much information. Most interesting is what he has to say about the acquisition of the manuscript for *Long Day's Journey*.

f. Theory and Criticism.   *Tekst og Trope: Dekonstruktion i Amerika*, eds. Lars Erslev Andersen and Hans Hauge (Aarhus: Modtryk, 1988), is a general introduction to American deconstruction in criticism and a presentation of the so-called Yale school. In their choice of *Text and Trope* as their title, the editors want to emphasize the main contribution to critical debate of American deconstruction, i.e., the focusing on the *rhetorical* moment in both literature and theory. In an opening essay Hans Hauge tells the history of the movement, explains the doctrine and its method, and deconstructs a classic Danish poem as an example. There are individual essays on Paul de Man, M. H. Abrams and J. Hillis Miller, Harold Bloom, Geoffrey Hartman, and others. The editors hope that the collection will help introduce deconstructive criticism and prepare the way for a postmodern hermeneutics.

Odense, Uppsala, Oslo Universities

20. General Reference Works

David J. Nordloh

The computer continues its advance into the reference room. The latest of the traditional resources to make the translation into electronic form is "Twayne's United States Authors Series," the 30-year-old series of monographs on individual writers great and small. *DiscLit: American Authors* (Hall) is a CD-ROM "product" featuring the full text of 143 of the most important titles in the original series—including those on Poe, Hawthorne, Dickinson, Crane, Langston Hughes, and Mailer—together with a related bibliography of 127,000 books, serials, audiovisual materials, manuscripts, and other items derived from the OCLC electronic catalog of library holdings. Using search software suitable for the personal computer, *DiscLit* provides the capability to search both the TUSAS volumes and the accompanying bibliography by word and phrase, a feature that might make it attractive even for those with access to the more cumbersome print resources of the research library.

From the disk to the handbook. Tradition is the first but by no means the only strength of *Sixteen Modern American Authors, Volume 2: A Survey of Research and Criticism Since 1972*, ed. Jackson R. Bryer (Duke), which supplements rather than replaces the 1972 revision of *Sixteen Modern American Authors* (1969), that indispensable paragon of collections of bibliographical essays. The 16 authors—for those who have been in a cave all this time—are Anderson, Cather, Hart Crane, Dreiser, Eliot, Faulkner, Fitzgerald, Frost, Hemingway, O'Neill, Pound, Robinson, Steinbeck, Stevens, William Carlos Williams, and Wolfe. As Bryer points out, the passage of time has also been marked by the deaths of four of the original contributors. Bernice Slote, Reginald Cook, Frederick J. Hoffman, and C. Hugh Holman had written the original essays on Cather, Frost, Hemingway, and Wolfe, respectively.

The second edition, revised and enlarged, of *Handbook of American Popular Culture*, ed. M. Thomas Inge (Greenwood), in three volumes, represents the continuation and expansion of another well-established bibliographical tool. As in the original, each chapter consists of an overview essay on a topic followed by a selected bibliography. The sections in the first edition most obviously pertinent to our needs, including the chapters on literature, poetry, and drama, have been moved out of this work—which carries the title of Inge's original enterprise—and into his *Handbook of American Popular Literature*, published last year (see *ALS 1988*, p. 560). Still, there are several chapters covering topics of some relevance: Faye Nell Vowell, "Minorities" (pp. 745–70); Jeanie K. Forte and Katherine Fishburn, "Women" (pp. 1425–58); Anne E. Rowe, "Regionalism" (pp. 1185–1202); and Richard A. Schwarzlose, "Newspapers" (pp. 817–49). And the discussion of definitions and methods in the appendix by Michael J. Bell, "The Study of Popular Culture" (pp. 1459–84), is worth a look.

The *Dictionary of Literary Biography* program published by Gale—in its various manifestations it is more than a series—relentlessly masses itself on the shelves. *American Short-Story Writers, 1880–1910*, ed. Bobby Ellen Kimbel with the assistance of William E. Grant (*DLB* 78), is the second volume on this genre, an earlier one having dealt with writers prominent before 1880 (*DLB* 74). Among the 31 writers here treated in biographical-critical essays and the other standard *DLB* apparatus are Lafcadio Hearn, Mary Wilkins Freeman, Willa Cather, Stephen Crane, Jack London, Edith Wharton, and Owen Wister. It is to be expected, in a volume like this one made up of essays by different hands, that there will be unevenness; the Hearn essay is barely satisfactory, for instance, and the Freeman very substantial. The illustrations are uniformly effective. Another addition to a subset is *American Magazine Journalists, 1850–1900*, ed. Sam G. Riley (*DLB* 79), carrying on from the earlier *American Magazine Journalists, 1741–1850* (*DLB* 73). The 50 entries here reflect the centrality and diversity of the magazine medium in American national life, with such figures as James Russell Lowell and W. D. Howells on the high edge, Frank Leslie and John Brisben Walker on the low, and Bret Harte and Victoria Woodhull somewhere between. *Chicano Writers, First Series*, ed. Francisco A. Lomeli and Carl R. Shirley (*DLB* 82), is a new topic for the series and a departure from its typical pattern. In their preface the editors argue that "Chicano literature, the aesthetic principles that define it, and the body of criticism that supports it resist comparison to what may be called mainstream American literature," and indeed by its addressing its own audience and their needs may be "often elusive" to other readers. Acknowledging this separateness, the volume consists not only of the usual essays on individual authors—52 of them, including Eusebio Chacón and Miguel Antonio Otero—but general essays on Chicano history and language, and even an essay on literary works about Chicanos written by non-Chicanos, Antonio Márquez's "Literature Chicanesca: The View from Without" (pp. 309–15).

Dictionary of Literary Biography Yearbook: 1988 (Gale) evidences the ongoing evolution of this particular beast into a not-quite-almanac, not-quite-review. There are two new major sections, one covering the year's literary events and topics, the other obituaries and tributes. These join the usual annual reports on literary biography, book publishing, poetry, and fiction, and reports on book reviewing, new literary periodicals, the Nobel Prize. There are a list of awards and honors, a checklist of new works in literary history and biography, and a necrology. But there is also a biographical-critical essay on the Nobel laureate, Najib Mahfuz, accompanied by the text of his Nobel lecture, accompanied by an essay by Jeffrey Meyers on the Nobel Prize and literary politics. There are obituaries (including a very touching one on Nancy Hale) and essays celebrating the centenaries of Raymond Chandler, T. S. Eliot, and Eugene O'Neill. In sum, a frustrating—and expensive—mix of the essential and the ephemeral.

The last *DLB* item this year, *Hardboiled Mystery Writers*, ed. Matthew J. Bruccoli and Richard Layman (*DLB* Documentary Series 6), is consistent with the pattern of this series-within-the-series and fascinating as a "look" rather than a "read." The mystery writers in this instance are Raymond Chandler, Dashiell Hammett, and Ross Macdonald, and the emphasis really is on documents—photographs, facsimiles of letters and manuscripts and other handwritten authorial items, and reproductions of newspaper, magazine, and scholarly assessments. The editors offer no biographical-critical essays, no long introduction: only a brief preface and extensive caption commentary, most of it biographical in nature, on the items.

Though *DLB* is the most prominent of the Gale publications related to American literature, it is not the only one. *American Dramatists*, ed. Matthew Roudané, volume 3 in Gale's "Contemporary Authors Bibliographical Series," offers primary and secondary bibliographies together with essays commenting on the major secondary works for 17 authors, among them Albee, Baraka, Hansberry, Rabe, Shepard, and Tennessee Williams. Similar to it in focus, but by another publisher and treating a greater number of authors, is *American Playwrights since 1945: A Guide to Scholarship, Criticism, and Performance,* ed. Philip C. Kolin (Greenwood). Forty playwrights, in alphabetical order from Albee to Zindel, with Robert Lowell, Arthur Miller, and Arthur Kopit among others between, are accorded analytical bibliographical essays followed by checklists of the items discussed. The essays address five topic categories: achievements and reputation, primary bibliography, production history, survey of secondary sources, and future research opportunities. Despite differences in organization, these two volumes seem evenly matched in their value as reference resources. In the same general area but with a more biographical and less scholarly orientation is *Contemporary Theatre, Film, and Television,* ed. Linda S. Hubbard and Owen O'Donnell (Gale), volume 6 of which was published this year. The series is a continuation of *Who's Who in the Theatre,* which went through 17 editions before the transition. It is possible to find some writers here (William Link and Neil Simon among them), but not easy: with no index, a prefatory list indicating who is to be treated in coming volumes, and entries in alphabetical order, the reader must thumb and hope.

William McPheron and Jocelyn Sheppard have compiled *The Bibliography of Contemporary American Fiction, 1945–1988: An Annotated Checklist* (Meckler). This selective list identifies a total of 613 items divided between multi-author and single-author studies, with the latter category subdivided by authors. The volume includes subjects and author indexes; it excludes poets who also wrote fiction, since these are covered in McPheron's *The Bibliography of Contemporary American Poetry, 1945–1985* (1986). A very different kind of book covering part of this same period is Karen Hinckley and Barbara Hinckley's *American Best Sellers: A Reader's Guide to Popular Fiction* (Indiana). Concentrating on the period 1965–85 and the 468 books and 216 authors, American or not, identified by the *World Almanac* as highest in U.S. sales, the Hinckleys provide a master list of them all, arranged by authors first and then best-selling titles in alphabetical order, including brief biographies and notes on the genres of the works. Then follow chapters on topics drawing on that information: the characteristics of best-selling authors (their ages, experiences, educations, other jobs, and so on), the popularity of certain genres, characters, themes, and trends. Appendixes record awards and distinctions, pseudonyms, books made into movies, books by year of publication. Though not the most toughly scholarly stuff and written in a style part sociology and part soap opera, this book is both cultural groundwork and great fun.

A step up in seriousness and concerned with form rather than popularity is Susan Garland Mann's *The Short Story Cycle: A Genre Companion and Reference Guide* (Greenwood). In pedestrian prose that never quite settles on a satisfactory working definition of this genre upon a genre, Mann provides essays and bibliographies for nine "representative" cycles, all 20th-century, including Faulkner's *The Unvanquished* and Updike's *Too Far to Go: The Maple Stories,* and then lists, by authors, other 20th-century examples. Despite its limitations, her study has its interest and could be a productive beginning for research and teaching.

Three very different volumes concentrate on aspects of women's writing, one of those more narrowly with "women of color," and a fourth deals with black writers male and female. Gwenn Davis and Beverly A. Joyce have compiled *Personal Writings by Women to 1900: A Bibliography of American and British Writers* (Okla.) to "demonstrate something of the variety of women's literary activity before the twentieth century and to enable readers to find and rediscover their work." The crucial content here is an alphabetical list by authors, then titles, unannotated, the whole elaborately cross-indexed by maiden and married names and pseudonyms. An appendix identifies these women writers by chronological periods, an index cites major topics and genres, and the introduction surveys the writing by periods. Bernice Redfern's *Women of Color in the United States: A Guide to the Literature* (Garland) stresses publications mostly since 1975 in almost every field of scholarship—literature, politics, sociology, education. Redfern divides the work into separate chapters on Afro-American, Asian-American, Hispanic American, and Native American women, and offers in each instance a brief overview of the significant kinds of discussions about these groups followed by an annotated bibliography divided by intellectual categories ("Literature and the Arts" among them). Of a total of 636 items, the majority—377—deal with African-American women. And Nancy K. Humphreys's *American Women's Magazines: An Annotated Historical Guide* (Garland) lists writings about such periodicals, dividing the record of 888 items between alternative and mainstream publications and concentrating (with the exception of *Elle* and *The Lady's Magazine*) on American publications. Excluded from the record to hold down the volume's length are discussions appearing in mainstream newspapers. The introduction discusses only the compilation, the sources, and the format. *Black Writers: A Selection of Sketches from Contemporary Authors* (Gale) lists 400 writers, all 20th-century. The introduction does not quite make clear whether all of these writers also appeared in *Contemporary Authors*; it does say that more than 100 entries have been written for this volume. Both Americans and others are represented, and so are people not primarily known as writers (e.g., Roy Wilkins).

I count among general reference works bibliographies of individual authors. The most noteworthy among those published this year is Edwin T. Bowden's *Washington Irving: Bibliography* (Twayne), a volume in "The Complete Works of Washington Irving." This is both an exhaustive primary bibliography and a fine model of its kind, sensitive to the difficulties of the mode, advising readers of alternative methods and interpretations, shunning jargon and speculation for clarity and good sense. Bowden's record of the book publications (he devotes 523 pages to just 25 titles) reflects his use of the research done in the editing for the "Complete Works". He notes not only editions, impressions, and states, but representative variants that enable users to quickly distinguish among the possibilities in actual copies. My sense is that this volume establishes a new standard for its field. Of more strictly workmanlike quality, but sufficiently representative of the demands of the genre, are Elisabeth C. Foard's *William Saroyan: A Reference Guide* (Hall) and Jack Bales's *Kenneth Roberts: The Man and His Works* (Scarecrow). The former sets out a preliminary list of Saroyan's own works and then organizes its annotated secondary entries by years, carrying the full record through 1985 and books only through 1986. Foard "intends" the list to be comprehensive. Her introduction traces Saroyan's reputation on the basis of the record. Bales attempts a more ambitious biographical essay on Roberts, then proceeds to the annotated record of reviews, articles, and essays, biographical and bibliographical studies, theses and dissertations, obituaries, and whatever is left over. Several appendixes set out additional research information. John Tebbel, who knew Roberts, supplies a foreword.

Elizabeth Wiley has prepared—apparently using the computer but in an astonishingly primitive way, without benefit of any of the number of programs developed for the purpose—a *Concordance to the Poetry of Edgar Allan Poe* (Susquehanna). The information is in the

KWIC (keyword in context) format, with lines keyed to volume I of Mabbott's *Collected Works of Edgar Allan Poe* (1969), and a table of frequency counts follows. The concordance is the indispensable tool of the annotator, and at $85 and 746 pages this one is a substantial bargain. Oh, and "quoth" occurs nowhere but in "The Raven."

I can't end on that somber note. So I'll cite two essays qualifying by their topics as reference works: Ludwig Deringer, "The Pacific Northwest in American and Canadian Literature since 1776: The Present State of Scholarship" (*Oregon Historical Quarterly* 90:305–27); and Margaret Perry, "The Harlem Renaissance: Source of Information for Research," pp. 297–315, in Amritjit Singh et al., *The Harlem Renaissance: Revaluations* (Garland).

Indiana University

Author Index

Subject Index

DATE DUE

GAYLORD   PRINTED IN U.S.A.